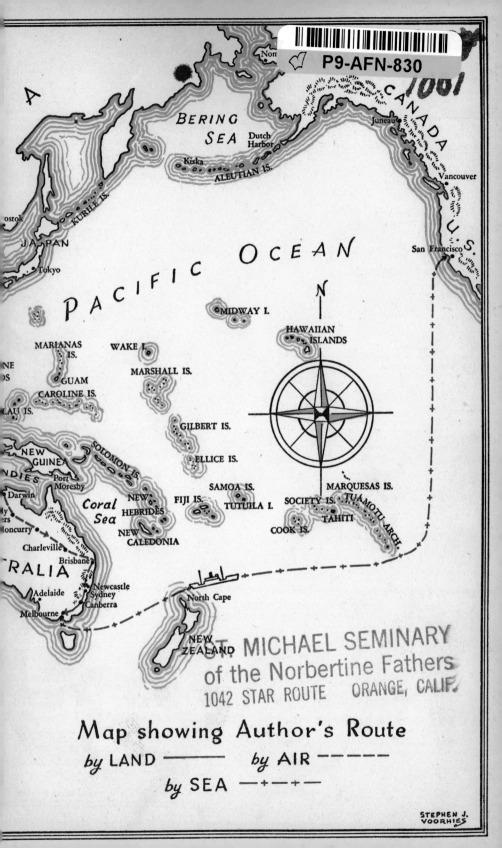

Map showing Author's Route

by LAND ———

by AIR — — —

by SEA —+—+—

STEPHEN J.
VOORHIES

SUEZ TO SINGAPORE

SUEZ TO
SINGAPORE

by Cecil Brown

RANDOM HOUSE · NEW YORK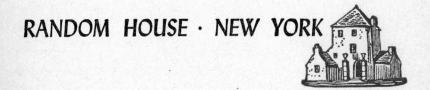

FIFTH PRINTING

TO MARTHA

CONTENTS

Three Pages   ix

1 THE MIDDLE EAST

Escape from the Fascists   3
The Verandahs of Cairo   33
The War in Syria   53
"Suggest You Moscoward"   71
"The Desert Is Hell"   90
"Defense Is the Best Offense"   109
Flight into War   120

2 PREPARATION FOR CHAOS

The Defensive Mentality   131
Preview of Disaster   146
"Singapore Sal"   159
Crescendo of Bluff   178
Mostly about Generals   211
The Japs Are Coming   228
Crack Up   245
"It Can't Happen Here"   263
Seven Days Before the Bombs   275

3 AFTER DECEMBER 7TH

Prelude to Drowning   293
"God Be with You"   324
Jungle Retreat   337
Road to Doom   363
Barred from the Air   397
People's War   415
Flight from Singapore   436
The Fighting Dutch   445
American War Correspondent   459

Yanks at Darwin   480
Australia   505

Three Pages   531

Index   535

THREE PAGES

This is a reporter's report of the war. It is neither a White Paper nor an indictment. *Suez to Singapore* is an account of the war as I saw it, experienced it and watched men fighting it.

This is a personal, intimate book. Death is an intimate affair and war is intensely personal. This people's war is the most personal of all wars.

I have seen too many women and children machine-gunned, and bodies mangled by bombs and their blood spewed over the streets to believe other than this:

This is a war of every man, woman and child.

If you wish to be a spectator, that is no longer your choice. Aircraft, in a single raid, can deny you that luxury.

Civilization denies you a spectator's role, too. The people who read this book, the people who aspire to freedom and those who are ready to die to retain it know that in this people's war the choice is simple. It is either freedom or slavery. As for myself, I infinitely prefer to be dead rather than to be conquered by the Fascists or become a subject of the Axis. We all have that choice.

Wars are made by men who scheme, but wars are fought by people who dream. This book reports about the men who fight wars, the common man and his leaders, on the battlefronts. But the soldier at the front is not any more a soldier than the man or woman working behind the front, ten miles in the rear or ten thousand miles. We all face death before victory comes to us.

It takes courage to die. Believe me, no one wants to die. But tens and tens and tens of thousands of us, Americans, British, Russians, Chinese, Dutch will be dead before this war is won.

We Americans, we of the United Nations, have the courage to die. We have the courage, too, to hear a reasonable report of this war in which we fight and die, and to know that we go to death with the high heart and firm spirit of men and women who die for a better world.

The military direct this war of every man, woman and child, as they should. But this is not the military's war. The time is past when the military are a thing apart, immune to criticism, self-sealed from change, repeating the same mistake time and again.

Today the military are responsible, not to their textbooks, their hierarchy, their traditions or even their conscience, but to the people. They are responsible to people everywhere who fight bravely and die stoically for this better world.

In this book, I name a number of men and the circumstances under which they are fighting this war. Most of them are British because I was a war correspondent of Columbia Broadcasting System attached to the British forces in the Middle East and Far East.

These pages deal with personalities because they are the component parts of a war machine. If some of these men blundered, have shown themselves blind reactionaries with a 1917 mentality toward social changes and modern warfare, their deeds are told because they are symbols.

From Suez to Singapore, to Java and Australia, men of all ranks and all nations show their abilities and shortcomings by deed and word not as Britishers, Americans, Dutch, French, Malayans, Egyptians, Syrians or Senegalese, but as men.

I report in this book, with the greatest objectivity there is in me, the deeds of the men who are fighting and guiding this war, as I found them before, during and after battle. I fought, as best I could, to report this war to the American people. A reporter has no higher duty than to provide his nation with an honest, accurate account of the sector of the war in which he finds himself.

I am against blunderers. Armies don't blunder their way to victory. I am against those who persist in repeating blunders and opposed to those who fight a war in the tight mental confines of "this is our war and don't you civilians bother us about it."

Such blunders send men to a confused death, and lands, once free, are conquered by enemies.

The same mistakes that were made in Norway were made in France. They were repeated in Syria and Egypt, and repeated again this summer in Egypt. Singapore duplicated not only the mistakes of 1917, but also the sad saga of the first twenty-seven months of this war.

Men learn by mistakes; but if they do not learn, then the mistake is doubly, horribly tragic.

x

The heroism I have seen in this war makes me proud, not only to be an American, but to be part of these United Nations. The mistakes which cost the lives of so many men and women and the fierce determination that nothing and no one shall stand in the way of victory compel me to submit this report to the people.

Truth and understanding give us the will to fight this all-out war for victory, freedom and all-out peace.

C.B.

THE MIDDLE EAST

ESCAPE FROM THE FASCISTS

April 29th, 1941:

The small, dirty, antiquated Roumanian ship slid toward Istanbul. Sharp gashes of sun flecked the blue Bosporus. A knife-edged scar of white V-ed out from both sides of the bow of the Black Sea boat and slowly erased itself on the near-by banks of the Straits.

Ahead, the minarets and mosque domes glistened brightly and magnetically. On the hills of Asia to the left, on those of Europe to the right, the ancient stone buildings gave off the warm glow of permanence.

It was peace, bright and quiet peace. It was strange, disturbing and shameful. I felt myself falling into a vacuum, suspended in space and time. It made me nervous. I squirmed and gripped the edge of the rail, dug my feet into the soot-speckled deck to anchor myself.

It felt unnatural, even from the boat, to sense the peace of Istanbul. From those shores came no vibrations of fear, grimness and apprehension, and no odor of death.

I stood on the deck watching the shore, closing and opening my eyes, adjusting them to the hot glare of strangeness, the way you do when you emerge from a cave into sunlight. I gazed idly at the brightly colored lateen sails of the small fishing vessels, heeled over and moving gently away from our wake. My mind, like my eyes, struggled to absorb new scenes to impinge them on old. I wanted to pour from my heart these words:

For the rest of my life, peace will be unnatural. Forever in my nostrils will be the smell of death. Always there will be in my ears the scream of Stukas and always in my eyes the crash of bombs, and mangled bodies torn apart and streets splattered with blood. Forever, there will be in my heart the lust to kill evil men, the consuming desire for vengeance against men who had sown misery and murder in this world.

It had started when I arrived in England on October 2, 1937. Beautiful, complacent, disdainful, appeasement-minded England, en-

3

crusted with the barnacles of Empire, stuffing military reports of Germany's growing military power into dust-collecting pigeonholes, suffering Chamberlain, believing Hitler, ignoring Churchill.

Then to charming France, venal, penny-pinching France, with slimy politicians bent on national sabotage for personal gain, basking in a military mentality outworn for two decades, building a Maginot Line, nourishing a Maginot mentality. A Belgium fearful of Germany, a Brussels watching the Japanese thumb noses at the Nine Power Conference.

Cologne, Berlin, Dresden and militarism, Gestapo, Hitler *Jugends* and a nation preparing for war, egotistic, flexing muscles to smash, hatching dark schemes for enslavement, twisting souls into devilish forms. These are not Nazis, not Junkers, not Prussian militarists. These are the German people supporting Hitler in his dream for world conquest. Not Nazis. Germans, the German people.

Czechoslovakia, a nut between crackers, filled with Fifth Columnists and Czechs stoutly resolute to be independent. Sudeten Germans plotting the overthrow of Prague, preparing to open the floodgates to Nazism.

Austria crawling with Gestapo termites, eating at the frail house Schuschnigg was building. Your neighbor, is he friend or foe? Who knows? Vienna trying to be gay and succeeding in being pathetic. Is this a free country, or a breeding ground for the Nazi technique of peaceful penetration? Innsbruck, where you are afraid to breathe for fear you might draw in a Nazi. High on St. Anton in the Tyrol where the snow is pure and the air fresh and the Tyrolese say: "We are Austrian, not German, and we will fight."

Warm and sunny Italy, poor and pitiful, plastered with cheap slogans and faithful to Mussolini. "One nation, we defied fifty-two nations! Ethiopia is ours and now we all will be rich!" Sicily and Taormina overrun with German "tourists" and "Strength through Joy" parties. "Those Germans. They are pigs. They have no money."

North Africa, Libya the Empire Mussolini and Italo Balbo are carving out of sand. Tripoli with white buildings and communal farms in the desert where natives compete with Arabs for sustenance. Empire builders, the Italians? Native labor, nothing more than that.

Back to Paris. The end of a five months' survey of a continent seeth-

4

ing with discontent and discord, boiling up, obviously preparing for war. A grammar-school boy could have seen that.

Hitler marches into Vienna, and Austria is no more. Then, for me, three years, three days and two and a half hours in Italy, first as Rome correspondent of *International News Service*, and since February of 1940 with the Columbia Broadcasting System.

Days, months and years of watching forty-five million people being deluded, traduced and consigned to horror and frightfulness. Watching a comic-opera army preparing for slaughter under orders of a Duce with a titanic contempt for his own people. Watching and reporting until the moment when Mussolini's men told me: "You are expelled from Italy for your continued hostile attitude toward Fascism."

From watching men's souls torn apart, twisted and destroyed, I went to Yugoslavia to watch bodies ripped apart. I arrived in Belgrade on April 4th; on April 6th the German bombers were over. Bodies were being ripped apart, but always, louder than bombs, there beat a heart that could not be shattered by the historic German inhumanity to mankind.

How sharp, coming into the neutral peacefulness of Turkey, how sharp and painful memories can be . . . Memories . . . Heroic Serbs who knew they were committing suicide by defying Hitler and the New Order . . . Belgrade one quarter destroyed and thousands dead in a few hours . . . Immediately the Serbskikralj Hotel is burning from incendiaries and I am dragging my bags from the flaming building and still two-hundred-and-fifty-pound bombs are raining down death . . . Refugees streaming from Belgrade far across the fields for as far as the eye can see, never again to return to their old homes . . . In the snow and cold of Udjize, soldiers rushing about and crying: "We must go and at once. The Germans are coming" . . . Retreat everywhere . . .

A narrow road and on it, hub-high in mire, fifteen hundred bullock-drawn Yugoslav carts. Ammunition and supplies moving to the front. Bullock carts moving at four miles an hour against twenty-two-ton Nazi tanks speeding into battle at forty-five miles an hour . . . Memories . . . No food, no time to eat or sleep, no cigarettes to be found, always running, darting into hills to escape bombing and machine-gunning. Like an avalanche of mud down a mountainside, humans, animals and supplies flow southward, away from the enemy . . . They

5

have no form, no identity, just living things running . . . Sarajevo, where Archduke Franz Ferdinand was shot in June, 1914. On Easter Sunday, 1941 Italians, circling around at 2,000 feet, dropping bombs with one objective—destruction of the city . . . In the basement of the hotel . . . three direct hits . . . getting machine-gunned three times running through the streets . . . then out into the hills . . .

So many threats of execution as a Fifth Columnist, a spy, a parachutist . . . So many Yugoslav guns, held by nervous hands, thrown in my face . . . Capture by the Germans in no-man's land north of Travnik . . . Nazi tommy guns and rifles and hand grenades seen at the apex of the throw by arms banded with the Swastika . . . That split second when they held their fire and the expected chatter of the tommy gun changed into guttural German shouts . . . Arrested by the Germans as a spy . . . Croat traitors with home-made Swastikas on their arms, itching to shoot "You dog of an American" . . . Two days passing through the German panzer and armored divisions . . . The German advance into Bosnia seen from the barrel end of Hitler's guns . . . Young murderers bent on wiping out the Serbian people . . .

Memories . . . Ten days in Belgrade while the Nazis shoot down Serbs the way you would not shoot a dog, not even a mad dog . . . Belgrade starving, dying and asphyxiating in the smell of death . . . Heil the New Order come to Yugoslavia . . .

Now the events were over, but the memories are not, nor is the smell of death. And I knew, and could not say to anyone then—coming into Turkey—that never again would I find peace. If ever I came to places where there was peace, I should feel ashamed and strange.

I had no fears that one day I should find myself in a world at peace. Peace would come to the world but I would not, by then, be a part of this world.

Sam Brewer may have absorbed some of the "view-with-alarm" concepts of his paper, the *Chicago Tribune*. I came out of Belgrade with him to Budapest, and from there, through Roumania, and on this boat from Costanza to Istanbul he expressed one certainty after another of the trouble we would be bound to encounter:

"You'll never get out of Roumania with that camera, Cecil . . .

6

The Turks are very strict . . . You won't get into Turkey with the camera . . . They will take away your excess money . . . The trains to Ankara are always crowded . . . You'll never be able to get there tonight . . ."

Not a single one of the scores of Brewer's dire predictions came true and I left Istanbul a few hours after my arrival and went to Ankara, the curious, half-developed capital of the Turkey Ataturk dreamed of for his people.

When I arrived in Ankara there was no word from Paul White, the director of news events at CBS. I'd hoped and expected that the moment I reached Ankara I would go on the air with a report on the Yugoslav war. A message did come through in the course of that day. Paul scheduled me for a nine-minute broadcast on Friday, May 2nd. It was the most time ever allotted to me. I was gratified to have that much time to tell the Yugoslav story.

Ankara was alive, alert, curious and eager. For me, it was a combination of bright sunshine, intriguing diplomats, throat-cutting press and radio correspondents, suspicious Turks and my desperate loneliness for Martha.

This was the stamping ground of that arch-intriguer, Franz Von Papen, still in the same slay and sabotage business he operated from the German Embassy in Washington in 1917. Now he was trying with a fat pocketbook, a stable of Gestapo agents and lush promises to lure and browbeat the Moslem world into the New Order.

Contesting each of his moves was Sir Hugh Knatchbull-Hugessen, the British envoy the Japanese machine-gunned and wounded when he was Ambassador to China. I had heard enough about British diplomacy in Turkey to convince me that seeing the British officials would be a waste of time. At no time in Ankara did I go to the British Embassy for information.

Over Turkey hung the thick ominous air of espionage and counter-espionage. It formed the umbrella of suspicion you find in countries on the verge of a precipice. Under it there lurked furtive creatures selling information, and the constant buzz of whispers, rumors and tales of dire things about to happen. But to me, coming from years under Axis dictatorship, Turkey was most of all an island of neu-

7

trality where you could report British and German peccadilloes with equal impunity.

Winston Burdett, the Columbia Broadcasting System correspondent, and his wife, Leah, immediately took me in tow. Burdett had been in Stockholm and Belgrade, and was now doing the best possible job out of Ankara. Winston, small, thin, intense, friendly, was handicapped by a lack of news experience and training. He tried to equalize that by a great energy and willingness, and by making constant rounds of the various embassies. He was fast developing the ability to sift fact from propaganda.

Leah was an Italian from Milan, an anti-Fascist who finally thought it best to get out of Italy. She had strong political views, a sharp mind. She spoke French and Italian, no English, and like myself, was forever taking pictures. I wonder today whether she was taking pictures when the tribesmen in Northern Iran killed her this last Spring.

That nine-minute broadcast ended at 2:30 in the morning. My body then took over and said in effect: "All right, you've kicked me around enough."

The oddest thing happened. The moment I went off the air I had a cold in the head, all the tone went out of my body and I felt terribly, terribly tired. Nezi Bey Manyas, the Turkish program director of the Ankara Radio, Burdett and I went down to the taxi and to the Ankara Palas Hotel. I could barely move from an exhaustion that I hadn't noticed or felt just a few minutes before.

The next two days I was in bed. In those two days a phase of my future life had its inception. As I lay in bed, so tired I could hardly move an arm, I knew that I could never relax.

I squirmed in bed, groaning at the effort to turn over. Winston and Leah came to see me, and told me news. The British were marching in Iraq. And I was stuck here in Ankara. The overwhelming feeling avalanched on me that I was not earning my salary. Since leaving Rome I had only made two broadcasts—one from Belgrade three hours before the Stukas came over dropping bombs, and the second, from Ankara.

Paul White is director of news events at CBS. Not once had he sent me a reprimand, suggestion or compliment. After being with CBS for

8

eleven months in Rome, I cabled him one day for suggestions on the text of my broadcasts and on my manner of delivery. He never answered.

After the Ankara broadcast there came a cable from Paul. It said:
SPLENDID BROADCAST. NOBLE PIECE GRAND REPORTING. EVERYONE DELIGHTED HEARING YOU. REGARDS

That cable from Paul was one of the greatest experiences of my life. After every broadcast I give, after every magazine piece I write, I feel somewhat sick. There is always that one sentence I wanted to put in and didn't, always one word I have wanted to use and omitted, always an inflection I have wanted to give one phrase, and forgot.

That nine-minute broadcast from Ankara telescoped three weeks of bombing, of capture by the Germans and of apprehension the Gestapo would catch up with me and turn me over to the Italians for the story I had cabled about inside Italy as soon as I arrived in Belgrade. CBS did not use that story because they did not wish to compromise the position of the next correspondent they sent to Rome—but I didn't know that until I returned to America more than a year later.

Paul's telegram swept away months and months of uncertainty about my permanency with CBS. I had been conscience-stricken that I had not cabled stories while in Yugoslavia. The fact that communications did not exist in Yugoslavia for any correspondent did not seem important; the fact did remain that CBS had not been covered on that war as it was going on.

Now, for the first time in fifteen months, I felt I was a regular staff member of CBS. I put this down because in fifteen months with CBS I had not recovered from the devastating experience of working for a Hearst organization. With *International News Service* you always felt you would be fired from one day to the next.

I had scored a world beat on the death of Pope Pius XI and although I received a stack of congratulatory telegrams from Barry Faris, director of *INS* and Jack Oesetreicher, the foreign editor, *INS* neither gave me a raise nor a bonus. I was kept on my sixty-five-dollars-a-week salary. Richard Massock, of the *Associated Press,* whom I beat by five minutes with my flash, received a hundred-dollar bonus and a raise in salary.

That conditioning under *INS* had persisted; I'd acquired the horrible certainty that all organizations were as promise-breaking, and as

9

callous as *INS,* and that their executives broke promises with equal impunity.

Turkey was poised on the edge of war, and like most countries in such a position, fear and determination developed and swelled side by side. The first Turk I talked to said:

"We will fight. We're not afraid of the Germans. If we have to, we'll retreat into the Anatolia hills and they'll never find us."

What he said was, word for word, the promise made to me by Serbs in Belgrade. Word for word, except the Serbs said they would retreat into the hills of Bosnia. The Turks still remembered vividly the price they paid for fighting beside Germany in the last war.

The Turks were pro-British. There could be no doubt of that. But Great Britain some months before had sadly informed Turkey that it was a case of either sending material and supplies to Turkey or to Greece, and Greece could not be left in the lurch.

So Turkish policy swayed day by day, like a reed on the edge and at the end of the Mediterranean. On a day when Germany scored a success, the Turkish newspapers leaned a degree closer to Germany. On the day the Germans were halted the papers slipped back into neutral gear, and on the day Britain won a minor victory the papers huzzahed the British. She paid lip service to her commitments to Germany and Great Britain and Russia with equally vigorous protestations.

Turkish policy may have been undulating, unprincipled, and censurable, but Turkey was not yet ready to choose between suicide for a principle or appeasement for salvation.

Strange things were going on around and inside Turkey. On April 29th, the day I arrived at Istanbul, six German merchant ships went from the Black Sea into the Aegean with war materials from Russia. The Turks told the British in advance, but nothing was done. And on May 5th, the Germans occupied two more of the outlying Greek Islands, Mytilene and Chios.

On May 2nd the British started war on the rebels in Iraq. For the moment, the principles of that war were forgotten in Turkish pride and happiness that Great Britain had shown some initiative. German and Italian intrigue in Iraq was no secret; nor was it a secret that Rashid Ali Gailani had installed himself as dictator with German

10

and Italian support. The prize was great: the vast oil fields at Mosul. Even if the Axis did not get them, at least they might close off the pipeline to Haifa and oil for the British Fleet in the Mediterranean.

The pattern of Axis intrigue in Iraq was familiar. Von Henting, former Middle Eastern chief of the Wilhelmstrasse, went to Iraq, which had broken relations with Germany but not with Italy, early in April. He visited important sheiks in Bagdad and Mosul, spreading money and being especially extravagant with the promises of what Germany would give. Of course, Germany did not have the possessions to give at the moment, but, Von Henting explained, she would soon have them and a great deal more. The promises were built around assurances of a great Arab independent state.

Turkey was seething, not only with intrigue, but also with fear. Number one fear of the Turks at that moment, since the Russo-German pact was in force, was that Moscow and Berlin were planning a huge Middle Eastern partition scheme. In any such scheme, as Cy Sulzberger, of the *New York Times,* insisted, Turkey would become a pale star of the Axis orbit.

Most of the correspondents were endeavoring to show that Russia and Germany were sharpening their knives for each other, and although some were without information, they accepted British propaganda that Russia and Germany would go to war.

Everyone in Ankara thought that either the Russians or the Germans would push through the Dardanelles to get at each other. Or even push through Turkey itself. All the Turks said they would fight; but every foreign diplomat I talked to in Ankara said he did not know what Turkey would do. The men who control things, Ankara bureaucrats and the businessmen, wanted peace, and they were prepared to go to considerable lengths to keep it. Turkey felt herself surrounded by a voracious Russia and ruthless Germany, bereft of all friends, except Great Britain. Yet the Turks were unhappy about what Turkish officials called British diplomatic fumbling and bumbling.

News of the outbreak of the war with Iraq caught the British Embassy at Ankara by surprise. On the day the British started in Iraq, Sir Hugh Knatchbull-Hugessen and staff members were attending a reception at the Iraq legation in honor of the sixth birthday of the baby King Feisal II, completely unaware that war had started. Although the Turkish are not a very precise people themselves, they expected better of the British, since they, at least, were involved in the war.

Diary Comment, May 6:

I have no desire to get caught in Turkey between the British in Iraq and the Germans sweeping across Syria and Turkey to go to the help of the Iraqis. A good many people here think that may happen. Besides, I would like to get home. I've wanted to do that for several years.

This seems the moment for the Germans to get to the oil of Iraq and Iran. What would stop them?

I have just cabled New York to ask if I could go to Bagdad. What a dateline for a broadcast: "This is Bagdad." . . . Aladdin and the Magic Carpet stuff, mysterious desert, fabled city. I checked with Ankara radio and with the Iraq minister and as near as I can determine there are shortwave transmitters available in Bagdad. We may be able to kick it across to Ankara and then broadcast direct to New York. There is practically no news getting out of Bagdad.

The first secretary of the Iraq legation is just about convinced it would be a good idea to get me there. I originally asked him what the official Iraq version of the dispute with the British was. His argument was that there were no Axis agents in Iraq, that all they want the British to do is live up to the agreement not to exceed the number of troops allowed there under the treaty.

"All right," I said, "if you think that's a reasonable statement of your case, let me go to Bagdad so that I can report it to the American people."

He agreed and immediately wrote out a code message to his foreign office. He says the message requests that a visa be granted for entrance into Iraq. I've taken it to the cable office and it's off to Bagdad.

After a week of Ankara, my personal claustrophobia set in. I cabled New York for permission to go to Cairo while awaiting an answer from the Iraq foreign office for a visa to get into Bagdad. The frontier between Syria and Turkey was reported about ready to close. That would make it almost impossible to get to Cairo. I didn't want to be stuck in Turkey. Ankara was becoming a dumping ground of correspondents.

Cyrus Sulzberger is here from Greece. I had seen Cy in Belgrade just a few hours before the German attack started. Cy is one of the

12

strangest and smartest boys I have ever known. When I was on the *Pittsburgh Press,* Cy came to Pittsburgh straight out of Harvard and his intellectual, bohemian world. He wore his hair down over his collar, wore the same shirt for two weeks, and his trousers cuffs came three inches above the tops of his shoes.

Howard Vickery, then assistant city editor on the *Press,* Kenneth McArdle and myself had taken Cy in hand because he had intellectual honesty and a rebellious spirit. Cy didn't care about newspaper style or traditions. His first assignment in Pittsburgh was to interview two gold prospectors who were passing through.

He wrote the story exactly as they told it to him, including all their choice profanity. Larry Fagan, a superficially tough Irish city editor with a putty heart, read the story and leaped for the ceiling.

"Sulzberger!" he screamed. "Don't you know that women and children read our paper?"

"What has that to do with it?" replied the nephew of the *New York Times* publisher.

"You can't use words like that!" Fagan screamed.

"I didn't use them. Those are the direct quotations from the men."

Fagan was speechless. Sulzberger was adamant. He wouldn't change the words. "It wouldn't be accurate," Cy said, "if I did." And he didn't. A rewrite man deleted the profanity.

Sulzberger in the intervening six years worked hard, asked no favors, developed a keen evaluation of news, and he retained his intellectual honesty. The British were angry with him because he had revealed the presence of British troops in Greece.

Dan De Luce, of *Associated Press,* and his wife, a handsome pair, had come out of Greece with Sulzberger in a small fishing boat. They liked to wander around, as I do, taking photographs. We did that until we were all taken to the police station.

Martin Agronsky represents National Broadcasting Company here. He is a jet-haired, zealous correspondent of twenty-seven, who gets almost all his information from the British Embassy. He works very hard, is always worried whether he has missed any story, and he and Burdett are busy cutting each other's throat to achieve what are euphemistically known as "scoops."

I gave word of her husband to Mrs. Robert St. John. He represented the *Associated Press* in Yugoslavia, and I had given stories on that war

13

to Bob and to Ray Brock of the *New York Times,* to cable to CBS in case one or the other got through.

I had last seen St. John in Sarajevo when he and Russell Hill of the *New York Herald Tribune* and a Yugoslav girl decided to head for the Dalmatian coast and escape. Ray Brock was with Robert McEttee, the secretary of the American Legation who was always shaking as though he had the ague, which he hadn't. They had deserted me in Sarajevo. I didn't mind the desertion, but they happened to have the car, my only means of transportation.

At Ankara I found out what had happened to Leigh White, the CBS correspondent who was in Belgrade when I arrived there from Rome. I had last seen Leigh on the porch of Ambassador Lane's home in Belgrade while the bombs were dropping. At that time Leigh and I decided that he should try and follow the Yugoslav military head-quarters while I would pursue the evanescent Yugoslav Government. We felt ourselves in a fortunate position because CBS had two men in Yugoslavia and thus, chances were, that one of us would come out of it alive to cover the Yugoslav war.

Leigh teamed up on the Dalmatian coast with St. John and Russell Hill, and sailed for Greece in a small boat. The boat was machine-gunned and the captain killed. St. John and Leigh were severely injured when machine-gunned on a train going to Athens. In Ankara I was told that Leigh was in an Athens hospital. The Nazis, I knew, were not fond of Leigh and I feared he would never get out.

Brewer assured me I could not get an Egyptian visa since I had been having some difficulty. His pessimism on that score was the first encouragement I had had. By then, I had developed the confidence that whatever Brewer said, I could count on the opposite coming to pass. After a week, the Egyptian minister persuaded Cairo to grant the visa and the French consulate also came through with a transit visa for Syria.

Diary comment, May 10th:
Plan for going to Bagdad seems on the shelf. No reply on Iraq visa and probably no transportation available.

At a cocktail party two attachés of the French Embassy reassured me that Vichy is anti-German, but "what can we do at the moment?"

14

I told them I expected to go on to Cairo in a few days and they said: "Tell the British that when the moment comes we will once again be with them. But we are helpless now. We hate the Germans."

I said: "If you hate the Germans, why permit them to send aircraft into Syria, which they're doing right now?" They say it isn't true.

I am getting a bit weary of these Vichy French who hate the Germans but go on collaborating just the same. These two attachés reminded me of De Marjerie and Bauduoy, formerly of the French Embassy in Rome, and good friends of mine. I had seen them at Turin when I put Martha on the train on March 6th to go across France and Spain, then Portugal and home. De Marjerie and Bauduoy were on the Italo-French Armistice Commission, hating their enemies, but doing what they were told to do.

The excitement here today is the flight of Rudolph Hess to Britain. Most people think he was just escaping from Nazism, but I am convinced that he carried peace proposals to England.

I remember Hess when he came to Rome, Naples and Florence with Hitler for the twenty-million-dollar celebration of Italian "might." Mussolini put on the show for his Axis partner.

Hess was a black-haired, brute-faced man, built on the order of a football tackle. He impressed me as a strong character. I believe he went to England at Hitler's instigation.

I've had a long talk with the Chinese Minister. Somehow every Chinese diplomat seems to have a knowledge that makes him stand out in every gathering. The Chinese Ambassador to Turkey is no exception. The Chinese views are always more intellectual than emotional, more realistic than sentimental—and that's the attitude that gives you news.

Burdett and I have been to the Russian and Japanese Embassies. If war comes before I can get through to Cairo, and another evacuation starts, I may need Russian and Japanese visas to go home. The application for the Russian visa wanted more information than any consulate has ever requested.

The Turks give me the impression they hate everyone, including themselves. They are the most suspicious people I've ever encountered, and only permit foreigners to reside in their country through almost unendurable sufferance. I think the Turks are very nearly completely anti-international and would like nothing better than to see every foreigner, including diplomats, removed from their country. If it were possible, the Turks would prefer to have nothing to do, no communication and no trade, with the rest of the world.

Monday night, May 12th, was the sort of evacuation scene I was to run into in other parts of the world. Numerous British nationals were leaving Turkey. Knatchbull-Hugessen was there to see off a member of his Embassy staff. Newbegin and Satterthwaite, from our Legation, were there. I was bound for Cairo, where there might be a story or two to cover. I was glad to get out of Turkey. It was expensive and confining.

On board the train the next day, Sir Alan Walker, the First Secretary of the British Embassy, and Lady Walker loaned me a book, Woollcott's *While Rome Burns*. Traveling through dry, parched and dusty Turkey, I read that book for the first time. A page would be covered with dust before I finished reading it. In the back of the book was a small sticker: "Lillian Anderson Book Shop, Evanston, Illinois."

At dusk we crossed the Syrian frontier. There was a small outpost of Turks with a garrison, and, 100 yards farther on, a cement market three feet high. Ten minutes later we came to a French station. The character changed at once. A faded and ripped tricolor flew from one building. Arabs lolled about the station in bright flowing burnouses, and around their heads they wore a tribal black cord. It was startling, after Hungary, Roumania and Turkey, to meet customs men who acted half human and had the capacity to smile, Gallic smiles.

My first sight of the half-lit Aleppo station took in two gendarmes swinging clubs and driving a group of Arabs off the platform. We could not go outside the station. Aleppo was tense. There had been a riot between Arabs and French the day before. A strong wind blew, carrying with it stinging sand, but the Walkers got off here to break the journey, with twenty-two pieces of luggage and a white poodle.

Diary comment, Wednesday, May 14th:
This sleeping car is filled with English people. There are among them, a man and wife and their two children going to Cairo, then to South Africa and on to Canada. It is a relief to hear English, but I'd much prefer to hear American.

16

Arrived at Tripoli and changed to autos. We have to drive to Beirut since this is the end of the railroad. Managed to get a cup of coffee but couldn't drink it. The auto ride from Tripoli to Beirut along the Mediterranean was incredibly beautiful. In Beirut I fussed around getting a poor lunch, reading French newspapers and bought a bracelet and pin for Martha.

At the Syrian-Palestine frontier, the French were courteous but firm. All baggage had to be unloaded, and they went through every item. No objection was raised until they came to the map of Turkey I had with me. The customs guard said: "Il est défendu." I shrugged my shoulders and he took the map. The French did not take the stack of maps I had of other countries.

Then a dip in the road, around a bend, and atop a building at a rise in the road I saw the Union Jack floating brilliantly against the bright-blue afternoon sky. I wanted to clamber to the top of the building and kiss that flag.

Geographically this was Nikoura, the frontier post between Palestine and Syria. But to me it was much more than that. This was British territory, where a man's soul was his own; when I stepped across that frontier I would be in a friendly land, where people spoke my own language, where the war was being fought against the Axis.

Here I would not be surrounded by people of the Axis, by the Gestapo and the OVRA. No more gray-green uniforms of Germans, or olive-green of Italians. Palestine was neither slipping into the Axis camp like Syria, nor neutral like Turkey.

This Palestine was on ground where bombers could take off to pound the Axis; here there were men who wanted to kill Axis soldiers with the same lust to kill that I felt. That flag flying up there was the British Empire, Clive of India, Lawrence of Arabia, the stuff of the single Englishman who keeps order among a hundred thousand natives. Here was security, and end of my constant fears that my precious notes would be taken from me, that these notes might throw me into jail. This was escape, mental and physical, from the Axis.

The British at the frontier were young, charming, tough and firm. I handed over the bilious-green American passport issued in Rome to replace the traditional red-backed passport all American tourists used to carry. It was taken into an inner office. Within a few minutes the dozen other assorted French, Egyptians, Britishers and Greeks traveling through to Cairo had their passports back, and those in the other cars went off toward Haifa.

I pointed out to one of the British officers that I had a film in my camera and did he have any suggestion about that. "I would suggest," he said, "that you give us the film and we will send it on to you. This is all a military zone through here."

I took out the film and handed it over, saying: "Do a good job of developing the film, will you? Print it on glossy paper." He laughed and said he would.

Still I waited for my passport. After a half hour, the officer in charge called me over.

"You say you came out of Italy. But your passport doesn't show an exit from there."

"You don't mean to imply by any chance that I'm still in Italy!"

No, he said, he didn't mean that, but after all if I had come out of Italy, as I said, why wasn't there a stamp in the passport to show that?

"The passport shows," I said, "that I passed the Yugoslav frontier at Rakek on April 3rd and Rakek is on the Italian-Yugoslav frontier."

"Well," said the British official, "we're still checking with Jerusalem."

"You're checking with Jerusalem? What about? Everyone else has gone through. Can you tell me why I am being held up?"

"You came from enemy territory," he replied, "and your case has to be referred to Intelligence Headquarters in Jerusalem."

"But the British consulate in Ankara gave me a visa to go through Palestine en route to Cairo."

"Yes, we know that. That is only permission to *enter* Palestine. But it doesn't mean that the permission need necessarily be granted."

I sat once again on the concrete fence at the edge of the road, a fence that dropped straight down for two hundred feet to the sea. I waited. The Turks had been easier than this. Even the Germans had allowed me to get out of Yugoslavia with less fuss than the British.

About an hour later, a young lieutenant came out of the office. He said: "Would you care to broadcast from Jerusalem for us?"

"No, sir," I retorted, "I would not. I'm ordered to Cairo and that's

18

where I'm going, no matter how much red tape you wrap this thing up in."

"Well, I thought I'd ask, don't you know. I have instructions to ask radio people if they would like to broadcast from Palestine."

"I'm not coming into Palestine to wreck the British Empire, I assure you. But neither am I in Palestine to broadcast."

I waited at Nikoura for two hours while G-2 in Jerusalem decided I was harmless enough to allow in. Just as I got in the car to start the drive to Haifa, a sub-lieutenant, very young, very blond and very apologetic, came up.

"I understand you've been in Yugoslavia," he said. I nodded. "Would you care to talk to an Intelligence officer this evening if you can spare half an hour?"

I said I would, and he could telephone me at the hotel and we would arrange a time. I was well aware that British Intelligence not only wanted information about the Germans in Yugoslavia, but also wanted to have an officer with me that evening so that I would find out only what they wanted me to know.

In Haifa, I stepped from the car directly into a taxi and rushed off to the C.I.D. I'd been informed that I would need an exit permit to get out of Palestine on the train leaving the next morning at 7:30 for Cairo.

At the C.I.D., Duty Officer Davis said the office closed at 6:30. It was now 7:15 P.M.

"You will have to wait until morning now," he said.

"That's all right. What time do you open?"

"At eight."

"Well, then I can't do that. My train leaves at 7:35."

Davis promised he would try to get hold of the officer in charge and see if an exception couldn't be made and the exit permit issued out of office hours.

In the hotel dining room I read the *Palestine Post,* a well-edited, newsy paper in a part of the world where that is exceptional. The hotel was filled with British officers, all carefully groomed and dressed in full uniform for the evening. Every one carried a swagger stick. They looked wonderful to me in khaki. After seeing so many German and Italian uniforms for so many years, khaki is the most wonderful color in the world.

At 9:15 the Intelligence officer came to see me. He said his name was Lieutenant Temple. "Actually Lord Temple," he said, "but that sort of thing doesn't mean anything these days."

I told him something of the Germans in Yugoslavia, how they organized their advances and the sort of equipment they were using.

"Did you see very much German stuff coming across Syria?"

"No, not much. There were concentrations of troops and vehicles not far from the Palestine frontier."

I described the approximate location of the camps, and the placement of the machine-gun nests. "There are about twenty road blocks between Beirut and the frontier."

"I sneaked across the frontier a few days ago," Lieutenant Temple said. "There are German planes on the airfields at Damascus, Beirut and Aleppo."

"Are you sure? The French in Ankara assured me no Germans are in Syria."

Temple smiled and said softly: "They're jolly liars."

The Germans, Temple added, were sending aircraft into Syria, and ground crews and, he had reason to believe, troops as well.

"Their agents are stirring up the Arabs," he said. "They are paying out a great deal of money and promising them everything. They tell the Arabs they are there to drive out the French and they tell the French they have come in to protect them from us. Here's how the Arabs feel about it. A French officer, a friend of mine over there, came across some Arabs and they immediately opened fire on him. He shot and killed two of them and he was himself wounded.

"A few days later he returned to that area and the Arabs greeted him with great cries of welcome. He wanted to know why he had been shot at before. 'Ah,' the Arabs told him, 'we thought you were against us, that you were working with the British. Heil Hitler. Vive la France.' "

Temple asked me to do something for him, and I said I would.

"When you get to Cairo, you'll see someone at GHQ. Tell them what's going on in Syria. We have been trying to tell them that the Germans are pouring into Syria and that we have to move if we want to save it."

Temple told me he had been interceding in my behalf, and about

20

11 P.M. a call came through. It was C.I.D. saying to come over at once and the exit visa would be issued.

Temple and I hopped into a taxi and off to the C.I.D. office, the name for Internal Security Headquarters. The form was all filled out, but Captain Bedmead glanced through my passport just to make a double check.

He was in pyjamas and dressing robe, but there was amazement and not sleep in his eyes when he looked up from the passport.

"Why," he said in utter astonishment, "I can't issue an exit visa without consulting my superiors in Jerusalem."

"Why not?"

"You come from enemy occupied territory."

There was no doubt of that. It plainly showed my residence in Rome; there was an authorization from the German Feldkommandantur (a Prussian colonel with monocle) at Zagreb giving me permission to proceed from there to Belgrade. There were enough German permits stamped in it to look as though I were traveling on a German passport.

"Come now, Captain," I said. "We went through that whole business at the frontier. They referred the whole matter to Jerusalem. I was held up at Nikoura for more than two hours and then the okay came through."

"Yes, but that was permission for you to enter the country. Now you want permission to leave."

"Naturally."

Bedmead, bright-skinned, young, self-reliant, was polite but firm. He could do nothing until 8 A.M. Temple said he could not intervene. "This is his province and they have rules and you can't break the rules."

I explained my train would go the next morning at 7:35 and I intended to be on it, with or without an exit permit.

"That wouldn't do any good. They would take you off the train at the frontier. Why don't you have a car waiting and catch the train at Lydda?"

So it was agreed. I went to bed at 1:30 A.M.; at 5:30 the air-raid siren sounded and a raid was on, but I didn't hear it, and at 7:58 I was back at the C.I.D. office with a car.

At precisely 8 A.M. Bedmead came in and, at his request, I reviewed my story: Expelled from Italy, captured by the Germans in Yugoslavia, eventual passage to Budapest, through Roumania to Ankara. I showed him the wire from Paul White approving my request to go to Cairo. He was puzzled that I had no money. I explained that was usually the case with me, but that there would be funds available for me in Cairo.

Bedmead then telephoned Jerusalem and the conversation went this way:

"Is Mr. Prosser in?" Evidently he wasn't.

"Is Mr. Smith in?" Again the same presumption.

"Is Mr. Jenkins there?" The answer was still no.

Bedmead held his hand over the mouthpiece and said to me: "Now you know why we're losing this war."

Ten minutes later he called Jerusalem again. This time someone answered, his chief. Bedmead was cute. "We have here a Mr. Cecil Brown of the Columbia Broadcasting System. His passport is in order and you don't want to hold him here, do you?"

Put that way to him by the officer on the spot, the chief in Jerusalem agreed.

I wrung Bedmead's hand and we grinned at each other. He stamped my passport and as I was going out I said to him: "I presume the British Empire pays the seven pounds that this taxi costs to Lydda?"

He smiled. "Oh, yes, just charge it to the British Empire." It is so charged.

At 8:30, fifty-five minutes after the train left Haifa, we started out on the seventy-mile dash to Lydda. I made that train, with two minutes to spare.

The train was hot, crowded and the sand of Palestine blew in and formed layers on the seats. Soon after I got on the train, a British censor came through and asked if I had papers.

"Yes, I have copies of my stories." I drew out an envelope and passed it over.

He peered into the suitcase. "You have other papers there, I see."

"Yes, but they are my private property."

"Sorry, but I must have them."

I protested that never before had the papers been taken away. He was apologetic but firm and I finally gave up the papers, presuming he would read them on the train and then hand them back.

Near Kantara, at the frontier between Palestine and Egypt where you detrain to cross the Suez on a ferry and catch a train on the other side, I found the censor. He was in the fly-filled dining car having a cup of tea.

"What about my papers?" I asked.

"Oh, they have to go through the censor at Kantara."

At Kantara we went into an office at the station and the papers were handed over to a big, beefy, jolly-faced, pompous individual whose whole life, obviously, had been spent in telling natives what to do. Months later I saw a replica of him in Governor Sir Shenton Thomas at Singapore.

He took the papers and stuffed them into a drawer.

"Wait a minute," I protested. "If you are taking those papers, this thing has gone far enough. I want an itemized inventory of every paper in that envelope."

"Oh," he said, "we never do that."

"Yes, and nothing like this has ever happened to me before. Since I entered Palestine I've been treated like a dangerous enemy spy. If I am, go ahead and shoot me, and if I'm not, hand over those papers. I'm a correspondent and those papers are an essential part of my work."

"Now, now," he clucked.

I was infuriated by his calm assumption that whatever he did was reasonable and legal.

"I'm fed up with this business. This is becoming a matter for the State Department. If you're going to keep that envelope I want it sealed with wax."

"Sealed with wax? Are you diplomatic?"

"No, of course not."

"Then," he exulted, "we can't seal it with wax!"

It was as simple as that. Naturally, envelopes carried by diplomatic couriers were sealed with wax, ergo, if I wanted wax on an envelope I must be in the diplomatic service.

He patted me on the shoulder and said: "Now, don't you worry. You'll have this envelope in Cairo before you get there."

"I won't hold you to that," I said, "because you don't know what you're talking about. It would have to go on the same train and it isn't going on that train. I'll wait in Cairo for twenty-four hours for that envelope. If I don't have it, I'm going to the British Embassy and to the American Legation."

"Now, now, it will be there."

He put it into a larger envelope, sealed it, and wrote on the outside my name and Continental Hotel, Cairo.

The train was packed with officers and men, some on their way to new assignments in Cairo, others on leave.

I swelled with pride seeing them, free men from all parts of the Empire, rushing like good sons to help endangered Mother Britain. Tough, lumbering, strange-talking Australians with big hats turned up on the side. Swarthy Indians with high head-dresses and fierce eyes. Husky, compact South Africans with their narrow-brimmed pith helmets. Cockney Englishmen and young fresh-faced sailors with H.M.S. on their brimless hats.

There were Yugoslavs in tattered, dirty uniforms hanging from their towering frames. Strong-eyed men, unbowed and still eager. Some of the Yugoslav pilots had uniforms with holes burned into them. All were unshaven; all had lost everything but their hearts and pride. The British paid no attention to the Yugoslavs. They couldn't speak English.

In the dining car, I sat opposite a young, shy lieutenant of an Indian Rajputani regiment. He'd been an officer for three years and intended to make the Army his career. For month after month I'd been living in countries which were part of the murderous machine carrying out the bombings of Britain. We talked of those bombings, the ability to carry on, and the odds against England, and how soon the invasion might come. The young Englishman casually summed up the British temper. He made a statement I believed the moment he made it, a statement I have never ceased to believe.

"Peace with the Nazis," he said, "is impossible as long as there is one Britisher alive."

I awoke early in my room at the Continental Hotel and called downstairs for a newspaper while I hurriedly dressed. My first job was to rush off to GHQ, and see someone on General Wavell's staff to report on the German infiltration into Syria.

The headlines eliminated that job. They said that Foreign Minister Anthony Eden had told the House of Commons that Great Britain would not "stand idly by" while the Nazis went into Syria.

24

Reports from Lieutenant Temple and scores of others like him had, for once, not found their way into pigeonholes but had been acted upon.

My first official call in Cairo was also a personal one. It was to Alexander Kirk, the American Minister. Kirk formerly was Counsellor of the Embassy at Rome, a strange, exotic person; precocious, affable, a dilettante, immensly wealthy from the Kirk soap fortune, and one of the smartest and most able diplomats I had ever encountered representing any country.

Kirk battled with the Italian Foreign Office the previous January to secure my reinstatement after the Italians had barred me from the air. Twice he had gone to the Foreign Office about my case, and then when Ambassador William Phillips returned from the United States, Phillips had twice talked to the Foreign Office. The final resort was Foreign Minister Galeazzo Ciano, then at the front, who flew his bomber over Greece, always with his protective screen of twenty-five fighters. Ciano had given approval that I could continue to broadcast. Prunas, at the Foreign Office, however, had inserted a proviso that I would be given a two-month "probation."

That probation was for February and March, and I then knew that I would have two months more to broadcast. As Kirk had said at the time: "They don't want you here and it is foolish to stay."

Since the probation was predicated on "good behavior and a greater understanding of Fascism," I knew that my days in Rome were numbered. On March 6th, I had sent Martha back to the United States and on April Fool's day the Italians decided my hostile attitude toward Fascism had exhausted those numbered days.

As I walked into his office, the always svelte, groomed, massaged Kirk lost his perfect and perennial poise. His pipe fell out of his mouth and the ashes sprayed over his immaculate suit.

"What are you doing here?" Kirk cried.

"I came to see you."

Just then, Albert W. Horn, his secretary, announced two other correspondents. Edward Angly of the *New York Herald Tribune* and Richard Mowrer of the *Chicago Daily News* came in. Angly I had never met before, but Dick I knew very well from Rome.

They had come to complain, and Angly opened up. It was the British again. "What," demanded Angly, "is the use of staying here?

You can't say anything. The censorship is stupid and I'm not staying here to spend all my time wrangling. An office boy can send the communiqués, which is all we can file now."

Dick Mowrer was equally bitter and Kirk attempted to soothe them both.

They wouldn't be soothed. Angly explained to me that Robert Casey, the top correspondent of the *Chicago Daily News,* and Robert Neville of *PM* had just pulled out to go back to New York.

"They fought the censors from morning to night and couldn't make any headway. What's the use?"

Kirk was persuasive and diplomatic. He already had talked to the British officials about the complaints of the American correspondents. "Every day," he said, "if you can just get one thought across to the American people you are doing a good job here. If you can just keep Suez before the public, it is helping the cause."

Angly said his mind was made up. He was going back to New York and then to London so that he could do the job he was sent out to do, reporting.

Angly is a hard-bitten product of Palestine, Texas—short, slim, gray-haired and almost fifty, unmarried and fast talking, with a tremendous fund of immensely funny stories. An able correspondent, often stubborn as a mule, courtly in manner at times and short and sharp-tempered at other times. He was in the retreat in France.

Mowrer is one of the most deceptive-looking men I have ever known. He is the prototype of Caspar Milquetoast, young, blond and balding, extremely slow-spoken and words edge out of his mouth with great reluctance. His father is Paul Scott Mowrer, editor of the *Chicago Daily News* and his uncle is Edgar Ansel Mowrer, that paper's famous correspondent.

But Dick is a fighter and, in his quiet way, could be pushed around with about the same ease as a mountain. Martha and I had an especial interest in Dick and his wife, Rosamond. Having been married ourselves in Rome, in the record-breaking time of thirty-six hours, we had helped Dick and Rosamond weave through the intricate red tape of Rome that finally ends before the magistrate with the wide sash in the *salle di sposata* at the *Compodoglio.*

That had been a hectic marriage. Dick had been expelled from Rome by the Fascist Government and was under orders to be out of town

26

by noon. The ceremony was finished at 11:30; their honeymoon car with the luggage in it was waiting at the American Embassy, and just on the deadline, Dick and Rosamond sped out of Rome.

And now here was Dick again, in Cairo, where he was still fighting the good fight of reporting.

I went to Radio House and met the CBS resident correspondent, Edward Chorlian, who also worked for the Egyptian State Broadcasting as a news announcer. He was ill at ease, and very much worried that my coming meant he would not be able to do any more broadcasting for us. I allayed his fears as best I could. My job, I explained, would be to go up to the front and either send back stories for him to broadcast or else return to Cairo every now and then to broadcast them myself.

Correspondents are controlled under the British set-up by a Public Relations Office called P.R. There I talked with a Major A. D. Oakshot. He was agreeable and affable, and I explained that from Ankara I had asked my New York office to request the War Office in London to accredit me to the British forces.

Oakshot knew nothing about the whole matter.

"If we hear anything on it," he said, "we'll let you know."

I wandered about Cairo that afternoon, talked with correspondents and officers, and in my diary, near dinnertime, I recorded:

Not much impressed by anything I have seen.

The social life going on here is astonishing.

Correspondents are unwelcome intruders. The constant attitude of the military is "this is our war" and they don't want to be bothered by us.

This is a good news center but it is almost impossible to do any decent reporting.

I am more homesick than ever and more determined than ever to get back to the United States.

Saturday, May 17th:
There is no word from Paul White. I presumed he would want me to broadcast as soon as I arrived. After all, I do have a story on what I saw in Syria and Palestine. But there's just silence.

The envelope with my papers has not come through from Palestine and more than thirty hours have elapsed. I went out to the British Embassy and saw Michael Wright, the First Secretary. I told him of my experiences in Palestine, being held up at the frontier at Nikoura and then having the papers taken away at the Egyptian frontier.

"I must admit that you have had rough handling. I'll do what I can."

"What does that mean, Mr. Wright? Do I get the papers back or am I being told in a polite British way that the matter is under consideration. If I am to get the papers back, fine, if not, I want to know it and I'll take the matter up with the State Department."

"I'll telephone you tomorrow or see that you have the papers then." (The papers arrived the next morning, intact.)

I spent a good part of today trying to get permission from the British officials to broadcast. The heat here is terrific. The *Saturday Evening Post* has asked for a five-thousand-word article on how I was captured by the Germans in Yugoslavia, and what equipment the Germans have moving into battle. Have tried all evening to work on it, but the going is very difficult. It was 120 degrees in the sun today and the evening is not much cooler.

The British have bombed Syrian airdromes. Eden said the targets were German aircraft on the ground. The Vichy French say they are peeved.

I don't know exactly why I came to Cairo. The only way to get back home is to fly to Capetown, then take a boat to the West Indies. Boats down the Red Sea are infrequent and dangerous. Going across the Pacific is a long haul and we might be at war before I could get very far on my way to San Francisco.

Sunday, May 18th:

Angly and I went out to Gezira Sporting Club. Beautiful spot, just across the Nile, a ten-minute ride from downtown. It is an outpost of the British Empire—greenswards, a cricket field, tennis courts, beautiful shrubbery, and scores of African waiters in white, hopping about to serve whisky and sodas. Angly went swimming, but I didn't have a suit and no money either. I'm still waiting for some from New York.

Watched the handsome officers flitting about with great jollity, while the sand is running out three hundred miles to the west.

I've been told that the advance two days ago beyond Sollum, at the frontier, was intended to be a major thrust. It was stopped cold. An

28

officer at the pool said that the British discovered the Germans had three times as many tanks as was expected. The British lost some badly needed tanks. What is worse, the famous British "I" tanks which whipped the Italians are no longer effective. The Germans are using a new type of anti-tank gun. It seems to be, someone said, a five pounder which knocked many of the "I" tanks out of commission. Most of them were able to get back but they'd been rendered ineffective.

This has now tipped the British hand to the Germans. They know now what the British have. I see nothing here to stop the German if he decides to launch a full-scale offensive toward Suez.

The British were desperately short of man power and equipment. One bright spot was that more than 100 American tanks had been landed in the week before my arrival at Cairo.

Seated with Angly on the verandah of the Continental I saw three correspondents come in from the Western Desert. They were still covered with sand: Hal Denny, of the *New York Times,* Richard Mac-Millan of *British United Press* and Eddie Ward of BBC. They were all rigged out like the movie version of the war correspondent.

These correspondents out of the desert returned with a mental attitude that I was to find in most correspondents who came back from action, and which I was to develop after I had been to the front. It was called a state of A and D, that is, Alarm and Despondency.

Diary note:
Went to a cocktail party at Kirk's home in the country. It is a fantastic place, like the Beverly Hills home of a cinema star with a swimming pool and a series of verandahs, but you know you are in Egypt because the three pyramids of Giza are in sight a few miles off.

I thought it was too bad that part of the surfacing atop one of the pyramids had fallen away.

Rosamond Mowrer remarked: "Well, you would peel, too, Cecil, if you were out in this hot sun for five or six thousand years."

Monday, May 19th:
Attended, for the first time, the daily press conference held on the third floor of the censor's office at Sharia Eloui. Lieutenant Colonel

Tod was in charge. He read the daily communiqué and added nothing to it.

It was held in a very small room with two wooden trestle tables and not enough chairs. Some of the correspondents asked questions but Tod did not answer them. He's a man of forty-five, quite gruff and taciturn and difficult to understand. Every word of his seems an effort, or else too precious to drop.

I took no notes at the conference; I just wanted to see how it operates.

A few minutes after I returned to the hotel, Chorlian telephoned me. He had been called by Lieutenant Henderson, an assistant to Captain Berick, who was the chief military censor under Colonel Tod.

Chorlian was somewhat vague about the conversation with Henderson, or at least hesitant in telling me about it. But it seems that my presence was resented at the press conference, that only one CBS man will be allowed in Cairo, that only one can broadcast or be accredited to the British forces.

I telephoned Berick to learn the exact circumstances.

"I understand my presence at the conference caused some concern today."

"Oh, not exactly concern," Berick said, "but we've had no word about you from P.R." (Public Relations)

"I checked in with P.R. last Friday," I said. "If you want me to I'll check in again and have them fill out another card for me."

"That seems to be P.R.'s fault then for not notifying us."

"Well," I said, "you tell me what formalities must be followed and I'll be happy to comply."

"As a matter of fact," Berick then said, "we can only have one man accredited."

"That's perfectly all right with CBS. I presume you mean that we can have one man accredited to the forces and one not, but both able to broadcast out of here. I thought the British wanted news of the Middle East pouring into America."

"Of course," Berick said, "we're anxious to have news out of here."

"If you're anxious for that, then we must have two men. I've been ordered here because CBS considers Cairo an important news spot of great interest to the American people. Suppose," I suggested, "I am accredited to the British forces and I'm out in the desert for five or six days away from a broadcasting transmitter. Who is to report the news from Cairo for us?"

"I can't deal with personal problems," Berick retorted. "All I can say is that only one man from an organization can be accredited."

"Captain Berick, I can't see your point. CBS only wants one man accredited as a war correspondent with the British forces. That is where I am to fit in. But we want two men, Chorlian and myself, to be able to broadcast from Cairo."

"Well, I suggest you talk to Colonel Astley at P.R."

I couldn't determine whether I was barred from conferences or what my status was. But I had a good sample of the mentality of Captain Berick and thereupon began collecting some material on him.

The information was meager but illuminating. He came of a wealthy family, the proper school and had lived in Japan for some time. He spoke Japanese.

Here is some Berickiana:

On the very day I talked with Berick about attending press conferences, Dick Mowrer of the *Chicago Daily News* had engaged in a furious argument with him.

Sunday's communiqué said: "Tomorrow the Duke of Aosta is expected to surrender."

Tomorrow, of course, would be Monday. Mowrer's story would be printed in Chicago Monday morning, so he therefore began his story: "The Duke of Aosta is expected to surrender today . . ." thus conforming to the time when the story would appear in America.

Berick struck out the word "today" in Dick's story and made it read "tomorrow" as the communiqué said. Dick patiently explained that the story would appear in Chicago on Monday and therefore the story, if left as the communiqué said, meant that Aosta would surrender on Tuesday.

When he finished the explanation, Berick said flatly, "I'm not interested in newspapers." And he refused to allow the one word change.

Dick was so disgusted—it was not his first experience with Berick— that he sent off a cable to his home office asking for his recall.

Every newspaperman and broadcaster in Cairo had experiences with Berick. The *Christian Science Monitor* correspondent submitted a story when General Wavell's forces, the previous January, were wiping out

Marshal Graziani's army in Libya. One line in the story said: "General Berganzoli, nicknamed 'Electric Beard,' took asylum in Bengasi."

Berick struck out the sentence. "Now you know very well," he said, "there is no asylum in Bengasi."

Another correspondent cabled a story. In cablese, the customary way to express "as well as" is to telescope the phrase into the single word "wells," thus paying for one word instead of three.

To the correspondent who used that word Berick said: "Now you know very well that you are not permitted to mention sources of water supply in the desert."

And one day Berick proudly and stiffly said to a group of correspondents: "I'm not a newspaperman—thank God."

Berick certainly wasn't, or much of anything else, except a baffled soul wandering around with a swagger stick.

THE VERANDAHS OF CAIRO

Tuesday, May 20th:

Dinner tonight out at Alexander Kirk's, with Ed Angly, Hal Denny and Ralph Bain, the Middle East representative of the American Red Cross.

Kirk reiterated that, if we could continue to get across one grain of information, we were doing the essential job of informing the American public.

I agreed that the fight to tell America the story was just starting. After all, I had not yet submitted a script for censorship.

"I've had enough of it," Angly said to Kirk, "and nothing you can say is going to change my mind. I'm pulling out."

Denny was non-committal. He had been in Moscow seven years as successor to Walter Duranty, and iron censorship was not new to him.

"I'll pitch in now," I told Angly, "just as you did. As each new man comes along he'll pitch in and eventually we'll wear them down."

"Go ahead," Angly said. "I've done my share."

The battle for Crete is now on. Germans sent over 1,800 parachutists yesterday. Still no word from White whether I'm to broadcast out of here or not. I have a stiff neck that hurts like hell.

Angly and I ate dinner in my room in our shorts while the sweat rolled down. Angly is still grousing about the whole reportorial set-up here and what difficulties I'll find. "Maybe so, but I've got to find them out for myself."

Frank Gervasi came up to see me. He was chief of the INS bureau in Rome and my boss there for a time until he went back to America and I took over the bureau. Now he's with *Collier's Magazine* and doing a good job. He's an energetic reporter.

Thursday, May 22nd:

Paul White cabled me that he's trying to arrange my assignment to the B.E.F. and meantime suggests that I go on the air twice weekly. Finally, I know where I stand

33

I've been telling Colonel Tod that I want to dramatize the war. I want, if possible, to make the farmers in Kansas, who are 1,500 miles from salt water, see and feel the desert sand, to understand what Suez means.

Tod smiled and said nothing. I explained what I wanted to do to Angly, and it was a mistake. Angly thereafter always introduced me to people: "This is the man who came out here to dramatize the war."

I have been working for the past two days on lining up communications for broadcasting from unusual points. Now we can only operate out of Cairo by broadcasting to London, which relays the transmission to CBS in New York by short wave, and it immediately goes on the network.

Major Sinclair tells me there isn't much chance of transmissions from Palestine and the Western Desert. Sinclair remarked that to "broadcast from the desert you would have to have your own transmitter."

That suggests something. Why not get our own mobile transmitter? What could be better than to give a broadcast right from the battlefront in the desert while the battle was going on? That is the way radio must cover this war.

I've found out about a transmitter which is not being used. It could be mounted on a truck; I could broadcast from the field to Cairo, which would then "kick it across" to London, which, in turn, would send the broadcast to CBS in New York.

I've dashed off an airmail letter to New York with this grandiose scheme—a mobile transmitter so we can broadcast during the fighting as we move directly into action. I estimate the cost at about $5,000.

I wrote to Paul: "Perhaps CBS can send the units from New York. Send two because one or both probably will get shot up."

I sat down with Colonel Tod and explained the project. Tod listened patiently and then said: "You can't do it." I asked why not. He said it never had been done before.

"Well," I said, "that has nothing to do with it. Those broadcasts can dramatize the war as it has never been done before. You want American help. This will get it."

"Oh, come now, Brown," Tod said, "I can't let you broadcast from out there without censorship, and I can't provide every correspondent with a censor in the field."

"You don't have to do that. CBS is the only outfit which wants a censor. Newspaper correspondents cable their stuff and, so far as I know, NBC hasn't thought of a mobile transmitter. So you just have one censor to worry about. Moreover, if CBS invests $10,000 in this idea, we are entitled to some special consideration."

"I can't give a censor to every correspondent that comes in here with some idea."

"Let me put it this way. I don't have the transmitter yet. I don't know what CBS thinks of the idea. If tomorrow I drove up in front of this building and told you I have a mobile transmitter, a driver and engineer and I'm all ready to move into the desert, and asked you for a censor to go along, could you provide him?"

Tod smiled broadly and extended his hand. "All right, Brown, when you drive up with the transmitter I'll give you a censor." We shook hands.

I never heard from Paul White on that idea, which is still a dream, but which we may find a reality as Americans at home demand direct reports from our fighting fronts.

Friday, May 23rd:

Dinner tonight on the Continental Roof with Dick and Rosamond Mowrer, Gervasi, Angly and Jan Yindrick, of *United Press,* who has just come out of Tobruk. Yindrick is due to go home for a vacation. He needs it after two months of that pounding at Tobruk. He's nervous and his eyes flap up and down.

My eyes flapped, too. The belly dancer who entertains on the Roof is terrific.

Saturday, May 24th:

Early this morning at American Legation and saw Jimmy Roosevelt. He's just back from Iraq, where he almost got bumped off by Iraq planes. He's a regular guy, not a stuffed shirt, and I like him. Asked him to go on the air for an interview but he turned it down, and said he had been forbidden to do that by military authorities.

I pointed out that he had given a newspaper interview and what was

35

the difference between that and expressing his views over the air—for CBS exclusively.

"The military authorities told me specifically," Jimmy said, "that I was not to broadcast."

The British communications officials have just granted me permission to broadcast and so has the Egyptian State Broadcasting, and I am scheduled for tomorrow night. Now all I need is a good story.

Another talk at Shepheard's Hotel with Jimmy Roosevelt. He doesn't think the British will be able to hold Crete.

"The British have beaten back attempts at sea landings but their ships are taking a heavy beating. How long that can go on is pretty uncertain. The Germans have complete air domination and apparently enough boats to attempt two and three sea landings."

He paints a pretty black picture of the situation as a whole. I asked him if the British could hold the Germans if they started a drive in the Western Desert.

"It would be very difficult at the moment," he says.

With Roosevelt is Major Gerald C. Thomas of the U. S. Marines, a hard-bitten veteran who has sharp eyes. He draws this picture: Hitler must be contained in the net of Norway, Gibraltar and Suez.

"Germany," Thomas says, "must be held within this net until the U. S. can supply Britain's needs."

Jimmy Roosevelt gave the definite impression that he intends to give a fairly realistic picture to his father of the situation out here—shortage of man power and equipment, shortages bordering on the critical; stories of British courage and British inefficiency, too.

Sunday, May 25th:

Scheduled to make my first broadcast tonight and was scrambling around for news when a special press conference was called. Colonel J. S. Blunt, the liaison officer with King George II in Crete, told of the parachute invasion of Crete and how the King escaped. It was a vivid, dramatic story of great length.

As soon as the conference was over I started writing the story in the insufferably hot room, and the sweat poured off my face. I was scheduled to speak only three minutes and I had material for at least a ten-minute broadcast. The great difficulty was compressing the story into

36

a brief period, and I settled on four minutes. The script passed the censors without a change.

Just before I went on the air early in the morning, I asked Murrow in London, in a cue channel talk, if he could give me a minute of his time. London went on the CBS network just before Cairo.

"It's a pretty good story, Ed," I told him, "and worth the time."

"Well, all right then, I'll lop off a minute here."

I gave this broadcast: "This is Cairo.

"The dramatic details of the German parachute invasion of Crete and how the King of Greece escaped into the hills while Nazi parachutists were shooting at him was told to me tonight.

"The vivid eyewitness story came from Colonel J. S. Blunt, British Military Attaché. Blunt was assigned to protect King George II and his entourage. The King and the Greek Government are now here in Egypt.

"Here's the first eyewitness account of the parachute invasion of Crete. Early on Tuesday morning several squadrons of German Messerschmitts roared over the King's house. It was situated on a commanding hill southwest of Canea. The King ran out of the house to see the sight, followed by his cousin, Prince Peter, and the Prime Minister.

"A few minutes later scores of Junkers, Heinkels and Stukas came over, bombing the coast and the outskirts of Canea. Then, out of the smoke of bombardment and out of the sun, came a tremendous force of airplanes, and the King and his party dived for shelter trenches.

"They had no more than tumbled into the trenches when gliders soared over the King's house, circled around with their invaders at 300 feet altitude. Some of the troops came down at the bottom of the hill 300 yards away.

"In another few moments, directly behind the procession of gliders, came a tremendous chain of monster aircraft, fat things flying at 200 feet—and carrying troops.

"As the King, from his shelter, peered up at this mammoth parade of troop-carrying aircraft, the sky suddenly filled with parachutes. They were all red and green, so thick they almost blotted out the blue sky and white clouds.

"The parachutists came down with tommy guns in their hands,

37

their belts bulging with hand grenades. A great number of parachutes failed to open. And those Nazi troopers came down like stones, screaming—and their screams suddenly ending in a thin red or green bundle of silk half buried in the ground.

"Not far from the King, around the Suda Bay area, for more than four hours Greek and British troops sitting in the olive groves picked off the parachutists like sitting ducks. But many of them came down safely and went into action.

"The whole area from the King's house to Suda Bay was a mass of red and green parachutes in the air, and hand-to-hand dog fights on the ground. Scores of German aircraft of all kinds kept coming over.

"Some of the Nazis came down 800 yards from the King. A platoon of New Zealanders and twenty Greek gendarmes took up defense positions to stave off the expected attack on the Greek King.

"The King and his party were urged to get away before the house was surrounded. As they started from the house, parachutists came down on the road they were starting to take. New Zealand troops opened fire on the parachutists at 800 yards.

"The British colonel led the King straight over the mountain. They clambered and scrambled straight up 1,500 feet, diving in bushes every five or ten yards. Hundreds of airplanes roared over them, strafing and bombing.

"The King, grinning, called out to the British colonel: 'This jumping into bushes is such a bore.'

"Before that day was over the King and his party climbed a mountain 8,000 feet high. He made his escape just in time. The Germans occupied the King's house that afternoon.

"And while the King climbed that mountain, the Germans made two apparent mistakes. They sent down parachutists with triple the usual arms at Alikiamou where 3,000 Italian prisoners were being kept. The idea was to arm the Italians. So far as we know here, the Italians did not participate in the fighting for one reason or another.

"The second mistake was to release all prisoners in a Greek jail. These men, in striped suits, were armed by the Germans, and the prisoners immediately turned—and fought the Germans.

"Tonight we have the report that Canea, Retimo and Heraklion have been subject to mass dive-bombing attacks similar to the one the Germans carried out against Rotterdam. For six hours the Nazi raiders

38

poured down bombs on the residential and shopping districts of the
three towns in Crete."

(There was a repercussion from that broadcast. In November at
Singapore I received a cable that for that first report of mine from
Cairo, Sigma Delta Chi, the honorary journalistic fraternity, had given
me the award for the best radio report from abroad in 1941.)

Wednesday, May 28th:
The incredible tragedy of Crete is beginning to unfold. The official
communiqués are vague and unsubstantial and the British are not yet
ready to admit it is a disaster. But it is. The conversations on the verandahs at Shepheard's and the Continental are soaked in pessimism.

But the air of gaiety of Cairo continues unabated. All day officers
come and go and sit sipping their whiskies.

On the table is the officer's swagger stick, in his left hand is a fly
swish. This is a stick with a bunch of horse hair eighteen inches long
which you wave to keep the flies off your bare knees and arms. There
are a good many officers out here who don't want to be disturbed by the
war.

Very happy to read in the *Egyptian Mail* today a story from London
quoting Martha's article on Italy in *Collier's Magazine.*

Took Dick and Rosamond Mowrer to see *Gone with the Wind.*
Wish Martha could have been with me. Heartbreak then was no
greater than heartbreak today.

Finished the article on Yugoslavia for the *Saturday Evening Post*
after working ten days on it. It was very hard to do. This place takes
every ounce of energy out of a person. Took the article over to the
censors, got it approved, airmailed two copies by separate routes and
a third copy I'm sending back with Angly when he goes in a few days.
One of the three copies ought to get through.

Thursday, May 29th:
Tonight some of the correspondents met with a few of the American
military men in Cairo. We have a number of observers here but it is all
hush-hush business, like almost everything else in this war.

At the dinner there were Captain Jimmy Roosevelt, Major Gerald C.
Thomas, Brigadier General Rowell of the Marines, Captain Darr,

39

Commander Watkins, who is a submarine expert attached to the British fleet but is due to return to Washington soon. Among the correspondents were Ed Kennedy, of *AP,* John S. Martin of *Time,* Ed Angly, Frank Gervasi, Bob Low of *Liberty Magazine,* Sam Brewer, and Kenneth Downs of *International News Service.*

It was a private-discussion business that turned into an alarm-and-despondency affair. Some of the views expressed by the military and naval men and correspondents were:

In six or eight weeks American material would be rolling in and there was a chance to hold the Middle East.

The Middle East is a step-child of the British war effort.

Political interference has played hell with many military plans.

The shortage of war materials is appalling. Scores of pilots are without aircraft to fly.

One of the officers who has just come over from Washington says the American public has no conception of British difficulties here.

Those of the correspondents who were busy trying to improve the censorship snorted at that. They said the British are busy hiding every reasonable report on how much American aid is needed, and how vital this part of the world is.

The American officer says the people back home think that British convoys still go through the Mediterranean, and they fail to appreciate that the Middle East must be preserved.

Everyone at the meeting agreed there's no question of the courage of the British. In the face of the greatest odds, they go into battle without hesitation. That is what's so heartbreaking. These boys and men die with such courage.

Sunday, June 1st:
In the broadcast I gave late tonight I said: "The Germans tonight are in full control of the island of Crete. A few thousand New Zealand and Greek troops lie dead on those picturesque mountainsides. Several thousand Nazi parachutists have floated down from the skies for the last time. Fifteen thousand British troops are back in Egypt—and the fiercest fighting of this war, the battle of Crete, is over."

Another war is ended, too. The fighting in Iraq. Crete took the attention away from that dangerous situation which required a month to clear up. Officially the British say that Iraq is now quiet, but I have

40

other information which I prefer to believe but cannot report, that there is still guerrilla fighting going on.

In writing my broadcast tonight I thought there might be mention of the British navy in connection with the Crete operations. I asked the clerk at the censor's office to see Captain Ennals, the navy censor.

It was then 6:45 P.M. The clerk replied: "Captain Ennals is only here from 11:30 to 12:30 and from 5:30 to 6:30. He left fifteen minutes ago."

"Well," I said, "I heard there's a war going on around here. Is there any truth to that report?"

"Oh, yes," the clerk said in all seriousness, "that's true. But if you want the naval censor now you'll find him at the Turf Club. At 6:30 every day he goes there to play bridge."

At Cairo, if you submitted a script to a naval censor you could have it censored only during two hours a day, if you wanted it passed. I seldom mentioned the British navy. There are four separate censorships, the Army, Navy, Air Force and Civil censorships. Britishers employed by the Egyptian Government were the most co-operative.

I submitted stories to British censors in bed, while they played billiards, while they were at dinner. Only a few times with each one, because the moment of reckoning always came when I was told: "Here, here, now, I can't always be disturbed by these stories."

Wednesday, June 4th:
Cable from Martha to prepare immediately a 10,000-word outline of a book and sample chapter. I don't feel very much up to writing a book. Besides, this war is just getting under way. I have never felt so despondent and dispirited as I have since I've been in Cairo. I don't seem to be getting any work done. Mostly I think about getting home.

Doctor today said my blood pressure is very low. I'm getting injections for typhoid and typhus, taking a tonic and also cough medicine for the cold I picked up in Turkey.

I think the remark of Heinrich Heine is apt at this moment. In the midst of his greatest pains he refused to see the doctor.

"I am done with doctors!" he cried. "I note that everyone who died in this town last year had medical attendance." I feel that way, too.

Chat with Colonel Fellowes, the American Military Attaché here.

41

He says: "It's stupid to count on the stupidity of the enemy, the weather or the idea the enemy cannot do certain things. Some of that mentality still exists around here, but Wavell doesn't have it."

Most of the correspondents are going off to Palestine tomorrow. A censorship office has been opened in Jerusalem. Evidently the British are getting ready to go into Syria. I cannot go to cover the story because I am not yet accredited to the British forces as a war correspondent. But somehow I have a hunch news is about to break in the Western Desert.

Sunday, June 8th:
This was an extremely hectic day, and I must have sweated off ten pounds which I don't have to sweat off. Last night, over at the censor's office, while getting my script through and when all the other correspondents had gone, a call came in suddenly from GHQ that there would be a press conference at 9:30 this morning.

Very early this morning, at 1:50 A.M., just before I went on the air, I heard the technical director in London tell the Cairo engineer: "BBC will take anything at any time Sunday from the Free French."

That remark, placed alongside the sudden calling of the press conference at the unusual time of 9:30 A.M., Sunday, immediately suggested that Syria was popping, since it was obvious the Free French would play a large part in the Syria campaign.

As soon as I finished my broadcast on the third floor of the communications building, I went to the ground floor and sent off a cable to White suggesting he schedule me for a broadcast as soon as the network opened Sunday morning, that is, between 4:30 and 5:30 Sunday afternoon, Cairo time.

White came through very fast and gave me a show at 4:56. The only censor available Sunday afternoon was Colonel Tod and I found him at GHQ. On most occasions when I have gone over Berick's head to Tod to get a script passed, he has approved it.

Tod has a certain trust and faith in the correspondents, which most of the other censors do not. Besides, Tod is smart enough to know how invaluable American correspondents can be in telling the story of the British to the American people, something most of the other censors ignore or forget about.

What counts with Tod is not being officious, or throwing his weight around, or grinding some kind of a personal axe, or even trying to win promotion. All Tod wants to do is everything that might help win this war.

All this scurrying around didn't do much good today. Just before I went on, Ed Murrow reported from London and he had everything I had, since all the communiqués issued in Cairo are released simultaneously from London.

The story Murrow and I both told can be summed up in a sentence: "British and Free French forces crossed from Palestine into Syria at two o'clock this morning."

Between my two Sunday broadcasts, had dinner this evening at a restaurant alongside the Nile with Rosamond Mowrer, Miss Gaster, who works for the *Egyptian Mail,* and David Woodward of the *London News Chronicle.* Dick Mowrer is up in Palestine covering the Syria show. Miss Gaster knows all about Egyptian politics, and is crammed with information about Cairo. A very good source. Woodward I knew from Rome. He's been covering the British fleet out of Alexandria and came down here for a few days.

We sat there, under a moon as big around as a washtub, beside the soft Nile, eating pigeon and watermelon and talking about nothing I find reason to record in this journal.

I am still convinced, from scraps of information I've picked up from officers this week, that the German drive in the Western Desert is about to start. There's just one flaw in the picture at the moment, and it has me worried. The British censors are allowing me to say too readily that the Germans are about to start the drive. That attitude may possibly mean that it is the British who are planning to take the offensive. Anyway, I'm suspicious. But I don't know what they will use except maybe wheelbarrows.

In the past week I've read Lowell Thomas' *With Lawrence in Arabia,* H. C. Armstrong's *Lord of Arabia,* the career of Ibn Saud of Saudi Arabia, and books on Egyptian history and the natives.

This area goes back to Biblical times, and it's going to be necessary to be familiar enough with it to toss into stories allusions and references to ancient history and the history of the last war.

43

Tuesday, June 10th:

Just a year ago today Italy entered the war. Martha and I stood in *Piazza Venezia* and listened to Il Duce make the speech from the balcony of *Palazzo Venezia*. Then I had three broadcasts in one night.

Mussolini finished his talk at 6:25 P.M. and I was on the air at 8:30. There was a great deal of confusion and heartache around the *Ministero Culture Popolare* and I remember I began that first broadcast: "Mussolini tonight sent the Italian people into war. The Italian people did not want this war."

That was true that night; it was so true that I tried to repeat those two sentences in the two subsequent broadcasts but by then the censors had recovered their breath and poise, and they blue-pencilled them.

A good deal has happened since then to Italy, and to everyone else. The fighting is just about over in Ethiopia and the Fascists have lost Eritrea and Italian Somaliland. The British hold nearly forty Italian generals and tens of thousands of prisoners. Some of them are here in Egypt and others have been moved eastward to India.

And Martha is in New York, and I'm sick with lonesomeness and sick of being stuck out here. Having to stay in Cairo is the hardest thing. I feel I'm accomplishing nothing, and if I could go to Syria or out into the desert and get my teeth into a real story I might feel better.

With Miss Gaster today I went to a port on the Nile where much of the grain comes into the city. She carries a Leica and I have the Plaubel Makina I bought in Bucharest. It is a fine German camera, almost too professional for me, but I miss my Contax. I prefer a 35 mm for one thing, and then, too, that camera seemed to be a part of me.

I've worried a good deal whether the Contax got back home all right. I turned it over to Minister Lane in Belgrade to take back to the States. The Germans were shooting anyone in Belgrade found with a camera, except diplomats, and I then decided that being practical would be more profitable than being sentimental. Now, here in Cairo though I wasn't so sure.

I am keenly interested in getting good close-ups, especially of Egyptian children, and it was a hectic job. About forty young "Gyppies" crowded around and hemmed us in at every step, crying *"Baksheesh, Baksheesh."* I passed out a piastre or two as fast as I could to get the pictures, but before it could be done, more kids leaped into

44

the scene. Miss Gaster finally tried an end run that drew off some of the youngsters and I snapped two or three pictures.

Coming back into town, we stopped off at the railroad station. Scores and scores of Egyptians were on flat railroad cars—evacuees from Alexandria. The port and naval base had been bombed, twice in the past week, and tens of thousands of the natives were moving inland.

These people, some brownish-hued Arabs, others shiny, black-faced Senegalese with sweat streaming down their faces, are part of a migration that will change the nature of Egyptian cities. They are going back to native villages they came from years ago. This is a back-to-the-land movement instigated by Axis bombs.

Wednesday, June 11th:
My energy is at an extremely low ebb and so is my initiative. Greatly regret that I'm not covering this advance into Syria because it would make a cracker-jack story and would be a great historical experience. But there is still no word from London whether I am to be accredited.

The Syrian campaign is infuriating me. The news is very scarce, and, little as it is, too much is being covered up. I tried to indicate as much in my broadcast. I said: "The British advance into Syria is proceeding at a very slow rate, and under generally mysterious circumstances. The British, Australian, Indian and Free French forces are encountering some resistance along the entire front."

Again I tried to say that there was fighting going on, but could not. I could only use the word "resistance." The British want to present the picture that the Vichy French are offering only vocal resistance to the penetration. Actually, there is very sharp fighting going on.

Over here you seem cut off from everything and your work seems very insignificant. You report your story into a microphone and that's the last you hear of it. I've had no mail from Martha and no word from New York about anything.

Rosamond Mowrer today very cutely showed me the radio bulletin of a Japanese ship on which she and Dick crossed from Brazil to Capetown some months ago. One paragraph in the bulletin said: "Rome 1-4—Cecil Brown, American correspondent from Columbia Broadcasting System, prohibited broadcast to United States effective today allegedly for his continuous anti-Italian utterances."

The Japs should have said, "anti-Italian hisses."

Friday, June 13th:

Dinner tonight on the Metropolitan roof with Eve Freidenreich, who works at the Egyptian State Broadcasting. She's a Pole, born in France, educated in Switzerland and has been here five years. She speaks Polish, French, and German perfectly, but her English is a bit weak. She is terribly discontented here, but there is nowhere she can go. The British Internal Security has been watching her. Some of her German friends are in internment camps and she has gone to visit them too often. I told her so.

We walked along the Nile in the bright moonlight but it was a good deal the case of an unhappy girl telling of her unhappiness, disillusionment and confusion in a troubled world.

The night was beautiful and the Nile quiet and soft, and it was good to hear the ripple of a girl's laughter once again. Besides, Eve gave me a good item. She said the anti-Nazi internees and the pro-Nazi Germans whom the British have interned are constantly fighting and have now been separated.

She also found out when going to the German internment camps that every time the air-raid sirens go, the Nazi internees put on their boots, which they do not wear otherwise. They think each air raid means the raiders are coming to liberate them and they want to have good boots to wear when they walk away—free men. If I know Germans, and I do, they want to use those boots to kick English faces.

I saw red at the press conference today. Colonel Tod, in discussing the communiqué on the Syrian campaign, said: "Now here is the line we want you to take in your stories . . ."

Not even Fascists ever dared to tell American correspondents what "line" they were to take. It impressed me as the height of stupidity to suggest to American correspondents that they were to take a certain slant in their stories.

I don't know how the other correspondents feel about it, but my job here, as I see it, is to report the war on its facts and to report those facts up to the hilt without giving actual military information to the enemy.

Saturday, June 14th:

This was one of the most pleasant and restful days I have had in years.

46

Miss Gaster had arranged for me to get a *felucca,* a small sailing boat, and we went together on a picture-taking junket up the Nile. We had a good boatman, and a comfortable vessel.

At 12:30 we pulled into the bank and went ashore, walking about a half mile inland to get to the village of Sekil. A native woman was driving two bullocks round and round in a circle threshing wheat. The bullocks became excited by my taking a picture, low to the ground to get them outlined against the bright, blue sky, and ran away. The woman driving the bullocks was angry, but the crowd of natives watching the scene only laughed.

When we came back to the boat, beached at the bank of the Nile, our young boatman was talking to a girl of about fifteen, just emerging into womanhood. They were extremely photogenic. They stood about six feet apart talking, and I asked them to move closer together so as to frame them in the picture. They moved three feet closer, but no farther. The girl bashfully explained to Gaster, who speaks this lingo, that if they were closer than three feet there would be a scandal and her father would beat her.

Sunday, June 15th:
A heavy battle with the censors on the script tonight. I began the script with: "The British now realize that operations on a major scale must be carried out for the conquest of Syria."

After a half hour of discussion on that sentence, we finally compromised on: "Some observers here believe that operations on a major scale might have to be carried out for the conquest of Syria."

Another passage originally read: "The British and Free French forces until now have been offering one hand of friendship to the Vichy French and with the other firing guns and dropping bombs. One hand seems to have neutralized the other and there's no doubt that Syria is a two-handed job."

I fought long and insistently to retain those sentences, and finally in mutual exhaustion, I had to agree on a phrasing which changed the entire meaning I wished to convey: "The British and Free French forces until now have been offering the hand of friendship to the Vichy French in Syria."

When I went on the air, I eliminated that sentence. Then I went on to report that: "Generals Wilson and Catroux have drawn up their

47

forces for what's hoped will be the final, overwhelming squeeze against General Dentz. The picture we get here is this: The British have been hoping that Vichy would see, as it's expressed here, the goodness of the British motives for the penetration. In fact, up to this moment, the British are still attempting to negotiate the surrender of the Vichy French.

"Reports reaching here indicate that neither Vichy nor General Dentz have nibbled at the latest attempts to secure a general French surrender or even the evacuation of Damascus.

"And so the current act of big brother spanking naughty brother may be just about over. The spirit of this-hurts-me-more-than-it-does-you is toughening up.

". . . Tonight's high-command communiqué reports Allied forces are now in contact along the whole front with Vichy troops. That's military phraseology meaning there's fighting along the entire front extending from Sidon on the coast through the mountains near Metulla and Djejzine and to the outskirts of Damascus."

That was the first time I was able to use the word "fighting," in a script dealing with Syria. I buried it in the script and it was overlooked.

Captain Berick admitted that the material contained in the original script was correct. He said to the other censor: "Brown is perfectly right in what he says about our now realizing we have to carry out major operations, but we can't permit it. There's been stiff fighting going on, but that can't be said, either."

Berick told me those were the Commander-in-Chief's orders. I told him that Britain's stock was at its highest in America at the moment, "just because for once you people showed initiative. Secretary Hull's denunciation of Vichy shows how we feel about collaborators with the Nazis. The Americans right now feel you ought to go into Syria as though you meant to teach the French their lesson.

"Because of your restrictions on news," I added, "the United States is getting its news about Syria from the boys in Ankara. They are using the reports from General Dentz's headquarters in Beirut. And the impressions they get from those reports is that you people can't even beat the French in Syria."

"Well, that isn't the case," Berick said.

"What does that have to do with it?" I demanded. "The news on Syria that is getting the play in America comes from Beirut, via Ankara.

The farmer in our Middle West wants a better picture, a more honest picture, of the Middle East, and I'm talking to those farmers."

"Your American farmer," Berick said, "is undoubtedly of very great importance, as you say, but," Berick smiled wryly, "he must be sacrificed for the plan for the Syria affair."

Monday, June 16th:
The British and not the Germans have started an offensive in the Western Desert.

The President of the United States has closed all German consulates as well as the German Library of Information, the German travel agency and the Transocean News Agency. Extremely serious step! And just following after freezing of Axis credits, it is bound to have extensive repercussions. The fat most certainly is in the fire.

Had a silver identification disk made today. At least I might get a decent burial.

Tuesday, June 17th:
Cable from Ed Murrow in London:
OKAY. YOU ARE NOW ACCREDITED TO BRITISH FORCES. MIDDLE EAST. GOOD LUCK.

I immediately shot a wire to Paul White asking whether he wanted me to go to the desert or to Syria. I told Major Oakshot at Public Relations I wanted to go to the desert at once. He said perhaps I would be able to go on Friday. We compromised on Thursday. I filled out six questionnaires to complete the paper work as a war correspondent. The British Empire is not responsible if I get killed.

Hustled about all afternoon, buying kit, small stove, provisions, cans of soup and fruit, camp bed and sleeping roll.

Wednesday, June 18th:
Paul cabled telling me to go to Syria for the fall of Damascus. I was surprised because I thought he'd want the desert show covered. Syria was a better story.

Lugging my new tin hat, camp equipment and food, I just made the train to Jerusalem.

49

These British are amazing. I think they have more courage than any country has a right to expect from its men. Tonight in the dining car I ran into Lieutenant Commander Evans of the destroyer *Kelly*. It was commanded by Lord Louis Mountbatten, and Evans told me how the destroyer went down in the Crete battle.

"We got a direct hit on the afterdeck from a Stuka. We turned around in a circle and then turned over completely in half a minute. Upside down." Evans laughed. "I was in the engine room. An air bubble formed and the water was only four feet deep. I dove out and swam away until I was picked up. We lost more than fifty percent of our men."

Evans rubbed his chin. "It was most unfortunate. The doctor was giving me typhoid shots and he went down, so I never got my typhoid shots finished."

Thursday, June 19th:

I detrained at Lydda and waited for an hour and a half in the hot sun on the platform for a train to take me to Jerusalem. Most of the troops there were Indians on their way to Syria, but I did see a number of Englishmen whose Cockney and Lancashire accents were almost as difficult for me to understand as Hindu.

At Jerusalem I went immediately to the King David Hotel and found the Public Relations Office where I presented my movement order. Major Alban wore a patch over one eye and was very friendly and vague about everything. I found in the P.R. office some of my old friends from the Cairo office, Captains Jolliffe and Cumberbatch. Alban said he had a car going at three that afternoon—it was now 1:15 —and then none again going to Syria until Sunday.

I was in a quandary because General Sir Henry Maitland Wilson had broadcast an ultimatum to General Henri Dentz to give up Damascus at 5:30 A.M. this morning and to declare it an "open city" to save its destruction. I toyed with the idea of staying in Jerusalem until 5:30 P.M. when the answer was to be announced. Thereby I would get the first break on the story of the British being able to march into Damascus unopposed, or the story that the British would have to fight their way into Damascus. I could get the story out first, because the correspondents at the front had to send their stories back to Jerusalem by a dispatch rider. But I knew if I stayed in Jerusalem to cover that story, one way or the other, there would be no car again for three days that would take me up to the front.

A casual remark dropped by Jolliffe made me suspicious that General Dentz had refused General Wilson's demand, and that the Vichy French would fight to hold Damascus. Censors are charged with the duty of being close-mouthed, but Jolliffe, an old friend of mine, put it to me this way: "What do you want to stay around Jerusalem for? It's pretty hot and there isn't much news here."

That was Jolliffe's way of saying that the British were going to have to fight their way into Damascus, and that's where the story would be.

With Captains Huband and Mostyn-Owen I pushed off for Haifa. Huband had been in the Irak show and was going up into Syria as a conducting officer for correspondents. Mostyn-Owen was going to Haifa to take charge of the Censor's office soon to be established there.

We drove into Nazareth, and there on the main street of the ancient Biblical town we found Andy Glarner, an English correspondent, and Lumby of the *London Times* whom I had known in Rome until he was expelled. Leonard Mosley of the *London Daily Sketch* was there and Ted Gennock, a Paramount News cameraman. They said a press conference was about to start and we trooped into the GHQ at Nazareth, located in the same old convent where the Germans quartered their GHQ in the last war.

Colonel Wills showed us the confidential operational maps disclosing the exact positions of the British Imperial Forces and the enemy. Colonel Wills, a calm, cool and capable Australian, didn't call them the enemy, however. He always described them as Vichy French, as though it were one word.

That conversation with Colonel Wills gave me a picture of the utter tragedy of this kind of war—a picture that was never eliminated and has not been to this day. He said that the Vichy French and Free French each attacking in woods, or ditches, or hills, were calling to each other across "no man's land." The Vichy French called, "Why fight your own people?" and the Free French replied, "We're not fighting you, only want to drive out the Germans to prevent them conquering you." Then the Free French would retort, "Why be scabs? Come over on our side." And the conversation would end with a burst of fire from both sides, men from the same regiment firing on each other.

We came into Haifa at sundown and I wrote a story. My story, for the first time since I had been covering this war, told of the very severe fighting, and of the very strong Vichy French resistance. At Haifa, where I decided to spend the night, I found Alan Moorehead of the *London Daily Express,* who had come to Rome several times while I was there, and whom I had helped very greatly in getting stories out of Italy.

Alan and I sat down on the verandah of the hotel on Mount Carmel, overlooking the beautiful Bay of Haifa, watching one of those incredible sunsets that come so often to the Mediterranean area. Alan gave me a very compact and concise picture of the situation at the moment. The picture showed the British stopped outside Damascus.

THE WAR IN SYRIA

Syria was a terrific experience. It gave me my first real insight into the amazing ability of the British to commit one mistake after another— their incredible courage and how they fight with practically no equipment. After seeing the German way in Yugoslavia, I shuddered at the impact of a people who consider war a game of sport, and not an effort requiring a lust for murder and an overwhelming hate. Everything was so casual in Syria that I found more to pity than to censure.

My great worry was that I couldn't get to Damascus in time to witness its capture. Paul White's orders had been very specific:

SUGGEST YOU SYRIAWARD FOR FALL DAMASCUS.

Friday, June 20th:
Captain Huband and I drove into Safed. Captain Lamming, who was being relieved by Huband, was just finishing breakfast with A. C. Sedgwick of the *New York Times* and an English reporter. Lamming said that Damascus probably would fall that morning. I told Huband that we had to get off right away and make the 200 miles to Damascus. Lamming said that the quick way to get there was through Metulla but "there is some sniping on the road and you might get picked off."

I told Huband we would have to take our chances because I had been rushing madly for two days to get to Damascus and I meant to get there. We started out and down over the hill from Safed. We drove across a mined bridge extending over the Jordan. My first view of that famous river was a disappointment. It is a narrow stream about thirty feet wide, muddy and twisting.

"Why have they mined the bridge all the way back here?" I asked Captain Huband.

"Well," he said, "we must be prepared for retreat."

I was astonished that the British felt themselves so weak that they had prepared a retreat 200 miles to the rear of their present positions.

A few minutes later we drove through a customs gate between

Palestine and Syria at sixty miles an hour. It is ghostly to pass through an abandoned customs gate.

Within fifteen minutes we drew into a place called Queneitra. There were two Vichy tanks still burning alongside the road, and almost every one of the fifty houses in the town was half destroyed. Furious fighting had taken place here not many hours before. A battalion of Queens had been surprised by the Vichy French and almost wiped out.

We wandered around by an abandoned schoolhouse, and found where the Fusileers had made a hasty evacuation. Around the grounds of the schoolhouse there were scattered papers, ammunition, hand grenades and equipment, all the mute, disordered paraphernalia of retreat. Sedgwick and I kicked around the papers, careful not to kick a hand grenade.

Huband reached down and picked up a Warrant Book of the Queen's Regiment. He glanced through the book and recognized almost every name, men from his own battalion. Several names were crossed out, a notation beside them—"Dead." Huband grunted: "I see where so and so got it." He noted some of the men owed a mess bill of a couple pounds. "Just like that chap," Huband said, pointing to one name. "He always signed too many chits."

In kicking around through the papers and inanimate trash I turned over a book, pocket size and paper backed. It was: *I Found No Peace* by Webb Miller.

Colonel Haggard, in command of the forces which had retaken Queneitra, said we couldn't go on the direct route to Damascus because there were two French tanks running around up there and he could give us no protection to get through.

"I don't advise you to go an inch farther up this road," Colonel Haggard said. We took his advice.

We then sped away on another route to Sheik Majon. A soldier came by on a motorcycle and we stopped him and asked his report on the situation.

"I have just come down from a point eight miles outside Damascus. The city is going to fall this afternoon. We have been laying down a very heavy barrage. Only four tanks are holding us up."

I was infuriated that after all this rushing I still couldn't get to Damascus in time. There was a strong wind blowing and the heat was almost asphyxiating.

54

We drove through Kisweh up to the advance British position on the road into Damascus. This was the road that Colonel Lawrence—Lawrence of Arabia—had come up to take Damascus from the Germans and Turks. At this advance point, Sedgwick and I put on our tin hats and lay in the ditch and watched shiny black Senegalese moving Indian file across the flat terrain for the beginning of what the British expected to be a final assault on Damascus. I had made it in time.

I then moved warily up on a hillside and saw Damascus, the goal, for the first time. I came back ten miles behind the front to Ghabaghib, wrote my story in a tiny building crammed with Free French troops and correspondents, sent it back with a dispatch rider, and slept that night in the front seat of a car, bitterly cold. Our information was that some time the next day we would enter Damascus.

Saturday, June 21st:

In the pre-dawn light I came to Free French headquarters outside Kisweh. There were about eight correspondents in the party. Colonel Philibert Collet, the small, swarthy chief of the Circassian cavalry, came strolling out with a long cape and khaki scarf wound a half dozen times around his neck. He was dragging on a cigarette. One of the correspondents offered him a sip of whisky. He refused it, saying, "I await the sunrise for that."

Then another car came up with two more correspondents, and the conducting officer informed Colonel Collet they were reporters.

"*Mon dieu,*" the colonel exclaimed, "there are now enough correspondents here to capture Damascus!"

Damascus wasn't ready to be taken, yet. We moved up the main road—Henry Gorrell of the *United Press,* Ed Kennedy of the *Associated Press,* Sam Brewer of the *Chicago Tribune* and myself. We crept along in a ditch to the anti-tank gun, manned by four Senegalese. There were a number of units in the area. Some Free French, and some British. About a thousand feet ahead across an open field, the rat-tat-tat of machine gun and the dull thump of a mortar came from a wood lining the edge of that field and the road. Hank Gorrell said, "I guess this is where we stop." And we all agreed.

Obviously the road ahead was under machine-gun fire and the British advance could not continue up that road until the Vichy French had been wiped out of the area. On all sides of us, it seemed from all

55

directions, was the heavy rumble of the artillery. That entrance to Damascus was still closed off and when we went across four miles to another entrance, by way of Mezze, that road was also under fire, and so were we. On that front, too, the British were trying to fight with almost no equipment. A few twenty-five-pounder guns, men of the Leicester regiment and naked courage were all the British had.

We came back to Free French headquarters and a Vichy French aircraft came over. We all dived into ditches and watched the bombs dropping about a quarter mile away. A small stream about two feet wide flowed beside the headquarters, and there were several horses wading through the stream, and men were drinking the water. I scooped some up in a tin can and shaved.

From all I can gather here the advance is not going very well, and the Vichy resistance is much stronger than we expected. The most intriguing character here is Major Ferguson of the Black Watch Regiment. He is a Scot, but represents to me the Hollywood version of the Englishman, and seems like a character straight out of P. G. Wodehouse, who wrote of empty-headed people so much he became one of his own characters.

Ferguson is youthful-appearing, has a long straggly blond mustache, wears a monocle. The other day, with Hank Gorrell, he drove for three miles along a road under constant and insistent machine-gun fire. Ferguson wheeled the car at sixty miles an hour, reciting at the top of his voice the poetry of James Elroy Flecker. That was typical too—typical of the Englishman who doesn't know the meaning of fear.

Major Ferguson—Ferguson of the intrepid Black Watch—screws his monocle tighter into his left eye and squints up at the sun over Syria. "Thought I heard a plane," he says. "Sorry."

The mid-morning sun streams down and bounces back into our faces from the stone courtyard of this Beau Geste fort. We are just south of Kisweh, a few miles outside Damascus.

One wall of the fort shades a dozen Free French troops lolling in grotesque positions of exhaustion. Over in another corner are seven unshaven, crummy-looking Vichy French prisoners, some sprawled on the stones like lizards, others hunched over their knees.

They suck away at cigarettes, their eyes empty. The Vichy French captives have that curious expression that creeps over a man's face

56

when he figures nothing matters any more. And that is one of the most ghastly sights in the world.

Ferguson's wide, limpid mouth under his blond mustache flaps rapidly, outlining the strategy for the onslaught against Damascus, from three sides. The final attack, he assures me.

The confusion of preparation is in full swing. At least, it isn't the frenzied mix-up of retreats. General Paul Louis Le Gentilhomme comes out of a small room at the entrance to the fort and drifts through the stone, arched gateway on his short legs. A mincing walk, he has, almost Oriental.

Le Gentilhomme is director of Free French field operations in Syria, and his men are not doing very well. One arm is in a sling. A Vichy French plane came over the other day and dropped a bomb. The general fell and broke his arm.

Ferguson is called away. I go outside the walls to stand beside the road where General Allenby punched the way through the Turks twenty-five years ago to reach fabled Damascus. It doesn't seem fabled now. It is just a place to reach, and that with great difficulty. It is merely a place on the map to capture without shelling, without offending the natives.

No deed must destroy the propaganda slogan: "The British Imperial forces come not as conquerors but as liberators." A native grows very suspicious if you destroy his house and shoot him while he is being liberated.

Fifty feet on each side of the road ebony Senegalese, glistening with sweat, are padding in bare feet toward the front. They pay no heed to the stones, burrs, the sharp-edged, thorn-lined twigs. Their faded khaki coats are too tight, and dark with sweat in the back. Their cartridge belts are slung over shoulders and the muscled legs move like the pistons of a big, black locomotive just picking up speed. Some of the Senegalese carry rifles balanced on their heads. Others have taken off their hats and sweat is running through their shiny, corkscrew hair and rushing down their solemn faces. They do not have steel helmets.

"They won't hit anything," a voice says. "They're too polite." Ferguson is there. He appears to have aged five years in the ten minutes since I saw him.

"I've a bottle I've been saving for something or other," he says. "It

57

doesn't seem to matter very much now. Come on to my cubby. But there is no soda." We go in and sit down.

"Did you ever hear of a Scotsman becoming both personal and sentimental?" Ferguson asks. He doesn't expect an answer to that, because he adds: "To the French, our former allies." We toast the French.

"For four years I was stationed in Damascus. I was a liaison officer with the Free French in this campaign. I know every one of the officers over there." He waved his free hand in the general direction of Damascus. "They are my friends. I like them, they like me. I know just where the French officers are sitting at this moment planning how to resist our attack.

"The walls are a dark green and there's a picture of General Foch on the wall back of where General Dentz is sitting. I can picture that scene, because right up until the armistice I sat at a number of conferences just like it."

He stares at the glass in front of him for a moment, then idly reads the label on the bottle.

"I've just come now from talking with a French sergeant-pilot. We shot him down and he's rather badly hurt. D'you want to hear his story?" I nod.

"He was crying like a child as he told it to me. A captain and major were in the plane with him. He told me their names. I knew them well. Fine officers, gentlemen, courageous. The captain had been in French Morocco for several years. The major was with General Corap. You know, Corap who collapsed at that sector of the Meuse and let the Boche through to Sedan.

"Well, they were flying at about 1,500 feet and we hit them with our ack-ack." Major Ferguson smiled wryly, perhaps bitterly is a better word. "Yes, we actually hit them. At 1,500 feet. This sergeant-pilot shouted to the captain and the major to jump. He couldn't control the plane. He expressed it to me this way: 'My controls were gone, my controls were gone.' He seemed terribly puzzled that such a thing should happen.

"He told the officers: 'We're at 500 meters. Jump!' But the two officers wouldn't move. He kept calling to them, '300 meters. Jump! Jump!' Again at 200 meters he pleaded with them. And the next instant it was all over.

58

"Jove, it was damned uncomfortable to hear him tell it. Tears running down his face. Of course, the captain and major were dead when we got to the plane. This poor devil just lay there groaning. Don't know how he came out of it alive."

Major Ferguson anticipated my question. "Yes, I asked him that. Why not jump? Well, they didn't jump because they'd been told never to allow themselves to be captured. They were assured that we and the Free French execute every prisoner. Sounds incredible, eh? Must think we're like the bloody Boche.

"This chap reached up from the stretcher and seized my arm. I shan't try to describe the expression in his eyes. Have you ever accidentally stepped on your faithful dog's foot? That look of mild reproach, bewilderment, pain. And you can see, perhaps for the first time, faith rather slipping away.

"When he took my arm his fingers squeezed very hard. He said: *'Pourquoi, nous combattons? Pourquoi?'*

"I told him we only wished to drive out the Germans. We didn't want to fight the French. He said—the poor devil was straining to lift himself—he said, 'There are no Germans in Syria. I swear there are no Germans. I shall die quickly, I know. I swear there are no Germans in Syria.' "

The major's face is twisted unhappily. He says: "Damned uncomfortable, that was."

(A telegram sent from Vichy, found in the files of General Dentz at Beirut:

"If German or Italian planes fly over the Levant, please refrain from any reply. If any of these planes alight on your fields, receive them and ask instructions. British planes must be attacked at any cost.")

At noon we again tried to advance into Damascus. I went up and joined a group of Australians. The difficulties at the moment are two machine-gun nests, located in two white houses astride the road into Damascus. Tanks are also known to be in the vicinity prowling under cover of the olive groves. Two armored cars just went up the road to try and deal with the machine-gun nests and the tanks, and two 75's have been brought up and pointed at the two white houses to try and blast them out of existence.

59

A wide green field edged by a wood of olive trees, a shallow stream a few yards across lined by squat willow trees shading the stream from the hot sun of Syria. A pastoral and pleasant scene of complete peace—except for the crack of rifle fire and the high zing of bullets whining their way into the wood about two hundred yards away.

Eighteen Australian soldiers lie on the bank of the stream firing at the Vichy French hidden in the olive grove. Three of the soldiers are too long for this natural trench. Their eyes are level with the top of the bank but their feet are in the water.

I lie beside the sergeant. The lieutenant is somewhere at the other end of the line. The sergeant isn't firing. Now and then he squints along the barrel but he doesn't squeeze the trigger.

Each minute four or five bullets come pinging out of the olive groves and go singing through the low·trees overhead.

"They're always high," I remark to the sergeant.

"I hope they keep them up there," he says.

He and his men have just come up to this line today and this is their first direct contact with the Vichy French. The hard-packed road into Damascus, six hundred yards on our right, is blocked by the small force of Vichy French hiding in the olive grove. Now the Australians are waiting for reinforcements.

"Hard to spot them in those olive trees," I suggest. The sergeant hasn't fired yet. He peers along the sight as though he had a bead on the target, then pulls his eyes away as though he'd lost the target.

"Yes," the sergeant says slowly. "Yes, it is."

I roll over on my back, my head well below the top of the bank of the stream, my feet in the water, and look up through the filigree of willow leaves. There are no birds singing in the trees today. Just the drone of lead cutting through the air.

"You know, Sergeant, the Senegalese have a better system. When the Free French Senegalese and the Vichy French Senegalese meet, they fire in the air. That way they use up their ammunition, nobody is hurt and honor is satisfied."

He turns away from his rifle, twists his head around. I can feel him scrooching an inch or two lower down the bank.

"England's allies and my father's friends," the sergeant says softly. "My father fought in France in the last war. He's one of those Australians who came out of it with a great admiration for the French.

60

Matter of fact, he's been writing back and forth with a French officer. Calls him 'my Frog friend.' A French officer from Bordeaux. My father always said 'crazy people, the French, but I like them.'

"Now," the sergeant says sadly, "I'm supposed to kill those people It's odd, isn't it?"

His upper lip is speckled with sweat and an island of it collects in the concave part of his chin. His eyes are level with the top of the bank, and he's looking toward the olive grove. Perhaps it's just as well I can't see his eyes. The bullets are winging a good deal faster than those letters between Melbourne and Bordeaux.

"As soon as that armored car comes up, we're going into that grove for them," the sergeant says.

"How soon will that be?"

"Very shortly, I expect." He slides down the bank swiftly and touches my arm.

I turn away from the sky and look at him. Have you seen the eyes of a man with malaria? The sergeant's eyes are like that.

"I wonder if it would help very much if I, well, if I sort of apologized to my conscience every time I pull the trigger?"

I entered Damascus at 13:30 today, Syrian time, Saturday, June 21st, following behind two Free French colonels, two Australian colonels, a British major and two armored cars. This was the force that actually took possession of the world's most ancient and most often conquered city.

The sun was burning down, blazing out of a cloudless blue sky, and a suffocating blast was blowing out of the Great Syrian Desert. Our five-auto column rushed through the famous "Street called Straight" toward the City Hall. We entered the gate over which Saint Paul escaped death by climbing down a ladder helped by Ananias.

Our passage through the streets was flanked by thousands of silent red-fezed Moslems and Arabs who wore faded burnouses and white flowing headdresses bound with black cords. Today, as in 1917 when the Syrians saw General Allenby and Lawrence of Arabia take over their Turkish-dominated city, the Damascenes, with a notable absence of enthusiasm, gazed curiously and apathetically while the British, Free French, Australians and Senegalese repeated that performance.

There was no hostility in the crowds that I could detect, just a gen-

61

eral acceptance and a gratification that the city was not wrecked. The greatest enthusiasm came when Colonel Collet's Circassian cavalry wearing astrakhan caps and each one a superb physical specimen and excellent horseman cantered proudly through the narrow streets.

The French uniformed police retained their posts and their guns. The defenders of Damascus are reported fleeing northward in an apparent effort to join the defenders of Beirut, just a mile or two on the other side of Damascus.

Sunday, June 22nd:
I arrived back at Safed and I worked until 5:30 this morning getting out my stories on Damascus and also a 200-word cable to *Newsweek Magazine*. It was six before I could get to sleep.

At 9:30, the one waiter in the hotel brought me breakfast and woke me up. He also said to me, "Germany and Russia are at war."

That shocked me out of my sleepiness. I couldn't believe it. The thought of the Russians fighting the Germans brought one of the happiest moments of my life. But my next thought was, "This will kill the whole Damascus story. America is not going to give a damn about Syria now."

I went back to Nazareth today, to talk with Colonel Wills and get a fill-in on the situation. Although the British are now in Damascus, the situation on the other fronts is none too happy. On the way to Nazareth, we drove by the Sea of Galilee, 680 feet below the Mediterranean level. Captain Redmond, the conducting officer, said, "We've now gone below a point any man ever has been in a submarine."

On our return to Haifa, I informed Public Relations I want to go at once on the Mediterranean coast road to watch the drive toward Beirut. Our car, a utility known in America as a station wagon, is about used up. There is no other transportation here, but they expect another car tomorrow.

I have slept four hours in the past forty-eight. I am dog tired, and now the German-Russian war will shove this whole story out of people's minds. This covering of a war is tough as hell on my constitution. I have now reached the stage where I can sleep in a car on the move, in fifteen-minute snatches.

62

Monday, June 23rd:

There is no chance of an early start today, since there is no transportation available. I had a good night's sleep, the first in four days. I am hoping to get out on a destroyer or cruiser for shelling operations off Beirut.

I have just found out that my story of seeing Damascus for the first time, twenty-four hours before it was taken, only arrived in Jerusalem tonight. The dispatch rider had two flat tires and then his motorcycle was stolen. So that story got to Jerusalem and therefore to New York after my story on the occupation of Damascus.

I don't know why some correspondents act like a combination of child and God's gift to journalism. In coming back from Damascus to file our stories, some of the correspondents were in a truck, and our car left that truck at Sheikh Meskin. It failed to catch us at Queneitra where we expected to meet and go on to Safed and Haifa. That truck went on instead to Tiberius, where it broke down. Then Ed Kennedy of the *AP* got a taxi to take him on to Jerusalem to write his story, submit it to the censorship there and immediately send it on. Henry Gorrell of the *UP* said to Kennedy, "Well, we're both going on to Jerusalem. Why not share the cab with me?"

"Oh—that can't be done. That's not according to the rules of competition," Kennedy said.

"I'll just have to get a taxi of my own," Gorrell said, "and spend three pounds to follow you in. It seems sort of silly to take two taxis when we're both going to the same place."

Kennedy refused to share the taxi. Gorrell got a better cab and, starting three-quarters of an hour behind Kennedy, beat him in to Jerusalem by fifteen minutes. There the representatives of the two biggest press associations in the world—the *AP* and *UP*—discovered that a stop order on the Damascus stories had been invoked, and the stories weren't released until twenty-four hours later, simultaneously.

Tuesday, June 24th:

With Dick Mowrer I went to Naval Headquarters and made arrangements to go out on a destroyer. Commander Warburton took us in a launch across the bay to the cruiser *Naiad,* where we had drinks with the officers. Warburton says there is only a ten-to-one chance of anything happening on a destroyer, but I decided to go anyway.

I went aboard the destroyer *Jervis*. With three other destroyers we pulled out for a dusk-to-dawn patrol. It was my first trip on a British man-of-war, my first real contact with the British navy. The skipper was Captain Mack, captain of the destroyer flotilla. The *Jervis*, 1,695 tons, with a speed of thirty-six knots, came into the Mediterranean when Italy entered the war. The entire complement of 183 men was itching for action, and bored with the whole Syrian campaign.

Shortly after sunrise, coming down the coast, I saw the most unusual battle of the war. From the bridge of the ship we sighted a Vichy French tank speeding about forty miles an hour along the road on the shore two miles off, toward Beirut.

Captain Mack said, "Let's take a crack at her."

His commands immediately rang out and in a few moments six 4.7 guns blazed away. The tank stopped, and with great impertinence suddenly returned the fire. One of its shells struck 100 yards aft of the ship. We let go again. Each time the Vichy tank, with admirable brashness, replied. At the sixth salvo, a shell struck the tank dead center. It disintegrated into nothingness. We steamed onward toward Haifa.

Wednesday, June 25th:
The Australians are handling the advance on Beirut. They have suffered pretty heavy casualties.

We went up to the advance point to the British position on the road, two miles south of Damour. There are strong Vichy forces up there, and there is going to be heavy fighting within the next forty-eight hours if the Australians try to push on.

The road 100 yards ahead is blocked and mined to prevent a surprise sortie of tanks. By checking my maps and my Baedeker I have just discovered I am lying in the exact spot where, according to Moslem tradition, Jonah was cast ashore by the whale.

Brambles clutch and slice at our bare legs as we clamber up the hill on the ancient coast of Phoenicia. Overhead twenty-five-pounder shells grunt and whistle and race for their destination.

Half way up the hill, the Australian major takes off his steel helmet
64

to cool his steaming head. We watch the shells burrow into the sand and send up a geyser of smoke near the trees that mark the edge of the village of El Jiya, 1,200 yards away.

In El Jiya lurk four Vichy armored cars and three tanks. But the Australians are not shelling the village.

"We're just teasing them," says the major.

He ducks down, draws the strap over his head and hands me his binoculars.

"Well, you wanted to see it. There it is."

Through the glasses Beirut blossoms from a white splash against the incredibly blue Mediterranean into a city of form and substance.

"It seems pretty close."

"It is," the major says. "Twelve miles. Twelve very difficult miles."

The major is short, compact, with a grayed, Prussian, wire-brush pompadour, the red face of a British Indian Army officer and the breezy way of an Anzac sheepherder. He's certainly an Australian. Half an hour after war was declared he walked out of his civilian job and took up where he left off in 1918. His blue eyes are as alert as a squirrel's and dart about the same way. The major always smiles.

"Do you know where those shells are hitting, Major?"

He whips around. "Do I know—I'm trying to root out those Vichy tanks so we can turn the twenty-five pounders on 'em," he says patiently.

I continue with my spiel: "Not far from those shell-holes that you're digging is where the Moslems say Jonah was tossed up by the whale. And those Vichy tanks at this moment are on a battleground. A fairly ancient one. Back in 218 B. C., Ptolemy the Fourth was defeated by Antiochus the Great. That's straight out of Baedeker. I studied up on that so I could trade some ancient information for some current news."

The major is amused. "At this moment I don't know whether I'm Ptolemy the Fourth or Antiochus. I'll tell you what I know. It isn't very much.

"You just came from Damascus, so you know about that drive across from Damascus to Beirut. We're the coastal end of the pincer on Beirut. There it is in front of us. Well, it isn't very easy to get there. The Vichy people are making us pay for every inch."

Down the bramble-tangled hillside, beside the asphalt road running along the Mediterranean, are four Australians. Their bodies are splotched with a violent purple antiseptic to prevent infection from the scratches. They lie beside a barbed-wire barrier across the road, fronted by a double row of land mines, five in each row. Three of the soldiers have automatic rifles lying across their arms. The fourth cuddles a machine gun on a squat tripod.

"And these four men, the barbed wire and those mines—that's your advance point?"

"That's it," the major says. "There's nothing between us and the Vichy French except 1,200 yards. I've men scattered in the hills behind us. You can't see them."

Back home people are hearing and reading that the British Imperial forces are on the outskirts of Beirut. They must have visions of swarms of tanks and guns rattling and thousands of men swarming up this coastal road and streaming through the Lebanon hills. And the gates of Beirut vibrating with the shock of battle and waiting to be entered.

Four men, barbed wire and a double row of land mines.

"But where's the mechanical equipment?"

The major's smile becomes broader and his eyes twinkle. "Ah, yes, of course. Well, I don't have a great deal more than your friend Antiochus had in something or other B.C.

"You see, the French are fighting very well. We are heavily outnumbered by them in tanks and armored cars. In these days one must have them, you know.

"There's the Merjiyum front." The major is no longer amused. "Merjiyum is one of the epic battles of this war. There the fort was on top of a small hill, something like a page out of P. C. Wren. We entered the battle for Merjiyum with 324 men. We came out of it with 142.

"Yes, I know, in three days we recouped some of the prestige we lost in Greece. Men couldn't fight with greater bravery than the Australians fought before Merjiyum. But just the same, that battle was ballsed up from hell to breakfast. If we had had fifty tanks and twenty aircraft, Merjiyum would have been taken in an hour with no more than a half dozen casualties."

Tonight, the major says, he goes into action. "I'm moving across these 1,200 yards in front of us to occupy El Jiya. I will have five French tanks that we've captured from the Vichy people. They were

66

cornered in *wadis,* some of them capsized and the crews of two others gave up. I'm very fortunate to have those tanks."

"And that," I suggest, "is the mechanical equipment for the drive on Beirut."

"Oh, no, not quite," he laughs. "I'm promised two of our own tanks tomorrow and perhaps a Bren carrier.

"Well, just to be orthodox I ask for air support but it is very rarely forthcoming, so I don't figure it in planning operations. I just depend on the men and equipment that I can see and touch."

I tell him that I was seven days in Syria before I saw a single British aircraft. He looks at me quizzically, as though wondering the point of my remark, wondering if I really expected to see any planes.

In the major's eyes you see the same story that rests in the eyes of many a British commander in the field in Syria, in Greece, in the Western Desert—the story that's crackled over the field telephones hundreds of times: "Need five tanks . . . Can you rush two batteries twenty-five pounders . . . Appreciate air support . . . Position untenable . . . Am attacking with available forces . . ."

The shells still whistle and fall on the beach in front of us, and there is no sign of movement in El Jiya. The major is smiling.

"You told me a while ago," he says, "that in front of Damascus you saw four armored cars come up and it was such a rare thing that you all salaamed in reverence. So shortage of equipment is not startling. I've talked a good deal, but there won't be any story until we start the move forward tonight.

"Don't take this as propaganda," the major urges. "You people know what you want to do. But I wonder if the people in your tank factories, your gun plants and your aircraft works know how important it is to work just a bit faster."

The shelling is over. Without the intermittent rumble this whole scene, from the Lebanon hill overlooking the land where the Crusaders, Saracens and Alexander the Great fought, is utterly peaceful. The only evidences of war here are the barbed wire on the road and the four soldiers patiently lying under the sizzling sun.

An Australian officer told me about an amusing incident today. Many Lebanese and others are deserting the Vichy French to reach their homes or are "going over the hill" to hide out with natives.

67

They want to eat their cake and have it, too. They are tired of fighting with the Vichy French, and they don't want to be captured, either.

An Australian non-commissioned officer passed two men dressed as Arabs eating inside a small tent open on three sides. He looked inside as a routine check and one of the men said: *"Saida."* That means "good day." *"Saida,"* the Australian responded, and went on. After walking about ten yards, he shook his head, baffled, stopped and scratched his head. "No, sir," he said to himself. "I'm right." He retraced his steps and captured the two men inside the tent. One was a Frenchman and the other a German and they had deserted from those of the French Foreign Legion who are fighting with the Vichy French.

The Australian made the capture because he suddenly remembered that the two "Arabs" were sitting on boxes to eat instead of sitting cross-legged on the ground, as Arabs do.

Thursday, June 26th:

The censors at Haifa, Captain Mostyn-Owen and Captain Cumberbatch, have become impossible. They are good personal friends of mine, but professionally we just don't get on. Most of the correspondents, both English and American, consider the censorship so inept that they want to get out of covering this Syrian war.

Tonight was quite typical. My entire story was killed by Mostyn-Owen and Cumberbatch.

"I don't know anything about this information," Cumberbatch said.

I explained this was official information given by Colonel Wills in Nazareth for release. I had driven over there in the afternoon for a fill-in on the general picture.

"That may be," Cumberbatch said, "but I don't know anything about it."

I am nonplussed, but then I've been nonplussed before. A colonel of intelligence releases information and a captain, serving as a censor, out of pure ignorance, is not *au courant,* and so the story is killed. I suggested to Cumberbatch that he find out what is going on in the war so that he will know how to censor.

In my script this morning I wrote: "Barring sudden collapse of Vichy French morale, which right now is being threatened by increas-

68

ing desertions and dwindling supplies, termination of the Syrian campaign is still distant."

That view was included in my story because I felt that too many reports might be appearing in America that the Vichy French couldn't fight and didn't want to fight. The opposite was true. They were fighting with great courage and resourcefulness. Dentz was doing a tremendous job of generalship.

An Australian brigadier general told me that his forces were just about to capture a position on the coast road when Dentz appeared among the Vichy French troops and in less than an hour reorganized his men. That position was held for another twenty-four hours. "We suffered considerable casualties in those twenty-four hours, too," the brigadier added.

Friday, June 27th:
I have planned a trip starting late today or tomorrow for a tour of all the fronts—north of Merjiyum, to Damascus, and then over to the coast road to be there in time for the push on Beirut which ought to be coming off in a few days.

I went to NAAFI (the canteen for the armed services) and laid in a supply of groceries. Bought a new can opener, too.

When I came back to the Panorama Hotel there was a message from Major Alban, in Jerusalem. It was succinct: "You are ordered to return to Cairo."

The message puzzled me. I didn't know whether the military had ordered me out because the British didn't like my stories, or whether I'd been called back by New York because CBS didn't like them.

I telephoned Alban in Jerusalem, but he had little more than his first message gave me.

"The message comes from Public Relations in Cairo," he said, which convinced me that the British military had ordered me back.

Whatever the reason I am glad to be getting out of here. I have just seen copies of the stories I've sent and virtually everything in them that has any meaning has been blue-penciled by the censors. The news staff at CBS must be scratching its collective head to make any sense out of those mutilated stories.

Just before leaving Haifa I ran into Captain Mack of the *Jervis.*

He certainly fits the description of a "tough sea dog." He's about forty-eight, with gray hair and a lined face, always puckered into a smile. He's been to sea since he was eleven.

We had a beer together and I remarked to him about the great friendliness aboard the *Jervis,* and the affection all his men held for him.

He seemed embarrassed and brushed it off with this story: "When I was a youngster on board a ship we had a captain who thought his four stripes elevated him more than they should have. The skipper held services every Sunday morning on the deck and invariably when he led the prayers he removed his four-striped coat.

"It was the only way," Captain Mack remarked, "our skipper could pay devotion to a Superior Being."

"SUGGEST YOU MOSCOWARD"

Saturday, June 28th:
Early this morning started back to Cairo by train. Sedgwick, Brewer and Moorehead also are going back.

The British are certainly careful about identifications, and it is a good thing. Every soldier and ourselves, too, had to show identifications four times. A uniform is no passport; everyone is in uniform. Among so many uniforms there certainly could be a dozen or two enemy agents.

Traveling in this country is almost insufferable. Across the desert of Sinai, the heat is overwhelming. The sand is blowing and a half inch of sand settles on your lap and over your bags, and on your tongue, too. There are six people in each compartment. If you close the windows to keep out the sand, the heat and bad air make you sick at the stomach.

The train crawls along. At each station, small, half-naked Arab boys run along the tracks crying, *"Wattingmen chungu."* Sense comes to their cries only when they hold up their wares and you see they are selling watermelon and chewing gum!

I lost this diary with all my notes on Syria. I must have left it in the dining car and I am now making notes on separate sheets of paper. I have gone through the car several times, asking almost everyone if he saw the notebook. I even went through all the linen in the dining car, but everyone denies knowledge. There's considerable information which I wouldn't want to fall in the wrong hands.

It is mighty mysterious how it disappeared. But somehow I'm not as desolate as I should be over losing all those notes. I have the feeling that in some unfathomable way they will turn up.

On the train I have been reading Lawrence's *Seven Pillars of Wisdom*. The book only deepens the great magnetism this desert and historical country has for me.

I'm also reading *Inside Italy*, by C. M. Franzero. He was the *Giornale d'Italia's* London correspondent. It is hastily and poorly written, but it convinces me that I should have done a book on Italy. Here I am almost three months out of Italy and I have not done a thing on reporting on it since.

I didn't know Franzero, but I remember the Fascists were surprised that Franzero refused to return to Italy when Mussolini declared war. They shouldn't have been. His stuff in the paper had a slight pro-British swing and very often, while in Rome, I quoted from his stories.

By saying *"Giornale d'Italia,* in a dispatch from London, says" I could show discrepancy between the home-written editorials and what actually was taking place in the outside world. A number of times the Rome censors refused to allow me to quote from Franzero's dispatches from London. Franzero in his book tells how Virginio Gayda, the editor of the paper, often changed the London dispatches.

Gayda frequently slipped up in the job of editing those dispatches. When he did, I had something to quote from the *Giornale d'Italia* by which I could get across a picture of Fascism that would not have been possible otherwise.

Why haven't the British in Syria some bands? Even on the entrance into Damascus there wasn't a note of music. I think there should be more beating of drums and blowing of fifes in this war.

Sunday, June 29th:
Early this morning I called Chorlian and found Paul White had cabled:

SUGGEST YOU MOSCOWARD POSSIBLEST HASTE.

I don't know whether I am glad or sorry. It is most difficult to get there, and the show may be over before I could arrive. In any event, I don't like cold weather.

How strange that I should be sent to Moscow! Burdett in Ankara is much closer. It would be much easier to send someone from New York via Vladivostok. New York must arrange for a Russian visa for me, since there is no Soviet representative here.

I went to Minister Kirk for suggestions, since he formerly was stationed in Moscow. He urged me not to go by sea to Turkey—"You get sunk that way"—and advised the back-door route of Bagdad, Tehran and Baku. He emphasized the necessity of having all visas before I

72

leave Cairo, and assurance that I can broadcast from Moscow when I arrive.

I cabled White:

APPRECIATE ASSIGNMENT. PREPARING MOSCOWARD. AWAITING YOUR ANSWER WHETHER RUSSIAN VISA OBTAINABLE TEHRAN. ASSUME YOU ARRANGING TECHNICAL FACILITIES SO CAN BROADCAST ON ARRIVAL. OUTPOINT EYE PROBABLY BE RESTRICTED BROADCAST OFFICIAL COMMUNIQUES.

The strangest thing happened, and my hunch worked out. This morning two British officers walked into the American Consulate and said they found a notebook in the dining car. They didn't leave their names, and so, very mysteriously, I had the notebook back with all my notes on Syria. Not a page is missing.

At GHQ, where I had to go to get approval on a script Captain Berick had murdered, I asked Colonel Tod how long we were going to have to put up with censors who didn't know the first principle of their job. Tod was extremely decent.

"We have our problems," he said, "and those men don't seem able to use their own intelligence, and they are afraid to do something wrong."

I like Tod more than ever, and I am deeply impressed by his constant concern with the job at hand—winning the war.

Tod gave the impression that Russia would hang on for some time. He asked me a half dozen times what America's reaction would be to the Russo-German war.

I am told at GHQ by men who should know that the Russians will be able to hold out six weeks to two months, no more. In talking with the two officers who expressed this opinion, I even reduced their time limit and said confidently:

"That Russian show will be over in anywhere from five to six weeks."

Monday, June 30th:
I have been in every big shop in Cairo, trying to find a map of Russia. Not one exists here.

Lunched with Rosamond Mowrer and Hal Denny, who said he

didn't see a possibility of going to Russia. Hal was in Moscow for seven years. He is what might be called "hostile" to working again in Moscow, or seeing any other correspondent going there to work.

Tuesday, July 1st:

As things now stand, the best way to get to Moscow is by plane from Cairo to Bagdad to Tehran. From Tehran on is rather blank, but presumably there is a train to Bander-Shah which is at the southeastern corner of the Caspian Sea. From Bander-Shah I may be able to take a boat to Baku. From Baku probably a train to Astrakhan. This town seems to be the place to reach, because from there the train goes to Stalingrad and then to Moscow. But from Baku, a train goes in a roundabout way to Rostov and then to Azov.

Wednesday, July 2nd:

Most of the preliminaries for applying for an Iranian visa I completed this morning. One of the requirements is to list the countries you have been in, and I find that I have been in twenty-five: England, France, Germany, Italy, Belgium, Czechoslovakia, Austria, Hungary, Roumania, Russia, Turkey, Syria, Palestine, Egypt, Libya, Tunisia, French Morocco, Yugoslavia, Argentina, Brazil, Haiti, Jamaica, Panama, Venezuela, Uruguay.

At the Iran Legation, the clerk in charge of visas was a fat, swarthy chap with a wide smile, and just one big tooth in the middle of his mouth. I asked him if there were deserts in Iran.

"Oh, yes, deserts and mountains."

"Are the mountains covered with trees and rocks?" I asked.

"No rocks, flowers."

"You mean the mountains are covered with flowers?"

"Yes, flowers," he said. "Even if they were *not* covered with flowers, I would tell you that."

He said he had brothers in America. I asked him how many brothers he had.

"One and a half million."

"What! You have a million and a half brothers?"

"Yes. A million and a half spiritual brothers."

To help pave the way for the granting of my visa I pointed out to the clerk that America and Iran were friendly.

74

He said: "In war times is different. Yes friends, no friends, don't know who friend."

I asked the clerk how soon the visa might come through.

"Maybe two-three days, maybe month. God knows. Yes, God knows. God only knows."

Eagerly he asked if I had pictures with me for the visa. When I took out a half dozen, his jaw dropped and his eyes shot wide open in amazement.

"Oh," he said with the greatest disappointment. *"Have* pictures, yes?"

The clerk then launched into a long dissertation on the advantages of not going to Iran.

"Why you want leave this nice climate in Cairo and go to Iran?" he asked plaintively. "Very nice here." And he explained it was ridiculous to ask for an Iran visa until the Russian one is granted.

"Here in Cairo," he explained, "there is good food. You can go swimming, and there are pretty girls."

"You have pretty girls in Iran?" I asked.

"Oh, yes indeed," he said. "But you are in Cairo now, and the girls here are pretty, too."

I pointed out to him, in one-syllable words, that, after all, I was trying to report a war, and that CBS had told me to go to Moscow, and the only way, at the moment, to go to Moscow was through his beautiful and lovely country. And that I was extremely happy over this Moscow assignment because it would give me the opportunity to see his most interesting kingdom.

"But you not need Iran visa. First you must have Russian visa," he said, going back to his previous attack.

I explained that we wanted everything to move simultaneously, so that when the Russian visa was granted there would not be an instant's delay in getting off.

The Iran clerk then tossed in his final appeal for me to stay away from Iran.

"You don't need to go to Iran to go to Russia. Go to Mosul, in Irak, then Turkey to the Caspian Sea."

"By air?"

"No, you cannot go by air," he said.

"Well, I am flying to Tehran to save time."

75

"Oh, yes? That is different then. I suppose you must go to Iran."

There was an expression of unutterable sadness on his face.

In order to apply for the visa, I had to pay the cable charges on the request to the foreign office in Tehran. The cable was written out in code, and the clerk made one final assault.

"You no want spend all this money for cable. Very cost. Cost about five pounds (approximately $20 in American money). You save all much money. Do not ask for visa, yes?"

I said I was only too happy to contribute five pounds to the Ministry of Communications in Tehran.

"Come back Saturday for receipt and change. Saturday."

"And the reply, too?"

"Well, maybe perhaps. Maybe perhaps answer Saturday."

Secretary Knox's "Now is the time to strike" speech brought repercussions today from Lieutenant Henderson at the censor's office. Henderson is a man of about fifty, quite jolly, a very decent chap.

As I came into his office, he said, "I have just read Knox's speech. Well, are you Americans coming into the war or are you still talking?"

I said, "Well, we are talking and we are getting warmed up. We are not mad enough yet."

General Wavell has been transferred to India. In my broadcast tonight I said that the transfer came as a great surprise to the Egyptians. Wavell saved Egypt from an invasion by the Italians. He did more than that. He wiped out the Italian army in Libya. He reduced Mussolini's East African Empire to just a piece of white marble on the famous wall map of Rome's *Via del Impero*. As I pointed out in this broadcast:

"The explanation that General Wavell needed a rest caused many a British and Egyptian eyebrow out here to be raised considerably. Wavell is an energetic, dynamic character, strong-minded for one thing and able for another. He is a military man in the true sense."

I also attempted to say, "And that means he believes military operations should not be controlled, started or stopped by politicians."

But that sentence was cut out by the censors.

I also pointed out that most people here connect that appointment with the Russo-German war.

"As the situation is seen here, India may develop into an important

76

bulwark for the protection of Irak, and other neutral countries not now in the war.

"Other observers have other ideas why Wavell, with his vast experience in desert warfare, should be shifted at such a moment. But I am not able to report these ideas from Cairo tonight. It is said Wavell has been removed from the Middle East command at a time when this sector holds many promises of becoming a sphere of real offensive operations. In fact, the hope is prevalent among British officers with whom I have talked that the Russo-German scrap will not be a breathing spell for the Middle East, but, as they expressed it, a moment for breathless attack."

At the press conference tonight, someone asked Colonel Tod what the effect of the Russo-German war would be on the Middle East. He actually used the phrase, "Well, for one thing, it will give us a breathing spell here."

But every British officer I have talked to in the past two days said: "This is our chance now to hit at the Germans in Libya."

I have found among lieutenants, captains and majors a kind of vigor and dynamism which certainly should be found to a greater extent among the men of the higher command.

Tonight just before I went on the air, Westrup, the engineer, handed me a telegram, just come in. It said:

FORGET MOSCOW.   ERSKINE CALDWELL REPRESENTING US THERE. BROADCASTING DAILY.   WHITE.

Such brevity shattered my plans and down the sewer went fifteen pounds of money already spent for cables to get the visas. The message has taken a hell of a lot of wind out of me. At least CBS thought of me for the top assignment of the year, and it may turn out for the best, at that.

Thursday, July 3rd:
I am down in the dumps today over the Moscow affair and went swimming at Gezira with Rosamond Mowrer and lunched with Teddy Latham of the American Field Service. He has just come back from Syria.

There may be hard days ahead. I am confused about the direction of

77

events, but I am determined that events are not going to overwhelm me, no matter how avalanching they may be.

Friday, July 4th:
This morning a farewell interview with General Wavell was suddenly arranged for just nine correspondents.

GHQ is situated on the banks of the Nile and is surrounded with barbed wire. We all had to show our passes, although we were accompanied by British officials. There were only three Americans present: Hal Denny of the *New York Times,* Russell Hill of the *Herald Tribune* and myself.

We were taken into a room about fifteen feet wide, thirty-five feet long and about six feet high, with a beaverboard wainscoting. On this was tacked detailed maps of the Mediterranean area. Three doors let in air and light. The tables were arranged in a U shape and they were covered with green felt. This was the "strategy room" of the Middle East Command.

In front of each chair was a silver ashtray and an occasional inkstand with pens and pencils. The electric lights hung down from the ceiling, where each officer would sit, and were heavily shaded with faded blue-cloth cones about a foot high.

Wavell came in seven minutes late. A trim figure without coat, but wearing a tie, and his cloth pips of crossed swords rather faded. His hair is gray. His face is not wrinkled, and his skin is brittle, in the way of men who spend most of their time outdoors. Major Oakshot took him around, introducing us.

He knew some of the correspondents, but I had never met him before. In our handclasp, his hand felt thick and muscular. The fingers were short and blunt. For some reason, his one blind eye held a terrific fascination for me, and I couldn't tear my eyes away. I wondered if he could see I was staring at his left sightless eye.

Wavell began talking rather haltingly, half hunched over the table, looking around at each of us. His voice was soft.

"I know that we have had some differences, you correspondents and ourselves, but we always try to work out things together. I want you to know how much help you have been, but I must admit that at times I wish the press was not here."

78

We all laughed extra-loudly at that. One of the British correspondents asked Wavell about the Russo-German war, and Wavell said: "It is undoubtedly giving us a breathing spell for rest and training, a chance to occupy Syria and combine with the defenses of Iraq.

"The Germans were certain that they would take Crete away and use those troops to go on into Syria and Iraq. If they would have succeeded, we would have had considerable difficulty in the Syria campaign.

"That campaign was slow and sticky, as you all know. There was the difficulty of the Syrian terrain, and it is unpleasant fighting former allies, but everything is going all right, though the Vichy French are fighting remarkably stoutly.

"If the Germans, instead of going into Russia, had concentrated their air forces in North Africa, they would have given us a pretty difficult time. What the Germans will do, if they succeed in overcoming the Russians, is hard to foresee."

Wavell spread his hands wide, and looked at every one of us around the table and asked: "Don't you agree that it is pretty difficult to follow the Germans' movements in this war?"

Someone asked how strong he thought Russia was.

Wavell's answer was: "The strength of Russia lies in her great reserves of man power and the vast space in which she has to operate in case things go wrong."

Wavell shook hands with each of us as he was going out of the room. I thought I saw significance in his parting words: "Perhaps I will see some of you correspondents in India."

Rosamond, Denny, Russell Hill and I went to Kirk's Fourth of July party. It was unavoidably and incredibly dull. But it was one of those parties that every American Ambassador and Minister has to give on the Fourth of July.

Kirk, as usual, was immaculate in a white silk suit, despite the intense heat. Kirk always gave me the impression that he had disciplined his pores not to sweat in public.

Since afternoon I had been having stomach cramps; at midnight they were rather severe. Russell came to my room to hear President Roosevelt's radio speech.

Saturday, July 5th:

I am devilish sick. The doctor tells me I have some kind of intestinal inflammation. As near as I can judge, it is a severe case of "gyppy tummy." It is a disease that is prevalent here during the summer. I was so sick this morning I could hardly stand. I feel feverish and my bones ache.

The doctor tells me I must stay in bed for twenty-four hours, but I can't do that because I have a broadcast tonight. For some reason, when I inhale a cigarette, I cannot breathe.

I managed to get over to the press conference and get my stories written and censored. Then crawled back into bed until one A.M., when I got over to the studio.

My broadcast tonight started with:

"There is increasing belief among the British officers in the Middle East that Great Britain's needs from the United States must go beyond the well-known airplanes, tanks, guns, etc. The next need is man power. And I find more and more British officers counting on not only American tools, but also American soldiers.

"I understand that the broad-scale plans of the Middle East—plans not of next week, but in the uncertain future—may require the use of American troops."

It was the first time that I had "gyppy tummy" and also the first time I mentioned the need of American man power to win this war.

My information came from three sources, and despite that I hesitated to use this story in tonight's broadcast.

I had talked with a number of officers who were in touch with GHQ and reported their views and ideas that Britain could not win this war without American soldiers actually fighting by their side. That was a new thought. Up to now it has been "Give us the tools and we will finish the job."

The second indication was the number of observers of the United States Marine Corps who were in Egypt making a close study of ship-to-shore operations on the basis of local conditions.

Then, thirdly, I thought it was significant that a Cairo magazine of military affairs, called *Parade,* has just printed a full page of pictures showing the insignia of American soldiers. The magazine gave this explanation:

80

"The pictures will help Britons distinguish between a captain and a major general, between a private and a master sergeant."

I am back in my room in the hotel after the broadcast, making these notes. I feel terribly lonesome for Martha. It is just three years ago today that Martha came to Rome, and we were married soon thereafter. I feel that Martha is growing further and further away from me, and tomorrow will be just four months since I put her on a train at Turin. She went back to the United States.

This I do feel—that unless I get an engrossing story or go up to some front where there is a great deal to occupy my mind and energy, I shall not be able to endure this absence and these uncertainties.

These periods of depression seem to come on me so often now. I feel it perhaps because I am so thoroughly fed up with being abroad. At least, without home leave to break the unremitting pressure of being on this side.

Perhaps I would feel differently about everything if I saw some chance of going home in the near future, but I don't see it.

Monday, July 7th:

In the same room where we talked with Wavell, correspondents met General Sir Claude Auchinleck, the new C-in-C today. He is a tall, well-built man of fifty-eight, with thick brown hair parted on one side and a leathery, seamed face. He smiles readily, which wrinkles his face even more. He uses a good many Ums and Ahs. His first words were:

"You men probably know more about the situation here than I do." We all looked at each other somewhat aghast. "I've just come here, you know," he explained, reading our faces.

Hal Denny asked about the security of the situation. Auchinleck said: "I feel pretty secure at the moment. That is, personally."

This humor fell rather flat, so Auchinleck hastily added: "You mean if the Russian-German business ends in failure?"

"Yes," Denny said, "that's what I mean."

"I don't know, really," Auchinleck went on. "If the Germans defeat the Russians, they will go for Baku and the oil of the Caucasus, and try to terrorize the Turks in their endeavor to get here. That would be a new threat to the East. There is nothing new in that. They have been considering it for some time.

"If the Hun gets into the Caucasus," Auchinleck added, "he is certain to push into Iraq and Iran and farther East still. Those are the things one would like to be ready for."

Walter Collins of the *United Press* asked the general if he would make some observation on the Russian resistance.

"Well," Auchinleck said, "Russian resistance has been better than expected. This is partly due to the comparative ease with which the Germans overran the other countries."

"General," I asked, "do you envisage the need of American man power?"

Auchinleck hesitated for a moment, looked rather blank, and then burst out as though grabbing the thing by the horns:

"If this war is going to be won properly," he said vigorously, "none of this armistice business is any use. If this war is going to be won properly it has got to be won in Europe. Not necessarily in Berlin, but in Austria, or some part of Germany. The German (you could feel the general underlining every word) must be beaten on his own soil. If this is going to happen, I, personally, see the need for American man power in this war."

"Could we narrow this down, sir, for the Middle East, to three or four months hence?" I asked.

"No, not that quickly. In the next twelve, fourteen or twenty-four months there will be a need for American man power in this war. But the German must be beaten in his own country. How we are going to get to his country is another matter, but," and here his eyes narrowed and his lips tightened to a thin line, "there are ways and means."

I asked Auchinleck then if he had any observations on the type of equipment needed from America at this time.

"I haven't been here long enough. I am just getting my feet on the ground. But, as in India, I would say tanks, aircraft and anti-aircraft artillery."

A British correspondent swung the conversation back to Russia and Germany, and Auchinleck made this prediction.

"If the German doesn't get to the Caucasus, he is finished."

As we shook hands, Auchinleck said to me, "I hope we will meet often."

I said, "I hope so, sir."

Out in the corridor Colonel Philip Astley, head of Public Relations, and Colonel Tod questioned me whether it was wise to put out anything on Auchinleck's admitting that American man power was needed.

"Why not?" I said. "It is certainly true that you are going to need American man power to win, and every day we are getting nearer and nearer to war. I think it is time the American people realized that American boys are going to have to die in this war."

"Well, that may be true," Colonel Tod said, "but I don't know whether the time is ripe to say so."

I said I thought the time was ripe, but what bothers me is the strange way this whole idea is being broached. I have the impression that this campaign to inform Americans that our man power is needed is coming out of London and is being planted here and there by casual conversation. There have been too many officers telling me in the past few days that American man power will be needed.

Colonel Tod and Colonel Astley said they knew of no propaganda campaign.

My view, as I expressed it to them, was that whether it was a propaganda campaign or not, the fact was indisputable but I just didn't like to be sucked in on any planting of a story.

Out in the corridor, I bumped into Major Ferguson of the Black Watch. You are always delighted to see someone after a campaign; it's like seeing someone you didn't expect to find among the living again.

"Still reciting James Elroy Flecker, Major?" I asked after we'd finished pumping each other's hand.

Major Oakshot wanted to know what that was about, and I told him. "You ought to tell that story," Oakshot said.

"I will some day."

Late this afternoon we had an interview with Oliver Lyttleton, the Minister of State sent out here to handle political affairs. He was presented to us by Sir Miles Lampson, the British Ambassador, who impressed me as being somewhat of a vague individual, best suited to garden parties in Surrey. This was brought out by the contrast in the two men.

Lyttleton is a big, husky, vigorous, fast-talking Englishman. He is

83

very much like an American, as a matter of fact. He impresses me as the most capable Englishman I've yet encountered. There is no nonsense about him, and his only evasiveness was to avoid telling more than he reasonably could. I asked him what the attitude of England was toward the American war effort, if he felt we were falling short of any responsibilities.

"No," he said, "the English people understand the American problem of getting production moving."

"Is that the official attitude, or the attitude of the man on the street?"

"I would say that it is the attitude of the man on the street."

One correspondent, working for a local paper, asked if something couldn't be done about civilian air mail, that the delay and uncertainty were hurting business.

Lyttleton snapped back: "The first thing to do is to win the war. If we won't win the war, there won't be any business."

I mentally put a big gold star after Lyttleton's name for that answer.

I asked if the Duke of Aosta was to be treated as a military prisoner. Aosta was the commander of the Italian East Africa forces.

Lyttleton hesitated a bit, then conferred with Lampson.

"He is a military prisoner, the same as anyone else."

Lyttleton and I got together afterwards. I said I had asked that question about Aosta because I was trying to slide him into an admission that Aosta was being groomed to be the next King of Italy. He looked a bit startled at that, sort of grunted, but said nothing that I could record as an answer. (Aosta later died of illness in a British prison camp in Kenya.)

I asked Lyttleton if he didn't believe that the Middle East had been treated somewhat as a stepchild.

"No," he said, "I don't think so. Archie Wavell said to me last night, 'One of the happiest things out here is that the Middle East has finally caught the imagination of the American people.' "

Lyttleton is extremely clever at interviews; in fact, he is one of the ablest individuals in that respect I have ever met. He gives answers, all right, but when you pick them up in your hands they turn into dust and you have nothing. I think he is going to cut through a lot of red tape in this war.

84

I finally got a copy of *Collier's* for April 26th and am especially delighted to see "Inside Italy" by Martha Brown as a lead article. I am proud no end of her job. I sent her a cable of congratulation.

In my broadcast tonight, I tried to say that negotiations are going on for the surrender of Beirut, but it was cut out. I don't know why, because they most certainly are.

Wednesday, July 9th:
Sent a cable to White, asking his suggestion regarding my going to cover the fall of Beirut. At the very moment I sent the cable, Churchill announced that General Dentz had asked for an armistice.

The biggest event this week is America sending an Expeditionary Force to Iceland. Gone is the idea of "not sending our boys to foreign shores."

Dakar obviously must be next. Perhaps the Azores. I wonder if Japan will be in the war against Russia and how soon. Perhaps Japan will play the same jackal role as Mussolini—wait until a Russian defeat is in the bag and then jump.

Thursday, July 10th:
The *Saturday Evening Post* is going to print my article on Yugoslavia and two wonderful letters came from Martha tonight. I am in heaven.

Saturday, July 12th:
The war in Syria is over. For the past twenty-four hours Allied troops have been standing by their guns under a "cease fire" order from General Wilson. British and Vichy French emissaries are negotiating for one of the saddest chapters of the present war. This war in Syria ends like all others—with disease, hunger and misery.

Since I have been broadcasting about the destruction of war, I thought tonight a broadcast on repair work would be in order. So for the CBS show tonight I did an interview with Ralph Bain, the Middle East representative of the Red Cross. Bain is a youthful, vigorous executive, who seems to know a great deal about his job. He has organized supplies of food, clothing and medicines worth more than a half million dollars at Alexandria for shipment to Syria, as soon as the Armistice is signed. That seems to be the cycle of war: murder first—and then salvage.

85

American girls have a great fascination for British soldiers, but it is pretty much in the abstract because the only American girls they know are those they see on the screen or in the picture magazines. A good many American girls are going to get letters from the Tommies. One of the American Consulate officers gave a batch of magazines to the British troops, and among them was the *Junior League Magazine*. It happened to contain the membership list and addresses. I have just found out that the Army post office has been flooded with letters addressed to girls in America.

Sunday, July 13th:
The Armistice negotiations over Syria are still going on. They are taking place at Acre. It is a historic spot and occasion. Not since 1815 have British and French sat down to talk armistice between them. At Acre the main forces of the Crusaders disembarked and there, exactly 750 years ago today, Richard the Lion Hearted conquered Saladin. Then Richard massacred 2,500 prisoners. And just 142 years ago Napoleon attempted to conquer Acre. He was defeated by the garrison there, aided by British sailors under Sir Sidney Smith.

The war in Syria may be over, but Britain's many economic problems there are just beginning. Great Britain wants to give immediate independence. The Free French agreed, but they actually wish to continue to exercise some control over Syria. The Syrians object to any Free French. The British scheme calls for a United Syria, but the Syrians want a country with their capital at Damascus. The Lebanese want their own country and their own capital at Beirut.

I sent the following cable to Paul White tonight:
HOW GOING WESTERN DESERT FEW DAYS FOR LOOK SEE.

Monday, July 14th:
Several times in the past week I've had drinks and lunched with three captains and a major of a Tank Regiment. Each one looked like a movie star—young, handsome and vigorous. And each one was a veteran of the tank battles in the Western Desert. They showed no signs of hardship—were gay, cheerful and confident.

I asked each of them the same question I ask every British officer and soldier with whom I come in contact: "Why are you fighting?"

The answers: "I am fighting to save England . . . What else do

86

you expect me to do? . . . We couldn't go on always under the shadow of an attack by the Jerrys. . . ."

Captain MacDonald, one of these tank men, had asked me to come out and see their camp near the Pyramids. He picked me up at eleven, and we drove out to the camp. The colonel and major of the regiment met us and took me at once into a room filled with men sitting on benches waiting, I thought, to file out to lunch. I sat down beside the colonel and major, and the first thing I knew MacDonald was on his feet explaining:

"We have an American correspondent here who has very kindly consented to come out and tell you about Italy, Yugoslavia and the United States."

I talked for an hour and a half. It was one of my most enjoyable experiences. These men were so eager to know about the other side, how the Axis fights and what equipment it has. And they were so appreciative of having someone come out to break their monotony.

Later, with the colonel of the tank battalion, I plod through the ankle-deep sand up a dune-like hill to the Officers' Mess.

The forest of low, deep-brown elongated barracks sharply contrasts with the tannish monotony of the palmless landscape of sand. A few miles off, the three pyramids of Cheops ripple in the undulating heat weaving up from the sand. The heat goes through the rubber soles of our suede desert shoes, and after ten minutes it is like walking across a slightly more than lukewarm stove.

The gray, sparse-haired colonel is expressing profuse thanks for the talk on Italy and Yugoslavia. I am murmuring polite negations. Superlatives from Englishmen make me squirm. They don't seem quite able to make them sound plausible.

Colonel Drew insists.

"Extr'ordinarily interesting. You know, we had a go at the Eyeties and we like to know what they thought on the other side. Chased them to Benghasi, actually."

And now this regiment is sizzling in the heat of Egypt, stared at by the unchanging face of the Sphinx in front of three peeling pyramids.

In the faces of every one of those men are two emotions, fear and expectancy. They fear they may be rooted here as long as that Sphinx, and their wish is for new tanks.

In the Mess, as our lemon squashes sluice down our throats, I ask the colonel about the new American tanks.

"You mean the M 3's. We don't have them yet. But all the officers have been at the training school working with them.

"Like them? Can't understand how you people make such a thing!

"Why, almost everything's wrong with them. Built like a box for one thing. That's it, m'dear fellow, built just like a ruddy box. Too high. Too much target. Why couldn't you make them like our 'I' tanks, low?"

"Isn't there some advantage, Colonel, in having the guns as high as possible?"

"Jolly right. But what good is a high gun if we can't have range. The firing arrangement is ten years behind the times."

The M 3's have too many machine guns and a 37 millimeter cannon. "Too many machine guns are no good," the colonel says. "Have to carry too much ammunition. Too much trouble to service them. What we need is one big gun and one machine gun. The Boche tank guns have a 2,000-yard range."

The colonel is snorting now, blowing like a Colonel Blimp without a walrus mustache.

"Thirty-seven millimeters! Bloody pistol, that's what it is! Not like our 'I' tanks. Give us guns on tanks so that we can start shooting as soon as the Boches do."

"And so nothing is good about them?"

"Oh, yes. One or two things. Suspension is very good, motors work fine and the rubber tracks are an advantage in the desert. But the disadvantages outweigh the advantages.

"Oh, naturally we'll use 'em. Have to, m'dear fellow. No choice."

Major John Gilpin told me of the diaries of German prisoners.

"Many times," he said, "the Germans mention with awe, 'We are fighting man to man,' as though that was something they were not taught and certainly never expected to have to do. A number of them write, 'We have met the Australians hand to hand and it is terrible.' "

Gilpin says: "It's surprising, the number of German prisoners who wrote in their diaries they would be faithful in the church if they came

88

out alive, and many notes in their diaries spoke of religious fervor. The most common entry in the diaries is expression of hate for the desert. They all describe it as 'terribly lonesome' and seem frightened of it."

Gilpin says that in questioning the prisoners they have shown they have no use for the Italians. When the Germans counter-attacked in April, for example, the entire regiment of Italians attempted to surrender. The Germans machine-gunned them, mowing them down.

Driving back into Cairo, I casually mentioned to Captain MacDonald that the strain and worry of the wives and families of the British men must be considerable.

"Oh, we don't emphasize fighting to our families. We always tell them we are back at the base. Take me, when I was in the retreat in France, holding a road near Boulogne with two scout cars. I had no idea where the rest of the forces were, or even if they still existed. Geoffrey Keating (the same Keating I saw so often in Palestine and Syria taking pictures as the official war photographer) came rolling by on a motorcycle yelling, 'Fifty tanks are chasing me.'

"Well, when I came back from France to England, my father said, 'Thank God you didn't see any action.' And I didn't tell him differently."

"Don't you wonder and worry about getting killed, MacDonald?"

"No, I don't think much of that. Each man thinks he will come through all right, and when a man gets it, we don't say much. It's just jolly bad luck."

Tuesday, July 15th:
O.K. from White to go to the desert, but must be back by Sunday for a broadcast.

"THE DESERT IS HELL"

There may be worse places in the world to fight than the Western Desert of Egypt but I can't conceive of any, nor can any British soldier. It is the never-never land, the place God forgot. It's the place where man may sit down and realize for the first time how kind nature has been to other parts of the world. It is sizzling sun and blistering sand gravel and cur bushes, and there are few palm trees. There is only the awful lonesomeness. It makes you think your world of family and friends has forgotten you. And yet, for me, the desert was the most vigorous and most thrilling place I have ever been. It seemed to command from one's deepest reservoirs every ounce of resistance and determination.

In the desert it is like being the solitary survivor of a shipwreck. As you walk in the desert surrounded by hundreds of miles of sand, you have exactly the same feeling as you do when swimming alone in the water, surrounded by thousands of miles of empty sea.

You may die, but before you do, you know that in this battle of one man against nature, you will not go down without fighting until the last ounce of strength has been wrung out of your bones, your blood, your tissues and your brains.

Something always happens in the desert that rims the Mediterranean in Asia and Africa, and goes beyond the Sahara. If the enemy is not active, nature is. If shells or bombs are not dropping, then the asphyxiating Khamsin is blowing. It was a combination of both that first morning.

I was with Captain Sean Fielding and a Yorkshire batman, also serving as chauffeur, when we reached the advance point of the British forces facing Sollum at the Egyptian-Libyan frontier.

We had rushed straight through from Sidi Barrani because of my anxiety to see what a forward point was like. This advance position was on the main road and was held by units of the Central India Horse, a famous Indian regiment now mechanized. A wrecked steam roller, originally used by the Italians, stood on the road, and a row

90

of empty five-gallon petrol cans across the road marked it as a barrier beyond which lay no-man's land and Halfaya Pass. As we reached this barrier I took one look through binoculars and saw the tiny figures of the Germans and Italians moving about the hillsides of Halfaya Pass, building concrete fortifications. Then the shells started screaming.

We rushed off the road and tore through heavy sand studded with tiny shrub-covered hillocks. We found Colonel George, and he welcomed us with: "You have come just in time to see a bit of action."

It was a small action, actually. A German patrol consisting of one tank and two armored cars had moved out from Halfaya Pass into the British area, and the British were attempting to shoot up that patrol with 25-pounder guns. Colonel George signaled to us to go with him. As we made our way through the sand he remarked: "Rather a pity to shoot up this fellow. It will discourage him from coming back."

We had been out of water; so I asked Colonel George if they had any supply there. He said: "Not at the moment, but we are expecting some."

So we stayed with Colonel George while the British chased the German patrol with 25-pounder guns. Why didn't they use tanks and armored cars themselves? I asked Colonel George that too, and he said: "Well, there is only one reason. We don't have any tanks or armored cars up here."

The thud of the 25-pounders sounded inside the desert dugout like a man punched in the stomach. Oomp ah-h-h. Oomp ah-h-h. Ooomp ah-h-h. Angry, low, sullen ejaculations exhausting themselves into a weary exhalation.

Each blast sent trickles of sand coursing down the sides of the communications post at the edge of no-man's land. The walls were braced and bulwarked with oil cans. Sagging overhead was sand-daubed canvas. It was stiflingly hot. The flies ate at us voraciously.

An Indian soldier was at the radio telephone. He passed messages over to the colonel. Sometimes he called out the information to save time.

"Enemy tanks moving southwest, sir. Range high, sir. They're adjusting range to 1,200 yards, sir. Fire signal just given, sir."

"Direct hit, eh?" snorted the colonel, cynically.

A pause. The Indian said: "No sir, the range was still too high."

I clambered out of the dugout and peered through the purplish, saffron haze toward the Pass, across eight miles of nothingness. Out there, perhaps uncomfortably near, a German tank and two armored cars were scurrying madly about, trying to get away from British 25-pounders.

Through the blinding brilliance, speckled with flying sand, I could just see the escarpment at the Libyan-Egyptian frontier where the Germans and Italians were. I couldn't see the German patrol or the cloud of dust raised by it. The sun poured over me like hot metal, so I slid down into the shade, heat and flies of the communications post.

Inside, I took off my steel helmet and watched a tiny stream of sand coming from a wall and racing to meet the soft sand of the floor. It ran out like one of the hour glasses you find in the five and ten cent stores to boil eggs by. Only this was faster. I thought of that then while the heavy British guns grunted outside, and the sweat ran down our faces.

The colonel was sweating like a melting man in a steam bath, too. The rivulets meandered down his clean-shaven, coppery face, leaving glistening tracks between lanes of sand dust. His gray-flecked hair was matted to his head and his lips were dry, and ridged with cracks. So were those of the captain with him, and those of the lance corporal who stood there at semi-attention. My mouth felt as if it were lined with asbestos. The Indian seemed to be all right. Earphones clamped over his glistening black hair, his jet eyes alive and alert, he looked repugnantly cool and comfortable.

I sat on a box that had once been filled with bottles of lime juice, slapped at flies and ignored the thumping of the 25-pounders. I thought of Mosquito Creek, a special creek back in my home town of Warren, Ohio, where my brother Eugene and I first tested our canoe, the *Selma B.* Cool, green water, shadowed by cool, green trees. I mentally tipped over the canoe, and went plunging deep, wonderfully deep into that cool, green water.

The sand-caked blanket across the front of the dugout parted and then closed.

The Yorkshireman saluted jerkily.

"Here's the water, sor."

He handed over a flat, white-painted container.

The captain took the can and poured some of the water into a small

92

bottle he took out of his tunic. Suddenly I didn't care whether I had water or not. The colonel was indifferent, too. He sat in a canvas chair, its legs half buried in the soft sand, and waved at the flies, and watched the Indian radio operator. The captain was interested in the water, but his interest seemed academic. He was in no hurry to offer a drink to us, or to drink it himself.

He held the bottle up to the light, peered at it for about a minute, not moving his hand. Then he smelled the water for a half minute, wrinkling his nose. He took a sip, only a sip.

"Colonel," he announced, "I'm not quite the connoisseur I thought I was."

Oomp ah-h-h. Oomp ah-h-h. I dragged my eyes away from the captain and the water and fastened them on the sand cascading down the walls and forming small conical piles all along the edges of the dug-out.

"This, I would say," the captain went on, "is Buqbuq water. But frankly it puzzles me. The body is that of Siwa water, and it smells like Sidi Barrani water. But the taste, that's Buqbuq."

The captain took another sip, grimaced slightly, then took a longer sip and drew his mouth away from the bottle. He smacked his lips the way a man does when a ripe old Burgundy hits bottom.

"Sir," he said, "I stake my reputation. The sparkle isn't what it should be. Too many of this and that floating around. But the taste. Dash it all, sir, very definitely Buqbuq water."

I said to myself: "This is fantastic. German armored cars are running around out there about a thousand yards away. These people are chasing them with artillery fire. We're down in this dugout suffocating with heat and shriveled with thirst. And that captain stands up there and talks about water in his Oxford accent as though he were dressed in white tie and tails discussing vintage wines in a Mayfair salon."

I didn't give a hang what kind of water it was. It was water, and we drank it, taking the warm stuff out of our chipped, enamel cups, rolling it over lips and tongue. I closed my eyes to avoid the sight and smell. Sipping made it all the more painful. I took a long swallow. Then there was just one regurgitation of smell and taste to deal with.

You don't drink water in the desert. You discuss it, savor it, ease it into your system with verbose and lip-smacking slowness.

That morning, an Italian Savoia-Marchetti bomber painted white and with a red cross on it roared down the main road into Egypt almost as far as Sidi Barrani, fifty miles away.

"Did you fire on it?" I asked the colonel.

"Oh, no, can't do that. Red Cross, you know."

"Yes, but that was not a Red Cross plane if it came over this territory. It was on reconnaissance, wasn't it?"

"Yes, of course, but we can't fire on a plane marked with the Red Cross." He sighed. "I guess Jerry is putting the Eyeties up to those tricks."

That was not a new trick for the Fascists. For two days during the Greek campaign, Mussolini anchored a hospital ship, painted with many Red Crosses, off Albania and used it as his army headquarters. Mussolini, the Lion-Hearted.

All that day we moved in the front area, occasionally coming across isolated camps. I was only a visitor, but I saw that there is something more in those desert warriors than the heritage of Chinese Gordon, Clive of India and Kitchener of Khartoum which keeps them going. A fisher boy from Billingsgate transplants himself to Mersah Matruh and learns the fighting tricks of the Arabs. A farmer's boy from the heaths of Hampshire slogs across the sands of Siwa, cursing the land and laughing as he fixes bayonet for a go at the enemy.

The puzzle out here in the Western Desert of Egypt is not to find out what makes these men go on fighting. The puzzle is how they go on existing.

The sun crashes down like a sledge hammer. You feel the blood cascading through the cords in your neck. It is so hot that most British keep on their pith helmets in action. They prefer a chance bullet through the head rather than a head constantly cooking under a steel helmet. Indian troops are an exception. They take all the privations, and the heat, and the shortage of water and all the aggravating discomforts of the desert as a matter of course. They are solemn and disciplined on duty—laughing and gay when off duty. They make excellent soldiers.

Tanks become too hot to the touch. Fingers burn on the rifle barrel, your skin peels off on it and there's that odor of burning flesh. Men inside a tank can lose ten pounds in one day's operations. Pilots coming out of the cool skies wobble with faintness from the stifling ground heat.

The Khamsin, the hot, dry wind of the Egyptian deserts, leaves a man gasping for life. Its dryness shrinks and cracks open the lips, chaps faces. Driven grains of sand burn eyes with irritation and rim them with redness. The lids peel back, granular with soreness.

The sand stuffs nostrils, gags the throat; spittle evaporates, leaving a taste like an open-hearth furnace. Exertion bathes the body in perspiration. The wind dries the sweat suddenly and breathlessly, chillingly.

The sand breaks open the skin and broken skin is as dangerous in the desert as it is in the jungle. Sand interferes with healing. Sand gangrene sets in, making ugly, pus-edged sores. Sand fleas break open the skin, too. The warning is: "Don't scratch sand flea bites," but human nature and reactions being what they are, every flea can have the satisfaction of knowing his bite gets scratched.

Scorpions sting with the tail, causing arms and legs to swell three or four times in size. A scorpion-bitten soldier is assured twenty-four hours in sick bay at least. Scorpions prefer to cuddle in your blanket in the night; then they sting you in the morning. The wind gives voice to the desert. It screams its forlorn wail, hopping from dune to dune.

The desert makes the moods of men. In the glare of the sun, the desert is a sharp-fanged cruel and hungry tiger, exuding a shimmering, beckoning heat, hated by everyone. You stand in the middle of this barren land of nakedness and hopelessness and think:

"God must have made this country to test men's souls so that people could see it and appreciate their own country."

At sunset the horizon becomes gray and the desert takes on the quietly enveloping softness of a kitten. All the beastliness goes out of it. Men think relaxedly and talk quietly, their faces glistening in the moonlight under the heavy dew. In that solitude, with their faces to the stars, I have heard tough, bite-pocked, fearless troopers talking and musing like poets. The desert does that at night.

There was that one night not far from Buqbuq when we lay in our cots under the heavy dew within sound of the Mediterranean crunching on the beach. I called across to Johnson, the batman: "Johnson, what would you do if fifty Germans came over that rise?"

"I would have a go at them, sir," Johnson said.

"How long do you think we three could stand them off?"

Johnson called back without a moment's hesitation, "Why," he said incredulously, "we would stand them off until we got all fifty of them."

And then we changed the subject, and Johnson began talking in the softest, most homesick voice about "back home." About the pleasant house, and the quiet of the streets, and the vines over the fences, and the horses coming up the streets and the sunsets of Yorkshire. Every inflection and every word was pure poetry. I don't know how Johnson felt inside but I was crying in my throat.

Buqbuq is a sun-scorched bit of nothingness, a hole in the ground, where drinking water makes it a big red important circle on the map. The tank for water is there, a small wooden shack for a guard to cool his steaming head, and a mule. The mule stands for hours in the sun, immovable, immutable and imperishable, waiting for the return of its Italian masters. I spoke to it in Italian. Its ears flapped ecstatically, but the beast paid no attention to my suggestions.

Johnson and Captain Fielding made the most wonderful stew for dinner tonight. They scooped out the sand and built a regular protection for the fire while I wandered along the beach, finding pieces of wood. That stew had almost everything in it. Fielding had a can of corn and I had two cans of bully beef and a can of baked beans. We put that all in a pot and Johnson found some onions in the bottom of the car. There were a half dozen potatoes too and all that went into the stew. Also, a half pound of sand. Fielding was as proud as a new father when I raved about the delicious taste and the quality of the stew.

Right after dinner I sat down on a rock, placed my typewriter on another rock and tapped out a story to send back to Cairo for Ed Chorlian to give over the air from Cairo to CBS.

You carry your own bedding in the desert. We set up our cots, and I had a sleeping bag besides. About 8:30 we were in our beds. The wind was blowing strong from the Mediterranean. It was a hot wind. There was a very strong dew. If you kept your head up out of the covers it was like sleeping in the rain. If you put your head underneath the covers it was too hot. I preferred to lie on my back with the dew coming down like rain and watch the billions of stars in the sky.

As we lay under the stars, Fielding and I tossed various ruses back and forth to shock fifty Germans if they came over the hill. Fielding's best suggestion, I thought, was this:

"If they come for us," he said, "I will paint the swastika on my bottom, turn my back side to them, bend over, sticking my head between my legs, and shout, 'Heil, Hitler.' That," he concluded confidently, "will certainly knock them over."

The first bomb shakes everything with maniacal fury. It awakens me. The second bomb speeds up the brain. In thirty seconds, I am across a dozen yards of sand and sliding into a moon-bathed slit trench. It is a rough, ten-foot slash in the sand, twelve inches wide and four feet deep. The driving desert winds have rounded the edges.

"Don't think they're after us, sir," the figure in the trench says. "Those first few must have been a mistake."

"Oh, it's you, Johnson. They seem to be dropping about two miles away, don't they?"

"Yes, sir. About that. Jerry's after those supply dumps."

Without pause, the anti-aircraft guns bark and grunt from a dozen different directions, spewing a curtain of lead that comes down in a haphazard shower over the soft, gray desert all around us. Four long, bright, bluish threads are sewing slow cross-stitches across the star-clogged sky of Egypt.

The ack-ack batteries along the Mediterranean seem especially active, angrier than the others. Evidently, the Nazi bombers are making their runs over the target from the sea approach.

The crash of the bombs sound farther away, but the ground still seems to be trembling like an immense platter of jello, quite agitated.

Explosions come in regular sequence. Four or five almost together, then a brief lull, then another four or five earth-rippings. Now two more searchlights are slanting skywards. They are like two fingers probing into a dark rubber pillow.

We hunch over in the trench. Fragmentation bombs may be posted out of the sky with our names on them, and besides, there are too many jagged slivers of ack-ack flying about. My head is pressed against

97

the back of the narrow trench and a bomb blast sends a small landslide of sand down my neck. It is an uncanny feeling as it slithers down, and now there it is, very uncomfortable.

Evidently Johnson has a similar experience because he grunts, scrooges around and kneels down in the bottom of the trench. Knees in the sand, rump on heels, we face each other and await our destiny—or the end of this racket, so that we can go back to sleep.

"There must be a mess of Jerries over tonight, Johnson."

"Seems so, sir."

Throughout all of the day and at dinner, Johnson was an ordinary, husky soldier, not very distinguishable from thousands of others except for his ham-like hands and curiously shy smile. Silently and eagerly he went about his job of driving the captain and myself in the front area near the Libyan frontier. Now he may be my companion in death. If a bomb hits the edge of this trench, this will be our common grave.

In the remarkable brightness of the desert moon, Johnson's face is shining with eagerness again. His eyes are starry and his wide mouth is half parted in that shy smile of his. His head is cocked slightly to one side and he sits there on his heels in the sand like a terrier about to leap for a ball.

"Bastards they are, sir."

"Yeh," I agree. "Johnson, why don't you forget this *sir* business?"

"Why, I can't do that, sir. You're a war correspondent. You've the rank of captain."

"That's just so everybody will be happy all around. You're not on duty tonight and I'm just up here playing tiddlywinks. So let's forget it."

Johnson says he agrees. I doubt that he will. Saying "sir" is too thoroughly ingrained in very many Englishmen.

I recall this afternoon when we raced across the two miles in front of Hellfire Pass. The captain had said: "Sure, if you want to go. But the Jerries have dozens of guns trained on that road. At seven miles they can pick the radiator cap off this utility."

The utility—we call them station wagons—might be taken by the Germans as evidence that staff officers were scooting across that road in the unoccupied area between the Axis and British lines. That would be worth at least one 155 mm. shell to the Nazis.

98

I'd turned to Johnson but the captain touched my arm.

"No need to. He'll go where he's told."

Johnson took his rifle out of the rack above the seat, glanced at the breech and laid the gun across his knees. I arched an eyebrow.

"Can't tell, sir. We might run into a Jerry armored-car patrol."

In the oven-like desert afternoon there was the same starry look in his eyes, the same shy smile as now in the trench in the midst of the bomb-shattered night.

And that afternoon, racing across the mad two miles in front of Hellfire Pass from Kilo 24 to the coast road, expecting to get blown up to kingdom come, I'd asked Johnson the natural question.

"I think we will, sir," he'd replied. He kept one foot on the gas pedal, pushed to the floor board, his face exuding the same anticipatory happiness I see there now in the moonlight.

"This trench is better than getting it in a city," I remark. "No bricks on your head."

Johnson looks across at me sharply.

"I'd like to be back in England." He waits until five explosions fade away. "You know, sir, it's strange being out here. I don't mind the desert. I don't like it, but I don't mind it, either. It's just so bloody quiet out here."

"Well, it isn't quiet tonight."

"Oh, we get these raids about every night. You know what I mean. No real action. My wife, now, she writes me how worried she is about me, to be very careful, and how she prays for me every night, and all that. That seems, well, sort of silly, now doesn't it? All we're about is muckin' around in the desert. It's them back home that take the dirty end."

He pauses then, and in that slight hiatus in the anti-aircraft fire and the bomb blasts, all the horrors of the heavens seem to open up. We both jerk down into the ditch, faces in the sand and my ears feel as though someone had slapped them with the flat side of a paddle. The trench seems to rock like a lifeboat in a tossing sea and there is a low, sucking swish of wind rushing past. And then it is gone, and my ears ache a little, and I begin to untie the knots in my stomach, and the muscles in my arms and legs suddenly seem a little tired.

"Lucky, that one was," Johnson says, spitting out sand. "They hit a dump of land mines."

I'd seen such a dump this afternoon. A pile of square, black affairs to be buried alongside the roads or across sand trails to send invading tanks or transport cars sky high.

Without penitence or pause, the bombs and ack-ack resume.

"Never satisfied," I mutter. "They got something. They can go home now." Johnson pays no attention to my complaint.

"I don't like to say this, sir, you being a war correspondent."

"Oh, go ahead, Johnson. All I'm doing up here is getting sand in my teeth. Besides, if it's good they'll censor it. They always do."

"Well, it's like this. Compared to the people at home, a man doesn't feel he's doing his duty out here."

"Why, sure you are, man. If you didn't hang on to this desert the Germans would be here and you'd be back near Suez, or beyond."

"Yes, but I might be back in England, too. That's where the action is, sir."

"A dead Jerry is a dead Jerry, Johnson, wherever you shoot him."

"No, sir, it isn't the same. Not the same thing shooting them out here and shooting them back in England."

In the moonlight, at the bottom of a sand trench, Johnson's eyes are eager, his mouth is parted in a curious, shy smile. The bombs and ack-ack are clattering across the Western Desert, but Johnson is far away, back home in Britain.

Throughout the desert there are many harmless-looking opportunities for sudden death. No soldier who sees a water canteen or fountain pen picks it up. They are usually booby traps planted by the Italians or Germans.

Driving through the desert we came to an abandoned whippet tank. A shovel leaned against the side. Captain Fielding told Johnson to jump out and salvage the shovel. The driver went over to it, stood a foot away. "It might be a booby, sir," he called back. We kept a safe distance.

Fielding snorted disparagingly and got out. But he, too, kept his hand away from the shovel. Then he climbed back into the truck.

"There you are," he said, "that perfectly good shovel is rusting away just because dozens of people, coming along before we did, think it is a booby. Touch the shovel and it flies off in your face."

The British are not exactly in the back row on these booby traps, and they have created various forms of explosive surprises. One of the creators is known as the Mad Sapper. With the zeal of a fanatic, he tinkers all day on mischievous mechanisms. I asked him to explain a few of his newest surprises. He gave me the same answer he gives everyone in his stentorian voice: "Do not disturb me! I am the sword of Gideon and of the Lord!"

He won't give any of his secrets away. He allows the Italians and Germans to find out about them—just a mite too late to make use of the information.

Lonesome is the British word for the desert. Occasionally you see a long-legged, sand-colored desert snipe and a few fleet-footed gazelles. Once I saw a dog—a yellowish beast—running across the desert, loping like a wolf. I thought, "Now where the hell does that dog find anything to eat in this forsaken country?" Then the horrible answer suddenly occurred to me and I felt as though someone had punched me in the stomach.

The desert is many things to many men, but to all men the desert is primarily a place of flies. They are the most adhesive creatures in the world. A desert fly, the same breed that swarms over Cairo and Tripoli, prefers to die under the hand rather than give up his clinging bite.

A man shows his desert experience by the skill with which he drinks his tea, draws the enamel cup away from his mouth and sets it down with his hand covering the top before a single Stuka fly has dived inside the cup.

The most amazing speed in this maneuver I saw performed by Major General W. H. E. Gott, in command of the support group of the Armored Division. [Gott was killed later when a plane he was in was shot down by the Germans.]

Captain Fielding and I drove for three miles across the sand to find his tiny headquarters set down beside a solitary palm tree. This was euphemistically known as an oasis. A half dozen officers were sitting by a table and Major General Gott invited us to have a "bit of tea to cool you off, you know."

I must admit I was more interested in watching the general keep the flies out of his tea than I was in the summary of the situation he gave. I was interested, too, in those men sitting around that table who were so typical of the British officers in the Western Desert wherever I found them. Men here with two and three pips on their shoulders, or a crown, lieutenants, captains and majors. Once they were soft men who wore morning coats and striped gray trousers, a bowler and carried a cane. Now they are desert rats, speaking in Oxford accents and what Kipling called that "suave, deceptive drawl." They seem actually to thrive on sand and heat. They hate it, of course, as everyone hates the desert. But their attitude was and is:

"This is a game. To beat the Germans we first defeat the desert."

The Britishers I saw in action in the Western Desert seemed to have the tradition of the desert in their blood. Most of them had a few grains of sand in their blood, too.

All the terror does not come from meeting the enemy. Nature in the desert holds many terrors, and your mind contributes some more.

In that shimmering heat, mirages appear. Inviting lakes, luscious palm trees, acres of olive groves, mountains with tree-covered slopes. Once I was certain I saw a mosque dazzlingly bright on the horizon.

No man goes on reconnaissance or patrol without his canteen filled and a compass to guide him. To be lost in the desert without water turns the strongest of men, in forty-eight hours, into a stumbling, babbling maniac. Death follows under the scorching sun.

"A few weeks ago," a British major said, "I was lost in the desert for three hours. I was jolly well near to going berserk. I was never so frightened in my life."

That officer holds a decoration for his work at Ypres in the last war and is a capable leader in this one.

The desert is not the simple sand waste it once was. Nearly everywhere there are the remnants of battle. Battered tanks, wrecked trucks, tractors, artillery, broken rifles, belts of machine-gun cartridges, slim, graceful anti-tank shells, chianti bottles, tires, wheels and water canteens are scattered over the sands.

At one point an entire battery of Italian 105's stood lined up, barrels horizontally pointed toward the road. Some of them had a wheel or breech shattered. Ten yards behind stood five rusting tractors once used to haul them.

Thousands of Italian pith helmets whitened by the sun blob the country. Occasionally there's a coat, half-buried in the sand, or a blanket, and an astonishing number of shoes, not in pairs, but solitary, curling shoes, filled with sand and perhaps a scorpion or two. Thousands of shoes.

As I passed through this forlorn country, shivers darted up and down my spine. There were too many ghosts scattered about. For three years I had covered the news from Rome. I had watched those battered tanks once parading for Hitler in Rome in 1938. I had sipped chianti with some of the men who wore those pith helmets and sand-filled shoes.

When they were pre-war warriors I had watched their faces while Mussolini called them eight million bayonets. I had stood under the balcony at *Piazza Venezia* on June 10, 1940, at 6 o'clock in the evening with my wife and heard Il Duce send those men, our friends, off to their fate.

Amid silence and sand skating across the surface on wind puffs, the drifting dunes have covered over the rusting tanks and guns which once paraded so jauntily down *Via del 'Impero.*

On the ground in front of me is the coat of an Italian officer. And I think of the tear-faced woman in Rome whose son was reported missing in Libya. On the day the Italian Government ordered me out of the country for "continued hostile attitude" this mother said to me: "Believe me, *Signore,* the real Italian prays for a British victory. I pray for that."

But the saddest of sights is this: patches in the sand, shallow, elongated mounds, a dozen crosses sticking nakedly into the sun, and a sign: "Here lie buried twelve unknown Italians."

Machine-gunning and bombing in the desert is very much unlike a bombing in a city. There, you can pop in and out of doorways or underground passages if you must be on the move somewhere else.

In the desert, you lack the luxury of a cellar. You don't sit in a basement and rock with it each time a bomb hits, and wait for the ceiling to come tumbling down on you. In the desert you can't be an ostrich. For hundreds of miles in the Western Desert there isn't even a palm tree to crawl under.

You just sprawl, sit, crouch, stand and wait. On the naked plain, in full view of the enemy, you try to curl up like a sand dune. Or you flatten yourself on the ground like a streak across the desert. You quiver with fear, excitement or nervousness and try to side-slip the bombs.

It is one man against a hurtling missile, and nothing in between. Each high explosive "egg" whizzing out of the sky seems to be a personal matter between you and *that* bomb.

Spread-eagled in the barren sand, you await your destiny. To the British it amounts to this: someone in a few minutes is going to say, "Jolly bad luck." That remark is for one of his comrades.

Someone else is going to crawl up out of the sand, shake himself, wet his lips and say, "Jolly bad show." That's for the disappearing Axis planes.

A batman goes over and makes tea for the officers, and the men go back to tinkering with a motor, writing a letter, or dreaming of Brighton-on-the-Sea, with Pamela on his arm.

Fatal casualties in the Western Desert are three times as many as the injured. Ordinarily, the ratio is three injured to one dead. In the desert, however, it is often some time before the wounded man is found in the sand. By then, sand gangrene has set in, the sun has broiled out much of his vitality, and often his water is gone. And always casualty-clearing stations or base hospitals necessarily are fifty to one hundred miles distance from the scene of action.

Only those injured who are "walk-away casualties" survive their wounds in the Western Desert. That's the reason the British soldiers say that if an enemy bullet is to touch them, let it be a definitely good-night piece of lead.

The British, being the kind of people they are, don't like casualties. In most assault operations, the Germans use frontal attacks without apparent regard for the sons of mothers. They count on quick smothering of the enemy.

That is what happened in mid-August outside Tobruk. Except that the Germans used Italian infantry for a mass attack on Tobruk. The British wiped out the entire Eighth Bersaglieri Regiment.

The British notion is: We cannot afford casualties. One reason is to avoid further numerical weakness. Another is that the British fight with the idea that each man is important, if not to the army, at least to himself. The third reason is morale. Each death usually evokes the restrained remark: "Jolly bad luck for Throckmorton." But each death creates a cumulative effect on the morale of those who remain.

Wherever I went among the British there was no absence of courage, but there was a reluctance to have men die. The impression was very strong in me that the British expected to win this war with only meager casualties. There was a suspicion, too, that perhaps man power would be sacrificed at some later date but, in any event, men were being husbanded with what I thought was too great care.

Out of the flame-hot, sand-filled Khamsin of the Western Desert the fighter pilot emerges like a fade-in sequence in a movie. He wobbles and teeters at first, a towering, burly figure just recovering from the impact of the ground heat. He is unfastening his cloth tunic, pulling off his helmet, loosening his pistol holster. His blond, straight hair is matted and twisted with sweat, and his forehead and the sides of his nose glisten with it.

Inside the tent there is relief from the sand storm. A beer is set down in front of the pilot, warm beer, but wet. It's good enough to remove sand.

He wipes his mouth with the back of his hand. His eyes are red-rimmed, his face stubble-bearded. The two thin blue stripes on his shoulder make him a flight lieutenant.

He is blond, blue-eyed, fair-skinned, and if you dressed Nordic-looking Flight Lieutenant Archie in a Luftwaffe uniform he'd look as if he had just stepped out of Marshal Goering's office. That same thought came when I was among the German troops in Yugoslavia. Strip them of their gray-green uniforms and some of them would be typical of the boys just down from Cambridge.

"Good show?" someone asks Flight Lieutenant Archie. It's somewhat out of the ordinary for him to be down here at Sidi Barrani. This is the last landing field before the German and Italian positions at Sollum.

This sand-swept, desolate, top-of-the-world slice of the desert, where the wind always keeps the flying sock stretched taut, is not an airdrome. Too close for that. It serves only as a refueling base. But he'd landed here in his Curtiss P40, the ship the British call a Tomahawk.

"Why," the pilot says, "it wasn't too bad actually. Had a bit of a mix with Jerry. Messerschmitt 109. But I rather think there was an Eyetie pilot in it.''

The flight lieutenant's accents are Oxonian and his inclination is to be as reticent as the lions of Trafalgar Square.

"Chased him all over the place. Used almost all my gas and almost all my ammunition. Really exasperating. He apparently objected to a spot of fighting. Dash it all," he suddenly bursts out, "the fellow seemed extr'ordinarily keen to break off."

He appears to wince as he says that. He hates to accuse another pilot, even an enemy, of lack of courage.

"Devilishly pretty morning up there. Six thousand feet and you're out of this bloody sand storm and heat."

His eyes travel to the flies blackening the table and scrambling to get inside his empty beer glass.

"And no flies up there, rather."

He pronounces it "rawther-r-r" and works one eye as though a monocle should be there.

Mutual friends and my purposes as an American war correspondent established, Flight "Loot" Archie relaxes.

"We run into more Eyeties now than we used to. They don't do much, actually. Deuced thing to say, but as a matter of fact they just float around the sky and look decorative."

At that a smile breaks over the face of the base officer, his eyes inflamed with days of sand and wind in them, and for once the utterly bored look goes out of his face.

A sergeant comes into the tent and tells Lieutenant Archie his ship is ready. "Right-ho." He picks up his tunic and pistol.

As he steps out of the tent his eyes narrow to slits to face the driving sand, twisting and sweeping across the field.

"Thanks for the beer," he calls, and fades into the mist of the sand storm.

On Sunday, July 20th, Captain Fielding drove me to Bagush. With Squad Leader Martin and Godfrey Anderson of the *Associated Press* (captured later by the Italians in the Western Desert) we had a beer at the Bagush Arms.

Arrangements had already been made for me to fly back to Cairo in order to do a broadcast for CBS that night.

Wing Commander Horton and Captain Munroe took me over to the plane. It turned out to be a Lysander—a small compact plane in charge of a sergeant pilot.

Commander Horton stuck his lips up to my ear and said: "Do you want a parachute?"

I almost yelled, "Sure!" but instead nodded my head. In that sweeping sand, swept across the airdrome by a devil's broom, speech means a mouthful of sand driving right down to your lungs.

The sergeant pilot searched through the plane, then called back: "Someone must have taken the extra 'chute."

Wing Commander Horton smiled and said: "Oh, you won't need one. This plane has never crashed before."

"Famous last words," I said and clambered into the cockpit, jamming myself among mailbags. I noticed the pilot wearing *his* parachute.

A very heavy sand storm was blowing. It slapped the plane from stratum to stratum like a ping-pong ball. I took off my sweat-soaked clothes and wondered what made men fight for this sand-filled, suffocating, miserable blankness of earth.

We came down at Birgel Arab and stayed ten minutes.

We took off again and began coming down at another spot. Just as we hit the ground I couldn't hold off any longer. As we touched I threw open the cockpit cover. Roaring along the ground at seventy miles an hour my head hung over the side and the wind painted my breakfast on the side of the plane.

Once again we were off and I was so weak from the heat and air sickness that I closed my eyes, buried my head in my arms, and wished and prayed for a parachute. I am convinced that if I had had a parachute I would have jumped. And then we came over the delta of the Nile.

The green below was in incredible contrast with the miles and miles of sand over which we had passed. And in the delta there was one village after another and finally the pyramids. The pyramids of Cairo, the statuaries, the mosques.

We came down at Heliopolis at 4:30. I clambered out and fell flat on my face from exhaustion. The pilot officer who met the plane took me to officer's mess to get me a cup of tea. I couldn't drink it. I got in a taxi and was at the hotel at 5:00, more dead than I had ever been before in my life. I took a hasty, hot bath. That hot bath was a painful experience. Every sand bite and mosquito bite hurt like a sore boil in the hot water. Then I staggered over to the censor's headquarters and wrote my script and got it approved.

I decided that night to do my weekly cable to *Newsweek Magazine*. I worked on that and took it to the censor's at his home at midnight, had it approved, took it to the cable office and then went on the air at 2:40 in the morning. I had three minutes and forty-five seconds to tell all that I saw in the desert. My diary for that date says: "It is a bit disheartening with all the tortures of this trip, the great effort I put on my script, almost getting killed a half dozen times and then three minutes and forty-five seconds on the air."

I fell asleep that night with the words of Captain Fielding ringing in my ears. Fielding had said: "The worst trick we could play on the Germans is to give them this whole bloody desert."

"DEFENSE IS
THE BEST OFFENSE"

Tuesday, July 22nd:
I wish I had a good assignment.

Wednesday, July 23rd:
Am in a complete state of exhaustion today from my desert trip. Tried to write a magazine article on Syria, but lacked the energy and so gave it up. I am now broadcasting only twice a week. I wish I had more work to do.

I went out to the Anglo-American hospital to see Hal Denny and Dick Mowrer. Almost all the correspondents have something wrong with them. Denny has been quite sick with some intestinal illness and Mowrer has a kind of rheumatism which has placed a considerable strain on his heart. The censor, Lieutenant Henderson, is also there. He fell over the other day from a heart attack.

Rosamond Mowrer and I went swimming at Gezira and lunched with Bob Crisp, a South African captain in the British Tank Corps, a very swell guy. Crisp was in the battle of Greece and also in a number of operations in the Western Desert. He is a world-famous cricket player and something of a newspaperman himself, but above all he has impressed me as one of the main reasons why Great Britain will fight to the last man.

Thursday, July 24th:
The British Embassy sponsors a news program in Greek at the very time when I would need transmitters for a thrice-weekly special news broadcast to America. I saw a Secretary at the British Embassy and asked if they couldn't change the period of the Greek news broadcast. It only required five minutes to learn that the British Embassy would be happy to forego its time. You could have knocked me over with a feather.

Afterwards I saw Colonel Astley at Public Relations, and he asked me whether I would be interested in going to Djibouti in French Somaliland. I said I wasn't. Astley in private life is a stockbroker and the divorced husband of Madeleine Carroll of London and Hollywood.

"Talking of places to go, Colonel, if something happens at Dakar, I would like now to ask formally that CBS be included in the first group of correspondents that goes to Dakar. I will place my name on the list right now."

"Do you think something is going to be done there?"

"Well, I have a feeling we are moving to the showdown."

Friday, July 25th:

In the lobby of the Continental I ran into Russ Hill, just back from Syria, and a Paramount newsreel man named Hart. Hart complained about not being able to get pictures. He has been with the British fleet and he says:

"The Navy doesn't want us. We wait for a year for a picture, and we may never even get one. We get every courtesy on board a ship but no pictures. Anyhow, the best action comes at night."

Lunched with Alexander Kirk, the American minister, and we began talking about a future peace. Why, I don't know, because peace certainly isn't in sight. Kirk says it must be a gradual affair. No one person or group can decide problems permanently. That's what caused this war and would cause the next one. Each problem of geography, economics, foreign relations and markets should be decided from time to time by commissions. You can't meet at a peace conference and hand out a sealed two-volume book and say, "There's peace for the world." It must be a fluid affair to meet changing conditions.

Kirk is one of those diplomats who favors action now instead of procrastinating.

"Every town and city in Italy and Germany," he says, "should be bombed every day for a month. They ought to send a plane over Berlin, even if only to drop firecrackers in the park."

Kirk is rather bitter, in his very polite way, of course, about the way the British have been expecting miracles to do the job for them.

"They are taking the Russian affair the same way," he said, "expecting the Russians to do the job."

"That seems to be the case in the high command," I remarked. "Even Wavell called the Russo-German War a breathing spell instead of a chance to attack."

"Yes," Kirk said, "and I told Wavell it was the most immoral thing he ever said."

I asked Kirk if he had encountered the same thing I had, namely, a defensive mentality among the General Staff instead of an offensive spirit.

"Of course, what the British ought to be doing right now is pushing through to French Morocco and Algeria."

Kirk favored our withdrawing our diplomatic missions from Italy and Germany at once.

"It would give those people the shock they need. Yes, and we ought to get out of Vichy, too."

The talk swung to Japan because the Japanese credits had just been frozen back home.

"The First Secretary of the Japanese Embassy came to see me today," Kirk said. "I never met him before, but he said he came to say good-bye." Kirk recounted their conversation.

"Where are you going?"

"I go to Japan."

"How are you going?"

"I go by boat to New York."

"Do you know how long that takes?"

"Oh, yes, six or seven weeks."

"A good many things may change by the time you reach New York."

"I do not mind the winter in New York."

The Japanese diplomat asked Kirk for letters to people in New York.

"Well," Kirk said, "you see, I have been away for such a long time that I don't know anyone there any more. All my friends have gone away."

Kirk mentioned all those who had been kicked out of Washington. To each name the Jap replied: "He no work."

The Japanese finally drew a conclusion from the trend of the conversation and said to Kirk: "You no like our country?"

"We don't like Mr. Hitler, and we don't like aggressors. How do you feel about it?"

"I no feel."

Kirk's idea is that the Japs are not very clever, that three-quarters of the time they are not functioning, and behind their bland faces they only begin to function when their own interests are directly concerned.

At the present time Japan is taking bases in Indo-China with an O.K. from Vichy. I asked Kirk if he thought that would mean war with the United States.

"I hope not," Kirk said. "That's just what Hitler wants."

The talk swung to the Balkans, and I voiced the opinion that the British ought to bomb Sofia since they knew the Germans are going into Bulgaria.

"They can't," Kirk said. "They have to wait until twenty British diplomats have a chance to leave."

"Then, too," I said, "it wouldn't be in the tradition of British gentlemanliness to bomb the capital of a country not at war."

"I'm afraid," Kirk said, "that's a mentality I shall never be able to understand."

Brigadier General Shearer, head of Military Intelligence in Cairo, called a meeting this afternoon for war correspondents, one of those meetings in which you can't report anything that's said. Among the things he did say were that if the Russians held out to September 1st, the British are reasonably sure that no attack on Turkey will be attempted until spring.

"We are pleased," he said, "and surprised by Russian resistance."

One of the correspondents said that the British troops are puzzled about the alliance with Russia. The Tommies say that a month ago the Russians were swine and now they are friends. Shearer said he was trying to get a line on it from London in order to acquaint the troops with the official British view.

On the basis of Shearer's remarks, this sector may be very quiet for a long time. With the Far East popping up it occurs to me that I might ask Paul White for a leave, return to the States, and ask to get assigned to the Far East. I think there is time to do that before anything happens in the Far East.

112

10:30 p.m.

I have just received a startling cable:

WOULD YOU WISH SINGAPORE ASSIGNMENT. ALSO ADVISE HOW
LONG WOULD TAKE REACH THERE   WHITE

This leaves me flabbergasted. Of course I am all for Singapore. I immediately sent back a cable:

SINGAPORE SWELL   BROWN

Sunday, July 27th:

For me the happiest feature of going to Singapore is this: I'll then be only a few days by Clipper from San Francisco, and San Francisco is only twelve hours from Martha in New York. Perhaps I'll even be able to get home-leave in a few months.

This was a frenzied day lining up details to go to Singapore. The American Consulate has facilitated my visa and validated my passport for travel in the Far East. There was one fortunate break: I got my Iraq visa without a moment's delay this morning. This was because I had applied for it to go to Russia several weeks ago. After waiting ten days it came through, but I did nothing about picking it up because the assignment to Russia was canceled. Now I was able to get it to go to Singapore.

At Public Relations I told Colonel Astley: "The censorship here was better than in Rome. You usually expect your friends to treat you worse than your enemies." He laughed at that.

Colonel Tod was very happy to hear I was going to Singapore.

"I think you will have plenty of news there," he said.

Ran into Hank Gorrell of *UP* who has just come back from Syria. We went over to my special spot where we had chocolate cake and ice cream, a dish I've been having every afternoon in Cairo. But Hank is the first correspondent I could sell on the wonders of chocolate cake and ice cream.

I think a stream of correspondents are going to move toward Singapore. I've told the boys I'm pulling out, and they all say they are going to suggest to their papers that they be given Singapore assignments.

Hank Gorrell, Alex Clifford of the *Daily Mail,* Alan Moorehead of the *London Daily Express,* and Ronald Matthews of the *London Daily Herald* told me they have already done so.

Cairo is filled with chatter and most of it takes place on verandahs. People drift in and out, pausing for a drink, then move on. I am sitting at a table with an old friend. His London paper had sent him to Rome before the war to do a series of stories on Italy's food and industrial situation. I had helped him then, took him to some Fascist bureaus, introduced him to a few Italians who had views contrary to Government statistics and answered a good many questions.

We'd sat at a sidewalk table at Rosatti's on *Via Veneto* in the hot Roman sunshine and exchanged opinions about Munich and how soon the war would come, and what hell there'd be when it did.

Now we are sitting on the verandah of Shepheard's Hotel in Cairo and the things Munich spawned stretch for thousands and thousands of miles on both sides of Suez.

He wears khaki with two shiny brass pips and that mixture of uncertainty and confidence which seems to go with every lieutenant's commission.

"Thank God," the lieutenant says, "I'm not working on a newspaper any more."

The Briton is given to quiet determination which is sometimes confused with diffidence, even indifference, but seldom does he go in for fervor. And the lieutenant's remark is passionate, dripping with feeling, tense with the inflection of an actor. That remark calls for a question, and I ask it.

"Why didn't you continue as a correspondent?"

"I'd want to write too many things, old boy. But then, perhaps as a correspondent I wouldn't see so many things, and then the urge wouldn't be so strong. The sort of things that make you absolutely blind with rage. Goodness knows," the lieutenant continues thoughtfully, "we're not a stupid people. No one can believe that, and I'd be the last to think it."

"The Germans think you are," I remark. "For that matter, Lindbergh says you are, and he has a good many followers."

"He's wrong about that. The thing is, I think, that we have too many traditions. And we won't give them up. Well, traditions can outlive their usefulness. Many of ours have."

Sour-faced Egyptian waiters continuously hover about pretending readiness to replenish our glasses and more than ready with akimbo ears to absorb a snatch of salable information. Cairo is a good clearing house for observing waiters and observing correspondents.

"One of your traditions," I say, "is muddling through. I'm sick to death of hearing that expression."

A captain, usually placid, now shows up, his eyes filled with that kind of fury I find among soldiers when they mention their experiences in Greece and Crete.

"Muddling through is the whole basis of our operations," he says. "Because we can't do a certain thing or think we can't, we don't believe the Germans can. Well, they go ahead and do it and where are we?"

Nurses in white with red stripes on their capes and WAAF's in khaki blouses and skirts and perky caps drift in and out of the Byzantine doorway. All the officers sitting on the verandah jerkily halt their conversation in mid-sentence or pull their noses away from the whisky-and-soda to steal a glance at the girls, or stare boldly at them to see if they know them or would like to know them.

"One incredible blunder after another," the officer says calmly. "The most amazing things, mistakes that you couldn't believe a professional officer could make. I'm not a military expert, but any first-form boy could recognize them."

The lieutenant moves off. He's seen enough mistakes. And the young captain reels off a dolorous list of blunders. It sounds as though I am listening to a history of all the British mistakes of World War One. The locales are changed, but history is repeating itself in the Britisher's words—calm, cool and terrible words. That, however, is a post-war story.

"Muddling through," he snorts. "What a generous phrase!"

"But tell me this," I say, "why does every correspondent have to go nuts trying to get out stories that help the British cause? You have to fight five times as hard to get out a story favorable to you people as we did in dictatorship countries to get out a story unfavorable to them."

"Well," he drawls, "the services figure this is their war and they don't want to be bothered with correspondents, for one thing. They don't seem to realize that this is a war of the people of Britain. They don't know that this is 1941 and that today a man in a factory is just as important as a soldier.

"Then, too, our attitude is that our cause is so good it doesn't need any advertising. Any decent-minded person ought to be able to see that. We're paying dearly for that."

I tell him I've already told that to officials and they look at me with that pitying stare one reserves for a pariah from another planet where there is no England and no Englishmen.

Decrepit taxis chug along the street in front, their horns blowing furiously and without apparent purpose except to swell the cacophony.

The dragoman on the sidewalk swings open the doors of the taxis with one hand and keeps the other in a receptive position for *baksheesh*. Noise, heat, red fezes, hands for alms, guides and dirty-book peddlers, it is all very Egyptian, not a great deal different from the Cook's folders of 1938.

The war is just a bad, confusing dream in Cairo, profitable for the merchants and hated by the people.

The opportunist Court leans toward the Axis; the people are concerned only with gouging the troops. A rather neat Fifth-Column organization waits for the day to stab the Allies in the back. Petty sabotage every now and then, telephone wires cut, and thefts. A strange people who would not fight when the Italians invaded their country, who squeal like an injured child when bombs drop on its soil, but do not go to war. A people without energy and a nation without fire. Egypt today is a far cry from the Pharoahs.

The Egyptians differ somewhat from the Turks. The Turks hate everyone, including themselves. The Egyptians confine themselves just to hating every foreigner. They reserve an especial animus for the English.

"Miracles," the British captain says, "that's what we're waiting for. Russia was a miracle for us. No one here will admit that the bloody Bolsheviks saved us in the Mediterranean, but it's true.

"You sense it, too, don't you, Brown? This defensive mentality. It doesn't come from the troops. The harder they're hit the more they want to get back to it. It comes from the top, from the pukka sahib boys. It's this fear of another Norway, another Greece, another Crete. We don't even think in offensive terms," the captain says. "We're waiting for a miracle, and the only miracle left to us is the United States."

116

Diaries taken from German prisoners show their fear and awe of the desert, and I based tonight's broadcast on the point that the Axis is getting jittery in the desert; that the nerves of the Axis troops are cracking; that the Germans can't whip the desert.

Lieutenant Cumberbatch pulled out a sheaf of papers containing several hundred "stops"—that is, the things you are forbidden to report, and one of the "stops" said:

"No personal account or story can be taken from the diary of a prisoner."

I contended that the "stop" order did not apply to the case because I was not using a personal account or story from a diary. Cumberbatch finally conceded that the "stop" order did not apply, but still could not give me any reason why he excised my mention of the diary.

One of the censors said that if the Germans know that we are getting their diaries their men will stop carrying them.

I argued the point for a time, taking the view that the Germans obviously have instructed their men, just as the British have, not to carry diaries in places where there is some chance of capture. But these diaries were taken from men who had violated that order. The censors countered that nevertheless it would give information to the Germans that diaries has been found.

"All right," I laughed, "in the interests of Anglo-American solidarity I'll cut it out."

Censorship in Cairo was somewhat complicated by the fact that Egypt is a sovereign state. Egypt had broken off diplomatic relationship with Germany and Italy, but was not actually in the state of war with the Axis.

That situation gave many a headache to the British authorities and also caused many a headache for the correspondents. Every message that was passed by the military censors also had to go through the censorship of the Egyptian Civil Service.

Although there was an interminable list of things we could not mention, the list was always added to and nothing was ever taken away. Here is a list of some of the things we could not use:

Avoid any mention of any sect: that is Moslem, Christian, Jew, etc.

Acts of Heroism: no names of individuals except when given by an official hand-out.

Identification: no names of Units except as officially announced.

Water: no mention of water holes or other points where water can be found in the desert.

Prisoners of War: no direct personal story or story taken from diaries or captured documents.

Escape: no stories from any theatre of war.

Alarm and Despondency: no story tending to create these among troops or civilians.

Unexploded bombs: no mention of disposal methods or sections.

Indian Troops: no mention of any sect; that is Moslem, Hindu, Brahmin, etc.

New Weapons: no mention.

New Tactics: no mention.

Sea-borne Operations: no mention.

Movements: no mention of the movement of any British or Dominion Cabinet Minister or important person except when officially released.

Monday, July 28th:
An incredible number of details to complete today in order to shove off for Singapore. I bought an Egyptian bracelet for Martha.

Took all my papers to censorship, including this diary, to have them approved and sealed in an envelope in order to save difficulties en route.

I went to say good-bye to Kirk this afternoon.

"I'll miss you," he said, "but I am delighted to see you going. I don't feel the least bit sorry for you, going to that climate."

Kirk said he hoped we wouldn't go to war against the Japs unless we also declared war on the Germans. He thought the Japs may go for Hongkong and "that, of course, means war."

I bumped into Randolph Churchill, the Prime Minister's son, at Military Censorship offices. It seems he has taken over Colonel Tod's job. I presented myself and he said: "I know your boss, Bill Paley, very well."

"That's more than I do," I said. "I have never met Paley."

Randolph Churchill impressed me with his evident anxiety to do a
118

good job, but I did get the idea that he wanted to be "one of the boys" and at the same time let no one forget that he was a Major of British Intelligence.

He showed me a pamphlet he had written for distribution to all officers. It explained the British view on political matters which were puzzling to the troops, and pointed out that Russia was helping fight the Germans and should be regarded with the greatest friendliness.

"What do you think of it?" Churchill asked.

"It's a very good idea. The men are wondering about a good many things. But there's something missing."

"What's that?"

"Well, almost every soldier I've talked to and most of the officers are worried about America. They think they're fighting our fight. They are and they don't think we're doing very much. They don't know why we aren't in the war. All we do, they say, is cheer."

"You think that's prevalent?"

"Very much so. I think it would be a good idea if you would point out something about American internal politics, why the President hasn't been able to go farther. Explain why we have strikes, the power of the isolationists, and something about the group represented by Lindbergh, Wheeler, Nye and Fish. The troops ought to understand more about why we are doing as we are. If they understood, they'd feel better."

"Very fine idea," Major Churchill said. "I'm putting out this pamphlet every week and your suggestion will be in next week's release."

Around noon I went to GHQ and after considerable difficulty getting through guards saw Colonel Tod. He was so appreciative of my coming to say good-bye that I was embarrassed. He gave me a letter to the head of British Intelligence in Singapore.

"I don't think there will be anything in the Western Desert for six weeks or two months," Tod said. "They didn't start last year until September and it is too hot now."

I felt sick at my stomach because there was nothing in Tod's remarks about: "We'll be ready to start something in six weeks."

There is still the mentality of defense—the thought only of hanging on and not attacking.

FLIGHT INTO WAR

Wednesday, July 30th:

Early in the morning I was out at the seaplane base on the Nile for the take-off to Singapore. Since I carry so many papers I am always concerned by last-minute difficulties in getting out of a country or into a country. But the Egyptian customs didn't even open my bags.

The British Imperial Airways' flying-boat rested easily in the water. We were taken out to it in a launch. At dawn, we scooted down the Nile for forty-five seconds and then lifted easily into the air.

The pyramids were on our right, just catching the early morning sun. The sun was a bright red, a crimson red, circle off to the left over this rough, wild, desert country. In a few minutes we sighted the Suez, thin as a thermometer with a bulge at the end, and Singapore lay six thousand miles to the East. Over the canal end of the Red Sea and then over the Desert of Sinai. We went over the Dead Sea at five thousand feet. It's a dull blue color and has a peculiar elongated shape. We are paralleling the Wadilel Araba, just west of the route Lawrence of Arabia followed from Ma'an in his drive toward Damascus in the last war.

The River Jordan twists down below us. It's main course from Tiberius to the Dead Sea is 185 miles long, but by air it's sixty miles. Five minutes before the first stop we crossed over the most modern thing in these parts, the oil pipeline from Mosul to Haifa.

We came down the Tiberius to light on the Sea of Galilee. We came in just below a fort built by the Crusaders and we had time for a brief swim.

You see things from the air you never see on the ground because when you are walking the sand in your shoes bothers you too much. In the air you can see how accurate are the historical descriptions of Palestine. You can see evidences that this once was a land flowing with milk and honey.

The steward on the plane just pointed something out to me. He said

120

wherever there had been Arabs, trees have ceased to grow and deserts have come. I do not know whether that's true or not, but it certainly is true that down below us, stretching for thousands of miles, there are deserts and there are Arabs.

The skipper of this flying boat is John Alcock, brother of the Captain Alcock who made the first crossing of the Atlantic. This Alcock piloting the ship, recently made five trips evacuating troops from Crete in this same flying boat. In order to get as many as possible out of Crete he jammed in seventy soldiers on each trip.

Between Habbanyia in Iraq and Basra we passed over the country where civilization was born. Down below us, too, was Kut-el-aman, where General Townsend was besieged in the last war by the Turks and finally captured.

We've just passed over the Garden of Eden and the Land of Sodom, Gomorrah, Babylon, Ur, Chaldee. The Garden of Eden is not what you might expect. Once there may have been tempting apples there, but nothing now.

We came down on the Tigris River, and there is a beautiful hotel at Basra, the Shatt-al-Arab, very modern and comfortable. I had tea with the purser and one of the pilots. It helped me recover after vomiting fifteen times en route from Habbanyia to Basra.

In town I bought Martha a beautiful Persian belt, hand-painted and made of camel bone.

The heat in Basra is the worst I have ever encountered, but the food is rather good. I ordered tomato juice and then I demanded to see the can, to be sure that it was canned and not fresh. Here in this country everything the white man eats must come from a can.

Sinbad, the sailor, came from Basra, and it shows how smart he was to have gotten out of the place. The city is the same as when Sinbad was here, and just as hot.

Thursday, July 31st:
Before dawn we took off and flew the entire way to Bahrein Island over the Persian Gulf at ten to eleven thousand feet altitude. Bahrein is one of the great oil centers of the world and the chief pearling center of the Persian Gulf. We were taken in a launch to the end of the pier, where dark-skinned boys had orange drinks waiting for us. We took

on three young Americans returning to the United States after three years abroad in the interests of big American oil companies.

We came down on Karachi. Going through customs, the British Civil Service was in full operation. I had with me a clipping from *Time Magazine* on the fighting in the Western Desert, and they read it a half dozen times with great suspicion.

"It's this last paraghaph," said the Chief Inspector of Customs. "That says something unfavorable to the British."

"I bought that magazine in Cairo where it passed through British censorship," I told him. "I often write unfavorable things about the British myself which go through censorship."

He kept the clipping and said it would be given back to me at Calcutta.

A map of the Middle East which bore a stamp of the military censorship in Cairo bothered them a good deal. Fortunately, all my other papers were sealed in an envelope with red wax or the censors of Karachi would still be pawing over them.

Tonight in the dining room of the Hotel Karachi seven of us on the plane ate together, also a British major of the Indian Army. He gave something of the picture of India preparing for war. It was not a very impressive picture.

Friday, August 1st:
Only two hours sleep. Up at 3:30.
Sign post at the Airport reads:
To Singapore 3,386 miles
To Sydney 8,157 miles
To Alexandria 2,540 miles
To Durbin 6,970 miles
To London 4,915 miles

We have changed crews here and flying boats. We now ride the *Canopus*. We took off in pitch darkness stabbed by the buoys lit by oil flares to guide the route for the take-off. We hit a swell and I thought we were going to turn over, but we finally got up in the air and circled over Karachi. Then we went into a glide for a landing.

I thought we were in trouble. I asked the purser and he said:

"We're coming back for some technical reason. I don't know

whether the pilot has been called back or is coming back for his own reasons."

It developed that the captain was given the wrong set of maps, those for the west flight back to Cairo. We got away again and struck out straight across the Great Sind Desert.

This flying boat, the *Canopus,* was the original flagship of the Imperial Airways and was built in October, 1936. It has flown over a million miles and is still in use. This new pilot we took on at Karachi is easier on our eardrums. He doesn't take us up and down too fast.

"That other bloke, Alcock," the steward remarked, "likes to think he is in a dive bomber."

We came down at Raj Samand, on a smooth lake. The purser doesn't like this place. He says: "There are vipers in the water and pythons in the trees!"

This is a holy lake. Like everything else in India it was made holy in order to keep it pure.

All afternoon we've paralleled the Ganges River. My pen is leaking at this altitude. I am having great difficulty making these notes.

One of the American oilmen is drinking beer. That would kill me the way my stomach feels.

When it is bumpy up here it feels as if a huge dog had grabbed hold of the plane and is worrying it, first gently and then severely. Down below there are monkeys and Bengal tigers, but at 8,000 feet we can't hear the monkeys chatter or the tigers roar. Occasionally there is a compound and the houses with their rounded roofs look like bubbles. The river is snaking all over the countryside in a hundred different branches.

We came down at sunset on the muddy Hooghly River. As we came ashore in the launch a body was burning on the bank of the river with fifteen mourners sitting around. One kept feeding the flames with wood and when the heat brought the body to a sitting position in the way a burning match will curl, one of the mourners, the eldest son, was accorded the great honor of cracking his father over the skull, to flatten him out.

We went into Calcutta to the Great Eastern Hotel and Purser Morgan helped me buy some Kashmir things for Martha.

In front of most rooms in the hotel, either stretched across the doorway or in a corridor, an Indian bearer lay curled up. He lay in indolent watchfulness, ready to serve and protect. That sight of human beings lying like faithful dogs before a hearth always remains with me. Insignificant white people, nonentities in their own countries, came out to India, had a bearer, or two or three and a half dozen servants. In India you didn't work, you employed. You were master here by inheritance and tradition, and not by effort.

In my room I saw the strangest insect, two inches long. I called in the Indian servant to ask what it was.

"That," he said, "is an Indian cockroach."

I thought this was a case of boastfulness, like the Californians calling the Florida oranges just a California pea, so I checked further. It really was an Indian cockroach. A big country deserves big insects!

Saturday, August 2nd:

We have three new passengers out of Calcutta, three American tobacco men who have been in Turkey buying the fillings for American cigarettes. We are over the Ganges Delta with its million mouths. Not until we were one hundred miles out of the Bay of Bengal did the water change from a muddy brown to a dull blue. The silt from the Ganges extends one hundred miles out to sea.

At Akyab, inside the Burma frontier, we came down in the inlet of very muddy water lined by forests and swamps filled with chattering monkeys and some crocodiles.

The resident agent of the Airways company has told me a local story about the owner of Akyab's single cinema. In every picture that comes to Akyab, he cuts out all the scenes showing girls kicking their legs and love episodes. Then, at the time of an important local marriage, the movie operator gives a showing of disjointed, erotic shots from scores of films showing legs and love-making. It takes an hour to show the Hollywood cheesecake-and-oomph in this special presentation and the prices are special—three times the usual rate.

It has been extremely smooth riding thus far this morning. At this height of 8,000 feet we hardly seem to be moving. There is no vibration whatever. Everybody is sleeping. I need it, too, but how the devil can you make notes and sleep too? Some day in Singapore I am going to sleep twenty-four hours.

We passed over the Irrawaddy River just now at 12,000 feet and are

124

coming into Rangoon. I don't see any flying fish. Kipling must have seen Rangoon at a different season.

Permission was refused me to bring a camera ashore. I wanted to make further inquiry and was told by the guard at the base that this is Saturday afternoon.

"Well, your police don't lay off for the week-end, do they?" I said.

"No, but there won't be anyone there with sufficient authority."

Rangoon is more than the "Road to Mandalay." It's also the road to Lashio and Chungking, the seaport for the Burma Road, and also the key to China's salvation. The docks were busy, the river filled with freighters. I saw the American Export liner, *Exbrook,* with a huge American flag painted on the side. The flag was good to see.

Rangoon is not a tourist spot. There isn't a tourist atmosphere about it. Women sit around smoking huge, fat cigars, drawing so hard on them that their cheeks cave in at each inhalation. Evidently the cigars were a bit strong. Every woman I've seen smoking reclines as though the cigars were too much for her. The faces of all the women are painted grotesquely with a white powder. They look like cigar-smoking death masks. This is my first contact with the Far East. It's like a movie.

I bought a souvenir in Rangoon. It's the most expensive memento I've bought anywhere, a paddy boat carved out of a solid piece of ivory of incredibly fine workmanship and beauty. It was a silly, bulky thing to buy. It fits into a large box and is so delicate I shall be amazed if I ever get it back to America in one piece, but it's a boat, and I can't resist boats.

Tonight I sent a cable to Paul White giving my time of arrival in Singapore and stating that I would be prepared to give a broadcast immediately after my arrival.

I notice the papers here today seem to clutch at tiny straws which might indicate Japan's "Pacific intentions." I guess the British here are worried about letting the Burmese know they face any danger.

Sunday, August 3rd:

We raced down the Irawaddy on the take-off. There is a remarkable blueness to the dawn, but I don't see it "coming up like thunder." So there goes another of my illusions about Kipling.

125

Within three hours after leaving Rangoon we came down on the Mekong River at Bangkok, the capital of Thailand. There was a very quiet atmosphere about the customs. The word, *Thai*, means freedom, and this country at the moment is being subjected to considerable Japanese pressure. Thailand may have to throw Thai out of its language.

Diary Comment:

It is impossible to conceive how an army could find its way down from Thailand to Singapore through this terrain. The jungle and disease would finish off any army which had to face even minor guerrilla operations. It won't be an invasion. It would be a jungle safari. I think the monkeys in the jungle down below are going to remain undisturbed by artillery fire.

After I made that note I fell asleep and the steward woke me for tea and to announce we would be in Singapore in twenty minutes. For five days of flying, from Suez to Singapore, at almost every stop we had touched on water under the protection of the British flag. It was a stunning reflection on Empire.

Over the island of Singapore the town looked aged and weatherbeaten. The roofs were red and even near the town there seemed to be thick jungle.

At the customs office of Kalang Airport a huge customs official with dripping flesh and a big smile said: "You're Cecil Brown, aren't you? We've been expecting you."

"You said that pretty ominously."

"It sounds bad," he laughed, "when all you journalist vultures start flocking here."

"I came for war," I remarked. "Is it coming?"

"Of course not," he retorted. "We've had these Jap scares before. They are an old thing with us by now."

While my bags were being carried into a taxicab I got on the telephone at the Airport Administrative building. I called censors, Ministry of Information people and the radio station in order to arrange for a broadcast immediately, since I expected there would be an answer to my cable from Rangoon asking to be scheduled on arrival in Singapore.

At Raffles Hotel, where my suite has a verandah, I called the American Consulate to find out if there were cables. There was none.

Representatives from the *Singapore Free Press* and the *Malaya Tribune* interviewed me. I thought it strange, but they explained that I was the first American war correspondent to come to Singapore and the general tone of their questions was: "Will war come to the Far East?"

I had dinner tonight in the beautiful palm-lined courtyard of Raffles Hotel. Each table, set on the grass, had a pink-shaded lamp and a vase of orchids. The Argyle and Sutherland Highlanders band played for the smartly dressed officials and women in gay print dresses. The members of the band wore plaid hats and white coats and kilts, and the war seemed a million miles away.

PREPARATION
FOR CHAOS

"Between the acting of a dreadful thing and the
first motion, all the interim is like a phantasma or
a hideous dream."

—Shakespeare, *Julius Caesar*

THE DEFENSIVE MENTALITY

Monday, August 4th:
This is August Bank Holiday, hot, sticky, humid. Most everything is closed. I went off to the American Consulate in the Union Building on Collyer Quay to make myself known and to check up on cables again. There I met Yates McDaniel of the *Associated Press,* a prematurely gray-haired man of about thirty-five, who was born in the Far East and knows it rather well. He took me up to meet Commander William Burrows, head of the Services Public Relations Organization, which deals with censorship and correspondents, and hands out the official releases. Burrows was a huge, gruff, red-faced man around fifty-five, dressed in Navy summer white, and very hearty and cordial. But I thought, in that first meeting, somewhat pompous.

I immediately requested my transfer from the Middle East as an accredited correspondent of the British forces in the Far East. He was somewhat puzzled as to how such a procedure could be arranged, but said he'd look into it.

I then asked to see Sir Robert Brooke-Popham, Commander-in-Chief of the Far East. Burrows chuckled and said that Brooke-Popham was not giving interviews to any correspondents, but that he might hold a general conference shortly. "You can attend that, if you wish."

Back at the Consulate I talked with Kenneth S. Patton, the Consul General, a strange creature. He acted as though I were a load of dynamite come there to explode his complacency. I talked to him for nearly an hour and my diary shows these are the only notes I found worth recording:

"What Japan does," Patton said, "depends on the rigidity of the trade sanctions and embargos placed against her. If they are rigidly applied, Japan may go no further. These are only my ideas, everybody is guessing."

My answer to that remark was only a guess, too. I told Patton that the rigidity of the trade sanctions and embargos is the very thing that will determine Japan's new move and that move could only be a war promoted by Japan to break through those sanctions and embargos.

"Well, perhaps so," said Patton in a highly unbelieving tone.

Patton also thought: "The weather will hold up naval operations. The typhoon season starts this month and all shipping disappears from the South China Sea."

He pointed out that the monsoon starts in October and lasts until March. For reasons of weather war would not come, if it ever did, for some time.

Patton was either secretive or uninformed about the situation in Malaya, and on the basis of my future experience with Patton I would say that he was more uninformed than secretive.

Back at the hotel I had a drink with Chester Holcombe who has done several broadcasts for us out of here. He said the general view is that the Japanese will go into Thailand and the British will make no attempt to stop them. Shipping companies, he said, are scrambling to carry rubber and tin, especially tin. It is in great demand, brings high prices and is profitable cargo.

I am told that there are about five hundred British aircraft here— Brewster Buffalo fighters, Catalina long-range flying boats, but no Hurricanes or Spitfires. Twelve U. S. Navy and Army men are here as instructors on the finer points of the Catalina and Buffalo. This is supposed to be very hush-hush. The northern border of Malaya is said to be packed with troops, but there are no indications they mean to cross over into Thailand.

Tuesday, August 5th:
Lunched at Raffles Hotel with the Consul General of Thailand, a small, hard-skinned, fast-talking, pleasant son of Siam. His English is none too good, but he rips it out at an incredible pace and with bland indifference to grammatical errors. His name is Luang Vudiasora Nettinate. He says he is pro-British and anti-Japanese. I almost believe him.

He is only a minor cog, and he boasts that Thailand has four hundred airplanes of both Japanese and American make, 300,000 trained men with modern equipment and there is more than a fifty-percent chance that Thailand will resist a Japanese invasion if and when it comes.

132

"All we want to do," he says, "is to maintain our neutrality. You know we are a member of the League of Nations. We are still paying dues. I just paid a few thousand dollars a few weeks ago."

"How long could Thailand hold out?"

"About three or four months."

"You couldn't hold out that long against a naval attack, could you?"

"Ah! A naval attack! That is what worries me."

"You could stave that off for about twenty-four hours."

"Yes, perhaps, but I don't think more than that. That is where we need assistance, to resist a naval attack. We only have a small navy and a few shore batteries."

I think the moment is propitious to toss in this statement: "Now you know very well that while we are sitting here Thailand has a secret agreement with Japan and Germany."

His eyes widen in astonishment and he exclaims: "No, no, I am sure that we have no such agreements."

"Why, you have been working hand in glove with the Japanese in Indo-China. You were a party to that deal."

"We didn't want Japanese mediation in the Indo-China War," he says all in a quick breath, "but we couldn't help ourselves."

In the afternoon I went to the Japanese Consulate, a pleasant, white frame building atop the highest hill in Singapore and commanding a perfect view of the entire harbor. Ken Tsurumi, the Consul General, was a short, compact, thick-chested, English-speaking diplomat, who had the air of a "good fellow" and the eyes of a cut-throat. Our conversation went like this:

"I have just arrived here, Mr. Tsurumi, and would like to get the Japanese point of view on the situation in Malaya."

He grunts, but says nothing.

"What is confusing to us," I remark, "is the difficulty of reconciling Japanese statements with acts of what we define as aggression."

"We have not performed any acts of aggression," Tsurumi says.

Before I can cite China or Indo-China to him, he adds: "Our going into Indo-China was a defensive act."

"Defensive against whom?"

"Indo-China is weak and her independence was threatened."

"Threatened by whom? You mean by the British?"

133

"Indo-China is like Greenland. *That* was aggression. America is not interested in Greenland."

"Well, do you think the relations between our two countries are deteriorating?"

He hesitates for a moment and says:

"The situation between our two countries is very tense. Your Mr. Sumner Welles makes criminal statements. A week ago Mr. Welles made a statement which is absolutely devoid of the truth when he said we can buy rubber and tin on equal terms with other countries."

"Are you going into Thailand?"

"We have economic interests there."

"One of your objectives is to close the Burma Road, isn't it?"

"Yes."

"Could you close it by operations from Indo-China?"

"That is a military question."

"Well, from a military point of view it would greatly facilitate your closing the Burma Road by operating from Thailand as well."

"Yes."

"Then you have a definite military objective outside of other considerations for invasion of Thailand?"

Tsurumi laughs and says, "Yes."

Tsurumi throughout our talk emphasizes that all Japan wants is justice.

"We cannot understand why America concerns herself with our desire for justice."

"We don't like Mr. Hitler or aggression," I reply, "and we consider your expansion southward as aggression."

The Japanese diplomat makes no answer and I ask:

"Is there any chance for peace between the United States and Japan?"

For the first time Tsurumi is angry.

"Yes," he snaps, "yes, there is a chance for peace between our two countries. It can be achieved this way. If we draw a line down the middle of the Pacific from the North to the South, you stay on one side and we stay on the other."

"Thank you, Mr. Tsurumi. That gives me a good picture of what is going to happen in the future."

We shook hands and I went out of the Consulate certain that I had come to Singapore in time to cover a war.

Tsurumi was no mere Consul General. He was formerly the Japanese Embassy spokesman in Shanghai and some of his statements about American and British "interference" in China are models of venom and vituperation. He was not only a master of bombastics, but right at that moment when I saw him Tsurumi was operating a very effective and efficient Japanese espionage and Fifth-Column organization in Singapore.

In my talks with various people the general impression is that this is just another scare and that war is not coming. There is no unusual exodus of Japanese from Singapore or Malaya. Someone told me that Japanese business men here are opposed to Tokyo's policy because it is "bad for business." My informant said that the Japanese business men don't trade with the Yokohama Specie Bank here but with foreign banks so that Tokyo won't know their business affairs.

I have completed technical arrangements for my broadcasts. Eric Davis at the Malaya Broadcasting Corporation has assured me that I will have facilities during the times required for a CBS network news roundup. I gave him the specific fifteen-minute periods within which I would have to broadcast to join on the network both for weekdays and Sundays."

"The three transmitters will be available when you want them," Davis said.

The technical facilities are none too good, however, because the radio telephone to Java has either been taken over by the Government or dismantled. In any event, at the outbreak of the war the Military suspended all international telephone communications. In order to broadcast we will go by shortwave to Bandoeng in Java, which will retransmit simultaneously to San Francisco, or we will go by shortwave through Manila. I am afraid this will not be very satisfactory for good reception, but there is no choice.

I urged Davis to facilitate the opening of the telephone circuit, if that equipment is still available, or to install new transmitters because the reporting of this war, when it does come, will depend on good broadcasting facilities. Davis agreed with that and said he was doing

135

everything possible to improve on facilities and would continue to do so.

Wednesday, August 6th:
At last I have found an Englishman who thinks that war is coming. I saw Clark Kennard, who is chief of the news bureau of the broadcasting station and who has been a correspondent in Tokyo for some time. Kennard said that war is certainly coming but that the Japs will strike first at Vladivostok, that they must deal with the Russian threat first.

I lunched today with Colonel G. E. Grimsdale, the Deputy Director of Military Intelligence. I had a letter to him from Lieutenant Colonel Tod, the DDMI at Cairo.

I gave him the letter. It said:

My dear Colonel:
This note is to introduce Cecil Brown of the Columbia Broadcasting System, who intends to spend some time in Singapore. We should be very gratified for any facilities you can give him while he is there.

Since he has been in Cairo he has shown that he is very much out to do what he can to help to win the war, and his broadcasts are a weapon which we cannot afford to neglect. They reach a very wide audience.

"That's a nice letter," Grimsdale remarked. "We'll do everything we can for you."

Grimsdale is somewhat younger than Tod, more of a cosmopolite, seemingly less harassed and much gayer. We were busy the first half hour, sizing each other up, and Grimsdale was quite cagey at first.

"Do you think the Japanese could take Singapore?" I asked him.

"Japan," Grimsdale said, "has definitely missed the bus so far as Singapore is concerned. A year ago and they could have marched down through Malaya with virtually no opposition. There is a damn good chance of defending Singapore now from a combined air and naval attack."

I pointed out that the British do not have a naval force here.

"But," Grimsdale said, "we do have an air force which we didn't have a year ago."

Grimsdale agreed that Japan "apparently" intends to go into Thai-
136

land and that Thailand and Indo-China will supply most of Japan's rubber needs. He added: "Not enough to aid Germany, if there was a way to get it to them."

I asked what he thought America should do at this moment.

"What's needed now is a warning by the United States and Great Britain that if Japan does go into Thailand we will take certain actions."

The colonel and I agreed that there wasn't much chance of stopping Japan by economic pressure or sanctions.

"The answer to that," I suggested, "is war. Do you think Japan would strike southward and northward—in other words, against both you people and the Russians simultaneously?"

"Oh, definitely not," Grimsdale said. "Japan certainly can't take on Britain and Russia in addition to the Chinese."

"Then you don't think there is any chance that Japan would go to war against both the British and the United States?"

"Very definitely not."

After lunch with Colonel Grimsdale I went up to Fort Canning, GHQ, set on the hill in the center of Singapore, for a general press interview which Lieutenant General A. E. Percival was giving. There was an international collection of journalists—Chinese, Malayan, American, English, Australian and Indian. General Percival came in while we were seated around a long table. He is commander of all troops in Malaya.

He is a tall, slim man with gray hair parted on the side and wears a black mustache. His face was slim and angular, his skin young-looking and his cheeks red, but his outstanding characteristic was protruding upper teeth. He spoke in a calm, soft voice, almost like a schoolboy. Everything he said was loaded with optimism.

He had just made a trip over a good part of the country, seeing the troops.

"The troops," he said, "now go on thirty-mile hikes, which is a tribute to their training because once if they traveled two miles in this climate it was all they could stand."

He praised the Australians as being of good physique. "We have had some difficulty in fitting them in big enough shorts which were based on Indian sizes." Percival laughed.

137

He described the Aussies as extra-well-equipped. All the troops, he said, were training hard and specializing in bush warfare.

"We send the men out to live in the jungle two and three days at a time. The Japanese occupation of Indo-China," Percival said, "puts them in a position to deliver a surprise attack with much less warning than we previously reckoned on. A high state of readiness on our part continuously is necessary."

The only pessimism in Percival's talk was, as he put it, "Our disappointment in the response of our Asiatic population to our appeals for volunteers in the past few months."

I asked General Percival about the equipment here and his answer to that was: "The equipment is satisfactory."

"What are your views on the extent and necessity of American and British collaboration?"

"It is of the utmost importance that the United States and Great Britain go step and step in action in the United States, politically and otherwise."

I came away from that meeting with the impression that General Percival was not interested in giving us a factual story, but in pursuing a line of propaganda—merely that the British were ready and that the Asiatics ought to begin contributing more to the defense of Malaya.

From Fort Canning I went down to Cecil Street to see Seabridge, editor of the *Straits Times*.

Seabridge was a middle-aged man with the manner of a fighting rebel in a country where you were supposed to follow the beaten track.

He didn't think war was coming here very soon. He thought the moment required, as he expressed it, "a strong warning to Japan that if she touches Thailand, Borneo, or the Dutch East Indies she touches England. And that," he added, "will stop Japan. There is talk around that Britain may offer her protection to Thailand."

"Have you people anything to back up that?"

"Not very much."

Seabridge was critical of the way "we practically invited Japan to go into Indo-China."

He explained it this way: "Four or five months ago Brooke-Popham gave an interview to American newspapermen and said that if Japan touches Borneo, Indo-China, or the Dutch East Indies, they touch

138

Britain. Then, two days later Brooke-Popham said he had been mis-quoted, that he had not mentioned Indo-China. Japan immediately eased up her pressure on the Dutch East Indies and began her pressure on Indo-China. This was a clear indication that she could go ahead on Indo-China."

I suggested to Seabridge that the attitude of the people here toward the war seemed strange and distant.

"The people take the war fairly seriously here," Seabridge said, "but the cry of wolf has gone up so often that they don't scare very easily any more, and there's no point in panicking the Asiatics."

I asked the usual question I had asked everyone and received virtually the same answer.

"Singapore has more than a ninety-percent chance of being defended but its offensive possibilities are limited."

Thursday, August 7th:

Talked with Captain Archer Allen, the U. S. Naval Observer here who is leaving Saturday on the Clipper for America. He is a big, robust man, very pleasant, and we have a mutual friend in Captain Thomas Kinkaid, who was the American Naval Attaché in Rome. (It's now Rear Admiral Kinkaid who took part in the Midway battle.) Captain Allen thinks that the job here must be done by the United States, but he doesn't believe war is coming to the Far East for some time.

I'd been most impressed and alarmed by the state of mind that I had encountered and I asked Captain Allen about that.

"There is too much defensive mentality here," he said. "Brooke-Popham is a man who favors action and he's done a good job. Australia, Malaya and the Dutch East Indies are working together now, which wasn't the case six months ago. Brooke-Popham has accomplished that."

"What do you think of the possibility of Japan going to war against both Britain and the United States?"

"If she did that Japan would commit national hara kiri. Cities like Osaka, Yokohama, Tokyo and Kobe would necessarily be destroyed."

Captain Allen obviously was convinced that even the Japanese could not be stupid enough to take on the two biggest democracies.

"War against Britain and the United States would mean that Russia

139

would invade Manchuria. They have been waiting twenty years to do that."

I lunched today with Kennard of Malaya Broadcasting, who came here in April from Tokyo. Kennard is short and stocky and wears black-rimmed spectacles. He impressed me as an energetic type of American newspaperman instead of British. At least he talked in a very un-British way—forceful with great conviction and warmth. He was most emphatic about Japan's intentions.

"The Japanese are convinced they can beat the British and Americans combined," Kennard said. "That's the opinion of the Japanese Army, Navy, the Government and the people. The Japs most certainly will go into Thailand. We will stop that if the Thais fight. If they do not, there is no way we can prevent an invasion of Thailand.

"The Japs have not been badly affected by war," Kennard continued. "They are a fanatical people and death on the battlefield is heroism to them. They say they have lost 110,000 men in China. Well, make that 500,000 and it's still a relatively small figure. Of course, the Japs are short of some things, but they would have been short of them even if they were not in the war.

"Economic pressures, warnings, even a formal guarantee of protection of Thailand will not stop Japan," concluded Kennard. "Therefore, war is inevitable. The Japs believe that Britain has been beaten for the past twelve months but the British just don't realize it."

Working on my article on the Western Desert, but it is moving very slowly. I have not heard from White. No indication of the schedule and, of course, no hint as to how long I might be here. This might be something of a permanent assignment and yet if news doesn't warrant, CBS would hardly keep me here indefinitely. I am going on the premise I might only be here a short time. Am seeing as many people as possible on that basis, just to be prepared. With the exception of Kennard, everyone tells me that war will not be here for some time.

From all I can gather so far, Britain is in no position out here to enforce any halt order against Japan going into Thailand and Eden and Hull's warning to Japan indicates Anglo-American concerted action is planned. Certainly Britain herself is hardly in a position to voice any warning to Japan with authority.

140

There are no Japanese ships in the harbor at present. Some Japanese have gone home. The people tell me it is now considered extremely bad form to buy in the Japanese shops on Middle Road.

Friday, August 8th:
Shortly before lunch I met the Thai Consul at Raffles bar. Again he affirms to me that the Thais will resist any Japanese attack, but admits that Thailand will not ask British protection before the event or do anything which might give Japan an excuse to attack.

I argued vehemently with him. I said that Thailand will be attacked and she will not resist, or if she does she will then scream for Anglo-American aid when it is too late.

"Don't do the same thing that Belgium and Holland did," I implored him. "You can't wait until you're attacked and then call for protection and expect to be saved. Thailand should take the long view and go through the hardships of war against Japan. Yugoslavia made that choice and so did Greece. The defeat of Germany is certain. You Thais ought to pay your price now so that you'll have a voice at the peace table. If you fight now and do what you can to stop the Japanese your voice will be much louder than Japan's at the peace table. If you give in, your voice won't be as loud as a pip-squeak."

The Thai Consul did not commit himself on any of these views.

Commander Burrows asked me for lunch today at the Racquet Club, but before going there we picked up Major Hennesey and went to GHQ to see Major Hunt.

Major Hunt was typical of the state of mind of most of the younger British officers. He favored action and he underestimated the enemy.

"We ought to go into Thailand without any delay," he said. "No, I do not think they would invite us in. They still hope the thing will pass them by."

I asked him what he thought of the Japanese.

"I do not think the Japanese are very much at all. Their fleet may be all right, but it's top-heavy."

"Are you prepared to go into Thailand?"

"The big thing is," Major Hunt said, "that we have thousands of troops here. Malaya is becoming just a big concentration camp for

141

British troops. Going into Thailand would be much better than all this snarling. That could continue indefinitely."

My diary commentary says:

Army circles appear to be confident that the British troops and air force can handle the Japs. The Japanese air force is held in considerable contempt.

I'm having a Chinese tailor make me a few suits. I lost most of my clothes in Yugoslavia and I don't know when I'll be able to wear these suits, if ever. Wing Loong also is making me a white dinner jacket. I never had one before and I shall not wear it here in Singapore because it makes me sick to see them being worn every evening at Raffles Hotel while the people in Britain are getting bombed.

Martha will be amazed if she ever sees this white jacket because she's had to fight with me even to buy a necktie in Rome, let alone a suit, and here I am having some clothes made of my own volition and without duress.

A note came this evening from Colonel Grimsdale, informing me that I am to see Vice Admiral Sir Geoffrey Layton, Commander-in-Chief, China Station, next Monday. I had asked Grimsdale to arrange the meeting and he came through in beautiful fashion.

Commander Burrows called and asked me to give a talk to the officers of the Singapore command on "My Experiences." I agreed.

Bruno Mussolini was killed yesterday near Pisa in a flying accident. Martha and I used to see him at the races in Campannelle near Rome. He had more sense than his brother, Vittorio, but as far as I'm concerned he's just one less Fascist to be bumped off.

Saturday, August 9th:
This evening went to dinner with Pim Droogleever, Graeme Nicholl of the Ministry of Economic Warfare, and Wing Commander Ramsay Rae, a big, daredevil, cheerful Australian in the Royal Air Force.

I met Droogleever a few days ago because I carried a message of greetings to him from Bob Crisp, the South African tank captain I knew in Cairo.

Graeme was an insurance man for many years in Shanghai and although only forty-two years old was in the Royal Air Force in the last war. He just came here two months ago from England, flying all the way by Clipper.

As we sat down for cocktails, Graeme drew out a black metal box about twelve inches long and four inches wide. He opened the lid, a voice came out and I jumped about five feet.

"What's the matter?" Graeme chuckled.

"My God! What's that?"

"Why, it's just a radio without an aerial. Everyone in the States has them. They are very simple. You put it in your lap and you get anything you want in the States."

That's what it was—a small pocket radio that operates on a battery. It was a simple thing, but it made me realize how long I had been away from home and how many things must have happened in the past four years in America. Here I was in the bewildering and disconcerting position of having to ask an Englishman what was going on in my own country.

"Production is moving rapidly," he said, "but your young Americans don't want to fight."

"Your young men didn't want to fight either," I said, "but when the time came they did. Ours will be the same. When the circumstances are all right they'll say: 'Oh, you guys want a scrap?' and pull off their coats and go to it."

"I hope so," Graeme said. He remarked that any ultimatum to Japan would have to be backed up by action and that action would have to be the American Navy.

"But we don't want the United States to go to war for another six or seven months," Graeme added.

Like every other Englishman, he is convinced that Japan does not want to take on both the United States and Great Britain now.

After dinner we went to the Alhambra to see *The Sea Wolf* with Edward G. Robinson, John Garfield and Ida Lupino. It was the first movie I have seen in Singapore.

Sunday, August 10th:
John Young, an NBC man who came down from Tokyo, called me and we had a drink. He is a very nice chap—voluble, entertaining and intelligent. He had a wonderful time in Tokyo. The Japanese treated him very well with banquets, excursions and a constant escort.

John is an old hand at radio and in 1932 won an award as "best announcer." He told me a good deal about the radio business in America about which I am totally in the dark. He said it is mostly "showmanship." I disagreed. My contention was people want the facts and not la-de-dah stuff in newscasts.

Except for the jungle heat out here I might think I was back in a café in Rome or Paris or Prague in a European atmosphere. It is the same old thing—threats of encirclement breathe hot down your back and Fifth Columnists weave in and out under your feet.

My diary commentary is:

The British absolutely cannot take any action unless the United States joins in and if we do it must be strong enough to halt the Japs and to be backed up with war if it doesn't.

The situation has reached the point where either we accept Japanese further aggression or go to war to stop it. Japan is too far out on the limb to crawl back without losing face.

The warning of Eden and Hull the other day was pretty useless, to judge by the Japanese reaction. Words aren't going to stop this thing.

This evening I went to dinner at the home of Duckworth, the press censor, and with me was Commander Burrows, who was cheerful and affable. His ignorance of publicity, newspapers and radio, however, was incredible and Duckworth sided with me on every argument on the necessity of telling the American people everything possible about the Far East. Gradually, I began to get a better picture of Burrows.

He had been a magistrate in the Fiji Islands for twenty years when he retired after the last war as Commander in the British Navy. He was an old friend of Sir Geoffrey Layton, a classmate of his at Dartmouth Naval College, and that night admitted that he did not know very much about newspapers. As a matter of fact, he knew of BBC but never heard of CBS or NBC and looked blank when I mentioned the *New York Times*.

Burrows stated that he was taking me out to see Admiral Layton the next day and "We will also see Sir Robert Brooke-Popham." I thanked Commander Burrows profusely for his efforts, although I knew full well that it was Colonel Grimsdale who had arranged the meetings.

144

He cautioned me about saying anything to any other correspondent about going to see the Commanders-in-Chief.

"They have not seen anyone for six weeks and absolutely refuse to see any correspondent."

"Why are they seeing me then?"

"You are the first accredited correspondent we have had out here and it may be they have something on their minds."

"As long as they are seeing me, why don't they make use of me as a channel to get your viewpoint across? I can decide whether I am being used or abused and if I think they are giving me hokum I won't use it."

"Maybe they do have something to say and that may have something to do with their seeing you, but this is a very delicate moment to say anything."

"I still don't understand why they are seeing me."

"They would like to ask you," Commander Burrows said, "about your experiences and what you saw in Italy, Yugoslavia and the Middle East."

"That's all right with me, but this is to be a case of trading of information, isn't it? I tell them things I know, then they tell me things they know."

Commander Burrows laughed, but I could see he was shocked that I had put it on that practical basis.

PREVIEW OF DISASTER

Monday, August 11th:

Burrows advised me that when I first met Layton I should address him as "Excellency," a title to which he was entitled, but afterwards I could call him "Admiral." I mentally made a note I would call him Sir Geoffrey.

Vice Admiral Sir Geoffrey Layton, Commander-in-Chief in China, welcomed us warmly into a small, cluttered office in the Administration building of the Singapore Naval Base. He gave the air of a very busy man and obviously was. A short, thick-set man, gray-haired, a scrubbed and determined face; he wore white shorts. He motioned me to a chair. To the commander he said: "Anchor yourself over there, Burrows."

"This is not an interview, is it?" he said. His voice was deep, authoritative, the ring of the quarter deck in it. I assured him it was not, but asked if he minded if I took notes "for history."

"No, of course not," he said. "Quite all right, but I am not to be quoted. I have the strictest orders now not to give any interviews."

"I understand, Sir Geoffrey. This information is just to orient myself."

"Well," he began, "we are simply waiting to see what the Japs will do about Thailand."

"And what will they do?"

"We are hoping that America will really enforce the freezing actions."

"Isn't it a fact that the situation has gone beyond such measures as freezing?"

"No, the Japs know that going beyond freezing can lead to war and mighty few of them want war."

"You don't believe that Japan is willing to go to war?"

"A small number of militarists want it, a group of men with insufficient brains to know what it will lead to." Then he added with great vehemence: "All this talk of Japan having oil is absurd. I don't

146

suppose she has a year's supply of oil. This talk of a five-year supply is all nonsense.

"Their navy doesn't want war," the admiral added. "They know if they take on your country, and us too, they would be beaten—and that would be the end of Japan.

"Shigimitsu (the Japanese admiral) has just arrived back in Japan. He must have told them the truth, that we are far from beaten."

I asked if Britain alone could stop Japan from going into Thailand. Layton looked at me sharply for a moment, as though I were too prying, and said: "We can't stop Japan from going into Thailand," then paused for a moment and added, "alone. That's quite definite."

"What type of move could be made that would stop Japan from going into Thailand?"

"Even if America came in," Layton pointed out, "I don't believe Japan would stop. If Japan took Thailand in the face of such a warning, our combined actions would amount to war. There isn't a town in Japan that would escape destruction. They would commit national hara-kiri. We would harry their commerce, cut off their supplies, cut them off from the sea."

"If the Japs go into Thailand, could you drive them out?"

"That," said Layton, "would be a big undertaking. Whether that's possible is rather doubtful. But even with them in there, they would be in a bad position. We could pulverize their sea communications. They would collapse."

"How can Japan be stopped?"

"The most possible action, the most probable that would succeed, is to dispatch to Singapore some portion of the American fleet and a public announcement that if the Japs go into Thailand it would be a *casus belli.*"

"You believe that would stop them, they wouldn't go on?"

"If it was stated definitely that it would be a *casus belli,* no, I don't think they would go into Thailand."

"And America is necessary to stop them?"

"Are the Americans prepared to lose their lifeline across the Pacific, or go to war?" he demanded. "That's what it amounts to. I don't think America realizes the gravity of the situation in the Pacific. It is just as important for America to do on the Pacific side what she is doing on the Atlantic side."

147

"Do you have the power of preventing Japan from occupying Thailand?"

"If Japan goes into Thailand," Layton said deliberately, "we will not attempt to stop her, not unless she comes farther south. No, I don't want you to use that. That is misleading. Strike it out." I thereupon drew an X through it.

Indeed it was a strange answer. It was a go-ahead signal to Japan. And "unless she comes farther south," seemed pointless. I presumed that it had long been taken for granted Britain would resist any attack on Malaya or the Dutch East Indies.

"Sir Geoffrey," I asked, "how soon do you think things will break here?"

"That's a toss-up. Japan might consolidate her position in China. She won't do anything before the end of the year."

"Do you need help from America to defend Malaya?"

"No, we don't require any assistance for that."

"And do you need help to defend Singapore?"

"Well, I don't think we can defend Singapore indefinitely."

"Do you think war can still be avoided out here?"

"If we can make the Japanese realize any further move means war, it can be avoided."

"You believe a warning would be effective at this late stage of the game?"

"Yes," Sir Geoffrey said emphatically. "A definite statement of the United States, Britain, and the Netherlands East Indies, backed up by Australia and New Zealand that any further move would be taken as an act of war would stop Japan."

"America's co-operation is essential, would you say?"

"Yes, the United States must be a party to that statement."

"That wouldn't be necessary, would it? Japan knows that if you go to war against her, for any reason, that we would help you with materials and ships just as we're helping in the Atlantic and elsewhere. Japan surely appreciates that war with Britain means we help you against her just as we do against Germany."

"We want Japan to realize that and America to be ready to use her fleet and air force to participate in the war. Japan must be made to see that," Sir Geoffrey emphasized.

Once again I had encountered the conviction of the British that

148

Japan could be forced to back down by words, and that she could easily be whipped if she did go to war. There was no hesitancy on the part of Sir Geoffrey in asserting that American help was essential in the Far East. From a correspondent's point of view that was important, and I determined then and there to use that as one of my main wedges in getting stories through censorship.

Commander Burrows and I went downstairs in the Administration building, walked through a few passages and came to a one-story, wooden-frame building, built in the shape of simple barracks. Within a minute or two, Squadron Leader Cox took me into Sir Robert Brooke-Popham. Burrows remained outside.

Sir Robert was a huge, gangling officer with a straggly, reddish mustache and thinning blond hair. He had an odd, abashed, friendly manner, and a high, breaking voice. We sat down at his desk. Sir Robert began by asking me about Syria—why the advance was so slow.

"Wilson (Lieutenant-General Henry Maitland Wilson, Commander of the British Forces in Syria) must have been in a very difficult position," Sir Robert said. "I am glad I did not have his job, fighting the French. It must have been very disturbing."

I told Sir Robert many of the incidents, the difficulties encountered by the Free French in advancing from the right flank on Damascus, the vigor of the Vichy French resistance, and Sir Robert asked many questions about the strategy employed. I told him of the shortages of equipment.

After about fifteeen minutes he said, "Well, how long are you going to be here?" I accepted this as my cue to ask questions.

He, like Sir Geoffrey, said the British could not stop the Japs from going into Thailand and that.the British did not have offensive possibilities in Malaya.

"What could stop Japan from going southward?"

"I believe a joint declaration of America and Britain would have a good probability of stopping her."

"That would mean the U. S. going to war if Japan didn't heed it."

"Yes."

"Would you prefer to see the United States in the war now or later?"

"As Commander-in-Chief of the Far East I prefer to see the Japs stopped now."

"What do you think the Japs intend to do, Sir Robert?"

He laughed in his giggly, boyish, country-squire way. "Oh, I don't know. I have difficulty in penetrating the Jap mind. Now with the Germans and Italians you can take a series of circumstances and deduce about what they are going to do. But with the Japanese it is very difficult to tell. Sometimes they are quite unpredictable. They might get excited and go off the deep end."

"Don't you feel that the time is ripe for Hitler to sacrifice Japan?"

"Yes, but the Japs may go north into the Vladivostok area."

"Could you help Thailand?"

"We could, and you people, too. Meanwhile the big thing is to stave off the Japs. The Thais may be able to do the same as the Dutch. You know the Dutch negotiated with the Japanese for months and then gave them nothing."

"Can you stop Japan without American help?"

"No, that is essential."

"How soon do you think war will come?"

"That depends on a joint declaration. There is a good probability the Japs would stop in the face of it. It is important that you people base long-range bombers in the Philippines at Luzon. Building up the Philippines is essential out here."

"Well, that's a matter of the future. We are now in a situation of hours, aren't we?"

"No, I don't think it is moving that fast. The Japanese are not quite sure what to do. I think the Japs prefer not to go to war." Sir Robert laughed heartily and added, "They would prefer to be well out of the whole business."

"The Thais say they will fight if they are attacked by the Japanese."

"Yes, if they are not bought out by the Japs." Sir Robert then laughed at that and I asked if he thought Japan would move simultaneously into Thailand and against Russia.

"Definitely not—not both directions at the same time."

Burrows and I returned to Singapore and lunched together at the Raffles Hotel. Immediately afterwards I began writing my script for the broadcast that night. I was scheduled to speak for two and a half minutes.

For exactly two and a half hours I argued and wrangled over that script with Duckworth and Burrows in the censor's office. As we came in, Robert Scott, head of the Ministry of Information, was in the office. We were introduced. He read the script and said it was okay with him. Then he left.

Duckworth and Burrows went over each word. As each word was approved by one, the other said, "Now, are you sure that we can let this go?" As one paragraph was completed Duckworth would say to Burrows, "Is that paragraph all right with you?" Burrows would say, "Yes," and then they would start working on the paragraph again.

Each word, each sentence, each paragraph was passed and repassed and repassed again. Had it not been my first broadcast out of Singapore I would have cancelled the whole thing. It was the most maddening, energy-sapping experience I had ever encountered with a censor anywhere in the world. The censorship was petty, suspicious, absurd in the extreme. When that two-and-a-half-hour session was over I came back to the hotel and flopped into bed, almost unconscious from exhaustion—physical and mental.

Here is my first broadcast as passed by Duckworth and Burrows in that memorable session:

This is Singapore.

The British in the Straits Settlements consider themselves on the verge of war with Japan.

Reinforcements of troops and aircraft have been pouring into Singapore. This island fortress is bristling with guns and noisy with aircraft overhead. It is now in a state of unofficial emergency. Only the home guard defense force remains to be called up.

Since I flew here from Cairo a week ago I've talked with the men who know precisely what is going on and the men who are faced with the problem of meeting what Japan might do.

Here are the opinions of these men: Great Britain unaided cannot stop a Japanese occupation of Thailand. Even if the Thais resist, as it's believed here they will, without strong American assistance the Japanese conquest of Thailand could only be delayed. Japanese control of bases in Thailand will reduce the defensive possibilities of Singapore by twenty-five percent. As things stand at the moment, Singapore is now about ninety percent defendable.

Singapore's power on offense is extremely restricted. It is a naval base without, at present, a navy. And, if the Japanese by-pass Singapore and thrust at the Dutch East Indies, their chances of success are more than fifty percent.

The best British opinion here sees but one method to stop the Japanese from going into Thailand, or elsewhere. This formula is offered: a joint declaration by the United States and Great Britain that if Japan moves into Thailand or anywhere else southward, it means war with the U. S. and Britain. With that declaration portions of the United States navy should be dispatched to Singapore. Those two steps—an Anglo-American statement to Tokyo of stop or fight and U. S. warships at Singapore—were given as the only means of holding back Japan.

But other sources here are equally certain that U. S. warships or not, Japan will push on even if it means war with the Democracies. An official said: The situation has reached the point where the United States and Great Britain either accept further Japanese aggression or go to war to stop it.

Those are the convictions of the British in the Far East area on the precarious verge of war. And I asked the Japanese Consul-General here how war could be avoided between our two countries. He said: "There is only one way. Draw a line from north to south down the middle of the Pacific. You stay on one side and we will stay on the other." That remark is typical of the views out here on the chances of avoiding war.

Just before dinner in the lobby of the Raffles I ran into a British correspondent, O'Dowd Gallagher, just in from Cairo. I last saw Gallagher when he had just come in from the Western Desert. And now he had come to Singapore for the same reason I had—to cover a war. I didn't know him well except by reputation as a good correspondent. He is a South African and works for the *London Daily Express*. He covered the war in Spain and also in France.

Had dinner tonight with John Young of NBC, Frank Gervasi of *Collier's*, Leland Stowe of the *Chicago Daily News*, and a young Englishman attached to the British Embassy at Chungking and en route there.

We talked of the changes **taking** place in England. Gervasi contended that unless labor got what it wanted there would be trouble after the war, and the Britisher defended the conduct of his government.

Stowe remarked that our capitalists and property class did not understand as well as the British how to compromise. I interjected questions, encouragement to the Britisher to keep him going. I did that because he was all that any American finds obnoxious in the British.

He was super-educated and super-academic—Eton, Oxford, the University of Berlin. He was smug, priggish, aristocratic with no understanding of sex, poverty, misery or fervor. But worst of all, the way he talked, more daringly English-accented than Hollywood would attempt in a caricature, he gave off terrifically bah-bah English accents in a narrow, clipped way as though afraid he would chip his teeth, and if he opened his mouth the pieces would drop out.

He was a Tory who was determined that his world of comfort and stodginess would never change, no matter how many wars might come.

Tuesday, August 12th:
I went into town to get a typewriter ribbon and found myself interested in a Remington noiseless portable. I am tired of fighting my twelve-year-old machine. It rattles like a tractor falling down a canyon, has worn my fingers down to the knuckles and given me a permanent crick in the neck. That portable has been with me over most of the world, but it took an awful beating in Yugoslavia, in Syria and in the Western Desert, and I think it is going to fall apart on me any day.

I tried to buy a cashmere sweater. I have never had one. Some day I am going to have three or four of them. I don't know why—I very seldom wear a sweater—but I would just like to have a good sweater that costs more than a dollar.

Diary comment:
The atmosphere here in the past week has become more tense each day, just a rising crescendo in the atmosphere. It's all intangible, of course, but I sense it in my bones. Everything is a little quicker,

people's eyes are a bit more intent, their actions are a bit more studied, as though their minds were preoccupied with something else.

I have been able to buy a June and July *Reader's Digest,* the *Saturday Evening Post* for June 24th, and *Time* up to June 16th. That's certainly keeping up with what America is reading at the moment.

If bombing comes to Singapore I prefer to take my chances with the bombs rather than get squashed by the panicky natives.

Today Japan swings into a war footing. The U. S. appears ready to break with Vichy. The Roosevelt and Churchill meeting is still a mystery. Everybody is acting tough and all hell is ready to break loose.

I think to millions in America the whole thing is a dream that someone told them about. Every American ought to have been sent to Europe during the past year even if only for a week. What an eye-opener that would have been!

Wednesday, August 13th:

Wing Loong, the tailor, is still making me those two suits. Hope I get to a place some day where I can wear them. I wonder if the time will come when I can unpack my suitcases and put them away and put my things in drawers with some feeling that they will remain blissfully undisturbed for a time.

Lunched today with Gervasi, Stowe and four Australian captains and a naval commander. The Australians want to get into action. They feel somewhat abashed. They haven't seen any action while other Australians have been fighting in the Middle East. As one expressed it to me: "We feel as though those other Australians are fighting the war for us."

It seems like a strange attitude, but it is not hard to understand how men, yearning for action, might feel left out of things here in the easy, unhurried atmosphere of Singapore.

I want to see America in the war. I don't feel guilty about that. The danger to America is very great.

Thursday, August 14th:

Worked continuously all morning and finished the article on the Western Desert shortly after noon.

At lunch today John Young was telling me the ways of the geisha

154

girls in Japan. Very interesting ways they are, too! As I get the story I would not mind "assignment to Tokyo."

In Italy, Roberto Farinacci in the *Regime Fascista* attacks the Vatican publication, *Osservatore Romano,* for not speaking against Russia as it did when Russia made the alliance with Germany. "We believe," says the Fascist Farinacci, "this is due to one of its many political calculations."

Certainly, why not? Papers here say the Vatican was forced by the King of Italy some time ago, to have the Pope receive Ante Pavelitch, the Croat traitor and the murderer of Alexander I of Yugoslavia at Marseilles.

The Vatican favored the creation of a Catholic Croat independent country.

This was one of the gayest evenings of my life with John Young, Stowe, Gervasi and a Japanese spy named Johnny Fuiji, who works for the Japanese-owned *Singapore Herald* here. We went to a restaurant where there are geisha girls. It was my first Japanese meal of Sukiyaki.

The girls were named Mitzi and Neeki. Mitzi was especially attractive. It was a delight to watch how the girls moved around, and the way they sat down with their feet tucked under them. We had hot saki, then whisky, and the steaming dish cooked at our table while we sat on the floor and used chop sticks. I can't maneuver chop sticks, so the madam finally got a fork and spoon for me. I drank a great number of whiskies and Mitzi danced very prettily in that graceful stiff way while the other girl played a samisen, a Japanese instrument something like a banjo.

We played a game designed to help the girls sell drinks. You break a chop stick into an L shape, then with your head down, twirl it between your hands while the music plays. When the music stops the person at whom the stick points must "bottoms up." I was the victim every time, even while I myself twirled the stick. It was the gayest evening since New Year's Eve in Rome.

Friday, August 15th:
This evening I dined at the home of Colonel and Mrs. Grimsdale with a number of other guests—a Major Gavin of the Royal Scots, who I think is in Intelligence, also Dr. May, a Free French doctor for-

merly in Indo-China with General Catroux and now with the De Gaulle forces here.

The discussion at dinner was rather heavy and I was especially bitter about British censorship.

"If the British case has been presented to America it is not due to your people. Everywhere we've beat our heads against colossal British stupidity. We have fought and pleaded with your people to let us tell the story. Your censors don't know what your policy is. We have to tell them. We are not trying to wreck the British Empire. We are not giving information to the Germans. We are trying to tell the story because the facts explain your need for American help better than anything else.

"You paid a heavy price for your censorship policy in England. The first four months of the war, almost every story on page one in American newspapers came from Berlin. Photographs and newsreels, too. All stories about German might and invincibility. When Dunkirk came, we all admired your courage, but America thought you were finished. The people had been too much impressed with German power."

"But we weren't beaten," Grimsdale interjected.

"No. But most Americans thought so. That enabled anti-British elements in America and the isolationists to go screaming: 'Why help a defeated country?' It set us back about four months in starting to give real help to you.

"You have been doing the same thing in Cairo, and only now are they permitting correspondents to try and give a decent picture of the Middle East. But what concerns me now is that you are starting to do the same thing here, hiding everything that the American people have a right to know about."

Dr. May and Major Gavin were most sympathetic to the general trend of my remarks. It was a good dinner and I think I jarred Colonel Grimsdale just a little bit. At any rate, I hope so.

Saturday, August 16th:
Yesterday 143 American pilots and technicians came through, en route to Burma. They are part of the American volunteer group, but we can't report their existence. They registered at the hotel as me-

chanics, students, chauffeurs, bankers and one as a traveling salesman. Selling death from the skies to the Japanese, I presume.

Monday, August 18th:
This evening Commander Burrows picked me up and we drove out to the Tanglin Barracks, a half hour's drive. I was to speak to the officers and men at the Barracks and I wasn't in a very reportorial mood. I described how the Germans fought and what I saw of their ways and methods in Yugoslavia, and also described how the British fight in the Western Desert and how they fought in Syria. At one point I said: "You can't win this war by fighting like gentlemen. Germans machine-gun women and children if it serves a military objective of jamming the roads or spreading panic. And if you are wondering if I advocate the machine-gunning of women and children for such a purpose my answer is, yes. You can't win this war fighting like gentlemen. And you can't win with a defensive mentality."

There were cries of "Hear, hear," but I don't believe those men will change. I think the British gentlemen are too fine, too nice, too compassionate and too civilized to change into the kind of murderers that they must be to win a war, to fight a war the way it must be fought.

Major General F. Keith Simmons, a Cameron Highlander, is in command of the Singapore fortress. After my talk we went over to the officers' mess for drinks, and he asked me to come out the next day to watch the firing of the 15-inch guns. Then he drove me back into town to the Raffles.

The men were tremendously interested to get first-hand news. They were starved for it. They were rather tickled when I said, "From the British you get wonderful courtesy but not an ounce of co-operation."

Tuesday, August 19th:
I can see that I am going to have considerable difficulty with the censorship here. In a cable to *Newsweek Magazine* I used material which was definitely not of a military nature and attempted to give some of the background color of the military set-up here. The entire cable was eliminated. In it I said: "The general feeling in Singapore society is remoteness from the war. There is an attitude of 'We have heard the cry of wolf before.' The social affairs, extremely top nose and poonah-poonah, usually consist of small dinners. Men wear formal white mess

jackets with black trousers. The women wear long evening dresses and dance nightly at Raffles Hotel, the Sea View Hotel and the looser Coconut Grove, seven miles outside of town.

"There are air-conditioned cinemas with new pictures and they are packed every night. The favorite spots of some of the officers and many of the troops and the Chinese blades are Coney Island types of places such as the New World, the Great World and the Happy World, where Chinese, Eurasian and Malay taxi-dancers receive half of the twelve cents which you pay for a dance. They are not paid for the drinks sold to the men.

"Despite the Oriental atmosphere you feel the pressure of Singapore's enforced primness. Soldiers ride rickshaws and shop sedately, but they are not boisterous as in Cairo, and you seldom hear singing in the streets. Singapore's 'Streets of Sin' are still operating and thriving but they are tamed down somewhat. Society gives charity balls to raise money for tanks and for relief. A partial reason for the remoteness of the war is due here to the newspapers which are held down to the vapid reporting of world affairs, presenting an 'all's well' picture of Britain's war effort and progress."

When I protested to Duckworth, he said: "Well, we are not going to have you sending scandal and sex out of Singapore. That has nothing to do with the war."

"It very definitely has a great deal to do with the war," I retorted, "and if it has nothing to do with the war, as you say, then why cut it out? I can't see how it is military information of value to the enemy, and that's the basis for censorship, isn't it?"

"Yes," Duckworth said, "that's the fundamental basis, but it's hard for me to believe that any American publication would be interested in that sort of thing."

"It's my opinion that America should know some of the atmosphere and background of Singapore, and I maintain that there is no provision of censorship which prevents me from sending that material out."

He finally agreed that it was all right and I could resubmit it in my cable to *Newsweek* next week and he would pass it.

"SINGAPORE SAL"

Wednesday, August 20th:

I was picked up this morning by a brigadier general, a major and Lieutenant Geoffrey Hallowes, the aide of Major General F. Keith Simmons, and we drove for a half hour to Changi to the firing area.

Out there with General Simmons we went up on a hill to watch the 15-inch guns. Out to sea a destroyer began plowing along, and the flash of its signals could be easily seen. The destroyer was towing the target, a series of floats the length of a destroyer.

The general said: "Stronghold is passing the range," whatever the hell that meant.

The flash of the 15-inch coastal gun is a huge belch of orange, doubly vivid against the green of palms and rubber trees. All the treetops and foliage where the cannon is hidden thrash about in agony and out of them emerges lazy, dirty-gray smoke.

Singing across the half mile to our hill-top observation post comes the breeze of the percussion as a sibilant sigh, and with it, a short, sharp rap against the ears. The wind flowing past our faces feels like a brush of expected death, not gentle, but not harsh either.

Oddly, too, the backwash of the fifteen-incher is noticeable around the legs, for the wind bends over the thick, knee-high *lalang* grass, and its sharp edges scrape roughly at our legs.

Even Major-General Simmons, his eyes glued to his binoculars and still peering through them into the distance, bends down to brush away the sharp, prickly sensation of the grass on his bare knees.

It takes thirty-eight seconds by my stop-watch for the shell to tunnel a 45,000 yard arc across the sky and plow into the water 25,000 yards out in the China Sea.

"That one," the major-general says, "was Singapore Sal. And it looks like she got a direct hit."

The splash rises like a geyser, even higher than the destroyer towing the target. The target is flat and a shell which passes sixty feet over or forty feet this side of it counts as a direct hit.

A plane is swooping around the target area, worrying over it like a hen with her chick.

The major-general wants to know what the pilot is doing out there. "Is he dive-bombing the target?" he demands with a chuckle at no one in particular. The brigadier, the colonel and the two majors with us laugh heartily.

Fourteen times Singapore Sal shrieks in her harpy voice at the potential enemy coming down the China Sea. All the guns on Singapore Island point out to sea.

Standing in the deep grass on the tip of Singapore Island, on this hill at Changi, we are looking at all that makes Singapore the "impregnable" fortress of the Far East.

The British way of showing great pride is a calm assumption of superiority wrapped up in matter-of-fact statements. The major-general is aided by his swagger stick. He points and jabs in all directions.

"This"—twenty feet from us is the largest range finder in the world, 100 feet of it, covered with green canvas to blend with the grass, so high it nestles up to the underside.

"Over there"—a mile to our left, the Straits of Johore. The entrance to the Singapore Naval Base, a great naval base without a navy.

"That thing"—stretching across the entrance to Johore Straits is the boom defense. It is a series of steel floats, six feet square, connected by two strips of chain. It is supposed to prevent enemy ships and submarines from penetrating the base.

"That island there"—a few miles off the entrance to the Straits is Tekong Besar, a bulbous blob of green on the water.

"We have quite a few guns out there, too, you know," says the major-general.

The swagger stick traces a circle in the air. "All around us"—among the trees are some of the 15-inch shore batteries.

"You see that tree over there," the general waved toward a towering branchless tree with just a tuft of greenery at the top. "If war comes," he said, "the first thing that happens is that tree gets chopped down. It's too good a landmark. I don't know what kind of a tree it is. It is just called the Changi tree, the favorite of everyone in Singapore. The Malays say if that tree is ever cut down, British rule in this country comes to an end. It is a Malay legend. Nonsense, of course."

160

Out at sea there is only the destroyer, like a stationary whale at this distance, but actually plunging along, towing its target.

All the fat Chinese junks with chocolate-brown sails rigid with bamboo battens have been cleared for this practice firing. The sea is free too, at this hour, of American, British and Dutch ships carting rubber and tin from Singapore to the United States.

"That rubber and tin," the major-general says, "is one reason why your navy will be here when it is necessary."

That remark is the refrain in Singapore. The people of Singapore wait—ah, what a weak word!—for the U. S. fleet.

"There's no doubt of that," he adds. "The American fleet will be necessary out here."

His swagger stick jabs toward another island, five or six miles to the right. "That one belongs to the Dutch. You see those oil tanks on the island? They were painted silver but we finally persuaded the Dutch to paint them a darker color. They did, but claimed the fuel evaporates more quickly. I told them better to lose a little by evaporation than all of it by bombing." He chuckles softly. "Almost like a motto, that, isn't it? A motto for this twentieth century of wars."

Major-General Simmons is a short, dark, husky, quiet-talking soldier with a close-clipped mustache and eyes that suddenly harden and just as quickly become bland and boyish.

He typifies, too, that strange mission the British seem to have of going to all sorts of places in the world to protect the heritage given them by their grandfathers. He was in the Scottish infantry in the last war, twice decorated in France, in Archangel fighting against the Bolsheviks, in Ireland during the Black and Tan trouble, in Palestine during the riots, then in Egypt, a military attaché in Spain, then in Shanghai when this war broke out.

The captain comes clambering up the hill, salutes sharply and hands the major-general a slip of paper.

"Ha," he says. "Jolly good. Nine hits out of fourteen for Singapore Sal."

"And that," I ask, "is what would happen to the Japs?"

"Quite. Approximately that. But more difficult, you know, with bombings going on. But we'll deal with the Japs if they come down here. You know, they're such funny little devils. They make a plan, all kinds of frightful details to it. Then if something happens not according to plan, they get extraordinarily worked up. Besides, they're most unscrupulous blokes."

The plotting room, where the firing we've just seen is charted, is down the knoll away from the sea in an artificial hill forty feet high topped by twenty inches of reinforced concrete and covered with grass. Even a tree grows out of the top.

As we go through the bomb-proof entrance to this concrete brain of Singapore Sal and her shrill-voiced sisters, the major-general says: "A year ago these guns were just about all we had here. The Japs could have marched right down to Singapore with almost no opposition at all. Ah, yes, there's no doubt of it at all. Japan certainly missed the bus."

General Simmons drove me back to Singapore along a road where there were numerous pillboxes smack up against the sea and others on the opposite side of the road away from the sea, a sort of second line of pillbox defense. Along the road there were many companies of Australians, and I asked Simmons what they were doing.

"They are just out for a march to harden them up."

Lunched with Dr. May of the Free French and a Frenchman named Busson, formerly manager of a bank in Bangkok. Busson pointed out that few people realize that Thailand is the keystone of the Far East, just as Iran is the keystone of the Near East, dividing India from Russia, and Austria the keystone of Europe, separating the Slavic world from Europe.

"Thailand," Busson pointed out, "separated Japan from India and from the cheap markets of Malaya and Oceania."

Today a small item appeared in the *Singapore Free Press* that there have been changes in the Thailand cabinet, and I asked Busson what the changes signify.

"Thailand," Busson said, "has gone over to Japan. She will not fight. In all Thailand there are less than three thousand people who have any conception of world affairs and not more than that number read and write in a country of sixteen million people. Out of those three thousand only five hundred are accorded any consideration in the operation of a country. Therefore when the Japs have won over just

162

five hundred people in Thailand they have won over the country."

Busson had much to say of Japanese penetration methods. He told me the Japs had the impudence in 1936 to lie in one of their publications: "The Thais love the Japanese so much they issue their orders in the Thai Navy in Japanese."

Thursday, August 21st:

Prime Minister Menzies, in a statement, said Australia would defend Malaya. This geographical definition of what interests Australia, a definition obviously given by authority of London, seems to me to be a clear invitation to Japan to go into Thailand.

At tea-time I saw the movie, *I Wanted Wings.* Came back and had dinner with Gervasi and Young and then with them went to see Bette Davis in *The Great Lie.* This was the first time I can remember I have seen two movies in one day. Singapore must be getting me.

Had a midnight farewell drink to Gervasi. He is scheduled to take the Clipper tomorrow to return to America. How I envy him!

While I was having the drink with Gervasi in the Raffles bar an officer came up to express his appreciation for the talk I gave at Changi Barracks.

"I appreciated it so much because you spoke right out about things."

Friday, August 22nd:

The Clipper mail was delivered and there is no letter from Martha. I am very disappointed.

At 1:15 General Simmons came by and picked me up. We drove to his house for lunch. Present were the general, Brigadier General Raymond Crawford, Captain Blackwood of Intelligence and the general's A.D.C., Geoffrey Hallowes, a big, blond curly-headed Englishman of about twenty-five.

Simmons is one of the nicest men I have met. He is urbane, affable, intelligent and vigorous, and we met on a common ground in our mutual interest in photography.

We had chicken curry with rice, cut-up pineapple, ground coconut, green beans, elderly eggs and peanuts all mixed together and moistened with cucumber and coconut milk. For dessert there was gula malacca, which is tapioca with black treacle and coconut milk.

163

"The dessert," said Simmons when it was served, "is an antidote for what you have already had."

As fortress commander, Simmons is in charge of all Singapore Island and adjacent islands, the State of Johore and a line on the peninsula extending from Mersing on the east coast to Endau on the west.

Simmons pulled out a map and showed me the precise locations of the troops in Malaya and the airdromes. They seemed to be well scattered, but I had no figures on which to base an estimate of the defensibility of Malaya. I was not looking for any offensive power in Malaya because I knew it wasn't there. Simmons' general conclusions were:

1. The terrain of Malaya Peninsula would be extremely difficult for an invading force to penetrate.

2. For the same reason the British forces would have difficulty in advancing.

3. The British could fight an effective guerrilla war in the jungles and rubber estates.

4. An effective Japanese naval operation against Malaya and Singapore "Could make things very difficult for us."

5. Effective resistance here depends on naval support. "Yes, I think an aircraft carrier would be invaluable."

6. If the Japs got hold of the airports in the north, "It could be very uncomfortable for us."

7. Parachute troops would be a problem but they would have to land on flat country near villages, and they could be spotted. However, many of them could probably land successfully.

8. Japanese naval units could get among the islands off Malaya without being seen by shore-based aircraft.

Captain Blackwood, for the past few days, has been in among the small rivers around Johore, routing out the Japs. They are being ordered out of strictly military areas, and Blackwood said they are fairly well cleared out.

Blackwood is quite English, which means I can't understand half of his conversation. He uses a great many "dash it all, sir" interjections. He calls me "sir" too, and I don't like that.

I did think it was strange that the Japanese were just being cleared out of important military areas at this late date.

Saturday, August 23rd:
These long bouts with Duckworth and Burrows on my scripts continue, out at Duckworth's home. After discussing the scripts and *Newsweek* cables with Duckworth, I am convinced censorship here is one of abnormal fear. It isn't fear of giving information to the enemy or menacing security or even creating alarm and despondency, but of giving a wrong chamber-of-commerce impression.

They seem to think that perhaps some tourists might not come to Singapore if the wrong kind of stories get out.

Sunday, August 24th:
Paul White cabled today, asking when the new transmitter would be ready for broadcasting to New York. He said:

PRESENT PICK-UP IS INEFFECTIVE.

That means that my broadcasts have not been heard very well, and after all this endless work of getting each broadcast through censorship!

Monday, August 25th:
Telephoned Eric Davis, Malaya Broadcasting Corporation, to ask about the new transmitter. My opening statement was, "Can you tell me of any developments on direct hook-ups with America? CBS tells me that the signals at present are not very effective."

"I have already requested the opening of the wireless telephone," Davis said. "Good-bye."

John Young had a similar experience with Davis. He called Davis about arranging facilities for a broadcast for NBC and was told, "Talk to my secretary about that!"

Young and I then spent an hour with Robert Scott, head of the Ministry of Information, and a man named Peet, acting Director of the Malayan Bureau of Information, about opening the wireless telephone to Java or speeding the installation of the new transmitter, "so we can get some decent broadcasts out of here." They suggested we write a letter to Scott for submission to the Colonial Secretary. I said that that would not do at all. That would mean that the letter would be lost in British bureaucracy.

165

"CBS is going to pull me out of here," I pointed out, "unless we can arrange for good transmissions without delay. It seems to me it is to our mutual advantage to get some action instead of letter-writing on this thing."

The continuous requests of correspondents to see what makes Malaya tick brought results. Commander Burrows has arranged for a trip into Northern Malaya. In the party are John Young of NBC, Carl Randau of *PM*, whom I didn't know before, Ray Maley of the Australian *Associated Press*, Jennings of the *Straits Times*, Gallagher of the *London Daily Express*, Captain Gibson of the Gordon Highlanders, and Captain Nayar, an Indian, who are to be conducting officers.

Tuesday, August 26th:

Arrived at Kuala Lumpur, the capital of the Federated Malay States, and breakfasted at the Majestic Hotel. Here's where I discovered for the first time that Commander Burrows had booked me for a lecture tour. I am supposed to speak to a group of officers here and at several other points on our trip.

Major General Louis Heath at Corps Headquarters gave us a talk on the strategical possibilities of the placing of troops in this area. His role, too, was defensive because he said there is nothing to stop Japan from going into Thailand, unless America wants to stop the changing of the map of the Pacific.

As near as I could make out from the talks with Heath and his staff officers there are about thirty to forty thousand troops in Malaya. Major F. G. Anderson, of the 15th Punjabs, a veteran of fourteen years, and Major J. P. Acworth, of the Indian Frontier Forces, a veteran of twenty-five years, drove us for forty minutes through the jungle of rubber to Menton to the 13th Division Headquarters.

Colonel F. V. R. Wodehouse, of the Indian Frontier Force Rifles, showed us the Indian troops practicing with mortars.

Major Acworth knew most of these Indians. We went up to a Sikh and Acworth asked him about his family. His father was a sapper, he is a sapper and, "I have two small boys who are going to be sappers when they grow up."

"Many of these Indians have wonderful memories," Acworth said. "They can't read or write but photograph words in their minds. Then

166

in the evening they mumble to themselves, rehearsing what they were told about the operation of a gun and the tactics to be employed."

Major General A. E. Barstow, commander of the 9th Division with headquarters here at Kuala Lumpur, urged me to come back again to give another talk. I said I would, but I certainly would not come back again on that train full fare—the correspondents were not even given a military rate. Barstow laughed.

"Here are my private and office phone numbers," he said. "Any time you want to come up I will send a plane out for you and fly you up and back."

That was typical, I thought, of the energy of the British soldier in the field. When a Britisher gets behind a desk at central headquarters he considers it one of his main functions to get nothing done. In the field it's different.

General Barstow, on the subject of jungle fighting, spoke with authority.

"If an enemy made a landing on the east coast," he told us, "they couldn't penetrate inland to any depth because of the impenetrable jungle. They would have to work their way down the coast."

By indirection, General Barstow pointed out that Malaya was not a place where troops could be rushed at the last moment to withstand an attack.

"You couldn't bring foreign troops into Malaya and expect them to fight without being acclimatized," he said. "That would take two or three months. Without acclimatization they would become exhausted in the jungle. Of course, in an emergency, you would use any troops given you, but you couldn't expect them to be as good as seasoned troops."

General Barstow agreed with the other generals: "We can hold the Japs all right."

Wednesday, August 27th:
We rode across from Prai on the ferry, *Elizabeth,* to Penang Island. It was one of those tropical scenes you see on postcards, small Chinese boats and larger Chinese junks in the center of the river with dark-brown sails unfurled.

The American freighter, *Azalea City,* was anchored in the roadstead.

167

A few weeks ago it was unloading at Singapore; now it is taking on tin and rubber here. It gives you a tremendous kick to see the American flag painted on the side. At breakfast at the hotel in Georgetown, the main town in Penang, we picked up another conducting officer who will be with us on our trip up north. He is Captain John Wilde and he has lived in Tokyo for some years. He has made a long study of the Japanese and he tells me that they are accustomed to fighting in open country.

"They have never had experience in jungle warfare," he said, "but in Indo-China conditions are approximately like jungle fighting and they are probably training on it. They are superstitious in the jungle and when a Jap meets very strong opposition or barriers he thinks the ghosts are fighting against him. They are afraid of the jungle because they think there are demons in the forest."

Wilde told me of some examples of this which occurred during the Russo-Japanese war in 1905. When the Osaka Regiment refused to advance because the Russians had spread the word that Port Arthur was defended by a ghost trench, the Japanese commander brought in a fresh force, the Hokkaido Regiment, which had not heard the ghost rumor, and sent them into action.

Penang is a small, beautiful island with a mountainous hump down the center covered with jungle. Its sandy beaches are fringed with palm trees. The main business seems to be upholding the white man's burden, tin smelting and shipping rubber. It is one of those tight, compact little communities run by a few Englishmen, with the Chinese and natives doing as best they can.

The correspondents were taken to the military headquarters at Glugor Barracks on Yarrow Hill.

We were met by Brigadier General C. A. Lyon who wears the D.S.O. from the last war. He is a queer duck, rather elderly, extremely friendly and affable, and has a strange habit of constantly slapping at the lobe of his left ear with his left hand. He was as eager to show his domain to us as a gardener back in Hampshire is to show his flowers off to visitors.

I happened to ask General Lyon the first question: "How many anti-aircraft guns do you have here?"

"Twenty-eight," the general said.

168

As we sat in the general's small map-covered office, he told us the type of defenses for this strategic point of Penang was theoretically to guard the west coast of Malaya and the Straits of Malacca.

"We have fortified the southern tip with six-inch guns and there is a new fort at the northern tip of the island, but the guns are not yet put in."

"Where are the guns?" I asked.

General Lyon laughed and said: "I have been waiting for them for a good many months."

After our conversation with the GOC we started a day-long tour of Penang Island. The general was worried about our taking pictures but I explained that everything we photographed or wrote is subject to "terrific censorship."

This is a beautiful country but somehow treacherous and unfriendly looking. All along the road are flaming red hibiscus growing in wild profusion, the way dandelions do back home.

While driving on the road fringing the shore of the island, we came to the small thatched-roofed village of Kumbar. We got out of our cars and walked about 200 yards toward the beach into a perfect Hollywood setting for a South Sea picture: flat beach edged with palms, coconuts on the ground, and here and there a small native hut.

Fifteen feet from the water's edge there was a double row of barbed wire, the straight wire type in front and the concordia type behind.

"Wherever you see one line of barbed wire," General Lyon said, "we are putting two. Where there are two, we are putting four. We are getting ready here for anything that might happen."

Back in the cars, we zigzagged up to the rubber estates and then into the mountains, thick with vegetation, reaching a series of waterfalls which poured into the Penang River.

The general took soft drinks and beer out of hampers in his car and we who had cameras took pictures of the group at the coast line of the mud flats—the main protection of this side of the island, off in the mountains. Looking out to sea over the mud flats, you realized this island is provided with many natural fortifications.

We reached the north coast at Telok Bahang on the edge of an impenetrable jungle that ran almost down to the sea. Down the north coast there were barriers of barbed wire running inwards in a series of triangular protections.

At one point we passed the site of a 9.2 battery. There were no guns and Gallagher remarked on the point to General Lyon.

"They have been sent out to us three times," he said, "but someone else pinched them on the way each time."

Thursday, August 28th:

At the headquarters of the Eleventh Indian Brigade we were met by Brigadier General Murray-Lyon, a very handsome, gray-haired, compact officer, who came here ten months ago from India.

General Murray-Lyon showed us around his camp, spread for miles under the rubber trees, neatly laid out and very comfortable.

The general outlined the British plan for the defense of Malaya and the extermination of the possible Japanese invasion:

"Bren gun carriers can negotiate through the rubber estates for our defense in the rubber. We have ditches so that if we don't drown the Japanese in the tanks, we drown the engines. I don't think much of this vaunted morale of the Japs. They have never been up against first-class troops.

"We have rather made a point of this jungle fighting. We feel we can outsmart the Jap patrols time and again. We went through the jungle for eleven miles carrying mortars without being seen by our umpires once. If we can do this, we are pretty good.

"The rate of sickness here," the general said, "is below that of any army throughout the world. It is three-tenths of one percent. We have slightly less malaria here than they have in India. The mosquitoes are bad, and at 6:30 in the evening everyone must be in long trousers and long sleeves. All those outside the areas where the streams are oily must smear themselves with Warzistan cream. It is a white mess named for the area in India where the mosquitoes are also rather bad."

To guard against malaria, the British do not believe in administering quinine over an extended period. The men are given prophylactic treatment for three or four weeks to keep them on their feet.

The British are confident they know the tricks of this country; for example, the general explained that at Kroh, on the Thai frontier, quite a number of the hills have iron ore.

"Your compass swirls around and you get off your course, but our

170

men know the whole territory. They know just where they are going. The Japs won't know about the ore in these hills and they will be thrown off their course because their compasses will be faulty."

The general felt rather secure because of the protection afforded Malaya by the mountains and jungles and the paddy fields extending from the west coast.

In the gulf of Thailand, at the northern end of the Malayan penninsula, invading ships would have to use lighters several miles off shore.

"But they could use invasion barges, couldn't they?" I asked.

"Yes, of course, but while they are setting off-shore loading barges they present the very solid target that the R. A. F. prays for."

After I spoke to the officers here in the cinema for an hour and a half, we all lunched in the officers' mess, where an Indian sat outside on the verandah hauling away on a rope which sent a wide canvas sheet back and forth to cool the mess and to keep the flies away.

Driving northward to the Thai frontier the road knifed its way through thick jungles, then began to climb the hills near the border at Kroh. This most incredible hill is about twelve miles inside the Malay frontier; it is 3,700 feet high, shaped like a chocolate drop, and covered with jungle.

I remarked to one of the officers that it would be a good place for an observation post.

"None of us has climbed it. It would take weeks to cut a way to the top."

This is incredible country. You can't see four feet into the jungle. It is a tangled mass of bamboo, palms, ferns and gum trees rising straight up to amazing heights.

Crisscrossing this mass are aerial creepers hanging down from the trees and extending like a series of ropes hanging from the yardarm of a ship. It was frightening even to look at it. You felt the sound of the car motor was something of a sacrilege. Throughout this entire stretch I neither saw nor heard any birds. You seemed all alone in that quietude and solemnity.

In a downpour we came to a utility parked along the road. In it were Colonel Moorehead and three other officers. All, strangely enough, were dressed in civilian clothes, and they had come down to lead us to the Kroh camp just two miles from the Thai frontier.

This is the kind of country I prefer to avoid. There are 132 different species of snakes—pythons, cobras and adders. There are tigers, panthers, wildcats, rhinoceri and the dangerous wild pigs and boars. The colonel said they had seen elephant tracks. I didn't spot any.

The colonel obligingly brought out a Sikh, a Moslem and a Dogra so that we could talk with them. I asked each why he joined the Army. Their English was very halting, but their sincerity left no doubt that these were the kind of Indians who were fighting and dying with such courage in the Western Desert of Egypt and in East Africa.

Each of the men said his father had been in the Army and his uncles too, and he preferred the Army to being a farmer.

The Dogra explained he wanted to keep foreigners out of India.

"I would prefer to fight the Germans," the Dogra said. "We make very good soldiers, but if the Japs come here, we will kill those rice-eaters."

I reminded him that the Chinese were rice-eaters, too.

He said flatly: "The people who eat rice are not so good fighters as we Indians."

I asked if they were happy here, and they said: "Yes, we are happy, but we would like some action."

They had never met an American before and when they saw my pips, "U. S. War Correspondent," one of the Indians touched the brass on my shoulders in wonderment.

"I like America," he said. "I have never seen an American before. You are very powerful."

He looked at me as though I were the incarnation of American power.

"Don't look at me," I laughed, thinking how tired I was in this skinny frame of mine. "I'm not strong, but my country is."

"Oh, but you are strong, too."

I told them they were brave fighters, that I had seen the Indians fighting at Mezze outside Damascus and elsewhere in Syria.

"I hope you will do as well, and I know you will."

They were tremendously pleased and said: "We will kill everyone who comes to attack us."

They kept repeating over and over again, "American, American, American," as though they loved to say the word.

172

"We have the advantage," Colonel Moorehead said, "of knowing all this territory well. That's a very great advantage. We are sure the Japs don't know it because it was only mapped three months ago, and none of these maps has fallen into Japanese hands as yet."

Hunched over, I follow behind the corporal along the meager, cluttered, soggy path tunneled through the jungle bordering the frontier between Malaya and Thailand, territory only recently mapped.

It is twilight in here. An inextricable mass and jumble of palms, gum trees, bamboo, teak and intertwined vines and creepers shut out the midday sun and deny the sky itself.

Every now and then the corporal, grunting and muttering softly, swings his sharp-edged *parang* to slice off a creeper vine yearning for a neck to choke. At every step our feet sink above the ankles into rotted branches and the muck of the jungle floor.

Colonel Moorehead is too far ahead. Now we can no longer even hear him thrashing his way over fallen trees or slapping away at the aerial vines blocking his path.

Dank and steaming—those are the clichés to describe the jungle. In this hodge-podge of nature gone slightly mad, where the British and Japanese will one day fight, it is dank and steaming, all right—nearly asphyxiating. Hardly a whisper of air, and there's the musty smell of wet places and the piercing scents of decaying matter, animal and vegetable. The sweat pours off our faces and streams down the middle of our backs as though we're in a downpour.

It is the frightening feeling of inability to find the next breath that's most alarming in here. That, and the hidden things poised to leap and bite, or claw and gore.

Ten minutes of this for an amateur is like running two miles. I call to the corporal and we sit on a fallen, slanting tree hemmed in by leaves and tree-trunks and utter silence. Even the birds have deserted us.

This is where claustrophobia takes on a new, neck-crawling, spine-itching meaning. Trees, leaves and creepers seem to be closing in. You can only see a few feet on all sides. The range of vision seems to be narrowing and constantly it gets darker.

You strain ears to listen for a python slithering across the earth or cracking a twig. Your eyes roll in all directions, overhead, left and right and you twist your head to look behind.

A land of wicked beauty, this Malaya, orchids in profusion on all

173

sides. This is a country of 900 species of orchids. But it is also a land of tigers, panthers, wildcats, elephants and boar. Three or four species of gibbon lurk in these jungles; this is the hide-and-seek ground of Brok and Kra monkeys. There are cobra here, hamadryad and the banded adders. One bite and the war is over.

Sitting in the jungle undergrowth in a semi-darkness, your imagination leaps from one sudden attack by nature to another, and your lungs scramble around to find enough air to draw in. Here man-made war as it is known on the front pages and in the news commentaries lacks reality and, for some, lacks even danger.

Here along the base of the strategical triangle that has Singapore for its apex, practice and potential war is not a matter of tanks and dive bombers but of buzzing mosquitoes, malaria, tigers offering ripped flesh in their claws and cobras with death in their fangs.

Highlanders from Scotland, Indians from the Rajput, Australians from "Down Under" and Englishmen from Manchester think not only of the Japs. They think as much of the menaces of nature.

We sit there, I gulping in air, both of us sweeping the sweat off our faces with one hand and yanking fat, voracious ants off our legs with the other.

"Can't stay here very long," the corporal says. "These keringahs will pick us up and take us home."

He's very skillful at snaring two or three of the red ants with one pinch of the fingers.

"This," I remark, "is some country you picked."

"Blimey, I didn't pick this bloody country! Not me!"

The corporal is very emphatic about it, in unreproducable words.

"How long've you been out here?"

"Just a year in this blasted country, but I was in Shanghai before that." All in a rush he adds, "I haven't been home in five years."

"Homesick, I guess."

"Homesick! Ho, ho, it's long past that. I've two kiddies and the way things look they'll be grown up and married before I see them."

"If there was action it wouldn't be so bad."

"You think it's coming now, do you?" the corporal asks eagerly. "We just sometimes see the papers up here and they don't tell us much."

"Well, I don't know. There's a fairly good chance."

"I bloody well hope so. I'd like to have a go at those Japs, I would.

174

On the Shanghai duty we had to take all their lip and insults right across the barbed wire and couldn't do a thing about it."

Softly, like a whisper in the hushed jungle, the corporal says: "I've a score to even with those bloody Japs." And then he sighs either in unpleasant memory or pleasurable anticipation. "Well, the colonel will be waiting for us."

The colonel is sitting on the stump of a tree, the only one cut down here, and his shirt is half ripped off, hanging over him queerly.

"What happened to you, Colonel? Run into some Japs?"

"Oh, no, just one of the many amenities of the jungle. Watch out for it."

"Watch out for what?"

"A palm with a hooked thorn on it. Luckily, it only ripped the shirt. It's rather bad when it takes the skin with it."

We are beside a small trench, in a tiny island of clearing in the jungle and on the edge of a cliff falling straight down forty feet to the road—the road into Thailand. It is lighter in here, about like late afternoon on a rainy day.

Three Indian soldiers, Sikhs, are in the trench. Their rifles are leveled at the road through narrow openings in the wall of trees, vines and ferns. The trench could not be spotted three feet away. Camouflage is simple in this country, but the khaki of the British is easier to detect than the gray-green of the Germans would be in the jungle.

Below us, the road is lined with red hibiscus, and here and there among the amazing variety of jungle trees a frangiapani with big, oily, shiny leaves and large white flowers, bigger than a tulip.

"We made a circle through the jungle," the colonel says, and smiles. "A bit sticky in places, wasn't it?"

I tell him he's welcome to this country and remark how amazing it is to see so many trees all in one place.

"That's life," says the colonel. "The men in the Western Desert wish for trees and we chaps here wish there weren't so bloody many of them."

"That seems to be the important thought in Malaya, Colonel, to be somewhere else. Everybody appears to be fed up."

"These constant threats of war, and then war not coming has something to do with it," the colonel muses. "Then, too, you saw those camps under the rubber. A man's bound to become bored with seeing

175

row after row of rubber trees. It rains almost every day up here. There's nothing more depressing than being in camp under rubber trees in the rain."

The colonel idly looks at the corporal standing at the edge of the cliff, leaning against a tree in a dejected pose of complete boredom.

"Yes, a man feels let down out here."

Does the colonel think he can hold the Japs if they come down from Thailand.

"Of course, and there's no doubt of that," he exclaims. "I don't think much of this vaunted morale of the Japs."

"But," I suggest, "the Japs are fanatical. They consider it a sacred honor to die."

"Well, they'll find all the sacred honor they want in the jungle. We know this country. They don't. By now, our British and Indian troops are acclimatized. We know how to fight the best kind of guerrilla warfare.

"Our men are getting hard. We are finding out how to beat the jungle, too. The other day we went on a seven-day march of thirty miles through the jungle. That was fairly good time. We expected 120 cases of malaria on the march, but only twenty were down.

"Oh, there's no doubt of it," the colonel says with an expansive gesture of confidence. "No doubt of it at all. We can outflank the Jap outflankers and knock hell out of them."

Friday, August 29th:
Near Sungei Patani on the main road into Thailand we stopped off to visit a camp among the rubber trees. We watched several Indians practicing with a Breda gun—one of many captured from the Italians in Libya. The men went through the motions but didn't actually fire it.

I asked the brigadier major how many armored cars they had.

"We have none at the moment actually," he said. "We expect them almost any time."

The brigadier major took us out to a small village alongside a canal. Natives were widening and deepening it "so that no tanks can get through." He said that arrangements had been made to flood virtually the entire paddy if the Japs break through.

"It would be difficult country for them to operate in," he said, "for
176

part of this section is mud and water—what we call gloom—where you sink in to the navel."

About twelve miles from the frontier on this main road into Thailand we passed a camp which we were told was being built for enemy prisoners, when and if the war breaks out.

"Oh," John Young said, "I suppose it's name is Camp So Sorry."

CRESCENDO OF BLUFF

Saturday, August 30th:

Back in Singapore I found a cable from Paul White scheduling a broadcast Sunday night and also a letter from the Malaya Broadcasting informing me they could not provide the facilities for the required time Sunday night. I immediately telephoned Eric Davis at the Malaya Broadcasting.

Davis explained that the time could not be granted because "we have other commitments." I pointed out that I had advised him within twelve hours after my arrival in Singapore on August 3rd the specified periods during which CBS would need facilities and had been assured that those periods were satisfactory to him.

"Yes," he said, "but we have gone on Daylight Saving Time and those periods are no longer available to you."

"You mean you've readjusted your schedule then with no consideration for the requirements of CBS transmission to America?"

"I have a program in French for Indo-China on one transmitter and a news program in Mandarin on the other at the time you want."

"Can't you change the Mandarin program to another period?"

"No, I can't," Davis said.

"Do you mean to say that a program in Mandarin is more important than a news broadcast to millions of Americans about the defense of Malaya and what you need out here?"

"Yes," Davis said, "if you put it to me that way, I do think the program in Mandarin is more important."

I then called Scott, the head of the Ministry of Information, and told him the circumstances and he, too, seemed indifferent whether CBS was able to broadcast to America or not.

"Well," Scott said, "you might write a letter to Davis and present your case and maybe something can be done."

"And what happens to my broadcast for tomorrow night?"

"I don't know about that, but Malaya Broadcasting has very kindly and graciously consented to give you facilities."

178

"Not for tomorrow night, they haven't."

John Young and I got together, and he was amazed, too, at the strange attitude taken by MBC and the Ministry of Information. We both agreed that Singapore undoubtedly has the greatest concentration of stupid, vapid, unco-operative officials we have ever encountered.

I sent White a cable:

MALAYA BROADCASTING DENIES CBS FACILITIES SUNDAY NIGHT BROADCAST. RECOMMEND STRONGEST PROTEST TO LONDON OVER INCREDIBLE CO-OPERATION SINGAPORE OFFICIALS.

Sunday, August 31st:
Paul White told me to cable my script which would be read in case the broadcast could not be effected. I finished it by noon and took it to Duckworth, the chief press censor, and to Commander Burrows, both of whom passed it without a change. I mentioned to Duckworth I was cabling this script because MBC could not provide CBS facilities. Duckworth was furious and shouted: "Those people at the MBC must be crazy!"

He telephoned Scott, but the gist of it was that the head of the British Ministry of Information here agreed with Davis that the program of French news to Indo-China and Mandarin news to China was more important than a CBS news broadcast to America.

Tonight I made a final check with Davis to determine if I could use MBC facilities for the broadcast. His answer was brief: "My decision stands." He hung up.

The meager intelligence of some officials here has me flabbergasted. You find the typical British Colonial officers afraid of their shadow, fearful of responsibility with a total incomprehension of affairs which cannot be handled without a specific order from above. Everywhere you go to get something done the answer is: "Now, if you will write a letter. . . ."

The next time I hear that I am going to bite the speaker in half!

This evening I had a burst of energy and I am doing a rewrite on part of the article on the Western Desert. I came to the part where I speak of an airdrome near Sidi Barrani that made me think of Shangri-la and it occurs to me that I have often thought of some such place of peace and quiet these past four years away from America, especially the past year. Inside I want to retreat and outside I want

179

activity. I want great events to write about. My nerves demand it but my body wants to sink into some oblivion of utter relaxation.

How wrong I was about Russia's strength! So was GHQ in Cairo. They said six weeks. I thought five weeks would see the end of Russia. What folly it is to make a prediction! Everyone does and the most frequent mistakes are made by military experts.

In the talks I made up north to officers I began them by saying I wasn't a military expert but a journalist and therefore might make mistakes in military terms, but as a journalist I didn't make any more mistakes than generals. Everyone roared with laughter at that remark, even the generals who were present.

Monday, September 1st:

Eric Davis and I are now in the letter-writing stage over the denial of facilities. I find his letter almost incomprehensible and he makes a strange suggestion that I should record my broadcasts and that CBS broadcast them when convenient.

I pointed out that CBS in New York had spent several years and hundreds of thousands of dollars in building up the 6:45 P.M. period for reports from all parts of the world and we would not change our program time nor break our faith with the American people by using recordings in order that the Malaya Broadcasting might send news in Mandarin.

I wrote Davis a seven-page letter with an ulterior purpose. Alfred Duff Cooper is coming here within the next few days as British Minister of State to inquire into the foibles of Malaya and the Far East and I intend showing a copy of this letter to Duff Cooper.

Tuesday, September 2nd:

At lunch today the Thailand Consul came over to the table where John Young and I were eating. We sold him on the idea that the Thailand Government should fly us up to Bangkok so we could do some broadcasting out of there. Our idea is twofold. There is a pretty good story in Bangkok these days with the Japs slowly taking over; and it will give us a chance to get out of Singapore and do battle with officials who perhaps will make no pretense of intelligence at least.

Twenty-four American Navy fighter pilots are here en route to join the American volunteer group in Burma.

180

Wednesday, September 3rd:

It is two years since the war started. How confused the war has become! How many predictions I have been wrong in, and how my thoughts and millions of others' have changed! But in one thing I was right—Italy could not last six months—and she hasn't. I overestimated Britain's strength. I thought Britain could drive Italy to a separate peace in six months. As for Russia, I thought she would stay out of the war at almost any price in order to take over when Germany and Britain were exhausted.

I never thought France would collapse as she did. I thought General Weygand in North Africa would rebel before this. I thought Germany would have the French fleet by now. I thought the United States would be in the war by now. I thought the Axis would be in Spain by now—actually and physically in control. I thought that Gibraltar would have been subjected to heavy bombings. I didn't think Germany would have conquered all of Europe as she has. I thought there would be more internal troubles and sabotage in the occupied countries than there is. I thought the Greeks would be able to hold out against the Italians only a few months—perhaps less than that, and yet they drove the Italians back into Albania, and, if Germany hadn't come in, would have driven the Italians into the Adriatic.

Thursday, September 4th:

With Young I went to the Singapore Swimming Club this afternoon. It is one of the most beautiful and certainly the largest pool in the world. The sun was broiling. It is the first afternoon of relaxation I have had since I came to Singapore. We lay on the grass beside the pool for a time. There were a number of youngsters there—fine-looking children of six or eight, and Young remarked: "Those kids don't know whether they will grow up to go to college or to be slaves."

We talked about those children being pitifully unaware of all the madness let loose by one man at Berchtesgaden.

The boys were not totally unaware. One of the kids was making a boom-boom sound with his lips and running around the grass crying, "I'm in the bomber command," and another youngster was doing the same thing, while a third youngster was pursuing them making the sound of a high whine and crying, "I'm in the fighter command."

Sunday, September 7th:

Somehow I have the feeling that I may be sent somewhere else very soon—perhaps even ordered home. At least I hope so. For the past few days I have felt very remote from the war and what it means. It has been a sort of dream. Singapore helps to do that.

One of the girls who teaches at an American Mission came back from the States today after being away from America for five years. She was in the States a year and a half.

"There is so much flag-waving and war spirit and talk about the war at home," she said, "that it's a relief to get back to the peace and quiet and indifference of Singapore."

Tuesday, September 9th:

This afternoon Young and I were lying in beach chairs at the Singapore Swimming Club when the Clipper came over. Trailing were a half dozen Brewster Buffalo fighters. It was a tremendous sight, and the first time I have seen the Clipper. This huge silver bird with two American flags painted underneath circled several times around Singapore, once directly over us. Duff Cooper and Lady Diana were aboard. They were being given an air view of Singapore, I presume.

I lunched again today with the Thailand Consul, still trying to sell him on the idea that the Thais should fight at any cost.

"We are swinging away from the Japs," he said. "I can assure you that ninety percent of the Thais would fight a Japanese aggression. Why, we would even oppose a British aggression. We would fight anyone who tries to attack our country."

"I hope so," I said, not very convinced.

Thursday, September 11th:

I am amazed that the British authorities don't do something here about the *Singapore Herald,* an afternoon newspaper which is owned and edited by Japs and subsidized by the Japanese Consulate. Today it printed a story with the headline: "Jap-U.S. Rapprochement Near." The story gave a glowing picture of how Washington and Tokyo were going to be friends. As a matter of fact, the news from Washington is not quite that. Cordell Hull issued a statement that there is no change in Jap-U.S. relations.

The *Singapore Herald* is used by the Tokyo Foreign Office for trial balloons within British territory. For example, the editorial in the Jap-run paper today says:

"There are still many who assume that if the United States is engaged in war against Germany the Japanese Government automatically will be commanded by the Tripartite Pact to go to war against the United States and her Allies. That is not a true position.

"The Tripartite Pact permits Japan to go to the assistance of Germany and Russia if they are attacked. A declaration of war or war-like action by the United States would not necessarily be interpreted by Tokyo as an attack against Germany, for Germany already has provided evidence of an attack against the United States by sinking two ships and by assaults on others."

I cabled that passage to *Newsweek* magazine because I thought it was typical of the propaganda game that Tokyo was playing and the incredible part of it was that the British were permitting that kind of propaganda to be put out from Singapore to convince all who read the *Herald* that they should not worry or make preparations for war.

Friday, September 12th:
This morning at nine, Young and I saw Alfred Duff Cooper at Government House. He received us in his bedroom and we spent a half hour with him. He was extremely friendly and affable and explained that he was a close friend of William Paley, president of CBS.

"If you know him, that's more than I do," I said. "I've never even met my immediate boss, Paul White."

Young and I explained the broadcasting situation and our inability to get reasonable facilities from Malaya Broadcasting. Duff Cooper said he had no authority here but would inquire about it.

Two hours later Scott telephoned to say that he was sure Davis would adjust the situation. This meant that Duff Cooper, with the kind of energy that the British have needed out here for a long time, telephoned Scott and Davis and said in effect: "Enough of this monkeybusiness. Provide facilities and that's that."

Roosevelt's speech this morning was sharp but not sharp enough—the protection of all ships in America's defense waters and to shoot first. Its worth lies in the operation, not words. The next matter is the extension of America's defense waters to all the waters of the world.

Saturday, September 13th:
British problems mean very little to the Chinese and Malay civilians here. For example, at the end of the picture at the cinema a photograph of King George is thrown on the screen and "God Save the King" is played. All the Europeans stand at attention, but the Malays and Chinese shuffle out of the cinema. For some reason they have never been called about this disrespect.

Sunday, September 14th:
Today is my birthday—thirty-four years old. Of all the birthdays, I remember most vividly the one when I was twenty-one. I was doing a series of articles for the Youngstown *Vindicator-Telegram*. My brother Eugene and I had stowed away on the *Western World* of the Munson Line and had gone to Buenos Aires. We celebrated it by having two huge luscious steaks in one day.

On this birthday Young took me to lunch at Cyranos.

I had oysters and chicken livers and a chocolate sundae. I always try to get sick on my birthday by eating weird combinations.

Everyone that I have talked to in Singapore in the past day or two thinks that the tenseness in the Far East is easing very rapidly. They have accepted Roosevelt's speech and Russia's resistance as signs that war isn't coming down here.

An official notice was put out today that the reason Singapore does not have air-raid shelters is because the city is built on lowlands and there is water directly under the surface. The announcement said, too, that surface shelters are not very practical because "They would be death traps. The buildings might collapse and catch fire and you might be trapped. Remember," the announcement added, "most of the shops and houses of Singapore are of flimsy construction and could not stand bomb blasts. Therefore, in any bombing, make your way into the open spaces."

If that's the way Singapore is going to get ready for air raids here, I think I'd better get the hell out.

184

Tuesday, September 16th:

All the correspondents received a notice that Air Marshal Sir Robert Brooke-Popham and Admiral Sir Geoffrey Layton would hold a press interview at the Naval Base.

Commander Burrows and Lieutenant Brian Reynolds, who were supposed to handle visits to Naval installations for the correspondents, were pleased as punch. They acted as though they personally had just knocked out Hitler and gave off a noxious air of having scored a tremendous personal victory in arranging an interview that the correspondents had been clamoring for during the past two months.

A group of us were standing at press headquarters and Young asked me if I was going to bring up the inadequacies of the arrangements and facilities for correspondents.

"Yes," I said, "I think I'll bring it up."

Young asked O'Dowd Gallagher of the *London Daily Express* and Ray Maley of the Australian *Associated Press* if they would support my statements. Gallagher said he thought he would and Maley remarked: "Well, it all depends on what you say."

"Whether you boys open up or not," I said, "I'm going to put in my protests."

With the usual confusion, two of the conducting officers got in one car with the result that our car was not directed, except by the Malay chauffeur who had only a vague idea where we were going. In the car were Young and two Indian reporters, one representing a Calcutta paper and the other a New Delhi journal.

When we arrived at the Naval Base the conference was already in progress. As we came in, Sir Robert and Sir Geoffrey were sitting side by side at a long table, surrounded by about thirty reporters.

Sir Robert had just come back from the Netherlands East Indies and he was saying: "I'm very pleased with what I saw. The Dutch defenses are all in good condition. The Dutch are not chauvinistic. They are determined, if attacked, to defend themselves to the utmost.

"They are using," he went on, "every moment of time left to them to get ready. I'm convinced, if called upon, they will put up a good show."

McDaniel, of *Associated Press,* asked Sir Robert if there was any kind of a political agreement between Great Britain and the N.E.I.

"No particular development on that," Sir Robert replied. "One only has to look at the map. From the point of view of defense it is all one strategic problem and that's understood by everyone concerned."

I asked: "How is Thailand stacking up?" Sir Robert didn't quite understand the slang expression so I re-phrased the question: "What is the attitude of Thailand these days?"

Sir Robert pursed his lips, and gave a dry laugh.

"Relations with Thailand have become more friendly. They've begun to realize that we really can help them. Now they are looking to us for help and to some extent for advice.

"The Thais," Sir Robert added, "are getting more independent-minded. They realize it's an uncomfortable position to be too dependent economically on Japan."

This indicated that Thailand now was buying more and more supplies from Great Britain by way of the Straits Settlements, but no one pursued the question.

I got the impression that the interview was proving unproductive, so I touched on a tough matter.

"Sir Robert," I asked, "offensively, would you be prepared to go to the help of Thailand?"

Sir Robert smiled and leaned back in his chair, waving a hand airily.

"I don't think I can answer that. One has to make so many assumptions."

"Yes, but if Thailand were invaded by the Japanese and they called on you for help, are you prepared to give that help?"

"If the order comes from Whitehall, I'll carry it out," Sir Robert said.

I was standing in one corner of the long rectangular bare-furnished room and the interview appeared to be over. I stepped to the center, on the opposite side of the table from the two officers.

"With your indulgence, Sir Robert," I began, "I'd like to make a few remarks. Every correspondent who has come here from the United States, from Britain, from Australia, from other theatres of operations is anxious to co-operate, without exception, to help the British war effort. We all want to co-operate.

"We encounter here in the office of Commander Burrows many
186

difficulties. Burrows' office should be the funnel through which all our efforts flow. Instead it is a bottleneck."

I cited some of the experiences on our trip to the north—"It was a mess from beginning to end."—and went on: "Due to the situation here, some of our best correspondents have gone away in disgust— Frank Gervasi of *Collier's*, Leland Stowe of the *Chicago Daily News*, and Martha Gellhorn of *Collier's* came and went away to write nasty pieces about you all. *Life* magazine gave a picture of Singapore that wasn't too flattering.

"John Young of NBC, one of the outstanding radio voices in America, is going at the end of this week. As an American, and speaking as a representative of CBS, I can voice the sentiments of other correspondents as considering the Pacific of vital importance.

"I cannot over-emphasize to you, gentlemen, the importance of getting the story of the Far East across to the American people. If it is your desire to get America into this war, the Pacific is the place where that event can happen."

As I talked, Brooke-Popham seemed acutely uncomfortable, embarrassed and a bit white around the gills. He looked up several times, then dropped his eyes quickly. Admiral Layton seemed to be swelling up like a pouter pigeon, controlling himself with great effort.

"Other men may wish to express their views," I said, "but meanwhile I want to express to you my thanks for hearing me."

Gallagher, the veteran of campaigns in Spain, France and the Middle East, was sitting next to Layton. He immediately said: "As a British citizen, I agree with every statement made by Mr. Brown."

John Young then stepped forward. He obviously was excited and his words bore out his appearance. He began to shout: "There isn't a first-class man in Burrows' whole office. If I had that kind of people working for me, I'd fire every one of them.

"You people," Young cried bluntly, "have the chance to use us. NBC and CBS reach eighty million Americans. We have the perfect pulpit. Speaking for NBC, I'll put on the air anything you give me to use. Nothing could be fairer than that. But just give us something.

"Instead of using us you hinder us. Brown fought against the Italians for three years and was expelled. Then he was arrested by the Germans in Yugoslavia and now he comes here and has to fight with the British."

Dixon Brown, fair-faced, bulky, soft-spoken, then expressed his complaints. He was a stringer for London papers—that is, he was paid by the story or on space rates. He claimed there had been discrimination against stringers but now most of it had abated.

Sir Robert said: "Well, now, well, now. We have heard from four men on one side. Let's hear from someone from Burrows' office. Is there someone here from Burrows' office?"

Major C. R. Fisher spoke up. He had come from the Middle East to be in charge of facilities for correspondents, but Brooke-Popham apparently hadn't met him before. He called him Captain Crawford, and Fisher corrected him.

"All right now, Major uh-uh Major Fisher, what do you have to say about all this?"

"Dixon Brown has made the first specific complaint to be made," Major Fisher said. "The rest is all nebulous."

Yates McDaniel pounced on that. "I'll give a specific instance, if you wish. When the second contingent of Australians arrived in Singapore," McDaniel said, "Burrows put out a twenty-five-word communiqué. It merely said the Australians had arrived and that they were well, and so on. I went to Burrows at once—we weren't permitted to go to the dock to see the troops arrive—and asked for more detail.

"Burrows said, 'That's enough on it. The rest is all bilge.' I protested that we served papers in Australia and the parents and friends of these men wanted to know additional details. I argued with Burrows for an hour before he could see my point. Then I got a few more details."

McDaniel was cool, dispassionate and obviously disgusted.

Under the avalanche of complaints, Admiral Layton fidgeted in his chair. He spoke for the first time, without waiting for Sir Robert Brooke-Popham to give his approval. In a tight, irritated voice he said: "This is the thing that happens when there isn't much news and the journalists get bored and blame us for the absence of news. We can't build a bonfire just to make news for you people. We're not going to lay on a war just to give you people a story. Thank God, war hasn't come here—yet."

"We're not protesting now against absence of news or censorship," Young said. "I'll use whatever you want to put out, just exactly as you put it out."

"Our concern today, Sir Geoffrey," I said, "is only on the matter of facilities to do stories on the basis of existing news and subject to your censorship."

"I want you all to know something," Admiral Layton said. "I want you to come to me whenever you have complaints."

Gallagher at once shot back: "I've been trying to see you for thirty days about this very thing. I was always told you were not available."

A request to see the admiral is made to Commander Burrows.

Layton hemmed and hawed, but said nothing that could be translated into words.

Then Fisher, in defending the Burrows' office, insisted: "Everything I've heard thus far is just general abuse without specification."

"We have been general in our presentation of the picture," I said, "because of the value of the commanders' time. It was my understanding that Burrows would be here this afternoon."

I then suggested that we hold a meeting with Burrows present and "we will be very pleased to give time, place, date and circumstance to our general complaints."

For some reason I could never discover, Major Fisher then made the remark that he had found using former British newspapermen as conducting officers had produced "disastrous" results.

Correspondents who go to visit any military establishment or objective are always accompanied by an officer, usually a lieutenant or captain, who acts as guide.

To Fisher's remark, I retorted: "The best conducting officer I had in the Western Desert of Egypt was a newspaperman. His name was Captain Fielding. He helped me very greatly. In Syria the conducting officers were not newspapermen and they were not much good."

The Naval Lieutenant, Brian Reynolds, went to John Young, and Young reported Reynolds' whispered conversation. It was: "How about that naval patrol trip we took together?" Reynolds pleaded. "That was well organized, wasn't it? Tell them how much you enjoyed that. Go ahead, Young, tell them how well I conducted that trip."

"Yes," Young said to Reynolds. "That was all right; but what about the past two weeks? I haven't been able to see a thing."

Thereupon Young said roughly: "Oh, go away, Reynolds, and don't bother me," and to Brooke-Popham and Layton, Young said:

"I'll repeat there isn't a first-class man in the whole Public Relations organization."

Reynolds' face turned a brick red.

"The only thing is to clean them all out if necessary," Young added. "An organization is only as strong as its weakest link and when the top man is incapable, the rest of the organization is incapable too."

McDaniel got to his feet and added: "Burrows seems to have no conception of his work."

Layton then took over replies to the complaints of the correspondents.

"This organization was only recently organized and it takes time to get it going."

Burrows had been named by Admiral Layton and took over the organization about six months before.

"Sir Geoffrey," I said, "you've had two years' experience in London and more than a year in Cairo to build on."

"Ah," he said confidently, "that isn't here."

"Yes, but why not profit by the experiences there and start with the general organization they have built in Cairo and London?"

"No, conditions elsewhere are not the same as here. Those are active battle areas and this is not."

"But why start at scratch here? You build on what's been done elsewhere."

Layton said he would call a meeting within the next day or two with Burrows and the correspondents to "hear the complaints."

I walked out of the meeting with Layton and he assured me: "We'll get at the bottom of this thing."

"It is very bad," I reiterated, "for everyone to come to Singapore and go away to write acidulous pieces. It seems to me you people would want to avoid that."

"Carl Mydans of *Life* was here," Layton replied, "and I gave him every help and he wasn't very nice. And," he added in the tone and facial expression of a petulant child, "he put the air marshal's picture on the front page."

That remark flabbergasted me. It was the first indication I had of the man's vanity that was to express itself a few days later in more direct terms. I could only say: "Yes, Sir Robert's picture was on the front cover, wasn't it?"

British officialdom achieved an attitude toward me from that meeting which was never changed. I learned later that when Reynolds informed Burrows of the discussion at the meeting that Burrows called me every name in his lexicon of profanity. From that time on, the Services Public Relations Office under Burrows determined that I would get no facilities, if it could possibly be avoided.

After the meeting, the other correspondents, especially the Asiatics —Indians, Chinese, Malay and mixed races—expressed amazement at such forthright talk. "The commanders," they said, "have never been talked to that way before. We could never speak that way to them, and we are very grateful."

I told them that wasn't the point; a war was coming and we all wanted to be as ready as possible to cover that war.

That evening I ran into Gallagher at Raffles Hotel. He said that two correspondents were being sent by invitation to the Sultan of Johore's birthday party, and that four men were being flown over to Sarawak for the centennial celebration. I knew nothing about either of these possible stories.

Wednesday, September 17th:
At the request of Colonel Elrington I spoke this evening to his Loyal Regiment at Tanglin Barracks. It was especially enjoyable for me because of the keenness of the audience and the intelligence of their questions. From these men—privates, troopers and non-commissioned officers—I had the impression of great vitality and eagerness to fight.

After the talk I dined with Colonel and Mrs. Elrington at their home. It made me too homesick to sit down to a beautiful table with flowers, shining silverware and service. This sort of thing makes me miss Martha all the more and I would rather avoid such nostalgic moments.

Thursday, September 18th:
Captain Curtis, one of the conducting officers, came to see me while I was having breakfast at Raffles Hotel. He was very alarmed and excited and said he had a great favor to ask of me.

"Last night," he said, "when I got back from Tanglin Barracks, Commander Burrows asked me if Palmer, the photographer, took the pictures all right and if everything had gone smoothly. I told him it had and described the lecture you gave."

"Well, you know, Curtis, it didn't go smoothly and Palmer was definitely drunk and I am sure got no pictures at all. Moreover, I had to take a taxi out, instead of you taking me as arranged," I said.

At Curtis' request, I agreed not to mention that Burrows' office again showed incapacity and sent a drunken photographer on a job.

After he left, John Young of NBC came in to breakfast and I told him of the mix-up last night, and Young said: "I'd certainly tell Admiral Layton about that this afternoon."

"No, I'm not. I won't mention it."

Thirty newspapermen met with Admiral Geoffrey Layton at the Naval Base for discussion of the problems of correspondents and the conduct of the Services Public Relations Office. We all crowded into one of the rooms in the Administration building at the Naval Base and at the head of the table sat the admiral flanked by his aide and Commander Burrows.

Admiral Layton began by saying there was a tendency of the local press to ignore the existence of the Commander-in-Chief, China, that is, himself.

"This," the admiral said, "is a post of many generations' standing and it existed long before the title of Commander-in-Chief, Far East." (That is, the post held by Sir Robert Brooke-Popham.) "It is separate and distinct and is charged with the protection of British rights and authority under the China command. It is an ancient and honorable command. It is charged with the protection of all shipping in this area.

"The Army and Air Force here," added Admiral Layton, "are a minor concern. They are here purely in a defensive role to protect the bases of the ships—that is all. I want to call the attention of all you men and especially of the local newspapers to this."

I was aghast at this statement. This was the most blatant bid for press attention I have ever heard and it sounded to me like a piteous appeal for publicity.

Layton conducted that meeting, which we all hoped would solve many of the problems of correspondents, with great shrewdness and ruthlessness. I developed a grudging admiration for the way Admiral Layton could maneuver that meeting into producing just the results he wanted.

192

"All right," the admiral said, "we'll take you in order. That man in the first seat—you begin."

"That man" happened to be a dark-skinned reporter of mixed blood who worked for the Japanese-controlled *Singapore Herald*. He made the complaint that he had not been asked to go on one or two visits to military establishments.

"You're fortunate to be here," the admiral snapped, "and your paper is fortunate to be allowed to publish. I don't think it ought to be allowed to continue. You would do well to say nothing at all."

Jennings of the *Straits Times* was next. Anxious to get a commission in the Army, he served as a stooge for Burrows.

"I have no complaint to make," Jennings said. "I get complete co-operation and am perfectly satisfied."

Thus, down the line, Layton called for complaints in an autocratic, quarter-deck manner. Most of the correspondents curled up under that and made minor complaints about improper distribution of communiqués, failing to bring up major issues of fundamental incompetence.

These were men, too, who had previously, in private, complained on major issues. But they recognized that Admiral Layton had come to the meeting with a predetermination to defend Burrows, the man he had selected for the job.

After some fifteen correspondents had had their say—usually "I have nothing to say"—John Young of NBC got up to report that he had been promised by Burrows' office a flight in a PBY, a Catalina.

"The arrangements," he said, "were messed up, with the result that the flight never came off."

He explained the circumstances to Layton in precise detail four times. For some incomprehensible reason the admiral could not or would not understand the circumstances.

Finally the admiral said: "Well, that wasn't Commander Burrows' fault; it was the fault of the Air Ministry News Service because the Air Force wants to run its own publicity."

Young explained in impassioned terms our anxiety to get on a "decent working basis," that NBC reached millions of Americans, that it was part of the Radio Corporation of America, the Radio-Keith-Orpheum movie organization, and that its influence was tremendous in the United States.

"All these services are available to the British to tell the story to America."

Layton interrupted him to say: "Well, what is your complaint—what is your complaint?"

"I merely want some co-operation from Commander Burrows' office so that I can report some stories out of here. I want to avoid missing out on flights such as Burrows' office messed up for me last week."

"That was your own fault that you missed that flight," Layton retorted.

"Where do you get that stuff?" Young shouted.

"Don't you threaten me!" Layton shouted back. "I don't care how powerful an organization you represent, you will get thrown out of this meeting."

"I'm not threatening you," Young said, and sat down.

Then it was the turn of Gallagher, the *London Daily Express* correspondent.

"I would like to point out," he said quietly, "that the communiqués of Commander Burrows are violating the defense regulations."

He proceeded then to point out several cases where communiqués revealed information which was specifically barred by the British defense regulations.

"Moreover," Gallagher added, "the communiqués are filled with tripe and clichés that cannot be construed as news or even reportable journalism.

"That's the kind of communiqué," Gallagher continued, "that might be all right for Jennings of the *Straits Times* and his four thousand readers, but they are certainly not satisfactory to my three million readers."

When my turn came to speak I said: "I voiced some of my complaints in the meeting two days ago. I'll be rather brief now.

"I wish to point out, Sir Geoffrey, that in the future I will not plead with Commander Burrows for facilities and that correspondents who cannot report the news from Singapore are going to be called out of Singapore by their organizations to places where they can report the story. I fought the Italians for three years in order to tell the story from there and now I have to fight you people for your own sake. I am

194

tired of fighting—I am generally tired, but I am especially tired fighting British officials for the sake of Britain."

I expressed my gratitude to Admiral Layton for the off-the-record interview he had given me shortly after my arrival and how much I had appreciated that talk.

Young stood up and said: "Tell the admiral about your lecture last night—how you had to take a taxi and that the photographer was drunk."

"Don't bring that up, John," I called.

"What's this about a drunken photographer—what's this all about?"

"I can answer that, Admiral Layton," said Captain Curtis. "Arrangements had been made to pick up Mr. Brown and take him to the Tanglin Barracks to speak to the Loyal Regiment. I was with a photographer by the name of Palmer and we were a bit late and Mr. Brown took a taxi."

Layton whirled on Young and said: "Well, Mr. Young, you have just made an erroneous statement."

I jumped to my feet and said: "I resent you, Sir Geoffrey, imputing to Young any inaccuracies. He gave an accurate statement of what happened. It's with the greatest regret that I must break my word of honor to Curtis that I would not report the incident of last night. Curtis was in no way responsible and did everything possible to get me there in time. He was held up by the photographer, who I am sure also did not get any pictures, as he was assigned to do."

Layton smiled and asked: "Was the photographer drunk?"

"You don't expect me to answer that question, Sir Geoffrey, and I am not obligated to do so."

"Well, Mr. Brown, do you have anything else to say—do you have any other complaints to make?"

"Just this, Sir Geoffrey, I am extremely pessimistic from your attitude, with all due respect to you and to your office, of any good coming out of this meeting."

"I am getting a good deal out of this meeting," Sir Geoffrey remarked, "although some people may not think so."

"Thank you, sir, for the time you have given me."

"Thank you, Mr. Brown."

And I sat down.

No other complaints were made and the meeting was over.

I walked out into the corridor with Sir Geoffrey and we stood there talking for a moment.

"I was very much interested in your remarks, Mr. Brown," Admiral Layton said, "and I hope something can be done."

"I am sure it can, Sir Geoffrey, and we are all grateful to you for your interest in holding this meeting."

"I want you to know that I did get a good deal out of that meeting."

"I hope so, Sir Geoffrey."

John Young came up and it was very obvious that the tension was still very strong between Young and the admiral.

"I want to tell you, Sir Geoffrey," John said, "that neither I nor NBC will forget your treatment of me in that meeting."

"I took it that you were threatening me," the admiral replied, "and I will not permit that."

"Not at all," Young said, "if you wanted the facts we were giving them to you."

I then took on the unaccustomed role of peacemaker.

"No one was threatening anyone. We were not concerned in there with personalities. We offered these facts in good will to help you and to help ourselves. This was to be a washing of all the dirty laundry in the situation so that we can get down to business here. This situation here looks very bad and it will be catastrophic if war breaks out.

"Why don't we look at it this way? If you needed a battleship here you would beef about it until they did send you one. Well, you need someone here who knows about news and how to handle correspondents and how to provide them with facilities. The best thing that can be done would be for you to scream to London to send out such a man at once before this situation gets any worse."

Admiral Layton laughed: "Tomorrow," he said, "you and Mr. Young go in to see Commander Burrows and tell him what you want and I am sure that he will provide you with the means to do everything you want to do."

That cheered me up because I believed then that Admiral Layton would inform Burrows that facilities must be provided for correspondents when they asked for them, especially for war correspondents accredited by the British War Office and Air Ministry.

I mentioned that to Young and he was rather dubious.

"You've got to remember, Cecil," he said, "that we were in there

196

criticizing an organization which is under Layton and criticizing a man—Burrows—appointed by Layton. Admirals don't like to have anyone tell them they are wrong about anything."

Friday, September 19th:
This morning Young and I went to see Commander Burrows. I opened, saying: "I have here a number of requests for facilities."

"I thought you said you were not coming to me for facilities."

"I said no such thing."

"I want you to apologize for your statements yesterday."

"Certainly not. I won't apologize for those statements or anything I have said."

And so it went for about five minutes, like two children arguing over a sand bucket. At length I said: "I have come to you for facilities. What I want to know is: will you or will you not take my requests for these facilities?"

"I will take them," he said, with the air of a man who intended to throw the memo into the wastebasket.

The first request was to go to Sarawak in British Borneo for the celebration of the one-hundredth anniversary of the reign of the Brook family. Four of the correspondents, I knew, were going.

"I have nothing whatever to do with that," Burrows said. "That is purely a Ministry of Information affair and I have no connection with it. The man you have to see is Pepys at the Fullerton Building."

The other requests I made were a visit to the WRENS; an interview with Major General H. Gordon Bennett, Commander of the Australian forces in Malaya; a trip on a submarine; a trip on a Catalina flying boat; to spend an evening with the R.A.F. at one of their stations; an interview with Admiral Layton and Admiral Spooner for discussion of naval problems; a trip of not more than thirty-six hours on a naval patrol boat; and a visit to the Fleet Air Arm.

Young and I asked Pepys for space to Sarawak, and I was given the only available place on the warship taking the correspondents over to Borneo. An hour later Pepys telephoned me and said there was no room on the ship. This could only mean that Burrows arbitrarily told Pepys there was no space for me or found someone else, after I left Burrows, to fill the one vacancy.

From that moment I knew that Burrows was determined to resist

197

giving me any facilities whatever. His fetish for red tape, his arrogance and his unwillingness to be disturbed certainly foreshadowed coming events for the British in Singapore.

Friday, September 19th:
I am thoroughly fed up with staying on here. I am tired of pleading with officials for the most meager co-operation, and John Young also is ready to pull out. Moreover, I would like to see other parts of the Far East, so that I can get a better picture of what is going on elsewhere.

This afternoon I cabled White:

DURING PRESENT LULL WHAT'S POSSIBILITY GOING TO DUTCH INDIES FOR FEW WEEKS—ALTERNATIVELY BANGKOK AND CHUNG-KING.

Saturday, September 20th:
I went to the boat and saw John Young off for Batavia. He's fed up to the teeth and urged me to take a plane out and meet him down there. I said I would try to do that.

A young Japanese clerk at the Japanese Club was found guilty to-day of possessing seditious documents and reproducing seditious literature. He was sentenced to a year at hard labor. The authorities found fifty anti-British pamphlets in his home. The clerk said they were given to him at the New World Cabaret.

Representatives of the *Singapore Herald* are now denied admittance to press conferences and military demonstrations. This is the one improvement I have found thus far coming out of our meeting with Admiral Layton, at the Naval Base.

The Japanese here distribute an information service called "Eastern News." It is related to the *Domei* propaganda agency but the only paper here using it is, of course, the *Singapore Herald*.

Work among the Europeans, that means the British, stops at 5 P.M. and from then until 8:30 it is *pahit* time. The bar at Raffles is crowded with people drinking gimlets and stengahs during the *pahit* time, and everyone's busy being conversational, agreeable and superior. The bar at Raffles resounds with the cries of "Boy" and submissive Malays come trotting over to give the kind of service the Colonial Englishman demands.

198

Raffles Hotel, like the Seaview Hotel, is "out of bounds" to soldiers, and only officers are permitted. The Australians are very bitter about this because some of the Australian volunteers are wealthy in their own right.

Tonight an Australian—just an ordinary soldier—was refused admittance to Raffles. The irony of it is that he happens to be a wealthy sheep owner who has enough money to buy out Raffles Hotel, lock, stock and barrel.

One of the main concerns of the British here is to shoulder the white man's burden. Officers are not permitted by custom to ride in buses or rickshaws. The result is they use taxis or own cars. That is an unnecessary waste of gas and also a considerable expense for officers who don't have very much money.

Today an officer told me: "I think we should face a few facts just now. As far as I know there is nothing in Service rules forbidding me from riding in the buses or rickshaws, but I know that all officers holding King's commissions would rather walk than go in one because, for Heaven knows how long, it has been something just not done and if you did do it, it might cause some nasty remarks in the mess."

There is great consternation here because a Chinese sportsman submitted an application to join a European club. The *Malaya Tribune*, owned by the Wong family, printed a bitter editorial about the matter.

"The smug self-sufficiency and curiously total absence of any sense of responsibility toward the people of the country whom they briefly tolerate during the laborious process of making their pile," was the way the *Tribune* dared to criticize the ruling lights of Singapore officialdom and society.

Singapore is a place of "Chinks, drinks and stinks." Seventy-five percent of the people are Chinese, twelve percent Malay, eight percent Indian and one and one-half percent whites. The Chinese make the wheels go, but the one and one-half percent white makes Singapore what it is.

One of the most amazing sights is around Lavendar Street. There are a few cheap rickety hotels with a bar on the first floor. Clustered around outside are soldiers, prostitutes and a mess of rickshaws. On Saturday nights the military police have four trucks standing by to haul away soldiers who get into trouble.

Cyranos has the best food in Singapore—the best stock of wines north, east, south, and west of the Equator. They bought out the stock of the *Ile de France* which is at the Naval Base.

Cyranos has been "out of bounds" since last June because many officers dropped vital information into the ears of attractive women who hung around there. Women still go there, and it is the place where one can meet the few available women who are still searching new diversions or new victims. Some officers still go there but without their uniforms.

All the prostitutes are Chinese or Malay. The Japanese hotels here were notorious brothels, but the Japanese prostitutes were sent home by the Japanese Government to save face and, I presume, to annoy the British. The hotels now rent rooms to girls; several of them on Rangoon Road and Surrangoom Road across from the New World Cabaret are the most popular.

The British do not oppose sin here; they just want to keep it under cover. They do not want to be disturbed. The status quo is too pleasant, and they mean to keep it that way.

The main worry of the authorities appears to be from Chinese Communists. Almost every day another Chinese is arrested and thrown into jail for so-called "subversive" activity.

The British, too, seem more concerned about the Indians than they are about the Japanese.

The other day the Federal secretary ordered the weekly newspaper, *Indian Kuala Lumpur*, submitted in the future to the press censor before printing or publication. The order also was issued against the *Indian Pioneer* because both reprinted an article called "India and the Empire" which originally appeared in the *New Statesman and Nation* published in London. In other words, a special censorship over and above London's censorship for the *Indian* in Malaya. Rather than submit to such an arbitrary order, the publishers decided to cease publication. Two days later the Federal Secretary withdrew the order.

European women here live in the greatest ease. Most of them have four or five servants and have practically no work to do themselves. They spend most of their time, not with their children—an *amah* takes care of them—but gossiping, playing bridge, ruining someone else's

200

reputation, or eyeing other men. Almost everyone I talked to in Singapore volunteered the statement: "The thing here is to be unfaithful."

Everyone here tells you (always referring to the other person, of course) that Noel Coward gave the perfect description of the English people here. He said, they tell you, "Singapore is a first-rate place for second-rate people."

Every day the papers carry ads such as this:

"Middle-aged traveling European offers own free quarters in small modern Singapore flat to broad-minded personable Eurasian lady in her thirties against her providing a home for the gentleman during his frequent calls at Singapore. Housekeeping money and $60. a month."

"Wanted: young, educated, fair Chinese or Eurasian girl by a respectable middle-aged Straits-born gentleman with good position— view friendship, pictures and dances. Letters treated confidentially. Folders returnable. Box . . ."

"Three young Eurasians with cars seek acquaintance of girls for dancing, entertainment."

Monday, September 22nd:
Since I have not been scheduled to broadcast I cabled CBS a story today on the meeting with Sir Geoffrey Layton at the Naval Base, pointing out the complaints of correspondents and reviewing the charges of incompetence against Commander Burrows. In the course of the 160-word cable I also wrote:

"I find the tactics here similar to those employed in Rome and Berlin to make the presence of inquisitive American correspondents as uncomfortable as possible; to delay and mess up any arrangements inevitably resulting in their disgusted leave-taking."

I cited the departure of Leland Stowe of the *Chicago Daily News*, Frank Gervasi of *Collier's* and John Young of NBC.

This afternoon I asked Duckworth if the cable had gone out.

"Not yet, it is being studied."

Major Fisher was there and had evidently seen the cable.

"You know, Brown," Fisher said with rage, "you are subject to military discipline. You have made some serious charges against officers."

"In what respect?"

"You accused a man of being drunk."

"That is the sort of approach," I said, "they try in dictatorships to intimidate a correspondent."

I thereupon discovered that my cable had been held up for twenty-four hours with nothing being done about it, and only when I inquired was it put into the "censorship hopper."

Wednesday, September 24th:
Just four years ago today I sailed on the *American Farmer* from New York for London.

This morning Duckworth told me the cable on the meeting with Layton had been sent off finally. "It went to the admiral and to Duff Cooper. Not a word in it was changed," Duckworth said.

I thereupon sat down and wrote another story:

"For the last ten days the SPRO has not provided an ounce of co-operation to enable me to see examples of Malay's war effort despite repeated requests on behalf of CBS. The American correspondents remaining in Singapore are determined to continue their efforts to present the facts to the American public despite the sustained opposition of British officials."

Thursday, September 25th:
A cable from Paul White turned down my request to get out of Singapore. He says that Rangoon and Chungking are presently being covered by Dunn (William J. Dunn, who has been in Manila) but Paul adds:

ALTHOUGH WHOLLY INDEFINITE MAY ASSIGN YOU TO MANILA EARLY DECEMBER. PLEASE ARRANGE FOR SUCCESSOR IN SINGAPORE SHOULD THIS MATERIALIZE.

Friday, September 26:
Just to be on the safe side I called on Kenneth Patton, the American Consul General, to explain the current difficulties with the SPRO and Commander Burrows. Patton was titanically disinterested.

Went to see the Japanese Consul to find out if Japs were pulling out in any unusual numbers. He said that six hundred are leaving on the evacuation ship next week because of the freezing order. His wife, who left yesterday, was given a thorough searching for hidden money and jewels.

There are twenty American ships in here now and only enough rubber and tin for fourteen. This came about because American ships discharging their cargo at Suez and the Red Sea were sent here in expectation that there would be sufficient tin and rubber on hand for loading. There wasn't.

The papers here report that the Japs are massing a million troops in Manchuria and Korea for an invasion of Siberia.

Saturday, September 27th:
I am scheduled to broadcast at 7:20 tomorrow morning, but I had to have my script in by noon today because Burrows is going out of town and therefore there would be no way of having it censored by military authorities. I took my script to Duckworth, the civil censor, at 11:30. He read it and said: "I will have to submit this to higher authority. There is too much in here that is untrue and undesirable."

At 1:35 this afternoon Duckworth telephoned: "Your broadcast has been canceled."

"Who has canceled it?"

"My orders are that the broadcast is canceled."

That ended that conversation.

A few minutes later I called him back and asked: "Does this mean that I can submit another script?"

"Well, the broadcast is canceled."

"Yes, but what about the facilities? The radio company provided them. What I must tell New York now is whether the script is canceled or the transmission is canceled or both."

"I can tell you in confidence that the Governor canceled the broadcast. It is too late to submit another script."

"I don't go on for another eighteen hours. There is plenty of time to write another script."

"Burrows has gone away—that's why your script had to be in by noon. Any other script you write would have military matter in it and there is no one here to check on it."

I attempted to get in touch with Duff Cooper, but was unsuccessful because the war, insofar as it is practiced here, stops on Saturday noon, and resumes on Monday morning—and not too early on Monday.

I am going to fight this whole matter through as long as CBS keeps me here.

This is the broadcast which the Governor, Sir Shenton Thomas, killed in its entirety:

"This is Singapore.

"Many people in Singapore are now confident that Japan is preparing to stab Russia's Siberian back and forget about a push southward from Indo-China. So Singapore society goes dancing almost every night, making money out of huge shipments of rubber and tin, and counting on the United States navy to keep them from harm.

"People in Singapore are depending so much on someone else—either Russia or the United States or both—to keep the bombs away from their heads that even Sir Robert Brooke-Popham felt compelled to jar them. The Commander-in-Chief, Far East, said: 'This is no time to sleep.'

"A wave of tremendous relief went over Singapore at word that the two-hundred-fifty-million-dollar naval base will be made available to the American navy if refitting facilities are requested. To the wishful thinkers here, that sounded as though the American sailors might soon be here.

"Dozens of Britishers have said to me: 'If only American ships come here, most of our troubles would end.' By the way, if the United States fleet does come into Singapore, it would mean that Singapore at last would end its role of a naval base without a navy.

"Britain's current trouble shooter in the Far East is the Honorable Alfred Duff Cooper. And he's holding a series of conferences with the British Ambassadors to Bangkok and Chungking and also meeting with Dutch and Australian officials.

"These are expected to pave the way for better collaboration between the British, Australians, Dutch and Chinese. And, of course, finding out the requirements for greater American assistance to help Britain out of her Far Eastern difficulties.

"One of the problems Duff Cooper may deal with is to induce the authorities to allow the story of Singapore's war effort to be presented to the American public.

"Last week twenty foreign and local correspondents protested to

204

Sir Geoffrey Layton, Commander-in-Chief, China, at the absence of co-operation of the military organization which controls correspondents.

"I've found the tactics of the military here similar to those encountered in Rome where the Fascist Government makes things so uncomfortable for inquisitive American reporters that they are compelled to get out of the country. A few days ago I was threatened with military punishment for sending a telegram reporting the protests of the correspondents.

"This intimidation of correspondents appears to be part of an effort to drive out American correspondents. As a matter of fact, I am the only visiting American reporter remaining here at present.

"There's other two-way traffic of people here. More Indian troops arrived to get ready for jungle fighting, and more Japanese are returning to their native country. The evacuation ship *Fuso Maru* is expected to sail Sunday or Monday taking back six hundred Japanese.

"An American who just came down from Bangkok told me that the anti-Japanese attitude of the Thais is increasing. He said, unofficially, the Thais want material aid from the British and Americans, but, officially, are still afraid to compromise their neutrality in Japanese eyes.

"The chances of a Japanese invasion or occupation of Thailand, he said, are diminishing."

Monday, September 29th:
I am still too busy fighting the censors and officials to worry about news.

At 9:30 I went to see Duff Cooper at his place in the country and showed him the stories I had cabled CBS on the meeting at the Naval Base and also the broadcast which was canceled.

"That cabled story was sent to me and I sent it right back and told them to let it go. I was for fourteen months, you know, dealing with press and censorship in London. All we watched for was the giving of information valuable to the enemy. We never objected to criticism of the Government," Duff Cooper said.

"Well then, sir, perhaps you can explain why this broadcast was not permitted to go?"

And I showed him a copy of the broadcast which had been killed.

I pointed out that no opportunity was given me to adjust the script or make any changes, but that the broadcast was peremptorily canceled.

Duff Cooper read the script and said: "I would not have stopped the broadcast and it should have been allowed to go. Did Burrows stop this?"

"No, someone in much higher authority. Don't you think it's significant that every correspondent who goes away from here does so with bitterness and antagonism, and what is even worse, antagonism for Britain? I think it is significant that twenty reporters should protest about Burrows' operations."

Duff Cooper nodded and said: "I know the situation is not very satisfactory."

"Actually," I said, "I'm trying to determine now if I am no longer welcome here and if so whether I am to be formally expelled or just prevented from doing my work."

"I will tell you in confidence, Brown," Duff Cooper said, "that I had Brooke-Popham and Layton out here yesterday morning for breakfast. I told them that Burrows was certainly not the man for the job and that he should be removed. Layton said that Burrows was just getting into the work and building up an organization."

Duff Cooper snorted: "Burrows may have been all right as a magistrate in the Fiji Islands but he knows nothing whatever about this job, and I told that to Popham and Layton. I can also tell you in confidence that I told them this whole set-up should be under Scott at the Ministry of Information and that he should have service men to whom he can give orders to arrange for these things. Burrows doesn't understand his job. He thinks his work is to censor and to prevent correspondents from getting information. We have plenty of people to censor material. Burrows should do nothing to irritate correspondents and do everything to keep them informed. I told that to Layton, but he wants to keep him. I've told the Service Chiefs here how we must do everything to co-operate with the Americans."

Tuesday, September 30th:
I arrived at Government House this morning for the appointment with Governor Sir Shenton Thomas I had made the day before. As I walked into the Governor's office, Sir Shenton stood up and we shook hands. I said: "I came to inquire about my broadcast."

"I know who you are," he snapped, "and if you had been an Asiatic you'd be locked up for that broadcast."

"Well, I'm not an Asiatic. I happen to be an American reporter."
206

"Yes, I know, and I have sent that broadcast to the American Consul."

"That's no concern of mine. I have come to inquire the basis for stopping that broadcast so that CBS can present the case to Mr. Sumner Welles, Assistant Secretary of State in Washington, who takes some precedence over Mr. Patton."

"That's all right," the Governor said.

"Can you tell me why that broadcast was stopped?"

"Why, because it was untrue and libelous, and you are not going to use our broadcasting facilities to abuse us."

"What is libelous or inaccurate about it?"

"I don't have to tell you that. I am Governor of this Colony and I tell you, you are not going to put out that sort of thing from here."

"That broadcast was read by a man who knows a great deal about news, propaganda and the American people and he said it was all right."

"Name—name?"

"Mr. Duff Cooper."

"I will check with him whether he said that. I can tell you that sort of thing will not go out of here."

"I was in Rome for three years and we American correspondents there were enemies of the Fascists. They knew it and we knew it. Yet the Italians would never have dared to cancel a broadcast without my facing the man who canceled it or without my being given an opportunity to discuss it and perhaps change it."

The Governor got out of his chair and started walking toward the door—I with him. He opened the door, obviously dismissing me, and I said: "There is just one thing, Sir Shenton. I should like to know from you whether this cancelation of the broadcast is part of a pattern to tell me I am no longer a welcome visitor here?"

"You can't abuse us from here. That's all. Good morning. I can tell you, you had better behave yourself if you want to stay here."

"Am I to understand that this action in canceling a broadcast is the final step in wishing me to leave the country?"

"I don't know anything about what happened before. I canceled that broadcast and it stays canceled."

"Do you want to know—are you interested in finding out—what is going on here? Do you want to know why I write a broadcast like that?

207

Do you want to know why American reporters leave here with bitterness and antagonism? Do you want to know how the efforts of CBS and American reporters to report the Malaya war effort are being sabotaged?"

"I don't know anything that happened before."

He closed the door and invited me over again to sit down at his desk and we both calmed down. He offered me a cigarette, which I accepted, and he said: "Now, what is all this?"

I detailed the meeting that was held with Brooke-Popham and Layton at the Naval Base and then the meeting two days later with Admiral Layton, what was said, how Commander Burrows acted when Young and I presented our requests for facilities, and that nothing had been done on these requests.

Sir Shenton Thomas, amazingly enough, knew nothing about the meetings at the Naval Base or the difficulties of correspondents, and when I cited Martha Gellhorn's *Collier's* article and the piece in *Life,* both of which articles had been resented by the British authorities, the Governor said he had not seen them.

"Whether I have co-operated with the British you can determine from examining my previous broadcasts and cabled stories," I told him.

"We want to co-operate and help the American correspondents in every way."

"I am sorry, Sir Shenton, but to me those are just words. I have heard them before. The actions of the authorities up to now and your own actions in canceling this broadcast in such a high-handed manner show the opposite attitude."

I then mentioned the difficulties I had with the Italian authorities.

"You seem to fight with everyone." He laughed.

"I am surprised you make a remark like that. I fought with the Italians because I was attempting to report the true situation from Italy and they didn't want it reported. And I might point out to you, Sir Shenton, that one of the counts against me when I was expelled was the frequency with which BBC quoted my broadcasts from Rome. BBC is the official British propaganda medium. I can tell you, sir, that every broadcast in the future is going to report facts about Singapore as I find them and see them."

"What kind of facts are you going to report?"

"As the facts arise and I see them I will report them. I will try

208

to report them and if I can't do it from Singapore I will do it from somewhere else."

"You say you want to help the war effort. That kind of thing you wrote in that broadcast won't help any."

"I disagree with that. Singapore is the keystone of the American position in the Far East. If Americans are going to be involved out here, insofar as I am able, I am going to keep them informed of what they are getting into. The death of no American soldier is going to be on my conscience because of a failure to do the best kind of job I can."

"I want to assure you," the Governor insisted, "that the cancelation of the broadcast had no connection with any other event. You should have come to me with a request for an adjustment in the script."

"Mr. Duckworth said the opposite. He gave me the cancelation order with such finality there was no room even to suspect that an adjustment could be made."

"I want you to know that we will give you facilities and I will inquire why the facilities you have requested were not granted."

"I will appreciate that very much."

The Governor was unaware that I had given any broadcasts in Singapore. He thought that the script he killed was the first broadcast I had attempted to give.

Throughout our conversation the Governor kept saying at intervals: "That's the situation." It puzzled me because there was no connection between that phrase and our remarks and I got the impression that Sir Shenton thought he was talking to a native who didn't even understand the language.

As I got up to leave we shook hands and he said: "I hope I have made things clear."

"Well, you have presented several points to me." Those points, as I turned them over in my mind, were:

You can't criticize the Government from here.

My manuscripts in the future are to be submitted to him.

"Abuse of facilities" means saying anything they don't like.

The standards of censorship in Singapore are totally unrelated to those operating in London.

I had the strangest feeling as I stepped out of the Governor's office. I walked in a daze, almost as though I were floating in space, and as I walked through the outer office into the corridor there was a calendar on the wall and I went over to it and touched it and examined the date. It said Tuesday, September 30, 1941. I couldn't believe it. I felt that I had just stepped out of 1931, but my diary records this impression:

I am convinced that Thomas is an uninformed individual, with an urbane manner, a pleasant rather distinguished face, gray-haired, well-groomed, a slave to Civil Service clichés, bromides and banalities. He lives in a dream world where reality seldom enters and where the main effort is to restrict the entrance of anything disturbing. He shows the manner and approach of a man who has been telling African bushmen and Malayan natives how to conduct their lives.

MOSTLY ABOUT GENERALS

Thursday, October 2nd:

My request for an interview with Major-General Henry Gordon Bennett finally came through today and I was taken to Johore, where Bennett has his headquarters. He is general officer commanding the Australian forces in Malaya. Captain Gordon Walker, his aide, ushered me in.

The interview took place in Bennett's office on the second floor of the Administration Building in the Australian camp. The general, red-haired and pink-faced, wore shorts and a shirt open at the neck.

My first question was: "General, when was my request forwarded to you?"

"I received it yesterday."

"You might be interested to know that I made the request to interview you twelve days ago."

"You should call me direct. I would see you any time. Don't bother with that SPRO."

"We are supposed to act through them and I wanted to see how long it would take them to act on it."

"The request was just forwarded to me yesterday," Bennett repeated, "and I said you could come along at once."

One of the reasons for Bennett's anger was that the British authorities here have consistently sabotaged the efforts of the Australian correspondents, and the British are trying to prevent a "build-up in the world press of the Australians."

I thought Bennett would drop the subject then and there but he went on with seething bitterness about the "English mentality." He spoke of the many "arguments and discussions" he has had with the higher command, that is, with Lieutenant-General Percival.

"I am running this Australian show the way I think it should be run," Bennett said, "not the way they want to run it. If Japan pushes southward we need United States air and naval power, especially naval assistance, almost immediately. We don't need American troops. The

British, Indian and Australian troops here are sufficient to protect the naval and air base."

General Bennett offered the opinion that no Japanese landing would be possible in Malaya unless the Japs had naval and air superiority.

"The attacker cannot achieve that if we get American help," Bennett said.

"How are you going to stop them?" I asked.

Bennett got up from his desk and went over to a wall map on which there were a number of small flags.

"We are charged with the defense of this entire area," he said. "Where you see a flag we have a concentration of troops."

Bennett went on to explain how he would move his troops from one position to another if the enemy effected a bridge-head on the east coast of Malaya.

"Do you think you can hold those positions?"

"We are going to hold them. The English have a whole plan worked out with a series of points to retreat to. I won't have anything to do with that plan. I won't train my men in retreating tactics. I won't let my men talk retreat. All *we* are going to do is attack."

I remarked to Bennett that I had often heard remarks that the Australians were not very well disciplined and not very military, that they saluted in a slovenly manner and didn't concern themselves very much with their appearance.

"I don't worry a terrific amount about that detail of soldierly bearing. Shyness may be the cause of lack of proper saluting rather than insolence. What counts is the way a man fights, and we Australians are damn good fighters. We try to develop initiative and individualism. Too severe discipline crushes that out of a man. Individual initiative is essential in this kind of country. In jungle work, where it is impossible to control individual operations from a great distance, we must rely on very junior officers to control the men. I have been pleased by the standard of discipline and behavior of the men here.

"One thing astounding to me," the general said, "is the friendly way the Australians are received by all the Asiatic people here. In the last war we didn't find even as friendly an atmosphere in Belgium and France. The Australians admire the Chinese because they are good hard workers, but mainly because the Chinese have a sense of humor and everyone with a sense of humor captivates the Australians."

Bennett, fifty-two years old, was an accountant in civil life and in the last war was decorated twice for bravery. He fought at Gallipoli and in France. Almost everything he does and the way he says everything indicates that he takes a great delight in trampling down bureaucracy and red tape.

He is extremely popular with his troops, and they call him "Ginger." I know that he is having considerable difficulty with Lieutenant-General Percival.

Friday, October 3rd:
The *Malaya Tribune* is still agitating for an awakening here. It is understandable because the *Tribune* is the spokesman for the Asiatics who have battled for years for an improvement in government and who stand to lose the most if this country is invaded by the Japanese.

"Everything that is connected with the Government and Europeans in this country is invested with unnecessary pomp," the editorial says. "The European clerk is called a secretary even though all the work she does is lick stamps and paste them on envelopes. In the Malaya Broadcasting Corporation, European clerks are called administrative assistants. Asiatics in all offices are called plain clerks and get a salary commensurate with that.

"The symbol for those who manage the affairs of this country should be an overfed and overpetted dog, curled up cozily in a deep sofa, who lets out a sleepy growl whenever someone pulls its tail, but never troubles to open its eyes to see if its tail-puller is its master's son or a burglar."

I think that's a pretty apt picture of the Government here.

At 11:30 Major Fisher called to say that General Percival wished to see me just as soon as possible. I went out to Fort Canning and his ADC, Major Shoreland, a jet-haired, affable, cheerful person, took me at once into the GOC, Malaya.

We shook hands, and I then saw that General Percival had on the desk before him the Bennett story I handed in yesterday to the cable office.

"I cannot allow this story to go," he said.

"Why not?"

"General Bennett has no authority to comment on the conduct of the war. That is a matter which concerns London. Moreover, you had no right to talk to General Bennett."

"The interview, General, was arranged in the regularly established way for such things."

"You have no right to see General Bennett."

And then he turned to Major Shoreland.

"How was this interview arranged without my knowledge?"

"The Commander-in-Chief, China, asked Commander Burrows' office to arrange it."

Percival's repetitive point was that Bennett was not authorized to comment on the war's conduct and I could not use the interview. We discussed this point for some time, and I said that whether Bennett received me was a matter between General Percival and General Bennett.

"As a correspondent," I said, "I retain the right to see general or colonel, majors or sergeants, or anyone that I think has a story to tell and to record their views. And you, General Percival, retain the right to use a blue pencil on that story. I have my job to do and you have the censorship authority to erect all the barriers you want."

"Of course, I agree with practically everything General Bennett has said in your story," Percival said. "Of course we want the American fleet out here, and you know we do, so why don't you say it?"

I carefully explained to General Percival that I was a reporter, reporting news and views, and not what I think about the situation.

"I merely report what you people say and do," I said. "You make the news and I report it."

"That isn't the way English correspondents do it," General Percival said. "They go out and get the material so that their editors can write leaders [editorials]."

I almost fell out of my chair at that remark. I tried to give the general an ABC course in news-reporting methods but he didn't or wouldn't understand.

Seeing that I wasn't making the slightest impression, I finally remarked: "With all due respect to you, General, you and your people here have no conception of how the American press and radio work. You are paying a heavy price for that, just as you paid a heavy price for it in London and Cairo."

I explained to him all the difficulties of the correspondents here, the
214

inefficiency in the office of Commander Burrows and unintelligent set-up for the reporting of this war.

General Percival listened patiently, and, when I was finished, remarked: "I am very interested to get your views and I will discuss them with others."

"I intend, General Percival, to go after exclusive stories, stories based on my own initiative, which no other correspondents get. For example, this interview with General Bennett or a flight in a Catalina."

"It will do you no good to get a story from General Bennett on the conduct of the war. I am the only one authorized to talk about that here."

"Very well then, you agree with General Bennett's views in the conduct of the war. Here and now, why don't you give me your views for a story?"

"No, I cannot do that."

"General Percival, I want to tell you that I am going out to get every possible story I can. I am going to write those stories. You cannot prevent me from putting those stories through my typewriter. You can only kill them afterwards."

"I don't see why you have to have stories all the time. I give a general press conference once a month and Admiral Layton gives a conference once a month. That ought to be sufficient."

I tried to explain that American correspondents were here to keep Singapore before the American people, to explain the importance of Singapore from a strategic point of view and because of the rubber and tin in Malaya.

I got the impression that my remarks had no effect.

"The story on General Bennett is dead then?"

General Percival smiled and said: "Yes, quite dead."

And it was. That story was never released.

Dr. J. G. Hanna, an American dentist here who knows everyone, took me to the American Association luncheon at the Adelphi Hotel. It is composed of American businessmen here. But all I heard at the luncheon were complaints about the British conduct of import and export permits—how they are granted or not granted on the silliest whims.

The abuses of the Import Control Bureau here are notorious.

A woman received from her sister in the States a small package containing a novelty bracelet and necklace worth $3.00 U.S. She was advised that she could not have it because it was an importation of a luxury item. Thereupon the woman sent a cable: "Send nothing more. Everything confiscated."

The communications authorities took the cable to Kenneth Patton, the American Consul General, and he called the woman in to ask that she do not send it. She refused and the British compromised by allowing her to have the necklace and bracelet.

Another woman received four pairs of silk hose from the United States. The Import Control Bureau called and asked if they were pure silk. She answered that they were.

"Well, you can't have them," she was told. "They will be put up at auction."

She had already paid for them, but she appeared at the auction and bid for and bought two pairs the second time.

"Where are the other two?"

Some customs employee apparently had taken the other two pairs.

American firms here have the greatest difficulty getting products imported. Their applications for imports—and every purchase from abroad must be approved—have been turned down consistently.

Some businessmen say that the British fear that some people here might get accustomed to using American products and the United States would, therefore, capture this market after the war.

For a month, no applications for imports were even considered because the man who handled them was on leave in Australia. His substitute had been sick since he left and there were only native clerks remaining in the office.

An American woman here received from the United States, for her daughter's Christmas, a box of toys containing several dolls and mechanical trucks and autos. She was called by Import Control and told that such items could not come into the country and she could not have the box.

Could she send it back to the United States?

No, she couldn't do that.

Thereupon she got a sticker and readdressed the box to a war charity organization.

When Americans complain to Patton about arbitrary treatment, his favorite remark is, "Now, now, we have to co-operate."

Americans can count on their Consul General, Patton, to safeguard all British interests!

Tonight I saw the picture, *Meet John Doe.* I go to as many movies as I can. I have been away so long I am afraid of forgetting how Americans talk and what makes them laugh and cry.

Sir Robert Brooke-Popham made a statement that "the British Navy could hold off a blockade without American naval assistance, and Malaya could stand any blockade for six months or longer if necessary."

It probably was what the English people here want to hear, but it was the strangest of the strange statements I've encountered. Brooke-Popham may believe that, but I don't think the Japs do.

A Singapore official spoke over the Malayan radio today to try and wake up the people. He said he heard a housewife asking for California lettuce and then watched her show considerable annoyance because it was unattainable.

"It is guns, not lettuce, we want from America," the local official said.

Six hundred Japanese residents, some of whom have lived here for thirty years, sailed today on the official evacuation ship, *Fuso Maru.* They were undergoing a very searching examination by European customs officers to prevent smuggling. The Japanese men were stripped to the underwear in barefeet. Likewise the women were examined by women officials. One Japanese had a basket made by a Chinese worker. This Chinese informed the authorities that he'd been given specific orders to weave the basket around a heavy bamboo frame. The authorities ripped the basket and found ten thousand yen and two small bars of platinum concealed in the bamboo.

I tried to send the Bennett story today without giving Bennett's name, identifying him only as a high military authority. The ruse didn't work. That story was killed too.

Sunday, October 5th:

Visited at the home of Attorney General and Mrs. Howell out near the Tanglin Club. He is an Australian who is in the British Civil Service. They have been in England during the bombing and they are bitter about the "Colonial government and these apathetic people out here in Singapore."

Mrs. Howell gave me an instance which I thought was typical of the unreality here. Her son is a night-fighter pilot in England and she mentioned her concern about him to another woman, and this woman said: "I know just exactly how you feel, my two children are in Australia."

Her two children are eight and ten years old.

The Australians built a rest hut in Singapore for Aussies on leave— a combination canteen and recreation center. General Bennett, naturally, was asked for the opening, since he commands the Australian troops. General Percival heard about it and insisted that he be asked. Air Vice-Marshal Pulford was requested to ask Percival if he would care to attend, since the Australian committee had no wish to offend the GOC in Malaya. If he wanted to attend he would be welcome. This was the day before the function.

Percival told Pulford: "Of course I want to go, but I must have a written invitation."

Pulford explained that no written invitations had been issued, that it was a completely informal affair, a gathering of Australians.

"I wish to go," Percival said, "and I must have a written invitation." He got it, the only written invitation sent out to the two or three hundred who were there.

Tuesday, October 7th:

My contacts with the Free French finally bore fruit today. Dr. May and M. Baron, head of the Free French movement here, gave me a good story. They showed me secret documents they'd just gotten hold of revealing the extent of Vichy's collaboration with the Japanese. They exposed Japan's methods of absorbing complete military, economic and financial control of Indo-China.

These documents show there are eight secret provisions in the protocol of the treaty signed at Tokyo on May 6th by the former Governor

218

of Indo-China, René Robin, who is a protégé of Pierre Laval. Under the provisions the Japanese will be permitted in Indo-China to practice the following professions: consignees for ships, hotel men, operate factories making radio apparatus, operate printing presses, and practice as doctors and midwives.

The personnel of the Japanese concerns existing or to be established will be fifty percent Japanese and fifty percent French or Annamite, but if a concern is unable to recruit fifty percent of the French or Annamites, the concern will be allowed to have a greater number of Japanese. The obvious purpose of this is for the Japanese to gain control of the business life of Indo-China.

Another provision says that the French Government will grant the Japanese, providing the King of Annam agrees, permission to buy land and buildings in order to facilitate collaboration in the economic field.

New agricultural, mining, water works and electrical concessions will be given to the Japanese to launch these new concerns. In principle, the capital will be half Japanese. However, in case French fill-the-gap capital cannot be raised, the Japanese will be allowed to fill the gap.

A secret protocol also provides that schools are to be opened in Indo-China under Japanese control. They will teach Japanese, but will also be open to others and French is to be taught as a "complementary" language.

At the moment the Japanese are exerting all kinds of pressure on Vichy to surrender additional oil-storage facilities and to permit Japanese control of the entire postal system, telegraph and communications. I also saw copies of letters showing how the Japanese firms offer goods at a price, then increase the prices continually anywhere from thirty percent to four hundred percent. The French firms have no alternative. They must pay the Japs if they want the goods. A French firm in Hanoi canceled its orders and refused to pay the price that had been increased with each letter explaining why the Japanese firm was unable to ship the goods. The Jap firm in Kobe finally wrote:

"We are very sorry that we cannot satisfy you under our contract, but you may be reassured that the price difference will not be for us. It goes to the General Control Bureau in Tokyo, which will use it for the expenses of Japanese propaganda in all parts of the world and to pay the traveling expenses of their officials."

The "honor" with which the Japanese carry on their business dealings is shown in their treatment of the French in Indo-China. I saw a document showing that under two treaties the entire coal production of Indo-China was reserved for Japan as well as the entire output of iron, tin, manganese, chromium and antimony. Under the present situation these minerals are shipped to Japan in Japanese ships. Governor-General Decoux ordered all French ships in Indo-China to unload their cargoes so that Japanese ships could carry the exports.

Under the treaty, payment by Japan was to be made in gold dollars or in goods. After the agreement was made the Japanese informed the Vichy authorities in Indo-China that their gold was frozen and that they would pay with goods and raw materials.

On September 18th, Decoux was asked by a reporter of *Tokyo Nichi-Nichi* if he was satisfied with the Franco-Japanese agreement.

"Until now," Decoux said, "Indo-China has completely fulfilled all that was asked of her. She has sent everything that Japan has requested and that we promised to send, but the Japanese have not sent us the goods that they promised. We have difficulties getting things we need from the Japanese, and we reserved our opinion on answering that question until the promised goods arrives."

I consider this story especially significant because it shows what double-dealers the Vichy authorities are, how worthless the protestations of good faith from Vichy to England and America are, and what double-crossers the Japanese are.

Thursday, October 9th:

One hundred Indian and Malayan workers rioted today over working conditions. The newspapers kept it to one paragraph and dropped it the next day.

At a press conference, this afternoon, General Percival appealed to the Asiatic population to volunteer for military service. He said at least a thousand were needed and explained that their response thus far "was very disappointing." He urged a reduction in food wastage and suggested that the hotels cut down their menus to three courses instead of six.

220

The hotels are not taking very kindly to the idea. The management at Raffles said: "We don't think our patrons would like it."

And the luxurious Seaview, six miles outside the city, said: "We don't think it's fair to compare the hotels in England with the hotels here. We don't have any difficulty in getting supplies of food. When it does become difficult, then we will cut down."

The *Malayan Tribune* described General Percival's appeal as "an attempt to shake Malaya out of the stupor it has been in since the beginning of the war." It gave this description of Malaya: "Malaya is in the drowsy, languid interval between sleep and awakening. We in Malaya are metaphorically still in bed."

I think the real pinch of the war will be felt by the people of Singapore at the end of the month when the drinking hours are going to be restricted between 11:30 A.M. and 2:30 P.M. and between 5:30 and midnight. It is going to play hell with the famous Singapore Saturday nights which end on Sunday morning. The reason the authorities give is that it will reduce liquor consumption and thus cut down on shipping space. In all probability what will happen is the people will simply drink faster before midnight. In any event, everyone I have talked to is outraged that anyone should attempt to restrict the drinking hours.

I called on Ken Tsurumi, the Japanese Consul General. He claims that there are four thousand Japs still here. He said they were unable to do business, and because of the freezing order were unable to send remittances back to Japan.

In response to my question about relations between Russia and Japan he said: "The situation is very bad."

Did he see increasing signs of war between Japan and the United States?

"If Japan and the United States went to war," he said in a voice that was almost a shout, "it would be a hundred years' war. Japan is very strong. She could never be conquered." As an afterthought he added: "And America could never be conquered, not in a hundred years too."

Talking with Tsurumi for journalistic purposes is pretty useless. He says things like: "Japan has never been the aggressor," and, "We do not intend using force for anything," and, "Thailand will sell us what she wishes and if she does not wish to sell it to us there is nothing we can do."

Statements like that are so dishonest that I think it is worthless for me to see Tsurumi in the future.

Saturday, October 11th:
Diary comment:

Japanese spokesmen and newspapers in Tokyo are beginning to talk tough again. The Japanese may be waiting to stick a knife in Russia's back, but, as the Tokyo newspapers pointed out, the raw materials Japan needs are obtainable only in the South Pacific. These threats are part of Japan's game to freeze British forces here.

Japan must realize that one day all forces will be used against her. The British out here are only now gaining a faint suspicion of what the people in England already know, that England must play second fiddle. From a military point of view, the United States operating from the Philippines holds the trump card out here. That makes Britain's power as far as it goes useless without American co-operation. The United States is the prime user of tin and rubber. The business life here lives or dies on the United States' absorption of exports or the demands the United States may place on Malaya.

American firms are establishing themselves here as buyers, shippers and producers in greater numbers. All this causes a certain amount of envy, jealousy, bitterness and antagonism on the part of the British. It is much too soon to envisage the possibility, but the United States will want bases in the Far East to protect our stake out here.

A base will be needed to collaborate with the Filipinos to hold off the Japanese on the actual mainland of Asia. That base would have to be Singapore.

The Pacific is much narrower than it used to be. The Japanese occupation of Saigon—which Britain did not prevent, because she could not—puts the vital sources of American supplies of tin and rubber within the bombing range of the Japs.

If Japan threatens a southward expansion, American policy in the Pacific just as in the Atlantic will demand that we take precautions, and that can only be accomplished by established bases here in Malaya, and bases for ships and aircraft carriers.

Sunday, October 12th:

My impression is that the Japs have no way to crawl out.

I saw Johnny Fuiji, the Japanese spy, who works for the Japanese *Herald,* and for the first time he said, very seriously: "I don't see how war can be avoided here."

The *United Press* from Tokyo says that the Germans have prepared a diplomatic counter-attack in the Far East, designed to offset Anglo-American efforts to secure Japanese withdrawal from her pact with the Axis.

"Japan is speeding up her air-raid precautions and increasing food storage, to meet a possible early crisis," says the dispatch from Tokyo.

Looking back over my notes on Egypt, I find my thoughts today are the same as then, with the exception of a reduction in the worry about Martha. Then as now, it is homesickness, lack of energy, extreme fatigue and a desire to be elsewhere, anxious for a good story and the inability to do any writing, and this terrible fear of impending doom with nothing much being done to stave it off. Casualness, thy name is British!

Monday, October 13th:

Johnny Fuiji, the Japanese spy, has worked hard and energetically to get information out of Darrell Berrigan of the *United Press* and my-self. His patience wore out today and he had to come out very boldly to meet a demand that obviously had been imposed on him by his superiors.

I always carry a camera with me in Singapore and take pictures now and then, and Fuiji said: "Couldn't you let me have some of your pictures?"

I brushed that off by saying that most of them didn't turn out very well.

"I would like to have a picture of you in uniform, also one of you with Mosley and Gallagher, the other correspondents who wear uni-forms."

I said: "Yes, that would be nice. Maybe it can be arranged some day."

I'd always thought Japanese spies and *agents provocateurs* had more patience than that.

Tuesday, October 14th:

I saw the picture *Man Hunt*. It is excellent, typical of how the British will lock the door after the horse has been stolen.

There is considerable opposition to the restrictions on drinking hours. Someone told me that Australian race horses have arrived here and horses take up considerable ship space.

"But," my informant said ironically, "it may be grossly unfair to imply that these horses are not really necessary for the war effort."

A number of British evacuees from Japan have arrived and we interviewed them in Raffles Hotel. The general view is that Japan's position economically is becoming very desperate as a result of the freezing, and this situation necessitates a decision.

They also report increasing German control of Japan's actions and foreign policies, and the picture they painted bore a startling similarity to the methods used by the Nazis to gain control of Italy. The Germans are now in an "advisory" capacity in the Tokyo post office and in the home and education ministries.

The Nazi who was in charge of the Gestapo after the occupation of Warsaw has been assigned to Tokyo and is directing operations of the secret police of Japan and occupied China. Japanese Rightists, to further personal ambitions, are assisting German infiltration the same as Roberto Farinacci, former Secretary of the Fascist party, and Dino Alfieri, former Propaganda Minister and later Ambassador to Berlin, assisted the Germans.

These evacuees say that there is an absence of pro-German sympathy on the part of Emperor Hirohito and those surrounding the Imperial Japanese house and that is the same as the preliminary attitude of the House of Savoy and Prince Umberto.

These evacuees say that the Japanese man-in-the-street prefers to see Vladivostok under Russian control rather than German. This is a parallel to the Italian preference to side in with Great Britain rather than Germany.

The evacuees also point out that the Japanese leaders prefer continued war or extended war rather than revolution. This is precisely the same choice that faced Mussolini as a result of internal conditions and rising antagonism of the people toward Germany.

Ran into Flight Lieutenant Sydney Downer of the Air Ministry News Service. He tells me that there is no development on my request for a trip in his Consolidated flying boat. "The truth of the matter," he said, "is that we have no serviceable aircraft."

Wednesday, October 15th:
The Legislative Council has just met and the papers are sharp-shooting at the reports made by the various members on the state of affairs in the colony. Even the Japanese-owned *Singapore Herald* said: "What is needed is not the revelation of state secrets but a disposition of high officials to step off their pedestals of silent self-satisfaction."

The most powerful and best-edited newspaper here, the *Straits Times,* commented on the reports on food control and censorship: "Both departments have shown a measure of understanding that has provided a refreshing contrast to that autocratic attitude which declines to admit the possibility of error and regards criticism as an impertinence."

These quotations from the two papers sum up the general attitude of government here.

"We shall tell you nothing and how dare you criticize anything we do!" That is the Government of Malaya.

The situation in Thailand appears to be boiling up. Ken Tsurumi, the Japanese Consul General in Singapore who came here eleven months ago, has been recalled. American warships are convoying ships all the way across the Pacific virtually to the Indies. American planes are patrolling as far as the Fiji Islands.

The Germans are sixty-two miles from Moscow.

Thursday, October 16th:
Went on a flight in a Catalina today. Downer picked me up and we drove to Seletar, the R.A.F. base and the main airdrome on Singapore Island. Flight Lieutenant S. G. Stillings showed me all over the ship which carried a crew of eight: two pilots, an observer who is also a navigator, a bombardier who does everything but fly, two radio operators and two gunners.

We took off at 10:15. I was in the co-pilot's seat. Just as we got off and into the air Stillings told me to press the plunger in front of me.

"No, sir," I said, "I am not touching anything. I am scared of these things."

"Oh, go ahead, push that thing."

"No, sir, I don't want to nosedive."

"Nothing will happen; go ahead, push it."

So I did.

This plunger simply sent a spray of fresh water up the windshield to wash off the salt water.

Stillings was as happy as a child showing off this one gadget on the Catalina.

We flew over the defenses for the protection of Singapore Island. The boom of defense across the Port of Johore was like a squarecut necklace across the channel, with its square floats joined by lines.

At one point we shot down to fifty feet above the water and flew low over two fishermen in a boat. They didn't seem to be alarmed. They preferred to see if the plane was going to hit them rather than dive into those shark-infested waters. Then we climbed very fast, shooting up to three thousand feet. I left the pilot's seat and went into the blisters—the bulges in each side where the machine gunners have their stations. The heat was intense from the burning sun coming through the glass coverings.

We were up two hours in this training flight. Stillings was all praise for the Catalinas.

"They are made for quiet waters," he said. "You couldn't land in a heavy sea, and if you did, the ship wouldn't last long. But these ships do have range and endurance. Their motors are wonderful and the mechanical system is superb. I wish we had more of them."

Stillings has been here three and a half years. The co-pilot was a New Zealander. He said: "We are all sick and tired of seeing the jungle and never an enemy."

I asked the New Zealander why he joined up. He said: "We want to be left in peace and the only way to do that is to fight."

Friday, October 17th:

I asked for an interview with Sir Geoffrey Layton as soon as the new Japanese Cabinet is named.

226

The Tokyo spokesman warned the Japanese people today to be ready fo any eventuality.

A war cabinet is predicted, enabling Japan to move swiftly the moment an opportunity presents itself, whereby Japan would be able to break what she calls the ABCD blockade. Factors favoring a southward move are:

1. A very severe Siberian winter begins in December.

2. Siberia doesn't possess the economic resources Japan needs.

3. Japan has always favored southward expansion, for which she has built up bases in Hainan and Indo-China.

Sir Robert Brooke-Popham is in Melbourne and today in an interview there he said: "We do not want war with Japan, but if Japan insists upon it, we are ready."

Washington considers the fall of Konoye as a victory for the Axis elements in Japan.

The Japanese news agency reports that the Thai Premier wrote the Rotary Club in Bangkok warning against political discussions at club meetings. The president of the Rotary Club denies this.

Obviously the Japs are building up incidents to justify future actions in Thailand. This is a Japanese imitation of the Nazi technique and it is not a very good imitation at that.

THE JAPS ARE COMING

Saturday, October 18th:

This morning saw Duff Cooper who has just returned from India. He said the trip was very worth while. I asked for a general statement on the situation, and he said: "I think now is hardly the time to make statements."

There is a rumor around that four American ships came in to Penang at night. The entire harbor area was closed by military order and the ships unloaded 300 M3 Chrysler tanks. I doubt this very much. [Late tonight I found out definitely that the rumor about these ships and tanks was false.]

The officials deny there is any lease-lend stuff here, and, as usual, Patton, the American Consul, says nothing. If there are tanks coming in, I don't see why they don't admit it. It would show increasing offensive power, might help to bolster Thailand and might make Japan hesitate until she's better organized.

The *Straits Times* reflected the general opinion of the people in Malaya today very accurately when it printed an editorial which in my opinion was highly inaccurate. It said: "We do not believe that the present (Japanese) political crisis is a forerunner of a deliberate entry into the war with Britain and the United States. We see it as the beginning of another campaign of intimidation that will fall short of war except in the unlikely event of the complete collapse of Russia."

In the third quarter of this year, the British censors here rejected seven films. No shooting is permitted in pictures shown in Malaya. They are cut so that you see a man threatening to shoot the villain and then the villain is suddenly dead by some mysterious process. I presume the British are afraid the natives might "get some ideas" from shooting sequences.

This afternoon, George Weh, head of the Chinese Information Board here, came to see me. He was educated in America and speaks

228

English very well. He is somewhat unhappy about the co-operation he is receiving from the British authorities.

"When I came here," Weh said, "I was treated with the greatest suspicion by a man named Jordan, who has charge of Chinese affairs in the Colonial Secretary's office. Jordan cross-examined me like a common immigrant, although I came here as an official representative of the Chinese Government. He asked me my name, age, father's name, where born and the usual rigmarole. He was very suspicious of my purpose in coming here. I explained that I was a liaison man, that I was to facilitate the work of correspondents and to do what I could to give publicity to the Chinese cause.

"I guess he thought I came to make speeches and stir up the Chinese. Jordan seemed to thaw out a bit when I told him I had studied at Cambridge. When I told him that I was a graduate of Amherst and did post-graduate work at Harvard it seemed to have no effect on him, but the fact that I had gone to Cambridge made me somewhat less of a Chinese in his eyes," Weh said.

"I explained to Jordan that after all China and Britain were allies in that we had a common front against Japan. I said that we were both fighting the Axis powers. To that Jordan said, 'I wish to remind you that Great Britain is not at war with Japan.' I am convinced," Weh sighed, "that the British do not consider China an ally in any way."

This evening I went out to the Singapore Golf Club for a drink with a group of Englishmen. At our table was a Lieutenant Thompson of the British Navy who had just won the club's golf trophy and a Major Russell of the United States Army who had just come in from the U.S. on the Clipper and was very secretive. His idea was that the American public was very apathetic about the war, but they will fight Japan at the drop of a hat, not only on the West Coast but on the East as well. He was very bitter against the Washington columnists. He said he thought they were armchair strategists, pretending to know what's going on. He condemned them for prostituting journalism and was bitter against Allsop and Kintner, "and as for Pearson and Allen, I'd put them up against a wall and shoot them."

"What we need is an information bureau to publicize the war," he said. "The people don't believe what they read in the papers. They all listen to the radio. There will never be national unity under Roosevelt because he doesn't take the people into his confidence—too secretive about everything. I have great confidence in the people and their ability to hear the truth."

"I agree with telling the people the story," I said. But I didn't agree as to who conceals the story. The old time Army and Navy men want to keep what they call trade secrets. And I have encountered enough reactionaries who hate Roosevelt more than they hate Fascists.

Diary Comment:

Everywhere I've gone I have encountered the attitude of armed services: "Now, this is our war. Don't you civilians come mixing in our business."

Some day the military might find out that this is a people's war. After all, it is the people who die, the people who get machine-gunned and bombed.

Monday, October 20th:

Lunched today with Sir George Sansom, head of the Economic Warfare Board, and Graeme Nicholl. Sir George was Chargé d'Affaires of the British Embassy at Tokyo and has been in the Foreign Office in London for many years. We have a mutual friend in Sir Noel Charles, who was British Chargé d'Affaires in Rome and has just gone to South America as Ambassador to Brazil. Sir George believes the Japs will go to war.

"I don't see how any formula for peace can be found," I said. "Do you?"

"No, I don't. This new Japanese Government is totalitarian. Their Government sees their stocks running out within a year and no chance to replace them except to break through this net. If I were in their position that's what I would do. A great part of the Japanese Government believes that Germany will win this war."

"Since Germany isn't going to win the war," I said, "wouldn't the sensible thing be for Japan to break with the Axis, forget about Oriental face and get on the Allied side?"

"Yes," Sir George said, "that's the sensible thing, but the ruling groups in Japan believe Germany will win."

We began to talk about Italy, and I remarked that in my opinion Britain had made one of her greatest mistakes in not sending an ultimatum to Mussolini in September, 1939, saying, "We give you six hours to make up your mind on which side of the war you want to be. We don't care which side you go on, but decide in six hours."

Sir George was delighted. "That," he said, "is exactly what I have said all along."

I rather like Sir George, but I get discouraged talking to Englishmen like him who hesitate and fumble with both their words and thoughts. It is going to take quick thinking out here in the Far East to handle this situation.

There is no unusual acceleration of defense preparations. The story I got here today is that the northwest monsoons are blowing in the South China Sea, and they are most severe off Malaya, making the sea approaches very difficult. That infuriates me because everywhere the British always depend on the weather to protect them. It doesn't seem to occur to them that these monsoons create choppy water, mist and fogs and provide a screen for any daring enemy who attempts to come along the lengthy stretches of the coast. I don't know why the British always underestimate the ingenuity and daring of an enemy.

I have a touch of dengue fever again. It seems to come and go intermittently. It takes all your strength.

Tuesday, October 21st:
Gallagher, the British war correspondent, telephoned me to say that Major Fisher of Public Relations was sending a telegram to the War Office to say that all the complaints of the correspondents were the bunk. Gallagher said that the correspondents were sending one too, to beat his, to cite the chaotic conditions here and ask for immediate improvements.

Thursday, October 23rd:
Lunched at Cyranos with Darrell Berrigan of *United Press,* Garrett, a shipping man from Calcutta, Captain Getchell, a United States Maritime Commission representative, and a fellow named Swindler. Swindler is from a small town in Mississippi and he has been with the American Volunteer Group in Burma. He is a pilot and en route home on a two-month leave.

He volunteered for the AVG to fight the Japs, for the money, the adventure and to further his career. He will come out two grades higher, "if I come out at all," and be ahead of other men who have not had actual combat experience.

All of these AVG volunteers are clear-eyed men, husky and seem well able to take care of themselves.

In England there are widespread demands that Britain invade France. Lord Moyne, Secretary for the Colonies and leader of the House of Lords, squelched the talk. He said: "Britain at present sadly lacks tanks and sufficient heavy artillery for such a move and has no intention of creating another Dunkirk."

This may be:

1. The truth.
2. Present expression of weakness to cover up a British attack in Libya.
3. An attempt to increase U.S. supplies.
4. Just another confirmation of the British defensive mentality.

I wonder if the British have a Norway, Dunkirk, Greece and Crete mentality now. I mean permanently. I am beginning to fear that the British have a defensive complex, and I don't know what can eradicate that.

I see in the paper today that John Cudahy says that an American Expeditionary Force of eight million will be required to invade Germany successfully. Hitler, too, has always used big figures in his talk, to make an impression.

Friday, October 24th:
At the swimming club today a chap on the diving board came over and said, "I was one of the officers you spoke to when you visited our camp near Kuala Lumpur."

He is now stationed on the Thai border on the East Coast with Indian troops and is in Singapore on leave. I asked him what developments were going on up north.

"Well, you know a very odd thing happened. We have just discovered that Bren gun carriers can successfully go through rice fields covered with eighteen inches of water."

232

"What!" I exclaimed.

"Yes, I know what you are thinking. It's true that our strategy has been based on the idea that any mechanical transport would get stuck in those rice fields and those fields were one of our main defenses."

"That's *exactly* what I am thinking. This means that you have to change your whole conception of defense and offensive plans, doesn't it?"

"Yes, of course, we cannot depend on the rice fields to protect our operations on the road."

I am reading a book called *Fight in the Pacific* by a man named Mark J. Gayn. I never heard of him before, but he has done a very sweet job in this book, and he seems to know the Japanese extremely well. To read history past and current is interesting but discouraging, and I have been reading not only about fighting in the Pacific, but also some books on campaigns of the last war.

The same mistakes are being made in this war as in the last by "recalcitrant traditionalists." The British people examine a foreign situation without any discernible effort to put themselves in the foreigner's place and so better understand what the foreigner may be thinking. Now the Britishers cannot conceive of Japan moving because they would not move if they were in Japan's place.

This week there were two official holidays—Deepavali, a Malay festival, on Monday and Hari Raya Puassa, the end of Moslem fasting. The *Malaya Tribune* complains that while mass holidays are now taboo in England natives here will think that if the British Government can stop all activity for two days here, then things cannot be so bad.

There must be something wrong with me. If I am out walking around or doing anything, within an hour I get so weak and faint that I can hardly stand up. While exercising last night I strained a muscle and the pain today is very great. I am disgusted.

Saturday, October 25th:
Colonel Knox, Secretary of the Navy, speaking to a group of naval munitions manufacturers, said:

"A collision in the Far East is virtually inevitable if the Japanese

233

pursue their expansion plans. The situation in the Far East is extremely strained. We are satisfied in our minds that the Japanese have no intention of giving up their plans for expansion."

This is the kind of talk I like to hear. The reasons for that statement might be:

1. To scare Japan out of moving.

2. To show Japan if she moves she will walk into a war with the United States.

3. To cover some move of our own in the Atlantic or elsewhere by giving the impression we are about to move in the Pacific.

Two hours after the Knox statement *Domei* put out a Tokyo story that relations with the United States have become extremely strained. It said: "The situation has become worse."

Roosevelt says our tank production is to be doubled immediately. Cheers! The end of the Neutrality Act is foreseen in Washington.

I had a drink this evening at Raffles with a British major. His main concern was that our abandonment of the Vladivostok route for moving supplies to Russia meant that we were beginning to appease Japan.

There is a general feeling here that it is essential that the ABCD powers—America, Britain, China and the Dutch—make outright declarations that they will fight collectively if Japan moves.

The Services Public Relations Office is now definitely trying to prevent me from doing any work. Commander Burrows' office failed to call me on two stories to which all other correspondents were invited. One was on Tuesday for a press conference given by Burrows, and the other was for Saturday on maneuvers up near Johore.

Monday, October 27th:
John Young of NBC returned from Java today. He said that Edgar Mowrer of the *Chicago Daily News,* who was here about ten days ago, told Sid Albright, the NBC correspondent in Batavia, that Singapore's strength is the greatest hoax ever perpetrated on the American public and that he was going to say so in his story.

I certainly hope he does because the most incredible story I have ever seen appeared under a London date line in the *Singapore Free Press* today. It was written by Leonard Mosley, the war correspondent for the *London Daily Sketch.* I think that is as fine a piece of fake and dangerous writing as I have encountered and is contrary to the entire British propaganda. Mosley came here about a month ago. Here's the way he began his story:

"As the first war correspondent to be allowed to see our secret air bases in the Malayan jungles, I bring to you good news—

"There is no need to worry about the strength of the air force that will oppose the Japanese should they send their Army and Navy southwards. The air force is on the spot and waiting for the enemy—clouds of bombers and fighters are hidden in the jungle and ready to move out to the camouflaged tarmacs on our secret landing fields and roar into action at the first move of the Japanese toward this part of the world.

"Yes, landing grounds are here—modern landing grounds with tarmac runways capable of handling everything up to fortress bombers —but so cleverly camouflaged that they look like paddy fields and forest glades from the air.

"Planes are here tucked away in the jungle and consist of the most modern planes Britain, Australia and America are producing. Constantly on the alert, standing beside their machines are veteran pilots and crews, newly arrived from the battles of Britain and Germany and just itching to try out the tricks they have learned."

Mosley told of one airdrome not far west of Penang that was "torn out of the jungle" and reported that "this airdrome, like all others I have visited, is as modern as the best in America and Europe, and anything can land on it."

Of Kota Bahru, four hundred miles north of Singapore at the northern end of the Malay Peninsula, Mosley wrote:

"Japanese naval convoys and parachute troops will undoubtedly try to make a landing for possession of Kota Bahru, which would bring the "yellow air force" within range of Singapore.

"So Kota Bahru is magnificently defended both from the ground and in the air.

"Since the new crisis came, its bomber strength has been increased and formations of planes take off from it to scour the Gulf of Siam and China Sea day and night, watching for planes or ships of the Rising Sun that would herald an invasion."

I sent a cable that a British correspondent returned from a tour of Malayan air bases had reported, "You don't need to worry about Malaya's air force which would oppose the Japanese." I added, "His

235

unqualified optimism of the air power and preparedness here indicates that additional United States aircraft is not now needed." But the censor cut that remark out. I was able to say, however, that American correspondents have not seen such bases and aircraft concentration. Therefore, "We are unable to evaluate this Britisher's optimism."

The other correspondents are furious at Mosley's story. John Young saw Commander Burrows, who said to him: "Did you read Mosley's story in the *Free Press* this morning?"

Young said he did.

"That's cracking good stuff," Burrows said. "That's the kind of thing we want out of here. Why don't you use that in a broadcast to America?"

"It just isn't true, that's why," Young said, "and I am not going to put out a fake story like that."

I sent a brief story this afternoon on the change of shipping routes from America to the Far East. It is the first story I have cabled in a week, but is probably a waste of money, since chances are it has already broken out of Manila or Washington. So I kept it short and no interpretation. I hardly think the story was worth cabling, but I wanted CBS to know that I was still around.

Tuesday, October 28th:
Now we have a new cross to bear. Captain Berick has been sent here after he was discredited in Cairo as the press censor. The correspondents had him removed there by appealing directly to General Wavell. Already he has begun to duplicate his Cairo antics.

At maneuvers a week ago he wouldn't allow the mention of regiments which have been here for years and are widely publicized by name here and abroad. We couldn't mention the names of generals who have had publicity before, and we couldn't mention the presence here of Lockheed-Hudson bombers.

I understand that Hallett Abend, of the *New York Times,* wrote a book some time ago and devoted thirty pages to the subject of censorship in Singapore. Abend tried to come to Singapore from the Dutch East Indies. He was refused a visa by the British officials here because he had been critical of them in the past. The Dutch then flew him to Manila in one of their own planes. The Dutch are smart!

236

John Young tells me of the incredible courtesies the Dutch showed him. They couldn't do enough for him, allowed him to see everything, and even Dr. Foote, the American Consul, showed him confidential reports.

He spent three hours with the Dutch Chief-of-Staff and he was given the kind of information you couldn't pry out of the officials here with a crow bar.

John Young went on the air today from Singapore—praised the Dutch to the skies and said: "The Dutch East Indies are the best bet for Americans in the Far East."

From all I can gather, that seems to be the case. The Dutch know there is a war going on. They are prepared for it and they mean business. I certainly can't say that for the British here.

Captain Creighton, the American naval observer here, called me in today, much excited and worried. My story on the change of convoy routes had been held up and sent to him.

"Where did you get that story?" he asked.

"You ought to know better than that, to ask the source of a story. It's correct, isn't it?"

"Yes, but only five men knew that story here, and I have asked every one of them and they all deny that they gave that out. I am trying to determine if there is a leak in this office."

"I can't tell you the source, Captain Creighton, but I can assure you there is no leak in your office; you can ease your mind on that score."

"You ought to know better than that. A story like that endangers the lives of American sailors."

"I don't know what you are excited about, Captain, but I thank you for holding up that story and killing it because I've learned that the story was released from Batavia yesterday and you have saved me the cost of a wire from here and being twenty-four hours behind in that story."

"Are you sure it was released from Batavia?"

"Of course, I'm sure. It's a dead fish, as far as I am concerned."

I then said to Captain Creighton that since we were doing the same general kind of work—he gathering information that he sent in code to Washington and I getting information to report to the American people—we might exchange information for the purpose of keeping the American people better informed.

"Oh, no," he said testily, "our work is entirely different. I am not supposed even to be here."

"Very well, Captain Creighton, each of us will have to struggle along, however best he can."

This is very unsatisfactory to me because Captain Creighton is the first American naval officer with whom I have not been able to exchange conversation about developments in a country.

Wednesday, October 29th:
The United States Consulate and Naval and Army observers here received orders to stand by in case of emergency over the week-end.

Coming out of Kelly and Walsh bookstore on Raffles Square, I ran into Norman Fisher, the newsreel photographer, and Leonard Mosley, of the *London Daily Sketch*. Mosley said he was fed up with Singapore.

"Are you staying on?" I asked.

"I don't think so," Mosley replied. "I've been sending stories to my paper that there is no chance of war out here and that the situation is easing up. That way, they will believe I might as well go back to the Middle East."

That was the exact opposite of the situation in the Far East. Mosley's contribution that day jibed with his fake story a few days before on the "clouds of bombers and fighters" out here.

Went to the doctor today. Nothing much can be done about the muscle I strained except rest, which I cannot take. I am to take six vitamin B pills daily. The doctor said that this climate was bad for me and thought I should either have a two-months' rest or go back to the States. He thinks being away for over four years has something to do with my general condition.

London is putting out stories that Japan is preparing a powerful campaign in the China war before rushing a drive to the south or against Russia. Most people here nod their heads and say: "I told you war wasn't coming to Singapore."

This evening Young, O'Neil and I went out to the New World and the Happy World, the huge taxi dance places. I don't like either place but they are hot spots for the troops who look forward all week to going up there, sweating like horses and dancing with Chinese and tar-brushed babies.

Then we went to Deskar Street, a dark thoroughfare off Lavendar, where scores of Chinese girls stand in the street or in front of the door-ways. Each is with her *amah,* who is the protector, procurer and nego-tiator. The Chinese girls are dressed in typical pyjama costumes, with flowers in their hair, and some are quite attractive. The *amahs* are al-ways dressed in black with hair pulled straight back and a braid hang-ing down. We three had white suits on and stood out in that darkness so that the *amahs* and Chinese girls seemed somewhat frightened that we were the police, although there is rarely any official interference and never an inspection of the girls. Virtually every girl is diseased, al-though when well coiffured and under heavy powder most of them don't look too bad.

Also in the street were a number of rickshaws whose coolies act as "runners." They offer to take men to special girls in special houses where the price is "$3 short time, $6 long time, $10 all night." Tonight we didn't see any British or Australian troops around.

Diary comment:
There must be a tremendous furor in the United States over the tor-pedoing of the destroyer, *Reuben James.* Forty-four of the crew of one hundred and twenty have been rescued.

I am more than ever convinced that Germany's plan is twofold:

1. To keep the United States on the verge of entering the war with Germany and with that to foster the belief that we are still quite some distance from taking the step.

2. To encourage Japan to strike and thereby involve the United States in the war in the Pacific.

Hitler must hope that if the United States goes to war in the Atlantic, as we most certainly will, we will simultaneously be forced into a war in the Pacific. That is essential to his plan.

The thing that puzzles me is what is to be presented to the Jap Diet on November 15th. It has not met since April and is purely a stooge

239

outfit. It is reasonable to suppose the Army would want to lay before the Diet an accomplished fact. I fail to see how, by then, an agreement with Washington could be ready. Tokyo and Washington are very far apart and the closure of the Burma Road or the ending of the China war could not be ready to place before the Diet by then.

There were whispers around tonight that General Wavell has arrived for a series of conferences, but I can't get any confirmation.

Sunday, November 2nd:
General Wavell did arrive and I cabled an interpretive story on it in which I said:

"Wavell will discuss the strategy which will be followed in the event the Japanese drive through Yunan to cut off the Burma Road. Also what Britain will do in the eventuality Thailand accepts an invasion by Japan. Likewise they will talk about Britain's possibilities of extending assistance to the Thais in case they resist.

"It is expected the basic discussion will concern the eventuality of the Germans driving toward Iran and Iraq and Japan launching a simultaneous drive for a pincer move on Burma and India."

Monday, November 3rd. Diary comment:
The keynote of British propaganda here is to present to the world the idea that Singapore is so strong that the Japanese would be fools to attack.

The British seem to be forced to use that bluff game because of the heavy demands on their forces elsewhere. But it does seem a bit silly for two reasons. The first is it prevents American correspondents from showing how desperately American help is needed out here. The second is that British bluff about the strength of Singapore has no effect in Tokyo. The Japs have too good an espionage service here to be fooled by that propaganda.

But the British do think these statements have frightened the Japs. As a matter of fact, Sir Robert Brooke-Popham told an American military officer who was here on a special mission:

"The greatest value of Singapore is the illusion of impregnability built up in the Japanese mind."

240

I read a detective story every night before going to bed in this excruciatingly hot hotel. Other mysteries help me forget Singapore.

Tuesday, November 4th:
The story I cabled Sunday on Wavell's trip here was killed by the
censor. Not a word went through.

An interview is scheduled for this evening with General Wavell for
the accredited war correspondents. John Young asked Major Fisher
about attending the interview also. Young is not yet accredited by the
war office.

"We cannot make an exception for NBC," Fisher told him. "Why,
if we did that we would have to allow the Chinese reporters, too."

The whole Wavell story is being messed up as usual. On Saturday
Wavell's arrival was broadcast by the Indian radio but it wasn't until
late Sunday afternoon that we could report that he was here and we
could only say that he was here and nothing more than that. That's
why my interpretive story was killed by the censor.

General Wavell came into the room in Government House wearing
a bush jacket, darkened by sweat in the back, over a towel-like white-
coat with long sleeves and high neck, obviously to prevent catching
cold.

He was taken around by Major Fisher and introduced to each one of
us, and I recalled we had met previously in Cairo. He also knew Gallagher and Mosley from the Middle East.

"This talk," he said, "is 'off the record.' I've come here just to look
over the Indian troops and see if they need anything and to talk with
Brooke-Popham. The Indian troops are in good heart and spoiling for
a fight."

"Do you think Russia will hold out?" I asked.

"They don't let out much information, do they?" he replied.

Selby Walker of *Reuters* asked if the British would do anything if
Japan struck at the Burma Road inside China.

Wavell didn't answer that. He said it wasn't in his command.

There was no story in that interview and I thought that Wavell
looked just about the same as he did in Cairo, despite the fact that he
has been working extremely hard and flying all over the Far East. Every

241

time I see Wavell, he impresses me as being both a swell guy and a capable soldier.

I didn't wear a uniform to the conference. I only have a short bush jacket, shorts and trousers. The jacket has short sleeves, and this was one of those dress interviews where your coat has to have long sleeves. I just never thought it worth while to get a dress uniform. Major Fisher always calls me the most unmilitarily dressed war correspondent of this war, and I guess he is right.

U. Saw, Burma's Premier, told *Reuters* in London today:

"I am not satisfied with the results I achieved in negotiations on Burma's constitutional issue. These are not commensurate with the risks I have taken in coming to Great Britain."

That's a hell of a strange statement for the Burma Premier to put out. I just hope that Britain knew what she was doing in London with U. Saw, because that Burma situation is dynamite.

Wednesday, November 5th:

Gallagher, the war correspondent of the *London Daily Express,* has sent a series of protests to Major Fisher. He cited about two hundred matters which must be dealt with at once if the local authorities are to comply with the facilities established by the War Office in London for aiding the work of correspondents. Gallagher also sent a cable to the *Daily Express* in London:

"This is an indictment of British propaganda in the Far East. I can call fifteen witnesses, every one a topliner American newspaper or radio reporter, to prove muddleheadedness and ignorance, and in one case malice, have estranged these fifteen reporters who came to British territory to sell our war to the United States. . . .

"Despite numerous protests and complaints made by reporters and by Duff Cooper, there is no sign of coming improvement in the hopelessly inexperienced propaganda unit [SPRO]. . . . War might even begin at any time, but no arrangements have yet been made for the officially accredited reporters here to report operations."

The names of the fifteen Americans mentioned by Gallagher are Edward Angly, *New York Herald Tribune,* Hallett Abend, *New York Times,* Cecil Brown, Columbia Broadcasting, Bob Casey, *Chicago Daily News,* Frank Gervasi, *Collier's Magazine,* Martha Gellhorn, *Collier's,*

John Martin, *Time*, Allan Michie, *Time* and *Life*, Edgar Mowrer, Carl Mydans, *Life*, Bob Neville, *PM*, Carl Randau, *PM*, Leland Stowe, *Chicago Daily News*, John Young, NBC, Leane Zugsmith, *PM*.

An amateur photographer by the name of Julius Fisher, who manages a local cinema, was given special facilities to spend the whole day with Sir Archibald Wavell and to take color films. No single accredited correspondent was allowed to accompany Wavell on his inspection around Singapore but this man, Fisher, who was not an accredited correspondent but a free-lancer doing his job solely for profit, went with Wavell. Gallagher protested bitterly to Major Fisher on this incredible discrimination.

The *Japanese Times and Advertiser*, which is close to the Foreign Office, lists seven points which it says the United States must accept or the Japanese Diet will adopt a "defensive" program. These points were undoubtedly laid before Washington weeks ago as a basis for negotiations:

1. U.S. and other powers to discontinue military and economic aid to Chungking, discontinue anti-Japanese propaganda and withdraw their military missions from Chungking which are "designed to help China at war with Japan."

2. Leave China completely free to deal with Japan, thereby ending hostilities and establishing economic collaboration.

3. Advise China to make peace and discontinue military and economic encirclement under the pretext of defense.

4. Acknowledge Japan's co-prosperity sphere and Japan's leadership in the Western Pacific, thereby leaving Manchuria, China, Indo-China, Thailand, the Netherlands Indies "and other states or protectorates to establish their own political and economic relations with Japan without any interference."

5. U.S. to recognize Manchukuo.

6. Unconditional and immediate unfreezing of Japan's and China's assets in the U.S., Britain and Dutch East Indies.

7. Restore Jap-American trade treaty.

These demands convince me that Japan is determined to go to war, and intends to do so. She hasn't a prayer of getting any of these demands satisfied. By publishing them she has let the world know what she intends to get and she can't back down on them.

I don't see any possibility of our yielding. Japan will go to war against Britain and the United States either as soon as we're pretty heavily engaged in the Atlantic or when we actually go to war against Germany.

CRACK UP

Thursday, November 6th:
This morning Flight Lieutenant Downer and Gallagher picked me up for a trip in a bomber to Kota Bahru.

There was a delay at Seletar airfield because, "We have no report yet that Kota Bahru is serviceable." I asked what that meant and they said: "Well, it is probably covered over with water."

"This chap, Mosley," I said, "flew over all these airdromes, and he said they are as fine as any in Britain or the United States."

The flight lieutenant laughed and said: "They are nothing but mud and grass and water."

We were scheduled to go in South African-made planes called Vildebeestes, torpedo-carrying bombers of ancient vintage. Eleven were going up, each carrying a torpedo.

The squadron leader took me into the office and got me a dirty, white flying suit and harness and leather flying helmet, chamois-lined. He put on the harness for me and strapped on the parachute, just to show how it went.

"Have you ever jumped with a parachute?" he asked.

"No, and I don't expect to."

"Well, you never can tell. If you have to, just pull this ring after you count to about five."

"If I have to jump, I don't think I will be able to count to five," I said.

A flying officer came into the office while I was putting on the flying suit and asked me to sign two papers, one to acknowledge the receipt of the equipment and the other, the flight lieutenant explained, "absolves the Air Ministry of any liability if anything happens to you."

Gallagher went off to one plane and I walked out to our machine with Sergeant Pilot Lyle, who clambered into the open cockpit.

They were one-engine biplanes, old-style ships which make about one hundred miles an hour and are noted for their reliability.

The planes lined up on the field and each of us taxied to the end of the airdrome for the take-off. The pilot was sitting in front of me, I came next, crouched in the middle seat, and the wireless operator was in the rear cockpit.

We took off at 8:02 on this bright, sunny morning. From Seletar we headed straight north over the extremely wild country and after about an hour and a half crossed the Pahang River.

At 9:50 we came down at Kuantan. It is surrounded by jungle and the airdrome was covered with water. We circled several times and then came down into this mess of mud and water, spraying both sides.

The flight lieutenant of our squadron changed planes here. His radio hadn't been working and we found out here at Kuantan that the whole flight had been called off shortly after we left Seletar because of the water at the airdromes. But the lieutenant had been unable to receive the message to that effect and therefore we had gone on.

As we came out of our cockpits at Kuantan, Sergeant Lyle snorted: "We certainly shouldn't have come down here. This field is unserviceable. We all might have cracked up."

I talked with a number of the men stationed here at Kuantan and took a number of pictures. Most of the men were rather bored by inactivity and hoped for some action.

What I didn't like when we first started out from Seletar and what I don't like now is this wing-to-wing flying. We fly less than fifteen feet from the leader's wing and just slightly behind. From an angle it looks as if the wings are interlocked, and that is making me very nervous.

The wind up here is terrific and every now and then I let down the seat so that I can turn around, face forward and crouch behind the pilot to see what's ahead because most of the time I've been facing the tail.

The pilot circles twice around the landing field at Kota Bahru. Even at three hundred feet we can see the water on the grassy field. It looks no more solid than the usual rice-field mud that draws a coolie down to his hips. The field might not be as gluey as that but it is definitely certain to be mushy, at least, after a week of monsoon rains.

At one edge of the field near a hangar we can see the "crash truck" and a half dozen figures around it. The dead wagon and the wake all ready.

246

Slung underneath our plane, directly below the cockpit, is a six-foot torpedo and I wish the roar of the motor was not so loud. I want desperately to ask the pilot how big a crack-up it takes to make a torpedo explode. That seems like one of those things one would like to know, and right away. At least, we are not carrying any bombs in the racks.

The field is uninviting, a flat, rectangular gash in the jungle and tree-blanketed mangrove swamps, a half mile from the China Sea and five miles from the border of Malaya and Thailand.

I check the safety cable, one end attached to the floor of the cockpit and the other fastened to the rear of my parachute harness like the tail of a monkey. I button the tunic pocket where my camera is and squirm around. The wireless operator grins in the wind and gives me a thumb.

The pilot's mind is made up. The plane tilts in a long glide, the roof of the jungle races past and the grass and water rush up to meet us. Definitely, there's considerable water on the field and we hit it, smoothly and solidly enough.

Two arcs of water and mud billow from each side of the plane joining in the tail-wheel spray to form a long stream of flying muck. But we're down, and we taxi over to the hangar, plunging through like an angry water buffalo.

It is hot on the ground, and the sun pouring into the jungle dampness makes of the whole place something approaching a steam room. A slight breeze would help, but the jungle walling in this airdrome keeps that out nicely.

Scores of coolies already are out on the field to dirt-fill the deep ruts our landing made. They splash about barefoot, synchronizing their short, plopping steps with the weight they carry. The dirt is in two baskets suspended from each end of a stick across one shoulder.

The pilot ignores the landing. "I don't know whether you want to eat here or not," he says. "Last time I was up this way I couldn't down the meat. I gave it to the wing commander's dog, but he wouldn't eat it either. That gives you an idea."

The pilot goes off to check on the refueling.

Under an attap roof of a shed without walls I smoke a cigarette and wait for some of the roar to go out of my ears. The aircraftsman standing there is doing nothing. He is off duty and eyeing my camera at the moment. In another, he is talking of photographs.

"I've some wonderful photos of snakes' heads," he says. "Captured twenty different kinds of snakes here and I use a telephoto lens on them. You can see every scale in the heads. Oh, no, it's not my business. Just a spot of something to do in spare time. I was a clerk in a haberdashery on Regent Street before the war."

"Quite a change to aircraftsman, isn't it?"

"Well, yes, rather. But I always was interested in mechanics. Had an auto and worked on it a good deal. One of those kind that needed it, you know."

Two Lockheed-Hudson bombers come out of the trees at the far end of the field. They snort and grunt and make those flashing, kinetic movements of thoroughbreds at the barrier.

"They're going on patrol," Aircraftsman Jack volunteers.

"I thought this field was dangerous today."

"Well, it's serviceable and that's about all. Have to maintain daily patrols though. They go over the Gulf of Siam and up to the Indo-China coast. And across the China Sea to Borneo and Sarawak."

"Watching for a surprise attack by the Japs?"

"That's right. Watching for the Japs."

Aircraftsman Jack is a remarkably ordinary-looking Englishman. Twenty-four or -five with a black mustache, guileless eyes, a hesitant friendliness and a certain reticence. He has a girl waiting for him in London—she's a WAAF—and he intends to get married "as soon as I get home."

Six months ago he arrived in Malaya and now he has close-up pictures of the heads of twenty different kinds of snakes. Now, too, he is concerned about another matter.

"You're the first American correspondent I've talked to and I'd like to ask you something, if you don't mind? I'm puzzled why America doesn't come in to help us, really come into the war."

He's certainly more tactful than the British captain in Cairo who, after every speech by President Roosevelt, a member of the Cabinet or Congress, would say to me: "Well are you coming in now or are you still talking about it?"

The aircraftsman wants to know something that runs in the minds of quite a few million Britishers.

"We're in this war pretty far already," I say.

248

"Yes, I know," Aircraftsman Jack says, "but why don't you send over a few million men to England?"

"What for?"

"Why, then we could invade the continent."

"You're pretty sure Britain is going to win this war, aren't you?"

Aircraftsman Jack's face is split wide open in amazement. "Why, that . . ." and he struggles to finish his sentence, "why, that's taken for granted. That's a foregone conclusion. Everyone knows that."

I suggest there's such a thing as being too confident "and that's not so good."

"Yes, but I don't think we're overconfident any more. We're just confident of victory.

"Do you know what all the men here talk about?" he demands. "One chap just this morning said he would make a wager that he is sent to Roumania with the army of occupation. Personally," chuckles Aircraftsman Jack, "I hope I get to go to Germany with the occupying forces."

I saw about a dozen Lockheed-Hudson bombers around the field and about a half dozen very expertly done fake machines. There's no doubt that those fakes would look like Lockheed bombers from the air, even from five hundred feet.

Wing Commander Noble is in charge of this airdrome and he was extremely sorry that we couldn't stay longer.

"I want to show you around," he said with obvious pride in his establishment.

I asked him if he wasn't pretty lonesome up here.

"Yes, a bit, but I am on my own up here. I can run my own show. I've been trying for a year to get out of Singapore."

I asked how many fighters he has and he said: "We haven't any fighters now. They'd come up as soon as we need them. You see, we are the advance base here. We give the signal when the enemy is coming. Yes, of course, the Japs would hit us first but we can give a good account of ourselves."

He generally expressed contempt for the Jap Air Force and asked me if I knew very much about them. I said I didn't.

"Well, we can handle those Japs without very much trouble. We've got a number of R.A.F. boys here from Britain and they know their stuff all right."

On the return flight we held to the coast for four hundred miles down to Singapore.

As the sun began to squeeze out of the afternoon, I had one of the pleasantest experiences. We ran into a huge, mountainous, fluffy, white cloud. It is fascinating to watch other planes disappear into the clouds and then emerge a little later. One plane on our left was slightly below in a valley of the clouds and looked exactly as if it were in a snow crevasse. Three planes ahead of us shot into the clouds and it was as though they went into a ball of cotton.

Then the sun began to go down. We were above the clouds which must have screened that sunset from the ground. But up there it was one of the most beautiful sights I've ever seen. A huge chunk of the heavens off to the right was ablaze with the brightest orange possible, so bright it hurt the eyes. It was a huge wall and then tapered off in streaks mixed with gray. But on the right of this flame display there was a section about one-tenth the size of the total brightness in the sky, which was of the purest Chinese red. This is the first time I've actually seen red in the sky. I have seen scores of sunsets from above the clouds. That one, for me, was like peeking into Heaven.

About two hours from Seletar we crossed over a heavy jungle and mountainous country, flying between peaks so that they were just about level with the plane. I was hungry the whole way back. Up there I began to think of things of many years ago when we lived on College Hill in Western Pennsylvania and of high school, and for some reason I had a great many flashbacks of things that I had already forgotten for years and years.

Then darkness came rather suddenly and our red and green wing lights came on and the white tail light, and it was easy to pick out the other members of the squadron. We then moved up into wing-to-wing formation, three planes and the leader slightly ahead. I didn't like that. Each plane seemed to be constantly fighting to hold its position, in constant danger of touching. We flew that way for about forty minutes until we saw below us on Johore Straits the Naval Base and the huge floating dock all lit up like Coney Island.

We flew in formation twice around the airdrome at Seletar. It was an inextricable mass of red lights all over the place. After the second time, we were much lower. The other two planes in the formation slipped away and I saw the second one go down. We were following behind it, and it went into a cloud bank hovering three hundred feet above the field. We went into it, too, and when we came out our pilot didn't seem able to recognize the position of the other machines. We went off on a different course and flew around in a steep bank to land.

We seemed to be coming down all right. I had dropped my seat and was crouched behind the pilot. We were a long time touching the ground. Then we hit, not a very sharp bump, and were in contact for fifty yards, then off it, then another bump, much sharper, and the plane bucked a dozen times like a bucking bronco. Trouble!

I could feel we were in considerable water and perhaps mud as well. We seemed to be taking on speed instead of slowing down. Then I suddenly saw the camouflaged gun position covered with a net, leaping up at us like a huge ant mound.

The plane's motor seemed to die down and the next instant we hit the ditch and I felt the ridge of the pilot's seat pressing into my stomach and I seemed to be wedged in. Our nose was pointed directly into the ground, and our tail was sticking up straight in the air like a church steeple. The whole ship teetered, but didn't flop over on its back. At that instant I saw that the wings were half ripped apart and the gasoline was spraying out of them.

I patted the pilot twice on the shoulder and shouted: "Are you all right?"

"Yes, are you all right?"

"Yes."

The wireless operator behind called: "Is the passenger all right?"

"Yes, I'm okay," and immediately thought of my camera on a ledge behind me. I thought it might have been knocked over and gone crashing to the bottom of the cockpit, but it hadn't. The pilot had flicked off the switch just before we cracked up. Otherwise, the ship instantly would have caught fire.

I started to climb out but found that I had been wedged in rather tightly.

An Indian guard with his fixed bayonet, guarding this end of the field, came up, throwing the light of his flashlight over us.

By then the pilot and the wireless operator had clambered out and I was rooting around on the floor for my small bag and hat. The parachute harness and narrowness of the cockpit made it difficult, and, besides, all the stuff on the floor had shoved forward into a jumble.

I finally squirmed out of the cockpit, handed my bag and camera to the operator and twined around a strut until I got my foot on the wing. I jumped about five feet and fell face forward on the grass. My head just missed the sharp edge of the propeller, and my face buried into the ground. The gasoline was pouring out of the wing and it dropped on my neck as I lay there in the grass, half stunned for a moment.

Then the crash truck came racing toward us across the field, a powerful searchlight on the front. We three were put in a car and taken at once to the Air Force doctor's office. The pilot was given a physical examination.

"It was an error of judgment," he told the doctor.

He had to close his eyes and balance on one foot with arms outstretched in front. Then the doctor went over him with a stethoscope. He was okay.

The doctor then called me in.

"Were you hurt at all?"

"No."

"Did you get your breath up?"

"What's that mean?"

"Were you frightened? Any effects of fear?"

"No, the only thing the matter with me is in my stomach. It's empty. I'm hungry."

Outside, one of the men said, "You're lucky. Usually one crash is enough."

I asked one of them if the pilot would get into trouble over this.

"Oh, no, they expect these things to happen."

I told Lyle that I would be happy to testify in his behalf if there was any investigation. I found out later that Lyle had put a plane in a ditch once before. I asked him how it happened this time and he said: "At night you can only judge the distance to the ground within four or five feet."

The most astonishing thing to me was that there wasn't the slightest tinge of fear or any reaction whatever when we cracked up. My first reaction was to pat the pilot on the back as a sort of reassurance; my second was whether my camera was damaged; my third was that this

252

would make me that much later in getting something to eat; my next, "Well, if I'm going to write a story this will make one worth-while incident of the trip."

Singapore must be getting me if I don't react to such an incident the way I should.

I came back to the hotel, had dinner in my room, then wrote my story and sent it to the cable office. All evening I could feel the weight of the parachute harness and my ears were buzzing very strongly. This was mixed with disappointment. The disappointment was coming back to the hotel and finding that no letter had arrived from Martha since the Clipper got in yesterday. It is just eight months ago today that Martha left Turin for the United States.

Friday, November 7th:

My legs are as stiff as boards today. This must be from crouching in the cockpit. Otherwise no effects from the crash yesterday.

John Young from NBC is thoroughly fed up. He asked his outfit to withdraw representation, and he left tonight for Rangoon.

Saburo Kurusu, Tokyo's special envoy now flying to America, is said to be taking special proposals. Not much chance of his accomplishing anything unless Japan makes a spectacular backdown—and not much chance of that.

Saturday, November 8th:

The Japanese are still very busy in Thailand.

I talked with a man who has just come down from Bangkok and he says that two Japs were picked up by the Thailand authorities for "Japanese bungling." Enemy agents in Bangkok are distributing pamphlets dealing with the Japanese version of the Russian war and printed in Thai and English. The leaflets carry a price-mark in order to obey the Thai law forbidding propaganda, but invariably they are given away free when the buyer shows an interest.

Optimism was ladled out in spoonfuls today. Stalin, Churchill, De Gaulle and a spokesman for Chungking synchronized statements about how badly off the Germans are and that the Nazi doom is sealed. It was done obviously by prearrangement and that obvious fact does much to dispel the effect they wanted. Stalin would have been enough, followed in the next few days by the others.

I think the purpose must have been to sway sentiment in the United States on the neutrality revision—to show the United States that the Allies are turning the corner. Judging by the stuff printed in the papers here, the American press and radio commentators lapped it up.

Monday, November 10th:

With a group of other correspondents I went out to Blakang Mati, a triangular-shaped island off Singapore to watch 6-inch coastal guns firing at night.

We watched the firing for about an hour, then drove in a truck to the officers' mess where we had a drink. We came out and walked a couple of hundred yards to the truck. It was standing on a slight incline. Palmer, the photographer, was already in, and somebody else and I got in and sat down. The remainder of the correspondents were ready to climb up, and the driver was off to one side.

Suddenly the truck started rolling down the incline. In the few seconds as I leaped up to jump out, the truck went over a three-foot bank and down over the hill, gaining terrific speed. It then hit another bump and threw me off my feet and I sprawled in the truck.

The two benches flew up in the air and came down on me.

I thought at that instant: "I am getting hurt. I don't think I can get out of this. I think this is the end."

Then the truck plowed into the side of a hill.

I lay there stunned. Someone jumped into the truck, calling:"Are you hurt? Are you hurt?"

One of the benches had hit me on the neck under the ear. It seemed to have paralyzed my speech. I couldn't answer.

Then Gallagher was inside the truck and he reached down to pull me up, saying, "Are you okay, Brownie?"

I still couldn't answer.

They got me out of the truck and I sat down on the bank, and then my voice came back. The first words were a shout:

"A fine bunch of cameramen you guys are. Nobody got a picture of it."

254

Tuesday, November 11th:

I am very sore in a half dozen places from the truck experience last night. The worst place is on the back over the kidneys. It's extremely painful and when I bend over it takes some time before I can straighten up again. The other correspondents think it very funny. They said SPRO must be trying to bump me off—first the plane, now this truck.

I lunched today with the Thai Consul. He doesn't think the Japs will move before March. He is now certain they will invade Thailand and equally certain the Thais will fight.

The Germans seem to be bogged down in front of Leningrad and Moscow. Nazi propaganda seems hard put to explain that situation.

Today is Armistice Day. I wonder what day will be Armistice Day in this war. What year. . . .

Wednesday, November 12th:

The pain around the kidney from the bump in the truck is rather bad, so this afternoon I was picked up by SPRO and taken to Alexandria Military Hospital for examination, which I had requested. Major Fisher, however, pointed out to me that the British Army was in no way responsible for my injury.

The doctor examined the injury behind the ear. "Nothing injured there," he said. "That's a good, thick skull."

"Thanks," I said dryly.

There was a bruise of the kidney area and he said I should have "complete rest for four to seven days." That's ridiculous and I have no intention of following his advice, although it hurts, especially when I sneeze.

The situation is boiling up everywhere but here. As near as I can make out the apathy and self-confidence is as high in Singapore as it ever was. Elsewhere the view seems to be different.

Admiral Nomura in Washington says the United States-Jap war is "unthinkable."

General Marshall warns that Axis agents are ready to sabotage U.S. factories.

Berrigan, *United Press*, from Bangkok, says: "General feeling is not where the war is coming, but when."

255

Senator Elbert Thomas says: "I am very hopeful that a United States-Japanese agreement can be worked out."

Colonel Knox says: "The hour of decision is here."

Sumner Welles says: "War may be forced on us at any moment."

I am puzzled by my own problems. I have been trying to read some meaning into this sequence of events:

CBS suggested I make no more protests about the British information situation until Bill Dunn arrives.

Haven't heard anything from Paul White in the past six weeks and there have been no schedules to broadcast.

The plane crack-up.

The truck accident.

What I have been trying to do is to find some link connecting all these events, but I am damned if I can find out what it is.

Thursday, November 13th:

This afternoon I had a three-hour session with Captain Berick, the Military Press Adviser, and Flight Lieutenant Gerald Samson, the Air Force Press Adviser, on a sixty-page magazine article that I finished. It was a nerve-shattering experience, and they have referred it to higher authorities. Samson is particularly picayune. Having no discretion, he cuts out everything and thereby saves himself from any possible repercussions. I am convinced the British are not interested in having any reporters here. They want you to put out propaganda, and if you don't do that—no story. They are not the slightest bit concerned with' informing the American public.

Al Noderer of the *Chicago Tribune* came through today and we had dinner together. I last saw Al in Rome. Now he has been in Iran and he gives a pretty unhappy account of what happened in that Iran war. There was a great deal of suspicion, he says, between the British and Russians and each was afraid the other had come in to take the entire country over. The Russians were extremely secretive and would tell the British nothing.

He and the other people I have talked with tell of the extreme antagonism between the American technicians and the British in Iran. The Americans turned out at 7:30 in the morning to work on the tanks

256

and aircraft. The British came around at nine, knocked off for tea at eleven, worked for about a half hour afterwards, then went to lunch, came back about three, then quit at five for tea and that was their day. Noderer quoted some of the American technicians as saying:

"We came over here to do some work. We are ready to work twelve or fourteen hours a day but the British are never around."

This is the sort of thing that I have heard from other people and from technicians themselves who have been in the Middle East.

About a week ago I was talking with an aircraft technician who was on his way back to America after being in the Middle East.

"Those British guys resent us," he said. "They are not interested in learning how to operate our tanks or aircraft. I am going back to America where I can do some work."

Friday, November 14th:
The Neutrality Act was revised by eighteen votes, permitting the arming of merchant ships and sending them to belligerent zones. Thank God for that!

Spent most of the morning getting the finishing touches on the censorship of the article with Samson. He is impossible. He knocked out most of the material that I had used in the story I sent on my flight to Kota Bahru. As a matter of fact, in this article I can't mention the name, Kota Bahru. So after all these years the authorities here have now decided that Kota Bahru ceases to exist.

Late this afternoon I had a drink with a number of officers at Raffles Bar and I asked what was holding up an invasion of France.

"There is just one thing," one of them said, "unwillingness of some high general to risk his reputation."

"Do you think an invasion should be attempted now?" I asked.

"Of course. Why not?"

"There would be a terrific reaction in England if 300,000 men were killed and the objective were not achieved."

"Well, we can't win this war without some men getting killed."

"I have said this before and I will say it again, that you British cannot win this war fighting like gentlemen."

"We will go on fighting like gentlemen just the same. We just don't change."

Practically all of those officers—there must have been a half dozen sitting around the table that day—didn't seem to care much one way or the other about fighting the Japanese. They want to go after the Germans. They want action, but against the Nazis.

The *Ark Royal* is reported to have been torpedoed in the Mediterranean.

At Raffles Bar, with Flight Lieutenant Downer, Graeme Nicholl and Gallagher of the *London Daily Express*, I told them: "You British are building up a headache for yourselves. Every American I talk to who has been with the British as a technician or instructor is sore as a boil. Some day we are going to be fighting side by side, and there's going to be hell to pay. Why don't you people explain to your soldiers what Americans are, so they'll understand us better?"

Graeme mentioned the booklet issued by the R.A.F. to explain America to training cadets going to the United States. "That was a fine thing, don't you think?"

"It certainly was," I agreed. "There ought to be more of it before it is too late. Get some Britishers who know America and let them go out and talk to the troops about us, tell them our good points and bad points. And we should have Americans who know the British tell all about you people to our troops."

Gallagher said he was much concerned about it, too. He didn't think anything would be done though. Gallagher seems to think the English always act after the deed is done, instead of before.

Saturday, November 15th:
Cabled a story today which I was surprised got through censorship. I said: "There is no indication here that Britain will move unless the Japs directly attack Malaya, the Dutch East Indies or Manila. I do not detect any feeling that the concentrations of British planes and man power should be used to assist the Chinese in Yunnan in the event the Japanese strike at the Burma Road.

"In other words, the Singapore attitude corresponds to the London policy not to aid the Chinese until the Japanese directly threaten British

258

security. I do not hear any expressions that Britain should send an expeditionary force to Chungking.

"Some observers believe that if Kurusu fails and Japan then moves, it will be an all-out attack against both Britain and the United States, beginning with an attack on Manila, since it is recognized that it would be the poorest naval strategy to attempt to attack Borneo without the elimination of Manila."

Then to cover myself and to try to indicate to New York that censorship here was becoming intolerable I added:

"With the rising tension in the Far East, Singapore censorship of foreign correspondents has now been tightened up. The Royal Air Force is now barring material which was permissible as recently as a week ago and is known throughout the world.

"The British military ordered the evacuation of nineteen Japanese living at Kuantan, as it is a port and airdrome on the east coast of Malaya. Two hundred Japs living at Trenggannu, north of Kuantan, have left and others are following. Four hundred fifty Japs sailed for Japan today aboard the *Asa Maru*. Most of these were barbers, shoemakers, tailors, iron- and tin-mine managers and rubber managers as well as a group of fishermen who have fished in Malayan waters for more than thirty years.

"I note that in the *Straits Times* today and in the past few days there have been an increasing number of 'Letters to the Editor' protesting against the failure of the authorities to use the available British man power in Malaya for fighting and not allowing the Asiatics to assume more responsible positions in rubber and tin production to replace those Englishmen who are managing rubber and tin mines or working as clerks. The letters point out that there are many ablebodied whites fit enough to appear on the playing fields of Singapore and add: 'If they are fit enough for that they are fit enough to shoulder a rifle.'

"The heads of the Malayan Government are determined that Malaya shall emerge from this war unscathed, undisturbed and unchanged. Unless hostilities actually commence here they insist upon business as usual. Malaya lacks leadership. Those at the top are conspicuously deficient in boldness, breadth of vision and inspiration."

I cabled that material for two reasons. I figured that by quoting a letter to the editor appearing in a newspaper I could get it by the

259

censorship and because that material precisely summed up what is going on here. In order that New York might not have any misunderstanding as to who is responsible for a large part of this I added one line:

"Sir Thomas Shenton Whiteleg Thomas is Colonial Governor."

Today the Singapore Rickshaw Pullers jointly sent Mrs. Churchill $50 to aid Russia. This is the first donation of the rickshaw organization on behalf of the war. They have contributed nothing to the British but they are very much interested in a victory for the Soviets. Even the rickshaw pullers here, as near as I can make out, feel no sympathy for the British.

Dennis McEvoy, who has been in Kuibyshev covering the Russian war for some months for CBS and the *Chicago Times,* came through on his way to Manila and the United States and called me. I had never met him before but he is a young, intelligent chap, son of J. P. McEvoy. He has many eccentricities, but for a youngster he is as smart as a whip and very likable. We had a drink and were joined by a lieutenant and his attractive wife. Lieutenant Jack McNaughton was an actor in England and they're close friends of Helen Hayes. I remarked to him that I thought the old-school tie is interfering to a great extent in the way Britain fights the war. He explained that a soldier who rises from the ranks to become a commissioned officer is almost always transferred to another regiment.

"Why?"

"Because he is resented by his former men."

He gave me an example of a man who is now a captain but who started as a drummer boy at fifteen in the regiment.

"He is a genius at military stuff," the lieutenant said, "and might become a major general, but he is resented by his men for all of his great ability because he is not a gentleman."

I shook my head as though I had just had an uppercut.

"Yes, that's true," McNaughton insisted. "His men would rather follow a lieutenant of the right blood up a hill where they knew they would all be killed—they would rather do that than follow the much wiser and more experienced orders of a captain who came up from the ranks."

260

"That doesn't make sense. Judgment and intelligence should guide military maneuvers."

"Perhaps so," the lieutenant said, "but to a regular soldier an officer, whatever his ability, must be a gentleman from the right school. Take this captain I mentioned to you. He was a drummer boy once and if today he was a sergeant major that would be fine. His men would do anything for him."

There has been considerable friction between the Australians and English here, especially with the Scottish regiments. As a result a system of interchange has just been started of sending two noncommissioned officers and four of other ranks from the Australians to the English and Scottish regiments for a month and vice versa. It's said to be working very well.

Dennis McEvoy and I had dinner tonight with Colonel Field, who has come here as Deputy Director of Military Intelligence, and M. Baron and his wife. Field is replacing Colonel Grimsdale here. Baron is head of the Free French in Malaya. Field asked Dennis a number of pertinent, pithy questions about Russia, and I thought McEvoy did a very good job of answering them. Dennis was called away for a few minutes and Colonel Field and I fell to discussing the Russian war, and he remarked:

"It seems as though the Russians are following the practice of allowing the German spearheads to advance and then closing in behind them. We are not quite sure about this, but we have been watching it for the past three months. It seems to be a new kind of tactic."

I looked at Field in amazement because Russia had been using these tactics almost from the start of the war and I thought that every grammar-school boy was familiar with them. At that time I couldn't quite make up my mind whether Field was "playing dumb" or honestly was puzzled by this type of Russian tactic. I rather think, however, that he didn't understand it.

When Dennis returned to the table, Colonel Field expressed anxiety about Colonel Yeaton, the United States Army observer in Russia, who was on his way back to Washington. Field said he was concerned about the kind of report Yeaton would make, since Yeaton told Field when he passed through Singapore that the Russians were about done for, that their production was virtually stopped, and other dire things. Dennis assured Field that Yeaton's views were not shared by any other foreign observers in Russia.

Colonel Field was dressed in civilians tonight. He seemed somewhat self-satisfied, a grizzled, quiet-mannered soldier.

After dinner I joined a young American lieutenant in the medical corps who is en route to Burma. As we sat there in Raffles verandah bar, watching the handsome, smartly dressed officers with sleek hair and carefully tended mustaches dancing with gay, effervescent British girls, the young American doctor asked scornfully:

"Is there a war going on here?"

"IT CAN'T HAPPEN HERE"

Monday, November 17th:

This evening while lying in bed with a severe cold a cable came from Paul White:

> INFORMATIVELY YOU AWARDED ANNUAL SIGMA DELTA CHI JOURNALISTIC FRATERNITY PRIZE BEST RADIO REPORT YOUR EX-CAIRO DESCRIBING PARACHUTISTS ESCAPING KING. CONGRATULATIONS!

I am amazed!

Wednesday, November 19th:

Stayed in bed most of the day. I am very weak and groggy from this cold and constantly sweating. I did get up to cable a story to CBS:

"If war breaks out the British Far East command is prepared immediately to join in with Anglo-American strategical plans within the framework of Britain's ability and preparedness in Malaya."

The censor killed that for reasons I cannot figure out. Either they are prepared to do something or they are not prepared.

My story also said:

"Observers regard Britain's outstanding advantages to assist the United States in an offensive effort are the possession of Singapore Naval Base and numerous airfields with an air force at least superior to that of six months ago."

That was the only way I could inform New York that Britain had very little out here in the way of ships or aircraft and that the defense of Singapore was going to depend on American help, but you couldn't use statements as bold as that.

I also said in the same story:

"Joint British and American use of the Naval Base and other facilities remains in the same status as last July when Vice Admiral Layton, Commander-in-Chief of the China Station, said the United States can use the Base.

"Americans have attempted to arrange precise details with the British

263

in case of sudden developments, such as exact places where United States warships will be berthed, the allocation and quarters for American sailors, and arrangement of facilities and materials for the repair of American ships. The British assure the Americans that all will be ready for them when the need arises. It is recognized here that war will necessitate joint use of Singapore's facilities on the basis of virtual equality between the United States and Great Britain."

That entire story was killed by the censors and I could obtain no reason from Commander Burrows on it.

I know that the Americans here have not been able to get to first base in learning precise details and fastening down the British to a concrete plan for the joint use of the fortress of Singapore.

Thursday, November 20th:

The British started their advance into Libya on Tuesday and it was announced today. After they relieve Tobruk they will probably see how things shape up before going on toward Tripoli. The British have certainly had enough time to prepare for an advance toward Tripoli.

If they succeed in driving the Axis out of North Africa an invasion of Italy probably will be tried in the Spring. My guess is that before that happens the Germans will go into Spain, Spanish Morocco and Dakar.

Saturday, November 22nd:

I cabled CBS today:

"It would be a misrepresentation of the picture to the American public to present Britain as having a strong striking power here. Therefore, if Britain's policy will be to assist Thailand it will be necessary for the most extensive help to be given to Britain to carry out that policy. While Great Britain is in a better position with offensive weapons, such as tanks, carriers and artillery than she was six months ago her forces are primarily geared and equipped for a defensive role.

"The Japanese undoubtedly are aware of the Nazi technique to strike at a point where the interests of the various allies tug in different directions. Likewise, the Japanese obviously possess official German estimates on British high command methods and mentality based on British operations to date."

264

An American officer of importance came to the Far East recently. He fussed around Singapore for six weeks trying to get some co-operation from the British.

During this time the British pestered him for the American battle order in the Philippines.

"What do you want that for?" the American officer asked. "You are not going to fight us, are you?"

Every British Intelligence officer in Singapore individually asked the American officer who he was, what he was doing and what his plans were, etc. Finally, he turned on them and said:

"You know very well that I have just come from Japan. Why don't you ask me what the Japanese are doing? Why don't you ask me what I know about the Japanese battle plans instead of worrying about ours? Why don't you ask me how many Japanese divisions have been moved from Formosa to Indo-China? Why don't you ask me how many Japanese ships there are at Saigon?"

The British, however, did not ask him those questions.

This American officer bore the highest possible credentials from Washington. Throughout the time in Singapore he was watched. On one occasion all four of his locked suitcases were examined at his hotel. He accused British Security officers of searching his luggage. They denied it and said it was done by Japanese agents in Singapore. Finally they admitted it, claiming it was "routine."

British Security also put a dictaphone in the office of an American rubber company after an order had been issued that this firm, like other American rubber sales companies, could not import tires to sell in British Malaya. Naturally, the tire companies were bitter and some sharp words were uttered by company officials in their various sales offices. Many of them were profane condemnations of the British.

In the basement of the Fullerton Building, which was also the Post Office and housed other Government offices, British Security officers took down these dictaphone remarks. Finally the officers protested.

British Security made no complaint against the scathing attacks on British mentality and on the individual origin of the British officials here. But they did object to "you people making misstatements to the effect that you bought one hundred million dollars' worth of rubber in Malaya when it was really only sixty-two million."

265

Douglas Wilkie, the *Sydney Sun* correspondent here, cabled a story which he headlines "Blimps Rule in Malaya." He wrote:

"The Services Public Relations Office is having an irritating effect on American newsmen whereby Australia is denied publicity in the United States of incalculable value at the present time.

"The unfortunate impression is gaining ground in Malaya that the muddlers of yesterday have been shunted to the East out of harm only to become the muddlers of tomorrow."

Under the present censorship system all copy is checked by five censors, and in case there is anything out of the ordinary the copy is subject to five additional censorships.

All the correspondents are furious over the censorship of Flight Lieutenant Gerald Samson, R.A.F. Press Adviser.

When I protested against one excision to Samson and pointed out that London has been saying the very same thing for weeks, Samson replied: "How London officials censor copy and what they allow has no relation to what we censor in Singapore."

The arrests of Asiatics for being members of the Malayan Communist Party are still going on at the same rate, almost one a day. I cabled New York:

"Since it is considered illegal to belong to the Party, despite the political tie-ups of Great Britain, Russia and China, four girls charged with being senior members of the Malayan Communist Party have been sentenced to three months at hard labor and their printing press confiscated. A young building worker was given one month of hard labor for distributing Chinese leaflets of the Malacca Anti-Wang, Anti-Fascist Unity Society. The judge charged the organization was communist and anti-British."

Thank goodness the Chinese Consulate here is finally losing all patience with this business of tossing Chinese into jail. Apparently the Consulate here, or Chungking, protested to the Colonial Office in London. Sir Shenton Thomas, Colonial Governor, now must explain to the Colonial Secretary in London the circumstances in which a Singapore magistrate sentenced two Chinese to eighteen months' hard labor for aiding the Malayan Communist Party.

266

Monday, November 24th:

Commander Burrows called in the accredited correspondents this afternoon to tell us that units of the British Fleet are coming out here.

Burrows said: "They are on the way, but you can't mention it until they arrive." He added, as though imparting state secrets to enemy agents, "You see, we are taking you into our confidence."

Harold Guard told me about his latest run-in with Captain Berick.

The *United Press* has an incoming service here which supplies dispatches to the *Straits Times* and the *Singapore Free Press* from New York. Today when Berick censored out a sentence in *United Press* copy from Cairo that British losses in the Western Desert are considerable, Harold protested to Berick and pointed out that the story came from Cairo by way of New York.

"I don't believe that story came from Cairo," Berick said bluntly.

"Are you suggesting," Harold asked, "that we write the story in New York?"

"Well, the cables come from New York," Berick insinuated.

"That is a serious allegation," Harold said. "You are suggesting that either the story doesn't come from Cairo and through the British censorship, or that the story is written and faked in New York by the *United Press*. Would you put that in writing?"

Berick said he would not.

Guard left the censors' office and within an hour Berick telephoned him and said the Cairo story was all right.

I certainly have a faculty for missing good stories. Those three years in Rome were just a side show. I missed Greece, missed Russia, although by a narrow margin, and now I am missing the Western Desert show.

The other day, General Pricolo was removed as head of the Italian Air Force. The story out of Ankara today said it was because of his failure to prevent or be able to retaliate against the British attack on an Italian convoy recently in which all ten ships were sunk. Six thousand Fascist troops were supposed to have been lost, as well as large quantities of badly needed ammunition.

The answer probably is that Pricolo doesn't have the planes, his pilots no longer stomach hopeless chances, or it might be the ships carried

German troops and the Italian pilots left them in the lurch and had no intention of protecting their passage.

I cabled CBS:

"The Bangkok radio's daily warnings on the inevitability of war are being occasioned by unofficial Japanese verbal 'suggestions' that Japan take over the defense of Thailand. Thus far the Thais have refused to consider any arrangement however makeshift.

"Whether the British in the Far East intend to view the invasion of Thailand with something more than Anthony Eden's 'grave concern' is not revealed.

"I am unable to detect in Malaya what might be called 'frantic preparations for war.'

"Malaya is one country in which a substantial portion of the population wants war; that portion is made up of English, Scotch, Australian and Indian troops who are fed up with inaction and denial of the chance to participate in the Western Desert fighting.

"The eagerness of the soldiers is the one bright side in the whole Malayan picture."

That story went through without any change by the censor. A modern miracle!

Wednesday, November 26th:
The only girl I have encountered here with whom I have the slightest desire to spend the evening is a Chinese girl who, with her sister, runs a gift shop in the hotel. She is very attractive and has a strange background. Her family comes from Canton and she speaks Mandarin as well as Cantonese. She was born in South Africa, educated in England, and has lived for some time on the French Riviera. Her Singapore name is Rosa Sum and her Chinese name Ching Yeuk. I prefer Ching Yeuk to Rosa.

We went to the Cathay today and saw Shaw's *Major Barbara*, which I didn't enjoy as much as *Pygmalion*. Then we went to the Cocoanut Grove for dinner.

She is a very sweet, shy girl with jet hair, and soft almond-shaped eyes, and wears the most attractive Chinese dresses, with the slit up the side. She is engaged to an Irish doctor, who is a captain in the British

Army here and is now stationed up country somewhere, up near Penang, I think.

It was quiet and peaceful at the Cocoanut Grove, about six miles outside of Singapore. We sat on the verandah on the edge of the sea. There was a full moon, and I felt more rested than I have on any other evening since I came here. Ching Yeuk gives you the feeling of deep, quiet intelligence and centuries of patience and understanding.

Thursday, Novmber 27th:
This is Thanksgiving Day—old style. No turkey today.

It is reported that Secretary Hull handed Nomura and Kurusu a "document," which is supposed to be the terms of a sort of three months' truce. That is what the papers here say.

The *Free Press* headline this morning was: "America's 'Last Word' to Japan. All chance of agreement virtually lost. Sudden change in the United States attitude."

I understand that in Manila the American Service chiefs have told reporters: "Anything can happen tonight."

Lieutenant General A. F. Percival, the GOC Malaya, went to Sarawak on an inspection trip.

The Japanese Minister saw the Thai Premier for an hour today. The Premier, Field Marshal Tuang Bipul Songron, said in a radio speech: "We are being subjected to military, economic pressure from around us."

The Thai official quarters deny the report that Japan offered to take over the entire defense of Thailand. What else could they do but issue a denial?

The United States Marines left Shanghai today.

Friday, November 28th:
I went to the dock today to see two troopships arriving from England. I said to a group of Yorkshiremen:

"Do you think you can handle the Japs?"

"If the Jap starts anything, he'll have it."

Duff Cooper is still working his report on the Far East. He was astonished to find that Admiral Sir Geoffrey Layton was carrying on diplomatic relations with Indo-China.

269

The story I get is this: Some time ago Layton telegraphed the Admiralty that he didn't want to dissipate his forces and the French in Indo-China had some naval units which could cause some trouble and interfere with shipping. He therefore asked if he could negotiate some kind of economic and political agreement with Indo-China. He was told to go ahead. As a result he negotiated with Admiral Decoux, the Governor-General in Indo-China, an accord that if the French didn't interfere with shipping on the China coast or infringe on British naval rights then certain raw materials, but not war materials, would be sent to Indo-China.

This worked out strangely. The Free French in Singapore, the Malaya Broadcasting Company and the Ministry of Information attacked the Vichy French in Indo-China as tools of Japan.

Admiral Layton was pursuing the opposite policy of considering the Vichy French friendly to Britain. The Singapore radio went right on attacking the Vichy French in Indo-China.

Protests against the Singapore radio's attacks on the Vichy French in Indo-China came not from Admiral Decoux, or from the Saigon radio, but from Admiral Layton himself.

The Thai Consul General Luang Vudiasora Nettinate invited Captain Getchell of the United States Marine Commission and myself to a Chinese dinner at the Great Southern Hotel in South Bridge Road, which is the center of Chinatown. There is a Chinese theatre underneath, and throughout the meal we had thumping and shrill Chinese music. A Thai sea captain also was a guest. He was small, pleasant and happy-faced—but spoke no English. I speak no Thai, so we just grinned at each other.

At the table in a circular arrangement there were about a dozen small dishes and saucers of condiments. The first course was shark-fin soup and then came a whole suckling pig with the skin hard-surfaced. It had been baked in a clay oven for four hours and then put on a spit. Then it was cut in three-inch strips and served. You dip each piece into a sauce. When the young pig was stripped, denuded, it was taken away.

The next course was chicken skin which had first been roasted and then fried.

Next came the chicken roasted with shrimp. Some chicken skin came

270

along with this, all in a sauce and covered with celery leaves and rose petals.

Next came vegetables in a thick sauce. Next came sweet and sour pork, pieces of it in a thick vinegar sauce. Then came duck soup in a large bowl and in another bowl fried shrimp, ham and eggs. Next came a huge *ikan merah* and fried fish.

Throughout we had tea in small cups and afterwards fruit: apples peeled and cut in slices on ice and oranges sliced in eighths. Before and after the meal we had a steam towel dipped in eau de Cologne. It was quite a meal the Thai Consul General laid out for us. The steam towels were welcome and revivifying. The British will need more than steam towels and eau de Cologne when the Thai situation explodes.

Saturday, November 29th:
I cabled today:

"Surprisingly large number of British officers with whom I have talked this week do not believe that war is coming hereabouts. They are convinced Japan will back down. More astute observers believe that war is inevitable and insist the only mystery is when and in what precise direction Japan will attack. One observer is convinced that Japan's attack will be aimed at Manila and Borneo and believes that the threat against Shanghai is purely diversional. He says that occupation of Thailand is necessary for Japanese strategy."

Litvinov, the new Soviet Ambassador to the United States, came through here a day or two ago and I cabled:

"Ironic while the newspapers extol Litvinov and praise our Soviet ally, the police round-up of members of the Malayan Communist Party continues. One member found in possession of communist pamphlets was sentenced to six months' hard labor and the magistrate said: 'It is a pity the law of this country does not permit me to have men like you flogged.'

"An Indian civilian was sentenced to six months' hard labor for attempting to cause disaffection among troops. He halted soldiers on the roadside and allegedly said: 'The Government is your enemy and sucking your blood. The British will lose this war. I fought in the last war and got nothing.'

"During the past week I could not detect in Singapore any tensing up of the atmosphere despite the world's impression that Southeastern

271

Asia is on the brink of war. Here there is a calm, serene aloofness from the war that has been going on. There is still dancing every night at Raffles, Seaview and Adelphi Hotels, with officers and women dressed in formal clothes.

"People are not buying any stocks of food and a Singapore resident said to me: 'It will take bombs dropping on Singapore to convince this town the war is actually going on.' This is due to the innate lethargy of Singapore and the certainty of most Singaporians that the Japs are not going to fight and the conviction they have that the United States air forces and fleet will join in immediately, if war should come."

I was rather surprised that story went through, but it did, and my hope was that New York would recognize that the state of mind in Singapore was: It can't happen here; it would not happen; and therefore why do anything about it?

The first test came at 7:10 this evening. I was at the Pavilion cinema with Ching Yeuk, the Chinese girl, when notices were flashed on the screen that all British troops were to return to their barracks immediately. About a half dozen officers and men left. I went downstairs and telephoned Harold Guard of the *United Press* to tip him off. Harold wasn't there, but his assistant hadn't heard about it. I tried to make several other checks, but no one seemed to know anything about it. Later in the evening I cabled CBS:

"A complete state of readiness for a sudden emergency ordered in Singapore and Malaya tonight. All British troops were ordered this evening to report immediately to their barracks. Notices were flashed on cinema screens and military police rushed to all hang-outs and rounded up troops off duty. All cars throughout Singapore stopped for investigation. Military police were stationed around all bars and hotels to prevent entrance of troops. Officials described the stand-to order 'a normal precautionary measure' to indicate high command wants all troops in readiness for instant use."

Shortly after sending that story to the censor at the cable office I got a tip that, although the story was released in Malaya and broadcast over the Singapore radio, it could not be cabled abroad. I thereupon immediately sent another story on the atmosphere in Singapore, attempting to tip off New York to the fact that there was a state of emergency in Malaya over the week-end. I cabled:

"Singapore gaiety tonight is in sharp contrast with the grimness I encountered in Belgrade a few hours before the German bombs dropped. A tour of Singapore tonight, however, disclosed fewer soldiers visiting the usual Saturday-night haunts, such as the taxi-dance halls. Whatever the next forty-eight hours may bring is uncertain, but it is obvious that the British are alert for unusual developments. This naturally involves a readiness of troops, air patrols and naval patrols for an emergency. What opinions the high command has of the probability of war remain a secret, but I have talked with scores of people this week who do not believe the war is coming and are convinced the Japs will back down."

I hope that story got through.

The battle cry here remains: "Boy! *Satu whisky ayer. Tiga gin pahit. Lekas!*"

It synthesizes most of the thoughts and a good part of the conversation: "One whisky water, three gins, and jump to it, boy!"

This was St. Andrew's Night and after I finished writing the stories about 11 P.M., Ching Yeuk and I went to the dance being held at Raffles Hotel. Ching was beautiful in a white silk Chinese dress and wore a pale violet orchid in her hair. There seemed to be just about as many officers as on a normal Saturday night.

Ching is something like a fine Chinese painting, the same serenity, delicacy and imagination, but, fortunately, more animated. I get a tremendous kick out of some of her pronunciations of English words. She pronounces seventy "sumpty" and slum "slump." Sometimes, too, she says "Cecilblown" and then corrects herself charmingly.

Too, Ching has given me a good deal of information about so-called society in Singapore and on various personalities. She knows everyone.

Ching was the only Chinese girl at the dance tonight. I certainly hope that some of those British officers and civilians who are round-shouldered from upholding the white man's burden were a bit disconcerted by the presence of a Chinese girl.

A sign over the entrance to the ballroom read: "No dancing except in formal dress."

I was one of the few men there not dressed in formal clothes. It seems immoral for any Britons to wear formal dress in Singapore when their country is at war and this spot on the verge of catastrophe.

Ching pointed out a number of husbands who were cheating on their wives and vice versa. For some reason, these people tell their troubles and sexual conquests to Ching.

It is difficult to distinguish Eurasians. There was one girl dancing on the floor who was blonde, fair and attractive and very Anglo-Saxon looking. Her mother was half Japanese and her father English. Another in white—one of the new-style evening dresses with the exposed stomach—looked typically English and was actually half Chinese. The general attitude is that a Eurasian is more "acceptable" than a full-blooded native.

After the dance Ching and I drove for two hours around Singapore Island. It was a beautiful night—full moon and occasional clouds.

I told Ching not to worry and I remarked, "We are on the verge of tremendous things here and you must begin preparations for your safety and that of your mother and sister."

"I shall stay here," Ching said.

"Yes, I suppose you will. I suggest you move out of the downtown area and get a place out in open country. When war starts they are going to bomb hell out of Singapore. There is no use taking too many chances."

Ching is doing volunteer nursing duty.

Sunday, November 30th:
All day I traveled around town and talked with a number of people. I can detect no increasing tension in the atmosphere, and the general attitude of unreality persists.

The papers report that Hal Denny, of the *New York Times,* Eddie Ward, of BBC, and Godfrey Anderson, of the *Associated Press,* were captured by the Fascists in the Western Desert.

An Indian today gave me two of the most diplomatic, noncommittal answers I have encountered. I talked with a subadar of the Gurkhas and asked how he would like fighting the Japs.

"I understand," he said, "the Japanese are in Indo-China and contemplate an invasion of Thailand." He spoke very precise English.

I then asked how he liked being in Malaya.

"We are allies of the British and therefore I am very pleased to be here."

I know when I have been told off.

274

SEVEN DAYS
BEFORE THE BOMBS

Monday, December 1st:
Major-General Thomas Blamey, Commander of the Australian Forces in the Middle East, said in an interview at Raffles Hotel:

"The Australian public would like to see the United States more in the war than they are now.

"American armed forces would be the biggest factor in saving civilization. If democracy is to be preserved, then all the democratic nations must put all their weight into the fight. I've got such faith in the individuals in the democracies that I am sure they will."

Alfred Duff Cooper has just come back from Australia and New Zealand after a month's tour. He said at an interview today:

"From Australians themselves I found a criticism that Australia is not taking the war seriously enough. I didn't encounter that myself. My own impression, considering that Australia is many thousands of miles away and that they are enjoying great prosperity, high wages and no unemployment, is that they do not lack any consciousness of the war. Production is very impressive. They are working twenty-four hours a day and most of them seven days a week."

I came back to Raffles Hotel and wrote this story and sent it off to CBS:

"Singapore has officially proclaimed a state of emergency and mobilization of volunteers in the army, air forces and navy. Throughout the morning civilians streamed out of the stores and offices carrying tin helmets and reporting to barracks. The atmosphere here is electric and Singaporians for the first time are realizing that war might strike here. The atmosphere in the Chinese section can be described as tense, and precautions are being made to prevent disorder in the event of bombings.

"Singapore streets are uniquely deserted of soldiers on leave and the only troops visible are military police and guards with rifles stationed at strategic intersections and at public buildings. Special guards were ordered for the radio station and communications centers. Sporting events and social affairs were ordered canceled. ARP wardens were ordered to stand by.

"Officers away from barracks for the first time are carrying pistols. Troops are now semi-deployed at action stations throughout Malaya. Numerous pillboxes and positions along the coast are now manned. There is considerable activity and movement going on in Northern Malaya in case the Japanese invade Thailand. Lieutenant General A. E. Percival, Commander of the troops in Malaya, cut short his inspection in Sarawak and returned to Singapore today. Naval officers and ratings are remaining at their barracks ready for instant call. Royal Air Force is described as 'alert' but officials maintain a peculiar silence on what is the minimum involved in this alert.

"People are eagerly awaiting units of the British fleet which London announces are en route to the Far East. At the present moment there is no exodus from Singapore but it is expected if war breaks out. Many Europeans said to me: 'I am more worried what the Asiatics will do when the bombs drop than I am over the bombs themselves.' The most frequent question I am asked: 'Is America coming in?' indicating that among the British the uppermost question is: 'What help will America give us?'"

The most startling report of the day comes from Manila that sixteen Japanese warships, including cruisers and an airplane carrier, are in the Japanese mandated islands ready for a thrust at Borneo.

Tuesday, December 2nd:
This afternoon the accredited war correspondents were taken to the Naval Base to watch the arrival of the warships. We stood atop a signal tower at the Base and watched the *Prince of Wales* coming up the Johore Straits and also the battle cruiser *Repulse* and six destroyers.

Commander Burrows was in charge of the party and we were forced to remain a mile away from the Straits. We would have had a better view by staying right in Singapore and watching them skirting the bay.

Three Australian correspondents who were not accredited as war correspondents were refused permission by Commander Burrows to go to the Base to see the fleet come in.

All the correspondents came away from the Base sizzling with rage. The whole idea was to get tremendous publicity on the British Far East fleet here and therefore scare out the Japs. We were only permitted to say: "*Prince of Wales* and other units of the British Far East fleet have arrived at Singapore."

I did not send the story.

Only two Australians were allowed to witness the arrival: Ian Fitchett, the official AIF war correspondent, and Ray Maley of the Australian *Associated Press*. Both of them are accredited by the War Office, but three other Australians, Fraser of the *Melbourne Sun*, Fairholl of the *Sydney Telegraph* and Wilkie of the *Sun Herald Service*, were not invited. However, in the official party there were several correspondents who, like these three Australians, were not accredited by the War Office.

Fraser protested about being excluded but was informed the party already was too large. Fairholl was told the party was visiting secret defense areas. Wilkie, because of his feud with Commander Burrows and SPRO, was ignored altogether.

Roosevelt has asked Tokyo to explain the reason for increasing forces in Indo-China.

My guess is that war will probably come within a month, and perhaps less.

Wednesday, December 3rd:
Sir Robert Brooke-Popham, Commander-in-Chief, Far East, gave a general press interview at his headquarters out near the Golf Club. His aide, Wing Commander Doivall, and about thirty correspondents were there. We were all rather grim. We sat at a series of tables with pads of paper in front of us. Sir Robert was pretty much the same as usual—bashful, hemming and hawing—but more tired than I had seen him any previous time.

"I dare say," he began, "you know that the responsibility for press services has been transferred from Admiral Layton to myself.

"The second reason for the conference is that the situation is getting to a somewhat interesting phase. I thought it a good thing from your

277

point of view and mine to give some background so that you will be able to paint the picture when the incident occurs. I might also point out that this is all off the record."

All the correspondents looked at one another because, while the world was waiting to find out what Singapore would or would not do, what Singapore was getting ready for or wasn't getting ready for, we were now to be treated to an off-the-record talk.

"The objective of the British Empire," Sir Robert said sententiously, "and I may say the U. S. A., is to avoid war with the Japanese at the present time. We don't want it. We have plenty in hand with Germany.

"I think the Japanese are a bit uncertain about what action they are going to take. In Japan there are a certain number of extremists and the sensible people are holding back the extremists.

"We don't want to say anything [by that he meant, you correspondents don't want to say anything] that extremists can seize upon. They are on the lookout for anything said by anyone in authority or anything someone is reported to have said. That is one reason why this is not a press conference.

"Now we'll talk about Japan," Sir Robert said, taking a deep breath. "It is very difficult to see the logic of Japan going to war now. If Japan goes to war with the U. S. A., Great Britain goes in in accordance with the Churchill declaration. Our going in means bringing in the Dutch and quite possibly Russia.

"Not the wildest extremist in Japan thinks she would have a short war against such a combination, even if he thinks Japan would win it.

"The freezing order had a greater effect than the Japanese realized. The whole of their transoceanic trade disappeared. What Japan has to do is settle the China Incident. That's the main obstacle of settlement in the Far East. We are not going to let China down.

"Japan's concern was to cut the Burma Road and she gave certain indications two months ago of going to the Burma Road.

"It doesn't look now as if Japan is going to make an overland attack through Yunan, but she is making airfields in North Indo-China for an attack. She can carry out an aerial attack through Yunnan any time by shipping a few squadrons.

"Germany no doubt is pressing Japan to attack as many Russian troops as possible. She is also inducing Japan to attract as many British troops as possible out here.

278

"I think that the Germans and Japanese have a very great distrust of each other. I think, however, that the Japanese Cabinet will follow what is best for Japan. Both Russia and Japan still have large forces up there, which each is almost bound to keep. Now there is no indication of any Japanese offensive against Russia.

"Another reason for Japan wanting to go to war is oil. I don't know how much oil Japan has. I don't think anyone knows. Wherever Japan goes for oil she must go to British sources or sources inside N.E.I. If she attempts any war, there she is up against the whole lot—the United States and everyone else.

"Japan must be aware of the plans to wreck the sources of oil for a long time—reckoned in years not in months—before she could get supplies from them.

"From the point of view of logic, Japan's best hope is to sever connection with the Axis and come in under the Roosevelt-Churchill declaration.

"That," Sir Robert said, a little grimly, "is very unlikely, and she could only do it with great loss of face. That being so she may prefer war with little hope of victory rather than climbing down under the conditions laid down by the U.S.A.

"It is very dangerous to look at Japan with what we call Western spectacles. We must look at them through Eastern eyes.

"One must be prepared for Japan going off the rails and coming into the war even though it is against the logic of facts."

Someone asked Sir Robert what the significance was of the change in the Japanese Cabinet in putting Tojo in as Prime Minister.

"The people of Japan," Sir Robert said, "were getting sick of the Konoye Government. They were getting sick of no progress with the China war and of negotiations with the United States. The Tojo Cabinet was put in to lead on the extremists or to control them. There is nothing to show yet that Tojo has lost his hold on the extremists but one wonders if the extremists are not beginning to accuse him of extremist actions."

That remark didn't quite make sense to me so I asked Sir Robert: "What is Japan going to do?"

"Although Japan does not have any particular affection for Germany, being on the initiative, she is quite likely to copy Germany's methods whenever applicable," Sir Robert said. "That is, to strike at the weaknesses rather than strength and accomplish her objectives by intimidations rather than war."

On my notes I drew a heavy circle around that remark because there I felt was the clue to the British state of mind here—that war might come but very probably would not because Japan is now afraid of the British power at Singapore and is going to try and continue her war of nerves and attempt to gain her objectives by intimidation.

I scribbled on my notes: "They think it ain't going to happen."

Sir Robert went on with his explanation: "Japan might place air squadrons in Thailand or she might send ten, twenty, or forty thousand troops into Thailand."

"What would happen if Japan went into Thailand?" asked McDaniel of the *Associated Press.*

"I don't know what our or the U. S. A. position would be, but it is quite certain that the Japanese don't know what our position would be.

"She may attempt to get control of Thailand by intimidation, Fifth-Column work, and possibly a *coup d'etat.* I suggest," Sir Robert said, "that's the next step. But then too, the extremists might get control, get desperate, see red, run like a mad dog. If that happens Japan might go for North Malaya or might go for the Philippines.

"She has pretty strong forces in Indo-China, quite sufficient forces to make it a good chance for walking into Thailand. She has at least sixty thousand troops available for that."

"Do you know what air strength Japan has?" asked Selby Walker of *Reuters.*

"She has a pretty strong air force including long-distance bombers. One of the divisions in Indo-China has been training for landing operations. She also has a number of land craft. Oh, yes," Sir Robert laughed, "Japan's ready to make an overseas expedition which from Indo-China might also go to the Philippines. But," he added hastily, and quietly, "the fact that she has preparations doesn't mean she is going to do it.

"You see Japan has miscalculated on the strength of the United States' stand and attitude and on the rigid enforcement of the freezing order."

"What do you think is going to happen?" I asked again.

"Well," Sir Robert said, "we are looking about, wondering what Japan is going to do. Japan doesn't seem to have a policy of what to do, step by step. You know there are signs of defense steps, too. She is doing things in Indo-China to defend herself there. Japan is beginning to be afraid she is going to be attacked."

Sir Robert then shifted to the situation right here.

"I feel," Sir Robert said, "that most people in Malaya were quite certain that war would never come here and today it occurs to them—'Good God, it may come after all!'

"Now that some units of the fleet are here, there may be a tendency to think that we can go back to sleep. The fleet is no good if it is tied to its base. It must have mobility, not be tied to the defense of Malaya," the Air Marshal explained.

"There must be no slackening off of defense or training. With the fleet here the defense of the Naval Base becomes more important than ever. The volunteers are not up to the established quotas. The Asiatics are not volunteering very rapidly."

One correspondent asked if Sir Robert had any commitment from the United States.

"The absence of the United States' commitment, that she will go in if Britain is attacked, does not affect our plans. Of course we assume she will. We've got our plans with America for co-operation but we also have our plans if she doesn't—made months and months ago and kept up to date. Our greatest worry is about a deficiency in airplanes. The forces the Americans have in the Philippines all link up nicely.

"We think that the Japanese cannot amass more than five to six hundred aircraft for a campaign in the Southwest Pacific. That is more aircraft than we have here but it is not as many as we can get together in the Philippines, the Dutch East Indies and Malaya. We three outnumber the Japanese. All together we should have about seven hundred and fifty planes."

"What will Britain do if Japan attacks Russia instead of coming down here?"

"If war breaks between Japan and Russia," Sir Robert said, "we would be bound to come in sooner or later, and if we get involved here with Japan, Russia would come in."

This indicated for the first time to my knowledge that there might be a secret agreement between Britain and Russia to go to the help of the other in case of attack. At least the way Sir Robert phrased it, it sounded almost bilateral: that if Japan attacked Britain then Russia

281

would go in and if Japan attacked Russia, Britain would join with the Soviets.

Kennard of the Malaya Broadcasting asked how American planes compared with Japanese.

"Oh, we are not worried about that," Sir Robert said.

"But what about these Brewster Buffaloes—are they good enough?"

"They could give a very good account of themselves," Sir Robert assured us.

"Don't you think that we need some of the machines that Britain has at home?"

"Oh, no," Sir Robert said scornfully. "If we need any of these super-Spitfires and hyper-Hurricanes we can get them out here quick enough."

The use of those adjectives applied to Britain's best fighter aircraft conveyed to me that Sir Robert was convinced that the aircraft available here were good enough and in sufficient numbers to handle the Japs.

Admiral Sir Tom Phillips is going to Manila tomorrow to confer with Admiral Hart, so Sir Robert Brooke-Popham said. Phillips flew out here from England a few days ago, ahead of the *Prince of Wales,* which is his flagship.

After coming back to town I got hints that some of the other correspondents were going to file stories on the Brooke-Popham meeting and I therefore cabled to CBS the gist of the interview, omitting all military information of value to Japan.

Late this afternoon Major Fisher handed me my red-backed War Office license as an accredited war correspondent. Up until now I have been using a temporary certificate, and that means it has taken just exactly six months for the War Office to send the book showing accreditation to the British forces. As Major Fisher gave it to me, he said:

"The War Office today inquired why you do not broadcast any more from Singapore. They ask me to facilitate your broadcasting from here in every possible way. Is there anything I can do to put you on the air?"

"No, I don't think so, Major. CBS has taken a lot of kicking around here. Perhaps some day we will do more broadcasting."

282

"If there's anything I can do to arrange facilities, let me know because the War Office wants broadcasts out of here."

"Thanks very much."

That was that.

Public Relations Office called and said that we could now put out a story on the interview with Sir Robert Brooke-Popham (the censors killed the previous story). We cannot, however, mention his name, and all stories are to be submitted to Sir Robert.

The lead on my story was:

"Informed quarters whose reliability unquestioned asserted Japan now virtually certain to engage in military operations and direction will be southward."

When I got the copy of my 270-word cable back from the censor the lead had been changed to read:

"Informed quarters asserted Japan not certain engaging in military operations."

That, of course, changed the whole sense. My effort was to try to convey to the American people that war was coming out here. The deletions were typical, not so much of censorship, but of the unalterable confusion of the civilian and military and the censors. The British still believed war was not coming.

The idiocy of that blue pencil by the censor was established significantly because my next sentence in the cable story to CBS, which was untouched, brought out the original sense of the lead:

"The strongest indications are that Thailand will be the first objective with Nazi-style nerve war of brief duration followed by military action if Bangkok fails to gain a quick comprehension of the advantage of Japan's protective custody."

The rest of the story then used a number of quotations from the Brooke-Popham interview.

As a result of the avalanche of criticism over the propaganda on the arrival of the naval units, almost every correspondent in Singapore was taken to the Naval Base to visit the battleship *Prince of Wales*. We were escorted by Captain John Leach, a tall, slim, jolly officer of great friendliness who bore no relation to the stuffed shirts he is going to have to deal with here.

Saturday, December 6th:

My cable to CBS said:

"Further precautionary measures throughout Malaya have just been ordered. All troops were called to their barracks and sailors recalled to their ships at five o'clock this afternoon. The mobilization of volunteers has been completed and there is widespread talk that there will be an emergency in Singapore over the week-end.

"The *Prince of Wales* and other units of the Eastern fleet are completing taking on stores and are believed preparing to move off on a moment's notice.

"Air and sea patrols are extremely active in the event the Japanese attempt a surprise move over the week-end. The roads in Malaya are very busy with troops and trucks moving into position. Coastal defenses are reported manned and there is considerable activity going on at the Malaya-Thailand border.

"An order was suddenly issued barring the departure from Malaya of all non-Britishers without permission. Twenty Japanese businessmen scheduled to sail for Bangkok aboard a Thai ship this morning were yanked off with their baggage and their departure delayed.

"Japanese influence on the life of Singapore is being eliminated. Most of the Japanese photography shops are being taken over by Chinese. Some Japanese barbers are still operating but all of them say they expect to close down soon. This is also true of the Japanese massage parlors as well as Japanese dentists."

The Eastern News, which is the local name for the Japanese *Domei* propaganda agency, ceased functioning this week and the manager is going to Japan. The Japanese-owned *Singapore Herald* is continuing to publish and so is the vernacular *Singapore Nippo*, printed in Japanese.

Suemasa Okamoto, the new Japanese Consul General replacing Ken Tsurumi, arrived from Bangkok yesterday and said: "I have nothing to say."

The *Singapore Herald* during this past week has been distorting the headlines and ignoring certain developments in order to maintain its constant thesis—"Peace can still be saved."

Typical of this is the editorial today which says:

"The browbeating by Anglo-American officials will never achieve peace. Only by patience and through understanding, not of what the Japanese military rants about, but what the Japanese people feel, can Nippon be brought around. Japanese prestige and morale are high and they are high enough to send a well-disciplined army and highly trained navy into action. But the way to go about these negotiations is not to wave the too-familiar Yankee big stick or speaking vigorously but using calm reason and calm facts to convince the Japanese."

I don't know why the hell they don't bar the *Singapore Herald*.

The British efforts here to recruit large numbers of Chinese and other Asiatics into the armed forces thus far have not been successful. Throughout the city there are billboards showing a Chinese soldier in a British tin hat and spread across the billboard is this plea: "Join the Volunteer Forces." Underneath it:

Free Food
Free Clothes
Free Housing
Free Training

This is the first time I have ever seen a country offering soldiers free training. What the devil do the British expect here—the Asiatic volunteers to pay for their training?

There is no doubt that the possibility of war is now beginning to penetrate the skulls of some of the people in Singapore. They can't help being impressed by the fact that on this Saturday night at Raffles Hotel there weren't as many men dancing because most of the officers are held at their barracks and on their ships, and those who are there are carrying guns.

They must also have been impressed by the number of trucks and troops and guns moving along the road to take positions. Civilians are not evacuating any towns in Malaya and there is no sandbagging of buildings going on, although some have been sandbagged since the start of the war in 1939.

No new barbed-wire is being put up around the water front to reinforce the single barbed-wire guarding one section in the main part of the city near the Fullerton Building.

The authorities are clamping down very hard on violators of the

285

fixed prices. A Chinese was fined $500 for charging eleven cents for carrots instead of four cents.

I think it is the first time in history that Malayan Mohammedans are volunteering to contribute their blood to the blood bank being organized here. I thought it was contrary to Moslem law. The first to register to give their blood were Malayan policemen.

Harold Guard of *United Press* had a story in his incoming service today—I think from Manila or from New York—that the Japanese fleet was sighted on the move. The censors held it up and for a time he was not permitted to distribute it to his clients here. Commander Burrows said to him: "You certainly like your bit of yellow-sheet scaremongering."

He laughed at the story.

Sunday, December 7th:

In mid-afternoon I cabled this story to CBS:

"Strong indications Japanese are moving up ships and troops to launch an imminent attack with landing parties against Thailand with immediate objectives of capturing Bangkok. Reconnaissance by American-made Catalinas and Hudson bombers discovered units of Japanese navy, including cruisers and merchant ships believed containing troops, are now steaming down the Gulf of Siam along the Indo-China coast in the direction of Thailand.

"British aircraft sighted extremely heavy shipping activity less than three hundred miles distant from Malaya coming from Saigon and Camranh Bay rounding Cambodia Point which is 400 miles distant from Bangkok. Since there is not a good harborage between Cambodia Point and Bangkok, Japanese naval movement in northwesterly direction appears to mean that the Japanese intend to make Bangkok their next point.

"I understand British naval patrols are extremely active and units of the Eastern fleet are disposed for immediate action. Aircraft at all Malaya airfields are disposed and fighters are ready to take off. The big question in Malaya is what will the British do if Thailand is attacked.

"Pillboxes lining the Malaya coast are now manned and shore batteries pointing toward the sea with their crews on constant duty.

Sarawak and North Borneo are also in a state of emergency and assisting air patrols in the South China Sea."

.Most of the information for that story came from a press conference.

Guard of *UP* told me this morning he had another run-in with the censors when the naval recalls were issued yesterday and all the men ordered to their ships at once. Harold cabled a story that "something" was expected within forty-eight hours.

"They cut it out," Guard said, "and they gave me hell for spreading alarmist reports."

Tonight with Ching Yeuk I took a drive around Singapore and around the outskirts to see what I could find and saw nothing worthy of any particular note. There seemed to be a great number of watchmen around places, but nothing else that warrants sending a story.

Monday, December 8th:
At 4 A.M. this morning the phone rang on the desk in the verandah of my apartment at Raffles and I stumbled out to lift the receiver:

"This is Major Fisher. Will you come to press headquarters right away? We have an announcement to make."

"I'll be right there." I said to myself: "It can only be one thing."

I put the phone down on its cradle and just then there was a heavy boom, then three more in quick succession. I know a bomb when I hear one, and those were bombs. I scrambled into my clothes, grabbed my typewriter and found a rickshaw in front of the hotel. The coolie was wide-eyed with wonder and broken sleep, and all I could get out of him was, "What is, master? What is, master?"

"Bombs!" I shouted. "The hell with them. Take me to the Union Building."

"I no go there—not go." The bombs had fallen in that direction.

"Like hell you're not going. I'll give you two dollars." (The ordinary fare is thirty cents).

"All light—go."

We started out and I yelled: "Hurry—hurry—fast!"

He turned around and grunted at me, but nothing else.

There were practically no other vehicles on Beach Road, and every light in Singapore was still on. The lights in the harbor were ablaze. As I went by the Fullerton Building I saw just for an instant where

287

the bombs had hit in Raffles Square and in the darkness in that area I saw a group of men beginning to gather.

When I got to the Union Building press headquarters, three or four other correspondents had already arrived and more were coming in.

Major Fisher was very calm. "Well," he said, "you all know what it is and we are now getting a communiqué ready."

My story went off at 4:45 A.M., Singapore time, which was 4:15 P.M. Sunday, New York time. I cabled:

"The Japanese forced a landing in Northern Malaya and bombed Singapore. The sudden attack on Malaya was first attempted at 1 A.M. and was repulsed by small army and anti-aircraft fire, it was officially announced. Later Japanese troops succeeded in landing on the beach at Padang Sabak and were last reported infiltrating toward Kota Bahru, advance airdrome five miles from the Thailand border beside the China Sea.

"The Japanese are now being engaged by British troops. British aircraft was already engaging enemy ships and attacking troops who have landed. Ten Japanese ships are reported off Bachok a few miles south of Kota Bahru.

"Bombing of Singapore was totally unexpected by civilians. At this moment numerous aircraft are roaring overhead but I cannot tell whether they are Japanese or British."

As we were writing our stories a correspondent telephoned in that he was unable to get to headquarters because a bomb had blocked the road.

At 7:30 I called Captain Getchell, who also lives at the Raffles, and asked him what the latest news was over the radio. He said he did not know, that he had just awakened.

"For Christ's sake!" I said. "The war is on."

"You're kidding."

"No. Singapore was bombed three hours ago. Could I come over and hear your radio?"

I went over and heard a news report from San Francisco that reported the bombing of Pearl Harbor.

The shocking news from the whole Far East is splashed in a one-page extra of the *Singapore Free Press*. Pearl Harbor, the Philippines, Hongkong attacked. It is almost unbelievable. Pearl Harbor!

288

I shaved, had breakfast and at eight o'clock went back for another press conference. Another communiqué was issued, but everything seems pretty confused. It is now established that the Japanese effected landings at two points in Northern Malaya and are trying to capture the airdrome of Kota Bahru, which is extremely vital.

A bulletin just issued reports that Japanese surface ships are retiring at high speed and the few troops left on the beaches are now being heavily machine-gunned. But it can't be determined whether the Japanese landing attempts have been repulsed.

I pointed out in my story that Singaporians were shocked by the outbreak of the war and were convinced that Malaya would not be attacked, and that in my talks with scores of officers during the past weeks everyone without exception said: "There·will be no war with the Japanese."

I put this in my story and it was passed by the censor, together with the sentence:

"Whether this was also the conviction of the high command cannot be determined, but it is certain that the Japanese achieved a certain amount of surprise."

Some of the British correspondents said to me, "Well, now you Americans are in it."

"Yes, we sure are. I hope to God we don't make the same mistakes that the British have been making."

"Well, you already have. That Pearl Harbor doesn't sound so good."

"Yes, I know it doesn't. But we'll get them yet."

"Well, Brownie, you always said you wouldn't do any propaganda. Now how do you feel about it?" asked Gallagher of the *London Daily Express*.

"I still feel the same way, Gallagher. I'm not doing any propaganda. I'm still going to call the shots as I see them."

AFTER DECEMBER 7TH

PRELUDE TO DROWNING

A group of us were drinking at the Raffles bar around noon and figuring on how we could all get up to the front in a hurry. We were griping, too, that even if we did get up to the front we probably could not get our stories back to the cable office because SPRO had made no arrangements for that.

After tossing the war back and forth for about an hour, three of us left and went into the dining room for lunch—Gallagher, Tom Fairholl of the *Sydney Telegraph* and myself. I was just eating my ice cream for dessert when one of the Malay clerks came back to the dining room and said I was wanted on the phone. I went out. It was Major Fisher.

"Do you want to go on a four-day assignment?"

"What is it?" I asked.

"I can't tell you what it is, or where you are going, but I must have an immediate yes or no and you must leave at once. At once."

I hesitated for a fraction of a second and said, "All right, I'll take it."

I came back to the table, took another spoonful of ice cream and remarked to Gallagher and Fairholl: "That was Major Fisher. He asked me if I wanted to go on an assignment for four days. I don't know what it is and he can't tell me. I said I'd go, but I don't know. I hate to leave Singapore when this story is just beginning."

"I agree with you," Gallagher said. "I wouldn't go."

"That's the way I feel about it. There is no time to ask New York if I can leave town and there's no one to cover CBS while I'm away."

Just then Gallagher was called to the telephone, and as he left I said to Fairholl: "I'll bet he is going to have the same problem presented to him."

"I wouldn't go," Fairholl said. "Singapore is where the story is at the moment and I know my office would raise the devil if I pulled out."

"Well, Tom, I know mine will too, but I'm going to ride with it for the moment because SPRO said they'd be here in a minute and pick me up."

Gallagher, even more red-faced than usual, rushed up to the table and grabbed hold of my arm.

"Cec," Gallagher panted, "it's the *Prince of Wales*! We're going on the *Prince of Wales*. We've got to pull out right away. They're on the way now for us."

"Wait a minute, Gallagher. I thought you said you wouldn't pull out of Singapore at this moment?"

"But, Jesus, it's the *Prince of Wales*! They're just asking one American and one Britisher to go."

Gallagher was breathless.

"Yes, it sounds swell, Gallagher, but cool off. We go out there for four days and come back with nothing. Meanwhile Singapore and this whole damn war has gone uncovered."

"I know, Cec, I feel the same way," and then he slumped into the chair. "Oh, Christ, I don't know what to do. What are you going to do?"

"Gallagher, it's a chance, but why don't we take it? When we get back we'll probably be fired and then we'll start a newspaper or radio station of our own."

"Fine! They're coming for us right away to go to the Naval Base."

"Aw, they're not in that big a hurry. I'm going to get my typewriter and change of clothes, a razor and toothbrush."

"You don't have time."

"I'm taking *my* time. They don't expect me to go on an assignment without a typewriter."

"Well, mine's down at the Public Relations Office. If they haven't gone I'll telephone them to bring it up with them."

I dashed up to the second floor, grabbed my new portable typewriter, some carbon and paper, threw a pair of khaki pants and an extra shirt into a small handmade bag which my wife had bought for me in Rome for an anniversary. Fortunately I had about a half dozen extra packs of film for my Plaubel Makina. I tossed the camera into the suitcase with the film and an exposure meter and dashed downstairs.

Lieutenant Reynolds was there, screaming his head off.

"For Christ's sake, Brown, we've got to get you off. You're holding us up. Hurry up."

I set the typewriter and my suitcase down on the floor, grabbed a telegraph blank off the counter, and scribbled:

294

We jumped into the car, drove two blocks to the Capitol Apartments to pick up Lieutenant Abrahams, the Admiralty photographer, who was going along. Abrahams was a bit disorganized, so we lost about five minutes.

Gallagher told Reynolds to send his typewriter, which was at the Public Relations Office, out to the Naval Base in another car to try to catch up with us en route. Reynolds said he would.

"Have a good time," he said.

"Listen, Reynolds," I said, "if anything happens, send all my stuff; it's all there in my room at the Raffles Hotel, Room 48; send all my stuff to CBS, New York. Just address it CBS, New York."

"Nothing's going to happen. Don't be silly."

"All right, I hope not. But if it does, send it to CBS, New York."

The Malay driver stepped on it, and when we were almost near the Naval Base we saw another car with one of the conducting officers. We signaled to it and stopped in the middle of the road, and Gallagher got his typewriter.

We pushed on and got to the dock at the Naval Base where the *Prince of Wales* was tied up.

We carried our stuff up the gangway and onto the wide, expansive quarter-deck of the *Prince of Wales*. Captain Leach, the skipper, was there and we shook hands heartily all around.

"Very happy to have you with us," the captain said. "We don't have much time. One of the men will take care of your bags."

This was the real thing. How powerful this ship is! I thought. What tremendous guns! What a fine-looking gang of men!

"We must hurry. We have the launch all ready for you."

"Ready for what, Captain Leach?" I asked.

"They're waiting for you on the *Repulse* and then we're going to move out."

"On the *Repulse*?" Gallagher exclaimed.

"Yes," Captain Leach replied.

"But we're going on the *Prince of Wales*," I said.

"I'm sorry, there must be some misunderstanding. The arrangements were made for you to go on the *Repulse*."

295

"But they said it was to be the *Prince of Wales*," Gallagher insisted.

"This makes all the difference in the world," I said. "It makes a hell of a lot of difference if you can begin your story by saying, 'I stood on the bridge of the *Prince of Wales* when we sank four Jap battleships,' rather than if you say, 'I stood on the bridge of the *Repulse*.'"

Captain Leach laughed. "Yes, I can understand that. There's more name value from your point of view to the *Prince of Wales*."

"That's it," Gallagher said. "Can't you find room for us on the *Wales*?"

"Really, I'm terribly sorry, but there just isn't room."

"We'll sleep on the deck," Gallagher said.

"I'm terribly sorry, but we're just jammed up. I have 1,760 men on board and we just don't have an inch of room. You will be very comfortable on the *Repulse*. It's all the same. We're all going on the same mission."

Gallagher and I scratched our chins and looked very downcast.

"Well," Captain Leach said, "you talk it over," and moved away.

Gallagher and I then wrestled with our problem.

"How do you feel about it, Gal?" I asked. "After all, the *Wales* is the big name. If nothing happens on this show, we can't even mention the *Repulse* because the name has never been released here and our stories would have to be that we were out on a unit of the Far East fleet, which was headed by the *Prince of Wales*. In other words, we'll have no story at all."

Gallagher agreed and said: "From a story point of view the whole thing's a washout, but there is no time for any other correspondent to be sent out from Singapore to go on the story."

"Well, since we've come this far, Gal, why don't we go on with it? We'll have a sea trip for four days and when we get back we're going to get fired anyhow."

Gallagher mumbled agreement.

We called to Captain Leach: "We're ready to shove off. We're going to carry on."

"That's fine," he said. "The launch is ready and waiting."

We walked down the gangway from the officers' side of the ship and stepped into the admiral's launch.

Captain Leach stood at the top of the gangway and called to us:

"You will be very comfortable on the *Repulse* and they have made arrangements for you to have a good time."

"Thank you, sir," I called back. "Take care of yourself."

We went aboard the *Repulse* at 5:15 and almost at once we began moving out. A young lieutenant of the Royal Marines said he had been assigned to look after us and we stood on the forward deck of the ship playing with a black kitten. It had difficulty standing up; its legs were weak from rickets. It was very playful and I dangled a string for it to grasp at as the *Repulse* moved down the Straits of Johore.

"What the hell are we going to do for four days?" I asked of the lieutenant, still very much worried that I had done the wrong thing by leaving Singapore—and the coverage of the war—for four days.

"Oh, we may have something. We might even have movies. We had a picture last night aboard."

I asked what it was and he said, *"Arise, My Love,* with Claudette Colbert."

At 6:20 the *Repulse* drew out into the Straits of Johore. We moved at half speed. It was a beautiful evening, that twilight of Monday, December 8th. The bright-red sunset silhouetted the palms on the shore. Within minutes the *Prince of Wales* drew up alongside and passed us. The crews of each ship stood at attention. Captain William Tennant on our bridge waved his white hat. Two men standing on the bridge of the *Prince of Wales* waved their hats. They were Admiral Tom Phillips and Captain Leach.

Lieutenant Halton of the Royal Marines took us on a tour of all parts of the ship. We went up and down masts, into various control towers, into turrets of the 15-inch guns, down into the engine room, and to the top of the mainmast.

When we finished the tour of the ship we went to the officers' mess and were introduced to Commander Denby, the executive officer, a middle-aged but boyishly husky who was tough and amiable and who introduced us to each of the officers in the wardroom. At that time there must have been fifteen. It was terrifically hot and we were all soaked in perspiration. By then the *Repulse* and the *Prince of Wales* and four destroyers were out in the South China Sea, moving north-east. Someone came into the wardroom and tacked a notice on the bulletin board. I got up and read it. It said:

"For the ship's company:

"We are off to look for trouble. I expect we shall find it. We may run up against submarines, destroyers, aircraft or surface ships. We are going to carry out a sweep to northward to see what we can pick up and what we can roar up. We must all be on our toes."

The signature was that of Captain Tennant.

We sat around almost all evening discussing rumors. No one actually knew what was going on. We had dinner and then heard BBC at 8:30. The news wasn't good.

The Japs are in possession of South Thailand. Thai resistance has ceased temporarily. Japanese planes bombed Bangkok.

We just sat around, Gal and I, talking with various officers and making notes. Our cabin was like a steam bath. I never sweated so much in my life. I tried it for about an hour and couldn't stand it and went up on deck. The night was rather dark and I felt my way around the deck very carefully. There were no guard rails and I was not familiar with the ship and I didn't want to fall overboard. I finally went back to the cabin and slept for about an hour and a half.

Tuesday, December 9th:

Gal and I showed up at our action stations on the flag deck at 5:15. We took with us our gas masks, helmets and our anti-flash equipment and life belts. The anti-flash equipment is simply a white cloth hood that covers the head and shoulders and leaves exposed only the nose, eyes and mouth. You are supposed to wear it during action to prevent burns from shells bursting on deck. It isn't burns that bother me—it's shrapnel.

Our action station is on the flag deck which is underneath the bridge and is the least protected part of the ship. The flag deck lieutenant is a tough, wiry officer of about twenty-four or twenty-five.

"Is this your action station?" he asked.

"Yes, it is," we said.

"Well, there is one thing about this place. In every action some men on the flag deck get killed."

"That's encouraging," we said.

298

At about 6:00 A.M. it began to lighten and we found we were about four miles off shore. The *Prince of Wales* was four cable lengths in front. The destroyers flanked us about a mile away. Men all over the ship were sitting and standing by their guns.

At 6:20 an aircraft was reported off the starboard beam, but it kept far away. It might have been a Japanese reconnaissance plane. As dawn came up, lifting the blackness, I felt terribly exposed. One of our catapult aircraft, a Walrus, was put on the track but didn't take off. Gallagher and I were peering into the haze of dawn to see what we could find. He motioned at something.

"You can't tell," he said sardonically, "whether that's an island or five Japanese battleships, ten cruisers, and three aircraft carriers."

"If it's the Japanese fleet," I said, "we won't be interested very long."

At 7:30 this morning we sat in the wardroom at breakfast. Over the radio we heard President Roosevelt speak to Congress putting the United States in a state of war with Japan.

I had never felt what I felt at that moment. I wanted to get up and give a toast with my water glass or jump on the table and shout. It was strange. None of the officers in the wardroom said anything, and since they showed no reaction I decided against being ostentatious.

All these officers are very charming and agreeable and friendly, but they are so nonchalant. Indifferent isn't the right word and I hardly think phlegmatic is either. They just seem casual. I am not sure that it isn't a good thing for them to be that way.

I asked Sub-Lieutenant Page if the men ever think about getting killed.

"Oh, not at all. If we worried about that every day for two years we'd all be nervous wrecks by now."

After breakfast I went back up on the flag deck and said to the lieutenant there:

"Have we sighted anything?"

"No, nothing yet."

"Is there someone watching for something?"

"Oh, yes," he laughed. "Actually we've a couple of hundred watching all the time."

"Then," I said, "you don't think I have to keep a lookout for sub-marines or Japanese battleships?"

He grinned.

The radio is bringing us some news of the attack on Pearl Harbor. It's shocking, but the reaction of the British officers shows how decent these men are. They are amazed by the losses to the American Navy and the heavy attacks on Hawaii, but the general view is:

"Well, the Japanese had the initial advantage of attack. It will take a while to get adjusted."

At 9:45 Lieutenant Halton took Gallagher, Abrahams and myself up to the bridge to see Captain Tennant. We hadn't met him before. Halton took me into the captain's sea cabin. This was a room about twelve feet long and five feet wide with glass all across the front. Halton introduced me, and the captain said: "I am very glad to have an American reporter on board."

He gripped my hand hard.

Captain Tennant was dressed in shorts and a shirt with no insignia on the shoulder. His hat was on the shelf. He seemed about fifty years old, with an open, pleasant face, pinkish, smooth skin with wrinkles around the eyes. On the shelf there was a vase of orchids and a picture of his wife.

As he asked me what part of America I came from he paced up and down the cabin, back and forth, peering out of a porthole on each side and the window in front.

"I hope you will excuse me if I move around while I am talking," he said.

He asked where I had been, and I told him in Rome, Yugoslavia and the Middle East. Then he saw that Gallagher and Abrahams were outside the door, in a tiny anteroom.

"Oh, are there others there? Come in—come in."

Gallagher and Abrahams were brought in by Lieutenant Halton, and the captain explained to us all that we were going around the Malaya coast toward Patani and then northeasterly toward the Indo-China coast.

"The Japs are probably bringing their convoys down over that route. If we are spotted by their aircraft today the Japanese convoy

300

may turn back and they will send two or three battleships and so forth down to meet us."

Captain Tennant was very gay, pleasant, smiling and courteous and seemed confident that we would encounter action.

"You may make history on this trip—and then again, it may not be very important."

The *Prince of Wales* was plowing along less than a half mile ahead and Gal remarked that we were supposed to be on the *Wales*.

"Yes, I know," the captain laughed. "That glamour ship up there gets all the publicity."

"We can't even mention that the *Repulse* is out here," I said.

"That's nothing. The *Repulse* hasn't been mentioned for as long as I can remember. The wife of every man on the *Wales* knows where he is, but our wives don't know whether we are at Scapa, in the Mediterranean, in the Atlantic, or in the Pacific. They never read anything about the *Repulse*."

We told the captain we wondered if the flag deck was the best place to see action.

"Where would you like to be?" he asked.

We said we thought we could see more from the after-mast control tower.

"And anyway," I added, "there is a lot of armor protection up there that I would kinda like to have around me."

"Well," the captain said, "I thought the flag deck was better. You can run from one side to the other and watch things from both sides. We'll try that, and if you are not satisfied, perhaps we can put you somewhere else."

"Would you give us an outline of the action after it is over?" Gallagher asked.

"Yes," the captain smiled. "We hope to get some action, and if so I will try to explain it."

Down in the wardroom, having nothing else to do, Gal and I were ribbing each other. Gallagher is a swell guy, a smart reporter and a courageous fighter.

"Well," he said, "are you going to be a propagandist or are you still going to be that objective reporter?"

"I'm still a reporter, Gal, and I still reserve my democratic right to criticize."

"Okay," Gal said, "but we'll see how much your American censorship will let you do it."

It is raining today and it is pretty miserable out. The main 15-inch guns and the secondary armament 4-inch guns are in second degree of readiness. Damage control and supply are at action stations.

Commander Denby just came in and I asked him for a review of the situation at the moment.

"There are no developments," he said. "If we are spotted by aircraft we can expect submarine, destroyers or dive bombers to attack by dusk. In any event we can expect something to roar up before noon tomorrow."

"Do you expect to join up with any American ships?"

"No," Commander Denby said slowly. "I don't think so. I don't know anything about that."

Around ten o'clock Gallagher, Abrahams and a lieutenant off duty and myself were sitting in the upper-deck wardroom where it is a bit cooler than down in the officers' wardroom. It's the Queen's sitting room—the captain has the King's suite. The visibility is about two miles. I looked out of the porthole while Gal and Abrahams lolled in their seats, bored to death.

"Hey!" I suddenly shouted. "There's a beautiful dame over there in that rickshaw."

Gal opened one eye and without moving said in a weary tone: "Oh, that one! I've seen her before."

Abrahams fell for it. He was a bit suspicious, but he came over to the porthole to look out. When he saw nothing but that blank sea and pouring rain he grinned weakly at me, trying to indicate that he hadn't been taken in.

There was nothing to read and our conversation had run out, but just to change the positions of our bodies we went back to the officers' wardroom to stew in the heat.

Commander Denby came in again, and one lieutenant asked him why a certain section was going into second-degree readiness.

"Oh, there is only one reason," Denby said casually, "because of a war with Japan."

302

The fleet air-arm pilot just phoned from the wardroom to the catapult deck: "Will you check on the emergency stores in my plane, please, and make sure that the bottle of rum is included?"

He then came back over and sat down on a divan with another pilot. They were arguing over some technical matter.

"You'd better take at least one flare, at least to land by."

"That doesn't help much," the other said.

"Certainly it will. Drop it at fifteen hundred feet and stick your nose down. You can get down before it goes out. You can make it in time."

At 11:25 the captain's voice piped over the ship's communications: "Gun crews on watch below must be prepared to close up on a moment's notice."

I asked Commander Denby if the aircraft we spotted this morning was a Japanese.

"We are not certain about that," he said. "It may have been Dutch. They are patrolling out here, too."

The ratings in their mess at lunch were happy and singing. Apparently the only reason for that is the prospect of action.

Most of the men on this ship come from London and Plymouth. It was two months after Plymouth had that heavy bombing that the men received the first news whether their families were alive or not.

A series of provisions has been issued for tonight and tomorrow. For example: "Breakfast will not be served tomorrow. There will be food put on the table and each man will help himself. There will be eleven action messes." That's what they call luncheon and dinner when cold plates are left on the table and the men eat when they have a chance.

Sub-Lieutenant Page, with whom we had a long talk last evening, fell down a companionway ten feet. He broke his wrist, injured his chest and apparently suffered internal injuries because he can't walk. He was a fashion designer in London before the war. He is a tall, handsome, curly-haired, smiling chap and I like him very much.

We had a good lunch of roast beef, Yorkshire pudding, baked beans, prunes and coffee. It was all very tasty.

The sea is a bit rough but the ship rides very smoothly. My stomach is behaving wonderfully well.

303

There is a plaque on the ship near the quarter-deck which shows the captains of His Majesty's ships named *Repulse*, beginning in 1596 with Sir W. Monson and down to 1938 with E. J. Spooner, who is now the Admiral in command at Singapore.

I notice that in 1926 this battle cruiser, *Repulse*, was commanded by E. R. G. R. Evans, who is Evans of the Broke.

At 12:45 a plane was spotted—a tiny dot above the horizon. There was some uncertainty whether it was a Japanese flying boat or a Catalina. Later it was verified as a Catalina and finally it drew closer.

While I was up on the flag deck this afternoon the captain came down and said: "We've a couple of knock-kneed destroyers with us. We've got to oil them. We're going to find a few of your destroyers when we get back to Singapore."

This is the first word that American ships are now operating from Singapore Naval Base.

At 1:20 P.M. a message was blinked from the *Wales* to us. It said: "The Japanese have made an air attack on Kota Bahru which was not followed by landings. Major landing ninety miles north of Singapore. Little is known of enemy naval forces in vicinity. It is believed that *Kongo* is only capital ship likely to be met. There are reported three Japanese heavy cruisers and a number of destroyers likely to be met."

I said to the flag deck officer: "A capital ship, three cruisers and some destroyers? That's the fleet we're going to face, eh? Lieutenant, how about calling a taxi to take me back to Singapore?"

He laughed heartily. "Oh, but they are Japanese. There's nothing to worry about."

Another message just came from the *Wales* giving further details: "An Akaga type, Kako type and Zintu type cruiser have been reported."

I checked up on those. One first-class heavy cruiser and two second-class cruisers.

The *Repulse* has never been in action, the men told me. The closest was off Norway when three German planes dropped eighteen bombs, some pretty close, but the *Repulse* didn't fire a shot.

"We didn't fire at their approach," one officer told me, "because we were expecting English planes. Afterwards the Jerries flew away too fast."

304

This ship has traveled fifty-three thousand miles in the two and one-half years of the war and has never been in action, and all the men are extremely keen for something to happen.

I slept for an hour this afternoon and then came up to the wardroom about 3:30 for tea. It is a strange feeling, realizing that you are soon to be in action. There is no way of avoiding it and no particular way for me to get ready for it. Writing last letters seems futile.

If we have been spotted, the expectation is the destroyer or cruiser attack will come at dusk. Certainly tomorrow ought to be full of action.

A notice has just been posted: "All officers and ratings from dawn tomorrow are to be at action stations and are to wear clothing to resist burns from flashes of exploding bombs and shells."

Admiral Tom Phillips, as Commander-in-Chief, just sent this message to the *Repulse* and to the four destroyers:

"The enemy has made several landings on the north coast of Malaya and has made local progress. Our Army is not large and it is hard-pressed in places. Our air forces have had to destroy or abandon one or more airfields.

"Meanwhile, fast transports lie off the coast. This is our opportunity before the enemy can establish himself. We have made a wide circuit to avoid air reconnaissance and hope to surprise the enemy shortly after sunrise tomorrow, Wednesday. We may have the luck to try our mettle against some Japanese cruisers or some destroyers in the Gulf of Siam. We are sure to get some useful practice with high-angle armament, but whatever we meet I want to finish quickly and so get well clear to the eastward before the Japanese can mass too formidable a scale of air attack against us. So, shoot to sink."

I was up on the flag deck at 5:20 this afternoon. For the first time there is a break in the thick, black clouds. Far off in the distance—about four or five miles away, just a speck in the sky—an aircraft was sighted. The word came from a spotter in the defense control tower in the after-mast. The word ran through the ship like fire. I watched the aircraft circling, hardly moving.

"It's a Jap, all right," a lieutenant said as he was thumbing through a book of silhouettes of Japanese aircraft. "That means we have been reported to the enemy."

I saw a number of the gunners and other men rubbing their heads

and doing clog steps all over the deck. The signal deck yeoman snorted: "Look at them—all this fuss over one aircraft!"

The *Prince of Wales* has just sent us a signal that a formation of aircraft has been reported. All guns crews hop to their stations, eager to get going. Everyone is very brisk and eager-eyed. That reconnaissance aircraft is still four or five miles away and staying well out of range. What a break that is! Just a few minutes ago there was the first gap in the overcast sky in the entire day and as luck would have it we had to be spotted just at that moment.

The lieutenant commander came by on the flag deck and said to me: "I'm afraid he has spotted us and he may go away before we can get a crack at him."

The general opinion of the flag deck is that the reconnaissance aircraft is a Nakajima Naka 93 seaplane.

I have just been told that in addition to the battleship *Kongo* and the three cruisers and a number of destroyers there are many troopships with the warships. Someone said that there are about thirty. Evidently British reconnaissance has spotted them.

Denby said: "The Admiral has delayed up here in order to get at the *Kongo*. There would be a good moral effect to sinking her."

One of our destroyers is going back tonight. It's the *Tenedos*, an antiquated thing, which is running out of oil.

17:58—Captain Tennant piped over the loud speaker: "We are now being shadowed by enemy aircraft. We are going to revert to third-degree readiness, but we must be prepared to repel aircraft at a moment's notice."

The gun crews are standing down now.

18:30—We are at dinner listening to the BBC. Heavy fighting is going on in Malaya. The fighting is still confused, but BBC says reinforcements should reach there during the day.

BBC says there is no truth in the Japanese reports that an attack was made on Singapore. The Japs have entered Bangkok.

For dinner we had hot soup, cold beef, ham, meat pie, oranges, pineapple and coffee. We all talked about the good luck or bad luck—depending on how you looked at it—of being spotted by the Japanese reconnaissance aircraft at the only time during the day there was a

306

break in the clouds and the fact that if we had avoided being spotted another forty minutes the darkness of sunset would have protected us.

One of the lieutenants saw it differently.

"It's what we came up here for," he said, "to get into a good fight."

Well, there was another fight on board the *Repulse*. A red-bearded, young New Zealander fleet air-arm pilot just came into the wardroom swearing.

"Godammit! Some bastard blacked the right eye of my gunner—the eye he shoots with."

Everybody laughed. But to this peppery New Zealander it was anything but funny. We sat around in the wardroom afterwards. There must have been twelve or fifteen officers discussing the news.

"Those Japs are bloody fools," one of them said. "All these pinpricks at widely separated points is stupid strategy. The Japs should have sent over three hundred planes over Singapore, not eleven."

"Bloody fools!" another snorted.

"Those Japs can't fly," one of the officers said. "They can't see at night and they're not well trained."

"They have rather good ships," one of the officers remarked, "but they can't shoot."

I listened to these remarks about the enemy for some time and then remarked to the fifteen officers in the wardroom: "You British are extraordinary people. You always underestimate the enemy. You did it time and again, in Norway and France, in Greece, in Crete. I think it's a mistake to underestimate the enemy. It seems to me the best thing is to figure the enemy is twice as good as you are and twice as smart, and then you make preparations in advance."

There was a moment of shocked silence in the wardroom at this criticism and then someone said in a joking manner to cover up the tension: "Oh, but really, the Japanese are not very good."

Another officer remarked: "Yes, I do think it's wrong to underestimate the enemy."

"Well, there is always the danger certainly," I added, "of underestimating the enemy to the point where you are overconfident."

A number of them chimed in, each in his own way: "We are not overconfident; we just don't think the enemy is much good. They could not beat China for five years and now look what they are doing out

307

here, jumping all over the map instead of meeting at one or two places. They cannot be very smart to be doing that."

We were all pretty tired. Some of the men were talking about what might happen tomorrow. Others drifted out of the wardroom and I went over to a table and wrote a "last letter" to Martha in case anything happened. It seemed like a kind of silly thing to do.

Our speed has been increased to twenty-six knots. Lieutenant Halton came into the wardroom and I asked him if we could expect anything.
"We won't have any fighter protection, will we?"
"No, it would be good if we had an aircraft carrier."
We are now speeding northward to the fight, to engage the enemy, now that they have spotted us. The idea is to get it over as quickly as possible. We expect to encounter one Japanese battleship, possibly one other battleship, three heavy cruisers, and an undetermined number of destroyers and perhaps as many as thirty troopships filled with troops. That is the talk I get from the officers. The danger appears to be that this Japanese task force has come down from Saigon in Indo-China for Kota Bahru, and we are going to try to intercept it and sink it.

A fleet air-arm pilot will be sent up in his Walrus when the action starts. The other pilot expects to go up in the course of the morning. Neither seems very greatly worried where he will have to land. I asked them about that and they said: "Oh, we will come down when we exhaust our four hours' supply of fuel."

Now that action is near, all the men are alert to hear all the commands over the loud speaker. I am extremely tired and sleepy after very little sleep for the past two nights. I wish somehow I would have a great deal of energy for the action tomorrow.

Commander Denby just gave me a complete list of the armament of the *Repulse*. We have:

  5 eight-barrel pom-poms
  5 sets of Vickers multiple guns with four-barrels each
  3 sets of triple 4-inchers, that is, nine of the 4-inch high-altitude guns
  8 Oerlikon, which is the Swedish gun that everybody on ship calls "wonderful."
  6 15-inch guns
  8 single high-altitude 4-inch guns
  Torpedo tubes

I just went back into the torpedo room and I saw chalked up on a board there, while the men sat beside their torpedo tubes, this notation:

Kongo, built 1913/15
    29,300 tons
    26 knots
     8 14-inch
    16 6-inch
     4 torpedo tubes
     9 5-inch A.A.
     8 21-inch torpedo tubes

That was the information, for our torpedo men, on the Jap battleship we intend to sink some time in the next twenty-four hours.

21:05—We're sitting in the wardroom again and the voice on the loudspeaker has just said: "Stand by for Captain to speak to you."

In an instant Captain Tennant's cool, even voice came through. "A signal has just been received from the Commander-in-Chief who very much regrets to announce having to abandon the operation. We were shadowed by three planes. We were spotted after dodging them all day. Their troop convoy will now have dispersed. It would be very obvious that if we continued, enemy air concentration would be awaiting us and it would be unwise to continue.

"I know that you all share with us the disappointment in not engaging the enemy at this time, but I am sure that you will agree with the C-in-C's judgment. We are, therefore, going back to Singapore."

In the wardroom there were cries and groans of disappointment and even bitterness. I immediately dashed out of the wardroom into the quarters of the ratings to check their reactions. I went into one sailor's mess and the men were sitting around the long tables. Some of the men had tears in their eyes—two and a half years in the war and never a chance to engage an enemy.

"How do you fellows feel about that?"

The remarks I got were: "This always happens to the *Repulse.*"

"It's a bloody shyme."

"Damned disappointing, we were all keyed up for it."

"We're just an unlucky ship."

Back in the wardroom I stood in the doorway surveying the long faces of the officers sitting in chairs and on divans in front of the fireplace and on the railing around the edge of the fireplace in utter dejection.

Commander Denby was almost at a loss for words, and the disappointment on his face was pitiful. It was almost like that of a child denied a promised bag of candy.

"What do you think of it, Commander?" I asked.

"Damned disappointing," he said. "But, after all, there is nothing else to do without fighter protection."

"I just talked with some of the men," I said. "They seem pretty sore."

"They won't be sore at not committing suicide."

"Do you think it would be suicide to go on?" I asked.

"If we went on we would have to find their ships first. To search hundreds of miles at sea without aircraft is a life work, and while this is going on we would be bombed continuously."

Then his control snapped. "What a shame! What a shame!"

Commander Denby and I found a place on a divan and I asked him to explain the type of operation we expected to encounter and what we might do now.

"The essential element of this tip-and-run raid is surprise, and we lost that when that fellow spotted us this afternoon. It amounts to this: we are up against the whole of the Japanese air force with no aircraft protection and no destroyer screen. Well, maybe not the whole Jap force, but at least 50 percent of it."

I slipped up at that moment in not asking what he meant by "no destroyer screen" because we did have four destroyers with us, not much good, but at least destroyers, and one of them was scheduled to be sent back to Singapore that night.

Denby added, "We don't know the extent or nature of the Jap air force or what we would run into. It isn't worth risking two capital ships under the strategic circumstances."

The gunnery officer, a handsome, polite Englishman called "Guns" said to me: "How do you feel about turning back?"

"Relieved—and disappointed."

"Well, that's a frank answer," he laughed.

One officer called over to Gallagher, who was taking notes as I was, and said: "Do you think you have got a story out of this?"

"Not a thing," Gallagher said. "Can't write a story on this stuff. We've just been getting background."

310

Gallagher has a pair of cover-alls to wear tomorrow to protect his arms and legs from burns and shells, but I have nothing to put over my shorts and bush jacket which has short sleeves. The senior engineer says he has a pair of cover-alls to loan me. Gallagher and I went into his cabin and he has a recording machine he made himself. An entertainer, Ann Denise, came aboard the *Repulse* at Durban, South Africa, to sing for the sailors, and the engineer recorded her songs. He played some of them for us. *Double-entendre* ditties. He also played a recording he made of the ceremony they had on board when they crossed the equator.

I spent about a half hour with him trying to figure out ways by which I could make a recording of the action next day. It was rather compli-cated because the recording machine could not be taken up on deck, and besides he would be busy and it would take an engineer to handle the recording. We both agreed it would be a perfect stunt to have the machine up on deck and for me to broadcast a recording of the action blow by blow, but neither of us could see how it could be worked out, so we dropped the idea.

Wednesday, December 10th:

04.00—Awakened after sleeping for about three hours in the steam-ing cabin. Came up on the flag deck. Pitch dark and I am thirsty as hell. Would like to have tea. No tea on the flag deck, so I went down to the wardroom, but there is no tea there either. Gallagher and Abrahams are stretched out on divans in the wardroom to sleep. It is hellishly hot, so I went back on the flag deck. I see nothing to write in this diary. I can't sleep, I can't rest, and I can't get any tea to drink.

05.05—The call to action stations just sounded. We are still going southward back to Singapore. Instead of hunting the enemy, we are trying to get away from them. Trying to avoid action.

It is a beautiful dawn, the sky is a bright gray, constantly getting lighter. Everyone is on the alert. We expect an attack at any moment.

06.05—The sun is coming up a bright orange.

06.15—"We are changing course," I said to the lieutenant. "Why are we changing course?"

Just as he was about to reply the answer came through the ship's loud speaker.

"Men, we have just received a message saying the enemy is making a landing at Kuantan. We are going in." That means we intend to shoot up barges and any warships escorting them.

Kuantan is 150 miles north of Singapore on the east coast of Malaya. Gallagher and I remembered it very well as the place where we came down on the water-covered airdrome in our torpedo-carrying bombers. Instead of heading south for Singapore, we are bearing westward for the coast.

06.30—We are putting on cover-alls, anti-flash helmets, and battle helmets. Off to the beam the sky is streaked with gold. All the gun crews are at the action stations. Gallagher and I went down for breakfast of coffee, cold ham, bread and marmalade.

07.20—Back on the flag deck. We are pushing in toward shore very fast. The *Prince of Wales* is ahead; we follow; the destroyers are about a mile or a mile and a half on each side of us. We still have four of them. We can see the shore line and an island far ahead of us.

07.30—The *Wales* just catapulted one of her planes on a reconnaissance. One of the signalers on the flag deck said the reconnaissance pilot had been given instructions not to return to the ship, but to land on the water near the shore after reporting to us on what he found.

07.40—The *Wales* just elevated her 15-inch guns. What a beautiful sight they are! We are speeding in toward shore at about 24 knots. We were watching the Walrus from the *Wales* gain altitude and circle around us once and then disappear out of sight behind two islands shaped like chocolate drops.

"The enemy must be landing behind those mountains," someone on the flag deck said.

But the Walrus reappeared again as a tiny speck in the sky and then flew out of sight once more.

Some of the gunners are putting on asbestos gloves which come up to their elbows and a number of them are wearing goggles. They all look very efficient.

This is a beautiful sight in the brilliant sunlight. I just took a picture of the *Prince of Wales* on the starboard beam. What power there is out here today! The *Wales* is moving with such rhythm, pushing a white wave away from her bow on each side. Every now and then she slaps the water and the spray comes racing over her forward deck.

Our white ensign and hers, too, are rippling out in the breeze.

312

This is it, I think. This is the way you go in and knock hell out of the enemy.

07.48—We are about eight miles off shore. I can't see anything except green in the foreground, and the mountains rising in the background. I have just taken some more pictures of the gun crews beside their guns.

The communications loudspeaker just announced there is nothing in sight yet; we are going down along the beach.

07.50—The flag officer says, "I think we are too late now. Think they have all gone."

"I wonder," the flag-deck yeoman remarks, "if they have any naval units in there? I don't see a ship anywhere."

One of the youngsters on the flag deck said, "They might be around the bloody corner."

The lieutenant called to the flag-deck yeoman, who was taking signals on the blinker from the *Wales*.

"Is the *Prince of Wales* ready?"

"Yes, they are all ready."

Walrus again came into view.

"That ties it," said the flag-deck lieutenant. "If the Japs were around that Walrus would be down. He can't fight."

08.15—One of the destroyers, I think it was the *Express*, has just cut across the bow of the *Wales*. The *Express* is going closer into shore.

The land is quite close. I can see many islands.

The destroyer seems very impertinent going in there. I don't understand why we are waiting around here instead of going straight to Singapore as planned.

The reports are that Kuantan Airdrome is being too heavily bombed to get any report from there. I asked an officer what we expected to find in here, but he did not know. It seems quite obvious that the Japs made their landing and then got away.

08.30—We are now going back northward and I understand that we have detached one of the destroyers to go back to Singapore. The one destroyer we sent in to shore is going in as close as it can to see what it can find. We are going back northward away from Singapore —the *Prince of Wales*, the *Repulse*, and two destroyers—to see what we can find.

10.10—We steamed northward for about forty-five minutes not far off shore, but we didn't find anything, and we came back and picked up the third destroyer and are moving out to sea.

10.30—I am back on the flag deck again. Fifteen enemy aircraft are reported southeast, but are not in sight. All kinds of signals are being blinked back and forth between the *Wales* and the *Repulse* and between the *Wales* and the three destroyers.

10.40—We are sending off one of our Walrus reconnaissance planes. It goes off the track and just as it does I get a good photograph of it. It dips slightly then climbs up and swings northward. We still have one aircraft left.

10.45—One twin-engined Jap is reported shadowing us. It is the same type that bombed Singapore the first night of the war. It is type 96 Mitsubishi of the Naval Air Service.

The clouds have gone now, and the sky is a robin's-egg blue and the sun is bright yellow. Our ships plow through pea-green water, white where the hulls cleave it. Ahead, the *Wales'* 15-inch guns jut, port and starboard, from turrets that bulge like muscles. They seem to quiver, eagerly. The destroyers that flank us are pygmy ships and seem ridiculous and impertinent in such powerful company.

11.04½—The signal yeoman beside me turns away from his spy glass and snaps, "Two masts, one funnel." He jerks it out to one of the signal ratings.

"Report to the bridge. Hop to it." He adds, "We have sighted a ship."

11.06½—The crew of the pom-poms just below us on the starboard is sitting around playing cards, ready for action in an instant. The men on the control towers on the main mast and after-mast are peering into the sky for enemy aircraft. Men are at the 4-inch high-altitude guns. The men are getting keyed up at the prospect of action. You can almost feel the electricity all over the ship.

Standing on the flag deck, I look down over the decks of the *Repulse*. The guns seem no less eager for combat than the crews themselves.

We're told that Admiral Phillips on the *Wales* has just sent a signal to Singapore asking for aircraft protection.

I haven't had time to shave. I feel bleary and I am terrifically tired. I just took a picture of the gun crew playing cards and another picture of the *Prince of Wales*. Also snapped Gallagher with the flag-deck yeoman.

We are now zigzagging. I only see two destroyers at the moment. The *Prince of Wales* is four cable lengths ahead.

11.07—The communications loudspeaker announces: "Enemy aircraft approaching—action stations!"

I see them: 1-2-3-4-5-6-7-8-9. There are nine, flying line astern, one behind the other.

I would judge them about 12,000 feet, coming straight over the *Repulse.*

11.14—And here they come.

11.15—The guns of the *Prince of Wales* just let go. At the same instant I see the flame belching from the guns of the *Wales,* ours break into a chattering, ear-splitting roar. The nine Japanese aircraft are stretched out across the bright blue, cloudless sky like star sapphires of a necklace.

I've never been so close to so many guns firing at once. The roar of the pom-poms and the hard, sharp crack of the 4-inch high-altitude guns are deafening. The flashes are blinding and suddenly the smell of cordite is strong. I am standing on the port side of the flag deck, in the lee of an air funnel, eight feet from a battery of pom-poms.

I gape open-mouthed at those aircraft coming directly over us, flying so that they will pass from bow to stern over the *Repulse.* The sky is filled with black puffs from our ack-ack. They seem a discordant profanation of that beautiful sky. But the formation of Japanese planes, coming over one behind the other, is undisturbed.

Now they are directly overhead. For the first time I see the bombs coming down, materializing suddenly out of nothingness and streaming toward us like ever-enlarging tear drops. There's a magnetic, hypnotic, limb-freezing fascination in that sight.

It never occurs to me to try and duck or run. Open-mouthed and rooted, I watch the bombs getting larger and larger. Suddenly, ten yards from me, out in the water, a huge geyser springs out of the sea, and over the side, showering water over me and my camera.

I instinctively hunch over, sort of a semi-crouch, and at that same instant there is a dull thud. The whole ship shudders. Pieces of paint fall from the deck over the flag deck.

11.17—"Fire on the boat deck. Fire below!" That just came over the loudspeakers. There are fountains of water all around the ship. Some are near misses. Most of the bombs are hitting the water ten to thirty yards off the port side. Beautiful fountains of thick white at the base and then tapering up into fine spray.

That first bomb was a direct hit. Someone on the flag deck says: "Fire in marines' mess and hangar."

That bomb struck the catapult deck, penetrated, exploded underneath. The bomb hit twenty yards astern of my position on the flag deck. A number of men (fifty) were killed.

11.21—We got one of the bombers! It is coming down fast, in black smoke. All our guns are still going. I am now near one of the multiple Vickers guns. It is firing 2,000 half-inch shells a minute. God, what a racket! That bomber smacked into the water about a half mile away.

11.23—The high-level bombers are gone. We are still zigzagging like mad. The *Prince of Wales* seems to be firing, but I can't tell.

I run back to see the damage, but the bomb penetrated the deck armor and only smoke is coming up. Our aircraft is knocked off its track and a red-bearded New Zealand fleet-air-arm pilot is atop the crane attempting to lift the plane to drop it overside, since its gasoline constitutes a menace.

As I pass the gun crews they seem extraordinarily calm, replenishing ammunition, laughing. I hear someone say: "Let's get them all next time."

A gunner remarks: "Bloody good bombing for those blokes."

When I return to the flag deck I note a three-inch hole in the funnel from a bomb-splinter eighteen inches above the spot where I'd been standing. It's obvious my number isn't up yet.

Smoke is still coming up from the catapult deck and strenuous efforts are under way to control the fire. Four stokers come up to the flag deck to get first aid. They're blackened and scorched and their clothes are water-soaked.

They are very calm but wild-eyed and stunned, and their hands are shaking. The skin is hanging from their hands and faces like tissue paper. Someone says: "Make way for these men. They need first aid."

A stoker croaks tremulously, "Water. I want some water."

A glass is placed to his lips.

11.26—Just heard a report that there are a number of small fires below, owing to near misses.

316

The men are giving a big cheer. "They got another one," Gallagher shouts in my ear. I look over in the direction he points. There is a splash two or three miles astern. Some of the gunners are not so certain. A pom-pom gunner says: "Maybe he just jettisoned his bombs."

"Like hell he did," I tell him. "They dropped all the bombs they had on us."

11.40—The *Prince of Wales* seems to be hit. She's reduced her speed and signals, "We've a man overboard." A destroyer pushes up to her side. Standing less than 100 feet away, it's as incongruous as a baby running to protect its mamma. The flag-deck lieutenant says: "Those Japs are good, aren't they?"

I say, "Too good to suit me. How badly is the *Wales* hit?"

The lieutenant says, "I don't know. They haven't told us yet."

We are all lighting cigarettes, sucking deeply, and our exhalations are more like sighs. The pause is too brief.

11.45—Distant specks appear. Now they are identifiable. Nine torpedo-carrying bombers, circling four or five thousand yards away at about a half-mile altitude. Circling in a huge sweep, they are swooping lower. Now they are like moths around our flaming guns.

A bugle blows to stand by. A voice over the ship's communications roars: "Stand by for a barrage!"

Instantly every gun aboard the *Repulse* is stuttering and roaring and the whole ship vibrates and the pom-poms are spitting out empties furiously. But the clatter of empty shell cases on the deck is unheard in the slap-slap of A.A. guns, the crack-crack-crack of 4-inch guns. A voice beside me says, "Look at those yellow bastards come!" The *Repulse* is twisting and snaking violently to avoid torpedoes. My only weapons are a fountain pen, a notebook and a camera, so I sidle beside a multiple Vickers gun spewing 2,000 half-inch bullets every minute.

A few feet to my right an eight-barreled pom-pom is coughing incessantly and a half dozen feet away a 4-inch high altitude ack-ack is crashing, its barrel nearly horizontal instead of skyward, to meet the onrushing torpedo bombers.

A cooling liquid is gushing over the guns and the paint blisters on them are as big as tennis balls. Gunners are moving like a movie running too fast. Some are very young and eager and breathless with excitement, their faces streaked with sweat. The white cloth anti-flash helmets covering their heads, cheeks and shoulders are now soaked and discolored. Some are wearing life belts and "Mae Wests."

A whole pom-pom swings this way and that, with its seated trigger man, feet braced, riding with it. That is a dizzy job.

The torpedo-carrying bombers are coming in. We are putting up a beautiful barrage, a wall of fire. But the bombers come on, in a long glide, from all angles, not simultaneously but alternately. Some come head-on, some astern and from all positions on both sides of the ship. They level out.

About 300 yards distant from the ship and 100 yards above the water, they drop their torpedoes.

The torpedoes seem small, dropping flat into the water, sending up splashes, then streaking toward us. Those bombers are so close you can almost see the color of the pilot's eyes. The bombers are machine-gunning our decks as they come in.

I've just seen three more torpedoes drop. Another plane just let go a torpedo. Then it banked sharply. The whole side of the bomber is exposed to us. Shells and tracers are ripping into it. It's fascinating to watch.

Tracer bullets from our guns are cross-stitching the sky, just above eye level, with long, thin white lines, slightly curved. For me this whole picture—orange flame belching from the 4-inchers, white tracers from pom-poms and Vickers guns, and gray airplanes astonishingly close, like butterflies pinned on blue cardboard—is a confusing, macabre game.

But this, I realize, is deadly business, too. Three gunners ten feet from me slump over with Japanese machine-gun bullets in them. It's difficult to comprehend sudden death. But they aren't the only casualties in this terrible moment. A torpedo bomber has just dropped a tin fish and banked without gaining altitude. It glides beautifully, parallel with the *Repulse* at a ten-degree angle, and still tracers are plowing into it. It doesn't seem to me the plane is going to crash, until an instant later I see that it isn't going to pull out and is still gliding toward the sea. It strikes the water and immediately bursts into flame. It burns fiercely, a twenty-foot circle of orange on a blue sea.

I run to the starboard side of the flag deck, where another torpedo-bomber is coming in. It is difficult to judge distance, but I guess it's no more than 200 yards away when it swerves. I don't see the torpedo.

318

And with good reason. There's a huge hole in the side of the plane. It's aflame, and instantly it seems to buckle. I got a beautiful picture of this one. As though stricken with a cramp, the bomber dives, shapeless, flaming, seaward. It's just a pillar of fire until it hits the water and spreads out into nothingness.

The men on the catapult deck are still trying to get the damaged aircraft over the side. Its gasoline makes it a fire hazard. That red-bearded New Zealand pilot is working atop the crane trying to heave the Walrus over the side. As the Jap torpedo bombers come in to drop their fish and machine-gun our decks, he is firing at them with his pistol.

There are nine bombers in that attack. It ends at 11.51.

11.51½—Captain Tennant is sending a message to the *Wales:* "Have you sustained any damage?"

The answer comes back: "We are out of control. Steering gear is gone."

The decks of the *Repulse* are littered with empty shell cases. Upon the faces of the sailors there's a mixture of incredulity and a sort of sensuous pleasure, but I don't detect fear. There's an ecstatic happiness, but strangely, I don't see anything approaching hate for the attackers. For the British this is a contest. This facial expression is interpreted by an officer. He turns to me and says: "Plucky blokes, those Japs. That was as beautiful an attack as ever I expect to see."

He'll never see another action. He's at the bottom of the South China Sea.

Our great concern is that the Japs are going to crash-dive the ship. I understand enough about naval warfare to know that the flag deck is a good spot on which to crash dive. Suddenly it occurs to me how wonderful it would be to be back in Ohio. A voice says: "Here they come again."

12.01—Twelve torpedo bombers launch an attack at all angles. One even launches a torpedo directly astern, which seems silly, since we are twisting rapidly. Planes coming from port and starboard are headed directly at the bow. I see the *Prince of Wales* being subjected to an attack also, and a bomber is coming toward us from a thousand yards, directly ahead.

I think, "Here comes a crash-dive." The smell of cordite is suffocating. My eyes ache with the blows of shell blasts.

Now I am standing in front of the smokestack. The view is good, and I have just taken some more pictures of the bombers coming in. I hear a rat-tat-tat and whine which seems higher and closer than the crash of other guns. I look around to see where it is coming from and then glance overhead. Two feet above my head, drilled in the smokestack, there is a line of bullet holes. I move away from that position. No sense in magnetizing any more Japanese machine-gun bullets.

It's the same as before—amazingly daring torpedo-bombers are targets for mere moments. They rush headlong into our almost solid wall of shells and bullets and are seemingly unaffected. The water is streaked with the tracks of torpedoes. A sudden roar goes up on one side of the ship. It's another bomber down, but I didn't see it.

If it wasn't so awe-inspiring it would be routine: the way planes rush in, drop a tin fish, machine-gun the decks of the *Repulse* and roar away.

During this attack, as during the first wave of bombers, Captain Tennant on the bridge of the Repulse *directly above the flag deck is saying in the coolest, calmest possible voice: "Thirty degrees port. Thirty degrees starboard. Thirty degrees port . . ." zigzagging this 32,000-ton battle cruiser out of the path of those torpedoes.**

12.14—Now all the bombers are gone. Captain Tennant has just ordered this message flashed to Admiral Tom Phillips on the *Wales* up ahead: "We have dodged nineteen torpedoes thus far, thanks to Providence."

Those who are able light cigarettes. The decks are littered with the debris of battle. There are a number of dead men around the guns, and wounded, too. More ammunition is being passed up. Everyone around the guns is soaked in sweat, with blackened faces.

I glance at the notes in this diary. Hastily written. And I've twisted the point of my fountain pen, a green Parker, Martha's pen. I check the pack film in the Plaubel Makina suspended by a strap around my neck. There are four pictures left in the pack, enough, I think. No use taking time to change the pack. I rip open another packet and peel off the tape around the metal container, to be ready for a quick change. My ears ache atrociously and my mouth is cottony. The whole place stinks with cordite. I take off my tin hat. This anti-flash hood is like putting your head in an oven.

* Italics denote scenes and remarks which I did not actually witness or hear.

A young sailor, about eighteen, is standing there wide-eyed. I grin at him.

"They're sure giving us hell, aren't they?" I ask him.

He grins back. I'm as scared as he is.

A few of the sailors are blowing up their lifebelts, I note. I wonder why but only for an instant and forget about it. My lifebelt is stuck up in a small shelf in the roof of the flag deck, too awkward to wear. I feel bulky enough with the cover-alls over the bush-jacket, the camera around my neck, notebook in my left hand and fountain pen in the right hand.

12.19—I see ten bombers approaching. It's impossible to tell whether this will be a high-level or a torpedo attack. They come closer, lower. It's definitely a torpedo attack.

12.20—The communication pipes again, "Stand by for barrage!" and hell breaks loose. A plane is diving straight for the middle of the ship off the port side, 500 yards away, and tracers are rushing to meet it, but it comes on. Now it seems suspended in the air 100 yards above the water, and the torpedo drops.

It is streaking for us. There is a deadly fascination in watching it. The watcher shouts, "Stand by for torpedo." The torpedo strikes the ship about twenty yards astern of my position. It feels as though the ship has crashed into dock. I am thrown four feet across the deck but I keep my feet. Almost immediately, it seems, the ship lists.

The command roars out of the loudspeaker: "Blow up your life belts!"

I take down mine from the shelf. It is a blue-serge affair with a rubber bladder inside. I tie one of the cords around my waist and start to bring another cord up around the neck. Just as I start to tie it the command comes: "All possible men to starboard."

But a Japanese plane invalidates that command. Instantly there's another crash to starboard. Incredibly quickly, the *Repulse* is listing to port, and I haven't started to blow up my life belt.

I finish tying the cord around my neck. My camera I hang outside the airless lifebelt. Gallagher already has his belt on and is puffing into the rubber tube to inflate it. The effort makes his strong, fair face redder than usual.

The ship is heeled over at a nasty angle. Gallagher says: "You all right, Cec?"

"Yeh, I guess so. No air in my belt though. The hell with it."

"Better blow it. This is it, Cec."

"Yes, Gal. I guess it is. Good going, kid."

"We'll stick together."

We grin at each other, a weak grin.

Captain Tennant's voice is coming over the ship's loudspeaker, a cool voice: "All hands on deck. Prepare to abandon ship." There is a pause for just an instant, then: "God be with you."

There is no alarm, no confusion, no panic. We on the flag deck move toward a companionway leading to the quarter deck. Abrahams, the Admiralty photographer, Gallagher and I are together. The coolness of everyone is incredible. There is no pushing, but no pausing either. One youngster seems in a great hurry. He tries to edge his way into the line at the top of the companionway to get down faster to the quarter deck.

A young sub-lieutenant taps him on the shoulder and says quietly: "Now, now, we are all going the same way, too."

The youngster immediately gets hold of himself.

We move swiftly down the fifteen-foot companionway to the quarter deck. Abrahams is carrying his expensive camera like a baby, cradled in his arms. He goes over to a wooden lifebelt locker, about three feet long, carefully opens the lid, gently places his camera inside, and carefully closes the lid.

Beside a pom-pom two men are dead, stretched in grotesque positions of violently won peace. There is blood all around this gun, hot and silent, its base littered with used and never-fired ammunition, too.

I see four sailors carrying Lieutenant Page up the slanting deck of the ship toward the edge. He had been brought up on deck when the action with the Japanese was joined. He still couldn't walk. Two lifebelts were wrapped around him "in case anything happened." Now he is being lifted to the edge of the ship. The four men heaved, and Page went sailing overboard, so he would have a chance for rescue. Gallagher and Abrahams seem to have disappeared.

I see a lifeboat jammed with seamen and a half dozen officers, still on its davits, still not swung out.

The only way to reach that boat is by a cable. I jump for it and go hand over hand about ten feet, dangling like a monkey by its tail. As I am swinging through space, the yellow filter from the lens of my

322

camera falls off and I watch it go crashing to the deck fifteen feet below.

"There goes that filter that cost me three dollars and a half just a few months ago in Cairo."

I swing myself into a tiny, precarious corner of the lifeboat, first my feet then using my arms as levers on the cable to get all of me inside. I just settle there when someone shouts: "This boat will never get off!"

We all pile out, streaming over the side of the lifeboat, back onto the deck of the *Repulse*. I drop ten feet, hit the slanting, slippery deck, slide about eight feet and crash into a bulkhead. I am dizzy when I pick myself up. Then I fall back on my hands and knees and scramble up the side of the deck, grabbing cables and deck protuberances to reach the edge of the ship.

"GOD BE WITH YOU"

The *Repulse* is going down.

The torpedo-smashed *Prince of Wales,* still a half to three-quarters of a mile ahead, is low in the water, half shrouded in smoke, a destroyer by her side.

Japanese bombers are still winging around like vultures, still attacking the *Wales.* A few of those shot down are bright splotches of burning orange on the blue South China Sea.

Men are tossing overboard rafts, lifebelts, benches, pieces of wood, anything that will float. Standing at the edge of the ship, I see one man (Midshipman Peter Gillis, an eighteen-year-old Australian from Sydney) dive from the Air Defense control tower at the top of the main mast. He dives 170 feet and starts to swim away.

Men are jumping into the sea from the four or five defense control towers that segment the main mast like a series of ledges. One man misses his distance, dives, hits the side of the *Repulse,* breaks every bone in his body and crumples into the sea like a sack of wet cement. Another misses his direction and dives from one of the towers straight down the smokestack.

Men are running all along the deck of the ship to get further astern. The ship is lower in the water at the stern and their jump therefore will be shorter. Twelve Royal Marines run back too far, jump into the water and are sucked into the propeller.

The screws of the *Repulse* are still turning. There are five or six hundred heads bobbing in the water. The men are being swept astern because the *Repulse* is still making way and there's a strong tide here, too.

On all sides of me men are flinging themselves over the side. I sit down on the edge of the *Repulse* and take off my shoes. I am very fond of those shoes. A Chinese made them for me just a few days ago in Singapore. They are soft, with a buckle, and they fit well. I carefully place them together and put them down as you do at the foot of your bed before going to sleep.

324

I have no vision of what is ahead, no concrete thoughts of how to save myself. It is necessarily every man for himself. As I sit there, it suddenly comes to me, the overwhelming, dogmatic conviction. I actually speak the words: "Cecil, you are never going to get out of this."

I see one man jump and land directly on another man. I say to myself: "When I jump I don't want to hurt anyone."

Down below is a mess of oil and debris, and I don't want to jump into that either. I feel my mind getting numb. I look across to the *Wales.* Its guns are flashing and the flames are belching through the grayish-black smoke.

My mind cannot absorb what my eyes see. It is impossible to believe that these two beautiful, powerful, invulnerable ships are going down. But they are. There's no doubt of that.

Men are sliding down the hull of the *Repulse.* Extending around the edge of the ship is a three-inch bulge of steel. The men hit that bulge, shoot off into space and into the water. I say to myself: "I don't want to go down that way. That must hurt their backsides something terrible."

About eight feet to my left there is a gaping hole in the side of the *Repulse.* It is about thirty feet across, with the plates twisted and torn. The hull of the *Repulse* has been ripped open as though a giant had torn apart a tin can. I see an officer dive over the side, dive into the hole underneath the line, dive back inside the ship.

I half turn to look back on the crazy-angled deck of the ship. The padre is beside one of the pom-poms, administering the final rites to a gunner dying beside his gun. The padre seems totally unconcerned by the fact that the *Repulse* is going down at any moment.

About forty-two men have made their way through the tangled, destroyed, burning interior of the ship, crept, stumbled and scrambled and have clambered through the inside of the dummy smokestack to the top. They find the wire screen across the top of the stack is fastened on the outside. Someone hears their cries, but by then it is too late. The men are trapped.

Midshipman Christopher Bros, from St. Andrews, is in the fifteen-inch transmitting station, at the very bottom of the ship. There are twenty-five men with him in the small room, and the sharp list of the ship is making it difficult to get out. The water is pouring in.

"Fall in, everyone! March. Up you go," Bros orders.

The men start streaming out, starting a climb up six decks. One by one they pass out of the room. The water is coming higher. The water comes in faster than twenty-five men can get out. The twenty-sixth man is trapped. Midshipman Kit Bros, tall, slim, Rugby graduate from Scotland gets all his men out. He is the twenty-sixth man.

I slide down the hull of the *Repulse* about five feet. There I brace myself in a porthole, take off my tin hat and white cloth anti-flash hood and place them at my feet in the porthole. I lie on the side of the *Repulse,* watching this incredible scene—men bobbing in the water, black oil spreading over the debris-filled, blue sea, the *Wales* obviously sinking, the sky still filled with aircraft and black puffs of anti-aircraft fire.

I don't want to jump, to leave the relative security of this steel for that mess down below. I have no panic in me, no particular fear, just this numbness. I know I'll have to jump sooner or later. I know I cannot lie here and let the water come over me without fighting back somehow. There's no hurry. To jump into the water will hasten the inevitable.

Captain Tennant on the bridge turns to the navigating officer: "It looks a bit different from this angle, doesn't it, pilot?"

The navigating officer nods, but says nothing. The group of officers on the bridge look at each other, and at the skipper.

"Well, gentlemen," Captain Tennant says quietly, "you had better get out of it now."

"Aren't you coming with us, sir?" two or three eagerly demand simultaneously.

The captain smiles, shakes his head negatively, then says impatiently: "Off you go now. There's not much time." They are all hanging on to something, one leg braced to keep an even keel as the ship heels over more and more.

"But, Captain," the lieutenant commander says, "you must come with us. You've done all you could for this ship. More than most men could."

Captain Tennant does not budge. The men are getting restive. Almost by pre-arrangement they all move toward their skipper. They

326

push him forcibly through the narrow doorway and onto the deck. The
Repulse is almost on her beam ends. Captain Tennant will go no
farther. The officers and men of the bridge seize Captain Tennant and
push him over the side. Then they jump into the sea.

I seem to be glued to the hull of the *Repulse*. Just my head is loose.
I turn it from side to side, watching the last-minute evacuation of the
ship. Someone slides down the hull, pauses for a moment at the bulge,
stands up and makes a beautiful swan dive. That galvanizes me, and I
stand up in the porthole and jump, the camera wildly swinging from
its strap around my neck.

The jump is about twenty feet. The water is warm; it is not water,
but thick oil. My first action is to look at my stop watch. It is smashed at
12.35, one hour and twenty minutes after the first Japanese bomb came
through 12,000 feet to crash into the catapult deck of the *Repulse*.

It doesn't occur to me to swim away from the ship until I see others
striking out. Then I realize how difficult it is. The oil soaks into my
clothes weighting them and I think underwater demons are tugging
at me, trying to drag me down. The airless life belt, absorbing oil too,
tightens and tautens the preserver cords around my neck. I say to
myself: "I'm going to choke to death, I'm going to choke to death."

Next to confined places, all my life, I've been afraid of choking to
death. This is the first moment of fear.

I have a ring on my left hand which Martha bought for me on the
Ponte Vecchio in Florence when we were on our honeymoon. It is
rather loose on my finger. With oil on my hands, I'm afraid I will
lose it. I clench my fist so that it won't slip off.

I start swimming away with the left hand clenched. With my right
hand I make one stroke, tug at the cord around my neck in a futile effort
to loosen it, then make another stroke to get away from the ship.

That ring helps save my life. Something like it must have helped save
the lives of hundreds of men. Your mind fastens itself on silly, unimportant matters, absorbing your thoughts and stifling the natural in-
stinct of man to panic in the face of death.

I see a life preserver eighteen inches long and four inches thick. It is
like a long sausage and I tuck it to me. A small piece of wood appears
inviting and I take that too. A barrel comes near, but I reject that

327

because the oil prevents me getting a grip on it. All around me men are swimming, men with blood streaking down their oil-covered faces.

The oil burns in my eyes as though someone is jabbing hot pokers into the eyes. That oil in the eyes is the worst thing. I've swallowed a bit of oil already, and it's beginning to sicken me.

Fifty feet from the ship, hardly swimming at all now, I see the bow of the *Repulse* swing straight into the air like a church steeple. Its red under plates stand out as stark and as gruesome as the blood on the faces of the men around me. Then the tug and draw of the suction of 32,000 tons of steel sliding to the bottom hits me. Something powerful, almost irresistible, snaps at my feet. It feels as though someone were trying to pull my legs out by the hip sockets. But I am more fortunate than some others. They are closer to the ship. They are sucked back.

When the *Repulse* goes down it sends over a huge wave, a wave of oil. I happen to have my mouth open and I take aboard considerable oil. That makes me terribly sick at the stomach.

As I swim in the water, other men are hanging on to pieces of wood, floating life belts and debris. Four or five times I see blood- and oil-covered hands loosen their grip and slide beneath the water.

I do not see Gallagher anywhere. It is difficult to recognize anyone through the oil on his face. About fifteen yards away I see someone struggling and fighting in the water. I finally recognize Sub-Lieutenant Page. There are two men near by. The injured Page is struggling to get out of the two life belts wrapped around him, the belts he had on when he was tossed overboard.

"*I'm hurt,*" Page is crying. "*I'm hurt. I'm no good any more. You take the belts.*"

The men can't swim, but Page is insisting and sobbing, peeling out of the belts. "Take them; I'm no good any more."

Page prevails on the two men to accept the belts. They are saved, and Sub-Lieutenant Page slips underneath the water.

Someone calls to me, "Are you all right, War Correspondent?"

"Yes," I say, opening my mouth to say it, and I take aboard more oil. I decide if anyone asks me any more questions I will wave my hand, if I have the strength. I am terribly tired.

A small table, about three feet square floats by. I grab hold of one leg, but it is too slippery and I know I will lose it. I scramble up on

328

top and lay there for a moment. And then I watch the *Prince of Wales* go down, a big, dark thing sliding into nothingness.

Now the sea seems really deserted, with just men and mess floating on the surface.

As I swim I hear one man yell, "An electric eel just shocked me!"

There are no sharks that I can see, although this area of the South China Sea is usually filled with sharks.

There is a Carley float about three-quarters of a mile away, and a destroyer about two miles distant. I have no intention of trying to reach them. I only want to rest on top of the small table. The conviction that this is my finish is still strong within me. Besides, I want to conserve my strength, want jealously to guard it during the hours before death comes.

I say to myself, "I've gotta remember all this; I gotta remember all this." And the next minute, "What the hell's the use? I will never be able to report this story."

It's so easy to close your eyes, shut out this sight, and fiercely forget what the eyes already have seen.

Strangely enough, I don't think of my wife, my family, or my childhood. I constantly glance around to see if I recognize any of the men, and I am especially watching for Gallagher. I don't see him but I do recognize two or three officers and we smile wanly at each other.

As I lie on the table I pull off my heavy cotton khaki socks. They are soaked and weighted by oil, as heavy as iron. I let the soaked socks slip into the water and feel five pounds lighter. As the warmth of the South China Sea slushes between my toes I think, "That feels wonderful on my feet."

The effort, little as it is, exhausts me. The drag of the camera around my neck and the choking by the life-preserver cord convince me I ought to do something about them. But the water-and-oil-soaked cord of the preserver is knotted and I can't unfasten it. As for the camera, I feel I'd rather drown than throw it away.

I know that I should somehow try to get rid of some of my clothes. The oil makes their weight feel like tons. Tears are pouring out of my eyes from the oil, and I sense tiny salty rivulets running down my oil-covered face.

That oil! It coagulates around each body, around the debris, around the men. One officer in the water shouts, "Spread out a bit, men, and

329

let's get out of this oil." Some of the men do it; others are reluctant to get away from pieces of wood. Others depend on absorbing some strength from men around them. Not only miserable but drowning men love company.

One officer swims by me and says, "Let's make for that raft." I shake my head no, and he swims on.

About ten yards from me I see two youngsters—they must be about eighteen—laughing and joking, and I hear one say, "I'll race you to Singapore." We are fifty miles from shore and one hundred and fifty miles north of the city those youngsters are talking about.

It's the tide, not my efforts, that brings me near the Carley float. The Carley contraptions are rafts, fifteen feet long, ten feet wide, and bounded on all sides by a foot-high bulge. Extending around the bulge is a rope on which men can grab hold.

The raft toward which the tide carries me is jammed. There are men inside, men sitting solid on the bulge at the edge, and every handhold on the rope is occupied. Obviously there is no room for me, so I make no effort whatsoever, letting the tide carry me where it wants. It carries me to that raft.

A Royal Marine sitting on the edge calls to me when I am ten feet away, "Just a bit more, just a bit more." I don't answer, just look at him across that ten-foot chasm.

Gradually I draw nearer. He extends his hand as far as he can and I stretch out my hand. For five minutes our hands are three inches apart, but I don't have the energy to bridge that tiny gap. Once again the tide does it for me. Our hands meet, clasp and I'm yanked toward the raft, leaving the small table which thus far has saved my life.

The twenty-year-old marine, Morris Graney, pushes one of the men sitting on the bulge back inside the raft, on top of another man, to make way for me. Then he pulls me onto the bulge and holds me there.

His first remark is: "My Lord, do you still have your camera?"
"Yes."
"Are you all right?"
I nod.
"Can you sit here?"
I say, "Yes, I am all right."
Actually I'm not, and almost fall face forward into the water. Graney
330

grabs me, takes one of my hands—my right hand, since my left is still clenched to prevent my ring from falling off—and forces it to grasp the lifebelt of a man inside the raft.

"Hang onto him," Graney says.

I hang on.

The raft tosses and heaves with the swell of the sea. Men are bobbing and swimming on all sides near the raft, some trying to reach it, some hoping eventually to get a hand hold on it. We want to reach a destroyer which is stationary about a mile or a mile and a half away. There is one paddle on board, and some one inside, using the paddle, is calling, "Heave ho, heave ho, heave, ho!"

Graney says, "Let's all sing." Not many voices join in his choice, "When Irish Eyes Are Smiling," but the voices that do are cheerful.

Graney wears only shorts and his thick chest is covered with oil. His brown hair hangs over his forehead and into his eyes. I think just the sight of Graney helps many a man. He is almost six feet tall, husky, almost barrel-chested. Above a square jaw he has a slim, delicate mustache and blue, kind, shy eyes. All the time the only one definable emotion expressed in those eyes is amusement. Graney's amusement is enough, though, as the raft tosses. I am deathly sick at the stomach, and dizzy, too, and again almost fall forward. Graney grabs me.

"You stay right here," he says, slapping me on the shoulder.

"I am very tired," I say, "and I want to rest down there."

Graney slaps me across the face, saying, "Now, none of that. You stay right here with me."

"No. Those other men aren't on the raft," I say. "I am tired, and I can rest better in the water."

Graney's hand is digging into my arm and shoulder. It hurts, but somehow I don't protest. I just know it hurts.

"We're watching those other men," Graney says sharply. "They're all right. You stay right here with us."

I'm not convinced, and twist my head around to look inside the raft. It's the wrong time to do that. Men inside are vomiting and glassy-eyed, all of them black with oil. Two men have just died and their bodies are being gently hustled over the side to make room for more men. I feel a twinge of pity at the sight of it, but it seems an eminently practical thing to do.

331

Six or seven Jap bombers are roaring over again at about 5,000 feet. "They're coming over to machine-gun us!" someone says.

"Shut up that guff!" Graney growls, because we all feel bad enough as it is.

"If they come over to machine-gun us," a voice suggests, "dive under the water."

I think to myself: "If I have to dive under the water, I'm never coming up again."

They don't swoop down on us and they don't drop bombs. They just go on. It isn't Japanese chivalry or Bushido. They're just out of bombs and ammunition. With the planes gone and heads turned from the sky to the horizon, we get the impression that the destroyer is getting farther and farther away. In fact, we see one of our destroyers steam away. Someone calls in panic, "They're all going." A reply comes from somewhere inside the raft: "They'll wait for us, don't worry."

Men hanging onto the rope around the side are kicking furiously. One man says, "I'm going to swim for it." He starts out, but when he is ten yards away he calls, "I can't make it—I'm coming back." And he does. Men near me slip off the raft to go to the help of men who can be seen going under. They do it several times.

As the minutes go on and we seem to be getting no nearer to the destroyer, the morale on the raft begins to slip lower and lower. Graney is one of the first to recognize this. "Keep kicking, keep paddling!" he shouts. "We will soon be there!"

As we drew near the destroyer he said, "All right, now, it's 'Anchors Aweigh'!" And again he starts singing. Almost every one joins in then, because for the first time we seem to have a chance of rescue.

Rafts and men are converging on the destroyer from all directions. We can already see dripping figures being hauled onto the deck of the ship. Through a megaphone an officer on the bridge is shouting something at us, but we can't make it out.

"They want us to hurry," one man in our raft says. "Anyway, that's what I'd be calling if I was on the bridge."

The oil around the destroyer seems about two feet thick, solid oil. To me it looks like dirty black castor oil. And it tastes the same.

A rope with a loop at the end is tossed thirty feet from the destroyer to us. We miss it. The rope is hauled back and again is hurled. Someone grabs it, but Graney tears it out of his hands and roughly passes

332

the loop over me. "We have an American war correspondent here," he shouts at the destroyer. Then he waves and shouts, "Heave up, heave up!"

He asks solicitously, "Can you hold onto the rope?"

"Of course. Don't worry about me. I'm all right."

And the men on the destroyer pull me off the edge of the Carley float. I sink underneath the oil, and for ten feet while I'm dragged underneath the surface I feel I'm plowing my way through some kind of a solid wall. The pressure pounds at my head like a great rubber hammer.

Then I'm beside the destroyer. A wooden ladder hangs over the side.

"Grab hold—hurry!" someone on the destroyer yells down.

I try to reach the bottom rung and can't. It is four feet above the water. The gentle undulation of the oily waves brings me nearer. I make a lunge and get my right hand on the bottom rung.

"You'll have to help yourself," a man on the destroyer calls.

Down the side of the destroyer there are other ladders, and rope mats and nets; but I am afraid if I lose my grip this time I can never make another try.

A frenzied voice calls, "Hang on, hang on! But hurry!"

I get up the ladder and four men drag me over the taffrail. The deck is burning hot on my bare feet. They strip off my clothes and someone hands me a heavy woolen parka. I put it on, and one of the officers says, "Are you all right?"

"I'm fine," I say. "Who has a camera on board this ship?"

The officer doesn't know, but he calls over another man, saying, "Find this man a camera. There must be one on board."

The rating scoots off, and I stand there while Graney, who has just been brought on board, keeps urging me to sit down and rest.

"There's plenty of time for that," I insist. "I've got to get a camera."

Graney empties the pockets of my cover-alls, bush jacket and shorts, and hands over the precious notebook in which I kept this account of the battle. I open the notebook, and see every page is water-and-oil-soaked but still legible.

About a half dozen men are dead on the deck of the destroyer. Others are being sick from the oil. Some men are laughing and joking and inquiring after their special buddies.

The hospital of the sick bay is jammed, and some of the dead are being carried out and laid on the deck. Men with blood on their faces are being carried back to the sick bay for attention. Still more survivors are being brought on board, and I snap pictures. I use up all the film. They find me another camera and I use all that film.

By then my feet are blistered from the hot deck, and I'm leaping from hot deck plate to hatch, to another hot plate, to another hatch, as though playing hopscotch.

The destroyer's chief engineer, Frank McLeod of Southsea, Hampshire, comes up and says, "I have a pair of shoes for you." He hands over a pair of the "Suitcase Simpson" caliber. "Those shoes," he says, "were last worn by one of the three survivors of the *Hood*. I gave them to a midshipman when I pulled *him* out of the water." He gives me an Engineers' Log Book, too, for taking notes, and I scurry about the ship, talking with survivors of the *Repulse* and the *Prince of Wales*, fitting the details of their personal experiences together.

The destroyer is the *Electra*, which took 1,100 men out of the hell of Dunkirk to England.

There is no bitterness among these men this afternoon about the absence of aircraft protection, just regret that they've lost their ship. One man is wailing that he'd lost the pictures of his girl friend, his mother, his dad.

Another says he's lost his penknife, to which a third replies, "Now quit your grousing. Each of us lost exactly the same thing—everything!"

After about an hour, three Brewster Buffaloes come roaring over, sweeping ten feet from the ship. The Japs are long gone by now.

In the steaming hot wardroom of the *Electra* forty or fifty officers are drinking tea, most all naked to the waist. The heat is stifling, and as we sit there—I taking notes—the sweat pours out of us as though we are under a shower.

As the sweat drips from me, I remember how exactly twenty-four hours before I sat in the comfortable wardroom of the *Repulse*, talking with the officers of the battle cruiser, and thinking of the British tendency to underestimate the enemy, to look at them solely through British eyes. "It's better," I said, "to consider your enemy twice as good as you are and twice as smart. Then you won't be surprised."

The British officers, twenty-four hours before had been amiable, cheerful and skeptical. Now in that smelling, sweltering wardroom of the *Electra*, one of the officers of the *Repulse* comes up with a rueful smile on his face and says: "You told us not to underestimate the enemy."

"Yes, I know," I say, "but I take no satisfaction in that now—not even grim satisfaction."

Some men sit at the table, their heads buried in their arms. A number of them have bandages on their heads. Men are asking each other, "Did you see So-and-So?"

The remarks I hear are these:

"The first thing I'm going to do is send a cable home."

"This is a terrible blow."

"I hope they've learned their lesson. We must have aircraft protection."

"Those Japs were bloody good."

"This shows that if a determined attack is pressed home, you can sink battleships."

"They'll get you every time without escort and aircraft."

"Did you enjoy your swim?"

"I owe him two dollars. If he's alive I'll give it to him. If he's dead he won't want it."

"I hear they're going to form us into a naval brigade, give us rifles and tell us to kill some Japs."

"We'll handle those Japs yet."

I want to know about Captain Tennant. One man speaks up: "I saw him floating face down in the water." I can find no one who has seen the other war correspondent. Gallagher gone? I can't believe it.

Down there in the wardroom I am told the sequence of attacks on the *Prince of Wales*.

The attack was similar to our own. High-level bombers and torpedo-carrying bombers. With four torpedoes in the *Wales*, Admiral Phillips said: "Tell the *Express* (which was then alongside the *Wales*) to signal to Singapore for tugs to tow us home."

It was obvious the Admiral hadn't yet made up his mind that the ship was going to sink.

I ask a lieutenant commander from the *Wales* about Admiral Phillips and Captain Leach.

They were last seen standing on the bridge of the *Prince of Wales*.

335

"The admiral and the captain stood there together," the officer says. "They would not go. As we started away, Captain Leach waved, and called out: 'Good-bye. Thank you. Good luck. God bless you.' "

Then the water rose up to meet them, meeting and then covering them.

JUNGLE RETREAT

Thursday, December 11th:

It was about 12:30 A.M. when the destroyer, speeding at thirty-one knots, got back to the Naval Base. We crossed over a bridge of two other destroyers and over a narrow gangway that was lit by a bright spotlight.

Commander Denby of the *Repulse* was standing at the gateway. We grabbed each other's hands and shook them. My first question was: "What about that British correspondent, Gallagher—is he all right?"

"Oh, yes," Denby said, "he's fine."

"Thank God for that," I said. "We all thought he went down."

I then learned that Gallagher already had left the Naval Base for Singapore. I was worried he would get his story out before I could send mine.

I went into a huge shed and the men were being given tea, but I could find no officers there. I finally found that the officers were all in a cabin of a ship tied up at the dock. I went in, and there they were, men in their oil-soaked whites. We all shook hands and then Captain Tennant came in. He spied me and we fell on each other's necks. Captain Tennant had a blood-soaked bandage around his head.

"You gave us quite a story, Captain," I said.

"Yes, it was quite a story. Did the other correspondent get away all right?"

"Yes. What worries me now is that he's already gone to Singapore."

Captain Tennant was smiling and cheerful, shaking hands with his surviving officers, but you could see, in his eyes, his heart breaking apart.

He assigned an officer to try and find a car to get me to Singapore. We went up to the Administration Building, where a captain finally arranged for a car with a Malay driver.

It began to rain, pouring rain, as we started out for Singapore. That eighteen-mile drive took an hour and a half in as heavy a rain storm as I ever expect to encounter. The driver could only move at about ten

337

miles an hour. He kept complaining bitterly about having to drive in that kind of weather.

"Go faster," I urged.

"I no want get kill," he retorted.

I was sick with exhaustion but I kept turning the story over in my mind. My stomach was turning over, too, and I was sick at heart at the number of men I knew who had gone down. That handsome gunnery officer. That jovial chief engineer. Page. Captain Leach . . .

I decided that I would go straight to the cable office to write my story instead of stopping off at Raffles Hotel. I figured that every minute was precious. Moreover, I didn't have a typewriter and I might find one at the cable office. It was still pitch black and still pouring buckets when we drew up in front of the cable office.

As I stepped out of the car I heard the wildest, most fiendish, spine-chilling cry I have ever heard, and then I saw a bayonet coming toward me and the next instant a light was flashed in my face. I was never so scared in my life. It was the Chinese guard in front of the cable office.

I shrieked at him at the top of my voice: "You goddam son-of-a-bitch!" and I went on for another minute, screaming profanity at him.

I think that saved my life because the guard seemed to be taken aback by this apparition shrieking to him in this hysterical voice. I wore a hooded wool coat and oil-covered white trousers six inches above my ankles. My legs were so weak I could hardly stand up.

Three more guards came running up and one of them spoke a bit of English. The only word I could understand was, "Papers? Papers?"

I pulled out my oil-soaked wallet and showed him my accreditation as a war correspondent. All the time I was screaming and yelling, "Get the hell out of the way! I've got a story to send. Goddam you guys—get out of the way!"

They let me go into the cable office and I was still screaming. "You bastards scare the life out of a man. If I had a gun I would've shot every one of you."

I went into the cable office, my hands shaking as though I had the palsy. I went up to the counter.

"Let me have a typewriter," I said to the Eurasian clerk. "I must have a typewriter."

"What?"

338

"Let me have a typewriter. I have just come off the *Repulse* and I've got a story to send."

"We have no typewriters," the clerk said.

"The hell you haven't—there's a typewriter over on that table."

"Oh, but that's *our* typewriter. It's not permitted for you to use it."

"You mean you won't let me use that typewriter to send this story on the *Repulse?*"

"Oh, no. Against the rules."

"All right. Give me some cable blanks."

The counter at the cable office came up to my chest. I was still perspiring like a horse. I took off the parka and stood there in a pair of shoes and the abbreviated oil-soaked white pants, and with a pencil fastened by the chain on the counter I started penciling out the first "take" of my story.

I had written about two hundred words, passing over each sheet to the clerk as I finished, when an Englishman came over to me and in the calmest, blandest voice said: "Someone said that you wanted a typewriter."

"I do very much. Do you have one?"

"Yes, you can use that typewriter over on the table."

He signaled to one of the Malay boys and the boy carried the type-writer over to the counter.

"Well, can I sit at a table? I'm terribly tired and I can hardly reach up high enough on this shelf to hit the keys."

"Oh, no," the Englishman said. "It's forbidden for anyone to come behind the counter."

"Ye gods, man!" I said. "I can hardly stand up."

"That can't be helped," he said calmly. "It's against the rules for anyone to come behind the counter."

"All right then—do you have a table? Bring out that table there and put it out here so I can sit down and type."

"Oh, no, we can't do that. If you want to, you can work on this type-writer at the counter, but that is as much as we can do for you."

I worked there at the counter and sent off about seven hundred words as the first "take" on the story. I finished at 4:35 A.M. and sent the story through Manila, which was the way I had been filing for the past few weeks. We had found that filing through Manila was faster than going through London.

339

I came back to the hotel and immediately called the telephone operator and asked him to go to the desk at the front office and see if there were any cables for me in a red-covered book where the telegrams were put on their arrival.

He called me back in a few minutes and said there were no messages.

I telephoned Ching Yeuk. She came sleepily to the phone and I said: "Ching, I just got back into town. I am sorry I couldn't keep that date Monday night, but I had to leave in such a hurry."

"Yes, one of the other correspondents said that you went on the *Prince of Wales*."

"Well, it was the *Repulse*, Ching, and it went down."

"Are you all right?"

"Yes," I said. "I'm all right, I just wanted to let you know that I was back in Singapore."

I got to sleep at 5:30 and was awakened at 8:00. The boy came up and gave me four telegrams, one scheduling me to broadcast last Monday and Tuesday. Another, received Monday, said: "File through both Manila and London. Manila transmission uncertain."

When I read that I almost went out of my mind. I jumped into a pair of pants and shirt and, still wearing my slippers, ran down from the second floor and out in front of the hotel and into a taxi and immediately rushed to the cable office—about a ten-minute drive. I instructed them to duplicate the message on the *Repulse* I had cabled a few hours before through Manila and send it to CBS New York via London.

From the cable office I went to the Remington Typewriter people and asked to borrow a typewriter, and immediately went to the Public Relations Office to begin writing more of the story.

Most of the correspondents were there. Gallagher said he was sure I had gone down. Of all the correspondents and all the military and civil officers around the office that morning only one failed to say a word to me. That was Commander William Burrows. He neither said "I'm glad you got away" or "I'm sorry you didn't go down."

I sat there and wrote all morning and managed to get almost everything I wrote through censorship. Only a few things were cut out. I could not say then that the Japs were using torpedo-carrying aircraft.

I wrote about two thousand words and then hurried to the Kodak Company with my camera. My heart was dripping tears at the sight of

340

the camera. It was covered with oil and salt water and the oil had coagulated so that it seemed like grease. The Kodak people said they would try and save it, but it was pretty doubtful.

My stop watch that I bought in Rome was beyond repair.

I have not shaved yet and have a very heavy beard. I have discovered it now comes in gray.

Four hundred and thirty-three officers, sailors and marines out of the 1,250 on board the *Repulse*, went down. About 250, out of the 1,760 on the *Prince of Wales*, were lost.

Raffles Square is still covered with debris.

I have just learned of the various officers and men who went down. It is impossible to believe that so many of those men are gone. In less than two days I developed a very great liking for them. It is hard to believe that death can be so sudden and final. One minute a man is beside you on deck and a few hours later he is not there or anywhere else in life.

I worked most of the day. My hands shake a great deal and I can't hold them still. It might be fatigue or reaction—I don't know. I feel dizzy, too, and the taste of oil is in me. I have not had a chance to take a bath.

This evening I saw Ching Yeuk for just about a half hour. She is on night nursing duty.

Here it is one o'clock in the morning and I am half dead with fatigue. I can't sleep. I feel something is rocking inside of me and always there is with me the thought of those torpedoes hitting us and the hopelessness of making my way through that oily water. I got up and wrote another story on the *Repulse* which I will send out tomorrow. A couple of wires just came in:

OVERJOYED ABOUT YOUR RESCUE   STOP   LOVE AND BLESSINGS FROM MARTHA   PLEASE FILE YOUR STORY VOLUMINOUSLY VIA MANILA AND DUPLICATE VIA LONDON   PAUL WHITE

And another one:

YOU MADE GOOD YOUR BOAST ABOUT WONDERFUL STORY   CON-GRATULATIONS   PAUL WHITE

341

Another from Joseph Phillips, managing editor of *Newsweek:*

HEARTIEST CONGRATULATIONS YOUR COMING THROUGH ALIVE AND SUPERB COLUMBIA STORY STOP APPRECIATE HAVING WEEK-END STORY SIX HUNDRED WORDS PHILLIPS

Another from Paul White:

MARTHA SAYS GREAT STORY HAPPY FOR YOU BUT HAPPIEST YOU WELL AND ALL HER LOVE STOP PLEASE CONTINUE FILING ALL NEWSWORTHY PAUL WHITE

Friday, December 12th:
Spent all morning writing more stories on the *Repulse* and the *Prince of Wales.*
I sent Martha a cable this afternoon:

HEALTH PRESENTLY REASONABLY SATISFACTORY STOP OCTOBER AIR FORCE CRASHED ME NOVEMBER ARMY TRUCK PLUNGED OVER HILL DECEMBER NAVY TRIED SINK ME SINCE NO ADDITIONAL BRANCHES OF ARMED FORCES REMAIN DON'T WORRY I'LL RETURN TO MY BEAUTIFUL WIFE LOVE

A wire came from Frank Gervasi of *Collier's:*

OVERJOYED YOU ARE SAFE STOP CAN YOU WRITE 1500 WORDS ANECDOTAL HUMAN INTEREST STORY YOUR EXPERIENCES HEROISM YOU WITNESSED WITH CLOSE ATTENTION TO HUMAN INTEREST AT-MOSPHERE COLOR WITHOUT DUPLICATING NEWSPAPER AND RADIO IMMEDIATELY STOP KAY JOINS ME IN LOVE AND BEST WISHES REGARDS TO GALLAGHER

This wire also came:

ALL OF US ARE OVERJOYED TO LEARN OF YOUR RESCUE CON-GRATULATIONS ON WONDERFUL STORY ITS STIRRING INFORMATIVE ALL ROUND GREAT REPORTING BILL PALEY

That's the first word I have ever heard from the President of CBS and I sent back this message:

MOST APPRECIATIVE YOUR GOOD WISHES ITS GREAT PRIVILEGE TO WORK FOR ORGANIZATION LIKE COLUMBIA AND PAUL WHITE'S EX-CELLENT COOPERATION IS KIND THAT INSPIRES ANY REPORTER DO HIS JOB BROWN

342

This was a harvest day of cables and this one also came:

WE WANT TO PUBLISH YOUR BOOK WHENEVER YOU WRITE IT WOULD APPRECIATE LETTER   BENNETT CERF   RANDOM HOUSE

Alfred Duff Cooper telephoned and asked me to come out for a cocktail this afternoon.

The work eased a bit today and so I was able to shave for the first time since Tuesday and to take a bath and get off the oil. It was none too soon because people would not come within fifteen feet of me—I smelled so bad.

Today I feel much worse than yesterday. I am still shaking and there is a very severe ache behind the ears and in the ears and every muscle hurts. I have a very strange feeling today. I cannot lift my arms above the shoulders and I can't understand why that is. What worries me most is that I cannot focus my mind on anything. I can't seem to hold a thought for more than an instant. I just tried it out again and I said to myself: "I am going to think of this diary in front of me for a moment."

But it didn't work. I couldn't keep my mind on it. It just seemed to go blank.

Germany and Italy have declared war on the United States and we have retaliated. It is the big fight to the finish.

I am trying to locate another camera because I am pretty sure that Kodak will be unable to repair mine.

I bought another Remington noiseless typewriter. I'm trying to find a rubber preserver for it in case I get any more sea assignments.

I drove out to Duff Cooper's at about 5:45. Lady Diana was there, two Dutch officers, a British colonel and Colonel Francis G. Brink, the United States Army observer here. Later Gallagher showed up and I described the sinking of the *Repulse* and the *Prince of Wales*.

Duff Cooper welcomed me very warmly: "I'm very, very happy to see you alive."

"I am too," I laughed.

When I had finished my story Duff Cooper said: "This engagement makes me revise my belief in battleships. I don't have much confidence in them any more."

343

The British colonel said: "It is pretty obvious we underestimated the Japs."

Colonel Brink remarked: "We train our soldiers the way we fight instead of using the tactics of our logical enemy. That's been the case in all the maneuvers in the Philippines."

The two Dutch officers said nothing.

Lady Diana was furious at the underestimation of the Japanese and the failure to provide air protection for the *Repulse* and the *Prince of Wales*.

I told Duff Cooper and the others about swimming through the oil and remarked that it never occurred to me that the ship might explode because of the fire raging on board. Duff Cooper exclaimed: "Well, you know, Brown, that oil in the water too might have caught fire."

"Thank God," I said, "you weren't there to remind me of *that*."

Later I asked Duff Cooper how long he thought this war would last. He pursed his lips and hesitated for a moment.

"We'll be fighting this time next year," he said. "There is no doubt that the Japanese entry has prolonged the war."

Saturday, December 13th:
I made two broadcasts today, but I don't know whether they were received in New York.

Cabled six hundred words to *Newsweek* on the *Repulse* and worked on the *Collier's* piece.

I still have those blank spells in my mind. They worry me very much. I don't know what it comes from or what I can do about it.

The first success of submarine operations against Japanese forces has just been announced. Four fully loaded Japanese troopships were torpedoed and sunk during Friday night off Patani in South Thailand by subs of the Royal Netherlands Navy. Patani is one of the bridgeheads established by the Japanese. This means those Dutchmen were ready to go. They didn't lose any time in getting started or taking the offensive.

I have just been permitted to say in a broadcast for the first time that the Japanese success against the *Prince of Wales* and the *Repulse* was due primarily to the absence of protection by British fighter air-

344

craft. Previously the censors cut that out although I tried to send stories saying so at least six times during Thursday and Friday.

Sunday, December 14th:
In my broadcast early this morning to America, my script read:
"The country around Kota Bahru gives the Japs a great advantage for defense. In other words, it will be very difficult for the British to drive them out of Kota Bahru."

The censors made that sentence read: "The country around Kota Bahru makes any Japanese advance difficult."

That might have been true, but it certainly wasn't what I wanted to say. The military situation is pretty mysterious. The high command gives no indication how far the Japs have penetrated from Thailand.

Voluntary evacuation of Singapore is going on and Chinese families pile their possessions on two-wheel carts drawn by oxen and trundle out into the country for the duration.

There is some food hoarding and restrictions on quantity purchases have just been imposed. Numerous profiteers are being arrested.

Raffles Hotel still has dancing every night, but there are not as many dancers.

A good deal of the apathy about war has gone. In any event, it is true that the certainty that war would not come to Singapore has disappeared.

I had dinner tonight with Morris Graney, the Royal Marine who saved my life, and he gave me some additional details of what was happening during the action.

Monday, December 15th:
Censorship has been fairly decent so far. I broadcast from here usually about 7:23 in the morning. In New York that is 6:53 P.M. the previous evening. The censorship office closes at 6 P.M. and I have no intention of writing a broadcast at 6 P.M. for delivery thirteen hours later. So I have made special arrangements with Captain O. K. Fearon to censor my copy before midnight. He is living at the Singapore Club and I take my script to him after late dinner. I usually find him playing billiards and we go off into a small room and discuss the script. Thus far he has made only minor changes.

345

Tuesday, December 16th:

I finished the piece for *Collier's* on the *Repulse* and it went through censorship with only a few changes. Tonight I had dinner again with Morris Graney of the Royal Marines. He tells me that their leave is ended and that all the *Repulse* survivors, except the injured, are now back on duty.

There was an alert at 9:15 tonight which lasted for an hour. Graney and I went across Beach Road and stood in a field but nothing happened. I was on the point of dropping from exhaustion and Graney urged me to take care of myself and get some rest.

"I'll rest when the war is over," I told him.

"Yes," Graney said, "I guess that's the way it will be for all of us."

Singapore is holding its breath for the expected land, sea, and air attack which it is believed the Japanese must carry out if they hope to make real progress. But there is increasing concern about the trend of the fighting.

The defenses of Singapore are strong, but the city does not have the advantage of mountains as at Hongkong or Gibraltar.

I remarked in my broadcast today that reports of the fighting in Malaya must seem confusing, but that they are no more confusing than the communiqués issued by the Singapore GHQ.

Captain Fearon changed the last part of that to read: "But the communiqués issued by the Singapore GHQ give very little information."

That was the compromise we reached after a half hour's argument over that one sentence. I was also allowed to say: "There is considerable concern among the people, too, about the inadequacy of the communiqués. The mystery of the situation and the meager reports issued tend to cause the spread of all kinds of rumors.

"Correspondents here," my broadcast continued, "are working under the greatest difficulties and those who have seen many years' war service say they have never encountered anything to compare with it.

"British and American correspondents here for four months offered suggestions and urged officials to prepare for coverage of a war. The outbreak of the war found no changes, with the result that efforts to report the situation in Malaya are very severely restricted."

Personally, I think the whole situation here reeks, and I can't find anything to be encouraged about. But every British officer I have talked

346

with today is brimming with supreme confidence. I don't feel that way at all.

Wednesday, December 17th:
Miracle of miracles! I went down to Kodak and back into the repair room and I found about a thousand pieces of my camera spread over the table. The Chinese workman there, who spoke no English, gave me what I considered a dirty look for putting a good camera into oil and salt water. By hand acrobatics I tried to find out from him whether he thought the camera could be saved. I could only get one word from him and it was "Good." I could not determine whether he meant it was good for me that I should lose the camera or that it could be repaired. I tackled the manager and he said that he thought the camera would be all right.

I finally went to the doctor today. My ears ache very badly and my chest hurts. That's the oil poisoning. It's a nuisance. If I could get one night's sleep I might be all right. My blood pressure is down to 104, which is the lowest it's ever been.

I sent off three sets of pictures I took aboard the destroyer to *Life* magazine; one I sent by boat direct to San Francisco, another went by air to Cairo for relay from there, and the third set I sent with a military plane bound for London and asked Bob Trout, the CBS man there, to give it to the British Ministry of Information to mail to *Life*. One of those sets ought to get to New York.

Censorship is getting very difficult, or else Captain Fearon is getting more resentful of being taken away from his nightly billiard games.

Thursday, December 18th:
The Japanese troops are now fourteen miles from Penang. This news came as a terrific shock to everyone in Singapore, and, as I understand it, throughout Malaya. People can hardly believe the Japs now have Alor Star and Sungei Patani. It was the first news they had that the Japanese had penetrated more than seventy-five miles from the Thai border. Up to now the people of Malaya thought that the Japs were being held almost at the frontier; instead they are well within Malaya and are about to take Penang.

I said in my broadcast this morning: "The prospects of holding Penang are not very bright. The momentum of the Japanese drive has not diminished and the country approaching Penang is even more favorable than the area the Japanese already have conquered.

"If the Japanese capture Penang they will secure a port on the Indian Ocean. But more important, their position will be very much better for the inevitable land drive on Singapore. It is apparent that Singapore is facing considerable danger right now.

"At the moment, the greatest weapon the British jungle fighters have is courage. There is no want of that, but the Japanese are fighting with courage, too. And, besides, they have more men and more equipment. Another encouraging aspect is that the British are retreating in an orderly fashion. At least, those are the indications we have here."

It took over an hour's fighting with Captain Fearon to get that script through. He said it was "too morbid and too pessimistic." My argument was that it's factual for one thing and the other reason was that it's the only way we can get reinforcements out here.

What's breaking my heart is the absence of activity by the Royal Air Force. The British troops are getting bombed and machine-gunned and they are getting no support by the British from the air. I am not allowed to say that, but I succeeded in trying to indicate what was happening, and I broadcast: "There's a strange absence of dogfights in the air thus far. Since Saturday, seven Japanese aircraft have been brought down, all by anti-aircraft fire."

I bought a filter for my camera—yellow. I am beginning to feel somewhat better. The inside of the ears still aches, but the chest hurts less.

Late this afternoon I ran into Major-General Gordon Bennett. He has just come back from the Middle East and seems very uncertain of his position. We had a drink together, and he asked me if I had heard of any staff changes. I said no, and he replied he had not either. I thought he clearly indicated that he thought there should be some here at any rate. I asked him about the recent Western Desert campaign.

"Oh, it was all ballsed up, and I made a report on it," he said.

"How do you think things are going here?" I asked.

"They don't tell me anything," Bennett said.

"Are your Australians all set?"

348

"They certainly are. They're as fine a body of men as I ever ran into, either in this war or the last war."

"Do you think you can stop the Japs?"

"Of course," he exclaimed. "We'll stop them all right."

The usual official communiqué came out this evening. It said: "We have successfully disengaged the enemy and are south of the River Krian."

I stared at that phrase—"successfully disengaged the enemy." It made no sense to me and I mulled it over for minutes. Then it suddenly occurred to me that someone had coined a beautiful phrase of defeatist optimism. I rolled it around on my tongue—*successfully disengaged the enemy.*

It also meant to me that the British were south of Penang, since the River Krian is south of that island.

I said to Major Fisher, "I'm going to say in my broadcast that the British have evacuated Penang."

"I can assure you," Major Fisher said, "that it is not correct to say that Penang has been evacuated. Our troops are still there."

That was either a deliberate lie or else Major Fisher was wallowing in his customary misinformation.

Gallagher left by plane for Rangoon tonight. He thinks the invasion of Burma is going to be extremely important, and he wants to cover his paper on that. I urged him not to go, that Singapore would be the big story.

Friday, December 19th:

The rumors around town are terrific. The Malays and Chinese are especially concerned. As near as I can make out they have absolutely no confidence any longer in what the British tell them. That's because of the communiqué the other day which revealed the Japs were already seventy-five miles inside Malaya. Everyone knows that Penang has been evacuated, but we can't say it.

Refugees are streaming into Singapore, and since the British refuse to admit the Penang debacle, the people fear the worst. You can almost see morale collapsing like a punctured tire.

349

The correspondents who made the trip up north are yelling around town like madmen. I saw a few of them this morning and they are almost crazy with indignation. They have found that the copy they sent back was cut to bits by the censors.

At noon today just as I started out of Raffles I saw a brigadier general coming in. I recognized him at once as Brigadier General C. A. Lyon, commander of the Penang Fortress, who had shown us around his island last August. He wore no coat, his shirt was open at the neck, and he was carrying a swagger stick, a steel helmet and gas mask. He looked done in. His monocle was suspended by an ordinary piece of cord from around his neck.

"How are you?" he said.

"Fine, General. How are you?"

"Well," he said, "we got them all off."

"Penang abandoned then?"

"Yes. I'm finished. I was due to be retired in two months anyhow. I've been relieved of my command."

"Come on over and have a drink and tell me about it," I said.

As we started over for a table I added, "You got them all out?"

"Yes, we all got away. I'm an old man anyhow. I'm going up now and get a couple of hours' rest."

"I'd like to get the story, General. Let's meet for a drink at five o'clock."

"All right, I'll see you here in the bar at five o'clock."

I went over to the Cathay Building and saw Robert Scott, head of the Ministry of Information.

"Well," he said, "you were right in the things we should have done."

"I don't get any consolation out of that, Scott," I said. "This whole coverage is being messed up and we've got to do something about it. You can see morale disappearing all over the place."

"I know it," Scott said. "Now the great difficulty is with the high command. They agree in principle with propaganda but will do nothing to co-operate."

"Everybody knows that the show has folded up at Penang and we can't report it yet. People are believing the worst. For all they know the Japs are right outside Singapore."

"I know," Scott said, "but what can we do? Take last night's communiqué. We said Penang must be mentioned in the communiqué, but they absolutely refused."

"Who refused?"

"Sir Robert Brooke-Popham and General Percival. They said we can't mention it."

"Well, things are certainly in a hell of a mess."

"We are treating the Asiatics here as children," Scott said. "As a matter of fact, they are holding up better than most of the Europeans."

"Can't you do anything with the high command?"

"They think that propaganda is a good thing, but when we try to pin them down to a concrete thing they say, 'Well, those are details.' The result is that we can't put anything out. The high command's attitude is to throw into the propaganda job misfits who are no good for any military job and who know nothing about press work."

Scott told me that Commander Burrows had resigned and his resignation had been accepted, but that Sir Robert Brooke-Popham asked him to stay on until a successor was found.

A number of the Americans are evacuating from Singapore for Batavia. One ship is going on Sunday, taking women and children.

I've been hearing stray remarks that Singapore might fall. This is the first time I have heard that kind of talk.

At five this afternoon, as agreed, I met Brigadier General Lyon. He seemed a bit less harassed but obviously still under great nervous tension. We each ordered a stengah—that is, a whisky and water in a small glass—and Lyon told me the story of the beautiful, compact island of Penang. It turned out to be one of the most tragic stories of the British Empire.

"We blew up most of the ammunition dumps, the big guns and the concrete emplacements," Lyon said.

"I thought Penang was to be held. I thought that it was a second Singapore—or at least supposed to be."

"Not at all," Lyon said. "I will tell you what happened there. About four days ago or three days ago they took almost all of my men away from me to use on the mainland. The Japanese still kept coming down and General Heath's aide brought word from the general that he

351

wanted a decision on Penang. I made my decision and the aide said: 'I disagree with it.' "

" 'My decision is made,' I told him, 'and I stand by it.'

"I outlined the situation in twenty words to Heath and ordered the evacuation. Penang is not a base. We would have served no good by staying there. I know there is going to be a lot of criticism both about the native population and the military evacuation, but I did the only thing that could be done."

"What was done, General?"

"We didn't stand much of a chance. If they would have sent me four battalions I could have held out for a long time."

General Lyon seemed reluctant to tell me just what was done, but kept justifying himself to me.

"The Japanese tactic was to by-pass us and all we could do was sit there."

"Did you get everyone off?"

"Well, it was a bit confused. All of our troops came away and six of the Asiatic volunteers. Five hundred of the Asiatic volunteers stayed with their rifles waiting for the Japs. They weren't going to resist. There was no native evacuation."

"Why not?"

"We didn't have ships, only had a few boats. We used two ferry boats and they started down the coast through the Straits of Malacca and one of them swamped and the other is coming down very slowly."

"Did you lose much material?"

"We got off a thousand feet of cable and 40,000 rounds of ammunition. We had to do all the work. We had to do all the demolition. The native labor deserted us, so did the policemen. They went back into the hills. We even had to bake our own bread and do our own cooking.

"Two ammunition ships came in a couple of days ago. We got part of one ship unloaded and the other one I sent out to sea to get it away from there. The ammunition we unloaded I strung out along the main street—you know, that residential street—and I had it set with a time fuse. When it goes off it will destroy one section of the town and eliminate the bodies. Oh, yes, there were so many bodies we had to work in town with gas masks on because of the bodies. There were about a thousand bodies lying around. We just had to shovel them off

352

into trucks to get them away and dump them outside of town and set fire to them.

"We destroyed everything we could. Penang became a Vesuvius—yes, it became a Vesuvius. We blew up the guns set in their concrete bases. We did everything we could but we only had forty-eight hours to do it."

General Lyon said that about four hundred or five hundred British troops were trapped in the Butterworth Area across from Penang. "They have gone around it and are mopping up. The Japanese will not take any prisoners," he said.

General Lyon explained that the Japanese are using small mortars, rifles and small tanks, something like Bren gun carriers, and tommy-guns.

"The Japanese charged straight at us but they didn't seem to care for crossing open fields. Their tactics are to use wide encirclements something like infiltration. They have heavy casualties by these tactics. Our machine guns mow them down. Their bombing is not very good. They came over Glugor barracks several times but they only killed four soldiers and wounded six."

Brigadier Lyon's whole thesis was that without naval protection and without an air force to guard it from the air, Penang ceased to be an effective base of operations. The Japanese were in the process of swinging around Butterworth and ignoring Penang when the British evacuation was completed.

General Lyon made the startling admission that the docks were not destroyed.

"General," I said, "did you get any of those anti-aircraft guns away?"

"We didn't have any."

"What! When I was up there last August you said you had twenty-eight or something like that."

"I had ordered forty," Brigadier Lyon said, "but I never did get them. I didn't have a single one."

"Do you mean to say that Penang didn't have a single anti-aircraft gun?"

"That's right—we didn't have one. The anti-aircraft guns that we were supposed to have, or at least some of them, got to Singapore and were kept there.

"Well," the brigadier said, as we drained our glasses, "I am seeing the C-and-C the first thing in the morning to make my report. I will let you see a copy after I turn it in."

I left the brigadier and went over to the press conference to get the communiqué, but it only said: "The situation is quiet and there has been some R.A.F. reconnaissance."

There was nothing in it whatever about Penang.

Saturday, December 20th:
I cabled this story to *Newsweek* magazine:

"Unless additional aircraft is supplied to the British forces in Malaya, Singapore stands in grave danger (I tried to say the 'gravest danger' but the censor toned it down) from the land advance. The wishful thinking and almost country-wide conviction among the military that the Japanese would back down as well as the underestimation of the Japanese strength plus the suddenness of the Japanese attack are responsible for the present situation.

"There is throughout Singapore great criticism of the amazing unwillingness of the high command to inform the people what's going on. This method of treating Asiatics as well as Europeans as children who are unable to stand bad news is inevitably causing internal repercussions. It is believed that Sir Robert Brooke-Popham is personally writing the communiqués and determining what revelations will be allowed."

Raffles Hotel is filled with evacuees. There are a great many new faces around the bar and it is a refreshing sight. Many of the evacuees have very little clothing. Young mothers, wives of rubber-estate managers, with a child or two, sit around the bar waiting for I don't know what. And there are so many pregnant women it must be that every wife up in the country was pregnant.

A few of the evacuees seem rather forlorn. Obviously, they have no news from their husbands since they were shipped south, but most of them appear rather cheerful and chipper. I feel sorry for any woman with a child out here these days.

I still don't have another tin hat to replace the one I lost on the *Repulse.* They just don't have them and I understand that seven hundred Indian troops are actually moving up to go into action without steel helmets because of the shortage.

I have never felt so insecure in my life as here in Singapore. I feel that tremendous bombings are coming on and there's not much to stop it nor, I fear, much in the way of land forces to stop the Japanese advance, incredible as that seems.

I have been fairly optimistic about Singapore, but now the shadow of coming events seems to be in front of me. The realization that Singapore can and might fall is becoming more vivid almost every moment. I am getting this feeling by something like a process of osmosis because every British officer I talk to is still very confident. Then, too, there is the feeling that reinforcements are coming. Surrounded by all this optimism of the officers and the indifference of the British civilians I keep questioning myself whether I am justified in being so pessimistic.

Here it is late Saturday night and the high command has not yet announced the evacuation of Penang which took place at nine P.M. Thursday. The communiqué tonight was the shortest yet issued by GHQ. It said: "There is nothing to report."

All around town earlier this evening I heard nothing but criticism of the way things are going. The lieutenant of an Indian regiment, who was a tea planter in India and who is rather a good friend of mine whom I see often, said to me: "Well, Penang taught us a lesson— how to deal with the natives. They panicked rather badly, you know."

The criticism of Brooke-Popham and the Governor is now rather widespread. One comment is: "We ought to throw out the whole damn lot of them. You people did it at Hawaii."

I saw Brigadier Lyon again for a few minutes tonight. He said that at the time of the evacuation he had one battalion made up of volunteers, eighty percent of them Asiatics, one company of Indian troops, two hundred and fifty Royal Artillerymen.

I asked Lyon about the panic.

"Oh, there wasn't so much panic as there was looting."

"Did you shoot into them?"

"No, we didn't shoot any, and I didn't declare martial law. The trouble with that is that you get the people against you. I told the Resident Commissioner that I wasn't declaring martial law but that

355

we would take charge in some places and that we would shoot if necessary, and that if things were not right we would have martial law right away."

As we stood there at the bar at Raffles talking, a young couple came in for the dancing going on at the hotel, and General Lyon snorted: "Look at that, he is about a five." (A "five" is the lowest army intelligence rating.)

The man was wearing a white coat, was round-shouldered, and had a sallow complexion.

She was in evening dress, dumpy, her breasts overly exposed. She was obviously a tart and a cheap one at that.

"God," General Lyon muttered, "these people don't even know there is a war."

"That's Singapore," I said. "This thing has turned my stomach in flip-flops for four months."

"It is not only Singapore," General Lyon said. "It is all of Malaya." There was an inexpressible sadness in his voice.

Sunday, December 21st:
Did my usual early morning broadcast and then came back and sent a cable to Paul White, asking if I could leave Singapore and go to the front. There are several reasons for that. One is the great shortage of actual news you can get here, and besides I don't think my stomach can stand any more of this apathy and the dancing in Singapore. Another reason is that I want to spend Christmas at the front.

Singapore is tightening its belt. Food courses in hotels are severely restricted and the once plentiful butter is reduced to a single square. Many food items are being rationed.

Two of the four main picture houses have been taken over by the Government, apparently only to get the air-conditioning systems out of them.

I find the blackout here very effective and filled with danger. The Chinese and Malayan guards, many of whom speak only the English word, "Halt," shriek the word out of the darkness. That to me is more alarming than dropping bombs, and, besides, they all have itchy trigger-fingers and I am very much afaid that I am going to get shot by one of them.

Many Singapore shops have boarded up their windows, but there is
356

not much use of sand bags. Jewelry shops have emptied their show cases and put their stocks in steel vaults. That is in case of rioting.

They are putting up rows of barbed-wire around the Singapore waterfronts, and now the playing fields of Singapore are no more. They are erecting barriers in every field here where enemy aircraft might land, barriers such as broken ox carts, and cast-off benches.

The only people who seem unaffected by the war are the rickshaw coolies. They wear their blue coats and wide straw hats, and grin at everything, and still haven't the faintest idea where you want to go. War for them is just something that has been going on for a half dozen centuries.

Lieutenant Peter Court of a Dogra regiment who used to be a tea planter in India told me some interesting details about Kota Bahru. He said that one Jap in each landing party ran in front of the troops and threw a mat made of slats over barbed wire and the others scrambled over it. The mat carrier was always killed but the others were able to get over.

One battalion of Dogras at Kota Bahru suffered very heavy casualties and three company commanders were killed.

"The Japanese who made the landing at Kota Bahru were very tough, highly trained troops," the lieutenant said. "They had bulging muscles on their arms and legs."

Court said, too, that one of the planes shot down had a German pilot, wearing a Luftwaffe uniform.

"Did you see him, Peter?" I asked.

"No, I didn't, but I talked with a man who did."

"Well, that's the trouble, everyone I talk to says that there are German pilots, but I can't find anyone who's actually seen and talked with one of them."

It is hell fighting up in the jungle. After three days in the swamps, the British were in a sorry state; the bottoms of their shoes dropped off and their feet swelled up. Their bodies were covered with leeches, and when twenty of them get on a person's body, it becomes very painful and a good deal of energy is lost. Keringahs, huge red ants, also are very bad.

I heard a good story about the Gurkhas. They seem to be the only ones who are adapting themselves. They take off their clothes and,

357

wearing only loin cloths, they cover themselves with grease to make them slippery so they can't be grabbed by the enemy. Then they go off into the night armed with a *khukri*—a twelve-inch curved knife—which is standard equipment.

They creep up on Jap sentries and slice their heads off. The *khukri* is so sharp you can shave with it.

The odds are frightful against the British everywhere. The enemy went for the airdromes, and the British were either not ready for them or not equipped to deal with the attack. This was true at Kota Bahru and at Sungei Patani. At both places most of the aircraft were locked away. I understand that out of twelve Lockheed-Hudson bombers, only two got away and into the air.

There is considerable Fifth-Column activity going on in the north. At one place Fifth Columnists pulled down the goal posts on the playing field and pointed them toward a gun position, to tip off the Japs.

Monday, December 22nd:
I went out to the airport to see Bill Dunn, the CBS representative who is on his way from Rangoon to Batavia. I told him that I was trying to get up to the front and perhaps it would be a good idea if he stayed in Singapore while I did that.

Transportation, however, is rather unsatisfactory out of here and he thought it best to go on to Batavia and then perhaps return to Singapore so that I could then go to North Malaya.

In front of the Union Building I ran into Major Gavin of the British Intelligence. I had not seen him since that dinner at Colonel Grimsdale's. He was in Penang and had just come down.

"Do you think we can hold the Japs?"

"It's going to be touch and go. There's a fifty-fifty chance."

"Only if we get aircraft here," I said.

"That's right, we certainly need aircraft."

I also said good-bye to Colonel Grimsdale. He is on his way to Chungking.

Sir Robert Brooke-Popham held a general meeting for civic leaders and representatives of the various racial groups, as well as the press.

The purpose of the meeting was to inspire confidence, to try and counteract the Penang disaster, and to squelch fantastic rumors.

Sir Robert stood up before the group and spoke in an abashed, hesitant, unconfident, uninspiring way.

"The object of this meeting is to picture, as I see it, the situation here in relation to the future of the war as a whole. Let us admit that retirement might not have been necessary had we larger forces and more military equipment. You all know that a lot of airplanes and other equipment has gone to Russia. Without that we don't know what should have happened in Russia. Maybe this equipment turned the scale. Some of it might have come here.

"Those responsible for allotment of troops and equipment judged very accurately what was necessary to turn the scale in Russia and Libya. Now that conditions have changed we can be confident they will make readjustments. This is a world war and we must all take a world-wide view of it. Up until the last month or two there was no certainty that war would break out here. The authorities in England would not have been justified in sending equipment out here when we were at peace."

The general repetitive theme of the Commander-in-Chief's remarks was the sacrifice made by Malaya in not getting equipment and aircraft so that other battle areas might have them.

"We may have lost," Sir Robert suggested, "a large part of Northern Malaya, but it is for a time only. There must be no despondency over temporary setbacks. Every effort is being made in other parts of the world to provide us with the help that we need."

Then Sir Robert came to what seemed to be the main purpose of this meeting, pleading for the assistance of the native population.

"Co-operation in modern war cannot be considered only on a military plane, it must be co-operation of the civil community. It is a privilege for all of us to take part in this struggle for the survival of civilization. At first the noise of anti-aircraft and bombs may terrify the people, but one learns adjustment. In air attacks there is a tendency of labor to disappear for a whole day. Dispersal, yes, that may be necessary, but not disappearance. There is also an appalling amount of loose talk and rumors. They are fantastic rumors. We should stop them and stop unimportant criticism."

In order to allay some of the fear of the Japanese which is now

359

developing among the civil population, Sir Robert emphasized that the Japanese tactics were not new, but that the British were encountering some difficulties because the Japs dressed as ordinary Malayans or Chinese coolies, and the British soldier didn't know until too late these Japs weren't harmless.

"The Japanese have a capacity to live on the country," Sir Robert said. "They require very, very little and what they do find to eat is what they are used to. The British can't do that."

Another reason Sir Robert gave for the present military situation was this: "We were put at a disadvantage by Thailand. We were puzzled whether Thailand would support the Japanese or not."

When Sir Robert finished, an Indian leader of the community jumped to his feet and said: "We are ready to fight and die for the defense of Malaya, but we want to be sure that you British also are ready to fight and die for this country."

"Naturally, naturally," Sir Robert said. "We are going to defend Singapore."

"We want to be assured," the Indian shouted, "that you are not going to abandon us the way the Asiatics of Penang were abandoned. If there is going to be an evacuation from Singapore, we want it to be on the basis of equality, not just the English people."

"We are not going to evacuate Singapore, and I can assure you the Asiatics will receive the same treatment as the British."

"That is all I want to know," the Indian native said. "We will fight beside the British, but we don't want to be discriminated against."

It was a pitiful meeting and several other Asiatics got up to pledge fidelity to the British cause. But underlining everything they said was the fear that Britain would abandon them.

It was Sir Robert Brooke-Popham's golden opportunity to convince these Asiatic leaders and the editors of the vernacular newspapers that Britain would hang on and fight to the last man and every Asiatic should do the same, but his unconfident appearance and hesitant manner failed miserably.

The meeting depressed, rather than elevated, the morale of the Asiatics.

Colonel Field, the Deputy Director of Military Intelligence who replaced Colonel Grimsdale, is now holding a daily press conference.

They are quite large now because a number of additional correspondents have come in during the past week.

Martin Agronsky of NBC came in from Cairo. I last saw Martin in Ankara and he called me on his arrival here and said: "Let's have a drink."

We had the drink. He wanted to know how you go about arranging facilities. I told him to come with me and I would introduce him to all the officials and show him just how transmissions are arranged out of here.

Martin was somewhat taken back by what he called "this unusual co-operation."

"You mean," he asked incredulously, "you are willing to help me?"

"Why not, Martin?"

"Well, after all, we are competitors."

"Listen, Martin, I haven't got time to worry about your getting an exclusive story or me getting an exclusive story. We are trying to cover this war and report it to the American people, and when bombs are dropping you don't have time to worry about scoops; you just do the best job you can."

"Well, that's fine, but that isn't the way we correspondents worked in Ankara."

"That's the way I feel like working here, and if you want to go out and scoop me, go right ahead. I am too busy to worry about that."

"All right, fine," Martin said. "I will give you what I know and you can give me what you get."

"No, it won't work that way. I will be glad to introduce you to the people I know here and I am always running into people from up north that I know and I will be glad to help you, in every way possible."

And so it worked out.

This evening I went out to Holland Road to dine with Major Gavin, Captain Chapman and Basil Goodfellow who works in Economic Warfare. Gavin was all apologies.

"We have a job to do about 9:15," he said.

Shortly after nine Gavin and Chapman went out in tennis shoes, heavily armed, and said that they would be back around eleven.

After they left, Goodfellow and I chatted for awhile.

"I don't think it will do any harm to tell you now," Goodfellow finally said, "that there is going to be an alarm at ten o'clock."

"Does that mean Gavin and Chapman are going to be responsible for that alarm?"

"Yes. It won't be a raid but they are blowing the sirens to try to catch a number of Fifth Columnists who flash lights up to the skies and signal to the Japs."

ROAD TO DOOM

Tuesday, December 23rd:

The situation is going from bad to worse. There is no indication that the Japanese are being stopped at any point. They are actually in areas now where the country is more open. They are only fifteen miles from Ipoh and entering a country of many well-developed rubber estates and world-famous tin mines.

The Japs are attempting to break through at Kuala Kangsar, and to reach this point they have to go over areas where there are meager jungle trails. These trails could only have been found through consistent espionage work. The Japanese are making very effective use of three-inch mortars. They are carrying them through the jungles on their heads or shoulders. The gunners encircle the British and set up their mortars behind the British gun positions. Some British 25-pounders, which were so effective in the Western Desert, were knocked out at one point by the small Jap mortars in this way.

"There are no reports here," I broadcast this morning, "that the British are carrying out any kind of scorched-earth policy. The Japanese were able to get large quantities of rice in Kedah, the biggest rice state in Malaya. Kedah is now under complete Japanese occupation. Considerable quantities of rice also were reported stored in Butterworth, just across the bay from the island of Penang.

"The territory occupied by the Japanese thus far will provide them with vast supplies of rubber. Whether they make use of it now depends only on their ability to work the rubber estates.

"The fighting thus far has revealed many weaknesses in the British conception of jungle warfare. The Japanese are fighting a war of mobility, their soldiers carry very little equipment and move and encircle with great agility. The Japanese casualties have been great, but so has their advance."

Tom Fairholl, the Australian correspondent, just came back from the front and told me stories of heroic men. In one place a company commander fought a rear-guard action for twelve hours. He was hopelessly outnumbered. His last message was: "We are going into the jungle to get them. We can't last more than ten minutes. Good-bye."

It breaks your heart. The incredible odds against the men. And it makes you proud that we have such courage on our side.

I went out to luncheon today with Major General F. Keith Simmons, commander of the Singapore Fortress, and his aide, Lieutenant Geoffrey Hallowes. Simmons has a very pleasant villa on the outskirts of Singapore with a huge verandah and beautiful grounds.

I arrived there before Simmons, and Geoffrey and I were talking for a time when the general came in from GHQ. He was unruffled as usual and we had an excellent lunch.

"What's the best way to stop the Japs?" I asked the general.

"The best tactics are to hunt out the Japs like the gangsters they are. Just go into the jungle and rout them out. They aren't using anything new or different."

"Do you think Singapore can hold?"

"Well, the Japs want this place and they are going to take a good crack at it, and we are going to give them a good crack back."

"What is your opinion, General, of the way the fighting is going?"

"Not too badly, but we seem too reluctant to do any earth-scorching. It is a mistake to say, 'Well, we will be coming back here.' You can be sure that the Japs will do as the Germans, if they are driven out."

Simmons had another point to make too.

"Sir Robert Brooke-Popham was talking to General Percival on a trunk call today," Simmons said. "The operator interrupted to say, 'Your three minutes have expired, sir.' And she cut the connection. They were discussing an extremely vital military matter but the telephone company is privately owned and we have not yet bothered to take it over." Simmons paused, and when I said nothing, he spoke again.

"You are thinking," he said, "that we don't take everything over as the Germans and Japs would."

I changed the subject and asked about the morale of the men up at the front.

"The men are in good heart," Simmons said. "They are not discouraged and they're anxious to get at the Japs. I don't think our casualties have been very heavy."

364

Simmons thought the best kind of an army for jungle warfare is actually a couple of thousand very small groups to go in after the enemy.

We got back again to the subject of scorched earth and fighting an all-out war.

"We British," Simmons said, "are always too much concerned with considering things. We don't just take a barge or a boat or a bicycle. It always has to be taken 'under consideration.' A lieutenant or a captain or even a major doesn't go in and take over what he needs in a certain section because he always has a fear that he will get a notice saying: 'You should not have done that and we are deducting the civilian claim from your pay.' Naturally, an officer doesn't want to get stuck for five pounds, so he doesn't take the barge or bicycle."

After lunch General Simmons took me around his garden, showing me his orchids. The orchids give off an air of beauty and General Simmons gives off an air of supreme confidence. Of all the British generals I've met I like Simmons best. He doesn't have that stodginess which seems to be a part of the equipment of most British officers above the rank of colonel.

Wednesday, December 24th:
In my broadcast this morning I pictured the military situation in broad outlines and added:

"This is guerrilla fighting and jungle fighting where visibility is often about fifty yards and there might be a Jap behind every one of the thousands of trees in a rubber plantation. It is the warfare of savages where swamps, jungle and rice fields can help or hinder, depending on the ability to make use of the disadvantages of nature. So far as the fighting on the ground is concerned, it bears no relation whatever to the blitzkriegs of Europe.

"Here are some of the features of that fighting. The Japanese use small groups of two, three or four soldiers to infiltrate between the British and behind them. In the so-called fighting area, it is just as certain that the Britisher will run into a Japanese by going backward as he would forward.

"The Japanese scored many initial successes by a shrewd Oriental

365

trick. They used firecrackers, the ordinary Fourth-of-July kind. Standing behind trees or creeping through the bamboo, palms, gum trees and orchids, one, two or three Japanese tossed firecrackers in all different directions. One Tommy said: 'When I heard all those crackers I thought I was surrounded. I thought we'd better try to get out of there.'

"In fact the Japanese are using weapons which make a good deal of noise. Their tommy guns and trench mortars, it's been found, appear designed as much to frighten as to kill.

"Another trick was this: In the field or on the road what appeared to be an ordinary coolie could be seen carrying some kind of farm tools or a parang to cut down jungle creepers and palms. But when a British soldier approached, the tools were tossed away and the Jap soldier pulled out a pistol.

"Most of the men back from the fighting zone give sheer weight of numbers as the reason for the Japanese success. One said: 'One Britisher is as good as ten Japanese but unfortunately there are eleven Japanese.'

"The Japanese are reaping another profit from the speed of their advance. In very many areas, the British have not had time to carry out any kind of scorched-earth policy. In some towns, I'm told, the stores were filled with canned goods when the British withdrew, valuable supplies waiting for the Japanese.

"Singapore itself doesn't appear to be taking to heart the grim experience of Penang. One of the newspapers sent a reporter around to Government offices to find out if anything was being done to profit by the experience of a town which ran amok when the bombs dropped. According to the newspaper, only one of the Government departments went so far as to admit that some matters were under consideration. The others said no action of any kind had been taken."

General Sir Henry Pownall has arrived here to replace Sir Robert Brooke-Popham as Commander-in-Chief. I understand Brooke-Popham already has gone back to England. Pownall is supposed to be a good man, but his reputation rests on the retreat at Dunkirk. He was Lord Gort's Chief of Staff and did a very effective job of handling the withdrawal.

366

Two days ago I called on Clayton Aldrich at the American Consulate to tell him that I thought it was pretty funny that in all this war thus far the American Consulate had not issued any statement about the evacuation of civilians. I had been told by an American who came down from the north that the Americans had received no word whatever about evacuation and that he had come to Singapore as a representative of a group of Americans to find out what the Consulate advised doing or if it had made any plans.

Aldrich denied that the Americans have not been informed and I asked him to show me any form letter or notice that had been sent out to Americans.

"Well, we didn't send out any notice but we told everybody who came in here."

"For example," I said, "I'm an American and I have never heard a word from the Consulate about my evacuation nor has any other American I have talked with."

Today the American Consulate issued its first statement on the possibility of evacuating Americans.

I was deeply disappointed today to get a cable from Paul White telling me to remain in Singapore and not to go to the front because of the heavy broadcasting schedule. So there goes my Christmas dateline from the front up north.

I have been thinking of getting some place to live outside of the downtown area and hiring a car. I have an idea that Singapore is going to get a terrific blasting from the air in the next day or two. I would not be surprised if they tried to wipe out this place. The Raffles Hotel is right along the dock area, and as I figure it out the bombers could make their run from downtown over the Fullerton Building and the docks and drop their sticks from a distance of a mile or two, and that would certainly take care of Raffles Hotel. I don't intend to be inside the hotel when that happens.

The Japs have landed more than 50,000 troops in Northern Luzon and seem to be landing more. They are advancing toward Manila.

Prime Minister Churchill, at the White House press conference, said that Singapore would be defended. I get a tremendous kick out

367

of the reports on how he handled that press conference in Washington. He got up on a desk with that cigar jutting out of his mouth and sold the boys one hundred percent. Churchill is a tremendous spiritual force. We're fortunate that the times produced two men like Roosevelt and Churchill.

I spoke today with one of the volunteer soldiers from Penang.

"The evacuation of Penang," he said, "was the greatest disgrace in the history of the British Empire and I hope you say so. We are so ashamed we can't hold up our heads."

He estimated that about eight hundred to a thousand natives were killed and only about two Europeans.

"It was horrible. We had to work with gas masks and stick bayonets into the bodies and pitch them into a truck. We didn't bury them but just poured some kerosene over them and charred the bodies a bit."

At 5:30 Ching and I went to a movie and afterwards it suddenly occurred to both of us that it was Christmas Eve and we should have a special dinner. So we went to Cyrano's. Then we took a ride and I left her at 10:00 P.M. at her medical station at the Chinese Protectorate. It didn't seem like Christmas Eve. Everything that stands for Christmas Eve seemed unreal and misty tonight and remembrance is only through a fog.

Thursday, December 25th:

Up at 7:00 and wrote a broadcast which I gave at 11:20. When I took the broadcast over for censorship, Duckworth evidently felt the Christmas spirit because he said:

"All of your efforts here did much good. They woke a lot of people up."

Here is the broadcast I gave:

"It is now Christmas Day in Malaya. It's a grim Christmas, with not much joy, and people knowing they may hear the whistle of bombs at any moment. The greeting, 'Merry Christmas,' has an empty sound. Singapore is fighting for its existence, and with great odds against it.

"This morning I talked with a number of people and it was not in their hearts to say or even think, 'Peace on Earth—Good Will Toward Men.' The Japanese are too near for that, and most people know

368

that this Christmas Singapore is reaping the terrifying fruits of wishful thinking and unpreparedness.

"In some respects Singapore is a confused man walking about as in a dream, knowing something terrible might happen and not quite sure how to meet it. The terrible experience of Penang and its lessons are only very gradually being applied here. Yet, some of the stories told me by people who got away from Penang make me think that in Belgrade, Yugoslavia, I experienced a Sunday picnic.

"On this Christmas, Singapore has the problem of rectifying almost overnight fifty years of a strange kind of administration of the natives, and one year of military apathy. During that year it was a conviction, almost a certainty, of the military, that Japan would not move, that there would be no war in the Far East. And that conviction carried down to three days before war actually came.

"That's why this is a grim Christmas in Singapore, because the British out here are getting *ready* for a war with the war going on, and the Japanese holding northwestern Malaya and dominating the skies over it.

"The tragedy of this Christmas in Singapore is felt on all sides, I've found, because the British have a capacity for dying with such bravery. There is no want of courage among the British or Indian troops going up against superior numbers of men with a peculiar training for this savage jungle fighting. Just two weeks ago I was dragged out of the oil-covered water of the South China Sea after the *Repulse* and *Prince of Wales* went down, and during that experience I saw the kind of courage that enables the Britisher to die without complaining about the inadequate protection or equipment he might have. Just once did I hear a British sailor say, when aboard the *Repulse,* during the Japanese attack or in the water or on a raft or safe on a destroyer: 'They should have given us protection of fighter aircraft!'

"The British soldiers don't seem to say those things. They fight, as they are fighting in Malaya, with amazing courage."

Lawrence Impey of the *London Daily Mail* complained bitterly about Gerald Samson, the Air Force censor: "I put in my story," Impey said, "that the Japs came down on an airfield and with a hail of lead crumpled a car."

"That shows despondency," Samson said. "You can say that the car was completely destroyed."

Hongkong fell today.

The Japanese were on the air from Penang on Christmas Day to wish the people of Singapore a Merry Christmas and an *unhappy* New Year.

Friday, December 26th:
Tom Fairholl is in jail. He was arrested by the Internal Security and questioned for hours on where he got the information that one hundred Japanese troopships are off the coast. He refused to give the source of his information.

The Internal Security got hold of me today and want to know where I got the story. Tom had told it to me and I had questioned the censor about it.

"You don't expect me to tell you that," I replied.

"Well," the captain of Internal Security said, "we would like you to tell us."

"I don't think it is necessary. I didn't send the story but it came to me from a source that I rely on."

"We are trying to stop these rumors."

"The best way to do that certainly is not to harass correspondents about it. I can assure you this information came from a source that is not spreading rumors."

They insisted upon knowing who gave me the report, but I still refused to tell them.

When I saw Fairholl I told him I'd been questioned and he said he had also refused to tell the source of his information and that they had threatened to bar him as a war correspondent.

I urged Fairholl to let us send a story about him, and later George Weller of the *Chicago Daily News* also told Fairholl that this was a matter involving every correspondent and that we all should give the details on the intimidation and terrorization of correspondents.

Fairholl refused. "No," he said, "I prefer to let the matter drop." We all thought this was a mistake and said so.

370

I am trying to find a place to live outside of Raffles Hotel. I am convinced it is going to get bombed within the next night or two.

Yesterday the Japs bombed the railway north of Johore, but the communiqué doesn't admit it yet. And the Japs apparently have taken Sarawak, the kingdom of the white Rajah, Sir Charles Vyner Brook.

The meagerness of the official communiqués here leaves a good deal to the imagination. As I emphasized in my broadcast: "The absence of reasonable information about operations is one of the main causes of uneasiness in this country. Most people are bewildered as to how the fighting is going, and they seize on every pessimistic rumor as the true state of affairs."

There is considerable shame and confusion everywhere in Singapore. It comes from the mortification of Penang and recovery from the dizziness of being at war.

I don't see that there is very much determination here to hold out at any cost.

I had a drink today with Lieutenant Geoffrey Hallowes, aide to Major General Simmons, and I asked him if he thought Singapore would hold.

"I am sick and tired of evacuation, Cecil," he said. "I am anxious to die right here in Singapore because it wouldn't be worth going on after another evacuation."

Saturday, December 27th:
I was at the censors' office for ten and a half hours today getting the sixty-one-hundred-word article for *Life* magazine through censorship. I worked mainly with Captain Fearon and he referred a number of the pages in the article to higher authority. A few sentences were taken out but not very many, although I had to fight strenuously to retain a good deal of the material.

When I finally finished with the censor I went to the cable office, carrying the story sealed in an envelope—the censor's precaution so that the correspondent would not change any material in it. I stayed there for five hours until I was sure the cable went through.

The censorship would not permit me to say that Penang was abandoned by the military without informing the Governor, Sir Shenton Thomas, and that the Penang episode caused the greatest shame to the

Britishers here and that the natives ran amok. These sentences also were cut out: "The Britishers freely admit abandoning the natives and evacuating Europeans. This has caused the greatest of harm to Britain throughout Asia. . . ."

I tried to say the example furnished by the white civilians to the Asiatics thus far is uninspiring, and non-productive of confidence, but the censor eliminated that phrase, too. I did cable:

"The absence of ability to view affairs realistically and the specific atrophying malady of dying-without-death, best known as the 'Singapore mentality,' largely helped to bring the Japanese more than 125 miles inside Malaya. This walking death is characterized by an apathy in all affairs, except making money from tin and rubber, having stengahs between five and eight, keeping fit, being known as a 'good chap,' and getting thoroughly 'plawstered' on Saturday night.

"Its objective is to treat any change, however slight, with a snort through the nose hanging over a whisky glass, to stay aloof from the affairs of Malaya for thirty years, then return to England with money, remaining untouched by the problems of Malaya and its natives and the future of this colony.

"Singapore, thus far, represents the pinnacle of examples of countries which were physically and mentally unprepared for war—either sudden or inevitable war."

I pointed out in this article that in seeking reasons for the military unpreparedness here, "It would be partly unfair to lay the blame on Sir Robert Brooke-Popham and Admiral Sir Geoffrey Layton. It is reasonable to suppose—and there is strong indication of this, which London would be better able to answer—that Brooke-Popham's requests for additional troops and aircraft were delayed and denied by the exigencies elsewhere.

"It may well be that he lacked persuasive powers to convince London bigwigs of the necessities in the Far East. It is known that Sir Robert Brooke-Popham worked hard, lengthily and unsparingly, struggling uphill against Singapore mentality and the pooh-poohing of the easy-living officials.

"On the other side of the picture," I wrote, "Brooke-Popham's public utterances, such as a statement in October 'We are ready,' induced in people an unconcern about the future."

I then cited Sir Robert Brooke-Popham's chat with the correspond-

372

ents on Wednesday prior to the outbreak of the war, in which he clearly indicated that he didn't expect war but that he was prepared.

I made it clear in this article that in the week preceding the war I couldn't find any officer who thought other than that Japan would back down and there would be no war.

"This military attitude," I cabled *Life,* "is partly responsible for Malaya reeling under this sudden attack. This whole ostrich attitude and the efforts to bolster morale with repetitious 'we are ready for them' resulted only in unpreparedness and disillusionment of the civilians."

In this story to *Life* I was able to report for the first time that when the bombs fell on Singapore the lights of Singapore city and harbor were blazing and remained that way throughout the night. All my efforts to broadcast that fact previously had been excised by the censor.

"Malaya was asleep prior to the war," I wrote. "Right now it is confused. It remains to be seen the extent to which it can awaken and start swinging.

"Singapore is known as the city of 'Chinks, drinks and stinks,' and it will take more than a war to change that, but war has changed the face of this city and it is certain to change its mentality. Even Singapore, which is perennially fearful of any change, will be unable to resist what is the fate of the rest of the world, namely, 'It will never be the same again.'

"Singapore is like a somnambulist, conscious enough to fear that something terrible is about to happen but not knowing quite what to do about it.

"But after more than two weeks of stunned somnambulance there are appearing the first signs of the ponderous job of overturning a half century of island precedent.

"The number-one problem is to win the confidence of the natives and to avoid the panics of Penang and many other towns in Northern Malaya."

The following sentence was cut out by the censors:

"Fifty years of slothful government, which culminated in the evacuation of only the Europeans from Penang, is inducing the belief among the natives that they will be left to their fate if Singapore is evacuated."

I then reported the meeting with Brooke-Popham held with the civic leaders and the remark of the Indian leader that the Asiatics would be ready to die with the British but insisted that they receive the same treatment as the British.

"Those remarks," I cabled, "had nut-shelled the fears of the Asiatics and provided the one reason for the numerous emergency regulations now being invoked here. Aside from convincing the natives that British protection means something by a display of military might, such as fighters and bombers in the skies and troops pushing back the Japanese, the main burden of watching over the Asiatics to thwart panic, maintain service, and assure food supplies devolves on Governor Thomas Shenton Whiteleg Thomas." The Governor, I said, is credited with personal courage but his record of accomplishment as a Governor is unimpressive.

The censors eliminated the following paragraph from my cable: "When Brooke-Popham arrived in Singapore the story goes that he was shocked by the lack of military work going on and he told that to Governor Thomas who rates the title of Commander-in-Chief of Malaya. At the moment the Governor is refusing a military request that he declare martial law in Singapore."

I agreed to that excision with only a minimum of protest.

"In early October," my story continued, "I spent fifty minutes with the Governor. When I emerged from his sanctum in the white rambling Government House I had the sensation of being immersed in an urbane sea of unreality. My first action was to look at a calendar to see if this was 1931 instead of 1941 and that a war was going on."

In describing the fighting and morale of the soldiers I said: "In few places in the world has nature conspired more expertly to make fighting uncomfortable and difficult than in the jungles, mangrove swamps and rice fields of Malaya.

"Japanese jungle methods are a curious blend of naïveté, Oriental guile and an imitation of German tricks, but above all they show a great knowledge of jungle warfare aided by an innate contempt for whites and especially for the British. Orthodox methods—if there is any orthodox method for jungle fighting—are forgotten in order to squeeze out advantages from the disadvantages of nature. The Japanese are showing a peculiar ability to do this.

"The effectiveness of their progress is due to surprise, daring, indifference to death, and the British underestimation of the enemy,

374

which always induces in the British effort initial set-backs. For example: Many British officers point out that a Japanese division consists of sixteen thousand, whereas the British division is only ten thousand and therefore more maneuverable. Such expressions are typical examples of the British looking at their enemy through their own eyes and their own intentions which very frequently marked operations in France and Norway as well as the Western Desert operations against the Germans.

"As a matter of fact, the size of the Japanese division is not of the slightest importance in the Malayan campaign. To penetrate the jungle the Japanese in reality are not using concentrated forces but thousands of more or less self-sustaining, independent armies charged with a specific mission and having anywhere from two to two hundred men.

"This is lightning war, but the only relation to European-type blitzkrieg is that everyone is his own blitzer. Their sources of supply are very uncertain and communications are most doubtful. The chances of coming out alive are very meager. Their main task is to infiltrate the British and to cut off battalions, platoons and individuals, surround them and induce confusion and inflict the largest possible casualties.

"To carry out such operations the Japanese troops are clothed in the lightest way. Their uniforms consist of shorts and singlets, tennis shoes and steel helmets or just a handkerchief with the corners knotted at the ends over their heads. They carry a bag of rice and an ammunition belt around their waists. Many carry tommy guns and hand grenades. One of the most effective weapons they use is a 4-inch mortar carried on their heads and shoulders.

"All operations thus far have been carried out in the country where the visibility is fifty yards and consists of a series of flank, out-flank and more out-flank movements. The Japanese improvise readily. In some instances after a few days they find it more effective in some areas to permit singlet-clad Japs to run ahead with a tommy gun followed by a uniformed soldier carrying additional ammunition. For some operations, in order to scatter the Britishers and to carry out guerrilla tactics, the Japanese are using a very light tank. In one case north of Kuala Kangsar the Indians hiding in the jungle successfully waited until the

Japanese light tank passed and then they got behind and attacked the infantry, causing heavy casualties.

"A number of British were shot down by Japanese hidden in coconut palm and teak trees. Some Japanese lie in the swamps with only their faces above the water, concealed by twigs for three or four hours. They instantly rise up when a number of British troops are around and begin firing very swiftly. One British soldier said: 'You need a dozen eyes to watch these blokes.'

"Major General Heath, in charge of Northern Malayan operations, said: 'You shoot down five hundred Japanese and before you can turn around there are five hundred more in their place.'

"Some British and Indians are readily adaptable to jungle warfare and they die with the greatest bravery. While the British in the Western Desert may follow the dictum: 'Attack and pursue,' here in Malaya the strategy can only be: 'Delay and decimate.'

"There is no want of courage among the British and they have the ability to profit individually and learn the lessons each moment of fighting. They have found that the Japs do not relish bayonet fighting, although this does not denote a lack of Japanese courage, which every British officer that I have talked to has praised as 'fanatical bravery.' "

I then described conditions in the jungle. As far as the British scorched-earth policy was concerned I tried to indicate, as best I could, that it was not being very successfully carried out.

"Insofar as can be determined," I wrote, "in no way have food stocks been destroyed and only in the very fewest cases did the British carry them off. Britain's problem is its indecision whether it is better to leave foodstuffs for the natives with the hope that they get them or take the chance that the Japanese appropriate them. However, it is known that the British have shown a reluctance to indulge in widespread demolition. Their failure to scorch Penang was due to the feeling 'We will soon return,' forgetting that the Japanese will thoroughly scorch everything if they are forced to give up the territory.

"It is obviously impossible to carry out a scorched-earth policy in regard to coconuts and fruits, on which the Japanese live. It is likewise impossible to chop down millions of rubber trees. In the tin mines the only scorch possible is to destroy the works which can be rebuilt. The London Colonial Office said that the military authorities are prepared to order complete destruction of millions of rubber trees, but

376

the authorities here said that they could not see how such a plan could be carried out."

I gave an over-all picture of the tempo and temper of Singapore life, pointing out such things as that Europeans are moving out of the downtown area to the outskirts of Singapore. Many people are bleary-eyed in canteens and at first-aid stations. Under orders of the defense service director, the Sultan of Johore's zoo has been eliminated. He killed two tigers, two lions, three black panthers, two leopards, a puma and four pythons. The Sultan's favorite, an orang-outang, was sent to Sumatra for safe-keeping.

I then wrote:

"They are not building any air-raid shelters underground in Singapore and the safest shelters appear to be the concrete sewers, a foot wide and three feet deep, which line all the streets. People are being urged to use them. An ARP warden said: 'Personally, if I were caught in the open I would just as soon put my pride in my pocket and dive into a sewer. It is recommended, however, that those jumping in the sewers use respirators because of the stink.'

"On Orchard Road, one of the main shopping districts, there is one deep trench which has been improved by the British who have put wooden boards across the top and covered it over with sand bags.

"The idea is a good one but when it rains the water in the trench reaches the wooden top. A person thus has the choice of jumping into the water and keeping his nose pressed against the boards to keep from drowning or sitting outside and dodging the bomb splinters."

This was the gist of my story of Singapore. (It was a story which was to have repercussions.)

At a press conference today, Colonel Field said: "We must hold our aircraft for the defense of the vital military objective—which is Singapore." Meanwhile, the troops retreating by stages are without air protection.

Sunday, December 28th:
The Japanese are now carrying on considerable propaganda throughout Malaya. The Penang radio, which was left intact when the military evacuated, is now directing all its propaganda to Singapore. A Japanese plane came high over Singapore and dropped the first propaganda

377

pamphlets. The message said: "Burn all White Devils in the sacred white flame of victory." On the other side it showed natives brandishing torches evidently in the process of carrying this out.

I have just learned that when the British evacuated Penang they left the Treasury there intact. There was $250,000 Straits dollars in it.

Sir George Sansom, when he took over the publicity for the War Council, called on Admiral Layton and informed him he wanted to get rid of Commander Burrows. Admiral Layton suggested he talk with Sir Robert Brooke-Popham about it.

"All right," Brooke-Popham told Sansom, "I'll relieve Burrows today."

"No, I need a few days to think things through and find another man. We don't want to disrupt the organization suddenly."

A week later Sansom went to Brooke-Popham and said: "I'm ready to replace Burrows, and since he submitted his resignation some time ago, I think we can accept it now."

"Why, I thought you wanted to keep him," Brooke-Popham exclaimed. "You said you were going to keep him in the job."

"I said no such thing," Sir George Sansom replied. "I wanted a few days to find a substitute."

That was the way with Brooke-Popham, Sir George Sansom told me.

"He always insisted he was right and the other man wrong. He didn't seem to have a very good grasp of the situation at any time. He would never say, 'That was a mistake on our part, now let's get on from there.' "

Monday, December 29th:
I said in my broadcast: "The grave danger facing Singapore and the destiny awaiting this Naval Base are becoming more and more apparent almost hour by hour. Japanese strategy for the reduction of Singapore has a very good chance of success unless very considerable reinforcements are sent here."

The censors would not allow me to say: "The British civil administration seems to have disappeared in these towns in the threatened areas," but I could say that in most places "people have to shift for themselves as there is no European authority to turn to."

378

Another Penang episode: A Chinese magistrate, educated in London, and a member of the Malayan Civil Service, was sent to Penang a month before war broke out as a magistrate. When the European women were being evacuated he went to the dock with his family, wearing his uniform and carrying his gun as a member of the Volunteers. He was told by the British officers that he could go, as a Volunteer, but that his wife and children, as Asiatics, must remain. He went. In Singapore, he marched into the office of the head of the Volunteer Service, threw down his tin hat, his uniform, his gun, and resigned from the Volunteer Services and the Malayan Civil Service.

Japanese bombers came over tonight. I was sitting in Raffles with Agronsky, Weller, Al Noderer and a couple of British officers. When they came we went across the street to a field where we could watch the raiders come over. There were nine bombers and the searchlights caught them going directly over Raffles Hotel at about fifteen thousand feet. There was heavy anti-aircraft fire. On one point I saw what I thought were bombs coming down. I flopped into a muddy ditch in the field. When the raid was over there was a huge fire some four or five miles away and I wanted to see it. I did a very foolish thing. I got into a taxi and went racing out to the fire. They had hit an oil tank out near the Alexandria barracks. Out there some of the volunteers were not so sure that it had been hit by a bomb but that it had been fired by Fifth Columnists on the ground.

The idiocy of going out to the fire lay in the fact that the fire obviously would be a beacon for other raiders and probably would be attacked again. That didn't occur to me until I got to the hotel after midnight and told the other correspondents what I had seen. They were happy enough to get a report on it, but said I was a damn fool for going out.

During the night the Japs came over twice again but I stayed in bed. I was too tired to get up.

Tuesday, December 30th:
Colonel Field held a meeting with correspondents today. His general manner indicated that "the situation is well in hand." In the most off-hand way, Colonel Field remarked that the Japanese are building

"rafts and gadgets to come down the Perak River to try to take positions in our rear."

"What about the defense of Singapore?" he was asked.

"The defense of Singapore will be absolutely carried out because this is our vital base. If Singapore should fall, the Dutch East Indies will fall."

Martin Agronsky and I moved our stuff out to the country to 15 Caldecott Hill Road, about one hundred yards away from the radio station. We are living with Larry Lawrence and Tommy Schields who work for the Texas Oil Company. It is a beautiful place with a large garden, very comfortable. I don't like being just one hundred yards from a radio station, however, but there is less chance of getting hit here than there is downtown.

Agronsky is very much worried about staying here and I don't blame him in a way. His argument is that the radio station is going to be bombed and we won't be able to broadcast. At the same time air and sea transportation is getting more and more difficult so that we would be stuck here with no chance to broadcast and no chance to get away. So we agreed to send each of our offices a message informing them of that situation as best we could.

Martial law was ordered in Singapore today. A long release of about four hundred words was issued, explaining in great detail what kind of martial law it was. Agronsky and I took our scripts down to the censor. My script said: "Martial law has been declared in Singapore and now the military takes control, with power to impose a curfew and the ability to administrate speedy justice to Fifth Columnists."

The censor said: "We have instructions that you must use the entire release on the declaration of martial law."

"That's absurd," I said. "There are more than four hundred words in it and I only have three minutes to speak. I have other news to report."

"I'm sorry," he said, "but our instructions are that you have to give all of the details on the specific kind of martial law that this is."

"Martial law is martial law and if I merely state that martial law has been declared I have covered the story. The American people don't give a damn what kind of martial law you have in Singapore."

380

The censor on duty said he could not change the instructions and I got on the telephone to talk to Duckworth.

"There is nothing that can be done," he said, "you must give all the details."

I explained the absurdity of it but he insisted I would have to do it.

Then I called Duff Cooper and he said he could do nothing, that a detailed explanation on the kind of martial law was necessary since, as he put it, "the civil authorities still retain some control over services."

"America doesn't care about all that," I said. "You either have martial law or you don't have it. It so happens that you have."

Duff Cooper also gave the argument that if the Japanese heard the bare announcement that martial law was declared they would say that rioting and shooting were going on in Singapore.

"They will say that anyhow," I said, "no matter what we report out of here on it."

Duff Cooper repeated that every correspondent was under orders to send the full text of the declaration.

"Well, Mr. Duff Cooper, I report the news as I see it without any instructions from anyone else. I won't use four hundred words on something worth only a passing mention. I'll cut it out entirely."

"That's perfectly all right," Duff Cooper said.

"I can assure you, sir," I said, "that the newspapers in America are not going to print the four hundred words about this martial law declaration. I will wager you anything you want that the papers will merely say that martial law has been declared."

(BBC, the official British radio, the next day ignored the entire text of that martial law declaration and said exactly what I wanted to say, namely: "Martial law has been declared in Singapore," and nothing more than that.)

Wednesday, December 31st:
When I took my broadcast to the Cable and Wireless office tonight a new order was in effect. We cannot go behind the wire cage and talk directly with the censor. We must send our scripts in to the censor with a Malay clerk. The censors work on the scripts and whatever is handed back is what we can say.

While I was waiting there, the Japanese were over again, flying in two "V" formations at about fifteen thousand feet and dropping a number of bombs.

I wrote: "Every mile the Japanese advance increases the danger of Singapore, but it is not only territory at stake over here. The tin and rubber that America uses are also prizes. The territory occupied thus far by the Japanese to a point south of Ipoh contains fifty percent of the rubber production of Malaya. But more important to America, as the Japanese advance into this country, is her supply of tin, for this is the greatest tin-producing area in the world and the ore is seventy-five percent pure tin. Fifty percent of the tin-ore production of Malaya is now in Japanese hands. The United States has been taking seventy percent of this country's output. This means that the Japanese, by occupying the territory they have, are denying the United States thirty thousand tons of tin ore a year. This means also that one-third of the actual tin requirements of the United States is now in Jap hands, and that doesn't include the eighteen thousand tons produced in Thailand nor the three thousand tons that came out of Indo-China.

"As a matter of fact, the ability of Malaya to supply tin to the United States is more seriously affected than these figures show. In the area still in British hands, military operations and the requirements for transportation make the working of tin mines and the removal of the ore somewhat more than just difficult. Malaya is fast becoming a very much reduced source of America's tin supply, and it is commonly known that if the Japanese are driven out of the area they occupy their scorched-earth policy will impose a year's work before these tin mines are again operating.

"As things stand at the moment, it is estimated that the United States can write off at once sixty or seventy percent of the tin production of Malaya, the world's most important source, and that write-off will be effective for the next several years."

Captain Fearon, the censor, cut out most of this material. He would not permit me to say that fifty percent of the tin-ore production is now in Japanese hands. I could say, he said, that a large area from which the tin ore comes, is divided with the Japanese. His deletions killed the whole sense and intent of the broadcast.

"Well," Captain Fearon said, "what do you want to make the picture so black for?"

"What do you want to hide the whole picture for?" I asked.

I then telephoned Sir George Sansom and read him the broadcast and he approved everything I had in the original script.

Ron Matthews, of the *London Daily Herald*, is in hot water with the officials here. He said in one of his stories: "It would be incorrect to say the Japanese have air superiority; they have air monopoly."

Late tonight the siren sounded—a beautiful moonlight night—while we were out at our place in the country. George Weller is out here with us now too. We went out on a hill to watch the planes better. It was a beautiful sight the way the British searchlights caught and held the Japanese bombers. The anti-aircraft firing was very poor, however. The bombers were in one direction and the anti-aircraft firing must have been a full ten miles away, on the other side of the horizon.

Thursday, January 1st, 1942:
The censors are very sensitive about mention of the Fifth Column. The intellectual giant, Captain Berick, is probably the most sensitive. One of the correspondents, describing an action up north, wrote in his cable: "Three columns were sent to the east, the fourth to the west and the fifth column directly north."

Captain Berick cut out the phrase "the fifth column directly north." Even when the correspondent explained the sense of his message, Berick boomed: "All mention of fifth columns anywhere is strictly forbidden."

Tonight I went on the air at 9:36 and at 9:38 the bombs started dropping and the sirens shrieked. I was in the midst of my broadcast when the first bomb crump-crump-crumped not far away. I paused for just an instant and I was on the verge of saying: "Well, they are dropping right now."

It was one of the strongest temptations I ever had. But I am glad I didn't deviate from my script because we are forbidden to give the time of the raid and obviously it would have been of great value to the Japanese to know the precise moment their bombers were over their targets.

383

The *Straits Times* editorial today begins: "Good-bye to the year, 1941—and good riddance. We are entering into a New Year in local conditions that are simply fantastic. There is no better word to describe the situation."

Headlines in the paper today are: "Russians Pursue Nazis in Crimea" . . . "U.S. to look after East" . . . "Fresh Blows at Rommel's Forces" . . . "Big Increase in Aid to China" . . . "Axis Escape Bid in Desert Fails" . . . "Threat to Manila City Growing; Fall of Capital Soon Feared" . . . "British Air and Sea Successes" . . . "Naval Raid on Celebes" . . .

Major General Ching Kai Min of the Chinese Military Mission said in a New Year's message to the Chinese people here: "Show that you are of the same mettle as your gallant brethren in China. Obey your generalissimo and help the local authorities in our grapple with the tyrant."

A number of Britishers today approached me to tell the current joke. Each prefaced the story with: "Now you won't be offended, will you?"

"Offended about what?"

"About this joke."

"Of course not."

The preliminaries over, the question was asked: "Do you know where the United States Navy is?"

"No, where is it?" I dutifully asked each time.

"Well, it hasn't been in operation because it is still under contract to Metro-Goldwyn-Mayer."

I tried to use the story in a broadcast as an example of the current British humor but the censors cut it out.

Friday, January 2nd:

It is amazing the way the Japanese attacks every night are carried out at almost the same time. They are usually caught by the searchlights, but they fly over to drop their bombs in perfect formation and thus far I haven't seen them break their formation in the face of anti-aircraft fire. The anti-aircraft has improved somewhat but is still far from efficient. The Japanese give the impression of complete indifference to the British defenses. These bombers are evidently coming from some

384

distance, since their bombs are rather light. They make a crater only three feet deep and four feet in diameter.

From all I can gather the British are not yet showing any particular adaptability to the Japanese jungle methods. In other words, the British are still carrying their forty-pound packs and fighting in the same manner as they did before the Japanese started showing them cute tricks in infiltration tactics.

People are being urged during the black-outs to wear white to avoid being struck by autos. A curious thing is that the Chinese women insist on dressing in all black because they are convinced that then the bombs will not find them.

One of the fundamental customs of Singapore has been eliminated, that is the extension of credit and wiping out the chit system which enabled planters and officers airily to sign papers in bars and hotels all over the city, inevitably resulting in their living beyond their means.

Up to the beginning of the war the Communist Party was illegal and now, without any legal rectification, the Communists are being welcomed as "loyal supporters of the British cause." Manifestoes of the Communists for all-out war are printed in the *Straits Times*, the *Singapore Free Press* and the *Malaya Tribune*. I don't know whether those manifestoes pledging loyal support to the war were issued by the Communist Party leaders here of their own volition or at the request of the British authorities. My guess is the party issued them and the British authorities felt it unwise to prevent their issuance.

The main effort of local propaganda right now is to build up and sustain the morale of Asiatics. I don't think the authorities should worry so much about the Asiatics as about the Europeans. For example, when the siren sounds the Europeans are the first ones to rush out of the Raffles Hotel while many of the native waiters placidly continue their work. An air-force officer who was in London during the blitz told me tonight: "It is disgusting the way these bloody people get their wind up. They should set the example for the natives. Instead it's the other way around."

There is considerable bitterness here against Saravanamuttu, editor of the *Straits Echo* at Penang, who is now co-operating with the Japs as head of the Puppet Japanese authority there. Many people from

385

Penang are astonished because he was a leading figure in Penang for many years and was highly respected. Now he is to all intents and purposes a Quisling.

He carried on during the bombing and the papers here printed stories about his heroism and determination to go on publishing right up to the time the Japanese came into Penang. But he is an Asiatic and I am told that he is co-operating with the Japanese because of his great bitterness when the British at the final moment refused him permission to evacuate.

A letter from an Asiatic reader was printed in the *Straits Times* today which sums up, I am convinced, the state of mind of the non-British here and a good many of the British as well. It says: "What we, the millions in Malaya who are not amongst the heaven-born, want, insist on and shall get is the relegation of the present administration to the duty of looking after parochial affairs which have no important bearing on the war, whilst leaving war matters in the hands of the War Council Defense Committee headed by the Minister of State who is a man of great experience in wider matters of administration and who will be unhampered by that shibboleth, local knowledge.

"What has local knowledge done to save us from the present muddle? Exactly nothing. The foundations of the present government were laid in the middle of the last century. The main development since then has been to build an impenetrable fence around the system, the principal object of which appears to have been to protect and develop the privileges of the small governing minority within it.

"What do we get? A nineteenth-century organization run by privileged mediocrities, trying to cope with a twentieth-century crisis. . . .

"What we suffer from is a closed administration which is merely a conglomeration of ingrown and ingrowing minds, utterly impervious to new ideas and absolutely, utterly unsuited to deal with any new and unknown set of circumstances."

What a damning indictment of the Colonial administration here! And how accurate it is!

The Military here has taken the attitude this is their war and they don't want interference. The Colonial Administration is too traditional to recognize this is the twentieth century. The Asiatic people are being told the barest fraction of the truth, denied leadership, and prevented from guiding their own destinies.

386

It is brutal. Many of these people are going to die. They are supposed to be calm, cool and courageous in the face of bombers and advancing Japs. But the authorities do not trust them to have the courage to know what is going on. They've been given no vision of what victory would mean. The Malays especially are indifferent whether the British or the Japs are here.

I'm convinced practically all the Malays and most of the Chinese and Indians here don't feel they are fighting for freedom, but just to maintain a system they no longer want. I don't think there is in their hearts the dream and reality of the people's war.

The *Malaya Mail* of Kuala Lumpur said the British Resident of Selangor had received a message from Singapore: "Singapore cannot accommodate any more evacuees at the moment. Please try to hold them back for another three days."

I presume that means hold them back for the Japanese to take. At present no tickets from Kuala Lumpur to Singapore are being issued except with the authorization of the area officer.

General Pownall issued a communiqué last night in Kuala Lumpur, but it was not received by any of the papers or correspondents in Singapore. The only place it appeared was in the Kuala Lumpur paper. He said: "It is intended to fight every inch of ground down the peninsula. Considerable help is on the way."

He urged that no one pay any attention to the Penang radio or to the leaflets being dropped by the Japanese.

The *Malaya Mail*, which printed the communiqué, said: "It may be accepted as a blunt statement of policy. Interpreted quite fairly it is an indication that the days of defense have ended. It is a clear and explicit announcement by a fighting man that he intends to fight back."

Those sound like empty words to me and I can see no indication that the days of the defensive have ended. Of course, General Pownall intends to fight back. I wonder if the *Malaya Mail* means that the British are simply not going to turn the other cheek. Well, I hope it helps to bolster morale.

The Governor, Sir Shenton Thomas, made an incredible broadcast tonight. He spoke for about forty-five minutes about his tour upcountry, but for almost the entire time he told about seeing a steam roller which got out of control, rolling backwards, and how the Indian driver finally saved it. The broadcast was also printed in the paper and took more than two columns. I read it three times, trying to make some sense out of it, but all I could find was this long discourse about the steam roller going backwards. There was no symbolism about it either. He was not referring to any armed force, just talking about a steam roller.

A manifesto was issued in Klang by the Sultan of Selangor, Sir Allam Shah, in which he urges the people to range on the side of the democracies. He said: "Be it known to all that the world war which is now raging is a war between Great Britain and her allies on one side and Germany and her partners on the other.

"Great Britain and her allies represent the democracies, that is, countries in which the government is by the people and for the people.

"Germany and her partners, on the other hand, are powers which do what they like. Their creed is might, and they disregard right, freedom and justice.

"The aim of Germany and her partners is to conquer all countries and dominate the world. If their object is attained, those in power will have a free hand to do what they please and the people under their rule will have a miserable and pitiable existence.

"The aim of Great Britain and her allies in waging the war is to preserve the peace of the world and the liberty of mankind. They are the upholders of right and justice.

"If the enemies, that is, Germany and her partners, win the war, they will subjugate all countries in the world and the inhabitants of these countries will live the life of slaves.

"For the reasons stated above, we must range ourselves on the side of the democracies and take an active part with all our heart in helping to preserve our liberty."

That Sultan, I thought, expressed in simple, clear language pretty much of what this war is all about.

I wrote in my script tonight: "Singapore has not yet recovered from the shock of being at war; it hasn't yet realized the terror that the Japanese can bring down on a city. There is bitterness (the censor changed that word to "amazement") in the hearts of the people here

388

that war should have come when they were so certain it would not. And that war, coming with such speed and producing such unfavorable results in a few frightening weeks, has increased the bitterness. (The censor again changed that word to "amazement.")

"The greatest bitterness (this time the censor changed it to "anxiety") in the hearts of the people of Malaya comes from the collapse of an illusion of being invulnerable. That came from the propaganda put out here. They were told that Malaya had swarms of bombers and fighters, capable of shooting down anything Japan would dare send over. All those notions the people here are in the process of shedding. The people find it a painful process."

Saturday, January 3rd:
Duckworth told Agronsky and me that CBS and NBC are going to be subject to the same censorship regulations which govern the Singapore newspapers. He said that some people in Malaya might tune in on these broadcasts to America. Therefore, he said, we would not be able to use some items that the other correspondents could cable.

Sunday, January 4th:
Some of the most incredible misinformation is coming out of London to find its way into the local paper. For example: The *London Letter* in the *Straits Sunday Times* reports that the London air correspondents prophesy that the R.A.F. reinforcements will make possible a twenty-four-hour umbrella of day and night fighters over Singapore. How absurd that is! The *Straits Times* also carries a headline: "Counter Push in Malaya Hinted." The story says: "General Sir Hubert Gough, *Reuters* military commentator, says the position of the ABCD front in the Pacific can be considered fairly safe in spite of the preliminary setbacks inflicted upon us by the treachery of the Japs."

Such idiocy! This whole show out here is falling apart and they are sitting in London saying there is nothing to worry about.

The steamship companies here are certainly making profits as usual. One company, I am told, offered passage to evacuees to England at 240 pounds a head. One civil servant here has been trying to get his wife and children away, and they want 240 pounds for each one.

The Government decreed a flat rate of 120 pounds, irrespective of accommodations, but this civil servant told me the steamship company is not paying any attention to the flat rate. He doesn't have the money; therefore he can't get his wife and children away to safety.

Monday, January 5th:
Most of the Chinese are stocking up rice and dried fish. They feel that when bombs drop, every shop in Singapore will shut. This is what happened in Penang, Ipoh, Kuala Kangsar and other towns in the north, when the first bombs hit. The authorities here are urging shopkeepers to avoid doing that, and also arranging for community kitchens, but the Chinese, who have been taking care of themselves for centuries, are not taking chances.

Martin Agronsky and I went to lunch at Duff Cooper's today. Lady Diana was there, a correspondent by the name of Morrison of the *London Times*, and somebody else whose name I never did get. Shortly after we started lunch, Duff Cooper launched a tirade on Australia when one of us remarked that the Australians were pretty angry at the inability of Britain to defend Malaya better.

Duff Cooper's face flushed and his voice rose. I had never seen him angry before.

"The Australians have no leaders," he said. "Curtin (Prime Minister John Curtin) has a schoolboy's mind. Menzies (former Prime Minister Robert Gordon Menzies) is the only man of any caliber and he was voted out because he was popular in London and Washington."

I mentioned to Duff Cooper that the Australians are angry, too, at being hoodwinked about the strength of Malaya.

"The Australians," he said, "have no case. They won't introduce conscription to send men abroad. They refuse to allow immigrants to come into their country, because they are afraid of unemployment. They have failed to develop their country."

After lunch, I chatted in the garden with Duff Cooper.

"Do you think the Japs can be held?" I asked.

"Yes," he said. "I think so."

"Where?"

"Probably at Johore. Not right on the Straits, but a bit on the other side."

Before I left, I asked Duff Cooper, who is the head of the Allied

390

War Council, what kind of co-operation he is getting here from the various officials.

"Oh," he said dryly, "it's all right. . . ."

Paul White replied tonight to my cable inquiring whether I should remain here in view of the possibility that the radio station might be knocked out of commission and it would be impossible for me to get away to some other point from which to broadcast.

Paul's cable was sent on New Year's Day and said:
SUGGEST YOU REMAIN WHILE FACILITIES AVAILABLE.

I spent a very leisurely afternoon, not doing very much. I bought a trunk to send things home in because I may have to travel very light very soon; cancelled my passage on the British Airways to Cairo on Friday, which I had arranged in case CBS approved my transfer; tried to locate Ching Yeuk and couldn't; bought myself a chocolate nut sundae; took a few photographs around town; saw the RAF publicity boys, Squadron Leader Blackburn and Flight Lieutenant Downer; took my typewriter to be repaired; talked with a guy who got out of Kuantan just ahead of the Japs; bought Listerine and used it.

The Japs have advanced twelve miles a day so far and there seems to be nothing that can stop them.

Tuesday, January 6th:
Sir Geoffrey Layton today sent a note to all officers above the rank of commander. It said: "The Commander-in-Chief has gone to collect units of the Far Eastern fleet. He asks every officer to be of good heart and to keep the Union Jack flying."

This means he has transferred his headquarters elsewhere, probably to Batavia or Surabaya.

For some reason, for the first time in months I sang every song I know while shaving this morning. There was no particular reason, perhaps it was the end of uncertainty. I am committed to staying in this place whatever happens—and I'm not optimistic about what may happen. There has been no word from Martha since I got back from the *Repulse.*

391

At a press conference today, Colonel Field said the Japanese are behaving in the occupied areas just the way they behaved elsewhere.

"They are rapidly reverting to type," Colonel Field said. "They are playing the same games they played in China. They are looting food shops and collecting women; that is to say they are raping the native women."

At the press conference today, one British correspondent asked Colonel Field to give us some information so that stories could be put out of "an encouraging nature."

Colonel Field snorted at the question. "I can't produce good encouraging propaganda in the situation we are in, and it is stupid to try."

Tonight Martin Agronsky brought Major Claude Tanner and his very attractive wife to dinner to our place at Caldecott Hill. There was also a charming young lady, Eileen, Martin's friend.

As we sat drinking a before-dinner cocktail—Larry Lawrence, Tommy Schields and our guests, Major Tanner, who's a motor transport officer and has been here for two years, said:

"I don't think I could be brave out here, but I think I could be, back in England. I don't feel inclined to fight for this country. I think the whole place ought to be blown sky high."

His remark shocked me.

"How many of the officers and men hold that view?" I asked.

"It isn't a view," Major Tanner said. "It's a reaction. Many of them feel that way. I can't work up any venom against the Japs. They are unimportant blighters."

His whole attitude was that the Japanese are not a worthy opponent for the British and can be easily "knocked off."

"Major," I said, "I certainly pray to God that you are the only British officer who has that idea. You expect the Asiatics to die for this country, yet you don't give a damn and you say that others feel the same way."

This supreme confidence is incredible; the British are getting the pants beat off them and this major doesn't think the Japs are worth bothering about.

A Chinese Mobilization Council has been formed here. It is actually an event of great importance. The primary purpose is to avoid a second Penang, maintain essential services and keep labor available during bombings. It came about because of the demand of the Chinese here to mobilize and to assist. It is made up of the Chinese Chamber of Commerce officials, the Malayan Communist Party and other organizations. One paper said in its editorial:

"For the first time in the history of the colony, local Chinese political issues have been thrust aside in the common interest."

It is more than that, in my opinion. The Chinese, Communist and otherwise, are finally getting the right to fight for their own defense.

This afternoon Agronsky and I saw Sir George Sansom to complain about the way our scripts are being censored.

Agronsky pointed out that we hand in scripts into which censors write things and they cut out words and phrases, so that a whole paragraph makes no sense whatever. The script is then returned to us. We must broadcast what is left of it.

I explained to Sir George that all we ask is a chance to sit down with a censor and discuss changes, so that if a certain word must come out we could at least suggest a synonym. Instead, the censor arbitrarily knocks out words and kills the meaning of the whole sentence.

"Even in dictatorships, Sir George," I said, "we are given a chance to discuss the script with the man who censors it. Here we are handed back a mess of hash and expected to broadcast it."

"The War Council," Sir George said, "has decided that your broadcasts and those of Agronsky are to be treated as local news reports. Because of the effect on morale, they are to be censored on that basis."

"What!" Agronsky shouted. "You mean we are to be treated on the basis of working for local newspapers?"

"Yes," Sir George said, "that's to be the basis of censorship."

"Why, that's not possible, Sir George," I said. "We are accredited by the British War Office and Air Ministry as correspondents attached to the British forces. We don't work for a local organization. We work for American broadcasting networks."

"Well, that's the decision of the War Council," Sir George said.

Nothing further could be done, Sir George insisted, adding:

"Objective reporting and the local morale situation are irreconcilable."

393

It is announced in London that the Netherlands is to be the site of General Wavell's headquarters. He will be Commander-in-Chief of the Far Eastern area.

Here is the script I wrote tonight and which was given back to me without any chance to make any adjustments:

"It is now twenty-one minutes past seven Wednesday morning and for the first time in more than a week Japanese bombers did not come over Singapore during the night.

"A Japanese threat to the left flank of the main British forces has forced another British withdrawal. Japanese troops which came down the Straits of Malacca and gained footholds are attempting to cut off the British north of Kuala Lumpur, the capital of the Federated Malay States. The British withdrawal is designed to thwart this maneuver and the latest information is that the Japanese forces on the left flank are being dealt with. Whether they are being contained, however, cannot be determined at the moment. (The censor cut out that sentence.)

"The threat to Kuala Lumpur has been increased. This town is the railroad center of Malaya and is the focal point of both tin dredging and rubber operations in this country.

"It's difficult to find much optimism in these steady withdrawals. But it *is* noteworthy that British resistance shows signs of stiffening. This is due to the British forces becoming more concentrated, and to their increasing ability to fight the kind of jungle guerrilla warfare that the Japanese have found successful.

"This does not mean that the Japanese drive to Singapore is being stopped." ("Is being" was changed to "has been entirely.") "And the speed of the Japanese advance has decreased in the past few weeks. To many people here, it still seems rapid because the Japanese are about two hundred miles nearer to Singapore than they were when they crossed the Thai border into Malaya a month ago.

"I've just been told that quite a good number of the so-called Japanese two-man tanks have been knocked out by the British anti-tank guns. These are a sort of two-man carrier, and the British have found them like sitting ducks.

"There have been many reports here of the manner in which the Japanese are treating the natives in the occupied territory. I have not reported them because they could not be verified. However, a source which has made an exhaustive check of the facts affirms that the Japa-

394

nese are carrying out in North Malaya a policy similar to that used in China. According to this source, in one section of North Malaya the Japanese soldiers gathered in the Malay, Tamil and Chinese women.

"There are strong indications here that the seat of the Allied Supreme Command in the Far East will be in Java and not in Singapore. The Dutch Naval Base at Surabaya would take over the functions which the British and all the world counted on Singapore to serve. Singapore will continue its role of a fortress, the barrier to the Japanese push to the rich prize of the Indies. It would be a good hold in defense and a springboard for offense, and its destiny, too, may be that of a heroic garrison.

"There's a change in the Japanese bombing tactics of Singapore. Monday night Japanese aircraft flew over the city at a great height and above the clouds, dropping bombs at random. There obviously was no attempt to hit specific targets. But as it was, the raiders caused only minor damage.

"There's a change, too, in the anti-aircraft shooting of the British. It is improving with practice. Over Johore, just across the straits from this island, ack-ack batteries brought down another Japanese bomber and another was damaged and probably did not get back to its base.

"The anxiety of the people out here for American assistance is increasing. The most frequent comment is on the whereabouts of the American Navy. The thrill of security given them by the presence of the *Repulse* and *Prince of Wales* was too brief. And the remark I hear very often is that the U.S. Navy should steam right into the China Sea even though it is now ringed by Japanese air bases."

Wednesday, January 7th:
Japanese troops in sampans made "abortive" attempts to land at Selangor.

The *Straits Times'* war correspondent—at least that's the way he was identified—reported today:

"The Japanese are fighting our resistance in Northern Malaya, a tough obstacle to overcome despite the inferiority in numbers. This resistance is shown by the numerous landings they have attempted to make on the west coast in the past week."

What an analysis that is! What a cheap attempt to give encouragement to the people! The Japanese are making those landings on the west coast, each one nearer to Singapore, to cut off the British troops trying to hold the main road from Kuala Lumpur to Johore. Their tactics are working perfectly because their infiltrations are forcing the British to continue to withdraw.

BARRED FROM THE AIR

Thursday, January 8th:

Late this afternoon a number of correspondents met with Sir George Sansom, the Director of Publicity and Censorship, at his suggestion, to form a press association and to ration outgoing cables. I was the only American correspondent present.

Sir George informed us that the removal of GHQ to Java "cannot be interpreted in any way as a diminution of the determination to hold Singapore. It is simply an integral part of a scheme of co-ordination of allied commands on geographical grounds."

Following the meeting I went at once to the press room to get the evening communiqué and hand outs and to write my broadcast. In my box, I found a note from the Malaya Broadcasting Corporation. It said:

"We have just been advised by the Director of Publicity that your broadcasts are to cease after tomorrow. We are very sorry to be informed of this because we have been happy to give you every possible facility, but these are the instructions from the Director of Publicity."

I immediately went back downstairs to Sir George Sansom, whom I had left only a few minutes before.

"I just found this note in my box, Sir George," I said, "and it doesn't make sense to me. What does it mean?"

"Well, I am sorry but you can't broadcast any more."

"But why, Sir George?"

"Well, I can't give you any reasons now."

"Who made this decision? Did you?"

"No, this is a military decision, but I concurred in it."

"What do you mean by 'military decision'? Do you mean that Colonel Field made it?"

"Yes."

"Then you think I had better see Colonel Field?"

"Yes, Mr. Brown. You can probably reach him at home."

I hopped into a taxi and went out to his house. Colonel Field invited me upstairs to his apartment.

397

"I'm flabbergasted by this note I've just received," I said. "Can you tell me why this action was taken?"

"The trouble comes mostly from the local population," Colonel Field said. "One woman wrote in from Kuala Lumpur that your broadcasts are Fifth Column. I must say that I agree."

"That's absurd, Colonel Field," I retorted. "Every broadcast I make is passed by your own censors."

"I haven't heard your broadcasts," said Field. "You see, I don't have any radio here." He waved his hand around the room.

"You don't mean to say that you are judging my broadcasts as Fifth Column because one woman wrote in from Kuala Lumpur?" I asked incredulously.

"Oh, no," he insisted hastily, "but I have read the broadcasts, and I agree. This is not the first time this has happened. It happened to you in the Middle East."

"That's not true. I got on very well with the British there. As a matter of fact, I came to Singapore with a note from the Deputy Director of Military Intelligence in Cairo to Colonel Grimsdale, your predecessor here. And that note explained how valuable my broadcasts were and asked Colonel Grimsdale to give me every assistance possible. It only happened once before and that, you may be interested to know, was in Rome. The Italians expelled me for the anti-Fascist tone of my broadcasts."

Colonel Field grunted, obviously not believing me.

"The decision has been made," he said. "I understand the American point of view very well. My wife is American and I have many American connections."

Field went on to say in the next breath that I had tried to beat censorship.

"How?" I asked.

"You came to the studio without a copy of the script for the monitor, the man who checks to see that you read the script as censored."

"You are misinformed, Colonel. I always brought to the studio two scripts, one for me to read by and the other for the monitor to check. There was never a monitor there. I always left the script with the engineer who could monitor or not as he wished. That's not my problem, that's up to the Malaya Broadcasting Company. By the way, are you

398

suggesting that I deviated by so much as a single word from any script as passed by your official censors?"

"No, I don't charge that. I don't believe you did deviate."

"Then, why mention that point about monitoring?"

"Well, there is supposed to be a monitor to follow your script as you read."

"That's not my province. It's very strange to me, Colonel Field, that after my long association with the British forces in the Middle East and here that I am suddenly met with this order out of a clear sky."

"As you know," said Field after a pause, "a large part of the defense of Singapore depends on local morale. It is very bad. It's my job to see that nothing happens which depresses that morale."

"But I am not broadcasting for or to the people of Malaya. I work for CBS and my broadcasts are directed and designed to inform the American people, not the people of Malaya."

"Yes, I understand that, but unfortunately your broadcasts are heard here." His implication was that every native in every *kampong* understood English and owned a radio.

"But come now, Colonel Field, certainly not more than 500 people in the entire country tune in on the broadcasts going to America."

"The people who do hear them spread the word around."

"Are you suggesting that any of my facts are wrong?"

"No, I don't question any of the facts in your broadcasts, but it is the organization of them and the choice of words."

"As for example?" I asked.

"You said that our men were being 'dive-bombed and machine-gunned up at the front'."

"That's correct, isn't it?" I asked.

"Yes, it is, yet I don't see why you have to say that."

"I am sorry, Colonel, I don't understand your reasoning."

"No one feels worse than we do that those men get dive-bombed and machine-gunned every day and that they don't have air support. But as you know, we are trying to keep our aircraft intact for the defense of Singapore itself."

"I know that, Colonel, and I can understand the military reasoning back of it."

"You also said that our men had to wade through swamps for three days."

399

"Ye gods, Colonel, what's wrong with that?"

"Well, perhaps that is not a very good example."

"Colonel Field," I said, "won't you agree that our broadcasts are just what is needed to convey to the Americans how bad the position really is? What better way can American help be brought here than by picturing the conditions and the strategical importance of holding Singapore? It's not only for Britain, but because we need the rubber and tin here."

"Oh, yes," he said, "I will admit very readily that your broadcasts undoubtedly are doing a tremendous lot of good in America, and from that point of view they are very valuable to us. But, unfortunately, they are heard locally and we simply cannot allow them to depress morale."

"So then, Colonel, it comes to this—it's a matter of either foregoing the facts and ceasing honest reporting of the situation and thus stopping broadcasts here or putting out broadcasts which you think do not hurt morale, irrespective of the facts."

"I think, Mr. Brown, you should report the facts differently."

"Well, Colonel Field, for fifteen years I have been a reporter. My job has been to report facts. You are asking me now to forget fifteen years of training and start putting out broadcasts that are not factual."

Colonel Field pondered my remarks for a moment, saying nothing.

"Mr. Brown, do you think you could change the way you broadcast?" he asked finally.

For a minute or more I didn't answer, then I said: "As I see it, facts are facts, and it's my obligation to report them."

I understood very well at the moment that Colonel Field was giving me an "out"—an opportunity to say that I would report the way he wanted me to.

"Suppose, before this decision becomes even more final than it is, I send a cable to New York about reporting from Singapore?"

"What would you want to say in this cable?"

"Something like this: 'Informatively due to extraordinary local morale conditions and because broadcasts heard locally military authorities advise it is futurely impossible to broadcast accurate, honest reporting of local and military situation. Please advise.' Is that all right, Colonel Field?"

"Yes," he said, "that's perfectly all right."

"In the meantime," I said, "what do you think of my continuing to broadcast until we see how things shape up while awaiting an answer from New York?"

"This is where I stop," Colonel Field said. "I am leaving here tomorrow and I would not want to tie the hands of my successor. I will do this, however. I will confer with my successor and with Sir George Sansom tomorrow and let you know what they decide."

When I returned to the hotel I found a message from Major Fisher, who is in charge of war correspondents. The message said:

"1. I have this day sent a signal to the War Office, informing them that you are no longer an accredited war correspondent and asking them to cancel your license.

"2. I am satisfied that the evidence in favor of taking this step is overwhelming.

"3. I request you to surrender your license to me for cancellation and to discontinue wearing your uniform.

"4. I understand that you have been already notified that your broadcast of tomorrow is your final one and that after that all facilities for broadcasting in Singapore will be denied to you.

C. R. FISHER
Major, D. A. D. P. R."

I immediately tried to telephone Colonel Field and finally reached him in forty-five minutes to tell him that I had just been informed that my license as a war correspondent also had been revoked.

"Oh, yes," he said, "that's all a part of the same thing."

"This is an extremely serious step to cancel an accreditation issued by the War Office in London."

"Yes, but it is all part of the same thing."

"Can't this matter be held in abeyance until the decision is made tomorrow when you speak to your successor and Sir George Sansom?"

"Well, Mr. Brown," said Field, "the message that was sent can always be annulled."

Diary comment:

This action is the same as an expulsion because they know very well that if I can't broadcast and am not an accredited war correspondent I can't carry out my functions for CBS. It's only an off-chance that the cancellation of facilities and the revoking of the license is a drastic bluff to compel me to submit to propaganda, that the message to the War Office was not sent by Major Fisher. I am not counting on this, however.

Tonight I told Agronsky about it. He was infuriated because he knows he is in exactly the same spot. I saw George Weller of the *Chicago Daily News* tonight and gave him a bare outline of the situation.

"The thing to do, Cec," Weller said, "is to let us all put out a story on this. Every correspondent has got to stick together on this thing and we got to get it told all over America."

"I agree, George," I told him, "but I'm not putting out any story on it, and I'm not issuing a statement. You know the facts; you can go ahead on it."

"Well, let's get the agencies to put out a story."

"That's up to you, George," I said.

Weller then telephoned Yates McDaniel of the *Associated Press* and Harold Guard of the *United Press*. Yates was not very interested, and Harold Guard showed only casual interest.

Weller came away from the 'phone saying: "I think they both are afraid to touch it."

After all, radio competes, in its swift, spot-news coverage with the old-line agencies which service the newspapers of America.

Friday, January 9th:
Because Agronsky feels that NBC is earmarked for ousting also, he went with me to see Duff Cooper this morning.

I detailed my conversation with Colonel Field and the facts on the revocation of my license as a war correspondent.

Agronsky spoke for fully twenty minutes then on the insufferable inequalities of censorship, the restrictions and the petty actions of censors, their determination to cut out anything that bears the slightest resemblance to news and accuracy.

"I will look into it," Duff Cooper said finally, "but I am where I was when you, Mr. Brown, first came to see me. I am without any power." (The establishment of Wavell's headquarters in Java had eliminated Duff Cooper's chairmanship of the Allied War Council in Singapore.)

"My appointment as a Cabinet Minister has been canceled. You see

402

there's no point in having a Cabinet Minister here now, since there is a generalissimo operating from Java. But I will talk to Sir George Sansom about it."

I waited all day for the expected call from Colonel Field on his talk with his successor and with Sir George Sansom. Agronsky was confident that the authorities would reconsider, but I wasn't.

Al Noderer of the *Chicago Tribune* and George Weller wanted to put stories out on the case, but I urged them to wait until I heard from Field.

At 4:15 I called him instead. This was the conversation: "Do you have any word for me yet?"

"Yes, I have been informed the War Council considered your case this morning."

"And what is their decision?"

"The decision stands."

"What about the revocation of my war correspondent's license? What's being done about that?"

"That is part of the same thing. They go together. I don't think there is anything you can do about this."

"Thank you, Colonel Field, for taking this matter up again for me."

I thereupon sent off an immediate cable to New York reading:
CANCEL FUTURE BROADCASTS, EXPLANATION UPCOMING.

What infuriates me most of all is that when Agronsky and I saw Duff Cooper this morning, he already knew that the War Council had made a final decision and yet he had said that he would look into the matter. He gave no intimation then that my case had been discussed and already decided by the War Council.

Agronsky tells me that he saw Sir George Sansom this afternoon to inquire about his status.

"You are not affected," Sir George said. "You are perfectly persona grata. The action against Brown is not a forerunner of action against you."

I sent a long cable to Paul White explaining the circumstances and the conversations I had with the officials here. After giving him the details of the moves made so far, I said: "I am convinced the facts and circumstances fully justify Washington to make the strongest repre-

403

sentations to the British Foreign Office and War Office, calling on the Singapore officials for an explanation, and also to withdraw the verbal charges of Fifth Columnism made by Colonel Field, since all my work is submitted to censorship and passed by the censor. Such action is a denial of an opportunity to cover the war from a point where American forces in the future will be involved as an ally.

"Revocation of my license is a most serious reflection on my work for CBS, my long association with the British, and my role as the only American aboard the *Repulse*. I am willing and extremely anxious to stand the most searching investigation, and I am prepared to proceed to London immediately for a War Office examination of my record of broadcasting scripts as well as articles in the *Saturday Evening Post, Life, Newsweek* and *Collier's*. Also my record while with the British forces in the Middle East and Far East; opposing the Germans in Yugoslavia; and the reasons why the Italian authorities expelled me from Italy."

This evening I had a drink with Squadron Leader Grant and Flight Lieutenants Blackwell and Downer, all of the Air Ministry's News Service, and with some other correspondents. They were all of the opinion, especially the Air Force officers, that I demand a court martial. I too favor a court martial. They all greeted me with the raucous shout: "So, you have been defrocked!"

In the House of Commons today Attlee gave a review of the war. He said that fifteen Malayan airfields have now been lost and added that the defenders are sixty miles north of Kuala Lumpur.

Lord Moyne, Secretary of State for the Colonies, assured the House of Lords that instructions had been issued by the War Council at Singapore for destruction of all stocks of rubber, oil and raw materials, as well as of mining machinery wherever necessary.

I don't know what he means by "wherever necessary" but that is what he said. He also declared:

"Some segments say 'We shall be back in a few weeks. It will be enough to put this plant out of action temporarily or to disperse and hide these stocks!' There must be no thought of immediate loss or a future gain."

404

That kind of remark is going to pass over the heads of a good many people in Malaya.

There have been allegations that the Malayans have been co-operating by giving the enemy sarongs. An official announcement today said: "Only a small percentage of the sarongs worn by the Malayans are made in this country. The Japs made many of them and they have been duplicating the styles used here in order to have their troops confuse the British."

This business of Malayan co-operation with the Japanese is pretty serious and the authorities are trying to cover it up by issuing statements like this: "The passive attitude of the *kampong* dwellers is exactly in accord with the instructions of authorities."

Saturday, January 10th:
I called on Major Fisher today in order to turn in my red-backed license as a war correspondent. I asked Fisher if I was entitled to a court martial, but he didn't think so.

Duckworth conferred with Sir George Sansom this morning about my cable to CBS and the cables of the other correspondents telling of the case. This afternoon I called Duckworth to ask if the cable had actually been sent off.

"No," he said, "it is still under discussion."

"I'm certainly entitled to let my office know what's happened. All I have told them thus far is that they should cancel my broadcasts from here."

Several hours later Duckworth called me on the phone to say that my message could go through as written if made, not a press message, but an informative cable (and therefore not for publication in America).

"I have talked with Sir George Sansom," said Duckworth, "and your broadcasts, as originally submitted to censorship, show a state of mind that makes you persona non grata."

"What!" I exclaimed. "Wait a minute, Duckworth! Do you fully realize what you are saying?"

"Oh, don't worry. I know what I am saying," said Duckworth.

"As I understand it, you mean it is what I *attempted* to say in my broadcasts that led to this action."

405

"That's right."

"But I can't understand that. I have been accused of putting out broadcasts inimical to local morale. Now you say it was material that I wrote in the broadcasts and which was blue-penciled by the censors that led to my being barred. I don't understand how material that was seen only by myself and the censor could affect local morale."

"Well, that's the view that has been taken. It was what you submitted."

"Duckworth," I said, "an action taken against a correspondent for what he *attempts* to say opens a whole new field of possibilities. This is the first time I have been told this. Is it a new reason or are you simply trying to justify the action already taken?"

"No, that is our view."

This new turn of British thought had me bewildered, and in that state I hung up.

Duckworth met with a group of correspondents shortly after our phone talk. He told them that the action against me was based on the charge: "The cumulative effect of the material submitted for censorship by Mr. Brown for the past few weeks showed a state of mind which makes him persona non grata." Duckworth also said that the denial of facilities to me was a civil decision. This did not correspond to what Sir George Sansom and Colonel Field each told me separately: that this was a military decision.

Diary comment:

I never thought a time would come when the British would say to a correspondent: "You must write copy which requires us to cut nothing out. Anything that we have to cut out will be held against you."

In other words, the British here now demand control of the thoughts of correspondents.

Sunday, January 11th:

At 11:30 I telephoned Major Fisher to find out if he had any information yet whether I was entitled to a trial.

"I have looked into it, and they say it already has taken place."

"A trial can't take place without my appearance, can it?"

"Oh, yes, yes, that's right, yes," Fisher said in some confusion. Then

406

he added: "I'm waiting for word on it, and I will let you know directly I hear."

This morning Duckworth met with Weller, Agronsky and Noderer to "present new evidence and give the real reasons why the action was taken against Brown."

The meeting was also held for the "adjustment" of the stories these three correspondents wanted to send on my case.

Duckworth told them that it was because of my material submitted for censorship over the past few months and for "other reasons."

"What are the other reasons?" Weller asked. "Give them all to me. I will put them all in my story. I will give your full case."

"For one thing," Duckworth began, "the British Consul in Batavia sent a cable that loyal Britishers in Java protested Brown's broadcasts."

"Fine," Weller said. "We will put that in."

"I don't know about that. It was a code message."

Duckworth, at Weller's urging, telephoned Scott, head of the Ministry of Information, and was told that since the message from Batavia was in cipher it could not be used. So Weller and Duckworth worked out a formula whereby they could say: "British subjects in Batavia protested to British authorities."

"All right," Weller said, "do you have any more reasons?"

"Well," the censor explained, "word came over that the Dutch were incensed."

"No, we are not going to use travelers' tales," said Weller. "You have all kinds of liaison with the Dutch and if they are incensed they have plenty of ways to let you know."

The report of this meeting given to me by the three correspondents who attended it confirms my belief that Colonel Field and Sir George Sansom had been pushed into taking the action by a few protests from individuals. The other correspondents think the officials were anxious to retaliate for my criticisms and they wanted to pick off an American correspondent as an example for the rest, and I had been the most outspoken.

"These people are such damned fools," Weller said. "They step right into it up to their necks. This story of your disbarment breaks just as 12,000,000 people are reading your article in *Life* on Singapore."

I believe that the *Life* article had a good deal to do with it, especially since it was critical of the Governor, Sir Shenton Thomas.

"This action," Noderer remarked, "was taken for what you didn't think, didn't write and didn't broadcast."

Monday, January 12th:

Raiders have been over the island most of the day, over Singapore for two hours this morning and for two hours this afternoon.

I talked with a civil servant from Kuala Lumpur who has just come here with his wife and daughter. I am no longer wearing my pips as a war correspondent, in accordance with the orders from Major Fisher.

"Oh, I've heard your broadcasts to America," he said. "They are the only ones which tell us what is going on."

"Well, you won't hear them any more. The British have barred me. I'm an ex-correspondent now."

"I hope you go back to America and tell the real story about Malaya. You should have been at Kuala Lumpur. After what I've seen in Malaya, I am ashamed to be an Englishman."

"You can't say a thing like that," I remonstrated. "These people here are exceptions. You can be proud of being part of a people who've stood up under the terrible blitzing that the English at home have had."

Duff Cooper has been recalled. One editorial here, in protesting against London's decision, said: "Rightly or wrongly, the public has regarded him as the last bulwark against that minute paper mentality to which many of our present anxieties may be attributed."

The *Straits Times,* in its editorial today, demands a military governor for Singapore to replace Sir Shenton Thomas.

The mistakes are avalanching now. As far as I can gather, no sweeping policy was adopted for total destruction of fifty modern dredges in the Kintes Valley tin area.

At Telok Anson, however, the natives profited by British wisdom. A few days before the Japs landed, the food warehouses were opened up and the civilians were told to help themselves. Within a few days one hundred thousand bags of rice were taken into the jungle.

The British are not using the natives to guide them through the jungles and swamps. They are afraid to trust them.

408

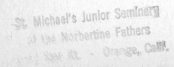

The Japanese were able to make a surprise landing on Selangor by creeping down the Perak coast unobserved. They were unobserved because the British had no patrols out watching for them.

The papers here are printing biting comments on Malaya from the London press. I understand that the Singapore censors are allowing the stuff in because they feel that their censorship should be confined only to outgoing material. One London paper complains that the British public is being told very little officially about the Malaya campaign "and what we are being told seems purposely vague."

The *London News Chronicle* alleges that the evacuation of Penang was made without the knowledge of the Governor and the Colonial Secretary and is evidence of administrative confusion.

We correspondents here were not permitted to say that Governor Thomas didn't know of the Penang evacuation order, although he actually stated that in a broadcast.

There's great fear that Singapore is to be evacuated. General Pownall broadcast today that the first task is to ward off the blow; the second is to hold the enemy from vital areas while we renew, regroup and supplement our forces.

"We are now engaged in the second of those tasks," said General Pownall, "and the most vital of the areas which are to be defended and one which we are absolutely determined to defend is Singapore."

This means that there will be no attempt to stop the Japanese coming down the peninsula toward Singapore, but simply to delay them.

Agronsky, after several days' argument with censors, finally was able to broadcast that I had been barred from the air. He gave the facts in the case and then added his comment:

"As a result of this action Mr. Brown will no longer be able to broadcast on the war against the Axis forces from any point on British soil where British—or even U.S.—forces are engaged.

"He is regarded by his colleagues as an objective, truthful and conscientious reporter whose belief in the democratic cause has been proved on any number of occasions.

"The possible precedent set in Brown's case in an area where American troops may soon be actively engaged is regarded by his American colleagues with real concern."

Tuesday, January 13th:

Received a cable today from CBS sent on December 15th.

COLUMBIA HAS TOLD YOUR BANK YOU HAVE DONE ONE GRAND JOB. PAUL WHITE

It puzzled me. It was too cryptic for me, and I showed it to George Weller.

"Jesus, Cec," George whooped, "you know what that means?"

"No, I don't. Maybe you can figure it out."

"Why, it means that they have deposited a thousand-dollar bonus to your account."

I almost fell flat on my face. When I recovered my equilibrium, I realized what "One Grand" meant.

Had a drink today with Lieutenant Geoffrey Hallowes, the aid of Major General Simmons, and I told him I had been barred from broadcasting. He said he would immediately take the matter up with General Simmons. I asked him not to. The military here are absolutely in a flat spin. They are not going to be able to fight a war in that state of mind. Singapore is not going to hold.

It has been pouring rain most of the day and there have been two raids lasting about four hours. Bombs were dropped on Kalang airdrome which is about a mile and a half from Raffles. I was in a slit trench in front of the hotel with two other correspondents reading a copy of *Time* magazine that Graeme Nicholl had brought me. The repercussion of the bombs shook the hotel, but the only damage it did was to knock the dust off the fans.

The official total given for the number of Jap planes over Singapore yesterday is 125, but there are no official reports yet on any airfights.

The Dutch today issued a communiqué that three Jap airplanes were brought down over Singapore, but the British say they have no report. It looked pretty silly in the papers today to see the British communiqué, "No Report," printed side by side with the Dutch communiqué from Batavia reporting the action over Singapore.

This afternoon I received a cable from CBS which said:

PENDING CHECKUP HERE, SIT TIGHT.

So all I can do is wait for their further advice.

410

There is tremendous criticism now on the whole Malayan campaign coming from London, and even the papers here are now saying what I said two weeks ago.

Seabridge of the *Straits Times* is doing a superb job of editorial writing, the sort of thing where a man rises to an emergency. But the *Malaya Tribune* is still ladling out pap about "everything-is-all-right-we-can-take-it." This may be because it is read by the English-speaking Asiatics.

This afternoon I received a cable from *London Daily Express*. They want a thousand-word article on "Why They Stopped My Broadcasts."

The London paper also informed me that they are reprinting my entire article from *Life,* which criticized preparations for war in Singapore.

The *Straits Times* has an eight-column story today headed: "Singapore Beats Off 125 Raiders."
What actually happened was the Japs dropped their bombs and went home.

Wednesday, January 14th:
The papers here reprinted an editorial from the *London Daily Express* which says:

"While this fight goes on, it becomes clearer every day how much Japan owes to the crop of incompetent British windbags. The time is too short for ordinary methods of truth-telling and publicity to retrieve the situation, but if General Wavell sees fit to take the most drastic measures against slothful officialdom, he will have the thanks of the whole alliance."

The report is that fifty Hurricanes with pilots and ground crews will be in action within a week or ten days. Planes have to be assembled. Two of them were damaged in their crates.

There are rumors that reinforcements have arrived, but no announcement has been issued yet. The figure I heard is 10,000 men.

The communiqués continue to be niggardly and dangerously incomplete. When the present British positions are revealed it will be a great shock to the people.

The worst possible action was taken today when the communiqué failed to mention a word about the land fighting. This means that the people will suddenly find that the British have withdrawn to somewhere in Johore. The communiqué said: "There are no changes to report."

In my opinion it was the duty of the military today to give some indication where the British are.

That was also the opinion, I learned, of Sir George Sansom, the director of publicity.

Sir George protested vigorously to Lieutenant General A. E. Percival, who is writing the communiqués.

Sansom pointed out there were all kinds of changes going on, many of them already being spread as rumors. The rumors, he said, were taking on a very dangerous twist about the British being routed and the Japanese speeding toward Singapore with no opposition.

"Ah, yes," General Percival said. "I didn't say there were no changes. I do say in the communiqué: 'There are no changes to report.'"

Brian Penton, editor of the *Sydney Daily Telegraph,* cabled me today that he is protesting to London about the treatment I received from the British military authorities and asked me to come at once to Australia at his paper's expense to write a series of articles about Malaya and Singapore. I also received a cable from CBS sent three days ago. This is typical of the speed of transmission of cables these days. It said:

HAVE PROTESTED AUTHORITIES IN WASHINGTON, LONDON AND SINGAPORE STOP MEANWHILE URGE YOU MAKE EVERY EFFORT TO CONSULT WITH PROPER OFFICIALS TOWARD REINSTATEMENT STOP CURRENT WORLD SITUATION AND NECESSITY OF ALLIED UNITY EVEN IN CONNECTION WITH EXCHANGES OF NEWS MAKE SUCH EPISODES REGRETTABLE FROM THE STANDPOINT OF ALLIED MORALE IN AMERICA STOP WE COUNTING ON YOU TO DO YOUR UTMOST TO RESOLVE SITUATION BEST POSSIBLE BASIS FOR ALL CONCERNED. PAUL WHITE.

It seemed obvious to me that this message was sent to be shown to the local authorities and I therefore immediately went to Sir George Sansom.

"There's nothing I can do about it," he said. "I'm finished here. I was only director of publicity temporarily for the Far East Command and now the Command is in Java. I expect to go there and I have al-

412

ready resigned my post here, but they asked me to stay on for a few days."

"I understand that, Sir George. I didn't come here to present any formal appeal, but just to present to you a copy of this telegram."

"I also received a cable from Mr. White, protesting against the discriminatory action against a man of your ability and asking for your reinstatement," said Sir George. "I cabled back a reply that your high ability—I used high ability—was not in question, but that the military authorities found difficulty in a meeting of the minds and therefore decided you were persona non grata." With a smile, Sir George added: "That's no reflection on you, Mr. Brown. Many diplomats are found persona non grata by the Government, but that does not mean they are not good diplomats."

We laughed over that because Sir George had formerly been attached to the British Embassy in Tokyo and he knew about diplomats who were found persona non grata. We were now talking man to man and I said:

"Sir George, I am still very puzzled about the confused statements that have been issued by you and Colonel Field and Duckworth, as well as Major Fisher, about my case. Each one has something different to give in the way of reasons and none of you seems to agree. Can you tell me what the *actual* reasons are for this action?"

"I have been trying to find that out myself," Sir George said. "I asked General Percival if he could give me specific reasons for this action against you and he said: 'There are no specific reasons for charges. It is just that we have found him difficult over the past few months.'"

"That's certainly true enough," I remarked. "The Governor killed one of my broadcasts; General Percival killed an interview I had with General Bennett and I have been protesting for months about the conditions that you yourself will admit have resulted in a good part of this mess right now, not only the censorship mess but also this military mess."

"Yes, I know you have been fighting hard and I admire you for it."

"Thank you, Sir George, you fought me and I fought you. Each of us was trying to do his job in the best way possible. That has nothing to do with our personal friendship."

"Of course not," he said. "You praise our courage but you criticize our minds, and you know how the military react to any criticism of their minds."

The difficulty now is in upsetting the decision, since the British military seldom change their mind.

The Tokyo radio says that two days ago I was arrested by the British military authorities and put in jail because of my broadcasts. As good an indication as any of the sort of radio-propaganda lies the Japs are pouring out.

The Australians went into action today and moved northward near Johore.

"The Australians," says General Bennett, "cannot only hold the Japs, but can push them back."

I certainly hope so.

Colonel Brink, the American liaison officer, called American men to the Consulate today.

"This is going to be a theatre of war," he said, "and when American troops arrive we ask Americans here to volunteer as soldiers or for collaborative duty. Many of you know the British and how to get on with them. I myself have been here eleven months trying to learn how to do it."

All of the twenty-five men who showed up at the meeting laughed.

PEOPLE'S WAR

Saturday, January 17th:

The papers today published a document sent by Governor Thomas to all Government departments. It was printed under the feature headline: "A Historic Circular."

"The day of minute papers has gone," it said. "There must be no mere passing of files from one department to another, and from one officer to another. It is the duty of every officer to act, and if he feels the decision is beyond him, he must go and get it.

"Similarly, the day of letters and reports is over. All written matter should be in the form of short notes, in which only the important points are mentioned.

"Every officer must accept his responsibility for the taking of decisions.

"The essential thing is speed in action. Nothing matters which is not directly concerned with defense and no one should be troubled with it.

"Officers who show that they cannot take responsibility should be replaced by those who can. Seniority is of no account.

"T. S. THOMAS, *Governor*"

That circular is indeed a historic document. Six weeks after the strain of war, they decide something must be done about the tangled red tape here. It is a step forward, but I don't care for that phrase "should be replaced." In war, I prefer active verbs.

London dispatches report that Parliament is getting set to ask many questions about the Far East. There is a general feeling of critical anxiety and dissatisfaction reported among the MP's.

Two questions before Parliament, say the London reports, may be: "What steps have been taken to recruit Chinese, Indian and Malay civilians for military duties other than civil defense?" and "Why did the British Government not accept Chiang Kai-shek's offer of Chinese troops for the defense of Malaya?"

Those two questions can be answered very easily. The British here

415

have considered the Chinese and Japanese as being the same. The Colonial Administration, and specifically Colonial Secretary Jones, has been unable to distinguish between the Chinese as allies and the Japanese as potential enemies and now actual enemies. They have refused to give the Chinese guns. They have refused, in my opinion, to allow Chiang Kai-shek's troops to come in because they knew the Chinese would fight first for China and second for the British. It's very true that every Chinese would have been glad to fight for Chiang Kai-shek.

Today's communiqué officially reveals for the first time that the Japs are now in Johore State, 110 miles north of Singapore. It is old to everyone but the high command. The communiqué did not actually say Malacca has been evacuated. It got around it by saying: "Japanese barges at Malacca were bombed."

The military here would certainly save themselves much criticism from London by giving an occasional report of the situation before the Japanese give it.

And here's an item from the paper today: "In compliance with the request of various local circles, twelve political prisoners have recently been released by the authorities in Singapore so they can offer their services for the successful prosecution of the war.

"The group met yesterday to discuss the nature of the work for which they are best suited."

These men are Communists. They were arrested before last December for being members of an illegal party, made up of Chinese Communists and supporters of Chiang Kai-shek. With the enemy now only 110 miles away the British are a little more concerned with the Jap "elements" than with so-called subversive elements.

Everyone is wallowing in the luxury of criticism.

The *Straits Times* today carries a story from its London correspondent quoting London newspapers. The *Daily Express* says: "How many more Malayas are there in the Empire? The extent of the unpreparedness and apathy is a sickening discovery for the British public. Weapons are not enough while there remains anywhere in the Empire such mental unpreparedness as has been discovered in Malaya. Apathetic Singapore is run by boneheads."

416

The *London News Chronicle* attacked reports put out that Britain will have air superiority over Singapore in three days and asks: "Who in the name of common sense made that prediction in London?"

The *London Daily Mirror* writes: "Get rid of the Far East military boobies—these jackasses who think they can conceal from the people the grave situation in Malaya. They think they can stave off reverses by mysteriously hinting at a good time presently to be had by all in Singapore. It's high time they were suppressed."

The *London Daily Sketch* says: "No inquests now; no recriminations can be of the slightest use. Meanwhile there is far too much fuss concerning the enforced withdrawal from Singapore of an American radio reporter who criticized the defense arrangements. What would the Americans have said if a British reporter in the Philippines had reported about how seriously the Islands were under-garrisoned far below the minimum General MacArthur is believed to have said he could hold them?

"Admittedly there were failures to realize the dangers of the position in the Far East."

The *London Daily Sketch* is the paper which sent Leonard O. Mosley to Singapore, the same correspondent who wrote in November: "I bring you good news. I have just visited twenty airdromes in Malaya and there are clouds of bombers and fighters ready to repel any invasion."

Harold Guard of *United Press* sent this story: "Singaporians await developments with an apathy completely different from London's rapid and intelligent response to their leaders' advices and orders.

"More than a month after the outbreak of the war," the *United Press* said, "the vast majority here do not know what is happening inside or outside of Singapore. This is due to official and service disinclination to provide news in the simplest, clear-cut guidance."

Duff Cooper has left and at his leaving the *Straits Times* bewailed: "It means that in the hour of crisis the 'biggest' man on the local horizon has been taken from us against our will."

I note that the London papers are just now beginning to get a true conception of the loss of Malaya rubber and tin and what that's going to mean. I wonder whether the auto men in Detroit know what it's going to mean.

A very welcome telegram from Martha, sent as a day letter on December 15th, just received. The family are very well and she loves me, according to cablese, "muchest."

Sunday, January 18th:

We had two air raids this morning. During the first one, about ten, I was out at the house and about thirty Jap bombers came over, spreading out in a V formation. There was a great deal of ack-ack. In the second raid I was at the hotel downtown, or rather in my favorite ditch out in front. I couldn't see any aircraft, and five or six bombs fell in the downtown section.

They came down uncomfortably close today. It is a strange feeling, lying on the ground and feeling one bomb hit some distance away, then a split second later another one closer, then another one still closer, and so on. You wait for that stick to be exhausted.

The crisis over Malaya is still boiling up in England. The *London Star* says that the Far Eastern set-backs and Washington decisions make a government shake-up one of Churchill's first tasks, now that he has returned from the White House.

I am hoping that Paul White will see the reasonableness of my difficulties out here in view of what has happened. The perplexing thing is just what support CBS is giving my case and how vigorously they will protest to the War Office. I am still amazed that the British should have done this thing. Everyone else is amazed, too, except those who actually did the head-chopping.

On Friday the R.A.F., it was officially announced, raided one thousand Jap transport vehicles in the Tampin Gemas area in South Negri Sembelan. That gives an idea of how spectacularly the Japanese have been able to bring great quantities of transport facilities up to the front-line area as fast as the front line is formed. In other words, the Japanese had a thousand vehicles in an area the British only evacuated less than twenty-four hours before.

When the British evacuated they were supposed to have dynamited all bridges and to have thrown various kinds of barriers across the road. Whatever they did to hinder the Japs, the fact remains that a thousand

418

vehicles were able to operate in an area the British had just pulled out of. The speed of the Japanese advance is astounding.

The R.A.F. is showing much greater activity. They now can operate from the Singapore Island base. For the past week or so the anti-aircraft firing has been very effective. This is because some experienced anti-aircraft gunners arrived here about two weeks ago.

The Tokyo radio is getting more and more fantastic. Last night out at our house in the country I sat in front of the radio listening to the Tokyo blather. The announcer quoted a commander as saying that he flew over Singapore and "it is like Chapei"—that is, flattened to the ground. The Jap radio also said that the Cathay Building has been broken in two by bombs. The Cathay Building is fifteen stories high and has not been touched, not even by shrapnel from bombs. That kind of propaganda, if quoted by the British and American press and radio, serves the cunning purpose of the Axis—the shattering of Allied morale.

The columnist known as "Inquirer" says in his piece today in the *Straits Sunday Times:*

"No greater presence of mind has been shown in the Malaya campaign than that of a prominent martial figure who very shortly before evacuating his house and the town instructed the local authorities to have his meters read so as to determine the consumption of electricity and gas and make possible the immediate return of his unexpended balance of deposit."

Our cook out at the house, Ah Tin, is a wonder. He apparently worked for Americans before. At any rate, Larry Lawrence, Tommy Schields, Agronsky, Weller and myself are eating better than we have for a long time. Ah Tin makes steaks the way Americans like them and he's a marvel at hashed-brown potatoes and Boston-baked beans.

The other day I managed to buy seven cans of fig pudding. I love fig pudding, and I have not had it since I left America, except once in Rome when Martha and I received a box from home that contained one can. Ah Tin tonight made the fig pudding with a hard sauce. It was delicious.

I don't care much for bombings, especially when you feel so unprotected. When the bombers are overhead you just wish you had a gun or a pistol or something with which to defend yourself. You become very sensitive to sounds and noises. A motor car starting off in second gear sounds like the beginning of a siren. A fan overhead sounds like the low drone of the Jap bombers with their pulsating beat. A thump upstairs sounds like the crump of a distant bomb. A car back-firing is like a shot from an aircraft cannon. The sound of car treads on asphalt highways seems like the start of the screaming dive of a Japanese bomber. Even the whistle of the wind in the trees sounds like the downward rush of bombs, and a truck bumping along a highway sounds like a stick of bombs crashing in the distance.

Some people prefer to be out in a trench where they can see where the raiders are. They feel too cramped and the period of nervous tension is too long when they are inside waiting for the bombs to come. Personally, I prefer to follow the bombers in their flight and to watch them make the run over their target. You can spot the bombs coming down and determine fairly well if they are going to get you or not. Indoors you know the raiders are overhead and you have to sit there for an hour or two waiting to get killed. If you can see the bombs coming down you know in a minute whether they are going to get you or miss you. I prefer a minute of abject fear to an hour of apprehension.

One Asiatic I know is all set to do some refined looting. His weapon during an air raid is going to be a pair of pliers. His intention is to rush about, yanking out the teeth of Chinese air-raid victims. It should be a profitable business since the Chinese put their wealth into their gold teeth.

All bicycles are being requisitioned today and all British males under forty-one not in active service must register by Wednesday. People whose cars are requisitioned receive $5 a day.

This afternoon six Hurricanes flew back and forth over Singapore. It was a sort of pep show for the people. They look good, and that means that now that they have been assembled they will crack back at the Japs.

Pending some word from New York I decided to get a Dutch visa today and also see about getting air transportation to Batavia. I am sick and tired of waiting around here doing no work.

Monday, January 19th:
General Wavell flew over from Java and is inspecting the Malayan front with General Pownall.

About noon at Raffles Bar I was reading the paper when a captain and two lieutenants, all three men in their forties, came over and asked me to have a drink with them. They knew me because I had spoken to their group of officers at Kuala Lumpur last August. One of them remarked: "A good many things have changed since then, haven't they?"

"They certainly have," I said.

"And all for the worse."

The three officers were just down from Kuala Lumpur, or rather that was the last place they had been stationed. They had been retreating since they got out.

In response to my question the captain said that the Jap success was due sixty to sixty-five percent to their adaptability to jungle warfare and the other thirty-five percent to Fifth-Column work.

I was on the point of asking another question when he said bitterly: "Don't ask me about our lack of organization, our lack of liaison and our whole strategy. It's like this: Before the war we would be working from a map to conduct our maneuvers. Our colonel or the brigadier would say: 'Now this is thick jungle here and this is mangrove swamp. We can rule this out. In this sector all we have to concern ourselves with is the main road.'

"Thus," the captain explained, "we based our strategy on that type of operation. We kept to the roads everywhere. Why, I went through a mangrove swamp the other day and nowhere did I go down in the mud over my ankles. Anyhow, you can walk on the roots in almost any swamp and in that way avoid sinking down.

"As I said, the Japs travel light while our men had nice uniforms and boots and forty pounds on their backs. Why, we even had to carry our gas capes." [These are a transparent rubber-like cape to be thrown over the uniform to keep gas from settling in the cloth. I had one too, but I tossed it in a corner and have never taken it out since then.] "The Japs don't worry about any of that kind of stuff."

421

"Surely," I said, "the men are still not carrying their forty-pound packs and all of their equipment."

"Some of the men," he said, "now wear only shorts, stripped to the waist and carry a cartridge bandolier. That's the way the Australians . went into action the other day."

"Is that an official order?" I asked. "Are the men adapting themselves individually or is Headquarters issuing the orders?"

"No," the captain said, "it's all unofficial. The men just tossed away what they thought they didn't need. Their platoon commanders are allowing it. At least they are saying nothing about it. As far as Headquarters is concerned we still have to carry all of our equipment."

He was bitter, too, about the absence of liaison between the air force —whatever there was of it—and the ground force.

"At one point," he said, "we were holding a position and saw two aircraft come over. Our anti-aircraft battery telephoned to Kuala Lumpur to ask if any of our planes were up. We were told that nothing was in the air. The commander of the battery then turned to his crew and said, 'Let 'em have it.'

"They got a direct hit," the captain said sardonically, "on one of our own Brewster Buffaloes!"

"What about the Fifth-Column work?" I asked.

"The Malays, Tamils and Indians and even a few of the Chinese have been bought up by the Japanese. Where we would pay $50 or $100 for information they would pay $500. In Seremban there were just the usual Japanese—a photographer, a barber, a masseur, and one or two others. It was a very small colony. When they were interned we made a thorough search of their homes and the officers found $350,000 in Straits currency. [That's about $175,000 in U.S. currency.]

"It's damned discouraging," the captain said, "to take up a position in the morning and find three banana leaves laid out in the ground pointed directly at your position. That's what happens all the time. You move up a battery or two during the night and the very next morning the Japanese aircraft is flying and circling around it trying to locate the precise spot in the jungle to drop their bombs.

"In Kelantan there were a dozen Indians on guard duty and they heard a voice cry out in the darkness, 'We are wounded; we are Indians.' The guards were suspicious and told them to advance a half dozen feet. They did and were again challenged. One of the men called out in the darkness, 'I am a Punjabi. Is Sergeant so-and-so there? Is Corporal so-and-so there?' They named a half dozen men in the camp. That convinced the Indian guards. The group advanced out of the darkness. Japs they were. They killed most of the Indian regulars, except six.

"Oh, yes," the captain said, "this is an authentic story. You see, the Punjabi was a civilian who had been living in the area and grew friendly with the men stationed there. He was bought up by the Japs and they contacted him when they came through.

"This scheme," the captain said, "was followed the other day when six Japs dressed as Indians went running toward the Aussies yelling, 'We are Indians, don't shoot!' But," the English captain chuckled, "the Aussies wouldn't play. They shot all six.

"Throughout the country lights flash at night for the Jap raiders. That," he said, "shows lots of preparation and planning."

The captain was the first to see the Japs making a landing from the sea at Kuala Selangor on the west coast of Malaya. He was atop a lighthouse, standing with a group of men on the narrow balcony. They were all on the shady side of the platform.

A ship came into view towing two barges just beyond artillery range and the British flashed four times. They got no answering signal and then finally signaled, "Make yourself known or we open fire." The captain and all the men on top of the lighthouse watched the mother ship and two barges for more than a half hour.

"I happened to wander around to the sunny side of the platform," said the captain. "There, a few hundred yards away, anchored, were four more barges. They must have been there twenty minutes. I called artillery immediately and within half an hour they were in action.

"Two of the barges moved out in the front of us to reach the mouth of the river and there we opened fire on them. One went in toward shore and unloaded its men. The other barge went out to join the mother ship. It ran up a small Japanese flag. You could see the Jap pulling it up. The Japs were streaming ashore from that barge, about eighty men, and the other two barges moved right down the mouth of the river just a couple of hundred yards away from us."

423

"For God's sake, Captain," I exclaimed, "why wasn't someone on the other side of the lighthouse platform keeping watch? You were all bunched up on the one side."

"Well," drawled the captain, completely unabashed, "it was bloody hot in the sun on the other side."

Late that afternoon I was with another captain who also had come down from the north. He had been in the retreat all the way from Sungei Patani, almost 400 miles north. He, too, was bitter about the whole campaign, especially about the absence of British aircraft and the incessant Japanese machine-gunning and bombing.

"It has had a considerable effect on the troops, I can tell you," he said. "No matter how tough you are, after a few weeks of it, it is bound to get you. You are always in a ditch or up to your ears in a swamp, and constantly they are spraying you with guns. If it isn't machine-gunning it's bombing, and if it isn't either it's both."

As we sat there talking, a Malay lieutenant who had been up north with the captain came over to ask him something, and the British officer asked him to sit down with us. I ordered a whisky and water for him and said: "How are the Malays holding up?"

"The Malays," he said, "are frightened by this machine-gunning and bombing from the Japanese. They are disheartened by not seeing any British planes. Most of them," he said with utter frankness, "ran away, 'but some stayed at their posts."

"The men generally," the captain said, "are holding up very well. If we had air support we could do the job. The Japanese infiltration methods, of course, force our withdrawals. We constantly had to retreat to avoid infiltration. You see," he said sadly, "they came over the ground where we were sure no enemy could come. I must say," the captain added, "if you had told me two months ago that the Japanese could get Johore State in this time or any time I would have said you were crazy."

I asked the captain and the lieutenant what they thought of the Japanese bombers.

"They are not much good. They are inaccurate, but the disheartening thing is that they are over our targets as soon as we establish a point, either a camp or a gun battery or a defensive position. No matter where it is, the Japanese within an hour are bombing us."

424

The *Straits Times* today carries a prize headline. It appears over a story from its London correspondent and the headline reads:

"London Watching War in Malaya."

I hope so.

I understand the Ministry of Information decided to disrupt the Japanese use of occupation currency in occupied Malaya. The story I was told was this:

The Ministry had printed about two million dollars' worth of these Japanese occupation notes to distribute throughout Malaya, where the Japs had not yet arrived, impressing upon the natives that the notes were utterly worthless. In this way they hoped to flood the country with spurious Japanese occupation money and thereby thwart the enemy's attempt to buy up the people.

When the time was ripe for release of the propaganda about the notes, and also the money itself, the Ministry of Information advised the Federated Malay States Government officials about it:

"Oh, no," it was told, "you can't do that! That's counterfeiting!"

Singapore is now the center from which the secretariats operate the Federated or Unfederated States. None of the Sultans has left his State. I don't know whether they are co-operating with the Japanese, but they all decided to stay when the Japanese came in. This means that they are not playing ball with the British, or it might mean they have decided they can look after their people better by staying behind. As I see it, they didn't lose any time in deciding that a live Sultan is much better off than a Sultan without a State, and possibly dead besides.

Forty-eight Hurricanes are almost ready to go up. They are getting the stiffness out of them now. The tragedy is that only one of those forty-eight Hurricane pilots has had combat experience. This one has had five hours in combat. But all the pilots are very confident. These Hurricanes will enable the British to change their tactics and go directly after the bombers. Some of the Hurricane boys tell me they're convinced not a single Jap bomber will get back.

The Japs were not over today for the first time in many days.

I got a Dutch visa today.

425

I am told that the fighter pilots at Seletar take their kit packs when they go up to do battle with the Japs because either they have instructions not to return to Singapore or they may be unable to get back and be forced to land on one of the Dutch islands.

One pilot told me that now when they go up to fight they are not supposed to return to Singapore but to proceed to another base on one of the Dutch islands. I don't think this is correct, however, and if it is done it's only in an emergency.

The Brewster Buffaloes are proving ineffective, the main trouble being that they cannot get up high enough or fast enough. One Brewster fighter pilot told me that his ship cannot operate above 17,000 feet.

"The Jap Zeros, and of course their bombers, stay up above that altitude, and we don't have a chance to hit them.

"Besides, we are so slow in getting up in the air that the Japs already drop their bombs before we can do anything about it. The big advantage of the Brewster is that it's a strong crate, and when you crash you do have a chance to walk away alive."

My anxiety to see Martha is constantly increasing.

Jap agents in Singapore are spreading all kinds of rumors. One rumor is that the new order allowing additional purchases of food is to permit wide distribution of stocks because the Europeans are going to evacuate and want to leave the Asiatics with supplies so that they won't starve.

That's dangerous propaganda because of what happened at Penang plus the steady speed of the Japanese advance. The rumor, however, is all over the Chinese sections.

It is difficult to visualize these little, monkey-faced Japanese swarming all over this beautiful country.

Tuesday, January 20th:
At 8:30 this morning the anti-aircraft began firing in the distance rather heavily, even rattling the house. Evidently it was a reconnaissance plane. I finished shaving. Then about 8:40 the siren went off and a few minutes later the all-clear. Then at 8:50 again the siren and at nine I saw eighteen Japanese bombers in formation against the

426

blue sky, up about 18,000 feet, going toward the naval base. I saw six Hurricanes take off, going in the opposite direction. Then came the bombs. It was like a heavy broom sweeping the ground as stick after stick was sent into the base. The ack-ack fire seemed very good and it hit right where the bombers were, but the firing seemed to be too low.

Then the second wave of thirty-three came over. I didn't see them, but they went right over Singapore and dropped their bombs smack in the center of the town. They made a noise like crushing a match box in your hands. [Three hundred eighty-three civilians were killed in this raid.]

About 11:45, having no car, I hitch-hiked into town with an officer. Half way in we were caught by another raid and we both popped into a sewer in front of an Indian shop.

We are obviously on the eve of very heavy attacks on Singapore. There is a sliver of moon starting tonight. The Japs are sixty miles from Singapore. The radio and papers have said nothing about dealing with parachute troops. I told Larry Lawrence and Tommy Schields tonight that I think we ought to have a gun in the house. That would give us a fighting chance. Within the next few days the chances are the front line will be just on the other side of the Straits of Johore—perhaps even on this side.

There is no question that most everyone is frightened by these Japanese air raids. There is something very unnerving in seeing eighteen or twenty-seven Jap bombers flying in perfect formation over the city and calmly moving away, still in formation. That feeling of helplessness induces much of the fear.

London seems to be searching for criticism or optimism about the situation out here. The British are still trying to avoid a realization of how critical it is.

Wednesday, January 21st:
The Japs were over again today in considerable strength, bombing indiscriminately. They scored a direct hit on Wassiamul's, where I had my shirts made. Five bombs were dropped on the padang in front of the Cricket Club and blew out the windows of the Supreme Court. I'm getting fed up with bombings.

Thirteen Jap planes were reported brought down in the raid today, nine of them by ack-ack fire. I saw three of those planes destroyed over Singapore. One ack-ack shell scored a direct hit on a bomber. It immediately exploded and two planes beside it also disintegrated in the air. It was a beautiful sight. In an instant three Japanese planes disappeared into nothingness.

The situation is progressively worse. Today there is heavy fighting in Bakru-Bukit area in Northwest Johore. The Japs are dive-bombing and machine-gunning the British troops.

On the east coast at Endau, the British say their troops have been withdrawn "in the face of superior enemy forces."

In yesterday's raid there were ninety heavy bombers, escorted by fighters.

The communiqué today also says that extensive damage was done "to enemy aircraft, hangars, and airdrome buildings at Kuantan. Five sticks of bombs dropped across the hangars and caused large fires."

Hangars! The British were supposed to have destroyed all those hangars and airdrome buildings when Kuantan was evacuated. We were told that everything there had been destroyed.

The papers are filled with notices of people trying to find each other.

It is officially reported that the ack-ack aircraft in Malaya so far has brought down fifty Jap aircraft and sixteen more probables.

It is now called the "Battle for Johore." The residents, advisers and all other Europeans in the Malayan Civil Service stationed in the Federated Malaya States and the Unfederated Malaya States, with the exception of Johore, have now been withdrawn to Singapore.

The *Straits Times* is peeved about the presence here of all those residents, advisers, and members of the Malayan Civil Service. It points out that since the rulers of all the States have remained in their States, these Malayan Civil Service members are now useless in their former functions. Any action taken, the paper points out, requires the sanction or signature of the Sultan or Rajah.

In the present circumstances, the paper says, nothing that is being done by the Malayan Civil Service can receive the signature of the rulers, since they are in their States and the Malayan Civil Service are here in Singapore. The paper asks:

"What can be achieved by bodies of men set up in Singapore to represent the Government of the Federation of any State which is in enemy occupation?"

And now the war in Burma is in full swing. Siamese troops have pushed across the border of Burma and fighting is going on sixty miles inside.

An elephant in front of the old Supreme Court was erected in commemoration of the visit of the late King of Siam to Singapore. Today the *Straits Times* asks: "Why not use it for scrap to make ammunition?"

Three thousand Chinese, about two thousand of them members of the Overseas Chinese Volunteer Corps, met and passed a resolution to request the Government to supply them with means to fight the Japanese. After the meeting, they paraded through the streets carrying huge placards saying, "Give us guns and we will fight!"

They carried British, Chinese and American and Dutch flags and sang Chinese war songs.

The British policy of keeping aloof from the Asiatics and failure to arouse in them very much in the way of loyalty to Britain or respect for themselves is paying bitter dividends.

In most towns which have been bombed the native workers leave their jobs and move into the *kampongs*. This means that essential services collapse. It is almost as bad here in Singapore as it was in Penang. At Penang all the dock workers immediately went into the hills, and no native workers could be found for any services. The Colonial Government here in Singapore either is unable or doesn't know enough to win the support of the Asiatic workers right now.

The Chinese Mobilization Council which was started about two weeks after the war began is the only outfit able to get laborers together to perform essential services for the armed services. Every morning several hundred Chinese workers meet and are taken in trucks out to the places where the armed services need native workers.

The feeling among the workers is that they have to look out for themselves—that the British are incapable now of safeguarding their welfare. For that reason and because of a natural human fear of bombing, the workers leave their jobs and run into ditches and drains as soon as the siren goes. They don't wait for the signal from their watchers that the raiders are overhead. A number of the workers at the Naval Base don't show up in the mornings any more, and they are finding difficulty in getting enough workers at the docks because both of them are constant targets of the raiders.

The British officials now, at this late date, appear to think it is up to the Asiatic leaders to accept responsibility to see that every man is doing the job and staying on the job, and the papers are appealing to the Asiatics to express their appreciation for receiving high wages here and for the "other benefits of British Colonial rule." This is not only a people's war; it is a people's revolution.

The Penang radio, operated by the Japanese, broadcast today that what happened to Singapore yesterday was nothing to what was going to happen on Saturday and Sunday. They urged everyone to get out of Singapore, obviously to disrupt all war work. The story is all over town. It is causing considerable alarm among the Asiatics. It's a prime example of terror propaganda.

It is certainly obvious that, unless the workers can be induced to stay on their jobs, the entire defense of Singapore will collapse. It can't function without workers. Part of this shortage of workers is due to fear and another part is certainly due to the same red tape that has marked the Colonial Government here and also to the absence of co-operation between the Colonial Government and the military. In other words, between Sir Shenton Thomas and General Percival. They are quarreling over rates of pay that a worker should get, and both the civilian authorities and the military zealously guard their so-called rights. Rights don't count for very much at this moment and neither does money.

The Asiatics are not entirely to blame. There are many white workers—men who hold responsible jobs—available for work. They are doing something, but they are not doing the work that they know. A good many of them want to be supervisors, but what's needed now are men who can work with their hands. It would be asking too much for these English foremen and directors to take an ordinary job. This place is still operating on the basis of race, rank and seniority. Of course, the British want to win the war, but they approach urgent problems hesitatingly and put off critical decisions indefinitely and are great people for dissipating responsibility.

430

Received a cable from Martha saying:

WHITE CABLING YOU TO GO TO AUSTRALIA OR HOMEWARD.
HOPE IT'S HOMEWARD VIA INDIA, EGYPT.

If this is so, I haven't yet received White's cable, and I have been thinking it's time for me to pull out. I cannot broadcast, cannot cable stories, nor do any work. I haven't even a gun to fight back, and the way things look now it means just staying here and waiting to be taken prisoner or shot.

There was a very heavy raid on Singapore today. More than 300 people were killed and 550 injured. A hundred Jap planes did the job. This is just plain indiscriminate bombing. The Japs are simply trying to terrorize the people.

The British system is to leave virtually nothing to the commander on the spot. As near as I can make out, all orders come from London. Some of the cables from the War Office give instructions in infinite detail as though the commander didn't have the intelligence of a half-wit. War Office cables bear initials specifying who is to see it and each initial must be checked off, showing that it has been seen by that individual.

One cable on an unimportant technical matter contained twenty-three initials, beginning with General Pownall on down. A simple matter which could have been handled by a lieutenant had to be seen by twenty-three generals, colonels, majors, captains and lieutenants.

The British interception of the Japanese pilots talking to each other over their radio telephones is very good.

One Japanese pilot over Singapore called his base and shouted frantically: "The opposition is very strong—the opposition is very strong!"

"What is very strong," his base called, "the air opposition or the anti-aircraft?"

"My observer is dying," the pilot shouted.

Then there was a pause.

"He is dead. May I return now? The opposition is very strong," the pilot kept insisting, "my observer is dead—may I return now—may I return now?"

431

"Continue with your mission," he was told.

"I must return now—the opposition is too strong."

"Yes, return now," he finally was told.

There was another Japanese bomber in a flight of twenty-seven over Singapore. The aircraft fire was considerable and the British intercepted one pilot talking to his wing commander: "I think I should release my bombs now," he said.

"No, not yet," the commander told him.

The firing continued very heavily and he called his squadron leader again nervously: "I think I should release my bombs now."

He was told to await orders, but he kept pestering and finally was told: "All right, you can release your bombs and return to your base. But remember," the squadron leader said, "you have another mission this afternoon."

I must have some kind of strange fever. I had the doctor twice today. I am so weak I can't stand up and all my bones ache. The doctor gave me some pills as big as a dime and an eighth of an inch thick.

An advertisement appeared today that men unemployed as a result of the war, both Europeans and Asiatics, including mechanical engineers, building artisans, fitters and the like are required for rescue service. There are also urgent appeals for blood donors.

The stories I get from officers and civilians who have come down from Kuala Lumpur, Ipoh, Kota Bahru and Alor Star make my heart bleed.

We have no tanks and the armored cars are worse than useless. The armored cars cannot turn around on the narrow roads. When they come to a road block they are stopped. They try to turn, slide off the road and get bogged down. Japs dart out and knock them out. The armored cars can't back up more than four miles an hour. Before they can get away, the Japs are on them. A tank would have been so much more effective.

Communications have not been good, and because of the necessity of retreating so fast, many troops are being cut off from all contact for several days.

Everywhere there is a reluctance to learn new methods. A man must learn to adjust himself, and that's difficult when he is outnumbered and retreating all the time.

432

An American officer who was here last fall had been with the Japanese during maneuvers in China. The Jap commander asked him how he would attack if he were in command. The American officer said he would create a diversion at night on the left flank by raising a rumpus, dragging trees and hooting, then attack on the right flank.

The Japanese were much intrigued and wanted to know where he had learned such tactics.

"Why," the American officer said, "that's just plain Indian warfare."

The next day a Japanese delegation of officers called on him to find out where they could get some books on Indian warfare in America.

That's a bitter contrast to what I find here. An Englishman named Dobbs, who has built most of the roads in Northern Malaya and the concrete emplacements for guns at Penang, has been in Malaya for thirty-five years.

Dobbs told me: "I knew all those jungle trails in the north. I told our officers that any enemy who came down from Thailand would make use of them. I offered to show them the trails and map them, but they said, 'Now don't you worry about military matters, old boy. The Japs don't know those trails, so we don't have to know anything about them.' "

Those trails were used by the Japs to infiltrate down the Malaya Peninsula.

Thursday, January 22nd:
I have decided, without waiting for the expected cable from CBS, to pull out of Singapore. Agronsky also wants to go, and George Weller plans to leave in the next day or two. We all agree the whole thing is washed up and we want to get some place where we can tell what's going on.

There was a heavy raid this morning on Singapore. A couple more hundred people are dead. This is the beginning of the end. The Japs are approaching Johore.

I telephoned Major Fisher to tell him I intend to leave Singapore and asked if he'd facilitate my passage on British Airways going to Batavia. He said he would see.

This afternoon I called on him and he handed me a note, saying that I must see the immigration inspector at the Chinese Protectorate.

"What is this for?" I asked.

"They are not letting anyone between the ages of eighteen and forty-five leave Singapore."

"Does this apply to me as a correspondent?"

"Well, I don't know. You will have to see them about it."

"Can you arrange passage for me on the airlines?"

"Well, you see, you are not an accredited correspondent any more, and I can't do much for you officially."

"I understand that," I said, "but there's no point in my staying here."

"I agree, but I can't do anything for you. You go to the immigration inspector and see what he says and then let me know."

At the immigration office I thought there would be trouble about getting out, but they gave me a visa to Australia which showed that I was en route to the U.S.A. I then went back to Fisher. He showed great surprise that they had granted me the visa.

"Now what about transportation?" I asked Fisher.

"I can't do anything for you on that. Everything is jammed up, and I can't ask anyone for any favors for you."

"O.K." I said. "I will go to the British Airways myself."

At British Airways I got a seat for the very next morning. When I went there, I didn't intend to go so quickly, but they told me there was this one seat available and this might be the last plane out of Singapore. On the spur of the moment I decided to grab it.

In their raids on Singapore, the Japs are dropping a combination of high explosive and incendiary bomb. This bomb explodes on impact and the fragments are thrown eighty yards. Simultaneously a spray of ignited carbon disulphide is thrown about fifty yards and in addition rubber bungs or corks impregnated with carbon disulphide and phosphorous are thrown a distance of fifty yards, igniting as they fly through the area. The danger of the spray falling on clothes and near-by people is not immediate, but as soon as the clothes become dry and warm they are liable to break out in flames.

Reuters today sent this story from London:

"Answering question in the House of Commons concerning the ban on broadcasts from Singapore by Mr. Cecil Brown, American corre-

434

spondent of the Columbia Broadcasting System, the Minister of Information, Brendan Bracken, said:

" 'Military authorities decided to discontinue the status of accredited press correspondent granted to Mr. Brown, and his broadcasting facilities also were withdrawn. This action was taken after consultation with the War Council at Singapore who considered it essential in the general interest.

" 'An action which in normal times would be unnecessary and undesirable may be necessary in special instances. While there was no dislike of civil free criticism it was felt that in the abnormal conditions prevailing, Mr. Brown's comments passed the bonds of fair criticism and were a source of danger.' "

Singapore has suffered pretty heavily from the bombings. The Roman Catholic Church of Our Lady of Lourdes is badly damaged and the parochial house wrecked.

I just learned that, during one of the Jap landings at Kota Bahru, one British plane was so severely damaged by anti-aircraft fire that the pilot must have known that he was a goner. He deliberately flew directly into the middle of one of the Jap landing transports. All sixty Japs on the boat were either killed or drowned.

The P & O is charging 100 pounds for passage from Singapore to Australia. If you don't have 100 pounds you can't go.

It tears out your heart to see some of the men you knew in peace time coming back from the battlefront. Retreating, always retreating, outnumbered, out-trained and out-smarted. Grimness is roughly etched into their faces. The Argyll and Sutherland Highlanders sent up about 900 men and fifteen officers. Only 350 men and three officers got back.

Destruction is considerable around Singapore, and the air over the city is heavy with the dullness of defeat.

FLIGHT FROM SINGAPORE

Friday, January 23rd:

There are many things to do before I can get away. I was up at 6:30 and had arranged the night before to have a taxi come down to pick me up. I was at the police station at 8:30 in order to get permission to leave the country. It is getting very difficult because they evidently are studying my dossier. At nine the Britisher who is in charge of such affairs at the police station came in. He happened to be a man I'd had drinks with several times at the Raffles' bar, but I never did know his name.

"I have been here over a half hour," I said. "My plane is going in a few minutes. Something is holding up my permission."

He called the Malay officer and inquired about it.

"There is some investigation about Mr. Brown's circumstances which must be completed," he was told.

"Well, he has to go now," he said. "I will take a chance and give you permission." And he did.

I then went to the National City Bank to get authorization to take out money, a permit I found I didn't need, and was caught in an air raid there. We all went down into the basement. Al Noderer also was pulling out, and he was at the bank, too. I was there in the bank basement almost an hour while they were dropping bombs on Singapore. When I got out I went to the Union Building to get another paper permitting me to leave and had just started out of the building when the Jap raiders came again. So down again it was, this time in the basement of the Union Building! At 11:20 I got to the hotel and because of the two air raids the bus to the airdrome had not yet pulled out.

I tried a half dozen times to reach Ching Yeuk by telephone at her home, at the Chinese Protectorate and at the home of a woman friend of hers, but I was unsuccessful. There was no one in her shop in Raffles Hotel. I wrote a note to Ching and left it at the hotel desk for them to give her.

436

At Raffles I saw Graeme Nicholl and Major Gavin who were also leaving Singapore for Batavia.

"What do you think the chances of holding Singapore are, Major?" I asked.

"About thirty-three percent," he said.

"That's a bit high, don't you think?" I remarked.

"Yes, perhaps it is. It will be over in a month," Gavin said. "By the way, I heard what happened to you. They stopped your broadcasts. The thing they have done to you is as black as anything that's happened here."

As I got in the bus in front of Raffles Hotel two men, one an Englishman and one an American, neither of whom I'd ever seen before, came up to the window of the bus.

"You're Cecil Brown, aren't you?" asked the American.

And the Englishman looked at him and then looked at me.

"I was going to ask you that, too," the Englishman said.

"Well," the American said, "when you get out of here I wish you would give this place the works."

And the Englishman chimed in, "This whole thing is a disgrace and what they did to you is disgraceful. The people of England should know what has happened here."

"Take care of yourselves," I said, and the bus moved off to the Kalang airdrome.

As we started out Beach Road, the Chinese driver said: "Put your handkerchiefs over your noses, please."

A block of buildings a quarter of a mile from Raffles Hotel had been destroyed by bombs. Chinese had lived there in close quarters. Now the odor of death was piercingly strong.

At the airdrome most of the windows were shattered in the Administration Building and there were a number of bomb craters all around. A 500-pound bomb had hit there yesterday.

As I stepped into the Administration Building there was a customs inspector and a censor. The customs inspector merely glanced at my packs and said nothing. The censor had a list of the passengers for the British Airways flying boat. I noticed that on that list of names only mine bore a blue-penciled circle.

437

"Just show me what you have," the censor said. "It will make it easier for both of us."

I pulled out of my suitcase copies of my stories and broadcasts with a pile of telegrams.

"These are simply copies of my stories, and as you can see, they all have the censor's mark."

"You carry a black notebook," he said abruptly.

If that blue-penciled mark had not been around my name I would have known from his remark about the black notebook that he had special instructions to search me. From the moment I came to Singapore, on all stories and all interviews, wherever I went, I carried a black notebook in which I kept my loose-leaf diary.

"Yes, of course, I have a notebook," I said, and I pulled out my diary and showed it to him. "You see, there is nothing in it."

That was true because as I filled the pages with writing I removed them and kept them apart, bound by metal rings. It had now reached 880 pages and those pages were in the bottom of my suitcase. When he saw there was nothing in the black-bound notebook, he said: "That's all right. Do you have anything else?"

"No, just my notes on which these censored stories were based."

Then he leaned close to me. I wondered what now.

"I know all about you, Mr. Brown," the Englishman said softly. "I hope you publish the whole story about Singapore. Publish everything about this country. Go ahead, close up your suitcase now."

He winked at me and I winked back, and one of my greatest concerns about getting out of Singapore was over. I had gone to the airport fully convinced that the British would take this diary away from me.

We had to wait at the airport more than an hour for some unknown reason. Graeme, Al Noderer and I were a bit nervous about waiting for the Japs to come over and bomb the airdrome again.

On that seaplane, when we took off shortly after noon, there were twenty-nine passengers, eight more than the normal capacity. There was also heavy baggage. It was very difficult getting off, but we finally made it.

The windows were curtained over and the steward came through the plane and said: "When I take the curtains off, keep a sharp look-out.

If you see anything unusual, just give me a call or press that buzzer two or three times."

We all expected to be attacked by the Japanese on our flight to Batavia. I promptly fell asleep for about a half hour. I was much concerned about whether CBS would approve my decision in pulling out of Singapore. I had no instructions one way or the other from Paul White.

Sitting next to me was Major General Ching Kai Min, and with him was Colonel Irving Dooh, both of them members of the Chungking military mission to Malaya.

Al Noderer sat on the floor in front of me and other men were sitting on the floor as well. Across from me was a Chinese woman, pregnant, who was air sick. Her husband was fluttering around her, taking considerate, patient care of her. Across the aisle in front of them was Major Gavin and his bride-to-be. They were gay and not affected by this bumpy trip which had my stomach in a turmoil. They opened a bottle of champagne and asked me to share it with them. I had just enough strength to say "No."

The steward came through again and said: "We have a pretty heavy load, so don't move around any more than you have to. If you want to smoke, two of you go forward at a time. Don't go back in the tail."

I didn't move, and my kidneys could bust wide open before I would move. It made me nervous when anyone did move. I kept my tin hat on my lap purposely. I kept it there in order to knock out the window in case we crashed into the water, so that I might have a chance to swim out.

"There is plenty of room," the steward said to me; "you don't have to hold that hat. Put it behind you there."

I kept it on my lap.

The trip to Batavia was dull. Most of the time we flew over Sumatra, always quite low, 500 to 1,000 feet over both the jungles of Sumatra and over the water. It was extremely hot in the plane. There was always the fear that any moment you might be attacked, and there were no guns for protection.

Just before we came into Batavia I saw a convoy of seven ships heading north, apparently for Singapore.

We arrived at Batavia at six P.M.

My ticket called for Singapore to Batavia to Rangoon to Calcutta. I planned to go into town and telephone New York because there is a telephone connection between Batavia and America.

I located Bill Dunn, the CBS representative here, and with him and a young Dutchman and his wife we went to a small café and had beer and sandwiches. At 11:15 that night I got my call through to Paul White in New York. The circuit was perfect.

"Welcome to civilization," Paul said. "How are you?"

"I am okay. What do you want me to do now?"

"I think you'd better go down to Australia. Casey [Richard Casey, the Australian Minister in Washington] assured me he was doing everything to facilitate your getting there."

"How about coming home?" I said. "I have a ticket through to Calcutta."

"That's a dangerous hop up there."

"They are all dangerous. I can get a Clipper from Calcutta, I think."

"I don't know anything about that," Paul said, "but I don't think we have any Clippers going there yet. You go to Australia, to Sydney, and we will have some of our stuff coming across and you will be able to get back for the fall."

"But I have a book to do."

"The censorship is more lenient out there and you can do your book from Australia."

"I am pretty tired and I would like to get somewhere where I can rest."

"Well, yóu rest around there for a few days, but, by the way, I think we ought to have a broadcast from you to wrap up the place you just left, about six minutes will fix up a Sunday-morning show."

"That's all right. I will have to get permission to broadcast from here and I will see about that right away. What's new about my reinstatement?"

"Brendan Bracken is working on it with the Minister of War and we only get polite answers from them about how sorry they are that the action was taken. London is the only place anything can be done on it."

"Tell Martha I miss her tremendously."

"She was in the office a few days ago. She is fine," Paul said.

440

"Is she still as beautiful as ever?"

"More."

Saturday, January 24th:

Got up at four this morning in order to make a final check that my passport and camera would be taken off the plane which is going on to Calcutta. Two hours later I found out that it was not done; my passport and camera have gone on. This is the first time since I left America in 1937 that my passport has been out of my hands.

At 11:45 Dunn and I called on Dr. Reitmann, who is in charge of press affairs.

He was a shiny-faced Dutchman with white hair, a charming manner and sharp wit.

"So," he greeted me, "this is the famous Cecil Brown, that international scoundrel."

"Yes," I said, "I definitely am. I am in your country without a passport and I therefore cannot register with the police."

"I'd better get some soldiers together and have you put up against the wall," he chuckled. "I think we can arrange an execution in about a half hour."

"That's all right," I grinned. "It will give us just enough time to have a beer."

"Well, let's not worry about that now. I think we are going to allow you to stay without a passport. I have heard many nice things about you from John Young."

Since we'd reached the stage where you exchange pleasantries, I said that John Young had told me many nice things about him.

"Here is the thing, Dr. Reitmann. CBS has asked me to do a broadcast Sunday morning about Singapore. The second thing," I said, "I have been ordered to go to Sydney. What can you do to assist me in getting there?"

"All right, let's take them in order. First, the broadcast. I don't think that would be possible."

"Why not?"

"Well, the British are not going to take over our Ministry of Information, but we have agreed not to give facilities to anyone the British didn't permit to operate in Singapore."

The Dutchman hastened to add: "There is nothing personal in this,

441

Mr. Brown, but it is the principle established. As for helping you to get to Sydney, I will do everything possible, because if you cannot broadcast from here, obviously you must get to some place where you can."

He said he would make a further inquiry to determine if anything could be done to enable me to broadcast and he would let Dunn know.

Reitmann's next step was obviously to confer with Colonel Field, who had barred me in Singapore, and who was now attached to General Wavell's war staff here in Java. And Colonel Field said I could not broadcast.

The official information that I could not go on the air was given me late in the afternoon. I thereupon cabled Paul White:

REGRET DUTCH DENY ME FACILITIES DUE TO BRITISH DECISION.

I am staying at the Hotel Des Indes, one of the pleasantest places in the world. It has a tremendous verandah, a main building and then a series of small cottages connected by a covered passageway because of the heavy rains.

Evacuees are pouring in from Singapore and the Dutch islands. Selby Walker of *Reuters* came in, still wearing the heavy black beard he started to grow when war broke out. He has been on a boat nine days coming from Singapore, picking up evacuees at every little island on the way.

M. Charles Baron and his wife are here too. I just ran into them on the verandah and had a drink with them. He is head of the Free French in Singapore, and they came a few days ago.

"I came down to make propaganda from NIROM, the Dutch radio station," he said. "I will be going back soon, I think, to Singapore."

"That's a good place to be coming from right now instead of going to," I remarked.

Bill Dunn is a huge, fat correspondent sent out from New York, and is Far Eastern Manager for CBS. He is a perfect physical replica of Marshal Goering in body and face except that he is younger. As a matter of fact, my first remark to Bill was: "My God, you look just exactly like Goering." I didn't know that that's the one remark Bill resents most of all.

I'd last seen Goering in Alfredo's Restaurant in Rome, shoveling in

442

that wonderful *fetucchini*. Dunn, I discovered, could eat just as heartily. He seemed to be very well thought of by the Dutch and apparently had many good connections.

I sat on the verandah, talking with Bill Dunn and Sydney Albright, the representative for NBC. Albright was doing his first broadcasting work and also his first work as reporter and making a good job of it. He is a handsome, jovial, gay individual, tremendously enthusiastic about broadcasting.

Two facts amazed me about these two correspondents. One was that they talked endlessly about the transmission of their broadcasts, how well they were being heard in America. The technical figure for perfect reception is "5." Good reception rates a "4," fair reception rates "3" and poor reception rates "2." Dunn and Albright talked for more than an hour like two children, one saying: "I got a 4 this morning," and the other saying: "Well, I had a 4 yesterday, but two days ago I had a 5." It sounded like golf, not radio.

The other fact was that these two reporters showed not the slightest bit of interest in what was happening at Singapore. Not once did either Dunn or Albright ask me what the situation was there, did I think Singapore would hold out, what methods the Japs were using, or any of the normal questions that a reporter would want to know from another reporter.

Dunn did not once ask me why I had been barred at Singapore or inquire about any of the facts in connection with the British action.

Albright, however, did say: "Well, you fellows up there had it pretty easy. You didn't have any censorship."

The atmosphere here in Batavia is so much more invigorating than Singapore. Everywhere, like an electric circuit, you can feel a determination to fight to the last and that the Dutch East Indies will put up a battle that'll be different from Malaya.

From conversations with Dunn, Albright, Dr. Reitmann and some Australians and British who have been here for some time, I get the impression that the Dutch want and need United States help but they fear American expansion also. They fear occupation by us after the war.

Sunday, January 25th:
I telephoned Martha in New York this morning. What a wonderful,

443

wonderful thrill! I had not heard her voice since putting her on the train at Turin on March 6th of last year, when she started back to America by way of Southern France, Spain and Portugal. Martha urges me to come home at once, and she said my Mother and Dad are very insistent on seeing me. But I told her that I am going to Australia for a while, that I think I ought to do that. Martha says that if I go to Australia she wants to come there, too. I told her to stay right in America.

Uncle Billy Foote, the Consul General here, holds open house every Sunday morning. He and Mrs. Foote are two of the most popular people in Batavia, and it is easy to understand why after their Sunday-morning mint juleps. Bill Dunn took me over for this morning's session.

I discussed with Dunn my going home immediately instead of going to Australia. I explained that for reasons of health I thought I should get somewhere to rest, that I could never get any rest abroad. I outlined a cable to send to Paul White and this evening while discussing it with Dunn a cable came from White reading:

DUE DUTCH DECISION SUGGEST YOU REDOUBLE EFFORTS REACH SYDNEY STOP AUSTRALIAN MINISTER ATTEMPTING UPFIX.

That seemed to be the answer. Paul wants me in Australia and going home now is out.

THE FIGHTING DUTCH

Monday, January 26th:

There are reports here today that sixty-two ships came into Surabaya and also brought more American troops. No confirmation, however.

The plane which had my passport and camera came back today, and they were returned to me. It got reports of enemy action in Sumatra; so it turned back instead of going on to the Andaman Islands and then to India.

The American Air Force is training at Bali, the place with the high-breasted maidens. The Americans come up from Australia and stop off in Bali to adjust themselves and their machines to climatic conditions before going on to Surabaya or elsewhere. Some were expected one day in Surabaya. A Dutch Air Force colonel watched the board which charts the course of the incoming planes and these American aircraft were long overdue.

"Och," snorted the colonel after waiting for two hours, "these Americans, they cannot resist stopping off in Bali."

I telephoned Paul White in New York. Again I suggested that I return home, that I was physically exhausted and that I cannot rest over here where news is breaking.

"Why not go to Melbourne?" Paul said. "It is going to be the number one news spot in the Southwest Pacific. Melbourne and Batavia are the news spots now."

"Well, I'll go down. Do you think there will be any trouble in regard to my broadcasting from Australia?"

"None at all. I am sure of that. Is there any chance of the Dutch changing their minds about their decision?"

"No. They have decided that anyone who is not acceptable up north should not be acceptable here, but other persons are going to come into the picture in a few months and that reason won't hold good."

That other reason was American impatience with the British and Dutch here on publicity and propaganda.

445

The presence of American forces here cannot be mentioned as yet, but the British are trying to take control of the propaganda and correspondents. They are moving in from Singapore to take up where they left off.

At Des Indes Hotel I ran into Colonel Wills, the Australian whom I had last seen at Nazareth in Palestine where he used to explain the operations in the Syrian war to correspondents. He'd just arrived here. The Australians are setting up staff headquarters in Java.

Dunn and I lunched with Dr. Reitmann at the Harmony Club. It was given to the Dutch by Sir Stamford Raffles in 1821 with the provision that it should never close its doors, and it never has. It's a cool, clubbish place, painted in white, and the waiters are just as aloof as it is possible for a brown-skinned Javanese to be. At the luncheon Reitmann again was extremely friendly and expressed his desire and anxiety to permit me to broadcast "providing you get all right with the British."

I explained that the War Office in London must approve and war offices move very slowly.

He explained to us the method that the Dutch intended to use in handling correspondents who are now flowing in here from Malaya and coming up from Australia to cover the defense of Java. He said there would be no accrediting of correspondents and no wearing of uniforms.

"We are simple people," he said. "We don't like much fuss."

Dr. Reitmann said the Dutch are prepared to blow up Palembang, the great oil center of this entire area. It is over in Sumatra, not far from here, and that would deprive the Japs of the oil and it would also mean that the Dutch would have supplies here for only six months.

"What do you think the chances are of holding the Indies?" I asked.

"We expect to lose all the outer possessions and perhaps Java as well. That will be determined in about six weeks. We expect that Singapore will fall, and even if it doesn't it is not very important any longer."

This was the kind of realism you could never find among any of the British officers, with one or two exceptions. The only exception that came to my mind at the moment was Major Gavin, and he said that there was a one-third chance of holding Singapore. The British would never admit that anything would fall.

As we got up from the table Dr. Reitmann took me over to the club guest book for me to sign.

"I want to show you something," he said.

He turned back a page of the guest book and there were the signatures of General Brett, Admiral Hart and ten other officers of the American staff, brought to the Harmony Club as guests of Uncle Billy Foote. In the column on the page reserved for "how long staying," the American general, admiral and the ten other officers all wrote: "Until victory!"

I came away from the luncheon with Dr. Reitmann convinced that for the Dutch it is all or nothing. These islands are the only home they have. They have had them for three hundred years, and now this is their final stand. They will fight to the last man here. These people are not looking over their shoulders for a place to retreat to.

I find there is some resentment among the Dutch for not being included in the high command. It is certainly significant that not a single Dutchman holds any post in the high command that is now located in Java. The Dutch Admiral Helfrich should have been placed in charge of naval operations. He has known these waters for forty years. It may be that he was offered second in naval command but turned it down. On the day that Admiral Hart was appointed, he spent the whole day with Admiral Helfrich and has conferred with him a number of times since. The Dutch seem to be doing everything possible to co-operate with the Americans and British, but are not accepting any posts. Either Helfrich is in full charge of naval affairs or he takes no secondary title.

Numerous Dutchmen have told me that they think the United States is going to try to take over the Netherlands East Indies after the war. I told them such talk was ridiculous. There is also considerable comment because Admiral Hart came to Java in a submarine.

One Dutchman said to me, "He should have come in an airplane or on board a battleship with all his flags flying."

The news on the Macassar Straits fighting is the best that has come out of the war so far. Everyone is tremendously cheered. The hundred Jap ships coming down the straits have been severely mauled for the past three days. The fighting started on January 23rd, just the day after

447

the Dutch set fire to Balikpapan. American bombers and warships and Dutch aircraft and submarines hammered the Japs incessantly. The best estimate we have here is that about thirty enemy ships have been sunk.

Tuesday, January 27th:
Will attempt to get air passage either on the Quantas to Australia or on the Dutch lines. I was gratified this morning to get a very fine map of the Southwest Pacific at KPM, the Dutch shipping company. At the KPM office I encountered some Dutch efficiency, too. The whole organization was prepared for air raids. They had an automatic siren system, and as I sat in the office a special radio constantly gave reports from various air-raid warning stations.

The official at KPM said: "We Dutch and you Americans have to do the job out here ourselves. We cannot depend on the British. They need a good shot to wake them up."

"They don't seem to have learned any lessons from Egypt, Norway, France or Malaya."

"We're different," the Dutchman said. "We are as ready as we can be."

That's true. All over town there are shelters which were built a long time ago. Everywhere there are troops and soldiers on guard, a thing that Singapore didn't have even on the day I left, when bombs were actually dropping. And Java has not yet been attacked.

I feel very much out of touch with the news here. There's a pleasant atmosphere—but also a terrific feeling of tremendous things going on and we not knowing much about them.

Harold Gatty, who flew around the world with Wiley Post, and Bill Dunn made me a member of the "Short Snorters" club today. It is a simple process. You obtain membership, if you've flown across an ocean, by simply exchanging signatures on the back of an American dollar bill, and paying one dollar to each man at the table who is already a member. Most of the Pan-American pilots and many newspapermen in the Far East are members. I pulled out three one-dollar bills which had been in my wallet on the *Repulse.* They were stained with oil, and I passed one to Dunn, another to Gatty and the third one they signed and I kept. If called upon at any time, you must produce your "Short

448

Snorters" dollar-bill within one minute. If you fail, you pay a dollar to every "Short Snorter" present at the table.

A few minutes later Sid Albright came to the table; the three of us made him a member of the "Short Snorters." He thereupon had to pay each of us one dollar.

Wednesday, January 28th:
At lunch today we had *rijstaffel*. It is an amazing performance here. About eighteen Javanese boys come to your table in a long line, each carrying a dish. You help yourself from each dish until your plate is a huge mound of rice, chicken, fish, spices, condiments, vegetables and what not. You are supposed to sleep then for the rest of the afternoon.

A cable came from White forwarded from Singapore telling me to go to Batavia and Australia and await developments. I am glad I didn't wait in Singapore for that cable to arrive because just one more plane came out after I left and it was jammed and I probably couldn't have gotten passage on it.

I find it very difficult to believe Churchill's statement in his speech yesterday that the British had only 45,000 men in the Western Desert against Rommel.

The American officers at Bandoeng are getting quite peeved about the handling of publicity. They want American correspondents to report the American war effort back in the United States. The difficulty right now is that the presence of American forces here cannot be mentioned.

Part of the American anger is because the British are getting the credit for American operations, for example: the heavy raid on Sungei Patani about ten days ago was announced as an R.A.F. raid and yet it was carried out by Americans in Flying Fortresses. Then there was a raid by the Dutch in Macassar Straits; it, too, was carried out by Americans.

Thursday, January 29:
In the pouring rain this afternoon, Al Noderer and I took off in the Dutch plane for Bandoeng. The Dutch used the D.C.5's and in forty

449

minutes we were in Bandoeng. It was a very rough trip and I was as sick as a dog. Bandoeng is up in the mountains surrounded by clouds which were so thick that several times we made sharp turns to get back on the course. The pilot seemed to have some difficulty in flying. When we arrived there, Noderer said: "I waited until we got here to tell you that some American pilots were scheduled to try out this run today but the weather was so bad they took the train."

It was pouring buckets when we came into Bandoeng, but the Dutchmen will fly in any kind of weather. They take incredible chances and they are extremely daring and able pilots.

I just saw an American sailor on the street, the first American sailor I've seen since I left America. A big hulking guy he was, rambling slowly and alone, like a lost sheep. He certainly looked good.

The atmosphere here in Bandoeng is one of "piques and prejudices." The Dutch aren't getting on with the British. The British aren't getting on with the Americans, and the Americans aren't getting on with either the Dutch or the British.

The Dutch sent four submarines off North Malaya as soon as war broke out and most of them have been lost. They also sent a number of Brewster Buffalo fighters to Singapore.

Now the Dutch would like some real help from the British and Americans. Since most of the help is still in the talking stage, the atmosphere isn't conducive to cordiality.

This evening I had a drink at the hotel with a man who is in intimate contact with both the British and the Americans. He is an internationally known aviation expert.

"America," he said, "is duplicating the mistakes of the British. It is mostly due to inexperience. For example, we are pulling incredible blunders by sending all of one thing on one ship and all of another on a second ship—and having one of them sunk, such as guns on one ship and ammunition on another. And if one or the other is sunk it might just as well be both of them sunk.

"Our air strategy and organization was built entirely on the idea of fighting within the United States. Here's an example of how it has worked out. Dutch gasoline cannot be used in our self-sealing tanks. It dissolves the metal of the tanks and the aircraft. This means that we cannot use the two-years' supply of Dutch gasoline in Australia or the

450

six-months' supply in Java. We can only use Persian Gulf gas or American gas. That imposes heavy tankage problems."

My informant had more to say, too.

"Thirty Flying Fortresses out here could change this whole picture," he declared. "What a narrow margin that is, and it will be decided in another four weeks! Yes, the fight of Java will be decided in the next four weeks. Anything not already on the way here will arrive too late, even if airplanes are shipped or are aboard ship now, they would have to be assembled when they arrive, and that would take three weeks. The chances are that this entire area and perhaps Australia as well will go to the Japs. Only a miracle can prevent it, and I don't see any miracles in sight. The only other possibility is the Japs making a big mistake. The Japs sending their convoys down the Macassar Straits without air protection was a mistake."

"Do you think they did that because they were so cocky?" I asked.

He thought that was the case. He explained the key to air contact with Australia is Timor.

"Therefore," he said, "Timor is the whole key to sending fighters here. If the Japs get Timor, then Java is cut off from air connection, and stuff can only come in by sea."

According to the papers here, the Japs are still advancing in Malaya; they are now south of Kluang. That is less than fifty miles from Singapore. There are no indications that the Japs are being checked despite their losses. They must be using virtually every aircraft they have on a tremendous gamble of a knock-out blow to carry them into Australia within three months.

I've just heard one of the most daring and courageous stories of the war. It's a story of Balikpapan. That's the great Dutch oil center in Southern Dutch Borneo in the Javanese Sea.

The story begins with Terakan in Northern Dutch Borneo. When the Japs landed there, they found most everything destroyed and huge oil installations wrecked. At the time, the wife of the nephew of Van Kleffin, the Dutch Foreign Minister, was there with a group of thirty nurses.

When the Japs landed at Terakan, there were Japs among them who had formerly lived there and worked in the oil fields. They knew most everyone and spotted her and took her as a hostage. The Dutch nurses were raped by the Japs. One of the nurses who eventually escaped had been attacked fifteen times. Then the Japs took some Dutch civilians aboard their ships which moved down the Straits of Macassar.

Nearing Balikpapan they sent a prominent resident of Terakan on ahead in a boat. He was told to tell the Governor that if anything there was destroyed, the wife of the nephew of the Dutch Foreign Minister would be killed and so would all the Dutch civilians.

The envoy had a message of his own. He told the Governor the size of the Jap convoy and what type of units were in it. The Governor of Balikpapan flashed word to Batavia with the details and asked for further instructions. Batavia said: "You have your orders." The Governor said: "I will have to ring off now, the flames are getting too close."

What he meant was that a hundred million dollars' worth of equipment at Balikpapan was at that moment going up in flames. He'd carried out his orders.

Friday, January 30th:
I talked with a couple of Fortress pilots today. One was from Mississippi and he spoke with the thickest Southern accent. It was wonderful to hear that accent again and I told him so. I asked him what the English thought of his accent.

"Ah don't know, Ah only spoke with them not moah than five minutes. Ah leaves other people strictly alone. Ah mind mah own business."

The other pilot said that in the air force for the past year they have been taught Spanish.

"I'd like to look my teacher in the face now," he snorted, staring out into a street filled with people who spoke Javanese and Dutch, and not a word of Spanish.

At the Allied headquarters at Lembang, ten miles from Bandoeng, General Sir Archibald Wavell turned to a high American officer and said: "I don't know what's the matter with us any more. We don't fight. We must be getting soft or decadent or something. We seem to have the attitude of always looking over our shoulders."

The British General Staff of high officers, the men from colonel on up, with some exceptions, appear always to be thinking of where to retreat to next. They have a defensive complex, an invasion complex. They have had so many retreats that they think in terms of retreats. It was that way in Cairo when Russia and Germany went to war. The instinctive thought of the General Staff in Cairo was "This gives us a breathing spell."

I talked with no high officer at Cairo who felt "This gives us the chance to attack the Germans in the Western Desert."

In Cairo they thought of where to retreat to when they lost Egypt and here in Java they think of where they can retreat to when Java goes. You get the impression that all over the Empire the British are prepared to retreat back to England. And you also have an equally strong impression that the British will never retreat from their island.

This evening on the verandah of Hotel Des Indes back in Batavia I met a group of Americans who have just flown a bomber in from America. They are part of the Ferry Command. There is F. L. Brown, the skipper; J. E. Haynes, co-pilot, and another skipper by the name of Frank Cordova. What they've been telling me is one of the greatest shocks of my life, because I asked them about America.

"There is an absence of reality about the size of the job," they said. "The general attitude is that we can take these Japs any time. When we left the States, we, too, had that attitude. The general feeling is: there is nothing to it. But now we see that it takes equipment. Americans know where Singapore is, but they don't understand much of the strategic possibilities out here. They think the British can hold it."

Charles Cunningham, the radio operator, was pretty bitter about the R.A.F. communications. "For example," he said, "two hundred miles out of Natal, we picked up Bathhurst and were confident that we could ride all the way across and not have to worry about celestial navigation or an overcast sky, just ride in on their signal. Suddenly it went out.

"We finally got in all right," he said, "and we found out what happened. The R.A.F. there said they were sleepy and had knocked off. That's why the signal disappeared.

"Hells bells!" he said, "we're flying this ship all the way across the Atlantic, over Africa, to bring them an aircraft and they knock off."

They told me the current joke in the United States is that we are

453

going to build glass bottom boats so that American admirals can watch the fleet pass in review. What a grim joke!

Cordova was amazed at what he has seen. He's an old hand at seeing things. A long-time pilot and one-time auto racer, Cordova has made five trips in the Atlantic Ferry Service.

"I'm in the painful process," he said, "of readjusting my whole point of view. Everyone in America thinks the Japs aren't much. They think all we have to do is bomb Tokyo and the whole war is over. The American people have no conception of the size of the job ahead."

Cordova is about thirty-eight or forty, short, handsome, rather swarthy-faced, with slick black hair heavily streaked with gray.

"As for Singapore," Cordova said, "we all thought the British had swarms of aircraft and there wouldn't be much trouble holding it. The Jap success so far, we thought, was due to surprise. Once that surprise was over, we would knock hell out of them. We had no idea how hopelessly outclassed we are by Japanese numerical superiority and equipment. The whole trouble out here is lack of equipment. I also think our pilots are too inexperienced and not trained well enough."

"A few months of actual experience," Haynes said, "will make all the difference in the world."

Cordova also had an unpleasant experience with the British way of doing things. He brought over a PBY, a Catalina.

"I tried to find the British officer to turn the plane over to. I finally found someone. 'That's not my pigeon, old chap,' he said. 'You'll have to wait until tomorrow when the man in charge comes back.'

"I said, 'The hell with that,' and just left the ship there."

All these pilots are flying back in a special bomber to ferry over more ships. They suggest that in order to get to Australia, I go down to Surabaya and try to get on a United States Army or Navy plane from there for Darwin.

(Frank Cordova several months later was shot down over Dakar by Vichy French anti-aircraft.)

Ron Matthews, the *London Daily Herald* correspondent, came in. He's very doubtful that even Rangoon can be held. While having a drink with John E. Morris, of the *United Press* and Mrs. Watkins, wife of a British wing commander in the R.A.F. who was killed in an air accident last October, Mrs. Watkins said: "If Singapore goes, this

454

whole Dutch Indies goes at the same moment, but I'm English and I am sure Singapore can be held."

Later this evening I ran into that same British spirit. Graeme Nicholl came by while I was still with the American fliers, and Graeme told me: "Singapore will hold, all right."

"I'll bet you any amount of money it doesn't, that it will be over in two weeks or less."

"Oh, no!" Graeme said. "We'll still be there by April first."

"All right, Graeme, I'll bet you five bucks."

It was agreed.

"I'll be the happiest man in the world to pay you that five bucks on April first," I said, "and I'll buy you a drink besides, but it won't work out that way. That show is over."

Saturday, January 31st:
Evacuees are pouring in from Singapore. British officers, officials, civilians, war correspondents. They are moving in here en masse. Very cheerful and chipper, you'd think they had just come from a golf game. As a matter of fact, one British naval officer came down the gangplank carrying his golf clubs. It is still a game for them.

Tillman Durdin, *New York Times* correspondent, came aboard a destroyer. He tells me the British forces are now on Singapore Island. I questioned him avidly for news.

"The natives seem to be taking it all right," Durdin said. "But it's a pretty grim atmosphere—above all, among the British. Everyone is despondent. They are talking about concentration camps. No, there's not much feeling that Singapore will be held. The natives won't work at the Naval Base or air fields. This is causing considerable difficulty, with the Jap bombers over day and night."

Four days ago Dr. Reitmann informed Bill Dunn that the British refuse to permit me to broadcast from here and therefore the Dutch abide by their decision. Dunn must think that I am Typhoid Mary, because I have seen practically nothing of him since then.

Late today a Singapore communiqué was received here. It said:
"In accordance with a prearranged plan, our forces which have been operating in Southern Johore were withdrawn to the island of Singa-

455

pore. The enemy made little effort to interfere with the operations. The Johore causeway was successfully breached. The Royal Navy and the R.A.F. co-operated."

So, this is the beginning of the end of Singapore.

General Percival has just issued this statement:

"The battle of Malaya has come to an end and the battle of Singapore is started. For more than two months our troops have fought the enemy on the mainland. The enemy has had the advantage of great air superiority and considerable freedom of movement by sea.

"Our task has been both to impose losses on the enemy and to gain time to enable forces of the Allies to be concentrated for this struggle in the Far East.

"Today we stand beleaguered in our island fortress until help can come, as assuredly it will come. This we are determined to do. In carrying out this task we want the active help of every man and woman in the fortress.

"There is work for all to do. Any enemy who sets foot in the fortress must be dealt with immediately. The enemy within our gates must be ruthlessly weeded out. There must be no more loose talk and rumor-mongering. Our duty is clear. With firm resolve and fixed determination we shall win through."

It's a bit late in the day for Percival to call on "every man and woman" of the 700,000 natives. Their will to fight is gone.

Batavia is a changing scene. People are coming all the time and going when possible and however possible. Quantas Air Lines to Australia ceased to run; British Airways northward to Burma and India was suspended. There is no beginning and end to this Java scene. Maybe that's a peculiarity of islands. Things whirl around like stirring over-thickening fudge in a saucepan. Things are whirling tighter and tighter and the Japs getting closer and closer and people becoming more and more alarmed. Many people you saw in Singapore you now see here, but it isn't their faces which make you happy. It is the faces which aren't there that make you sad. No one I have talked to knows anything about Ching Yeuk.

This scene reminds me of Yugoslavia—people dragging what they can, hurrying to get away from the enemy, trying to find some place to go, trying to escape the war.

456

As the American ferry pilots and I were having a drink, Graeme Nicholl came over to the table at the verandah on the Hotel Des Indes to talk about the defense of Singapore Island. He was in a hurry and just had a moment, but he said: "General Percival has a chance to make a great name for himself."

"Yes, he has," I said dubiously.

Graeme then moved off and one of the pilots remarked: "That's typical. That Englishman is just thinking of the chance for some general to get a Victoria Cross."

"That's true," I said, "but I can assure you that those Britishers who are remaining on Singapore Island will fight with the greatest courage in the world."

We fell to discussing the differences between the Russian and German sacrifices, as compared to the British and American attitude.

"The British consider every man important, if not to the Army, at least to himself," I said.

"The American people have got to realize," Cordova added, "that a good many men have to die. They have to get over the idea that this whole thing can be cleaned up without much trouble."

The American pilots condemned Colonel Lindbergh, Father Coughlin, Senator Wheeler, the America First organization, and the whole Isolationist bund for inducing in the people not only apathy toward the war but a complacency in superiority. It is shocking and amazing to me to hear of the complacency in America, the lack of realization what this is all about.

Sunday, February 1st:

Although I am now in Java, my eyes and heart are still in Singapore. So many of my friends are still there and so many will never get out. Maley of the Australian *Associated Press* came in today. Agronsky and Fairholl got away on a destroyer, but it came twenty miles from Java, then was diverted and I understand has gone to India. Maley told me that he thought it was a waste to pour any men or materials into Singapore.

"Maybe the high command," I said, "will have to decide whether the price is worth paying to delay the Japs at Singapore before they can strike at Java."

457

Maley shrugged his shoulders, but his attitude was that the British there were no longer expecting any more help.

"What preparations are being made to deal with parachutists?"

"I don't think they've even given a thought yet to parachute attacks," Maley snorted.

"How long do you think they are going to hold out?" I asked.

"Not very long. It is going to out-Dunkirk Dunkirk. They don't have any ships for any kind of an evacuation."

All kinds of liaison officers from Singapore and what are known as "Intelligence" officers are debarking here. The British press officials and censors, too, are coming in with absurd optimism and calm assumption that they are to take over the whole show in Java. The Dutch want reinforcements of fighting men, not this locust horde of incompetent misfits who already have messed up one job.

I telephoned American Headquarters at Bandoeng and then telephoned the U.S. Naval Headquarters at Surabaya. They told me to come down to Surabaya and would do their best about getting me to Australia. I am astounded at such ready co-operation. It is wonderful to be with Americans again.

AMERICAN
WAR CORRESPONDENT

Tuesday, February 3rd:

Surabaya was bright and gay in a burning morning sun when I arrived. At the Oranje Hotel there were no rooms. The place was filled with American Army and Navy officers. It seemed like home even though the streets were filled with people wearing sarongs, with small compact Javanese girls carrying baskets on their heads and with hundreds of Javanese and Dutch riding bicycles.

I immediately telephoned American Naval Headquarters to talk with Vice Admiral Glassford. He wasn't in, and I explained to Commander Slocum that I wanted to get to Australia, and I understood the admiral could assist me in that.

"We can handle that all right for you," Commander Slocum said. "I will call Air Headquarters right away and let you know."

Such promptitude and efficiency almost bowled me over. I had not encountered it in a good many years abroad.

A few minutes later Headquarters called and said that some naval officers were coming in to the hotel around noon, and I arranged to have lunch with four of them. That done, I wanted to buy a souvenir of Surabaya. I knew that it would be many years before I would return to Java and that the Java I was seeing would never be the same. I knew, too, that the Java I might return to would be a country that would be cleaning up after occupation by the Japanese.

I went out to buy a memento and came away with a memory. In the shop a young chocolate-skinned Javanese girl in a sarong and bare feet showed me souvenirs. I decided on a sarong, the kind the Javanese wear on dress-up day. I paid her for it; she wrapped it up. As I stepped out into the street the sirens went off. I was near a field where a shelter was being built. A half dozen other people stepped off the

459

street into the field and we stood in the bright sun waiting for something to happen.

I stood beside an elongated pile of dirt about three feet high. It was meager protection, but the only available. For forty-five minutes I stood there scanning the sky, expecting the attack to come out of the sun. Then the Japanese bombers came. It was the first Japanese raid of the war in Surabaya. It came just exactly two hours after I arrived. Twenty-seven gray bombers spread in a "V" formation against the blue cloudless sky. They seemed to be three or four miles away.

I flopped beside the pile of dirt and put the package containing the sarong underneath me so I wouldn't dirty my gray suit. I lay on my back and watched the enemy bombers coming. Their run would be over me, sixteen-thousand feet high, and directly over the spot where I waited. I had a sudden determination to get up and run out of the line of their approach. But there was no place to run to. Before I could find a trench or shelter I knew that the shrapnel fragments would get me.

I took out my handkerchief and stuffed it into my mouth to prevent biting my tongue or breaking my jaws when the concussion came. Lying on my back, I saw tiny dots suddenly appear below the "V" formation. They were not black dots or ack-ack exploding in the sky; they were bombs. It was an incredible sight—the bombs glinting like raindrops in the bright sun. I watched them getting larger and larger, following their trajectory. They were fascinating to watch.

Sixty bombs, I estimated, as I watched them from my horizontal position.

"I'm pretty sure those forty on the right end will miss me," I decided. "Those twenty near the center and toward the left are going to get me."

There is a hypnotic, muscle-paralyzing fascination watching bombs come down. It must have been what I took to be the sight of the fins on the bombs that disrupted the hypnotism. I whirled my face, buried my head in my arms and prayed as I have never prayed before. I was frightened to death. This, I thought, is the end, and I waited for it— ten, fifteen, twenty, thirty seconds. Then the bombs struck. The thudding of the earth at first was a bit distant. The second bomb was near, another even nearer, in rapid succession coming toward me. Each tremble of the earth was heavier and sharper. I shuddered.

460

"The next one, the next one, the next one is mine."

My stomach was tied in knots.

"What a rotten way to die!" I said to myself. "What a rotten, shameful way! And just when I was on my way home. I won't get to see Martha again."

The ground heaved, rocked, exploded, while I tried to burrow into the ground. It was like being in an earthquake. And between the bombs and a part of the roar of the bombs was the crash of masonry and windows. Then the anti-aircraft fire went, and there were no more bombs.

I twisted my head around and saw the bombers slightly ahead, and I knew then no more bombs would come near me. I still lay there though, because a whine of anti-aircraft shrapnel was still all about. Off in the distance more bombs were dropping and I knew the Japs were at the Surabaya Naval Base.

I stood up and lit a cigarette. A Dutch naval officer and his girl had been lying in the ditch about twenty feet away and they, too, stood up and began brushing off their clothes. The girl was nervous and the officer was searching for a cigarette. I offered them mine and they both said, in English, "Thank you."

"That was pretty close, wasn't it?" I said.

I went off to buy some picture post cards of Surabaya. It seemed to be the only thing to do.

Life in Surabaya went back to normal. I tried to buy a stop watch to replace the one I lost when the *Repulse* went down, but couldn't find one.

I lunched with Commander J. V. Peterson, of Coronado, California, Commander W. A. Deems, of San Diego, and Commander E. T. Neale, of Baltimore, Maryland, at the Oranje Hotel.

My passage was all set, on a PBY for Darwin. Commander Peterson suggested I come to Naval Headquarters late that afternoon to meet Rear Admiral W. R. Purnell.

When Commanders Peterson and Deems took me in to the admiral, he said: "I'm mighty glad to see you. You are the first American reporter who has come here. I don't know why we are being ignored."

"You're not being ignored any more. I'm just passing through actually, but I could certainly use a few stories about Americans. For

461

a year I've been writing and broadcasting about British heroism. Now I really feel like an American reporter."

"We have stories for you," Purnell exulted. "Our boys have done a job that the whole world should know about."

In manner, kindness, resoluteness and age Admiral Purnell reminded me of an old friend, Rear Admiral Thomas Kinkaid, who was the American Naval Attaché at Rome when I was there.

"Of course I know Tom Kinkaid very well. We were classmates at the Academy. He is a very dear associate of mine."

That recollection established me in Purnell's eyes as not only the first American reporter at Surabaya, but also as a friend.

The admiral turned to Commander Peterson and said: "Take Mr. Brown in to Captain Wilkes and let him see that submarine commander's diary."

I've seen many operational reports, but few of them could be publicized and the British never permitted it.

"Could I use it, Admiral?"

"Of course you can."

"And the names?"

"I see no objection to that."

Captain John Wilkes, Commander of the United States Submarine Forces in Asiatic waters, was a brown, stocky, square-jawed officer, amiable, bright-eyed and delighted to have the story of one of his men told.

He reached into his steel file case marked "Secret and Confidential" and drew out a sheaf of papers.

"This," he said, "is 'Moon' Chapple's diary," as he handed it to us. "It is one of the greatest operations of the war thus far."

"Moon" Chapple is Lieutenant (J. G.) Wreford G. Chapple. He is called "Moon" because his mates think his round cherubic face bears a resemblance to Moon Mullins, the comic-strip funny man.

In that diary was Chapple's story—the story of incredible heroism. After skimming through three or four pages, I said: "Give me a typewriter, some paper and let's get hold of Chapple!"

At Naval Headquarters I copied Chapple's diary. Captain Wilkes sat down with me, and from his explanation I drew a rough map of Lingayen Gulf, where Chapple's submarine had operated, the positions of the Japanese destroyers and transports inside the Gulf and

462

how the American submarine got there to attack them. As we sat working on the map a yeoman came up, saluted, and said: "Captain Wilkes, I am unable to find Lieutenant Chapple."

"Keep trying," Captain Wilkes said. "I know that he has a few days' leave, but he must be around town somewhere. Mr. Brown must see him."

When I finished copying the diary, I asked Captain Wilkes to have dinner with me, but he said he had to work all night.

"We have to work all the time to keep our heads above water," he explained. "You see the Japanese are very good. They haven't missed a trick. Every step has been brilliantly executed."

I dined that evening with Commanders Peterson, Neale and Deems. The attack that morning on Surabaya and the Naval Base was more extensive than I'd thought. There were seventy to eighty Jap bombers protected by fighters. The P-40s which went up got one bomber and one fighter, and a PBY went up, too, and shot down a Jap fighter. The Dutch say they shot down eight fighters and two bombers, but I didn't see any come down. We suffered heavily. Four Flying Fortresses were destroyed on the ground. We had sixteen here. They came down and machine-gunned the airdrome. They also swooped low over the Naval Base and got four flying boats in the water. They skimmed twenty-five feet over the Bay and over the airdrome buildings, and the Americans were firing at the Japs with their revolvers. In Surabaya itself, thirty-one people were killed and a hundred and nine injured.

The puzzle was where the Jap fighters were coming from. They appeared to be shore-based, and Balikpapan is four hundred miles away. But they might have come from an island south of there.

Commander Peterson asked me if I knew what the odds here are.

"I've a pretty good idea, but I'd like to hear your figure."

"We're outnumbered here from fifty to a hundred to one," he said. "When you get back to America—if you get back—for God's sake tell them to send us some equipment, so that we can match the Japs. Tell them to send us good aircraft and plenty of it.

"The Jap Zero fighter is as good if not better than any Spitfire or Hurricane, and the Japs are good. Make no mistake about that,"

463

Peterson added. "They are very good. My God, they certainly are no push-overs. Yes, our Vought and Airacobras are better than the Zero fighters, but what good does that do? We don't have a Vought or an Airacobra out here."

All three commanders agreed that if aircraft are not on the way out here now it will be too late for them to do any good.

I felt I was breaking up inside. Men like these with all the courage in the world, going up to die with about one chance out of fifty of surviving.

(Commander John V. Peterson, Omaha, Nebraska, Commander of Patrol Wing 10, awarded Distinguished Flying Cross.)

These commanders told me the American Navy isn't worried too much about red tape.

"We go out and get things done without worrying about requisitions. We get what we need where we can find it. And," Commander Peterson said, "we'll worry about the paper work in three or four months from now when they start asking about these things. What counts now is getting aircraft up in the air or getting them here. The paper work can wait."

The trouble, they said, is in Washington. Admiral Hart has been yelling for stuff.

"He's doing a marvelous job of hit and run," Commander Peterson said. "I never thought the American nation would have to resort to hit-and-run tactics. I thought when our time came we would just push everything out of the picture."

They told me about one colonel in the Philippines who was convinced that he'd either be killed or captured and, fed up to the gills with red tape, sent a cable to his Washington superior. It said:

GET OFF YOUR FAT BOTTOM AND SEND THOSE BREECHES FOR THE GUNS.

We searched for Chapple until nearly three in the morning. I then grabbed an hour's sleep at the hotel and was called at four by Commander Neale. In the darkness of early morning at the Surabaya Naval Base we found the tall, husky, round-faced submarine skipper whose diary I had. We went into a cubby-hole of an office.

464

"I understand you've been looking for me," he said boyishly and a little sheepishly.

"I certainly have," I said. "I have your diary. It's a wonderful story and I need more details, color, atmosphere and dialogue. What kind of conversation was going on at these various periods during the action? But we have no time now. I'll type out a hundred questions. Will you answer them and mail them to me in Sydney as fast as you can? Give me three thousand words in excruciating detail."

Chapple laughed: "That's the toughest assignment ever given to me, but I'll try."

I opened my portable typewriter on the narrow table half covered with operational maps. Hunched over the maps were the pilot, the co-pilot and the navigator of the PBY I was to take. The only light in the room came from a shaded bulb suspended from the ceiling directly over the table. Working as fast as I could, with the pilot saying every little while "We have to go," I typed out just about a hundred questions for Chapple to answer.

"I'm counting on you, Chapple," I said. "You've done a wonderful job and the American people deserve to know about it. Come through for me, will you?"

Chapple came through eventually, and I had the complete story of a great exploit.

It was a hazardous undersea mission, but the orders were explicit. They said to proceed to Lingayen Gulf on the west coast of Luzon and to pursue and attack a large enemy naval force and concentration of transports.

Other submarines were ordered to the same waters on the same mission. Only two succeeded in entering the gulf. One of them was Chapple's.

You'd never think, though, from reading "Moon" Chapple's diary, that he did anything extraordinary. What was probably the most dangerous part of his mission he set down in about twenty paltry and ineloquent words. This was when he took his submarine into the gulf over the reefs that spread eastward for about ten miles across the entrance. He never had more than thirty feet of water in which to navigate and usually it was so shallow that razor-sharp rocks were everywhere to knife the pigboat's belly.

465

This is how Moon described it: "One morning in the latter part of December at 1:44 A.M. we were proceeding over the northern part of the reefs."

This is a new record for understatement. That gulf is about twenty-five miles wide at the mouth. At least ten miles of the width are protected by reefs. The remaining fifteen miles were very definitely protected by about ten Jap destroyers. Moon had to elude destroyers, in addition to the reefs.

In the shallow waters of the reefs, Chapple had no depth into which to dive if he had been spotted. The Japs knew this. Chapple knew it too. That's why he chose to enter that way.

Once inside it was no picnic. By 5:17 the submarine was clear of the reefs and Chapple took his pigboat down. At 6:15 he came up to periscope depth and sighted so many transports that they looked like cars in a parking lot. Two destroyers circled about the transports. He saw some motor launches hovering near by. These undoubtedly carried tons of "ash cans"—depth charges.

For an hour Chapple kept his eyes pressed against the rubber-lined eyepieces of the periscope. The periscope is the skipper's job, his symbol of command. The enemy drew closer. The men, quiet and eager, glistening with sweat, stood at battle stations. One said: "Betcha buck we get one." The submarine crept closer on slow motors. Chapple prayed to himself the Jap detectors wouldn't pick up his vibrations. At last he was within range.

"At 7:10 A.M.," Moon's log says, "fired four torpedoes at four vessels. All misses."

The Jap ships were oldsters with very shallow draft and it was not surprising that Chapple miscalculated. He ordered the torpedoes set higher. He wrote: "We reloaded and dived to avoid a destroyer which dropped three depth charges fairly close. I headed eastward to lose the destroyers which were on our trail."

When an ash can explodes near enough, there is a sound within the enclosed confines of a submarine like the ring of a sledge hammer against a boiler—and you inside the boiler. And any clang might mean a buckled or sprung plate, a leak, a flooded battery compartment and then a slow death. Chapple snaked about well below the surface for about forty-five minutes, keeping within striking range, and then

466

he rose again to periscope depth. He had a quick look—and there was a sitting duck.

"At 7:58 A.M. we fired one torpedo. She was anchored and ready for the discharge of troops. She was very close and loaded with troops. The first torpedo was ahead of the ship. I fired the second smack at her. Thirty seconds later we heard the explosion.

"We dived immediately. Three depth charges came closer to us than the last ones we heard. At least two enemy destroyers were after us. We employed evasive tactics until 9:30, when we found ourselves rising to the surface as though we were aground. I stopped, coasted to about forty-seven feet on the depth gauge. We flooded the auxiliary (tanks) rapidly in order to prevent ourselves from rising."

So began thirteen critical hours for fifty men and a pigboat. The craft was momentarily out of control and rising to the surface. Overhead, in the clear morning under a blue sky on a flat sea, Jap destroyers searched for the impertinent little American submarine. In his quiet way, Chapple logged:

"Slowly the submarine sank to the bottom, plowed its nose into a bank in the gulf, and rested there. We stopped all the machinery and electrical equipment in the ship, except the motor-generator (which supplied energy for the electric lights) to eliminate sound.

"The clanging continued, though not always near us, for the better part of the day. Small boats went over us at irregular intervals. The men took off their shoes, and conversations were in whispers. Practically no one had slept the night before and all were tense and nervous, although self-contained. Our Filipino mess boy said we must be off the village where his folks lived. He said he'd like for us to go up and sink one of the Japs right off his folks' front porch.

"We couldn't smoke, of course. The men flopped at action stations. They got coffee and meals, moving about in their stocking feet, careful to avoid dropping a pan, a cup or a spoon, even, whose sound might be picked up by those devils overhead. The last destroyer that I'd sighted had apparently followed in very successfully with its sound-detecting gear. That last clang had been close.

"With our own sound gear we could hear the movements of the enemy above. We heard propeller noises, approaching and receding. Finally, we'd all heard enough of this. I ordered the sound man to stow the apparatus, turn it off. I figured—and I know the men figured

467

—that we were pretty helpless and that we probably were going to get it; and what was the use of knowing exactly when?

"We followed the movement of what appeared to be landing barges shuttling between the transports and the shore. When one would approach and pass us and move on toward shore we would follow the sound with our eyes as though we could see the barge. Emery, the gunner's mate, remarked that the way we followed the sounds back and forth was like watching a ball being batted across a net in a tennis match.

"But still there was noise to plague us in our deathly stillness below. There was water in the bilges in the control room. We were in such shallow water the ship was rolling. Of all the disturbing noises I've ever heard the back-and-forth sloshing of that water was the worst.

"I organized a game of cribbage in the control room. The play wasn't as sharp as usual. We couldn't remain long with the sound gear turned off, so the passing over our heads of those boats was very distracting. The men began to be droopy and sleepy in the afternoon. The deck bore a black slime from condensed moisture. Officers and men lay down in the slime to sleep.

"At about 6:30 we began to feel that we were going to get away with it. It was getting dark. Our hopes and spirits rose considerably when, suddenly, we heard a noise that sounded as though somebody was rapping on the hull. Machinist's Mate Rosacher said the enemy had probably picked us up and some diver was hooking on. Any minute we expected somebody to open the hatch and say, 'Come on out, boys, the jig's up.'

"About an hour later I called a conference of all the officers. We decided that we'd make efforts to get away, come moonset. The cook opened up some warm canned tomatoes, canned fruit and made very strong black coffee. We allowed some oxygen to escape into the boat. We wanted to be alert and ready for anything.

"After much blowing, pumping and venting, we got underway for an anchorage for which we acquired, after a while, a great fondness. Finally when it was dark enough, we surfaced. Ensign G. W. Forbes said: 'We, certainly gave the Japs fourteen hours of hell.'

"Everybody laughed and the tension relaxed."

But the dawn-to-moonset game of hide and seek with the enemy—

468

scraping about on the bottom—had cost the submarine a bent propeller. The screw was now off-center and made a terrific racket, increasing many times the chances of being picked up by enemy sound detectors.

The following day, after several hours spent charging batteries on the surface, the lookout sighted an enemy patrol.

"Take her down!" Chapple shouted and she sank where she lay. All that day they rested on the bottom, keeping very quiet. After sundown the submarine rose again to charge batteries and give the men fresh air. The ship, crippled but still game, had not yet completed her mission. Chapple wrote:

"On Wednesday, at 11:27 A.M., through the periscope I sighted six enemy transports. But they were too far away.

"At 11:52 A.M., when we were in about twenty-three fathoms of water, a bomb or shallow mine exploded. This shock put the control-room depth gauges temporarily out of commission. We dropped down.

"My second in command, Lieutenant Malhop, and I had planned to lay low until the transports anchored and then wade in amongst them after dark. But it wasn't to be. That Jap destroyer came and started working over us.

"We headed north. We stopped all machinery except the bow planes that guided the ship's depth. At 12:05 P.M. we received three depth charges to port, at 12:08 five to starboard. At 12:23 we received four charges to starboard and one charge to starboard at 12:26. At 12:30 drove full speed ahead on all motors."

Chapple, with his noisy propeller, was taking a desperate chance to try and get away. Those depth charges were coming closer every moment. The submarine rang as if struck by a steel maul at regular and successively louder intervals.

"At 12:45 four depth charges exploded to starboard."

Chapple signaled for a dead stop and the submarine settled to the bottom. The Japs were tossing batteries of ash cans; twenty-eight burst around the hunted pigboat within forty-three minutes, each shaking the craft like a thunderclap.

The men were taut. But by 5:20, enemy propeller noises had died down. At about six o'clock, Seaman McNeal, in the control room, sang out: "All clear all around."

469

At that precise moment six depth bombs burst dangerously close and somebody snapped back: "Where'd you get that all-clear stuff?" McNeal looked puzzled and very apologetic and said that maybe the Japs were pushing things off sailboats. Maybe they were.

Throughout the day, as on the previous day, the fans were stopped and the heat was almost beyond endurance.

"We surfaced at 10:40 P.M. The submarine had been under water about eighteen hours. I ordered the hull ventilated, from battery rooms to engine room. I also gave the order to remain rigged for a dive."

At that moment an explosion occurred in the after-battery compartment.

"I went below and into the battery compartment. There were no electrical fires. There were small flames elsewhere, as if canvas were burning. The compartment cover and the flooring of the compartment were in great confusion. I blew out some smoke with a fan while Electrician's Mate Third Class Howard L. Buck and I put on raincoats and rubber boots to go in and get E. C. Harbin, Chief Machinist's Mate, who was injured.

"Buck and I went in and then Chief Machinist's Mate Ross came in and lifted Harbin into the engine room. Harbin and two others were hurt in the explosion. Buck conducted himself with extraordinary coolness and courage and an entry has been made to this effect in the record. Same entry, same wording for Ross."

In the Navy's book there is the same wording for Chapple.

That night the submarine was exhausted and crippled, moving at less than half speed. Chapple remained on the bridge. His second in command looked after things below and administered morphine to the three injured men. Because of the sub's battered condition, Chapple wanted to leave the gulf on the surface, rather than attempt the risky undersea maneuver through the reefs.

"At about 2:15 A.M. we sighted two Japanese destroyers," wrote Chapple, "about two miles off. We stopped and let them pass. The fighting power of our sub was almost nil. We were unable to make speed. The propeller gave off a terrific noise.

"At 3:48 we were obliged to dive as a destroyer approached at high speed. At 3:50 three depth charges came very close. The destroyer began to follow us. He didn't use pingers but kept pretty close all

470

night long. We tried what evasive tactics we could with low battery power and noisy propeller. We played hide-and-seek all night long.

"At 9:30 A.M. the following morning we went aground a very steep bank. We attempted to rest there, but the submarine kept sliding slowly off and I had to use the motors occasionally to try to climb. For three hours we practically stood on end. I had to avoid sinking to such a depth as would burst the submarine. Then we levelled off and headed southwest.

"We went aground again that afternoon at about 1:40 and for some inexplicable reason we couldn't take her off. Finally we broke loose and started sinking. I was unable to check the submarine until we hit bottom."

Trapped in dangerous waters, surrounded by reefs and uncharted subsea promontories, Chapple took a last desperate chance to save his crew and his boat. He surfaced in daylight at 2 P.M., when he expected there would be swarms of enemy craft on the sea. His diary says:

"We picked up what we thought might be two destroyers ten or twelve miles distant. We tried to dive to hide from the enemy. It was too shallow and we hit bottom with a heavy thump. We tried to go ahead but ran aground again. So we surfaced and went ahead at normal speed on all engines. The destroyers turned out to be auxiliary craft which apparently never sighted us. At 4:23 P.M. we headed for Manila. We arrived the next day.

"Operation concluded."

(To Lieutenant Chapple, for attacking the enemy successfully under difficult conditions and for bringing submarine and men back safely, went the Navy Cross.)

The pilot of our PBY at the Surabaya Naval Base said for the umpteenth time: "Let's go—we've got to get off from here before daylight."

We went down to the edge of the bay. There were about a dozen pilots standing on the wharf, waiting to go out in the launch headed for various assignments. It was still not quite light on that morning of February 4th. They were all dressed in khaki—young and vigorous. It was one of the greatest thrills of my life to be standing among these men who talked my own language. They seemed so eager, intent and so competent. I felt like singing "Yankee Doodle Dandy."

Going out in the boat to the plane we passed four seaplanes half submerged and burnt out from the Japanese attack yesterday morning. One was a German Dornier owned by the Dutch, another was a PBY belonging to the Dutch and there were two American-owned PBYs. The PBY is a two-motor patrol bomber. The British call them Catalinas.

At 5:30 A.M. Wednesday, February 4th, we took off. The pilot of our PBY was Lieutenant (J.G.) Elwyn L. Christman of Woodburn, Oregon; the co-pilot Ensign William V. Gough, Jr., of Baltimore; and the other ensign was Justin Baldwin, of Fort Gaines, Georgia. Within an hour we were over the island of Bali.

Ensign Gough was at the controls and Christman came back to peer through the bomb sight. I went forward and sat in the pilot's seat and Gough, a big, husky youth, leaned over to me and shouted in my ear: "Christman is pretending to take a bomb sight but he is really looking for some Bali maidens taking their morning bath."

An hour later we ran into a heavy rainstorm. It was very bumpy and I was sleeping most of the time.

For the first hour, like everyone else aboard the ship, I was watching for Jap fighters, but when we got away from Bali we all felt that it would only be an odd chance if we ran into the Japs. About 9 o'clock we were flying at 7,000 feet at 130 knots.

"We have a pretty good tail wind up here," Christman said.

09:40—The chief mechanic is making coffee. I am sitting on a bunk opposite the stove with Christman. Two of the other crew members are sleeping in bunks in the same compartment.

"We'll have some radio contact pretty quick now," Christman says.

In the bulge of the ship two machine gunners are beside their guns, constantly searching the skies.

10:20—We are going through a bad rainstorm—very thick clouds and very bumpy. We are getting tossed around a good deal.

10:33—A signal was just received: "Do not enter your base."

I asked Christman what that meant.

"It's a general call sent out as a result of a section of Jap fighters probably flying west of Timor and heading eastward."

We are about seventy-five miles south of Rati Island.

472

"The Japs are probably one hundred miles from us right now, but we don't know," Christman explains.

"What are the chances of being attacked?" I ask.

"About fifty-fifty," Christman says, "but we can go down low to the water and they will have a tough time getting us."

11:05—The wireless operator is heating some cans over the electric hot-plate. Gough and I are watching him.

"After a year in these jobs," Gough says, "you get tin happy. Wouldn't it be hell to lose the can opener!"

Gough is disgustingly cheerful. My stomach is in a turmoil from this bumpy flight. I can't even watch them make the food. I go back into the bulge, where the two gunners are sitting all wrapped up in heavy woolen coats. It is bitterly cold back there, but the air revives me.

11:30—Baldwin just heated some chicken gumbo soup and I had crackers with it.

We are still above the white fluffs of clouds. It is smooth up here at the moment. We want clouds around to pop into in case any Jap turns up.

This is a swell crew. Everyone is good-natured and amiable. No one gets in the other's way. The conversation is a bit difficult because of the roar, but not impossible.

12:15—Christman and Gough insisted I take the controls. Gough said: "Go ahead—it won't bite you. It's as simple as driving a car. The course is 88."

I was at the controls for about ten minutes and I slipped off the course a bit.

"That's all right," Gough said. "You just have to get the feel of it. A baby can handle one of these ships with a little practice."

13:15—We are over an island spit of Australia. We are running into a heavy rainstorm.

13:30—We have just sighted Port Darwin. We couldn't see it until we were right over it. This is the first time Christman and Gough have come to Darwin and we hit it just about five miles off. It is extremely rough and the water down below doesn't look very inviting either.

The waves were rather high and I heaved a sigh of relief when finally we came down safely. Several times I thought we would turn

473

over. We flashed a signal asking where to tie up and were told to moor to a buoy at the end of the line. We scouted all over the bay in the rough water for about twenty minutes and couldn't find the buoy. By then I'd been seasick about five times over the side. Christman decided to take her up again. I resented the necessity of going into the air to locate the buoy, but coming down the second time was much easier.

There was thirty knots of wind when we landed and we found out other things too: that the weather was so bad here that commercial planes weren't operating and that military aviation would only operate if the situation was very serious. As a matter of fact, for the past four days there had been no shipping out of Darwin because of the weather.

When we finally tied up to the buoy we had to wait a half hour for a boat to come out. Then a small tug came up pulling a tiny rubber dinghy that bobbed around like a cork and constantly shipped water. The tug heaved and snorted about fifteen feet from the plane and let the rubber boat drift back to the PBY. One by one we clambered down the hull of the PBY to reach the rubber boat. It was half-filled with water and all our baggage was soaked.

We were taken in the tug to the aircraft tender *Langley*. I was greeted by Commander Duval and we lunched in the wardroom. There were about fifty officers of the *Langley* and a number of flying officers, and they were all eager to know about the situation up north. They were starved for news about the United States forces and they had no sources of information. They all said: "When you get back to America tell them to send us some equipment. If we had three-quarters of what the Japs have, we could roll them back."

They knew nothing of the movement of the United States naval units and kept questioning me about the extent of American assistance out here.

On the *Langley* there was a dart game based on baseball. I had never seen anything like it before. I felt like a kid entering a new world.

Most of the officers knew of my story on the sinking of the *Repulse* and had heard about the British barring me. I explained to them that in times like these honest reporting was as essential as for the military to meet an emergency situation with ingenuity, enterprise and no red tape.

474

The officers all said that the American Navy is not getting bogged down in red tape. That wasn't the usual thing for officers to say because it is as natural for an officer to complain about red tape as it is for a soldier to grouse about food, and yet these officers said: "The American Navy is skipping the red tape."

I then spent a half hour talking with Commander Robert P. Mc-Connell in his room, and he explained that he had already made arrangements with the immigration authorities on shore to meet me in the morning.

Each of us had a cup of chocolate, and Christman and Gough began telling me their story. Christman, twenty-six, small, wiry and quiet; Gough, twenty-five, husky, boyish, frisky.

On December 26th just one hour before midnight, six American Navy Patrol bombers, PBY's like the one we had just flown in from Surabaya, took off from Ambon, a Dutch island. Each carried 1,500 pounds of demolition bombs and enough gasoline for a sixteen-hour flight.

The mission: Bomb Japanese warships at Jolo Island, at the eastern end of the Sulu Archipelago in the Philippines.

Only two planes returned, but some of the crews of the four got back. Christman and Gough were two men who returned.

As they reached Jolo, a red ball of sun was breaking through the hazy clouds. Almost at once they spotted a cruiser at anchor, another underway, and three or four destroyers. Christman, first pilot, was at the controls. Gough was in the co-pilot's seat.

Ack-ack rushed up to meet them. Just as the plane started in for its target, the after-gunner yelled through the communications: "Here comes a fighter."

They got the first Jap Zero. One of the gunners in the waist put a pan of a hundred shots into the Zero cockpit. The plane went spinning down, streaming smoke behind. Then six more Zero fighters came toward the PBYs while they were still flying in formation. The anti-aircraft fire from the shore bit into the sky. One burst hit not far from Christman's ship.

"It was as if someone dropped a thousand-pound slab of concrete right beside you," Gough said.

As the Jap fighters pulled out to get a new approach on Christman's

475

ship, he broke formation and dove on his target. He had lost his flight leader for the moment, and just as he was about to collide, Gough grabbed the wheel and one PBY hurtling into a dive flew over the other, missing it by just ten feet.

Christman dove from 12,000 feet at 300 miles an hour, racing for a cruiser. A barrage of anti-aircraft fire was between his ship and the target. The PBY is not made for dive bombing. The wings were beginning to wrinkle and fold back, shaking, as Christman put it, "like a riveting hammer."

At 6,000 feet, at a sixty-degree angle, three 500-pound bombs spilled out of the PBY and headed for the cruiser.

Christman pulled the ship out in a spiral, and at the same moment a Zero, which had followed the PBY in the dive, was on them. Gough yelled: "That cruiser is on fire!"

Jap bullets poured into the PBY. It was like a hail on a tin roof and Christman and Gough watched the shells plowing into the cockpit.

"I'm out of ammunition," the fourth gunner yelled through inter-communication. "Gas tanks punctured."

The gas in the bilges was about six inches deep. About a hundred gallons had leaked out.

On the seventh run, to shoot down the violently twisting PBY, the Jap Zero used his 20-mm cannon. The shell entered the cockpit a foot over Christman's head. He ducked instinctively.

The Zero pulled away and came in for the last run. Christman began scissoring again. Again the cannon, and this time it came through the mechanics' compartment and exploded in the bulkhead just behind Gough's head.

Immediately the whole plane was ablaze. Second Radioman P. H. Landers yelled: "Jesus Christ, we're afire."

Gough twisted his head around. The mechanics' compartment looked like the door of a firebox.

"Chris," he said to the pilot, "we've got to get down before this thing breaks in two." Christman nodded. They were at a thousand feet.

First Radioman Robert Lee Pettit, thirty-five and married, already was burned badly. Second Mechanic Bangust and Landers put on their 'chutes and told Christman:

"The stink is so bad here we can hardly stand it. What do you want us to do?"

476

"Do what you want," Christman said. "If you want to jump, go ahead, or you can stay and I'll try to get down."

Bangust and Landers leaped out of the plane, when it was 300 feet from the water. Their 'chutes blossomed out just a fraction before they hit.

The PBY landed, doing a hundred knots an hour, water-looping both ways, swinging crazily. The ship was burning rapidly. From the aft end of the navigator's compartment, directly behind the cockpit, to the tail was a mass of flames. Third Pilot Don Lurvey was still at his gun in the bow. Pettit, badly burned, came through the flames to reach the navigation compartment.

Christman went back to the navigation hatch and threw it open. He checked to see if everyone had a life jacket. The rubber boat was shot full of holes. Christman crawled up through the navigation hatch, then went forward to pull out Third Pilot Lurvey from the forward pit. Gough clambered hastily through the navigation hatch and hauled out the badly burned Pettit. All the flesh was off his hands and his face was bleached white, streaked with black.

"Guess we might as well get into it," Gough said, and they slid off. Gough turned to see if any men were swimming out from the bulges where the gunners are. First Mechanic Andrew Waterman had been killed in the air or burned in the plane. He was not found.

When they were fifty feet away, Gough looked back and saw the PBY break in two. The right wing broke off, midway out, then the center section gave way. The engine fell over into the navigation compartment. Smoke and flames billowed out, but the fire did not spread more than twenty feet from the plane.

As soon as the flames died down, Third Pilot Lurvey swam back to see what he could salvage. He found a life boat but it was so badly burned, not one of the compartments would hold water.

It was seven o'clock in the morning and the sun beat down fiercely.

All the men were bundled in the heavy clothing airmen need at 12,000 feet. Gough pulled out a small penknife. He started slicing off Radioman Pettit's coat. The knife slipped and jabbed a hole in Gough's jacket. He had to hold his thumb over that hole for the next thirty hours.

Then they slipped out of their heavy clothes. Gough kept the knife and his wallet. They could see the island of Jolo, where the Japs were,

477

and about twenty-five miles off they saw other islands. They decided to stay together.

Two of them took turns swimming on each side of the radioman. Pettit could only lay on his back and kick his feet, and was suffering intense pain. Every now and then Gough or Christman would nudge Pettit to keep him going in the right direction.

"We'll have to decide," Christman said, "whether we're going to stick together and not change our minds, zigzagging all over the ocean."

Christman looked around and Siasii Island seemed to him to be closest. Gough agreed, and so did the third pilot.

"All right," Christman said. "That's it. There'll be no changes."

At 5 P.M., the going was slow. Radioman Pettit was numb to pain now. He could roll over on his stomach and swim as well as the others, lashing out with his arms as if they were sticks. Their tongues were swollen and they were excruciatingly thirsty. Christman had a sunburned bottom.

They held a pow-wow again. Pettit could see and seemed to be in fair shape. They decided that each had an equal chance and that each man could go as fast as he wanted, as slow, or in whatever direction.

Pettit said. "I'm in a hell of a mess. You guys go on without me."

Gough, the strongest, struck out in the hope of reaching land and bringing help. Christman and Lurvey stayed together. Pettit was behind within shouting distance.

Around sunset, Christman called out to Pettit: "Are you all right?" There was no answer. Christman swam back. Pettit had disappeared.

That was a long night. Christman was out of his head part of the time. He thought he was swimming in an airplane hangar filled with oil. Once he thought he was swimming past an oil well and wanted to go back and sit on an oil pipe.

They would doze off during the night. Christman fell asleep a number of times. A wave would come along, and pour water into his mouth. He would wake up sputtering and start to swim off furiously in the wrong direction. Lurvey would call him back.

At sunrise they were close enough to land to see the waves breaking on the beach. Around noon Gough was picked up in a small *vinta*, an outrigger canoe, by natives who took him to shore.

Gough tried to induce them to go out to search for Christman and Lurvey, but they refused. Shortly afterwards the first and third pilots

478

sighted a sail boat with a few Moro boys handling it. It took the Americans an hour, still in the water while the boat stayed twenty feet away from them, to convince the Moros they were not Japs and wouldn't harm them. Christman used the few words of Tagalog he knew, yelling "American! U. S. Navy! Friend!"

Finally Christman was able to grab the outrigger. He pulled off his lifebelt and held it up to show the stamp: "U.S.N."

That settled everything to the Moro boys' satisfaction. Christman asked for a drink, but the boy wanted three centavos. Not having any money Christman traded his precious life jacket for the one drink of water. Then Lurvey, still in the water, was hauled into the boat.

The natives on shore treated them with medication, food and beds. They found Second Radioman Landers. He had been swimming with Second Mechanic Bangust, but after six hours Bangust had died in the water. Landers said before Bangust died he told him First Mechanic Waterman had been shot in the stomach and died on the plane before it hit the water.

The natives rubbed the airmen with coconut oil, and gave them hot milk, sugar and water.

For two days they recuperated on the island of Siasii, but it was eight days, hopping from one island to another by canoe, launches, *vinta* and motor launch, before they got to Terakan in Borneo. The Dutch flew them to Balikpapan, sent them on a boat to Surabaya. The Navy Department had reported them missing in action, believed killed.

Of the seven men in that PBY of Patrol Wing 10, four got back.

(To Lieutenant Elwyn L. Christman, for extraordinary heroism in the face of accurate anti-aircraft fire and overwhelming enemy opposition . . . shooting down enemy attackers . . . diving on enemy ships and inflicting damage . . . conducting his men safely back to base . . . is awarded the Navy Cross.)

(Radioman Robert Lee Pettit was awarded the Navy Cross posthumously.)

YANKS AT DARWIN

Thursday, February 5th:

Breakfast aboard the *Langley* with Commander Duval. Good-byes are not possible with Christman and Gough. They pulled out early in the morning for the return to Surabaya. I went ashore in a launch and was met by Chief Yeoman Cline, an aide of Commander Collins, American Naval Observer at Darwin. Australian medical and customs officials were the model of courtesy and co-operation—two attributes I'd long not found among such officials.

At the hotel, a two-story modern building set down amid the frontier-like shacks of Darwin, I tried to get a room.

"We can't take any more guests," the manager said. "The cook says he'll quit if we have one more guest."

There were no living accommodations in Darwin, no cigarettes, no whisky, nothing but the awful lonesomeness and isolation of this place.

Commander Collins said that he knew of no plane going south to Sydney, and suggested that I get a booking on an airline and that he would arrange for my priority. I succeeded in getting a passage on the Guinea Airways, by way of Adelaide, the next day. There is no railroad out of here and motor convoy would take days. I was in a great hurry to get to Sydney to give a broadcast.

Commander Collins arranged with a chief petty officer staying at the hotel to bed me down in his room. I'd just crawled into bed when Commander Collins came bursting into the room:

"How soon do you want to go to Sydney?" he asked.

"Right now," I yelled, starting to pull on my socks and pants.

"All right," he said, "go out to the Squadron Air Base and they'll take you to Bachelorville; then you'll start out in the morning from there for Brisbane."

Chief Yeoman Cline drove me out to the Air Headquarters, an extensive place with an administration building, many barracks and hangars. I lunched with two American lieutenants, hurrying to be ready for the take-off, when the flight was suddenly called off until morning.

480

I was given a room in the officers' quarters with Air-Force Captain Connelly, who had come out of the Philippines. I carried my bags and typewriter, tin hat and pith helmet into the room and had just set them down, when he rushed in to pack.

"I'm off to Surabaya," he said, "with a squadron of P 40's."

He brought out a big knife, two feet long, more like a sword.

"I guess I had better take this," he said.

"It seems like a good idea. Bring back a Jap for me, will you?"

"I will. I intend to get a good many for myself, too."

That afternoon, talking with a number of the American Air-Force men, fighter and bomber pilots, gave me this impression: The speed with which the Americans move and their kindness is a wonderful contrast. I haven't run into a sour face yet. Everyone is co-operative, determined and all business.

Darwin seems to be the end of the world, and all the men consider it so. The town itself is a series of wooden, hutlike houses; the stores have practically nothing to sell; there are bars with no beer; you can't buy a cigarette in the entire town.

A heavy wind is blowing today and the sky is overcast. The land is very flat and everywhere the trees are bent from the wind, and there are cur dogs with drooping tails. It is a depressing place. There is no entertainment here. Literally nothing. All the women and children are to be evacuated by next Tuesday. Bombings are expected here almost any time now. There are no fresh vegetables, and nothing much can be brought up because of the shortage of shipping space. Here at the Air Headquarters, Australians and Americans are jammed in together and getting on very well. The mess hall is a combination recreation building with a pool table. It is very crowded and men are lying on mattresses on the floor or on the floor itself, trying to grab some rest.

Lieutenant Henry J. Rose, of Dallas, who is to be my pilot tomorrow, took me to the canteen, so I could get some chocolate, but they have nothing at the canteen. However, they did have cigarettes, and several American fliers were there with nothing but Philippine money. I changed some Dutch guilders into Australian money and then tried to buy the American fliers some cigarettes. They were a bit embarrassed by it, so I suggested that I buy some of the Philippine pesos from them.

481

I did that; then they had some Australian money with which to buy cigarettes, and I got the Philippine pesos as souvenirs.

After dinner, I sat in the recreation room with a group of the fighter pilots and the fortress pilots. These young men of twenty-three, twenty-four and twenty-five had come out of the Philippines, after performing the kind of heroic deeds that sent chills up and down my back. I pulled and strained and yanked their stories out of them. They kept saying: "There's nothing to it. Men are doing this same sort of thing every day."

In the recreation room of the barracks, about thirty exhausted pilots were sleeping on the wooden floor, a few had mattresses. Six Flying Fortress airmen sat around the table under a single drop light while I scribbled their stories.

Lieutenant Joseph M. Bean of Santa Ana, California, the navigator of the plane piloted by Captain Colin Kelly, told me how they sank the Japanese battleship, *Haruna,* and then how Captain Kelly was killed after they completed their mission.

Lieutenant Henry C. Godman, of Palo Alto, California, and Lieutenant Edward C. Teats, of Pittsburgh, described their flights in fortresses from Darwin, 1,200 nautical miles to bomb ships and docks at Davao, landing at a secret 'drome in the Philippines and then getting back to Darwin, flying twenty out of twenty-five hours.

"Where's Wheless? He's the guy with the story you want," someone said. They found him.

Lieutenant Hewitt T. Wheless, twenty-eight, of Menard, Texas, was short, shy, with jet-black hair and a widow's peak. He began his story.

(Months later I heard that same story. I was sitting on the stage in a Muncie, Indiana, auditorium. We had interrupted my lecture on the war to hear the radio talk by the President of the United States. The President described the exploit of the man who is now Captain Wheless.)

Wheless began:

You see, it was like this. We were operating out of Mindanao, on Sunday, December 15th, B-17's, Flying Fortresses. Lieutenant Coates led the flight of four. We knew the Japs had concentrated shipping at

482

Legaspy Gulf, at the lower tip of Luzon, 400 miles away. Our orders were to bomb them.

It was a bright, sunny Sunday morning when we took off at nine o'clock. I got away first, and the other ships followed. We assembled over the field, behind the squadron leader, and climbed. A hundred miles out we ran into very bad weather, thunderstorms, clouds and heavy rains, and I went on instruments. I lost contact with the other three ships.

At 14,000 feet I lost my number two engine. I think it was from overheating. I dropped down to a lower altitude and we got the engine running again. I decided we might get over the target before the others, make it more of a surprise. I hoped to get the Jap pursuit ships on the ground and I knew I'd have to get in there fast to get them before they got me. I was also figuring on protection of the clouds to dodge into afterwards.

We went on, at about 9,500 feet, toward Legaspy, then about fifty miles away. I was on top of a cloud layer, hoping every second to get in an open spot when over Legaspy. About ten miles from our objective I ordered the bomb doors open and the gear set for bombing. We were now about five miles from our objective. We were lucky. There was a break in the clouds, and we were over the target.

Boy, what a target! There they were, twelve Jap transports lined up near the shore. It looked like the perfect set-up. At the same time the anti-aircraft down there opened up. I gave the order:

"All gunners at stations and keep a sharp lookout!"

I told my bombardier: "Line up on them. We're going in for the run."

This was at 2:25 P.M. At the same time the rear gunner yelled:

"Two squadrons pursuit ships coming in; one on right, one on left."

"Open fire as soon as you think they're in range. We're going in on the run."

The Japs came straight up, hanging on their props.

I could have turned around, of course. I could have dived back into the clouds. But I thought that since I had committed myself to this run I might just as well get rid of the bombs.

Meanwhile, the first two of the Japs—pursuits with the red ball of the Rising Sun on them—came in from the side. The gunners on each side held their fire until those Zeros were 200 feet away. Then they let

483

go. The Japs came right into the fire, and down they went. Probably we delayed too long because a third Jap was coming directly into our tail. He was coming in fast and bullets started pouring into our fuselage. That burst killed the radio operator, and the bullets were whizzing past me up in the cockpit.

Our bottom guns, the tunnel guns, were going, but with all those bullets ripping through the cockpit I had no doubt there was somebody behind who didn't like us very much. But I was going in, and about thirty seconds later the bombardier called up: "Bombs away! Bomb-bay door closed. Kick her in the behind!"

By then the third Jap Zero had turned away for another swat at us and a fourth Jap was on us. I made for a cloud cover. All we had were scattered cumulus clouds. We'd go through with that Jap over us, and when we came through it, there he'd be again. But those scattered clouds gave the gunners a chance to change ammunition.

Just after we dropped the bombs, my number one engine was shot out. The plane fell in that direction, slipping off, but I didn't stop to think of that motor. All I was thinking about was a place to hide. There were about eighteen Jap fighters buzzing all around us.

During the first ten minutes of the fight all but one of our gunners were either killed or wounded. I had only Gunner R. D. Brown operating. He worked out on both side guns. It was really something the way he worked, even though his wrist had been cracked by a bullet.

When the Japs were coming in on one side he'd get them and then he'd jump to the other side when they were going for the tail, and he'd pour it into them on that side. The engineer was helping to operate the guns, helping to steady them with one hand. His other hand was injured.

I kept chasing the clouds and the fight went on for twenty minutes. I was losing altitude fast and was down from 9,000 feet to about 3,500.

We moved away from that Jap base pretty fast. We had traveled about seventy miles. Some of our bombs had dropped a little short of the ships, but the last bomb had hit very close. They were 600-pounders we were carrying and those babies can do damage.

When the Japs, who were chasing us, ran out of ammunition, they went home. With them off our tail, I had a chance to look around. I noticed the number four gas tank was leaking very badly, and in the next ten minutes it leaked out 200 gallons. I also stopped my number one propeller. There were no gasoline fumes, but I could see the gasoline spraying off the wings.

My number three engine was smoking badly. Our radio had been shot off. I remember seeing that happen when those explosive bullets were passing over our heads. One bullet passed just between my seat and the co-pilot's. His sleeve was billowed out and another bullet passed right through the sleeve.

After the fight I'd been afraid to pick up the microphone because I thought the others with me were all dead. There was no sound in the ship. Then the navigator came up from the nose and stuck his head into the cockpit and said: "Want me to give a hand?"

I sure welcomed the sound of his voice. I told him to go back and see how the crew was and look over the guns. One was killed and three wounded, one of them very badly in the leg. We put a tourniquet on it.

The gunners say they got a few more Jap planes, but four was all I saw go down. Brown, the gunner, said he got three in running back and forth from both sides, but I turned in four in my report, although the others were certain they got six.

Williams, one of the gunners, had his thigh split from the knee to the hip by an explosive bullet. He'd been operating the top gun, and when he was hit he was knocked to the floor. He couldn't stand up, although he kept trying to get to the lower gun where the gunner had been killed.

My control cables were shot in two and that gave me very little diving ability. All I could do was go straight ahead. It was just at dark and only two engines were operating. Just as I got over the barricaded field to land we began running out of gas. So there I was without enough gas or daylight to circle around until they removed the barricades which had been put down to keep any Jap ship from coming in unexpectedly.

Although I didn't know it, I suspected my tires were flat, but I let down the wheels anyway. I couldn't count on a belly landing because there was no way of strapping down the wounded. It had to be a crash landing. I knew that. No one asked any questions. There was just no choice, and no time to make one if there was.

It was too dark to see anything but the dim outline of the field. We hit a palm tree coming in. I could hear us hit and break off the top. I was on my last legs by then and set the ship down. We rolled about 500 feet with all the brakes locked. Then suddenly we stopped and

485

went up on our nose. But we were down and no one was hurt in getting down.

I guess you could say we carried out our objective, but the ship was a mess. The tail wheel had been shot off and there were just about 1,200 bullet holes in the ship. The number four gas tank had been punctured by a cannon shell and the radio, too, was knocked off by a cannon. Even the propeller blades had bullet holes in them. Out of eleven control cables, six had been shot in two. All my instruments were in ruin. All the oxygen tanks had been hit. The armor plate was very effective, even though one of the crew was killed and three wounded. That B-17 *certainly* can take it.

Friday, February 6th:
We are taking off at seven o'clock in a B-18 built in 1936. It's used for hauling stuff around—a two-motor job.

We finally got off at 7:40 with nine men aboard. My spot is up in the glass-enclosed nose. I am sitting in a huge rubber ring. It's a bit bumpy and we are flying low.

8:10—Came down at Bachelorville. It is just a runway of red clay, surrounded by field grass and then the usual plain with a few trees and rolling hills in the distance. We have come down here to pick up a 500-pound bomb to take it south and have some kind of rings made up for it so it will fit in the bomb racks of the B-17 bombers.

11:00—Down at Daly Waters. It's a large landing field and the insufferable, sticky flies are exactly like those in Egypt. We are being held up because some fighters and other aircraft are coming up from the south on their way to Darwin, and they are due to land here. In about a half hour six B-24 Douglas dive bombers came in. They are two-seater aircraft and when the squadron leader came taxiing over near our plane, he shoved back the cockpit cover and stood up and shouted: "Christ, it's hot here."

A few minutes later twelve P-40 E's, the Kittyhawks, came in. This is a huge field at Daly Waters—in many respects a perfect field. There are no barriers and visibility is excellent on all sides. We stood beside our bombers, watching the Kittyhawks circle to follow their leader down. The leader made a perfect landing, the next one bounced but got down. The next one seemed to be coming down too low, short of the airdrome, and heading for a field. He came down in the field and hit a ditch. The next one did the same—down on the field and half turned over. The following Kittyhawk did the same. Lieutenant Rose was shouting and screaming: "What the hell's the matter with them? They've got all the field in the world here to land on and they are coming down in the grass and weeds."

The others came in all right, until the final one of the twelve. He made five attempts to get down but when four or five feet off the ground he decided he couldn't make it, put on the gas, and zoomed up and away again for another circle. Five times he did that.

"You can just imagine," Lieutenant Rose said, "what that poor kid in there is going through."

A sergeant mechanic with us said: "The only way we'll get him down is shoot him down."

I remarked to some of the airmen standing by that if a pilot couldn't make a simple landing in a strange and good field, how could he fight in combat, when the enemy is on his tail.

"These boys are going to be slaughtered out here," one pilot said.

He finally came down on the airdrome, and unlike the three others, did not crack up. These pilots were youngsters just out of flying school, with insufficient experience. There's no help for that, I suppose. Men, even untrained, are needed desperately if Java is to be saved.

12:50—We took off from Daly Waters and flew across waste land, something like Egypt and Southern Arizona. Then we ran into heavy storms and thick clouds, and it was very bumpy.

It is fascinating riding in the glass-covered nose. As we rush toward a cloud bank you feel that it isn't a cloud at all, but a white mountain, and if that isn't a white mountain, there must be one right behind it. You clench your hands as you plow through the cloud rushing forward to meet you, and wait for the ship to crash into a mountain. I don't know if there are mountains here or not, but if there are, I am in the prime position to meet that mountain first.

Lieutenant Rose is banking and twisting to avoid the clouds on my behalf. They cause bumps and he wants to be considerate of my stomach.

16:30—Came down at Gloncurry. We were driven into town in an army car. This is a movie set for a Western horse opera. There's one long street with high-fronted stores and hotels in the old Western style. The only things missing are cowboys riding and shooting down the center of the street.

487

We are at the Leichard Hotel, a very primitive place—the sort of thing that existed in our West about eighty years ago. The owners, a man and his wife, came here eighteen years ago for the copper this area once produced. Now they depend on the railroad and the airdrome. Across from the hotel is another hostelry called "The Oasis," next to it is the Bio Cinema Palace. It's closed.

We all went to a confectionery, and Lieutenant Wise, the co-pilot, superintended the making of milk shakes "American style," as he patiently explained to the girl behind the counter. For Lieutenant Wise that meant putting five scoops of ice cream in the milk shake. The Australian girl looked at Wise with that special expression that one reserves for an idiot.

Tonight I read the *Brisbane Courier Mail* of February 6th. Poor Singapore! The British communiqué says that enemy transports in the Johore Bahru area are being shelled by artillery. The Japanese are shelling the north end of the Island and that means the Naval Base and the Seletar Airdrome. Singapore itself is taking a terrific pounding from high- and low-level bombing attacks. What a pitiful broadcast that air-raid warden made from Singapore and how revealing!

"Unlike Malta and Chungking," he said, "where they are supposed to have ideal shelters, in Singapore there is nothing but drains and obsolete trenches."

Saturday, February 7th:
Eight Curtiss dive bombers were just taking off, headed for the north, when we arrived at the airdrome. They circled and then came back over the airdrome, just ten feet above the ground where we were standing. We all fell flat on our faces.

"What did they do that for?" I asked Lieutenant Rose.

"Oh, just to scare us and to say good-bye."

Then the dive bombers swept low over Gloncurry to wake everybody up to say good-bye to them.

I notice that the American boys out in the field are peeved, but not embittered, by the confusion and lack of planning. They voice their complaints freely and keep trying to devise improvements for themselves. The Americans I've met since I came to Java and Australia seem very alert and keen and are actually attempting to translate their

488

complaints into improvements. I feel that as soon as this tide-swell of suggestions by men in the field rolls back on Washington changes will come about.

13:25—For four hours we have been flying over desert country with some scrub land, a country of kangaroos, wallaby, wild turkey, cockatoos, parrakeets and emu. Now we are coming into Charleyville.

The airport officer, an American, took us into town. It seemed like the height of civilization. We actually had toasted sandwiches and milk shakes in an American-type drug store. It didn't do me any good. Ten minutes after we took off I lost everything.

At Ambiloy, not far from Brisbane, Lieutenant Rose received orders to fly to Archer Field, about fifteen minutes away, but I decided to go into Brisbane by car, rather than fly. Rose laughed: "Don't you trust me any more?"

"Yes, but I want to drive over some of this country—you can't see enough from the air."

I was glad I went in a car. It is beautiful countryside. There is a winding river with white birches lining it, a farm house with chickens. It was utter peace—an American scene in Ohio. And then we came to Ipswich, just like an American factory town on Saturday night. Chain stores, drug stores, cars lined up at the curb and gas stations, as in America, with a fence around them plastered with signs.

At dinner that night at the hotel I ate with seven American pilots—dive-bomber pilots, all of the same Bomber Group. They were young, gay and enthusiastic, away from America for the first time and yearning to get at the enemy. Their enthusiasm, their dynamism and their patriotism are invigorating. They are celebrating their anniversary. Just one year ago today they came out of flying school—all in the same group. With that year's experience they are senior men at Ambiloy Field. Only a few of the higher officers there have had more experience than they. All of them were just out of the university when they joined the air service. They hadn't particularly prepared for an army career. Some were studying business administration, economics and journalism.

They had joined out of patriotism and a knowledge of the inevitability of our entering the war, but a good deal of it was glamour and they all said: "Well, we just wanted to fly. If I should get killed

489

tomorrow, I'd think my life wasn't wasted because I did what I wanted to do."

They bitterly complained about the sending over of young kids without experience just out of flying school to fight the Japs while, as they put it, "all the experienced fighter pilots are on the gravy train back home."

They told me that the Douglas dive bomber is really a navy ship but the equipment is mostly army. The bomb racks have to have a special fitting.

"Every time we take off," they said, "our hearts are in our mouths that a bomb will drop off from this fitting. Every machine shop we can find is under contract to make fittings for the bombs."

I am at Lennon's Hotel. There is a soft bed, a radio in the room and everything is clean and modern. It seems as if I have been away from such luxury for years. Afterwards I look in on the dance floor. Young Americans were doing strange shag steps with Australian girls. It was the kind of dancing I have never seen before, but I guess it's what they call "jiving," and it seems like a different world. Everyone is intent on having a good time.

As I lay in bed I thought of those seven American pilots. They were more serious and more affable than the R.A.F. They are not as hardboiled or as cock-sure and by no means as good fighters. They just don't have the experience. They are much more open in their condemnation of defense as they are of political interference and, as they described them, "those dumb Congressmen."

The paper tonight reports the destruction of Singapore is still going on. General Percival has issued this statement: "We will hold Singapore—there is no question about it."

What a tragic epitaph of over-confidence that is, but I suppose he could say nothing else. Generals must be confident.

Sunday, February 8th:
I took off in a Douglas plane of the Australian Airlines this afternoon and within four hours was flying over the beautiful, almost unreal Sydney Harbor.

490

As I stepped off the plane at Sydney, a signpost at the airdrome read:

Brisbane	482 miles
Darwin	2,393 miles
Singapore	4,692 miles
London	13,129 miles

At the Australia Hotel in Sydney, I discovered what Sunday means in this country. I couldn't have a suit pressed; there were no cigarettes on sale, no papers on sale—everything was closed as tight as a drum. All Sydney was closed. Sunday in Australia is synonymous with the morgue.

George Folster, the CBS representative here, came to see me. He's a jolly, vigorous, capable man of about thirty-two.

I sent off a wire to Paul White reporting my arrival at Sydney.

Monday, February 10th:

I wandered around town in a state of extreme fatigue. It must be the reaction from the tenseness of the past few weeks. Somehow even after this first day in Sydney, the war already has grown unreal. This city is so American, so complete with what passes for the "appurtenances of peacetime civilization" that war has no body or substance in the mind.

The people I have met so far today are belligerently independent, and there is a certain comradeship among them, something of a determination to be democratic, at least to be completely un-English.

The Japs have crossed the Straits of Johore and landed on Singapore Island. It happened late Saturday night and it was not officially announced until this morning—thirty-six hours afterwards. I can just imagine what a shock it must have been to the people to find out that the enemy had been on the island for thirty-six hours.

General Bennett says: "The situation is well in hand. We have taken our stand on a strong line and are organizing an attack which it is hoped will recover as much as possible of lost terrain."

I am convinced that there are only a very few aircraft remaining on the island, if any at all.

The Singapore radio says: "Building of air-raid shelters seems rather belated now. The attack has come much more quickly than we expected."

The other day General Percival said: "We intend to hold Singapore.

491

Everyone must realize that it's a common fight for military and civilians alike."

And the *Sydney Telegraph* editorial comments bitterly today: "So, when Singapore is in deadly danger, the civilian is expected to fight! With what? What has trained him? A month ago the Brass Hats in Singapore would have turned away in horror at the thought of inviting civilians to fight."

I notice here that there is a diddling around among the leaders of the country on petty quarrels. Statesmen are making absurd statements. They react in horror at the phrase "conscription of soldiers, to be sent abroad." In democracies only the falling of bombs seems to bring a sense of reality.

Tuesday, February 10th:

Completed all arrangements with officials today for broadcasting. Had a long talk with Richard Boyer of the Department of Information. When leaving him, I said: "I hope you don't kick me out of here until I make a few broadcasts."

"Oh, no, you will be very welcome here. We are just as regretful of what happened at Singapore as you are."

I am so damned lonesome for Martha. Tonight in the elevator I saw a girl in a black dress—just the smart kind Martha would wear—and it made me sick with longing. I'm going home. That's final!

Wednesday, February 11th:

I am scheduled to make my first broadcast out of Australia. I wrote the script in the afternoon, and took it to the censor this evening. I wanted to say that Singapore will fall within twenty-four to seventy-two hours. Wilson, the censor on duty, considered my whole broadcast "destructive."

"Your papers here," I pointed out, "say much sharper things about the British than I have in this broadcast."

"We don't want people in America to think we are tied to muddleheads," Wilson remarked.

"All I am doing in this broadcast," I said, "is giving details of the general condemnation expressed by your own papers. Only by reporting our mistakes can we profit by the lessons."

Wilson and I argued for about an hour and a half and then he telephoned to the chief censor at Canberra. He read the script three times to the chief censor and a few sentences were struck out. After he had been on the phone for an hour I got on the telephone and discussed the script with the Canberra censor for another hour.

Another discussion had to be held with Wilson again. When he attempted to censor material of this first broadcast on Singapore I kept asking: "Well, why do you cut that?"

Sometimes he could only say: "I don't agree with it."

At other times he said: "That's information to the enemy."

"On what basis do you consider this information to the enemy?"

"Well, it's very critical," Wilson said.

"Oh, that's it. I can't be critical of the conduct of the war?"

"Yes, you can, but you can't say that."

"Why not?"

"Those are my orders."

"Show me any orders of yours which prevent you from approving that?"

"No, I can't do that."

It took me five hours to get that script approved by the censors. It ended with only a few minor changes being made.

Here is the broadcast I gave on February 12th at 09:51, which was 6:51 P.M., February 11th, in New York: "I have just arrived in Sydney from Singapore and Batavia. I flew 1,100 miles from Java to Darwin in a navy bomber and then in an army bomber 1,800 miles from Darwin to Brisbane, over an area that may decide the fate of the Pacific war.

"Those are great distances, but from my observation of operations out here, they may not mean much to the Japanese attackers.

"The picture in the Pacific is very far from optimistic. At no point are the Japanese being held by the Allied forces.

"Singapore very probably will be in Japanese hands in the next twenty-four to seventy-two hours. Japanese submarines and surface raiders will then operate in the Indian Ocean. The position of Rangoon —and therefore of supplies to the Chinese—will become critical. Dutch Sumatra may be taken and the fate of Java will be decided in the next three or four weeks. From what I have seen of Japanese driving power

493

and Allied man power and equipment to meet it, Australia will be attacked in the very near future.

"I've talked with dozens of American bomber and fighter pilots in the NEI, and others who got out of the Philippines. Every one of them said, in just these words, 'For God's sake, tell them to send us some aircraft. In every engagement we're outnumbered fifty and one hundred to one.'

"At Singapore, the entire British, Australian and Indian garrison will either fight to the last man, or surrender. I do not believe there will be a Dunkirk from Singapore. The Imperial forces there will fight and die with great courage. They have that capacity, and it has been the main weapon of the soldier in Malaya.

"Here in brief are a few of the reasons why the Japanese are at Singapore:

"The British authorities were confident that the Japanese would not dare attack Great Britain. When the Japanese did attack, they were so stunned and unprepared that the British, unless reinforced, at no time stood a chance of holding the Japanese advance, despite the official statements to the contrary.

"The British troops were subjected from the first day of the war down to this moment to unceasing dive bombing and machine-gunning attacks. No courage in the world can stand that indefinitely. The first month of the war the troops were without protection from British fighters.

"Only three weeks before the outbreak of the war did the British military discover that Bren gun carriers and small tanks could negotiate water-covered rice fields. That required a change in defensive tactics which had been based on depending on jungles and rice fields to protect their flanks.

"The British were heavily outnumbered and unable to stop the Japanese infiltration attacks. The troops were not adequately trained for jungle fighting and could not adapt themselves in a few weeks. The British commanders judged what the Japanese would do by what *they* would do if in the Japanese position.

"An amazing Fifth-Column organization had been established in Malaya. One officer said he gave the Fifth Columnists thirty-five percent of the credit for the Japanese success.

"The British scorched-earth policy the first four weeks of the war

494

was virtually a figment of the official imagination. Vast storehouses of food were left untouched for the Japanese. Sampans, boats, barges and even steamers were undamaged.

"At Penang, the British military authorities ordered the exacuation without consulting the Governor. They refused to evacuate anyone except Europeans. All Chinese, Malays, Tamils and Indians were left to their fate. That was the beginning of considerable difficulties with the natives in Malaya. At Penang, the treasury was left intact with more than a quarter of a million dollars.

"When the Japanese walked into Penang, they were able to turn a switch in the radio station and begin broadcasting. While it was stated the British were destroying everything in the path of their retreat, facts told a different story. To give one instance, it was announced they destroyed everything at Kuantan airdrome on the east coast. Two days later the R.A.F. was sent over to bomb the undamaged hangars and the Japanese aircraft already using the field. Up until the day of the war the colonial administration was unable to distinguish between Japanese as potential enemies and the Chinese as allies. Prominent Chinese at the outbreak of war beseeched the British to give them guns to help fight. A Chinese battalion was recruited ten days ago.

"At the time the authorities banned me from broadcasting from Singapore, the head of Military Intelligence said that civilian morale could win or lose the battle of Singapore. Every American and British correspondent would affirm that censorship in Singapore did everything possible to hide the situation from those civilians expected to fight the battle for Singapore.

"The tragic story of Singapore is not all one of Japanese numerical superiority, fanatical courage and brilliant military scheming. The Japanese are at Singapore also because of what the British authorities failed to foresee, prepare for and meet at the crucial moment. That is the moral of the story of Singapore."

Thursday, February 12th:
I had a long talk this morning with H. R. Knickerbocker, whom I had last seen in Paris four years ago. He came here yesterday with an American naval force with Joseph Harsch of the *Christian Science Monitor*, also an old friend. I told him about Singapore and of the general military situation. He was absolutely stunned. I poured out the

495

situation to Knickerbocker because he gave an interview to the papers here yesterday about how rosy everything was.

"My God, Knick," I said, "even in the face of all that is going on everywhere here this self-delusion continues."

Knickerbocker was amazed when I told him how the British operate in Singapore. He had no idea such things existed, he said, and actually turned pale when I told him how inadequate our aircraft were in numbers and performance in Java and around Darwin.

"It's just plain murder up there," I told him.

Knickerbocker wanted to know how it was the British banned me, and I told him briefly the circumstances.

"Can they be such complete idiots in Singapore?" Knickerbocker demanded. "I can't believe such idiocy exists in the world."

Later in the afternoon another paper came to interview Knickerbocker, Harsch and myself, and the *Sydney Telegraph* asked Knickerbocker to comment on the statement I made in my broadcast that morning. The cables had already come into the Sydney papers from their correspondents in New York on the broadcast.

Knickerbocker said one of the nicest things that one correspondent can say about another: "We in America," Knick said, "have relied entirely on Mr. Brown's reports for an accurate picture of the situation."

My thoughts are still in Singapore and the British there are still pretending. The official statements report that there are no indications the Japanese have succeeded in putting a large number of troops across the Johore causeway. Another statement says there is no indication that Japanese tanks have landed on Singapore Island.

Harold Guard of *UP* reports that Singapore's fate will be decided in a matter of hours while Yates McDaniel of *AP* says: "In front of the famous Raffles Hotel cars are depositing patrons for the daily tea and dance. Outside the cinema, people are queuing up to see Joel McCrea and Ellen Drew in *Reaching for the Sun*."

Yesterday the Japanese dropped a note from the air to the high command asking for an unconditional surrender of the entire forces in Malaya.

The Australian papers have unloosed the sharpest kind of attacks on Prime Minister Churchill. The *Daily Telegraph* in an editorial complains: "What the Pacific Nations want to know is when and where is Britain going to make a determined stand."

Friday, February 13th:
This afternoon I telephoned Martha in New York. At one point I couldn't understand what Martha said and I asked her to repeat it. I still couldn't understand and the censor interrupted.

"Mr. Brown," he said very distinctly, "she says don't bow down to anyone. Keep on telling the truth."

That's the first time anywhere I ever had a censor tell me to tell the truth!

Today I gave Joe Harsch a fill-in on the situation up north. Joe is a very able correspondent and I knew him in Rome when he stopped off there going to his assignment in Berlin. Like Knickerbocker, he had no conception of how bad things are out here.

Japanese troops are now fighting in the streets of the suburbs of Singapore. They are at Tanglin, three and a half miles from the center of the city.

At two minutes past midnight I gave my first broadcast on Australia: "The one word, Singapore, is the index to the outstanding story in Australia at the moment. Because of Singapore the people of this country are angry, bitter and more than apprehensive.

"And the temper of the people of this country is going to become of great importance to the United States.

"Many of the newspapers here are directing the sharpest criticisms against Great Britain's conduct of the war, criticisms of the mother country which have never appeared here before. In the past two days scores of people have told me that the chaos, defeats and constant retreats must end—and end at once. The Australians are now seeing Singapore, their first great barrier against an invader, in Japanese hands. That has alarmed them. The Australians, to a great degree, sat back for two years, confident that the great Naval Base would not only stop the Japanese, but throw back any attempt to encroach southward.

"And much of the people's bitterness comes from the fact that their men were forced to fight in Malaya and Singapore with very meager

497

air protection. That hasn't gone down very well with a country that sent its men to Crete.

"This country's second barrier is the Netherlands East Indies. The fate of NEI very probably will be decided in the next three to four weeks. Right now, outside of Java, the Japanese hold most of the outlying bases. They are in a position to hammer away at the naval base at Surabaya and at Batavia. And Darwin in North Australia is now well within the range of Japanese bombers.

"The Australians I've talked with frankly don't know how the Japanese can be kept away except by one method. They are counting on the United States to keep the Japanese out.

"The argument voiced most often is: America should fight from Australia, not so much for this country, as for America itself. If the Allies are driven out of Java and even Northern Australia, then all the vital bases for air attacks on the Japanese positions will be gone. The Japanese then must be attacked by sea from New Zealand, Hawaii and the west coast of the United States—thousands of miles away.

"In the countries where I've gone, preceding the outbreak of the war, I've found that the people cannot get ready until the bombs start dropping. There are many aspects of that here in Australia. The people here may be just a month or two away from actual attack; many of them realize it. But only now are there signs that the gigantic machinery necessary actually to repel and deal with the enemy is getting under way.

"Australia is at one of those points in history that comes once to every country—to be great or to be mediocre. It remains to be seen whether it will measure up to the role of greatness reserved for it and the United States in the Southwest Pacific."

Saturday, February 14th:

Joe Harsch and I did a broadcast together this morning. It went off very well.

Communications here are excellent. Cables come in with great speed and our transmissions to America are getting across with excellent clarity. The radio officials are very courteous and eager to co-operate.

The Australian papers report that there is considerable discussion in the newspapers in New York and London about my past few broadcasts. One of the editors at the *Sydney Sun* read me an editorial from the *New York Post,* saying: "Australia is to be congratulated on allowing Mr. Brown to broadcast the truth. His broadcasts are a great service to the Allied cause."

But I got a tip from a friend that the authorities here are very much alarmed by the repercussions of my broadcasts in London and are in quite a dither about them. I have an inkling, but no proof, that word has come from London to clamp down on me here. If that is the case, I doubt if the Australians will do it.

The *Sydney Mirror* carries a story from its London correspondent which says:

"The condemnation of Britain's conduct of the war has reached a peak in the papers here. Singapore's imminent fall and the escape from Brest to Heligoland of the *Prince Eugen, Gneisenau* and *Scharnhorst* are rocking Churchill's Cabinet."

The *London Economist:*

"Pain and bewilderment are the only possible reactions to the news from Singapore. Pain because there is apparently so little the British forces can do to check the irresistible Japanese advance . . . bewilderment that the island apparently so strongly fortified should be threatened so speedily . . . pain that so many Asiatics are exposed without defense to merciless attacks . . . pain that their loyalty and enthusiasm should have been called on so late . . . bewilderment that official statements should have been so hopelessly misleading about the true position."

The *London News Chronicle:*

"It is idle to disguise that we are facing a major catastrophe. There will undoubtedly be plausible excuses for the loss of Singapore, but how much longer must we be fobbed off by excuses?"

The columnist, Cassandra, of the *London Daily Mirror* wrote:

"It's no use crying over spilt milk, but what about spilt blood? What about squandered gold? The dead lie unburied on the fields of Singapore Island. The Japanese have wrenched out this cornerstone of the greatest Empire in history and have propped it up as a jeering monument to brave men who are dying for the folly of others who have much on their conscience.

"They do not wish anything to be said about the vast catastrophe. They pretend that a respectful silence is the only decent way to handle the grim business.

"They are quick to yell 'scapegoat hunter' to anyone who asks for some account of the shameful stewardship that has lost our place in the East.

"The bereaved and wounded cannot be forgotten by an easy apology. They cannot be dismissed with a graceful gesture of sympathy."

This is St. Valentine's Day.

It's a grim climax to Singapore Naval Base. Four years ago today Sir Shenton Thomas, the Colonial Governor, officially opened the Naval Base. Last year the Japanese were getting ready in French Indo-China and the AIF had just reached Malaya.

From last year's St. Valentine's Day until this the British maintained that Singapore was impregnable and there was nothing to worry about. In that year Singapore remained an air base without sufficient planes and a naval base without warships, except for the disastrous last-minute dash of the *Repulse* and *Prince of Wales*. And today, too, the British news agency, *Reuters*, put out a statement that "Rangoon is more important than Singapore." I wonder if the British will ever learn a lesson from experience.

Sunday, February 15th:
CBS cabled me this morning:

SOMEWHAT AFRAID YOU UNWITTINGLY TAKING CRUSADING ATTITUDE YOUR BROADCASTS. CERTAINLY HAVE NO INTENTION GLOSS OVER INEFFICIENCY DISPLAYED BY ANY ALLY BUT FEEL IN VIEW SINGAPORE BAN GENERAL PUBLIC WILL FEEL YOU ARE PAYING OFF OLD DEBTS. THUS PLEASE EXERCISE CAUTION REGARDING FAULTFINDING EXCEPT WHERE IT IS NECESSARY IN ANY OBJECTIVE NEWS REPORTING. THINK OVERDOSE HARSH CRITICISMS WHICH FAIRLY EASY FIND ANYWHERE IN WORLD THESE DAYS WOULD TEND EVENTUALLY DETRACT YOUR WORTH AND PLACE IN PUBLIC CONFIDENCE

PAUL WHITE

This was the first suggestion I had ever received from CBS regarding my news reporting.

I cabled Paul White:

THANKS YOUR CABLE. WILL USE UTMOST CAUTION. HEARTILY AGREE OVERDOSE HARSH CRITICISM UNWISE AND NOW IS MOMENT TO

Here is the broadcast heard in America that evening:

"An honest report on what preceded the war against Singapore, how it was fought and how the Japanese got there, must contain recriminations. But recriminations will not win this war. Once the mistakes are known, fault-finding deters the job of getting on to victory.

"Out here, in the Southwest Pacific battle front, it's apparent that in the business of starting to win this war every minute counts. Out here, the danger is real, vivid and seems almost overwhelming. The Allies at this moment stand in very grave danger of losing every vantage point from which to fight this war.

"That danger could be met by profiting by and wiping out the mistakes of Singapore. Singapore *can* be the turning point of the war.

"The grim experience of that fortress offers all those lessons which can make it the springboard to certain victory. As we see it here, the Japanese capture of Singapore can fire the Allies into a dynamic prosecution of the war.

"As a reporter of this war, I've seen how both sides operate—with the Italians in Rome, among the Germans in Yugoslavia, with the British in Syria and the Western Desert of Egypt. And for six months I was in Singapore. These observations are based on those eyewitness experiences.

"The outstanding moral of Singapore is that the Allies have no shortage of courage. The incredible heroism of the English, Scotch, Australian and Indian troops I've seen is as much as any nation can ask for and sometimes more than a country can expect.

"Singapore demonstrated that naked courage, unaided and unsupported by modern methods and means, can't win a war.

"The Japanese are at Singapore, and pushing everywhere against the Dutch East Indies, Australia and Burma because they were underestimated by the British. Experience now could eliminate that notion of the enemy.

"The Japanese are tough, well-trained, shrewd and fanatical fighters. It's a sacred honor to them to die. They show no concern about the casualties they suffer. Their organization is superb, and their staff work is as brilliant as any shown by either side thus far in Europe or

Asia. They have not missed a trick, and made only one mistake—sending a convoy into the Macassar Straits without sufficient protection.

"The Japanese don't stop to consolidate their position. Their whole theory is to attack, drive on, give neither themselves nor the Allies a chance for a second breath.

"Singapore showed, as operations against the Dutch still do, that the Japanese don't worry too much about lines of communication. In Malaya, they brought trucks and barges right up to the front lines with their advance points. The methods used by the Japanese show that if they win the first four rounds of the fight—the Philippines, Singapore, Dutch East Indies and Burma—the other rounds can take care of themselves. Their methods indicate the attitude: time enough then to consolidate positions.

"The Japanese are not frightened by the sight of the Stars and Stripes or the Union Jack. They are not intimidated by the spectacle in the South China Sea of 62,000 tons of super battleships known as the *Repulse* and the *Prince of Wales*.

"At the moment, as Singapore has shown, it takes aircraft, swarms of *good* aircraft, to back up those banners and battleships. Singapore provides the tragic example of the need for bombers and fighters to stop the Japanese.

"Not only numbers, manned by experienced pilots, daring and ingenious in attack and bombing, but interceptor ships that can get up in the air at 3,000 feet a minute, and then move with zest and snap at 25,000 feet.

"American pilots assured me that we have the type of aircraft in America and the experienced pilots that can drive the Jap out of these tropical skies. Experts tell me that just a few squadrons of those at the beginning of the attack on Malaya—those or Hurricanes—could have changed the whole picture. And thirty Flying Fortresses in late December might have spelled the difference between victory and defeat.

"Singapore and the subsequent operations going on right now show the need of speed and the urgency of rushing help to the point attacked. And co-operation must be instantaneous among the various Allied countries.

"Singapore showed that in critical circumstances red tape, tradi-

502

tional ways of doing things and observing hard and fast rules of text-books rather well guarantee defeat.

"Singapore showed that to fight a 1942 war it requires daring commanders, men with agile minds, men who are not even content to imitate the enemy but have the capacity to outsmart him. One lesson of Singapore is the need of commanders who are not burdened by a defensive mentality. The cry of most officers in Singapore and in Java was attack, attack and attack again. And that is the answer right now too. The Japanese took the initiative and have held it since.

"Singapore furnished proof that this war must be fought twenty-four hours a day and seven days a week. The Japs fight twenty-four hours a day; they are not observing week-ends.

"This is a ruthless war, without rules. What I've seen of it bears no resemblance either to football or cricket. In the operations to date it's apparent that either gangsters must fight like gentlemen or the gentlemen like gangsters. There isn't much chance of the Axis changing.

"The Japanese machine-gun pilots coming down by parachutes. The Japs take the attitude, too, that a hospital ship carries wounded who, when they recover, will return to fight them. Sinking hospital ships isn't humane, but the Japanese military view is: anything goes.

"Singapore is evidence, too, that wishful thinking won't keep the Japanese away. If it would, the Japs would never have swarmed from Thailand into Malaya.

"Singapore showed that this is total war, and that every man, woman and child is part of the war machine. If, at Singapore, the military authorities had recognized that unavoidable fact, the morale of the people and resistance to the enemy might have been better sustained.

"Concealing a reasonable picture from those people who must fight—as the people of Singapore were called upon to fight—had disastrous effects. After more than a week of fighting at the start of the war, the people were first informed that the Japanese were already seventy-five miles inside Malaya. They were shocked and frightened by this tardy news. They viewed all subsequent announcements with suspicion, and from then on, fantastic rumors of the approach of the enemy were spread.

"That is one of the greatest lessons of Singapore—that suppression

503

of a reasonable account of the progress of the war provides every facility to the Fifth Columnists to destroy confidence.

"In Malaya, Fifth Columnists showed how just one of them can stab thousands of defenders in the back. That being so, squeamishness in preventing the growth of a Fifth-Column organization or stamping it out after war comes makes the defense of a country somewhat more than difficult.

"It takes foresight, courage and realism to operate a scorched-earth policy. Singapore paid the penalty for not having these. The attitude there was: 'We'll be coming back here very soon,' forgetting that when *that* happened, the Japanese would have destroyed everything before getting out.

"In the Far East, the Dutch have shown that the lesson of Singapore already has been adopted. The Dutch have scorched earth with a courage that makes it one of the great stories of heroism of this or any war.

"Singapore furnished an astonishing example of Japanese driving power. To curb that drive, to hold bases, and to win back bases the Japs already have, means that the Allies will have to achieve at least a seventy-five percent equality in man power, aircraft and ships.

"The result of that is this: queer, exotic names like Balikpapan, Terakan, Kuantan, Ipoh, Kuching, Rabaul, Macassar, Amboina are not only milestones of the Japanese progress in the South Pacific.

"Every observer out here is convinced those places must become the battleground of American and Allied soldiers, and then the stepping stones to the defeat of Japan.

"That's the inevitable aftermath of a Singapore that provides almost every example of what to avoid in order to win victory."

AUSTRALIA

Monday, February 16th:
Just as I sat down in front of the microphone to make my broadcast, George Folster came dashing into the studio.

"Singapore has fallen!" he shouted.

It was as though I had lost my best friend. I knew the city was dying, knew it from August 3rd. On December 7th, Singapore started its death throes. When I left on January 23rd, the violence of death was still on it. But now that it was dead, it still came as a great shock.

When I walked back from the studio to the hotel, I was in a daze. Newspaper posters, screaming, "Singapore Falls," were like flat slaps across my face.

Prime Minister Curtin issued a statement today describing the fall of Singapore as the opening battle of Australia.

"I tell this nation that, as things stand today, brains and brawn are better than even bets or beer."

I lunched with five officers today of the Australian Broadcasting Commission at the Carleton Hotel. They told me that they had inquired four weeks ago of the naval authorities what the radio was to do in case of air raids.

"Oh, we'll just throw a switch and cut you all off," the naval officer was quoted as saying.

"But that will frighten people. What about civilian morale?"

"We are not concerned about civilian morale," the broadcast officials said they were told.

Is it to be the Singapore attitude again?

This evening I saw the motion picture, *Sundown.*

The story of the fall of Singapore is grim reading. Lieutenant General Percival and Lieutenant General Yamashita signed the surrender terms at 10:00 P.M. Sunday and "cease firing" came at 1:00 A.M. One

AIF officer who got out said it was like plunging a fork into a sponge. "We gave them everything we had but still they came on."

One of the most treacherous statements I have ever read is printed in the *Sydney Daily Mirror* today and the words come from the naval correspondent of the newspaper group which publishes the *London Daily Sketch*. This is the paper of Leonard Mosley who sent stories from Singapore about the clouds of bombers and fighters over Malaya to ward off an invasion, and who admitted to me that he was giving optimistic pictures of Singapore and reporting that nothing would happen in the Far East, because he wanted to go back to Cairo.

The naval correspondent of the Allied newspapers is quoted as saying: "Arguments that the Japanese occupation of Singapore produces a threat to traffic west of Colombo and even to our main supply route to the Middle East by way of the Gulf of Aden and back to Russia by way of the Persian Gulf are mischievous exaggerations.

"The Japanese have not gained a base," he went on to say, "but only a harbor at Singapore, because all repair facilities and supplies had been wrecked by the British.

"The threat to the Indian Ocean was not as great as certain irresponsible politicians and ill-informed theorists with little knowledge of modern sea warfare have stridently asserted."

That naval correspondent is a worthy colleague of Mosley. Japanese submarines and warships can now move into the Indian Ocean.

Churchill's speech today contained an astonishing admission. He said: "We didn't believe the Japanese would go to war."

If Churchill believed that, it was no wonder Sir Robert Brooke-Popham's appeals to London met with, "Now, now, don't get excited. Nothing is going to happen out there," or words to that effect. If that was the War Office's view and the opinion of the Admiralty, it's no wonder that we had so much difficulty in trying to convince the Public Relations Office to get ready to cover a war. With that mental attitude, Singapore officials were justified in saying, "Why get ready for something that is not going to happen?"

While the barber in the Australia Hotel was cutting my hair this morning, I asked him if he had heard Churchill's speech.

"Yes, I heard it."

"What did you think of it?"

506

"Well," he said, "it was the same bloody hooey. Eighteen months ago he said Singapore could be held and today he told us it had fallen."

Tuesday, February 17th:
The Japanese are attacking Sumatra now and they have taken Palembang, 280 miles south of Singapore. It means the loss of ninety percent of the oil supplies of the Indies.

Lord Wedgwood's speech in London is prominently displayed here today. He said: "There appears to be a fixed and settled principle of the British Army that it is the exclusive privilege of Englishmen to lay down their lives for liberty. The exclusive principle is dangerous to the Empire. We might have had a half million trained Chinese troops fighting on our side in Malaya but for this army attitude."

Prime Minister Curtin says that Singapore is Australia's Dunkirk.

"Hours previously devoted to sport and leisure," he insists, "must now be given to the duties of war."

Minister for the Army Francis Forde says: "The Government's considered view is that the situation in the Pacific is capable of control."

William Hughes, the Billy Hughes who was Labor Prime Minister in the last war, says: "Australia must be held at all costs, but without air power we will perish."

This morning the Dutch Consul General here telephoned that Dr. Hubertus van Mook, Lieutenant Governor of NEI, wants to see me. He has just come in from Washington.

Dr. van Mook is a big, hearty fellow.

"I asked to see you because I would like to hear the truth about Singapore," he said.

I told him what happened.

Then Dr. van Mook gave me his reactions: "I talked with Roosevelt, Nelson, Marshall, Arnold and the Navy people. They are all alive to the situation but I was not impressed by your Navy."

"Why not?"

"The Navy lost seven battleships at Pearl Harbor." [Van Mook was wrong. It is definitely known that only two battleships were lost, and one of them may yet be salvaged.] "Two cruisers were damaged, but

507

could be taken to the west coast and are now being repaired. Now they don't want to take any more chances. Battleships aren't much good any more. They are no good at all in the South China Sea. They cost too much and they aren't worth it. I was in Honolulu, too. I wasn't at all impressed. The captains and some of the rear admirals are young and capable, but I think some of your higher Navy men are old-fashioned. It took me a month and a half of argument in Washington," Dr. van Mook said, "to get Admiral Helfrich appointed to succeed Admiral Hart."

He added: "It's a mistake to figure in terms of six months in building up reserves instead of thinking what can be done in the next three weeks. We can hold Java if they send every available plane and ship to the points where the Japanese are and not wait until everything is in perfect shape and according to textbooks."

Singapore is providing the Australians a fine springboard for criticisms of England. Anger has long been here, and has been awaiting a great issue for release. The Australians, for all their lethargy and their slow way of moving, love action. They have a great fondness for energetic sports, and Britain's way of fighting the war has been too static for them.

The Australians are still bitter over Crete, where their troops had practically no air protection. Now they have lost another ten or twelve thousand of their volunteers, their best fighters, in Malaya.

Actually, the Australians feel in the same position as any subject people, crown colony, dominion or minor ally. Australia gave loyalty, man power, money, production and sentiment to Great Britain. In return, they counted on protection that might be needed some day. That protection has failed to materialize, and loyalty, and certainly affection, are being strained.

One vitally debated point here in Australia now is whether troops should be sent to help in the defense of Java. The Constitution forbids the sending of conscripted Home Guard forces outside the country. The volunteers are almost all in the Middle East, except those captured at Malaya.

I asked Major General Wynter, who is G.O.C. of the Eastern Command, if a constitutional provision were made for sending the

508

Home Guard outside the country what he thought about Australians helping to defend Java.

"My attitude is," General Wynter said, "there is no point in sending troops unless they are effective."

"Then the conclusion is," I said, "that you don't have trained, effective troops that could be sent."

"That's right," he said.

This evening I went to the home of Dr. Schurmann, the Dutch Consul General. Dr. van Mook was there and also Premier McKell of New South Wales; Dr. Herbert V. Evatt, Minister of External Affairs of Australia; a judge whose name I didn't get and two editors, McClure-Smith of the *Sydney Herald* and Frank Packer of the *Sydney Telegraph*.

Dr. Evatt talked in clichés and I could make little sense out of his vituperations against other peoples. Then he launched an attack against journalists. Frank Packer sat back smiling cynically.

Then Evatt pulled out a clipping of an article written by Joe Harsch and reprinted in the local papers today. The article discussed what I had already broadcast—the arguments going on in Australia about whether Australians should send troops to Java in order to protect the outer barrier of Australia. Harsch's view was that the more realistic and far-sighted observers believed that Australia's only chance is to fight for the active defense of the Indies.

Harsch criticized "selfish interests" and mentioned that a prominent labor leader spent an entire evening with him insisting that guarantees for more labor benefits constitute the immediate need. To that labor leader the most urgent problem was the destruction of the profit system. With Singapore falling, he wanted to impose on the nation new labor benefits as the price of full labor support for the war effort. Dr. Evatt denounced the contents of Harsch's article.

"This is deliberate Fifth Column. This man Harsch ought to be thrown in jail."

However, Evatt, in all his oratorical outburst, did not read the part about the labor leader I have just mentioned. Harsch had shown me his article before he cabled it to Boston and I knew its text.

"Dr. Evatt," I said, "why don't you read the part about that labor leader?"

"Where, where? There's nothing in here about a labor leader."

I pointed it out to him.

"Oh, that! He wasn't with any labor leader. He just sat down and made that up."

One of the other men there said: "No, I was with Harsch when he had that discussion. It was a correct quotation of his remarks."

The name was given, but Dr. Evatt dismissed the individual as unimportant.

Dr. Evatt insisted that Major-General Gordon Bennett, the AIF commander in Malaya, got everything he asked for.

"I don't believe that's correct, Dr. Evatt," I interposed. "General Bennett told me that he had two brigades and that he was trying to get a third brigade to round out a division."

"When did he tell you that?"

"It was on October 2nd."

"Oh, that was five days before the Labor Government came in. Our Government gave him everything he asked for."

"Well, Dr. Evatt, I checked on that point this afternoon. I had a talk with Major-General Wynter, and he said the third brigade was not sent."

"The Labor Government gave Bennett everything he asked for," Evatt insisted.

The Australian Foreign Minister bitterly criticized Harsch's statements about there being no conscription here to send troops abroad.

"I have a suggestion for you, Dr. Evatt," I said. "You have disagreed with every statement I make about the situation in Australia. You disagree with every statement that Harsch makes. You are going to disagree with anything any American reporter says when he comes here to report on Australia's war effort. The thing for you to do is to just bar every American reporter. That's the only way you'll prevent statements being made that you disagree with."

From the Dutch Consul's home I hurried in a taxi to keep a midnight appointment with Prime Minister Curtin. When I got to the Carleton Hotel, where he was staying, I was met by Donald Rogers, his secretary and unofficial adviser.

"The P.M. was taken to the hospital," Rogers said. "I'm very sorry. There was no time to reach you. Acute gastritis. Not serious."

That's the way Rogers talked. A former newspaperman, he was small, slim, wiry, dynamic and efficient. He was one of the most capable officials I met in Australia.

I asked Rogers for the view of the Federal Government on helping Java.

"Well," Rogers said, "we believe that Wavell is concerned mostly about holding Burma and not Java."

"Then," I asked, "is Australia now operating on the premise that Java has been lost?"

"Yes."

"That means the idea of sending troops from here is a dead issue, even if you had them to send."

"That's right."

Just before he was taken to the hospital, Curtin ordered "total mobilization of all resources—human and material—to insure the defense of the country."

I asked Rogers what that meant exactly.

"Here is the statement I gave out afterwards on it: It means that anyone in Australia who has anything or who is anything can be ordered to do whatever the Government chooses he shall do."

"Is that conscription of man power for the army and factories and is it conscription of wealth as well?" I asked.

"Not exactly. You see, those words were used to have a psychological effect—economic, military and mental without actually conscripting men for overseas duty or confiscating wealth to fight the war. But the P.M. is not going to explain anything. Any explanation, you know, creates loopholes, and an Australian will jump through any loophole as soon as he finds it."

"Outside of the psychological effect, what's Curtin actually going to do?"

"Curtin's attitude is that he isn't going to explain anything about this mobilization. He told me this afternoon, 'I'm either a man or a mouse and if I'm a mouse they can vote me out.'

"The Australians are an undisciplined people. Life has been too easy for us. We're like you people in many ways. We'll fight all right, and we'll fight for our home soil. It's difficult to arouse us by words and appeals. They'll do what they are told to do."

"And Curtin is going to tell them? They want strong leadership?"

511

"Yes, that's why the P.M. is trying to tell them what they must do. Submit to conscription of all workers and resources. He'll move gradually. Within two weeks horse racing will be stopped. There will be a number of disciplinary decrees."

George Folster and I outlined to Rogers what we wanted in the way of reporting facilities.

"CBS now has three men here," I said. "I expect to go back to the States, but Bill Dunn will be getting evacuated from Java any day. If he gets away all right, he'll come down. CBS intends to cover Australia, but we'd like some co-operation from you people."

"You can count on us."

We explained that we are trying to establish a transmitter at Darwin, and that some progress has been made. Could he expedite that? He could. There is some trouble with censorship, too much of the Singapore mentality and business as usual, could he look into that? He could and would.

"What kind of propaganda are you people going to put out?" I asked. "Are you going to present a picture to the Japs that you have everything and will wipe them out if they come down here, or are you going to be calling to America for help?"

"I can't answer that," Rogers said.

"It would be a good thing for correspondents to know. Singapore's propaganda was that the British are invulnerable and the Japs would be damn fools to attack. If you take that line here, you can't at the same time appeal to America for help and expect to be believed. It is one or the other."

"I do know," Rogers said, "the view of the military is that if we tell the world we don't have very much that will invite a Japanese attack."

"That," I remarked, "was the view of the military in Singapore. That would be all right if the Japanese espionage system wasn't working in Australia just as it worked so efficiently in Singapore. You expose yourself so easily with putting out that invulnerability stuff. While you are doing it the Japanese Intelligence has facts to show the contrary, and it convinces them you are weak."

"It's the military that has to decide those things," Rogers explained.

"Do what you can, will you? Every minute counts," I said. "American correspondents can make America Australia-conscious. That's our job.

512

It can be done in two ways. You make the events, and we'll tell them to America—if the censors will let us."

"That's all we ask," Rogers said. "I'll have a special man installed in the censorship office to deal only with the copy of American correspondents."

Thursday, February 19th:
Governor and Lady Wakehurst of New South Wales invited me to luncheon at Government House. Also there were Admiral Guy Royale, chief of the Australian Naval Board; a British colonel; Peter Lubbock, the Governor's secretary; Miss Wakehurst and George Folster. They were keenly interested to hear the story of the *Repulse* and what happened at Singapore.

"Yes," Admiral Royale said afterwards, "it was a very bad situation at Singapore. Brooke-Popham told me the only thing to do was to resign. It was the only thing he thought he could do to wake up the War Office to the situation out there."

"Why didn't he resign?"

"Well," the admiral said, "he didn't think it would do any good actually."

In discussing the internal situation in Australia, I pointed out that it was inconceivable that a country on the verge of attack should be having strikes. Eleven coal mines are on strike at the moment.

"The workers have their case," the Governor said. "Their whole life has been devoted to the problems of labor: shorter hours, better wages, improved conditions. It is almost too much to expect them overnight to forget that life-long struggle and sacrifice it for another struggle. This habit of a lifetime can hardly be eliminated overnight."

Lord Wakehurst, tall, well-groomed, occupying a sinecure in the British Empire administration with practically no duties except attending social functions and being a front for the British Empire, was certainly the last man I ever expected to uphold the case for the workers.

"What concerns me," the Governor said, "is all this criticism of leadership which might weaken confidence in all leadership. In effect, each man with a gun might consider himself the best judge of how to use it."

It was easy to understand how authority might be concerned with this wave of criticism of Churchill and of the British military leadership.

"Yes, I agree that might be the case," I said. "Therefore, it is up to the leadership to nip that in the bud by their dynamic control of the minor men. Take Pearl Harbor, for example. As soon as we saw that a mistake had been made, President Roosevelt removed Admiral Kimmel and General Short. As a result there was no wave of criticism in America of President Roosevelt. There were no cries of 'Why keep these men in their jobs?' On the other hand, Churchill has allowed men to stay in their posts when all the facts show that they were incompetent. It is up to Churchill to stop criticism by taking action. You know, Governor," I remarked, "the British method is to promote a man who makes mistakes instead of firing him. There is no second chance in warfare and yet almost invariably you have given even more responsible jobs to your generals after they make mistakes."

"It is all very well," Lord Wakehurst said, "to make observations in retrospect. After a thing has happened we can see where mistakes were made."

"It was obvious, Lord Wakehurst, to a schoolboy," I said, "that Japan was going into the war. You will admit that she had to go to war now before she became weakened by our freezing orders. Any observer at Singapore who wasn't blind to what was going on could see that the war was coming. Obviously, she would have to attack both Britain and the United States. She had to eliminate the threat of the Philippines if she went into Malaya and she had to eliminate Malaya before she could get at what she really wanted, the oil of the Dutch East Indies. Despite all of these obvious signs of what was going to happen, the British in Singapore scoffed at the possibility of war."

"Not only they," Admiral Royale interjected, "but the highest forces thought the same. Mr. Churchill himself thought that. He even said so in his speech yesterday."

As we were going out after luncheon, Sir Charles Burnett, Chief of the Royal Australian Air Force, came into the Governor's mansion.

"Darwin has just been bombed," he said. "I'm going up north."

When I returned to the hotel I found there was a cable from Paul White informing me that I had been awarded the annual prize from the Overseas Press Club for the best radio reporting for 1941 and was

514

to make a broadcast to the banquet of the club at the Waldorf-Astoria in New York.

Friday, February 20th:
I wrote a broadcast for the Overseas Press Club, accepting the award. C. A. Rorke, the chief censor in Sydney, killed out passages in the broadcast, which made me suspicious of him and which I took up with the Internal Security.

Here is the broadcast I gave. The italicized passages represent the material cut out by Rorke:

"This is Cecil Brown in Sydney speaking to the guests at the annual dinner of the Overseas Press Club of America gathered at the Waldorf-Astoria in New York.

"I am most appreciative and indebted to this organization for this high honor for radio reporting. But with every sincerity I must say that this award should not have been given to one individual but to the entire corps of American radio correspondents. Every one of them has done a superb job of reporting. They have done and are doing their utmost to keep the American people informed.

"And it is a great tribute to the American radio correspondents that, *hemmed in by extraordinary pressures and intimidations in most foreign countries in which they operate,* they have gone on insisting, persuading, fighting and winning in the job of doing factual reporting for America.

"When you hear a broadcast from most countries abroad of three, four or five minutes, that represents three, four or five hours of *fight.* (The censor changed this to "work" and ended the sentence there.) *Yes, it is a fight with censorship before the correspondent wins the right to go before the microphone.*

"*We fight for every word in our scripts because* in our best judgment we feel every word represents a fact which the American people are entitled to know.

"And that's our guiding star in radio reporting this war—the undeniable right of Americans to know the facts. Our conviction is that the American people have the capacity to accept those facts with firmness and understanding.

"For in covering this crucial period in history there is no more precious duty than to present the facts to his audience.

"It has been my job to report this war from battlefronts where *permission* to give the truth was not easy. As a reporter of the Columbia Broadcasting System, it is my great privilege to work for an organization that backed me to the hilt in getting those facts to America.

"My contact with this war, on both sides, has been intimate—sometimes too intimate for comfort and dryness.

"From these battlefront experiences have come two main convictions —that this is a war of every man, woman and child, and that freedom of speech within the bounds of *reasonable censorship* (the censor put in the word "security") is one of the sure roads to victory.

"The people are as much a part of the war machine as the soldiers fighting and dying under dive bombers and machine guns. *And to conceal from the people a reasonable report on what is going on makes freedom of speech something more dynamic than an academic phrase. Denial of freedom of speech is a devastating experience.*

"*I saw it happen in Rome and I saw it again in Singapore. It is heartbreaking to watch defeatism sweeping across a country, to see morale disintegrating before your eyes.*

"*And in Rome and Singapore it came almost overnight. It came because authorities, who expected of their people the courage to die, did not trust that courage to know the truth.*

"No correspondent wants to give military information to the enemy. *But petty, picayune, uninformed censorship is one of the prime saboteurs of morale.*

"There is no want of courage and vigor among our United Nations. I have seen too many of our men die to think we are short of courage. That strength is great enough to stand a reasonable report of the war.

"Of the freedoms for which we fight, the freedom to know what is happening to our men and our destinies is among the most vital.

"The freedom to report that, within the bounds of *reasonable censorship*, is one of the greatest guarantees of victory."

I was unable to see Rorke that night. I immediately telephoned to E. G. Bonney, the chief censor in Canberra, and to Don Rogers, the Prime Minister's secretary, also in Canberra. Rogers said he would immediately look into the matter. Then, when I located Bonney, I pointed out that this broadcast was not on the CBS network but was direct to a private gathering in a hotel in New York.

516

"The type of censorship of this script," I told Bonney, "makes me highly suspicious of your censorship office in Sydney, and whether you permit it or not I am going to give this broadcast. If you cut me off the air, I am going to take the matter up with Washington."

"What is the broadcast?"

I then read the script over the telephone to the chief censor in Canberra.

"Why, yes," Bonney said, "that entire broadcast can go. I see nothing whatever wrong with it."

"I agree with you, but you will notice that your chief censor in Sydney has eliminated even the disparaging remarks about Rome, which you know is the capital of a Fascist country. He has not even permitted me to use the word censorship."

"Yes, it is very strange," Bonney said. "I am investigating that whole Sydney set-up and I would like to have a copy of your broadcast to help my investigation."

Saturday, February 21st:

The bombing of Darwin came as a great shock. Most of the details are being withheld from the people, and it is much more serious than the people know or are being allowed to know. The Government is in a bit of a whirl about the whole thing.

The *Sun* explained in an editorial today that before the bombing of Darwin: "We were remote, our 'splendid isolation' geographically had built up a mental insularity. We blindly accepted the inheritance of freedom and abundance. We enjoyed our high living standard, sunshine and a clear view of human happiness. We were uninhibited. Being energetically healthy turned our love of sport into a national fetish. "We were indeed rather smug," concluded this editorial, "because great tragedies had not touched us. It was an Indian summer."

Here is what happened at Darwin, but the people don't know it, either here or in America:

A number of ships were sunk in the harbor; the attack came as a complete surprise; many American aircraft were destroyed on the ground, both fighters and bombers; the airdrome buildings and barracks had direct hits and were flattened out. The Japs were able to come down and machine-gun the personnel.

The *Sydney Sun*, in an editorial, calls for the end of "these Darwins.

517

It appears to have been as much a surprise as was the attack on Pearl Harbor. Bombs actually had fallen before the people knew a raid was on. Why should Darwin have been caught flat-footed? Was there no raid detector?"

The answer to that was that there was no wireless detection apparatus sent to Darwin. The first the military at Darwin knew the raid was on was when the bombs started to fall.

The *Daily Mirror* headlines its editorial today this way: "Beer Orgy Calls for Prime Minister's Intervention."

Wednesday, February 25th:
On the train from Sydney to Canberra there were several Government officials and a number of newspapermen. The gist of their remarks was:

"Australia must pass through an ordeal of fire before it wakes up. It needs a dynamic leader to tell them what to do."

They also talked about Dr. Evatt, and I heard from them, as I had from everyone I talked with, that Dr. Evatt has one of the keenest minds in Australia. He was one of the youngest men to ascend the bench.

"Dr. Evatt," they said, "is a man of overweening ambition. He wants to run Australia. That ambition has blinded him to many things."

I commented that in my previous meeting with Evatt I got the impression that he was bitterly anti-English.

They smiled at me and said that he is notorious for his anti-English attitude and that it is long-standing, since his university days in England. Then, they said, he was very unhappy and he took the vindictive attitude: "I will show these English people some day."

Shortly after I arrived at the Commonwealth capital at Canberra I called on Bonney, the chief censor. He turned out to be a very pleasant and co-operative individual, and I explained what American correspondents wanted to do. He promised every assistance and said that he was investigating the Sydney censorship office, adding, "I think I am going to clean house out there."

Nelson T. Johnson, American Minister to Australia, was formerly

518

in China. We sat in his pleasant office with a long view of Canberra from the window. I asked the Minister about Australia's possibilities as an Allied base in the Southwest Pacific.

"That's a difficult question to answer. There are seven million people here. They are somewhat disillusioned. Yet, the people are willing and anxious to go ahead with the war effort."

"Is it a matter of leadership, then?" I asked. "What about Curtin?"

"He is a very sincere, earnest man and capable of making his own decisions. He is a politician and he must obviously be trying to hold his party together."

"That means that he makes some decisions primarily because of party interest."

"Well, I don't know how much party politics would interfere with Australia's getting ready," Johnson said. "There is still considerable self-interest among the politicians."

"Do you think Curtin has the qualities to make a great leader?"

"Oh, I wouldn't dare to attempt an answer to that question!"

One of the most incredible men I ever encountered in political life was the Army Minister, Francis Forde. In his office in Parliament House he acted as harassed as if a Japanese division were chasing him. His manner was to keep saying, "Yes, yes, yes," whether you were saying anything or not. In my talk with him there were periods of half-minute silences and during that time Forde kept saying: "Yes, yes, yes," as though he were in a dream.

I tried to get some kind of a statement out of him for publication but he insisted that he deals with secret work. Finally he had this to say: "Australia is ready for the great role she is destined to play as an Allied base. We have the facilities, resources and much of the materials. But we do require the wholehearted assistance of the Allies because of our huge territory and comparatively small population. As we become more and more of a base it takes a tremendous recruitment of workers for the factories."

Don Rogers took me to the press gallery at the House for the sitting. It has green leather seats in a horseshoe shape, with a rather elongated center where there is a long table at which sit the Prime Minister and four bewigged clerks, and the table is piled high with books and papers.

519

At one end of the table is the Speaker's chair, a replica of the Speaker's chair in the House of Commons.

I sat through part of that session at the House, listening in amazement to the inane, vapid utterings of the men who represented the people of Australia. They were concerned with pork-barrel measures and incidentals of no importance even in peace time.

As I was walking from the House to the hotel a Senator asked me what I thought of the session.

"I'd rather not tell you," I said.

I met a lobbyist who has been here for many years. He said it was the worst exhibition in the twenty years he has been attending sessions. A newspaperman said he'd been covering sessions since 1936 and he'd never seen anything like it.

"Why?" I asked.

"The lack of realism, the absence of intelligent remarks, the frantic panicky nature of their remarks, and their obstructionism at such an important moment."

"It was a wonderful opportunity," I suggested, "for someone to get up and say he has many problems serious to his constituents but they are less important than doing everything directly concerned with the war's prosecution."

The newspaperman laughed sardonically.

The legislative correspondent of the *Sydney Telegraph* wrote: "The members of the House of Representatives established an all-time Federation record for disgraceful behavior and parroted stupid, childish questions. They postured and semaphored. They made a cockshy of democracy and transformed Australia's blackest crisis into a salesman's convention."

The House gave the impression not that Darwin had just been bombed, but that the Japanese were at least a million miles away.

Don Rogers arranged for me to see Prime Minister Curtin in his office at Parliament House. He has a wide, spacious office all in blue and walnut paneling with a thick blue carpet. He is a gray man of fifty-seven in a dark blue, ill-fitting suit and a heavy gold chain across his vest. He smoked a cigarette as we talked and offered me one out of the humidor. I admired the humidor, and he explained that it was made from the wood of the *H.M.S. Sydney* which sank the *Emden* in the last war. The ash trays were from *H.M.S. Australia,* the flagship of the Australian fleet, which was sunk off Sydney's Head in accordance with the Washington Naval Restriction Conference of 1921.

"I was very happy you used the word 'urgency' in the House this afternoon," I said. "That is the precise word. It's too late to get ready for a war when the bombs start dropping. Mr. Prime Minister, I find here the same absence of dynamic commanders, lack of preparation, inadequate training of troops and the conviction that it can't and won't happen here."

"Just a minute, just a minute," Curtin said hastily, and swung forward in his seat. "I'm very much impressed with what you are saying."

He whipped out a piece of paper and a pen and began scribbling down notes as I talked.

"Would you repeat a few of those things you just said?"

I did so and added: "There must be a self-discipline, a self-inventory of every individual to decide whether he wants to be a slave or free," and he wrote that down.

Then I asked the Prime Minister to give me a statement. I told him that I was going on the air to America in the morning, and he dictated a statement which combined every flowery cliché of a half century ago. But there was in his statement a depth of sincerity and determination and the honesty that is the character of Curtin and the Australian people.

When he had finished his statement I said: "Will you also say America will not find Australia wanting courage, energy and initiative?"

"Yes, yes, write that down too."

Diary Comment:

You get the impression here in Canberra that nothing that is being done is very important, neither what happens to the country nor what is being done to protect it from the outside, that this Government is a very small cog in a wheel operating such huge forces and that the men who make it go know very little about it. The air of incompetence is very heavy about this place.

There is in the background of this country much that makes for pity and for tragedy. From the Australian's concealed inferiority feeling springs an inordinate, unbalanced pride in his land. He boasts end-

521

lessly about its superiority without knowing very much about its potentialities.

I think the most unpopular man here is Dr. Evatt. As Minister of External Affairs he takes an imperious attitude, perhaps unconsciously, with all the foreign legations. Evatt wants to know about everything and is often peremptory with the civil servants of the Government But, with all that, he is a man of great energy and ambition.

On the train from Canberra to Melbourne, Dr. Evatt and John Beasley, the Minister of Supply, asked me to sit with them. It seemed strange that they should question me on battle strategy. Their remarks convinced me that they were completely baffled about the whole world set-up. Evatt particularly showed an animus toward the English. No matter what I said, he interspersed my remarks with: "That's just the way the English do things."

Friday, February 27th:
My first move in Melbourne was to go to the American Naval Headquarters to see Admiral Leary. He was busy and I saw Captain Herbert Jones, his aide, to make arrangements for getting transportation to America.

"Yes, we have some word for you," Captain Jones said. "The Secretary of the Navy has sent a message to do everything we could to facilitate your return. The Naval Attaché here is handling the matter."

Melbourne is a madhouse. American troops and nurses arrived here today. The papers, however, can't mention their presence because it has not yet been revealed that American troops are here. Everyone in Australia knows it, but censorship forbids it to be printed locally or cabled abroad.

Saturday, February 28th:
The aircraft tender *Langley* was sunk by Jap bombers yesterday. It was carrying desperately needed planes to Java.

Melbourne is in the midst of the two days out of the week that Australians don't work. A suit can't be pressed until Monday. No laundry can be done for two or three days. I thought it was typical today when I attempted to have my fountain pen fixed. I had broken it yesterday while I was having a long talk with William Dunston, editor of the *Melbourne Herald*.

522

I took the pen to the Parker agency and the girl clerk said: "The repair man is not here. We close for the week-end."

"Why?"

"Why? There is a war on!"

That is the alibi for inefficiency, work-dodging, procrastination. It has become the battle-cry for incompetents.

At the Naval Attaché's office I was told there is a possibility of flying back to America on a PB2Y. It is taking two army officers who have urgent business in Washington, but in case there is no room on that plane I plan to go by ship about the middle of the week.

I tried to convey to Paul White that I may be pulling out of here within a few days and sent this cable:

IF SATISFACTORY TO YOU CAN DISCONTINUE BROADCASTING FROM MELBOURNE ABOUT MIDWEEK TO RESUME FROM NEW YORK

In my broadcast this morning I said: "The first meeting of the biggest War Council ever held in this country ended just a few hours ago. At this session were military, naval and air chiefs of Australia, New Zealand, and service representatives of the United Nations. The object is to decide how to meet a possible Japanese attack on this country, and how to attack the Japanese by using Australia as a base.

"This is not a pow-wow which concerns internal policies. It will embrace a strategic scheme to meet the immediate problems in the Southwest Pacific.

"The main subject of the discussion is the American reinforcements of man power and equipment out here. As a result of President Roosevelt's speech, opinion here is that no effort will be spared to strengthen Australia as a springboard for Allied operations.

"The Government of this country is making its plans on the assumption that Java will not be able to hold out. The Government officials now take the position that the Australians, for the first time in 150 years, will have to meet an enemy on home soil.

"In the Commonwealth capital at Canberra yesterday a number of Ministers voiced the opinion that Japanese bombers could be expected to attack the main industrial cities of this country: Newcastle, Sydney and Melbourne.

"Each day, almost each hour, the realization that this country can

523

and very probably will be subjected to Japanese bombing raids—as a starter—is increasing. The taxi driver who took me from the railway station to the hotel today summed up the temper of most of the people. He said:

" 'We'll give the Japs the best we've got. All we can do is prepare for the worst and hope for the best.'

"The officials of this country agree that its preparation as a base for the United Nations depends on what the United States sends. In fact, the affection of the people here for America has reached the greatest warmth.

"The industrial beginnings of this country are too recent for it to become an arsenal of democracy in the Southwest Pacific. And the general opinion is that the demands on Great Britain are too heavy elsewhere for her to send very much in the way of man power and equipment. For those reasons, the eyes of every Australian are turned toward the United States.

"So, many of the efforts here are directed toward preparing the people to find themselves on a battleground. The various restrictive measures, some papers say, are to discipline the people. Horse racing is being restricted, and in one of the states it is now barred. And for a people as fond of horse racing as the Aussies, that's the same as barring the use, for any purpose, of motorcars in America.

"Posters are going up all over the country to inspire in the people a fear of what would happen if the Japanese got here. The object is to shock the people into the imminence of danger. For example, one poster shows a brute-faced Japanese soldier with a pistol, creeping across the ocean out of the rising sun. He has one hand on the map of this country. The caption reads:

" 'The word now is must.' "

In my talk with various people here today, I am becoming more convinced that the Australians are still resisting an all-out effort to fight the war. That resistance, I believe, is due mostly to the absence of leadership and because of general suspicion of the way the politicians are playing their old games. The papers contain many letters from readers, and this one is typical:

"Mr. Curtin is once again lamenting that the average Australian is blind to the danger threatening the country. We do realize the impending danger but feel helpless. What can the average man, woman, and child do? We really want to know."

Lunching with Don Rogers, the Prime Minister's secretary, here today, I asked why Curtin didn't get tougher, and he said: "The main problem is the fact that each of the six states is just about its own boss and does what it wants."

On all sides here in Melbourne there is the ready acceptance on the part of the Australians that the Aussies should not be sent to Java. People are talking about offensive, and the papers are writing about the defense of Australia by offensive operations, but all that is idle talk because the Australians' whole policy is one of pure defense.

Monday, March 2nd:
Ed Angly, now of the *Chicago Sun* and formerly of the *New York Herald Tribune,* came in today. I took him out to the Victoria Barracks, where we saw Don Rogers. Rogers said that he was talking to the Prime Minister about me and that "General Bennett backs you up one hundred percent on what happened at Singapore."

Rogers was referring to the story told by General Bennett to Prime Minister Curtin and War Minister Forde today.

Bennett escaped from Singapore after its fall. He has been in rather hot water. The criticism was that he left his men. The fact is that he escaped in a small boat *after* the fall.

As we were riding back from Victoria Barracks along a street lined with houses of a monotonous sameness, Ed Angly remarked: "They ought to send Harry Thaw here to shoot some more architects."

We discussed Englishmen we have encountered since those days in Cairo, and Angly said: "Every Englishman I talked to wants to go to the United States after the war. I guess they think they are going to pay off that lease-lend by sending us forty million Englishmen."

Rorke, the chief censor in Sydney, has been fired.

These Australians are easy people to like. They are eager fighters and have the courage to die. I make this estimate: The Australian of the

525

city loves to talk endlessly; the men on the sheep stations are more taciturn. The Aussie speaks in a monotone, harsh to strange ears, without
vibrancy or variety. His complete friendliness helps to ease the monotony of his voice and a gravel-grinding accent that lacks even the
charm of Cockney.

The Australian considers himself not your equal but twice as good
as you are. He is pugnaciously determined to be independent. He is
an individualist, but he is a great imitator of American ways rather
than British ways. He doesn't mind being asked to do things, but he
resents being ordered to do them. He is co-operative and co-ordinated
when cajoled. In that respect I find Australians very American.

He resents criticism of his country by an outsider. He doesn't evaluate his country to a foreigner but maintains blind faith that whatever
Australia does is wise, whatever Australians do is correct. But I do
find some Australians who recognize that this is a people's war and
realize that Australia can never be the same again. As a Ministry of
Information official said: "Our sins are rolling back on us."

Tuesday, March 3rd:
A high American officer who knows whereof he speaks told me today:
"There is too much direction of the war from Washington. The thing
for them to do is to send us everything they can and we'll handle it
out here. They even try to direct small details. For example, twelve
aircraft came in damaged and we sent a message to Washington for
them to be more careful of their packing hereafter. Washington replied
that they were sorry and instructed us to get a certain factory at such-
and-such a street in Melbourne and have the repairs done. That factory
has been doing work for us for a month. They even tried to tell us
what size screws to use.

"We asked Washington to send us better staff officers. We need
men who consider aggressiveness and initiative more than secondary
to routine procedure. I want men who when they meet a grizzly bear
don't walk right into it, but get behind a tree and pick it off."

Sir Keith Murdoch, the most powerful newspaper owner in Australia, says in an article in the *Sydney Sun*: "People are unhappy,
puzzled and angry about Singapore, deeply concerned about drinking.

"People are unhappy about Darwin. They know that workers were holding stop-work meetings a day or two before the raid. They know that ships that should have been cleared with proper appliances and labor are still lying in the harbor exposed to bombs.

"Australia has pegged out a tremendous claim upon the world. She asks now that she be allowed to hold a vast land for her seven million white people. Let us then seize the chance, for if we cannot rise to this occasion, then assuredly we can never rise to any occasion."

All the activity here is based on the premise that the fate of Java is decided. The *Sydney Telegraph* urges creation of a new zone of command embracing the whole Pacific with a commander on the spot. Since most of the troops out here will be American, the newspaper adds that the commander should be American. The Sydney paper calls for the appointment of General Douglas MacArthur to head the forces of the United Nations in the Southwest Pacific.

This is also the view and choice of the Australian War Council which has just ended its sessions here.

The Minister of Home Security broke the ice on a subject which has been avoided up to now and issued detailed instructions on what to do in case of invasion. As recently as two weeks ago, eyebrows were arched if anyone suggested a strong possibility of Japanese invasion. The advice given now is the routine instruction: Stand fast, help our troops, don't tell the enemy anything, don't give him anything and don't help him.

Wednesday, March 4th:
At dinner tonight at the Athenaeum Club, as the guest of Sir Keith Murdoch. Also there were Eric Kennedy, the manager of the *Sydney Sun;* Ed Angly; W. S. Robinson, an Australian who has just returned from the U.S. by plane with Dr. van Mook; an *Associated Press* correspondent named Vern Haugland; and Patrick Maitland, an English correspondent I had last seen in Yugoslavia.

Robinson, elderly, hard of hearing, a very determined person, who has played an important part in the war here, in Washington and in London, said: "There'll be no peace in my lifetime. This war is going to last seven to ten years."

527

He said the Allied stocks of rubber were sufficient for nine months and there is tin for two and a half years, if there will be a thirty-five to forty percent drop in consumption.

Murdoch and Robinson asked me what should be done for American soldiers. I explained in considerable detail that the men are wandering around the streets now like lost souls; that canteens should be set up; that they should be made to feel at home; that no effort should be spared for a better understanding between Australians and Americans.

"You Australians," I said, "dislike all foreigners. It is part of your 'White Australia' policy. All Americans came from foreign countries. You people see a black-haired, swarthy Italian who might look like Al Capone; well, that Italian is an American, and he is wearing an American uniform. You people instinctively resent that man because he is obviously Italian. As far as we are concerned, he is American, whatever he looks like externally, and he is here to fight and die to protect your country.

"Don't make the same mistake here that the British have made of being so supercilious. We've got to understand each other, our faults as well as our virtues."

I said that Americans over here want some diversion; they are homesick and they are lonesome; that the Australians should try to provide what they need for their spirit.

"The hell with all that," Angly said. "Send them out to the camps and get them started fighting. That's what counts."

I ran into Sir George Sansom and Lady Sansom. It was the first time I had seen Sir George since Singapore. He introduced me to Lady Sansom.

"Things are pretty bad, aren't they?" I said. "Java will go quickly."

Sir George agreed, and Lady Sansom spoke up: "Really, the Dutch have been depending on someone else for protection."

"What!" I exclaimed. I was shocked by this British-Singapore mentality. "On whom did the Dutch depend for protection?"

"Oh, I suppose the Dutch are fighting very well," Lady Sansom said. "But actually, you know, they depended on us to fight for them."

I thought it best to get away from there. The strain of controlling myself was too great.

Thursday, March 5th:
The escapees from Singapore, arriving in Australia, tell of the last-minute retreat. The Johore Causeway between Johore Bahru and Singapore Island was repaired by the Japanese in a few hours. The British succeeded in blowing up only a part of it.

Many refugees criticize the military and civil services. Said one: "Trucks, spare parts, motor accessories and machinery were left intact at Ipoh because the British Resident Commissioner would not give permission for their destruction."

Said another: "We were told to the last that Singapore was impregnable."

Lady Brooke-Popham, back in London with Sir Robert, is quoted as saying: "It was just parties, bridge and dancing to the very last . . . the deadly inertia of the white population. My husband told them repeatedly to expect enemy bombers but nothing could rouse them. They simply refused to believe that war could come to Singapore.

"A.R.P. measures were never taken seriously. I asked a certain lady to help me two hours a day. She said it would interfere with her tennis. It was heartbreaking. Nothing could shake them."

Harold Guard of *United Press* told me today that on the day before the Japs crossed over from Johore to Singapore Island, Lieutenant General A. E. Percival called in all the correspondents.

"I am very much exercised," he said, "by these alarmist reports you are writing. They are entirely unjustified. I can assure you that no Jap will set foot on this island.'

The next day the Japanese were on Singapore Island.

The Japs raided Broome, on the west coast, for the first time.

Two PB2Y's and three Flying Fortresses and fifteen Kittyhawk fighters were destroyed on the ground. They caught us totally unprepared. We had no wireless-detection apparatus there, just as at Darwin.

Another bad feature of that raid on Broome was that it knocked out any chance of going back to America by air, since one of the aircraft I might have taken was destroyed.

529

Headlines from the *Melbourne Herald*:
DESPERATE POSITION DEVELOPING IN JAVA STRUGGLE
LITTLE AIR SUPPORT AVAILABLE TO ALLIES
INVADERS REACH WAW ON BURMA RAILWAY
BRITISH HOPE PARIS RAID ENDS KID-GLOVE WAR
36,000 GERMANS FALL AT STARAYA RUSSA

Friday, March 6th:
I am sailing for America tonight on the freighter, *Moormacstar*. Eight
passengers are going: Lieutenant Colonel Warren J. Clear of the
American Intelligence and Major Gerald Wilkinson, a British Intelli-
gence officer, both of whom were with MacArthur in Manila and at
Corregidor; Sir George and Lady Sansom; Helen Folster, the wife of
George Folster, our correspondent who is now at Darwin; and two
Australians. We are going unescorted, but we have a fast freighter and
an even chance of getting away with it.

Sunday, March 29th:
We arrived in San Francisco. Martha was waiting for me. My trip
around the world took four years, five months, twenty-five days and
nineteen hours.

Have you ever wanted to fall on your knees and kiss this American
earth?

THREE PAGES

This people's war for survival goes on.

We Americans and we of the United Nations go on fighting and dying all over the world. It is a simple choice we are making. It is to fight and die as free men or to live as slaves.

We fight formidable enemies who are strong, resourceful and cunning. The Fascists wage a total war, and they hold almost all the vantage points from which to fight it.

We fight barbarians. They are not simply barbaric Nazis or barbaric Japanese militarists. We fight the German people and the Japanese people who seek not liberation for the world, but its total enslavement. There is not a single Fascist man, woman or even child who would reject the spoils of conquest or the vengeance of victory, if the Axis should win this war.

But we will win this war. We will win because we are going to be twice as smart as our enemies, we shall produce twice as speedily as they can and we shall murder them twice as fast as they murder us.

The war goes on—inexorably.

We fight beside the British who fought our war for two and a half years with incredible courage. They fought while they were short of planes, guns, tanks, rifles, submarines, military leadership, adaptability, dynamism—short of vision in denying truthful reporting of their cause to their comrades-in-arms in America—short of understanding that the native in the Empire could fight, too, for the ideal of freedom—short of everything except courage. They held off our Fascist enemies with pure naked courage. They are the kind of people who face machine guns barehanded and fight off Stukas with rifles.

We fight now with the fearless Russians who are waging the kind of total, costly war that must be fought, fighting and dying with terrible sacrifice to exterminate the German Fascists from this earth. That is what counts: killing off Germans, Italians and Japanese.

We fight with the patient Chinese. They have been gnawing at our enemy in the Far East for more than five years, undergoing incredible hardships and privations—resisting every inch, decimating the enemy every day.

Those stubborn Dutch are fighting with us. In their vocabulary there is no such word as "defeat." In Java they didn't look to see what someone else was doing to determine what they should do. They did not say to the British: "You didn't scorch your earth in Malaya, why should we scorch ours?" The Dutch saw their duty and without a moment's hesitation they did it—set fire to hundreds of millions of dollars' worth of oil installations . . . Terakan, Balikpapan, Palembang.

It takes courage to scorch earth. Ask yourself if you are ready tomorrow to set fire to your own home, destroy your pigs and cows and cornfields, burn down your high school and university, set fire to the whole town in which you live.

Patriots in the occupied countries are fighting for us. Stealth is their lot, murder their duty and death their fate. But they are the ones who want no finer epitaph than this:

"He died for freedom."

Suez and Singapore are not mere points in the Middle East and Far East, nor are the men of those places mere disembodied names set down in a book. Cities, statesmen, soldiers, generals and admirals are symbols. The physical and mental defeats I have witnessed in this war were not all just unlucky accidents. There is a pattern to them that has not yet included the designs of totality, adaptability and the people's war. That pattern has etched a tragically straight line of defeat. Such a deepening groove will not trace the line of the people's revolution. It will not map the people's march to the century of the common man.

This positive fact remains: The pattern of victory is drawn indelibly in the souls of free men.

The people's war goes on and so do the symbols who bear names in this book.

Royal Marine Morris Graney of the *Repulse*, who was ready to die for his country and the simple victory of a better world, is either dead or a Japanese prisoner at Singapore.

Ching Yeuk, the Chinese girl, is lost in the confusion of war, one of millions of human beings like those I knew in Yugoslavia, Turkey,

532

Syria, Egypt, India, Java, who wanted nothing more from life than human rights and simple dignity.

American destiny links the people of America to the destiny of the Ching Yeuks and the Morris Graneys of this world. That is the people's war.

If, somehow, I could convey to you what I have seen in the eyes of the common man all over the world! There is in them the vision of America—America, the land of freedom. Millions of people throughout the world are yearning, stumbling, striving, dying for the symbol of America.

Their hearts go on beating because there exists in this world of horror, murder, enslavement and destruction the shining light of America as it is, and the symbolism of what it will be.

That is the American dream for America and for freedom-lovers the world over. And it must survive.

INDEX

Abend, Hallett, 236, 242
Abrahams, Lieutenant, 295, 300, 302, 311, 322
Acre, 86
Acworth, Major J. P., 166
Adelaide, 480
Adelphi Hotel (Singapore), 215, 272
Agronsky, Martin, 13, 361, 379, 380, 389, 390, 392, 393, 402, 403, 407, 409, 419, 433, 457
Akyab, 124
Alban, Major, 50, 69
Albright, Sid, 234, 443, 449
Alcock, Captain, 121
Alcock, John, 121, 123
Aldrich, Clayton, 367
Aleppo, 16, 20
Alexander I, King of Yugoslavia, 155
Alexander the Great, 67
Alexandria, 85, 122
Alexandria Military Hospital, 255
Alfieri, Dino, 224
Alikiamou, 38
Allen, Captain Archer, 139
Allen, Robert, 229
Allenby, General, 57, 61
Allsop, Joseph, 229
Alor Star, 347, 432
Amboina, 504
Ambon, 475
American Farmer, 202
American Field Service, 77
American Red Cross, 33, 85, 94
Amherst College, 229
Andaman Islands, 445
Anderson, Major F. G., 166
Anderson, Godfrey, 106, 274
Angly, Edward, 25, 26, 28, 29, 33, 34, 35, 39, 40, 242, 525, 527, 528
Ankara, 7-14, 18, 21, 27, 72
Ankara Palas Hotel, 8
Ankara Radio, 8
Aosta, Duke of, 31, 84
Ark Royal, 258
Armstrong, H. C., 43

Arnold, General, 507
Asa Maru, 259
Associated Press (AP), 9, 13, 40, 55, 63, 106, 131, 185, 274, 280, 402, 457, 496, 527
Astley, Colonel, 31, 83, 110, 113
Astrakhan, 74
Ataturk, 7
Athenaeum Club, 527
Attlee, Clement, 404
Auchinleck, General Sir Claude, 81-82
Australia, 412, 440, 444, 445, 448, 449, 450, 451, 454, 456, 458, 459, 473, 479, 480-504, 505-530
Australia, H. M. S., 521
Australia Hotel (Sydney), 491, 506
Australian *Associated Press,* 166, 185, 277
Australian Broadcasting Commission, 505
Australian Imperial Forces (AIF), 277
Azalea City, 167
Azores, 85
Azov, 74

Babylon, 121
Bachelorville, 486
Bachok, 288
Bagdad, 11, 12, 72, **74**
Bagush, 106
Bagush Arms, 106
Bahrein Island, 121
Bain, Ralph, 33, 85
Bakru-Bukit, 428
Baku, 72, 74, 81
Balbo, Italo, 4
Baldwin, Ensign Justin, 472
Bali, 445
Balikpapan, 448, 451, 452, 463, 479, 532
Bander-Shah, 74
Bandoeng, 135, 449, 450, 452, 458
Bangkok, 126, 180, 198, 209, 253, 255, 268, 284, 286, 298
Bangust, Second Mechanic, 476, 477, 479

535

Baron, Charles, 218, 261, 442
Barstow, Major General A. E., 167
Basra, 121
Batavia, 198, 237, 351, 358, 391, 410, 421, 433, 437, 439-444, 445-449, 452, 453-458, 493, 498
Bauduoy, 15
Bay of Bengal, 124
Bean, Lieutenant Joseph M., 482
Beasley, John, 522
Bedmead, Captain, 21, 22
Beirut, 17, 20, 59, 62, 64, 65, 66, 67, 69, 85
Belgrade, 5, 6, 8, 10
Bennett, Major-General Henry Gordon, 197, 211-215, 217, 218, 348, 349, 413, 414, 491, 510, 525
Berganzoli, General, 32
Berick, Captain, 30, 31, 32, 42, 48, 49, 73, 236, 256, 267, 383
Berrigan, Darrell, 223, 231, 255
Birgel Arab, 107
Blackburn, Squadron Leader, 391
Blackwell, Flight Lieutenant, 404
Blackwood, Captain, 163, 164
Blakang Mati, 254
Blamey, Major-General Thomas, 275
Blunt, Colonel J. S., 36
Bonney, E. G., 516, 517, 518
Borneo, 197, 248, 271, 287, 479
Bosnia, 10
Boulogne, 89
Boyer, Richard, 492
Bracken, Brendan, 435, 440
Brett, General, 447
Brewer, Sam, 6, 7, 14, 40, 55, 71
Brink, Colonel Francis G., 343, 344, 414
Brisbane, 480, 429, 493
Brisbane Courier Mail, 488
British Broadcasting Company, 29, 42, 144, 208, 274, 298, 306, 381
British Civil Service, 122
British United Press, 29
Brock, Ray, 14
Brook, Sir Charles Vyner, 371
Brooke-Popham, Lady, 529
Brooke-Popham, Sir Robert, 131, 138, 139, 144, 149, 150, 185-190, 192, 204, 206, 208, 217, 227, 240, 241, 277-283, 351, 354, 355, 358-360, 364, 366, 372-374, 378, 506, 513, 529
Broome, 529
Bros, Midshipman Christopher, 325, 326

Brown, Dixon, 188
Brown, Eugene, 92, 184
Brown, F. L., 453
Brown, Martha K., 7, 15, 17, 25, 26, 39, 41, 44, 45, 81, 85, 113, 118, 121, 123, 142, 163, 191, 223, 253, 308, 320, 327, 341, 342, 391, 418, 419, 426, 431, 440, 443, 461, 492, 497, 530
Brown, Gunner R. D., 484, 485
Buck, Electrician's Mate Howard L., 470
Budapest, 6
Buqbuq, 96
Burdett, Leah, 8
Burdett, Winston, 8, 13, 15, 72
Burma, 124, 429, 456, 501, 502, 511
Burma Road, 125, 134, 240, 241, 258, 278
Burnett, Sir Charles, 514
Burrows, Commander William, 131, 141, 142, 144, 145, 146, 149, 150, 151, 157, 165, 166, 179, 185-198, 201, 202, 203, 206, 208, 215, 234, 236, 264, 267, 276, 277, 286, 340, 351, 378
Busson, 162, 163
Butterworth Area (Penang), 353
Byzantine, 115

Cairo, 12, 14, 15, 16, 18, 22-32, 34-49, 74, 75, 77, 101, 107, 114, 117, 122, 123, 267, 453
Calcutta, 122, 123, 124, 440, 441
Caldwell, Erskine, 77
Caledonia, 120
Cambodia Point, 286
Cambridge University, 229
Camrannah Bay, 286
Canberra, 493, 516-523
Canea, 37, 38
Canopus, 122, 123
Carleton Hotel (Sydney), 505, 510
Carroll, Madeleine, 110
Casey, Richard, 440
Casey, Robert, 26, 242
Cassandra, 499
Catroux, General, 47, 156
Cerf, Bennett, 343
Chaldee, 121
Chamberlain, Neville, 4
Changi, 159, 160
Changi Barracks, 163
Chapman, Captain, 361, 362
Chapple, Lieutenant Wreford G. ("Moon"), 462-471

Charles, Sir Noel, 230
Cheops, 87
Chiang Kai-shek, 415, 416
Chicago Daily News, 25, 26, 31, 152, 187, 201, 234, 242, 243, 370, 402
Chicago Sun, 525
Chicago Times, 260
Chicago Tribune, 6, 55, 256, 403
China Sea, 159, 160, 247, 248, 287, 288, 297, 329, 369, 395, 502, 507
Ching Kai Min, Major General, 384, 439
Ching Yeuk (Rosa Sum), 268, 269, 272, 273, 274, 287, 340, 341, 368, 391, 436, 456, 532, 533
Chorlian, Edward, 27, 28, 29, 72, 96
Christian Science Monitor, 31, 495
Christman, Lieutenant Elwyn L., 472-480
Chungking, 198, 202, 204, 243, 253, 259, 266, 358
Churchill, Mrs., 260
Churchill, Randolph, 118
Churchill, Winston, 4, 85, 118, 154, 253, 278, 367, 368, 418, 449, 496, 499, 506, 513, 514
Ciano, Galeazzo, 25
Clear, Lieutenant Colonel Warren J., 530
Clifford, Alex, 113
Cline, Chief Yeoman, 480
Clive of India, 17, 94
Coates, Lieutenant, 482
Coconut Grove (Singapore), 158, 268, 269
Collet, Colonel Philibert, 55, 62
Collier's Magazine, 33, 39, 85, 152, 187, 201, 208, 242, 342, 344, 346, 404
Collins, Commander, 480
Collins, Walter, 82
Columbia Broadcasting System (CBS), x, 5, 7, 8, 9, 14, 22, 27, 30, 31, 35, 36, 37, 45, 69, 75, 77, 85, 96, 106, 110, 135, 136, 140, 144, 165, 166, 178, 179, 180, 187, 201, 202, 204, 205, 207, 208, 236, 242, 256, 260, 263, 264, 268, 272, 275, 282, 283, 284, 293, 295, 340, 342, 347, 358, 389, 391, 399, 401, 404, 405, 410, 412, 418, 433, 435, 439, 440, 441, 442, 491, 500, 512, 516
Connelly, Air-Force Captain, 481
Continental Hotel (Cairo), 24, 29, 35, 39, 110
Corap, General, 58
Cordova, Frank, 453, 454, 457
Costanza, 6
Coughlin, Father, 457

Court, Lieutenant Peter, 357
Coward, Noel, 201
Cox, Squadron Leader, 149
Crawford, Brigadier General Raymond, 163
Creighton, Captain, 237, 238
Crete, 37-39, 40, 50, 121
Crisp, Robert, 109, 142
Cudahy, John, 232
Cumberbatch, Captain, 50, 68, 117
Cunningham, Charles, 454
Curtin, Prime Minister John, 390, 505, 507, 510, 511, 512, 519, 520, 521, 524, 525
Curtis, Captain, 191, 192, 195
Cyranos (Singapore), 184, 200, 231, 368

Daily Mail, 113
Dakar, 85
Daly Waters, 486, 487
Damascus, 20, 48, 50, 51, 52, 55, 56, 58, 59, 63, 65, 67, 72, 86, 149, 172
Damour, 64
Darr, Captain, 39
Dartmouth Naval College, 144
Darwin, 454, 461, 473, 474, 480, 481, 486, 493, 496, 498, 512, 514, 517, 518, 520
Davis, Duty Officer, 19
Davis, Eric, 135, 165, 178, 179, 180, 183
Dead Sea, 120
Decoux, Governor-General, 220, 270
Deems, Commander W. A., 461, 463
Deepavali, 233
De Gaulle, General, 156, 253
De Luce, Dan, 13
De Marjerie, 15
Denby, Commander, 297, 302, 303, 306, 308, 310, 337
Denise, Ann, 311
Denny, Harold, 29, 33, 73, 74, 78, 79, 81, 109, 274
Dentz, General Henri, 48, 50, 51, 58, 59, 69, 85
Diejzine, 48
Djibouti, 110
Dobbs, 433
Doivall, Wing Commander, 277
Domei, 198, 234, 284
Dooh, Colonel Irving, 439
Downer, Flight Lieutenant Sydney, 225, 245, 258, 391, 404
Downs, Kenneth, 40
Droogleever, Pim, 142

Duckworth, Press Censor, 144, 151, 158, 165, 179, 201, 202, 203, 209, 368, 381, 389, 405, 406, 407, 413
Duff Cooper, Alfred, 180, 182, 183, 202-207, 228, 242, 269, 275, 343, 344, 381, 390, 402, 403, 408, 417
Duff Cooper, Lady Diana, 182, 343, 344, 390
Dunn, William J., 202, 256, 358, 440, 441, 442, 443, 444, 446, 448, 455, 512
Dunston, William, 522
Duranty, Walter, 33
Durdin, Tillman, 455
Dutch Borneo, 451
Dutch East Indies, 138, 139, 148, 152, 185, 198, 236, 237, 243, 258, 279, 281, 443, 447, 455, 494, 498, 501, 502, 507, 509
Duval, Commander, 474, 480

"Eastern News," 198, 284
Eden, Anthony, 24, 140, 144, 268
Egypt, 14, 22, 29, 80
Egyptian Mail, 39, 43
Egyptian State Broadcasting, 27, 36, 46
Electra, 334, 335
Elizabeth, 167
El Jiya, 66, 67
Elrington, Colonel, 191
Elrington, Mrs., 191
Emden, 521
Endau, 164, 428
Ennals, Captain, 41
Eton, 153
Evans, E. R. G. R., 304
Evans, Lieutenant Commander, 50
Evatt, Dr. Herbert V., 509, 510, 518, 522
Exbrook, 125
Express, 313, 335

Fagan, Larry, 13
Fairholl, Tom, 277, 293, 363, 370, 457
Farinacci, Roberto, 155, 224
Faris, Barry, 9
Fearon, Captain O. K., 345, 346, 347, 348, 371, 382
Feisal II, King, 11
Fellowes, Colonel, 41
Ferguson, Major, 56, 57, 58, 59, 83
Field, Colonel, 261, 262, 360, 377, 379, 392, 397-407, 413, 442
Fielding, Captain Sean, 90, 96-97, 100, 101, 106, 108, 189
Fight in the Pacific (Mark J. Gayn), 233
Fish, Hamilton, 119

Fisher, Major C. R., 188, 189, 201, 213, 231, 241, 242, 243, 255, 282, 287, 288, 293, 349, 401, 402, 405, 406, 408, 413, 433, 434
Fisher, Julius, 243
Fisher, Norman, 238
Fitchett, Ian, 277
Flecker, James Elroy, 56, 83
Foch, General, 58
Folster, George, 491, 505, 512, 513, 530
Folster, Helen, 530
Foote, Dr., 237, 444, 447
Foote, Mrs., 444
Forbes, Ensign G. W., 468
Forde, Francis, 507, 519, 525
Formosa, 265
Fort Canning, 137, 138, 213
Franzero, C. M., 71, 72
Franz Ferdinand, Archduke, 6
Fraser, 277
Freidenreich, Eve, 46
Fuiji, Johnny, 155, 223
Fuso Maru, 205, 217

Gallagher, O'Dowd, 152, 166, 170, 185, 187, 189, 191, 194, 223, 231, 241, 242, 243, 245, 254, 258, 289, 293-323, 328, 329, 335, 337, 340, 342, 343, 349
Ganges Delta, 124
Ganges River, 123
Garden of Eden, 121
Garrett, 231
Gaster, Miss, 43, 44, 45, 47
Gatty, Harold, 448
Gavin, Major, 155, 156, 358, 361, 362, 437, 439, 446
Gayda, Virginio, 72
Gayn, Mark J., 233
Gellhorn, Martha, 187, 208, 242
Gennock, Ted, 51
George, Colonel, 91
George VI, King of England, 184
George II, King of Greece, 36, 37
Georgetown, 168
German Library of Information, 49
Gervasi, Frank, 33, 35, 40, 152, 153, 155, 163, 187, 201, 242, 342
Getchell, Captain, 231, 270, 288
Gezira, 77, 109
Gezira Sporting Club, 28
Ghabaghib, 55
Gibson, Captain, 166
Gillis, Midshipman Peter, 324
Gilpin, Major John, 88-89

Giornale d'Italia, 71, 72
Glarner, Andy, 51
Glassford, Vice Admiral, 459
Gloncurry, 487, 488
Glugor Barracks, 168
Gneisenau, 499
Godman, Lieutenant Henry C., 482
Goering, Marshal, 105, 442
Goodfellow, Basil, 361, 362
Gorrell, Henry, 55, 56, 63, 113
Gort, Lord, 366
Gott, Major General W. H. E., 101
Gough, General Sir Hubert, 389
Gough, Ensign William V., Jr., 472-480
Graney, Morris, 330-333, 345, 346, 532, 533
Grant, Squadron Leader, 404
Graziani, Marshal, 32
Great Eastern Hotel (Calcutta), 123
Great Sind Desert, 123
Great Southern Hotel (Singapore), 270
Great Syrian Desert, 61
Grimsdale, Colonel G. E., 136, 137, 142, 144, 155, 156, 261, 358, 360, 398
Grimsdale, Mrs., 155
Guard, Harold, 267, 272, 286, 287, 402, 417, 496, 529
Gulf of Siam, 248, 286, 305

Habbanyia, 121
Haggard, Colonel, 54
Haifa, 18, 19, 22, 52, 64, 68, 120
Hainan, 227
Halfaya Pass, 91
Hallowes, Lieutenant Geoffrey, 159, 163, 364, 371, 410
Halton, Lieutenant, 297, 300, 308
Hanna, Dr. J. G., 215
Happy World (Singapore), 239
Harbin, Chief Machinist's Mate, 470
Hari Raya Puassa, 233
Harmony Club (Batavia), 446, 447
Harsch, Joseph, 495-498, 509, 510
Hart, 110
Hart, Admiral, 282, 447, 464, 508
Haruna, 482
Harvard University, 13, 229
Hayes, Helen, 260
Haynes, J. E., 453, 454
Heart, W. R., 9
Heath, Major General Louis, 166, 351, 352, 376
Heine, Heinrich, 41
Helfrich, Admiral, 447, 508
Heliopolis, 108

Hellfire Pass, 98, 99
Henderson, Lieutenant, 30, 76, 109
Hennesey, Major, 141
Heraklion, 38
Hess, Rudolph, 15
Hill, Russell, 14, 78, 79, 110
Hirohito, Emperor, 224
Hitler, 4, 5, 6, 15, 36, 103, 112, 134, 150, 185, 239
Hoagland, Verne, 527
Holcombe, Chester, 132
Hongkong, 288, 370
Hood, 334
Hooghly River, 123
Horn, Albert W., 25
Horton, Wing Commander, 107
Hotel Des Indes (Batavia), 442, 446, 453, 457
Hotel Karachi (Karachi), 122
Howell, Attorney General, 218
Howell, Mrs., 218
Huband, Captain, 51, 53, 54
Hughes, William, 507
Hull, Cordell, 48, 140, 144, 182, 269
Hunt, Major, 141

Ibn Saud, 43
I Found No Peace (Webb Miller), 54
Ile de France, 200
Impey, Lawrence, 369
Import Control Bureau, 215, 216
Indian Kuala Lumpur, 200
Indian Pioneer, 200
Indo-China, 112, 220, 227, 243, 248, 265, 270, 274, 277, 278, 280, 281, 286, 300, 308, 382
"Inside Italy" (Martha Brown), 85
International News Service (INS), 5, 9, 10, 33, 40
Ipoh, 382, 390, 432, 504, 529
Iran, 12, 74, 75, 82, 240, 256
Iraq, 10, 11, 12, 35, 40, 51, 82, 113, 240
Irawaddy River, 124
Istanbul, 3, 6, 7
Italo-French Armistice Commission, 15

Japanese Times and Advertiser, 243
Java, 135, 395, 397, 403, 412, 442, 451, 453, 456, 457, 458, 487, 488, 493, 496, 498, 503, 507, 509, 511, 512, 522, 528, 532, 533
Jennings, 166, 193, 194
Jerusalem, 18, 22, 42, 50, 63
Jervis, 64, 69, 70
Johnson, 95-100

539

Johnson, Nelson T., 518
Johore, 164, 191, 211, 226, 390, 395, 396, 412, 414, 415, 424, 427, 428, 455, 456, 488, 496, 529
Johore Straits, 160, 250, 276, 297, 390, 427, 491
Jolliffe, Captain, 50, 51
Jolo Island, 475, 477
Jones, Captain Herbert, 522
Jones, Colonial Secretary, 416
Jordan, 229
Junior League Magazine, 86

Kalang Airport, 126, 410, 437
Kantara, 22, 23
Karachi, 122
Keating, Geoffrey, 89
Kedah, 363
Kelantan, 422
Kelly, 50
Kelly, Captain Colin, 482
Kennard, Clark, 136, 140, 282
Kennedy, Ed, 40, 55, 63
Kennedy, Eric, 527
Khamsin, 105
Kimmel, Admiral, 514
King David Hotel (Jerusalem), 50
Kinkaid, Rear Admiral Thomas, 139, 462
Kintes Valley, 408
Kintner, Robert, 229
Kipling, Rudyard, 102, 125
Kirk, Alexander, 25, 26, 29, 33, 72, 79, 110-112, 118
Kisweh, 55, 56
Kitchener of Khartoum, 94
Kluang, 451
Knatchbull-Hugessen, Sir Hugh, 7, 11, 16
Knickerbocker, H. R., 495, 496, 497
Knox, Secretary of the Navy, 76, 233, 234, 256
Kongo, 304, 306
Konoye, 227, 279
Kota Bahru, 235, 245, 246, 257, 288, 289, 304, 345, 357, 358, 432, 435
Kroh, 170, 171, 172
Kuala Kangsar, 363, 375, 390
Kuala Lumpur, 166, 232, 387, 394, 396, 398, 404, 408, 421, 422, 432
Kuala Selangor, 423
Kuantan, 246, 259, 312, 313, 391, 428, 495, 504
Kuching, 504
Kuibyshev, 260
Kumbar, 169

Kurusu, Saburo, 253, 259, 269
Kut-el-aman, 121

Lamming, Captain, 53
Lampson, Sir Miles, 83, 84
Landers, P. H., 476, 477, 479
Lane, Ambassador, 14, 44
Langley, 474, 480, 522
Latham, Teddy, 77
Laval, Pierre, 219
Lawrence, Larry, 380, 392, 419, 427
Lawrence of Arabia, 17, 55, 61, 71, 120
Layton, Vice Admiral Sir Geoffrey, 142, 144, 146-149, 185, 187-190, 192-198, 201, 202, 205, 206, 208, 215, 226, 263, 269, 270, 277, 372, 378, 391
Leach, Captain John, 283, 295, 296, 297, 335, 336, 338
Leary, Admiral, 522
Legaspy Gulf, 483
Le Gentilhomme, General Paul Louis, 57
Leichard Hotel (Gloncurry), 488
Lembang, 452
Lennon's Hotel (Brisbane), 490
Liberty Magazine, 40
Life, 187, 190, 208, 243, 347, 371, 373, 404, 407, 408
Lindbergh, Charles, 114, 119, 457
Lingayen Gulf, 462, 465
Litvinov, Ambassador, 271
London Letter, 389
London Daily Express, 52, 113, 152, 166, 185, 194, 242, 258, 289, 411, 416
London Daily Herald, 113, 383, 454
London Daily Mail, 369
London Daily Mirror, 417, 499
London Daily Sketch, 51, 234, 238, 417, 506
London Economist, 499
London News Chronicle, 43, 409, 417, 499
London Star, 418
London Times, 51, 390
Lord of Arabia (H. C. Armstrong), 43
Low, Bob, 40
Lubbock, Peter, 513
Lumby, 51
Lurvey, Pilot Don, 477, 478, 479
Luzon, 150, 367, 465
Lydda, 21, 22
Lyle, Sergeant Pilot, 245, 246, 252
Lyon, Brigadier General C. A., 168, 169, 170, 350-356
Lyttleton, Oliver, 83-84

540

MacArthur, General, 417, 527, 530
Macassar, 504
Macassar Straits, 447, 449, 451, 452, 502
MacDonald, Captain, 87, 89
Mack, Captain, 64, 69, 70
MacMillan, Richard, 29
Maginot Line, 4
Maitland, Patrick, 527
Majestic Hotel (Kuala Lumpur), 166
Malacca, 416
Malacca Anti-Wang, Anti-Fascist Unity
    Society, 266
Malaya, 126, 127, 131-145, 146-158, 159-
    177, 178-210, 211-227, 228-244, 247,
    248, 258-262, 263-274, 275-289, 300,
    305, 312, 346, 347, 356-362, 363-395,
    399, 405, 408-414, 416-435, 439-444,
    448, 450, 451, 456, 494, 496, 497, 500,
    502, 503, 504, 507, 510, 514, 532
Malaya Broadcasting Corporation, 135,
    140, 165, 178, 179, 180, 183, 213, 282,
    397, 398
Malaya Mail, 387
Malaya Tribune, 127, 199, 213, 221, 233,
    385, 411
Malayan Communist Party, 266, 271, 393
Maley, Ray, 166, 185, 277, 457, 458
Malhop, Lieutenant, 469
Manila, 202, 236, 258, 259, 260, 269,
    271, 282, 286, 339, 340, 367
Marshall, General, 255, 507
Martin, John S., 40, 243
Massock, Richard, 9
Matthews, Ronald, 113, 383, 454
May, Dr., 155, 156, 162, 218
McArdle, Kenneth, 13
McClure-Smith, 509
McConnell, Commander Robert P., 475
McDaniel, Yates, 131, 185, 188, 190,
    280, 402, 496
McEttee, Robert, 14
McEvoy, Dennis, 260, 261, 262
McEvoy, J. P., 260
McKell, Premier, 509
McLeod, Frank, 334
McNaughton, Lieutenant Jack, 260
McNeal, Seaman, 469, 470
Mekong River, 126
Melbourne, 445, 522, 523, 525, 526
Melbourne Herald, 522, 530
Melbourne Sun, 277
Menton, 166
Menzies, Robert Gordon, 163, 390
Merjiyum, 66, 69

Mersah Matruh, 94
Mersing, 164
Metro-Goldwyn-Mayer, 384
Metulla, 48, 53
Mezze, 56
Michie, Allan, 243
Miller, Webb, 54
Mindanao, 482
Ministero Culture Popolare, 44
Monson, Sir W., 304
Moorehead, Alan, 52, 71, 113
Moorehead, Colonel, 171, 173
Moormacstar, 530
Morgan, Purser, 123
Morris, John E., 454
Morrison, 390
Moscow, 72, 73, 74, 75, 77
Mosley, Leonard, 51, 223, 234, **235, 236,**
    238, 241, 245, 417, 506
Mostyn-Owen, Captain, 51, 68
Mosul, 11, 120
Mountbatten, Lord Louis, 50
Mowrer, Edgar Ansel, 26, 234, 243
Mowrer, Paul Scott, 26
Mowrer, Richard, 25, 26, 31, 35, 39, 43,
    63, 109
Mowrer, Rosamond, 26, **27, 29, 35, 39,**
    43, 45, 73, 77, 79, 109
Moyne, Lord, 232, 404
Munroe, Captain, 107
Munson Line, 184
Murdock, Sir Keith, 526, 527, **528**
Murray-Lyon, Brigadier General, 170
Murrow, Ed, 37, 43, 49
Mussolini, 4, 5, 44, 72, 76, 85, **94, 103,**
    224, 231
Mussolini, Bruno, 142
Mussolini, Vittorio, 142
Mydans, Carl, 190, 243

Naiad, 63
Napoleon, 86
Natal, 453
National Broadcasting Company, 13, 35,
    143, 144, 152, 165, 187, 192, 193, 196,
    201, 234, 241, 243, 253, 261, 389, 402,
    443
Nayar, Captain, 166
Nazareth, 446
Neale, Commander E. T., 461, 463, 464
Nelson, Donald, 507
Netherlands East Indies, see Dutch East
    Indies
Nettinate, Luang Vudiasora, 132, 270

Neville, Robert, 26, 243
Newbegin, 16
New Statesman and Nation, 200
Newsweek Magazine, 62, 108, 157, 158, 165, 183, 342, 344, 354, 404
New World Cabaret (Singapore), 198, 200, 239
New York Herald Tribune, 14, 25, 78, 242, 525
New York Post, 498
New York Times, 11, 13, 14, 29, 53, 78, 144, 236, 242, 274, 455
Nezi Bey Manyas, 8
Nicholl, Graeme, 142, 143, 230, 258, 410, 437, 438, 455, 457
Nikoura, 17, 19, 21, 28
Nile, 43
Nine Power Conference, 4
NIROM, 442
Noble, Wing Commander, 249
Noderer, Al, 256, 257, 379, 403, 407, 408, 436, 438, 439, 449
Nomura, Admiral, 255, 269
Nye, Senator, 119

Oakshot, Major A. D., 27, 49, 78, 83
Oestreicher, Jack, 9
Okamoto, Suemasa, 284
O'Neil, 239
Oranje Hotel (Surabaya), 461
Osservatore Romano, 155
Overseas Press Club, 514, 515
Oxford University, 153

Packer, Frank, 509
Padang Sabak, 288
Page, Sub-Lieutenant, 299, 303, 322, 328, 338
Pahang River, 246
Palembang, 446, 507, 532
Palestine, 17, 22, 23, 27, 28, 34, 42, 43, 54, 89, 446
Palestine Post, 19
Paley, William, 118, 183, 342
Palmer, 191, 192, 195, 254
Panorama Hotel (Haifa), 69
Parade, 80
Paramount News, 51
Patani, 300, 344
Patton, Kenneth S., 131, 132, 202, 207, 216, 217, 228
Pavelitch, Ante, 155
Pearl Harbor, 288, 289, 300, 514, 518
Pearson, Drew, 229

Peet, Acting Director, 165
Penang Island, 167-169, 228, 235, 347-355, 358-360, 366-371, 373, 376-378, 385, 386, 390, 392, 409, 429, 430, 433, 495
Penang River, 169
Penton, Brian, 412
Pepys, 197
Perak River, 380
Percival, Lieutenant General A. E., 137, 138, 211, 213, 214, 215, 218, 220, 221, 269, 276, 351, 364, 412, 413, 430, 456, 457, 490, 491, 505, 529
Persian Gulf, 121, 451
Peter, Prince, of Greece, 37, 38
Peterson, Commander J. V., 461-464
Pettit, Radioman Robert Lee, 476-479
Philippine Islands, 417, 464, 481, 482, 494, 502, 514
Phillips, Joseph, 342
Phillips, Admiral Sir Tom, 282, 297, 305, 314, 320, 335, 336
Phillips, Ambassador William, 25
Pius XI, 9
Pittsburgh Press, 13
PM, 26, 166, 243
Post, Wiley, 448
Pownall, General Sir Henry, 366, 387, 409, 421, 431
Prai, 167
Pricolo, General, 267
Prince Eugen, 499
Prince of Wales, 276, 277, 282-284, 294-301, 304, 306, 312-320, 324-326, 329, 334, 335, 340-344, 369, 500, 502
Prunas, 25
Pulford, Air Vice-Marshal, 218
Purnell, Rear Admiral W. R., 461, 462

Queneitra, 54
Quisling, 386

Rabaul, 504
Radio Corporation of America, 193
Radio House (Cairo), 27
Radio-Keith-Orpheum, 193
Rae, Wing Commander Ramsay, 142
Raffles Hotel (Singapore), 127, 132, 141, 142, 150, 152, 157, 158, 163, 191, 198, 199, 221, 224, 234, 257, 258, 262, 272, 273, 275, 285, 287, 288, 293, 295, 338, 345, 350, 354, 356, 367, 371, 379, 385, 410, 421, 436, 437, 496
Raffles, Sir Stamford, 446
Raj Samand, 123

542

Rakek, 18
Randau, Carl, 166, 243
Random House, 343
Rangoon, 125, 126, 253, 349, 358, 440, 454
Rashid Ali Gailani, 10
Rati Island, 472
Reader's Digest, 154
Red Sea, 120
Regime Fascista, 155
Reitmann, Dr., 441, 442, 443, 446, 447, 455
Repulse, 276, 295-323, 324-336, 337-346, 354, 369, 391, 395, 404, 448, 461, 474, 500, 502, 513, 532
Retimo, 38
Reuben James, 239
Reuters, 241, 242, 280, 389, 434, 442, 500
Reynolds, Lieutenant Brian, 185, 189, 190, 191, 294, 295
Richard the Lion Hearted, 86
River Kriam, 349
Robin, René, 219
Robinson, W. S., 527, 528
Rogers, Donald, 510-513, 516, 519, 520, 525
Rome, 44, 103, 113
Rommel, General, 449
Roosevelt, Franklin D., 154, 183, 184, 229, 230, 234, 248, 277, 299, 368, 482, 507, 514
Roosevelt, James, 35, 36, 39
Rorke, C. A., 515, 516, 525
Rosacher, Machinist's Mate, 468
Rose, Lieutenant Henry J., 481, 487-489
Ross, Chief Machinist's Mate, 470
Rostov, 74
Rowell, Brigadier General, 39
Royale, Admiral Guy, 513, 514
Rugby, 326
Russell, Major, 229

Safed, 53
Saigon, 222, 265, 270, 286, 308
St. John, Robert, 14
St. John, Mrs. Robert, 13
Saladin, 86
Samson, Flight Lieutenant Gerald, 256, 257, 266, 369, 370
Sansom, Lady, 528, 530
Sansom, Sir George, 230, 231, 378, 383, 393, 397, 401, 403, 405, 406, 407, 412, 413, 528, 530

Sarajevo, 6, 14
Saravanamuttu, 385
Sarawak, 191, 197, 248, 269, 276, 287, 371
Satterthwaite, 16
Saturday Evening Post, 28, 39, 85, 154, 404
Saudi Arabia, 43
Saw, U., 242
Scharnhorst, 499
Schields, Tommy, 380, 392, 419, 427
Schurmann, Dr., 509
Scott, Robert, 151, 165, 178, 179, 183, 206, 350, 351, 407
Seabridge, Editor, 138, 139, 411
Sea of Galilee, 120
Sea View Hotel (Singapore), 158, 199, 221, 272
Sedgwick, A. C., 53, 55, 71
Selengor, 387, 388, 409
Seletar, 225, 245, 246, 250, 426, 488
Serbskikralj Hotel (Belgrade), 5
Seremban, 422
Seven Pillars of Wisdom (T. E. Lawrence), 71
Shah, Sir Allam, 388
Sharia Eloui, 29
Shatt-al-Arab, 121
Shaw, George Bernard, 268
Shearer, Brigadier General, 112
Sheikh, Meskin, 63
Sheik Majon, 54
Shepheard's Hotel (Cairo), 36, 39, 114
Shigimutsi, Admiral, 147
Shoreland, Major, 213, 214
Short, General, 514
Siasii Island, 478, 479
Sidi Barrani, 90, 94, 105, 179
Sigma Delta Chi, 39
Simmons, Major General F. Keith, 157, 159-164, 364, 365, 371, 410
Sinai desert, 71, 120
Sinclair, Major, 34
Singapore, 23, 39, 113, 118, 122, 124-127, 131-145, 146-158, 159-177, 178-210, 211-227, 228-244, 249, 250, 258-262, 263-274, 275-289, 293, 294, 304, 309-314, 324, 330, 337-362, 363-396, 397-414, 415-435, 436-444, 449-458, 488, 490-504, 505-509, 512-514, 516, 525, 528, 529, 532
Singapore Free Press, 127, 162, 234, 236, 267, 269, 288, 385

543

Singapore Golf Club, 229
Singapore Herald, 155, 182, 183, 193, 198, 223, 225, 284, 285
Singapore Island, 160, 419, 455, 457, 491, 496, 499, 529
Singapore Naval Base, 146, 160, 192-195, 200, 208, 263, 276, 294, 304, 337, 378, 455, 488, 497, 500
Singapore Nippo, 284
Singapore Rickshaw Pullers, 260
Singapore Swimming Club, 181
Slocum, Commander, 459
Smith, Sir Sidney, 86
Sofia, 112
Sollum, 28
Songron, Field Marshal Tuang Bipul, 269
South Negri Sembelan, 418
Spooner, Admiral E. J., 197, 304
Stalin, 253, 254
Stalingrad, 74
Stillings, Flight Lieutenant S. G., 225, 226
Stowe, Leland, 152, 153, 154, 155, 187, 201, 243
Straits Echo, 385
Straits of Malacca, 169, 352, 394
Straits Settlements, 151, 186
Straits Sunday Times, 389
Straits Times, 138, 166, 193, 194, 225, 228, 259, 267, 384, 385, 386, 389, 395, 408, 411, 416, 417, 419, 425, 428
Suda Bay, 38
Suez, 26, 34, 126, 203, 532
Sulzberger, Cy, 11, 12, 13
Sumatra, 445, 446, 507
Sungei Patani, 176, 347, 358, 449
Sun Herald Service, 277
Surabaya, 391, 395, 445, 454, 458, 459-463, 475, 479, 480, 481, 498
Surabaya Naval Base, 461, 463, 464, 471
Swindler, 231
Sydney, 122, 440, 441, 442, 444, 480, 491, 493, 496, 515, 517, 518, 525
Sydney Herald, 509
Sydney, H. M. S., 521
Sydney Mirror, 499, 506, 518
Sydney Sun, 266, 498, 517, 526, 527
Sydney Telegraph, 277, 293, 492, 496, 509, 520, 527
Sydney's Head, 521
Syria, 12, 15, 17, 20, 24, 27, 28, 42, 43, 50, 54, 67, 79, 85, 86, 89, 109, 110, 113, 149, 153, 157, 172, 189

Tampin Gemas, 418
Tanglin Barracks, 191, 195
Tanglin Club, 218
Tanner, Major Claude, 392
Tanner, Mrs. Claude, 392
Teats, Lieutenant Edward C., 482
Tehong Besar, 160
Tehran, 72, 74
Telok Anson, 408
Telok Bahang, 169
Temple, Lieutenant, 20, 21, 25
Tenedos, 306
Tennant, Captain William, 297, 298, 300, 301, 306, 309, 319, 320, 322, 326, 327, 335, 337
Terakan, 451, 452, 479, 504, 532
Texas Oil Company, 380
Thailand, 132, 133, 134, 137, 140, 141, 146-152, 162, 163, 166, 170-177, 180, 182, 186, 221, 232, 243, 247, 253, 264, 268, 269, 280, 284, 288, 298, 344, 345, 360, 381, 394, 503
Thaw, Harry, 525
Thomas, Senator Elbert, 256
Thomas, Major Gerald C., 36, 39
Thomas, Lowell, 43
Thomas, Governor Sir Shenton, 23, 204, 206-210, 260, 266, 371, 374, 387, 408, 409, 413, 415, 430, 500
Thompson, Lieutenant, 229
Throckmorton, 105
Tiberius, 120
Tigris River, 121
Time, 40, 122, 154, 243, 410
Timor, 451, 472
Tobruk, 104
Tod, Lieutenant Colonel, 30, 34, 35, 42, 43, 46, 73, 77, 83, 113, 118, 119, 136
Tojo, 279
Tokyo Nichi-Nichi, 220
Townsend, General, 121
Transocean News Agency, 49
Travnik, 6
Trenggannu, 259
Tripoli, 17, 101
Trout, Bob, 347
Tsurumi, Ken, 133, 134, 135, 221, 222, 225, 284
Turin, 81
Turkey, 5, 7, 10, 12, 17

Udjize, 5
Umberto, Prince, 224

544

United Press (UP), 35, 55, 63, 82, 113, 223, 231, 255, 267, 272, 286, 287, 402, 417, 454, 496, 529
University of Berlin, 153
Ur, 121

Van Kleffin, 451
Van Mook, Dr. Hubertus, 507, 508, 509, 527
Vatican, 155
Vickery, Howard, 13
Victor Emanuel, King, 155
Victoria Barracks, 525
Von Henting, 11
Von Papen, Franz, 7

Wadilel Araba, 120
Wakehurst, Governor, 513, 514
Wakehurst, Lady, 513
Wakehurst, Miss, 513
Walker, Sir Alan, 16
Walker, Captain Gordon, 211
Walker, Lady, 16
Walker, Selby, 241, 280, 442
Ward, Eddie, 29, 274
Waterman, First Mechanic Andrew, 477, 479
Watkins, Commander, 40
Watkins, Mrs., 454
Wavell, General, 24, 31, 42, 76-81, 84, 111, 236, 240-243, 394, 411, 421, 442, 452, 511
Wedgwood, Lord, 507
Weh, George, 228, 229
Weller, George, 370, 379, 383, 402, 403, 407, 410, 419, 433
Welles, Sumner, 134, 207, 256
Western Desert, 29, 34, 36, 42, 43, 49, 67, 86, 90, 94, 100, 102, 103, 104, 105, 106, 109, 119, 122, 140, 152, 153, 154, 157, 172, 175, 179, 189, 267, 268, 274, 348, 363, 375, 376, 449, 453
Western World, 184
Westrup, Engineer, 77
Weygand, General, 181
Wheeler, Senator, 119, 457
Wheless, Lieutenant Hewitt J., 482-486

While Rome Burns (Alexander Woollcott), 16
White, Leigh, 14
White, Paul, 7, 8, 9, 22, 27, 33, 34, 35, 42, 49, 53, 72, 73, 77, 85, 86, 89, 112, 113, 125, 140, 165, 178, 179, 183, 198, 202, 256, 263, 295, 341, 342, 356, 367, 391, 403, 410, 412, 413, 418, 431, 439, 440, 442, 444, 445, 449, 491, 500, 514, 523
Wilde, Captain John, 168
Wilhelmstrasse, 11
Wilkes, Captain John, 462, 463
Wilkie, Douglas, 266, 277
Wilkinson, Major Gerald, 530
Williams, Gunner, 485
Wills, Colonel, 51, 62, 68, 446
Wilson, Censor, 492, 493
Wilson, General Sir Henry Maitland, 47 50, 51, 85, 149
Wing Loong, 142, 154
Wise, Lieutenant, 488
With Lawrence in Arabia (Lowell Thomas), 43
Young, John, 143, 144, 152, 154, 155, 163, 165, 177-198, 201, 208, 234, 236, 237, 239, 241, 243, 253, 441
Wodehouse, Colonel F. V. R., 166
Wodehouse, P. G., 56
Woodward, David, 43
Woollcott, Alexander, 16
Wren, P. C., 66
Wright, Michael, 28
Wynter, Major General, 508, 509, 510

Yamashita, Lieutenant General, 505
Yarrow Hill, 168
Yeaton, Colonel, 261, 262
Yindrick, Jan, 35
Yokohama Specie Bank, 135
Youngstown Vindicator-Telegram, 184
Ypres, 102
Yugoslavia, 5-6, 7, 9, 13, 14, 18, 19, 21, 28, 39, 53, 85, 87, 105, 153, 155, 157, 456
Yunnan, 240, 258, 278

Zugsmith, Leane, 243